Manitoba Premiers
of the 19th and 20th Centuries

Manitoba Premiers
of the 19th and 20th Centuries

edited by Barry Ferguson
and Robert Wardhaugh

Printed and bound in Canada at Friesens.
The text of this book is printed on 100% post-consumer recycled paper
with earth friendly vegetable-based inks.

COVER DESIGN: Duncan Campbell, CPRC; series design, Brian Danchuk Design
EDITOR FOR THE PRESS: Brian Mlazgar, CPRC.
INDEX: Patricia Furdek, Ottawa, Ontario.
COVER PHOTOS: All photographic portraits are courtesy of the Archives of Manitoba, with the exception of the portraits of Howard Pawley, Gary Filmon and Gary Doer, which are courtesy of the Government of Manitoba.

Library and Archives Canada Cataloguing in Publication
Manitoba premiers of 19th and 20th centuries / edited by Barry Ferguson
and Robert Wardhaugh.

(Trade books based in scholarship, ISSN 1482-9886 ; 24)
Includes bibliographical references and index.
ISBN 978-0-88977-216-8

    1. Premiers (Canada)--Manitoba--Biography. 2. Manitoba--Politics and
government. I. Ferguson, Barry Glen, 1952- II. Wardhaugh, Robert
Alexander, 1967- III. Series: TBS ; 24

FC3355.M32 2010   971.27'020922   C2010-905938-7
10 9 8 7 6 5 4 3 2 1

CPRC PRESS
Canadian Plains Research Center
University of Regina
Regina, Saskatchewan, Canada, S4S 0A2
tel: (306) 585-4758   fax: (306) 585-4699
e-mail: canadian.plains@uregina.ca   web: www.cprcpress.ca

We acknowledge the financial support of the Government of Canada
through the Canada Book Fund for our publishing activities.

Canadian Patrimoine
Heritage canadien

Mixed Sources
Cert no. SW-COC-001271
© 1996 FSC
FSC

Contents

Acknowledgements. . . . . *vi*

Introduction   *Barry Ferguson and Robert Wardhaugh* . . . . *vii*

The Emergence of the Premiership, 1870–1874   *David Burley* 1

Robert A. Davis, 1874–1878   *Ruth Swan*. 29

John Norquay, 1878–1887   *G. A. Friesen*. 47

David H. Harrison, 1887–1888   *Karine Duhamel*. 69

Thomas Greenway, 1888–1900   *James Mochoruk* 79

Hugh John Macdonald, 1900   *Rory Henry*. 107

Rodmond P. Roblin, 1900–1915   *James Blanchard* 117

Tobias C. Norris, 1915–1922   *Morris Mott*. 139

John Bracken, 1922–1943   *Robert Wardhaugh and Jason Thistlewaite* 165

Stuart S. Garson, 1943–1948   *Raymond Blake*. 193

Douglas L. Campbell, 1948–1958   *James Muir* 213

Duff Roblin, 1958–1967   *W. F. W. Neville*. 237

Walter Weir, 1967–1969   *Scott MacNeil* 263

Edward Schreyer, 1969–1977   *Gregory Marchildon and Ken Rasmussen* 283

Sterling R. Lyon, 1977–1981   *David Stewart and Jared Wesley*. 307

Howard Pawley, 1981–1988   *Gregory Marchildon* 331

Gary Filmon, 1988–1999   *Barry Ferguson*. 355

Gary Doer, 1999–2009   *Karine Duhamel and Barry Ferguson* 391

Appendix. 420

Index 421

Contributors 448

Acknowledgements

Many people contributed to the completion of this project and deserve our heartfelt gratitude. Canadian Plains Research Center at the University of Regina is a wonderful organization to work with and we once again thank CPRC Press and Brian Mlazgar, publications manager, for his support and patience during the course of this project; thanks also to his staff: Donna Grant, senior editor; David McLennan, editorial assistant; Duncan Campbell, art director and designer; and Deborah Rush, sales and marketing manager. We also thank Natalie Johnson for stepping in to proofread the entire manuscript under a tight deadline.

We also want to thank all of the contributing authors, who interpreted our loose instructions in ways that have led to original and significant contributions to Manitoba and Canadian political history. They also were remarkably agreeable in accepting many of our editorial suggestions and sensible enough to resist some of them. While individual authors have acknowledged the help of research assistants and colleagues, we do want to especially thank James Muir, Jared Wesley and Rory Henry for taking the time to read and reread several of the essays.

Introduction

Anything But Bland: The Premiers and the Politics of Manitoba

Recent interpretations of Manitoba have often characterized the province's political life, past and present, as cautious, moderate, and even bland. In fact, this emphasis on the moderate nature of public life in Manitoba has become the dominant tone in the scholarly study of the province, as well as in journalistic accounts. The readers of this book, however, will find here a portrayal quite different from the current conventional wisdom. In recounting the political life stories of Manitoba's former premiers, the authors of the 18 essays in *Manitoba Premiers of the 19th and 20th Centuries* uncover a political history that is unique, contentious, innovative, *and interesting*.

There has been a strong tendency, particularly among political scientists looking at Manitoba politics and government, to emphasize the province's derivative political culture and uncreative ways. Nelson Wiseman's interpretation of Manitoba as a fragment of "Old Ontario" is a good example. Others have emphasized the absence throughout the 20th century of creative politics and distinctive policy-making. These political scientists have even at times questioned whether Manitoba possessed a distinctive political culture or institutional framework at all.[1] This body of work, however limited, does have a certain persuasive force; it does successfully capture the curious mix of dull public policy-making and volatile public debate that has characterized Manitoba's political history.

Manitoba's historians, though more cognizant of disruptions, have been struck by the long-term continuities and caution of the province's politics, particularly throughout the 20th century. This tendency is epitomized by the work of the province's most eminent historian, W. L. Morton.[2] Manitoba's 19th-century political history was characterized by Morton and others as an era of confrontation between the old and new settlers and between the province and nation. Morton contrasts the turbulent 19th-century experience with the increasingly centrist and cautious pattern of provincial politics over the course of the 20th century, up until the 1960s when his monumental history of the province was completed. Other historians of the 20th century have also been struck by the conservative provincial administrations and political culture.[3] Even historians reconsidering political issues in Manitoba have left the impression that decisive policies have more often than not been shown to have caused havoc at best and damage at worst.[4]

How accurate or complete are these depictions of a cautious, moderate, and bland political history? Even a quick glance at Manitoba's history indicates otherwise. As the essays in this book demonstrate, the province has often taken centre stage in many of Canada's most volatile political upheavals from the 1870s to the 1990s. These have been at least as frequent and turbulent as those experienced by any province in Canada, and include the Red River Resistance of 1870, the continuing conflict over Métis lands, the Manitoba Schools Question of the 1890s, the struggle against the CPR monopoly, the Western Immigration Boom, the Winnipeg General Strike of 1919, the emergence of protest parties in the 1920s and 1930s, the provincial response to the cataclysm of the Great Depression, the French language issue in the 1980s, and opposition to the Meech Lake Accord during the 1990s. In sum, almost all the crucial themes of economic protest against central Canadian domination, conflict over ethnicity, religion, and language rights, labour-business battles and class conflict, and the great rolling debates about the Canadian federal system, have been at the centre of the province's political history.[5]

Manitoba's political history has been anything but moderate and bland. The province's past has served as a battleground for many of the most important issues facing the nation. The outcomes have not always been admirable or decisive (examples include the disavowals of basic constitutional rights, the isolation and disregard for ethno-cultural groups, and the tedious slowness of public policy innovation), but the issues have been painfully clear throughout Manitoba's 140 years of political life.

These political struggles, as well as the broader continuities of provincial life, are made clear in the political lives of Manitoba's Premiers. The essays in this book encompass the full span of the province's political history, from the first tentative years of provincehood in the 1870s and 1880s, through the polarizing era of Manitoba's (and Winnipeg's) growth as a critical component of the national economy from the 1890s to the 1920s, to the long period of economic and social crisis and decline in the mid-20th century, and finally through the scramble to reshape the province socially, economically, and politically since the 1960s.

These 18 essays cover 140 years of provincial history. They serve as brief studies of Manitoba's governments as well as political biographies of Manitoba's Premiers. The essays are based upon the joint efforts of historians and political scientists. But while this work reflects the available scholarly resources, it should be pointed out that these resources are not particularly vast. Political history fell out of favour with academics in the 1980s and only recently has it commenced a slow return to vigour. The essays reflect an emphasis, rediscovered in recent political history, on both political institutions (including parties and governmental structures) and political culture (the beliefs and concerns that inform public life) as well as a greater interaction between political science and history.[6] They also reflect the singular importance of the Premier's office in all provinces under the Canadian political system, not just to shape policy but also to refract most social forces with the province. The office and the person of the Premier in every province are at the centre of provincial political life to a remarkable extent and the study of Premiers is the study of provincial public life.[7]

One lens for viewing Manitoba political and governmental history is through the political organizations that have shaped successive governments. Such a view allows a clearer picture of some the most influential characteristics of the province and its Premiers. The provincial party system in Manitoba has diverged sharply from the normative view of a two-party or multi-party system of long duration. Manitoba's party system has been as exceptional as any in the country.[8]

Manitoba began with a non-partisan, religious-ethnic political system from 1870 to the mid-1880s but shifted decisively to a version of the two-party system between 1888 and

1922. It then veered into a peculiar blend of non-partisanship and coalition from 1922 to 1958, and then has returned to the modern multi-party system since the late 1950s. An examination of the party system contributes to an understanding of politics and government as well as the ways in which politics reflected Manitoba's society and culture, including the role of political leadership.

Non-Partisan Politics

Between 1870 and 1888, Manitoba was governed at first by two Lieutenant-Governors (who controlled the first legislature) and then by four Premiers. Marc-Amable Girard was the first Premier, recognized by the Lieutenant-Governor in 1874, followed by Robert Davis, John Norquay, and David Harrison.

The emergence of normal provincial government under a first minister evolved slowly between 1870 and 1874. The first government of the province was controlled by the first two Lieutenant-Governors, Adams Archibald and Alexander Morris, who were, in essence, their own Premiers.[9] The hard-won triumph of legislative, non-partisan government followed from a deliberate attempt by the federal government of John A. Macdonald to create a local administration dominated by a federally-appointed and directed Lieutenant-Governor. It was Morris who recognized Girard's first ministership in 1874. Girard was the first "Premier," recognized by the Lieutenant-Governor as controlling the legislature and pursuing a legislative agenda. His putative predecessors, Alfred Boyd and Henry Clarke, were mere agents of the Lieutenant-Governors and not given the title of Premier in their day.

While scholars have long acknowledged the constitutional and governmental peculiarity of Manitoba's origins, the essays on Girard, Davis and Norquay emphasize the distinctiveness of Manitoba's original political institutions. There was no effective party system. Legislative representation was allocated on strict religious/ethnic lines with each of the Roman Catholic/Francophone and Protestant/Anglophone groups being assigned one-half of the assembly seats. This division reflected the deep schisms that had marred the Red River Colony during the period of Canada's "imperial" control, both prior to and after 1870. It also shaped approaches to politics and administration that emphasized two factors. One was the brokering of ethno-cultural differences, in which the ex-Quebeckers Girard and Davis demonstrated such skill; the second was the effort of Manitobans to avoid Ottawa's relentless political and economic bullying and even push back.

John Norquay's administration was notable for the Premier's persistent efforts to gain better financial terms from Ottawa and to challenge the CPR's monopoly over railway development. A most striking incident in this pattern of federal hamstringing of the province was the chilling blackmail of Norquay by Prime Minister John A. Macdonald, who used federal financial aid as his bait. Norquay, a leader of the English-speaking Métis community, appreciated the ruthless game of federal-provincial relations but he lacked the power to play against an unscrupulous foe. Norquay became Premier by balancing the many legislative factions, which reflected the social and ethnic divisions of the province. By the end of his regime, the outlines of a party system had emerged. Norquay's fleeting successor,

David Harrison, was a former Ontario Conservative who tried to manipulate his way into the premiership using his Ontario party ties, but he failed and left public life.

The political culture in this first era of provincehood reflected a society not just divided but balanced between ethno-cultural and religious groups. By the end of the 1880s, however, the balance was shifting decisively in one direction. The ascendant Protestant and British-Canadian population became a strong majority and asserted its dominance in public life. In this period, the province's economy began a 50-year period of robust growth, based upon the ascendance of agricultural settlement and the first phase of railway building. The little province built around Red River in 1870 became a more formidable geographical entity through boundary expansion farther into the prairies and northward in 1881, negotiated by Norquay, and the aggressive but failed pursuit of further expansion eastward into Lake of Woods where Manitoba expansionism ran into the forces of expansionist Ontario. Agricultural settlement was primarily undertaken by migrants from Ontario but it was leavened by the arrival of the first colonies of Mennonites and Icelanders. The burgeoning wheat economy supported the growth of Winnipeg from a small administrative town to a booming commercial city. The cultural expression of the agrarian way can be read in Manitoba's first generation of popular novelists. Both Ralph Connor and Nellie McClung, who were national as well as provincial figures, looked back on this period of settlement as a triumph of Anglo-Protestantism.

The backgrounds of political leaders in this non-partisan era were varied. Girard was a skilled lawyer as were Archibald and Morris, although Girard was trained in Quebec. The ministerial dupes of Archibald and Morris—Boyd and Clarke—were respectively a business promoter and a rackety lawyer. Davis was more typical of the frontier-era business speculator, later working on both sides of the international border. Although he had trained as a teacher, he made money in trade and real estate. Norquay was a successful teacher-farmer-businessman and singular in the 19th century for being a native Manitoban. Harrison was just as unsteady of occupation as Davis, abandoning his medical practice in Ontario for farming and banking, which he pursued in Manitoba and later in British Columbia.

The Two-Party System

Between the late 1880s and the early 1920s the two-party system was transplanted from old Ontario and four Premiers held office: Liberal Thomas Greenway, Conservatives Hugh John Macdonald and Rodmond Roblin, and finally Liberal T.C. (Toby) Norris.

The triumph of the party system was led by two political opportunists, Thomas Greenway, a former Conservative who became the first Liberal Premier in 1888, and Rodmond Roblin, a former Liberal who orchestrated the Conservative triumph headed by Hugh John Macdonald in 1900. Greenway's Liberals captured the energies of the majority Protestant Ontario farmers, and acted swiftly and ruthlessly to remake the party and legislative system. If Greenway was effectively subordinate to others, in particular the Machiavellian Clifford Sifton, his administration enacted what W.L. Morton described as the "triumph of Ontario democracy." Two enactments were politically brutal. The Greenway government (or the Greenway-Sifton regime as it was sometimes called) annulled

French as an official language in the public political and legal system, although it had been entrenched in the Manitoba Act. It also cancelled "separate" publicly funded Catholic and Protestant schools in the province, although that right also had been entrenched in the British North America [Constitution] Act of 1867 and the Manitoba Act of 1870. By this second action, the Greenway government created national convulsions. These acts worsened Catholic-Protestant conflict in a time of sectarian conflict, defied federal authority in ways that reshaped the federation, and helped to defeat a weakened national Conservative government. In addition, the Greenway-Sifton axis challenged Ottawa's economic development strategies in the courts and further established Manitoba as the main defender of provincial rights. Greenway carried on Norquay's campaign to achieve fiscal and constitutional recognition from federal governments that intended to maintain the Prairies as quasi-colonies of Ottawa.

Greenway's successors, Hugh John Macdonald and Rodmond Roblin, carried on the campaign to strengthen the authority of the province. Macdonald was a strange provincial force, serving both as Roblin's successor as Conservative leader and predecessor as Conservative Premier, a case that exposes the overt manipulation of political leadership. The Roblin administration not only rewarded its supporters through government contracts and public works but also built a powerful provincial institution in the Manitoba Telephone System as a response to the unpopular monopoly of the private Bell Telephone Company. It presided over the fulfillment of the province's bellicose protests against the CPR with the construction of two new national railways, the Canadian Northern and the Grand Trunk Pacific. Finally, Roblin's administration was rewarded for Manitoba's persistent demands to expand by the 1912 grant of boundary extension northward to Hudson Bay and the 60th parallel. Manitoba acquired its own economic hinterland.

The burgeoning farmers' protest against the national railway transportation system and the international grain trade swept the prairies and shook Manitoba politics during the First World War. In 1915 Manitoba's Liberals, under the lead of the farmer-auctioneer, Toby Norris, rode this agrarian wave to power. In the next seven years, the Norris Liberals enacted a series of remarkable legislative changes that made the province a model of reform. But reform meant not only such extensions of the liberal state as votes for women and a host of social protections such as Mothers' Allowances. It also included the final annulment of the constitutional rights of francophones, and the incidental recognition of minority languages, with the implementation of an English-only policy in the Manitoba school system, justified by the arrival of thousands of European immigrants. The legacy of constitutional illegality would strike back in the 1980s.

Winnipeg's urban society was increasingly contentious and divided as industrial labour, led by railway shop-craft and running-trades unionists, pursued both economic and political goals against obdurate and reactionary business owners and managers. All of this culminated in the General Strike of 1919. Since urban and federal politicians took the lead in confronting and breaking the radicalism of the strike, it appears to have had a surprisingly limited direct effect on the Norris government, but the battles certainly contributed to widespread dissatisfaction with the two-party system and its abolition in the 1920s.

Political life during this period reflected the aggressive cultural goals of the Protestant and British-Canadian majority in the province. The annulment of Roman Catholic educational rights and French language rights, despite their legal entrenchment, were the most obvious signs of British-Canadian hegemony. European immigration may have been a welcome aspect of national and provincial economic goals, but it also contributed to the anxiety of the dominant business and professional groups in the moment of their ascendancy. The outburst of labour radicalism and the persistent pressures and quiet successes of the women's suffrage movement only underscored the divisions that remained in Manitoba. The two-party system was increasingly unable to contain the divisions thus revealed.

The province's economy throughout this period continued to rely on its agricultural base, which was increasingly populated by Central and Eastern European settlers, and the explosive urban growth of Winnipeg, which became a transportation and industrial hub for Canada. Along with its emergence as the West's commercial metropolis, Winnipeg also became a multi-ethnic city and was shaped by socio-economic divisions within (the North End/South Side divide overshadowed the old St. Boniface/Winnipeg division) and the contrast between the industrial-commercial city and the agrarian countryside and towns. Cultural reflections of the new tensions may be found in the realist genre of Manitoba literature that emerged by the 1910s and 1920s. Among a growing list of popular writers, Frederick P. Grove and Martha Ostenso portrayed the hard slogging of farm life and the tensions within agrarian communities, while Douglas Durkin characterized the labour conflict in Winnipeg. The age of the agrarian idyll and evangelical fervour had begun to pass.

The political leaders of this era were drawn from the British-Canadian agrarian majority and all four Premiers were Ontario-born and raised. Greenway, Roblin, and Norris were all strongly linked to the farming community, although only Greenway tried to make his chief living from farming. Macdonald, an Ontario-trained corporation lawyer, was the exception and his clients included the CPR. Greenway's chief political allies, notably Clifford Sifton and Joseph Martin, were also lawyer-politicians.

The Quasi-Party System

Manitoba's populace and its political culture remained predominantly rural after the First World War. The province was mesmerized by the progressive and agrarian movements, as well as their faith in non-partisanship, meaning group, co-operative, and coalition government. It was not that parties and ideology did not exist but they were seriously attenuated, and the most active and successful politicians tried to mute if not destroy traditional partisan lines. During more than three decades, the province had just three premiers, John Bracken, Stuart Garson, and Douglas Campbell.

The strength of Progressivism in Manitoba politics was evident in the selection of John Bracken as leader of the United Farmers and Premier in 1922. Bracken held office under a variety of political and non-partisan labels for 20 years. His successor was Stuart Garson, who held office from 1943 to 1948, and for the most part, continued the non-partisan model during the wartime and early postwar reconstruction period. This model enjoyed amazing longevity, including the third and last Progressive, Douglas Campbell, who held office from 1948 until his electoral defeat in 1958.

Asked to assume the premiership by the executive of the avowedly non-partisan United Farmers of Manitoba, John Bracken brought formidable administrative acumen and considerable agricultural knowledge to provincial politics. Supported by the rural majority and the economic dominance of agriculture and related industries, and abetted by a majority wary of Winnipeg's spectacular growth and confrontational ethos, Bracken consolidated the farmers' central role in provincial politics. While other parties barely survived (Conservatives), were subsumed within the Progressive movement (Liberals), or grew from the scattered seed of social democracy (CCF), the predominant cast of provincial politics from the early 1920s to the late 1950s was distinct from the party system that existed at the federal level and in central and eastern Canada. Bracken's governments during the 1920s concentrated on agriculture, transportation, and hydro-electric development while trying to pursue the common Prairie political goal of gaining control of natural resources held by Ottawa. It also prepared the way—with Ottawa's agreement—for Manitoba's development of its northern hinterland without much concern for the local, predominantly Aboriginal, inhabitants' concerns. The crushing economic crisis of the 1930s reduced the province to fiscal desperation and the programs of government were reduced dramatically, as were public expectations, for two decades.

Bracken's lengthy hold on office relied partly on an electoral system (implemented in 1920 and surviving until 1958) that blocked Winnipeg's representation in the provincial legislature, through the systematic under-representation of the city and the use of one 10-member riding (expanded in 1949 into three four-member ridings) elected by the single-transferable ballot. This systematic means of limiting Winnipeg's influence was a remarkable case of containing the urban impact on political life. As of 1950, Winnipeg comprised nearly half of the province's population, but only one-fifth of the legislative seats.

Bracken's tactical success was based upon drawing almost all conceivable groups into various forms of coalition, citing fiscal crisis as the pretext for sustaining the non-partisan style. Although the Manitoba government became a vigorous proponent of the reform of federalism during the 1930s, through a more equitable division of revenues and recognition of provincial powers, Bracken himself jumped to federal politics in 1942, astonishingly as leader of the Conservatives (renamed the Progressive Conservatives at his insistence).

Stuart Garson succeeded Bracken and drew on his own experience as provincial treasurer and his legal skills to try to take advantage of the economic recovery that the wartime and post-war periods created. But his efforts at moderate reform of social policy and community redevelopment, desperately needed in many rural areas, met with strong resistance. Natural resource exploration in Manitoba's north was pursued during these years, but development was slow to occur. Ottawa was not prepared to engage in structural reform of the federal system in ways that would have strengthened provincial government resources. Garson succumbed to the lure of federal politics and became a major figure in the post-war St.

Laurent governments. He left the province in the cautious hands of Douglas Campbell, one of the original Progressives. Campbell was an advocate and practitioner of a style of limited government almost unknown elsewhere in Canada by the 1950s. Apart from fiscal probity, the one enthusiasm of the Campbell era was rural electrification, which unleashed hydrological planning and projects by Manitoba Hydro that would lead to vast changes to the north in subsequent decades.

During the 1950s, Manitoba's rural and agrarian political order was at last overwhelmed by the growth of Winnipeg and its concerns (the 1950 Red River Flood and its aftermath symbolized this new focus), overshadowed by the prospects for development of northern natural resources, and overtaken by swelling federal transfers directed at the provinces. The province became increasingly dominated economically by Winnipeg, which enjoyed its own reinvigoration during and after World War II despite being held down by the electoral system. The economy emerged with its characteristic "balance" between agriculture, industry, transportation and, at long last, northern resource development. Stable and steady economic performance rather than explosive growth was the hallmark of the province by the 1950s. The cultural changes in the province can be read in a literature that not only dared to mock its old rural ways in the satirical verse of Paul Hiebert but also began to reflect on the social costs of immigration and the limits of assimilation. The novels of writers like John Marlyn, Adele Wiseman, and Rudy Wiebe reflected in various ways how the mid-century consensus did not readily accommodate ethnic, religious, or gender diversity or even respect assimilation.

The three leaders of the non-partisan era were a professional agronomist, a lawyer, and a farmer. All three had rural/small town roots, all were Protestants in religion, and all were British in background. Bracken was oriented primarily by his career as an agriculture professor and president of the Manitoba Agricultural College. Garson started out as a small-town lawyer in Ashern and remained so while representing a rural riding until well into his political career, while Campbell taught school for a time but farmed and maintained his residence at Flee Island throughout his extraordinary legislative career, which lasted for 47 years.

The Third Party System: Multi-Partyism

Manitoba re-entered the world of conventional party politics in 1958 with Duff Roblin's successful rebuilding of the Progressive Conservative party and his election as Premier. Roblin was followed by the rise and swift decline of Walter Weir. In 1971 Manitoba joined the other western provinces in electing a new and interventionist government led by Edward Schreyer. This was followed by Sterling Lyon's single term as premier from 1977 to 1981. Howard Pawley's career followed but came to a surprising end in 1988. The NDP era was replaced by the Progressive Conservative leadership and governments of Gary Filmon between 1988 and 1999. The NDP returned to power for its most successful series of governments under Gary Doer, Premier from 1999 until his resignation in 2009.

Duff Roblin's skills in remaking the Manitoba Conservatives as a party that crossed the rural-urban divide placed him in position to govern from strength for a decade. His governments advanced economic development projects and Manitoba caught up with such "have" provinces as British Columbia, Alberta, and Ontario during the 1960s, almost as dramatically as Quebec in its Quiet Revolution. In this period, Manitoba expanded social institutions, including post-secondary education, and gingerly embraced national welfare institutions. Roblin's most notable public works project was the Winnipeg Floodway, implemented amidst great controversy and with considerable federal funding. The Roblin government oversaw major northern resource development including the mining and smelting operations at Thompson, further plans for northern hydro-electric and water management, and the construction of a forestry complex at The Pas, the latter of which nearly collapsed amidst financial irregularities.

When Walter Weir attempted to move the province back towards a more conservative and ruralist approach to government, he was unceremoniously defeated and the social democratic Ed Schreyer gained power in 1969. The governments he led were in the vanguard of confident interventionist regimes that came to the fore throughout western Canada during the 1970s. The Schreyer administrations worked hard to practice activist government in both economic and social policy areas, but the fiscal tide was beginning to turn as the long post-war boom began to fade. Schreyer nonetheless encouraged social policy innovation and Manitoba was for a time among the leading provinces in policy development, both economic and social, furthering a catch-up in governmental capacity begun by Roblin.[10] For his efforts, however, Schreyer was defeated in 1977.

Sterling Lyon represented a more effective conservative force than Weir, and he mobilized the ingrained conservatism of both the rural southwest and a segment of Winnipeg. His rhetorical initiatives may have been more powerful than his policy developments, but Lyon was consigned to the Opposition benches after one term. His opposition to Pierre Trudeau's federal constitutional initiatives of 1981 certainly had political traction in Manitoba, shown by the province's prickly reaction to Ottawa in many areas, but it was not enough to retain power or prevent reform.

Howard Pawley's government was a triumph of party rebuilding and a doggedly social democratic regime. He supported the positive state even in the face of certain weaknesses in public institutions and gave the opposition an ample target as the national economy softened throughout the early and mid-1980s. From his Opposition bench vantage point, Lyon vociferously challenged the Pawley administration and seemed delighted to condemn the government for its somewhat inept but well-meaning efforts to right the century-long blight on French-language and Roman Catholic educational services. The Pawley government's response to court decisions that condemned the province's annulment of French as an official language was fanned into a fire of popular resentment that was fed not only by criticism of government policy but also anti-French and anti-Catholic bigotry. Manitoba experienced a period of rampant sectarian conflict that put the lie to claims about the consensual basis of public life in the province. Pawley paid the price with defeat, albeit over economic policy, in 1988.

Arriving in office with a minority government that faced a stronger Liberal than NDP challenge, Gary Filmon was able to rebuild the Progressive Conservative party as well as to isolate its reactionary elements. Filmon inaugurated an 11-year regime by emphasizing a balanced and even nuanced approach to social and economic policy. Unlike such predecessors as Roblin and Schreyer, who narrowly won a first election but then strengthened their hold on office, Filmon was never able to build strong representation from all areas (agricultural south, Winnipeg, and natural resource north) of the province. But he did survive and he was able to corner the Liberals, who again faded provincially during the 1990s. The three-party system was never fully restored.

Filmon was able to use court decisions to enforce the reestablishment of francophone language and educational rights without appearing to be begrudging or pandering to any groups. His talent for balancing interests and calming passions was demonstrated most forcefully in his management of constitutional issues, notably the Meech Lake Accord. The government did less well managing the solutions to the isolation and mistreatment of Manitoba's Aboriginal peoples that was revealed courtesy of the Aboriginal Justice Inquiry inaugurated in its last days by the Pawley government. On economic matters, Filmon did lead Manitoba through the worst slump since the Great Depression without embracing the rhetoric of contemporary neo-conservatism, unless balanced-budget legislation is seen in that light. Although his governments did cut services, they did not exult in the cuts or threaten to remake the medical care or social welfare system. Filmon's one radical move was the privatization of Manitoba Telephones. His constant preaching and practice of budgetary caution—the balanced budget approach—was a success and adopted by his successor.

Under Gary Doer's patient and lengthy tenure in Opposition, the NDP not only took policy seriously but also the preparations for governing. When Doer won in 1999, he headed a government that took an incremental approach to policy. It used the rhetoric of the new social democracy of the 1990s but it also had the patience to develop policy initiatives. Doer's NDP was able to preside over the expansion of social policy spending in areas like medicare and welfare while taking advantage of more generous federal contributions. These expansions, however, were executed while ensuring the careful management that Manitobans had come to expect from their governments. The Doer government was successful in addressing Aboriginal matters and appeared to take seriously such environmental matters as water quality and farmland preservation. Even eternally-dissatisfied Winnipeg appeared to be addressing—but not obviously resolving—its problems of urban transportation, housing quality, and urban crime in concert with the province. The comparative weakness of the post-Filmon Conservatives in opposition throughout the Doer decade was a remarkable contrast to Doer's own record in Opposition. Doer left the premiership with a strong legacy and the province as a cohesive political entity.

Throughout the most recent period, Manitoba has remained a place of balanced and stable economic output while also being constrained by it. No sector—agriculture, resources, manufacturing, or transportation—ever really took off. At times the province experienced the frustrations of stagnation (agriculture) and the loss of capacity (transportation). Despite a strong core of resource industries and agricultural capacity, the province did not attract the large-scale immigration or even the sense of potential that other western provinces experienced. Yet, the greater diversity and the underlying prosperity found their expression in a robust cultural life. This vigour is found in such developments as the maturation of public institutions like the Winnipeg Folk Festival and the Royal Winnipeg Ballet, as well as the enormous success of the most recent generation of writers, artists, and film makers. The struggles of the old Protestant middle class as portrayed by Margaret Laurence, the clever urban social novels of Carol Shields, and the rueful humour in the work of Miriam Toews each present insights into a complicated Manitoba bereft of tidy social, cultural, and political resolutions.

Leadership from the Premier's office was more diverse than in the previous eras, at least in ethno-cultural terms, but gender diversity has yet to arrive in Manitoba. Although Roblin was from an established old-line family, he was in business rather than a profession. Weir also was a businessman, but of the small-town variety. Schreyer was a fledgling university teacher, but entered public life while still in his 20s and made politics his profession. He was notable for bringing the voices of multi-cultural Manitoba and the post-war generation to the forefront. His successors, Lyon and Pawley, were lawyers and, despite their differences in temperament and style, both brought an adversarial approach to public life as shown by the divisive politics of the 1980s. They were also members of the traditional socio-cultural majority Protestant culture that was being swept away by the new multi-cultural Canada. This new Canada was reflected in their successors, neither of whom was Anglo-Protestant in background. Gary Filmon, a North Ender, was educated as an engineer, but became a city businessman, while Doer was a public servant and labour leader. Both men spent a larger portion of their careers as politicians rather than their original lines of work.

Some Tentative Conclusions

The lives of the Premiers certainly reveal a basic and remarkable contentiousness to Manitoba politics and a surprising degree of political innovation, both belying contemporary interpretations of the province as moderate and bland, unlike the other Prairie Provinces. This characteristic contentiousness may wax and wane, but it certainly lies deeper than mere partisan labels as they have developed over time, or the efforts to avoid them in the non-partisan era. These divisions are found in sometimes-ferocious policy debates that punctuate the past 140 years. They emerge almost every time a government takes a strong position on critical issues, including cultural rights in areas like language and schooling or economic development ranging from transportation and trade to natural resources. Contention has also been expressed in the persistent divisions between social and economic groups, between the geographical-economic regions, and between Winnipeg and the rest of the province. These divisions are visible in the pattern of political support (between the rural south and the resource north, and Winnipeg itself divided between north, south, and suburbs).

The political system both reflects and also mediates the divisions that have been characteristic of Manitoba society throughout its history. The periods of party government have revealed the many ways in which the geographical-economic and the socio-cultural divisions in the province have found expression in provincial political life. But the periods of non-partisan government reflected the efforts of people in government and public institutions to contain these divisions in one way or another.

Manitoba's political leaders have either recognized or soon learned that decisive policies lead to explosive debates, whether within the province or throughout the country. Whether it has been challenges to national economic policy, reforms to the constitution and federalism, or major economic development projects, Manitoba's uniqueness in part consists in its peculiar resistance to the attempts by political leaders to rally and reshape the province, whether for or against Ottawa, or on behalf of a major economic or social development program. When major policy innovations are implemented, as the essays show, they come with a price in political conflict and often electoral defeat.

Provincial institutions have undoubtedly matured, especially since the 1960s, and political scientists, like historians, have discerned an increasing distinctiveness in Manitoba's political institutions and experience compared to the other Prairie Provinces. The increasing divergence of the Prairie Provinces, politically, economically, and socially, has been noted in the other two books in this series. In a sense, they all confirm an argument first made some years ago by Roger Gibbins about the contemporary shift from regionalism to provincialism. This view has support from such Prairie historians as G.A. Friesen and lucid theorization by David E. Smith in the case of Saskatchewan.[11] Whether there has been growing cohesiveness to Manitoba society, as historians often claim to discern, remains to be explored fully. Even the political skills and political prestige of the recent leaders—Filmon and Doer—did not mean that they could crusade on behalf of the province or lead the provinces in such matters as the fiscal or constitutional direction of the country.

The essays indicate how distinctive Manitoba has become in its political practices. There seems little doubt that, as Manitoba has become a more distinctive political unit, owing less and less to its identity as and identification with the other Prairie Provinces, it has also cultivated its own style of public life. It owes more to a consensual approach based on legislative hearings and public inquiries than virtually any jurisdiction in Canada. It also retains some features of the old "bias" of Prairie politics, above all an emphasis on politics as administration, that W.L. Morton identified some decades ago, and the tradition of dissent within the federal system that still prevails, as David E. Smith has observed.[12] In sum, one certain conclusion we can draw is that conflict rather than consensus, passion rather than blandness, and battles based upon both principle and venality, lie at the centre of Manitoba public life and have done so for the past 140 years.

Notes

Our thanks to James Muir and Jared Wesley for their thoughtful and critical readings of previous drafts.

1. Nelson Wiseman, *In Search of Canadian Political Culture* (Vancouver: UBC Press, 2007), Rand Dyck, *Provincial Politics in Canada: Towards the Turn of the Century* (Scarborough: Prentice-Hall Canada, 1996). A strong argument about Manitoba's relative moderate reformism is found in David Laycock's stimulating *Populism and Democratic Thought in the Canadian Prairies, 1910–1945* (Toronto: University of Toronto Press, 1990). A superb argument on this theme has been made by Jared Wesley, "Political Culture in Manitoba" forthcoming in *Manitoba Politics, Government and Policy in the 21st Century*, edited by Paul Thomas and Curtis Brown (Winnipeg: University of Manitoba Press, 2010). Dr. Wesley was good enough to allow us to read this chapter, which makes a strong counter-argument to ours. Forty years ago the standard view that Manitoba was riven by political conflict was argued by Tom Peterson in a series of scholarly and general articles. See, for example, "Manitoba: Ethnic and Class Politics in Manitoba," in *Canadian Provincial Politics*, edited by Martin Robin (Scarborough: Prentice-Hall Canada, 1972), 69–115.

2. W.L. Morton, *Manitoba: A History*, 2nd ed. (Toronto: University of Toronto Press, 1967). A similar emphasis is found in G.A. Friesen, *The Canadian Prairies* (Toronto: University of Toronto Press, 1984).

3. In addition to Laycock, *Populism and Democratic Thought*, cited above, see John Kendle, *John Bracken: A Political Biography* (Toronto: University of Toronto Press, 199), Mary Kinnear, *In Subordination: Professional Women in Manitoba 1870–1970* (Montreal: McGill-Queen's University Press, 1995) and *Margaret McWilliams: An Interwar Feminist* (Montreal: McGill-Queen's University Press, 1991), James A. McAllister, *The Government of Edward Schreyer: Democratic Socialism in Manitoba* (Montreal: McGill-Queen's University Press, 1984), and Jim Mochoruk, *Formidable Heritage: Manitoba's North and the Cost of Development, 1870–1930* (Winnipeg: University of Manitoba Press, 2004).

4. D.N. Sprague, *Canada and the Metis, 1869–1885* (Waterloo: Wilfrid Laurier University Press, 1988), Lovell Clark (ed.), *The Manitoba School Question: Majority Rule or Minority Rights* (Toronto: Copp Clark, 1968), Frances Russell, *The Canadian Crucible: Manitoba's Role in Canada's Great Divide* (Winnipeg: Heartland Associates, 2003), Raymond Hebert, *Manitoba's French-Language Crisis: A Cautionary Tale* (Toronto: University of Toronto Press, 2004).

5. Full citations to relevant works would be very extensive. Important examples are, in addition to works cited in the previous notes, Frits Pannekoek, *A Snug Little Flock: The Social Origins of the Riel Resistance* (Winnipeg: Watson & Dwyer, 1991), A. R. McCormack, *Reformers, Rebels, and Revolutionaries: The Western Canadian Radical Movement, 1899–1919* (Toronto: University of Toronto Press, 1977). A work that emphasizes the depths of social cohesion at least in Winnipeg is Jim Blanchard, *Winnipeg 1912* (Winnipeg: University of Manitoba Press, 2005).

6. Paula Baker, "The Midlife Crisis of the New Political History," *Journal of American History* 86, no. 1 (June 1999): 158–66, Ronald P. Formisano, "The Concept of Political Culture," *Journal of Interdisciplinary History* 30, no. 3 (Winter 2001): 393–426, Susan Pedersen, "What is Political History Now?" in David Cannadine (ed.), *What is History Now?* (New York: Palgrave Macmillan, 2002), Julian Zelizer, "Political History and Political Science: Together Again?," *Journal of Policy History* 16 (2004): 126–36.

7. The most recent and very persuasive explanation is in Graham White's book in the "Democratic Audit" series, *Cabinets and First Ministers* (Vancouver: UBC Press, 2005), Chapter 3, "The First Minister as Autocrat?". See also Christopher Dunn, "Premiers and Cabinets," pp. 165–204 in Christopher Dunn (ed.), *Provinces* (Peterborough: Broadview, 1996), and finally the not-unbiased account by Howard Pawley, "Governing Manitoba: Reflections of a Premier," pp. 118–33 in Maureen Mancuso et al. (eds.), *Leaders and Leadership in Canada* (Toronto: Oxford, 1994).

8. The most general account of this analytical approach for Canada is found in R. Kenneth Carty, William Cross and Lisa Young, *Rebuilding Canadian Party Politics* (Vancouver: UBC Press, 2000). The analysis has been adapted to Manitoba in Christopher Adams's important book, *Politics in Manitoba: Parties, Leaders and Voters* (Winnipeg: University of Manitoba Press, 2008). We have adapted the concept and used it far more descriptively than have the political scientists.

9. M.S. Donnelly, *The Government of Manitoba* (Toronto: University of Toronto Press, 1963), 14–25, John T. Saywell, *The Office of Lieutenant-Governor: A Study in Canadian Government and Politics* (Toronto: University of Toronto Press, 1957), 60–79.

10. An important overview of this process in Manitoba is in Christopher Dunn, *The Institutionalized Cabinet: Governing the Western Provinces* (Montreal: McGill-Queen's University Press, 1995) 107–99.

11. See Bradford J. Rennie (ed.), *Alberta Premiers of the Twentieth Century* (Regina: Canadian Plains Research Center, 2004) and Gordon L. Barnhart (ed.), *Saskatchewan Premiers of the Twentieth Century* (Regina: Canadian Plains Research Center, 2004). On Prairie political regionalism, see Roger Gibbins, *Prairie Politics and Society: Regionalism in Decline* (Toronto: Butterworths, 1982), G.A. Friesen, *The West: Regional Ambitions, National Debates, Global Age* (Toronto: Penguin, 1999), and David E. Smith, "Path Dependency and Saskatchewan Politics" in Gregory P. Marchildon (ed.), *The Heavy Hand of History: Interpreting Saskatchewan's Past* (Regina: Canadian Plains Research Center, 2005), pp. 31–50.

12. W.L. Morton, "The Bias of Prairie Politics," pp. 57–66 in *Proceedings and Transactions of the Royal Society of Canada*, Series III, Vol. 49, and reprinted many times. David E. Smith, "The Invention of Politics in the Canadian West," *Zeitschrift fur Kanada-Studien* 22, nos. 1–2 (2002): 74–84.

The Emergence of the Premiership

1870–1874

DAVID BURLEY

The Emergence of the Premiership, 1870–74

Manitoba became a province in 1870, but it did not have a Premier until 1874. In early July of that year, Manitoba's second Lieutenant-Governor, Alexander Morris, invited Marc-Amable Girard to form a ministry that would hold the confidence of the province's first legislature, which had been elected three and a half years earlier. Morris explained his action:

> In forming the Government I did so through the intervention of a premier thus introducing responsible Government in its modern type into the Province. The previous ministry was selected personally by my predecessor and none of its members were recognized as first minister.[1]

With Morris's act, the people of Manitoba finally possessed in parliamentary practice the constitutional principles of self-government associated with provincial status that had been promised under the Manitoba Act of 1870.[2]

Morris's predecessor as Lieutenant-Governor, Adams G. Archibald, had delayed responsible government because he anticipated that the supporters of Louis Riel might command a majority in the first legislature. While Archibald possessed considerable sympathy for the Métis, he worried that a government headed by Riel, or one loyal to him, would enrage the growing population of migrants from Ontario, which loudly demanded the prosecution of those responsible for the execution of Thomas Scott.[3] The loyalty of the Métis also troubled Archibald, and he noted the irony of provincial status:

> Half our people had been in rebellion. In the eyes of the law they were guilty of High treason, yet Parliament chose not only to give these people the elective franchise but to confer Responsible Government on the country.
> … I could hardly hope to engage any man who should have to proclaim it as his duty to hang men whose votes had raised him to office.[4]

The solution, he believed, was an amnesty for those who had resisted the transfer of the North-West to the Dominion, although Ontario's reaction made its timing highly sensitive.

As a closer colleague of Prime Minister John A. Macdonald, Morris knew that Archibald's recommendation was unacceptable. It might appease the French Catholic communities in Manitoba and Quebec, but Ontario and Orange Manitoba voters would surely punish any party that proposed it.[5] Instead, he concluded, responsible government would offer a local solution to the difficult question by making the provincial government responsible for the prosecution of those charged with Scott's murder, among other matters, and would remove some of the political pressure from the Dominion government.

Within the uncertainty of amnesty, Manitoba's Lieutenant-Governors had to introduce the first structures of government and to initiate the administration of governance in ways that would hold a basic, if qualified and tense, coalition of popular support. They also needed to be wary of the personal ambitions of local politicians, especially those claiming leadership of the French and Catholic community, Louis Riel, Henry Joseph Clarke, and

Joseph Royal. Politicians, community leaders, and the general public paid careful attention to the implications of the agenda of the first legislature, trying to discern the model for new provincial institutions and resenting measures that appeared to incline one way or the other. Was it Quebec or Ontario that should provide precedents for schools, municipal institutions, and real property law? Among the most difficult challenges confronted by the first legislature was the establishment of a system of transferable individual property rights. Such property law was essential to integrate the new province into an expanding national capitalist system. However, the Manitoba Act, by defining communal property rights for the Métis, created obstacles to a private market within which land was just another commodity to be transferred by pieces of paper. The allocation and administration of Métis land and land rights were responsibilities of the Dominion government and the Lieutenant-Governor, but the provincial legislature offered a forum in which those who viewed Métis lands as a homeland or an obstacle could voice their frustrations. Members of the legislature were limited, however, in the extent of the provincial protection that they could pledge since fiduciary responsibility remained with the Dominion government.

As the demographic balance of English and French shifted more and more in favour of the former with every year of migration, the mix of models that politicians claimed to seek and see in the legislative record became less and less acceptable to the growing English majority, especially concerning education. Where, they asked, was representation by population? The revision of electoral boundaries, acknowledging as it did that English and French no longer stood in political equality, provoked the final issue requiring a local solution and precipitated Morris's call on Girard to form a government.

Electoral Politics, Contending Factions, and Governing Coalitions

For more than three years, a coalition of uneasy factions assembled by Lieutenant-Governor Archibald, and continued by Lieutenant-Governor Morris, exercised government. Archibald's situation was an unenviable one, which he had accepted with some reluctance.

Adams G. Archibald was born in 1814 in Truro, Nova Scotia, the second son of Samuel and Elizabeth Archibald. Having practiced law for several years, Archibald embarked upon a political career, as his biographer has observed, "to promote his legal work." After holding several local appointments, he successfully sought election in 1851 to the Nova Scotia Assembly where he sat as a Liberal until Confederation. The only Liberal member to support Confederation, he was rewarded with a cabinet position as Secretary of State for the Provinces in 1867. Defeated in the anti-confederate tide that swept across his province in the first Dominion election, Archibald resigned his cabinet seat, although he did return to Ottawa after winning a by-election in 1869.[6] As an advocate of Confederation, his service to the government gave him a strong claim for some preferment, but no room remained in the cabinet. George Brown, no less, thought him a possibility for Lieutenant-Governor of Ontario.[7] Instead, George-Étienne Cartier, who was acting Prime Minister during Macdonald's serious illness in the summer of 1870, offered him the post of Manitoba's first Lieutenant-Governor.

Cartier had been impressed with his Commons speech on May 7, 1870 in support of the Manitoba Act.[8] Archibald declared, "I consider it sound policy to deal in a liberal spirit with the troubles we have so as to efface them at once and forever."[9] However, for him, clemency was an expedient to regain momentum for development, not the foundation for a binational North-West.[10] As he later explained to Macdonald, "The English element is inevitably destined to prevail in Manitoba. Immigration will fill it with English-speaking people; but for this, peace and good order are to be the first requisites."[11]

On June 24 the Legislative Assembly of Assiniboia cheered Archibald's appointment and Louis Riel, who presided over the session, observed, "There is great reason for congratulation in the selection of the Lieutenant-Governor."[12] Privately, Riel wrote to A.G.B. Bannatyne, "We will bring in Red River a responsible government."[13] Of course, he expected that his supporters would control the first legislature, with himself as the head of that government.[14] An old friend from the Collège de Montréal, Joseph Dubuc, who had come west in June 1870 at Riel's urging, summed up the hopes of Riel's supporters: "On a au moins en notre faveur le Gouverneur qui, il n'y a pas en douter, est parfaitement bien disposé."[15]

Joseph Howe, Secretary of State for the Provinces, directed Archibald to provide responsible government:

> In the Government of Manitoba you will be guided by the Constitutional principles and precedents which obtain in the older Provinces... . In dealing with the Province of Manitoba you will give your advisers the full exercise of the powers, which in the older Provinces have been so widely claimed and freely exercised, but you will be expected to maintain a position of dignified impartiality and to guard with independence the general interests of the Dominion and the just authority of the Crown.[16]

Archibald, however, disagreed with Howe and believed responsible government was impossible without amnesty:

> Was there ever before a responsible Ministry resting on a House, of whose constituents more than half were liable to be hanged or sent to penitentiary? ... You allow the electors to choose the members, and to make and unmake Ministries, but electors and members are to exercise their functions with ropes around their necks. To hang all, or to hang a few to whom the rest are blindly devoted, is much the same thing.... . You can hardly hope to carry on responsible Government by inflicting death penalties on the leaders of a majority of the electors.[17]

Instead, Archibald diplomatically attempted to assemble a government that would enjoy popular confidence, even if it were not strictly speaking responsible to the legislature. His challenge was to balance the different and contending ethnic and religious segments of Manitoba society, all the time being wary of the personal ambitions of politicians claiming leadership of one faction or another.

Ambitious, prone to violence, and unforgiving was the so-called "Canadian" or "loyalist" party of Ontarians led by John C. Schultz.[18] E.H.G.G. Hay, who voiced their concerns in the first provincial legislature, declared, "We have no union in this country. I can never unite with people who have been our enemies."[19] The vengeance that they sought for their treatment at the hands of Riel's Provisional Government, and especially for the execution of Thomas Scott, was expressed in their refusal to consider amnesty, in violent attacks against Riel's supporters, and in attempts to have warrants issued for Riel and others accused of Scott's murder.[20] Archibald observed to Macdonald, "There is a frightful spirit of bigotry among a small but noisy section of our people ... who really talk and seem to feel as if the French half-breeds should be wiped off the face of the globe."[21]

For the first few years after Confederation, as they confronted the growing and aggressive "Canadian" element, those of mixed ancestry, whether English or French, collaborated politically—just as they had under Riel's earlier leadership—because of common concerns over the security of their land and the future of coming generations. They might have had different priorities and favoured different tactics, but both mixed-ancestry communities knew that they had only a brief time to secure their interests before they would be outnumbered by new settlers.[22] Of greater immediacy to the French Métis was the amnesty issue. Even as "loyalist" insults and violence angered them, they restrained themselves from retaliation and deferred, not always in good humour, to the leadership of Archbishop Taché and the talented and ambitious Quebec lawyers whom the cleric and Cartier had persuaded to come west.[23]

In this context of anger and anxiety, Archibald sought political solutions and hesitated to fully establish order in law. Knowing that he could not restrain the "loyalists," he responded ineffectually to their violence against the Métis.[24] Later Archibald temporized by explaining that in the first years little could be done to enforce laws because the province had not passed legislation to create a functioning judicial system.[25] Until then no authority existed to convene a Grand Jury to issue indictments or a Petit Jury to try offences:

> From the time, therefore, when the Governor arrived, till the third day of
> April [1871] when this law passed, our tribunals had no power to punish.
> Offenders, to be sure, might be arrested; but they must have remained
> in prison or let loose again on the community without conviction or
> punishment.[26]

As well, knowing that the warrants obtained prior to his arrival for the arrest of Louis Riel, Ambroise Lepine, and W.B. O'Donoghue for the murder of Thomas Scott might, if ever served, inflame the French Métis to armed rebellion, Archibald persuaded magistrates not to issue further warrants.[27] Whether this calmed tensions, as he thought, or encouraged the "loyalists" to exact their own justice is debatable. The effect, however, was to make justice a matter for political negotiation rather than court action.

Negotiation and balance were implicit in Archibald's first Executive Council. On September 16, 1870, he appointed Alfred Boyd as Provincial Secretary and Marc-Amable Girard as Provincial Treasurer.[28] Capable as they both were, neither was closely connected to the factions that had been polarised during the resistance. That distance rendered their service inoffensive, but garnered them little depth of personal support.

Alfred Boyd was born in England about 1836 and was reported to be in Rupert's Land as early as 1858, initially perhaps as a "sportsman," but subsequently as a fur trader and merchant. Apparently successful and living in substantial residences, he was like most merchants of the day entangled in credit relations that could bring down even profitable operations if exceptional circumstances disrupted business. Indeed, his business was hurt badly during the resistance and he later submitted a sizeable claim for compensation. Describing him as "a merchant of good standing … [and] a man of fair abilities," Archibald judged Boyd to be "highly esteemed among the English party [while] he is not obnoxious to the French." Boyd had been one of the representatives of St. Andrew's parish to the convention of 40 called by Riel in January 1870. Playing a minor role, Boyd had privately expressed anti-Métis opinions and his public positions in the convention led Riel to judge him as "one of the most decided against us." Boyd's appointment drew some support from those who had remained neutral or opposed Riel's Provisional Government.[29]

Girard, who had arrived in St. Boniface just ten days before Archibald, was "a gentleman of some property, and of good standing … [and] the nominee of the French party." The son of a farmer, Marc-Amable Girard was born in Varennes, Quebec, in 1822. He attended the Collège de Saint-Hyacinthe, where he became friends with Alexandre-Antonin Taché, who later became Bishop of St. Boniface. After spending a year in Vermont to become familiar with English, he articled as a notary and was admitted to the profession in 1844. His practice was successful, as were his land speculations in Varennes. Closely associated with George-Étienne Cartier, Girard himself ran unsuccessfully for the Legislative Assembly and Legislative Council. He was more successful in municipal politics, serving as school commissioner, municipal councillor, and mayor of Varennes. Cartier encouraged Girard to move to Manitoba and no doubt his recommendation, seconded by Taché, influenced Archibald. Girard was less enthusiastic towards Riel than the other Québécois who came west in 1870 to enter Manitoba politics and, in the opinion of Riel's closest ally among that group, Joseph Dubuc, he was too interested in his own career—a "blockhead" and "a fool … [whose] first principle is to please the English."[30]

Having assembled his first Executive Council, Archibald's next task was to prepare for elections. Defining electoral boundaries and enumerating the population of the new province were administrative necessities easily resolved. At the same time Archibald proceeded expeditiously with preparations for the first provincial election, consulting regularly with Taché, Donald Smith of the Hudson's Bay Company, and even John C. Schultz, leader of the Canadian opposition to Riel, among other residents of the new province.[31] First a census had to be taken. Archibald assigned English and French enumerators for each parish. The results, different enough to indicate no collusion yet sufficiently similar to secure confidence, provided the basis for the subsequent demarcation of 24 electoral boundaries, which conformed closely to the existing 12 English and 12 French parishes.[32] On November 28, Archibald proclaimed an election and two weeks later made official the riding divisions. Plans were also implemented for the election of Manitoba's four members of the Dominion House of Commons.[33]

The campaign had in fact been underway at least from early November at public meetings throughout the parishes. Archibald needed little urging from Macdonald to take "a personal interest in the result of the election,"[34] as he worked privately to encourage his "central committee" of supporters—including such men as James Ross, Dr. Curtis J. Bird, Alexander Begg, A.G.B. Bannatyne, William Coldwell and Robert Cunningham—that voters should be persuaded to look to the future, rather than try to settle old scores. That advice was lost on Schultz's "loyalist" party, which vigorously and forcefully challenged the "central committee" at election gatherings. While a certain amount of pushing, shouting, and intimidation was exercised, the campaign appears to have been within the standards of contemporary Canadian political etiquette, rough and violent as the norm could be.[35] But important as the first election was, the province's small population and the restrictive franchise meant that few men participated in it. Not many more than a thousand votes were cast, with as few as 36 in Ste. Agathe and only in the riding of Winnipeg and St. John more than a hundred votes counted. Moreover, 9 of the 24 ridings, including 8 of the 12 French parishes, acclaimed their representatives.

In the French parishes, Bishop Taché[36] intervened on behalf of his favoured candidates recently arrived from Quebec and instructed priests to secure their success: Henry Joseph Clarke, Joseph Dubuc, Marc-Amable Girard, and Joseph Royal were all acclaimed. They recognized that the bishop could advance their careers in the new province and so heeded his advice and instruction. In fact, they needed little persuasion to accept Taché's vision, since building a "sister" province in the west for Quebec also presented them with opportunities to build political careers. For Clarke, ambition was a greater motive than that communal goal and over the next three years he attempted to build a political following.

Besides promoting his candidates, Taché advised Riel to keep a low political profile. Several Métis from St. Vital had pressed Riel to stand in their riding.[37] However, Riel knew that Cartier, speaking through Taché, hoped he would refrain from politics for a short time, just as Cartier had done following the Rebellion of 1837. Still waiting for the amnesty that the Bishop assured him was imminent, Riel acquiesced. Nevertheless, several allies (Louis Schmidt in St. Boniface West, Pierre Delorme in St. Norbert South, Joseph Lemay in St. Norbert North, and André Beauchemin in St. Vital) were returned in the election, although Riel's old opponent Pascal Breland defeated John Bruce in St. François Xavier East and another former rival, Angus McKay, was acclaimed in Lake Manitoba. The results of the election were gratifying for Archibald and promising in Riel's opinion.

Archibald drew together an Executive Council that he hoped would balance ethno-political interests. Boyd and Girard retained their portfolios. They were joined by Henry Joseph Clarke, an Irish Catholic lawyer from Montreal whom Cartier and Taché had encouraged to come west, and Thomas Howard, a captain in the Quebec Rifles sent out after the resistance to secure the Dominion's authority. The former became Attorney General and Government Leader in the Assembly and the latter served as minister of Public Works and Agriculture. (Shortly thereafter Boyd and Howard exchanged responsibilities.) Appointed Councillor without portfolio was James McKay, of mixed Scottish and Aboriginal ancestry, who became President of the Legislative Council after Archibald filled that house with his supporters on March 10, 1871.

The difficulty was that Archibald's ministers realized their positions depended upon the Lieutenant-Governor's good will and that they personally commanded little political following. Ambition dictated that they either closely adhere to their patron or try to carve out their own sphere of political influence. Girard chose the former tack and Clarke the latter. As well, selected to represent different constituencies, rather than common political positions or interests, they felt only conditional loyalty to their cabinet colleagues. Unity depended upon the authority of the Lieutenant-Governor. Archibald exercised this effectively. Later Morris, whose responsibilities had grown, found less time to manage the Council and decided that the collapse of the province's first government would force Manitoba's politicians not only to negotiate their own coalitions, but also to take political responsibility for popular and unpopular policies.

Archibald soon grew disappointed with Boyd's inability to hold the English-speaking community. Within his own St. Andrew's riding, Boyd suffered vigorous criticism from recent Ontario settlers, intent upon forcing Schultz's appointment to council. Charges that he had failed to secure much-needed local public works, while supporting measures in the interest of the Catholic Church, put Boyd on the defensive. Boyd's defence that cabinet solidarity demanded his support for measures unpopular with his constituents was belied by his willingness on other occasions to break with his council colleagues. Archibald, seeking someone who could stand up to Schultz, secured Boyd's resignation from the council on December 9, 1871. To offset the Orange demand for stronger Protestant representation, on December 14, 1871 Archibald appointed John Norquay, an Anglican of mixed English and Aboriginal ancestry and well-respected in St. Andrew's, to replace Boyd as minister of Agriculture and Public Works.[38] (Boyd remained in public life through the mid-1870s, but dropped from view thereafter. He returned to England about 1889, where he died in 1908.[39])

More satisfactory was Girard who by principle and to his personal benefit followed Conservative Party interests. On December 13, 1871, on Archibald's recommendation, he was appointed as Manitoba's Senator representing the French community. The Lieutenant-Governor explained, "The resident [Métis] population have nobody among themselves really fit for the position." Girard, though not the most popular among either the French of the English communities, "has been true as steel ever since he came here. He is a little out of the Bishop's good graces because [he is] not quite so pliant as he was expected to be."[40] At the time, it was acceptable to hold office at both the provincial and Dominion level and Girard continued to sit in the Manitoba Assembly, although he did resign his Executive Council position.

In his place, Archibald called on Joseph Royal, a close follower of Taché, who was publicly much more sympathetic to Riel, although in private, like Taché, he worried that the controversy surrounding the Métis leader hurt the Catholic cause.[41] But Archibald found in Royal someone who also objected to the ambitions of Henry Joseph Clarke and his divisive effect on Franco-Catholic unity.

Henry Joseph Clarke was born in Donegal, Ireland, on July 7, 1833, and immigrated to Lower Canada with his parents when he was three years of age. He was educated in Montreal and was called to the bar in 1855. Three years later his spirit of adventure led him first to California, where he became a journalist, and later to El Salvador. Returning to Montreal in the early 1860s, he became a criminal lawyer and later Queen's Counsel. In 1863 he unsuccessfully sought election as a Liberal-Conservative in Châteauguay, but remained politically active thereafter, working on behalf of his friend, Thomas D'Arcy McGee. A Conservative, bilingual Irish Catholic, Clarke was ambitious to be Manitoba's first Premier—and any other distinction he could claim.[42] That transparent ambition and the responsibility that he took in directing the government's legislation through the Assembly persuaded some at the time, and since, to consider him Premier, although he did not seek formal recognition of that role, initially at least. Archibald selected his ministers, set the legislative agenda, participated in Executive Council meetings, and intervened to maintain the direction he wanted. In sum, Archibald, like Morris after him, was his own Premier.

Not all went smoothly for Archibald with his Attorney General. Clarke tried to assert control over the legal profession, a useful tool for his ambition, by introducing legislation without Archibald's approval that would have required the Attorney General's consent for those seeking admission to the bar. Frustrated in his first attempt, Clarke tried again in the 1872 session and as well endeavoured to craft a provincial supreme court to which he hoped to be appointed. In exasperation, Archibald cautioned Macdonald in May 1871, "Bad as he is where he is, he would be greatly worse on the Bench" and later he exclaimed that he had "seldom seen a man so void of anything like discretion—or common sense."[43]

If Archibald's first appointments did not offend, neither did they inspire, and the lieutenant-governor continued to worry about the loyalty of the Métis. He learned in September 1871 that W.B. O'Donoghue, an Irish American who been a member of Riel's Provisional Government, was recruiting Fenian support to launch an invasion from Minnesota, which he hoped the Métis would join. In reaction, on October 4, Archibald called on all able men, "irrespective of race or religion, or past difficulties," to enroll in militia companies to defend the province.[44] Riel had little sympathy for O'Donoghue's design, but was reluctant to leap to the defense without some assurance that to do so would be to his benefit. After the intermediation of Father Ritchot, Archibald agreed that support during this crisis would entitle Riel and the Métis to "most favourable consideration." But, knowing he was negotiating with Riel, Archibald warned that with a quick decision "the more graceful will be their action and the more favourable their influence."[45] When approximately 200 armed Métis gathered in companies at St. Boniface on October 8, Royal and Girard invited Archibald to inspect the volunteers. During the review, Girard introduced Archibald to Riel, not by name, but as "the man whom the halfbreeds have chosen as their chief for the occasion." They shook hands. Archibald later denied that he knew he had met Riel, but Girard's meaning was hardly obscure and he was certain that the Lieutenant-Governor understood it.[46]

Militarily, Archibald's cultivation of Riel's support was unnecessary since O'Donoghue's Fenian adventure had collapsed on October 5, when American border guards captured his small band after they had crossed into Canada and seized a small Hudson's Bay Company post.[47] But, as Archibald forcefully argued, the failure of the raid could not have been predicted, especially without knowing the actions of the Métis. And the Métis response to his call for loyal arms, perhaps not so "graceful" as to appear spontaneous, nevertheless required his acknowledgement, with grace, that a choice had been made. Had he not done so, his insult might well have more seriously estranged the Métis.[48]

But the handshake enraged "loyalists" in Manitoba, who burned Archibald in effigy, and Orangemen in Ontario, who demanded his recall.[49] Sensitive to gusts of popular opinion, Macdonald bluntly let Archibald know that he had placed the Dominion government in a difficult situation, while Joseph Howe, Secretary of State for the Provinces, reprimanded Archibald for being duped by Riel, whose real intention had been to extort concessions on amnesty. To Macdonald, Archibald testily explained, "With you it is a question of popularity—of newspaper criticism—with me it is one of life and death."[50] To Howe, the old tribune of the people of colonial Nova Scotia, he served a lecture on responsible government:

> The people here must be allowed to be judges of how to manage their own affairs.... In my view you have to choose between revoking responsible government, and admitting that you cannot go back to inflict punishment for offences in which half the population were implicated, committed before responsible Government was conceded."[51]

Having defended his actions, Archibald tendered his resignation in December 1871, allowing Macdonald to accept it when most convenient politically. He then obtained a resounding expression of confidence from both houses of the Manitoba legislature, declaring that Manitoba had not demanded his resignation.[52]

In the uproar over the handshake, Clarke saw political opportunity and gambled that by opposing Riel he could win support from the Métis and others of mixed ancestry who had at best been lukewarm to Riel's leadership, as well as from the English community.[53] To that end, as Attorney General, he initiated prosecution in late 1871, and won a conviction, against a Métis implicated in the Fenian invasion.[54] The action greatly offended the pro-Riel faction, which had accepted that individual Métis would choose which side to support in the crisis. As a result, Royal was provoked to denounce Clarke in his newspaper, Le Métis.[55] In September 1872 Clarke decided to contest the Provencher seat in the Dominion election, even after Riel had expressed his interest in running. Refusing to choose a different constituency, Clarke criticized Riel for being "a fool who would not listen to his friends" and keep out of politics until hostility to him had blown over. He angrily confronted Riel on the hustings and even challenged him to a duel, leaving observers aghast at an Attorney General threatening violence. Clarke's and Riel's campaigns were halted when Cartier was defeated in his Montreal riding. Voting in the 1872 election extended over six weeks and, because Manitobans had not gone to the polls, Macdonald ordered Archibald to secure Cartier's election there: Provencher was the only constituency where the outcome could be assured. Clarke acquiesced to Archibald's instructions, while Riel, pressured by Taché, only withdrew after Cartier had pledged to defend Métis interests.[56] Despite his strained relations with Macdonald, Archibald had done as requested.

Macdonald then accepted Archibald's resignation and in December 1872 appointed as his successor Alexander Morris. Morris was born in 1826 in Perth, Upper Canada, into one of the province's most prominent families. He was well-educated in Scotland and at

McGill College in Montreal. For a time he was a law clerk for John A. Macdonald and later J.J.C. Abbott. In his own practice in Montreal he prospered. He entered politics in 1861 and became a vigorous advocate of Confederation and of Canada's westward expansion. Appointed minister of Inland Revenue in Macdonald's government in 1869, he nonetheless "gave the impression of being less partisan than many of his colleagues and was thus able to be a conciliator at a crucial time in Canadian history." In July 1872, for health and financial reasons, Morris resigned his seat, but accepted an appointment as Chief Justice of the Manitoba Court of Queen's Bench. When Archibald left the province in October 1872, Morris served as administrator of Manitoba and the North-West Territories until his own appointment as Lieutenant-Governor of both in December 1872.[57]

Unlike his predecessor, Morris saw little reason to maintain what he knew was a political impossibility: amnesty could never be granted by any government sensitive to Ontario opinion. His response to the contentions of Taché and the expectations raised by Archibald was the same as Macdonald's had been—to deny that any promises had been made and to maintain that since the execution had occurred while Red River was still under Imperial rule, only the Queen could offer amnesty without the case coming to trial. After the courts had decided on the charge, however, the Governor General could offer an amnesty.[58] Morris effectively closed private lobbying as an avenue through which the Métis might secure a general amnesty.

Thereafter, Riel pursued political action, first at the provincial level and then at the Dominion level. Riel felt encouraged and believed that his recent actions had placed the Dominion government and the Lieutenant-Governor in his political debt. His goal now was to force responsible government: getting elected would demonstrate the support of his community and the necessity of an amnesty. André Beauchemin, the MLA for St. Vital, agreed in November to resign so that his friend might win a by-election in the provincial legislature. Morris, who was then provincial administrator and not yet Lieutenant-Governor, told Beauchemin that he would refuse to call a by-election and warned him that if Riel contested a by-election, a warrant for his arrest for the murder of Thomas Scott would surely be issued. Indeed, Clarke, still prickly from his earlier contest, was determined to arrest Riel. On December 3 an attempt was made; though it failed, it sent Riel into hiding again—for a time.[59] Clarke then re-opened a case at which Riel was to be called as witness and issued a subpoena for his appearance. As well, he consciously appointed a magistrate who would agree to sign a warrant to arrest Riel and Lépine for Scott's murder. Again Riel fled before he could be served, but Lépine was arrested on September 16, 1873. Girard, among others, protested the proceedings, but Morris argued that the law must take its course.[60] Still, Riel reappeared to contest successfully the Dominion by-election in Provencher necessitated by Cartier's death in May 1873 and, in the general election called later that year, he was re-elected to the House of Commons.

Morris's denial of any knowledge about an amnesty and his decision to let charges proceed proved the first clever steps in resolving the Riel problem—at least in Manitoba politics. He made it clear that any political resolution rested with the Crown and the Dominion government, while the legal question was a matter for the courts to decide. Since criminal prosecutions came under provincial jurisdiction, leaving the matter with Clarke, his aggressive Attorney General, opposed as he was by Riel's equally assertive defenders, Dubuc and Royal, Morris effectively devolved responsibility to Manitoba politicians. From there it was only a matter of time until full responsible government followed. In fact, Morris was quickly discovering that an increasing number of responsibilities, from negotiating Indian treaties to advising on relations with the United States, left him insufficient time to juggle provincial factions. Politicians needed to form their own coalitions.

Clarke had long schemed to claim government leadership. In February 1873, he had persuaded the other members of the Executive Council to back his demands that Morris recognize him as Premier. The Lieutenant-Governor refused. Morris speculated that Royal, in almost constant contact with the "Rielites," had supported the move as an expedient, a step toward Clarke's defeat and discredit.[61] Indeed, Clarke's self-serving actions were gradually alienating more and more of the French community, which increasingly came to favour Royal.[62] As well, his personal life offended many, especially Catholics, since he abandoned his wife for the company of a married woman.[63] His service as Attorney General was questioned, too. The absconding impostor, "Lord Gordon Gordon," who was sought by American authorities on fraud charges in 1873, accused Clarke of trying to blackmail him.[64] Clarke became further discredited when doubts were cast about his expenditure of unauthorized funds for vaguely explained "secret service" activities.[65]

Recognizing his waning influence among the French Catholic faction, Clarke seized upon the contentious issue of electoral representation as a way to win support from the growing English population.[66] Several issues had antagonized migrants from Ontario for some time. The voters' lists, revised as of the first of April of every second year, imposed a one-year residence requirement and effectively excluded many migrants from voting for up to three years. That restriction had been one factor in the riots in Winnipeg and St. Boniface during the Dominion election of 1872.[67] The next spring English discontent focused on the distribution of provincial ridings.

The government first responded to the problem of representation for those areas of settlement, largely English, that were outside the old parishes, which had formed the first electoral ridings. A proposal, introduced by Thomas Howard, would have added the new areas to the existing parish-based constituencies—as had been done by the Dominion government for the 1873 election. Opposition members John Sutherland and E.H.G.G. Hay objected, arguing that the new population was sufficiently large to warrant a new riding in itself. Further, adding to the old ridings only worsened the disparities in population that had made the parishes ill-suited for electoral divisions even at the first election; all provincial ridings, they argued, should be redrawn on the basis of population. As Hay put it, "The English have the most wealth, the most population, the most enterprise, and they are only demanding their just rights when they demand to be placed on the footing of representation by population." Howard declared the government's refusal to change in the middle of the Parliament's life, but promised the matter would be bought back. As Joseph Royal elaborated, the government could not redraw boundaries yearly in response to population changes.[68] The measure passed, but the issue returned at the end of the year.

Complicating reconsideration was the prospect of enlarging the province and, possibly, creating new constituencies. In the spring of 1873 government representatives had pressed the Dominion government on the matter, hoping that more territory and greater population would justify an increased subsidy to the cash-strapped province. Provincial legislation requesting the boundary extension was introduced in November.[69] However, with a Dominion election imminent in the wake of the Pacific Scandal the issue was left hanging.[70] The Canadian party, led by Hay, worried that redistribution had been inextricably linked with the boundary question. His questioning forced government spokesmen, both Clarke and Royal, to declare their support for revisions based on population.[71] But then positions fell into chaos.

Having committed himself to the principle, however, Royal did not think that ridings should be redrawn until the province's borders had been decided. Further he objected to the draft bill that Clarke now introduced to the legislature in early November. It had been "concocted," he charged, in secret and came with no information or map in support of its proposed revisions. His criticisms were echoed by other French members, including Delorme, Lemay, McKay, Beauchemin, and Dubuc. Clarke dismissed Royal's umbrage at having been excluded from the drafting of the bill by denying that his bill was a government bill—even though he spoke for the government in the Assembly and had pretensions to its leadership. Further he condemned the government's "bastard re-distribution Bill" passed earlier. Opposition to the bill from Royal and others he attributed to clerical influence and he refused to put the government in "the hands of a few petticoated men across the river" in St. Boniface. Royal countered that the apparent efforts of those who redrew the boundaries to assure their electoral safety demonstrated just why the bill should have come from the government. Whether or not such personal allusions hardened positions, on November 8, in a division at which one third of the members were absent, the bill passed nine to six votes; that same day the Legislative Council passed the bill.[72]

For different reasons French and English opposition to Clarke had coalesced by the summer of 1874. When the Legislative Assembly met on July 3 to hear reports from delegates who had been in Ottawa seeking better financial terms for Manitoba, the leader of the English-speaking opposition, E.H.G.G. Hay, moved, seconded by Joseph Dubuc, "that the members of this House have no confidence in the present ministry." The motion passed 15 votes to 7, with all of the French members supporting it except Joseph Royal, who could not easily vote against a ministry of which he was a member, even though he had been instrumental in engineering the defeat. Indeed, thereafter in his newspaper, Le Métis, Royal applauded the replacement of the old ministry with one responsible to the Assembly.[73]

Clarke at first refused to accept the non-confidence vote, which, he claimed, had been arranged in the back room of a tavern. But Morris demanded his resignation and that of the other ministers. The Lieutenant-Governor felt unable to dissolve the legislature and call a new election, which would have been contested under a Redistribution Act that all considered seriously flawed and without an up-to-date voters' list. As well, since the government fell not on any piece of legislation or principle, but on a denunciation of its incompetence, Morris had some concern, in the absence of any formally recognized Leader of the Opposition, about calling upon Hay, as the mover of non-confidence, to form a new ministry.

After some consultation, he asked Girard to become Premier and put together an executive that would hold the Assembly's confidence. On July 8, Girard presented his ministry to Morris: Girard would serve as Provincial Secretary, Joseph Dubuc as Attorney General, E.G.H.H. Hay as minister of Agriculture and Public Works, Robert A. Davis as Provincial Treasurer, Francis Ogletree as minister without portfolio, and James McKay as President of the Council.

As the prospect of a provincial election loomed, the Girard government attempted to resolve redistribution.[74] The redistribution bill, which passed third reading on July 15, differed little from the controversial one of the previous session, but it had been drafted more carefully and its transparency drew more general legislative support.[75] Its effect, increasing the number of English-speaking constituencies to 14 and perhaps 15 and reducing the French to 10, acknowledged the shifting balance of population and demonstrated that representation by population could not be compromised.

Concerns of the French population were raised when Girard proposed the abolition of the province's upper house, the Legislative Council, on financial grounds. His government judged the subsidy from the Dominion entirely inadequate, but the new Mackenzie government refused either to extend the province's boundaries or to increase the subsidy. Aided by a new and open system of keeping the public accounts of Davis's design, Girard sought economies where he could find them. Abolition of the Legislative Council, it was argued, could save $5,000 to $10,000 annually. Royal, speaking in support of the measure, admitted that the Council's record, despite initial hopes that it would moderate legislation, did not inspire confidence in its ability to protect the interests of the French population. He hoped that justice would still be rendered, but he could not accept the cost to a poor province of retaining the Council.[76]

In what government members interpreted, probably rightly, as an attempt to embarrass the new cabinet and force Girard's resignation, John Norquay introduced a bill to prevent members of the provincial Assembly from sitting in the Senate. Norquay's high-minded protest that his intent was to establish the same principle that excluded members of the House of Commons from sitting in the Senate rather conveniently ignored the real principle in the Dominion prohibition, which was that a member should not have two votes on one piece of legislation. The principle of sitting in two different levels of government, provincial and Dominion, had been accepted from Confederation and in Manitoba had been practised by Donald Smith, the Canadian chief commissioner of the Hudson's Bay Company who served as MLA for Winnipeg-St. John and MP for Selkirk. That Senate and not Commons membership should be targeted demonstrated the partisan convenience of Norquay's motion. On July 17, the bill was rejected in a vote of 10 to 9 on a procedural amendment that split cleanly on ethnic lines. But the issue did reveal a lack of unity in Girard's cabinet. Despite his criticism that Norquay's real intention was to embarrass Girard, Hay supported the bill, as did Davis, the other English member of the government.[77] Later, on July 21, Norquay introduced a bill to abolish dual representation. It passed second reading, again on a clear ethnic split of nine to seven, but never received third reading before the Assembly adjourned.[78]

The double representation issue revealed the fragility of Girard's government, cobbled together, as it was, to implement electoral redistribution and to bring some order to the public accounts in the waning weeks of the first legislature. Disaffection grew among the English members through the late summer and into the fall as the trials of Lépine and Nault revived the French sense of betrayal over the failure of amnesty and the English frustration with delays in bringing Scott's murderers to justice. Adding to English discomfort, Girard, who was also the president of the Association Saint-Jean-Baptiste de Manitoba, convened a large assembly of delegates from the French parishes on November 22, 1874, to draft a petition to the Governor General calling for the release of Lépine.[79] Within a week the cabinet was in crisis. After several days of dispute, on December 1, Hay and Ogletree resigned, claiming that they could no longer accept French members holding the two most important posts of Premier and Attorney General—something to which they had acquiesced, of course, for six months. Girard submitted his cabinet's resignation to the Lieutenant-Governor and recommended that he call on Robert A. Davis, a Winnipeg hotelkeeper and the former Provincial Treasurer, to form a government.[80]

The Legislative Record

In the absence of responsible government, Manitoba's first legislature in some ways resembled a colonial legislature. Its head, nominally and in practice, was the Lieutenant-Governor who as representative of the Dominion government also held responsibility for various matters of national concern not normally assigned to a Governor General's provincial delegate. Its legislative agenda, functional in establishing the first apparatus of government, but political in balancing the contentions of differing ethno-religious communities, was communicated in throne speeches of the Lieutenant-Governor's own drafting. As well, the lack of responsibility and the Lieutenant-Governor's role as Dominion representative and provincial government leader gave provincial legislators, even executive councillors, the opportunity to criticize the Dominion government from the provincial Assembly and to pressure Archibald and then Morris for action on issues beyond their constitutional jurisdiction.

In his first Speech from the Throne on March 15, 1871, Archibald complimented the province for the ease with which he had been able to maintain "peace and order with scarce any of the institutions or aids of an organized society." But now the first legislature needed to create the essential institutions and practices of provincial government. Of first importance was the establishment of a judicial system to exercise the rule of law. Second, the rights of property required more precise definition. Archibald considered the two initiatives closely linked, their joint purpose being "to lay the foundations of property upon a basis of Law." Third in priority was the provision of institutions of municipal government.[81] In his speech, Archibald did not mention the fourth major institutional initiative—education—which was left to the next session for deliberation.

As first acts, Archibald urged "plain and simple," rather than complicated legislation, leaving amendment and finer tuning to subsequent legislatures as cause arose. And the first legislature followed that course, though often with fractious debate—as was revealed in the issue of electoral divisions already discussed.

Functional though much of the first legislation might seem, members of the legislature and the public watched carefully to discern the models being used. Some English critics feared that the *Code Civile* of Quebec would be preferred, since so many former members of the Quebec legal professions, including Clarke who introduced much of the legislative program to the Assembly, were active in Manitoba politics. In presenting the Supreme Court of Manitoba Bill, Clarke responded by defending the merits of the Quebec system, but he admitted that its bulk and extent were too large for introduction into a new province and it would be better for the province to build up its own legal *corpus* in response to needs as they arose. For the time being, he argued that in keeping with the legal tradition of Rupert's Land, the new system was intended to simplify litigation and thereby minimize expense. The act defining its procedures was "as simple as possible. All the old ideas of legal language and surplusage have been set aside so that any man reading it might thoroughly comprehend it."[82]

The Supreme Court Act provided not just the foundation for the court system, but also it was amended the next year to create county Courts of Session with, among other duties, jurisdiction over matters of municipal concern. Archibald, like earlier 19th-century politicians, considered municipal government an essential civic training ground "to create and foster public spirit and train the people to discharge the duties devolving upon them."[83] Indeed, the province possessed few sources of revenue beyond the inadequate transfer payment received from the Dominion government and so responded to the growing number of requests for various local improvements with advice that the Courts of Session might authorize a local tax levy to meet local needs. The Courts were to fill the gap until a more fully articulated municipal system could be legislated.

That stop-gap, however, did not satisfy the ambitious English boosters of Winnipeg, who appreciated the ability of a municipal corporation to advance private interests. After public meetings, a citizens' committee met to draft a charter, which was submitted to the legislature early in 1873. However, in a new province with few sources of revenue, the taxing power of a new urban corporation potentially diverted licensing fees from a provincial to a municipal government. As well, in a municipality in which much real estate would remain vacant for many years, the prospect of taxation for a variety of services frightened those who held large tracts of land—most conspicuously, the Hudson's Bay Company. These fiscal implications, plus the "loyalist" sympathies of the nascent city, generated little enthusiasm for the private member's bill submitted for Winnipeg's incorporation. Though passed on March 5, 1873, amendments proved offensive to its original proponents. The maximum rate of taxation was reduced significantly and Dominion and provincial property, much of which was rented from the Hudson's Bay Company, was exempted from taxation. As well, the corporation would be denied the authority to borrow money—its primary objective! Adding insult to injury was the change of the name, moved by Thomas Bunn and seconded by Dr. Curtis J. Bird, from Winnipeg to Assiniboia.[84] Quickly once the changes became known, the same day, an "indignation meeting," attended by "the whole male population [of Winnipeg], with very few exceptions," decided that the charter should be rejected and the government should be lobbied to restore the proposed bill. Its delegation, proceeding immediately to the legislature, found the Legislative Council in session and convinced it to amend the Assembly's bill. The amended charter necessarily was returned to the Assembly for approval. Bird, the Speaker, ruled the Council's changes unconstitutional since they addressed matters of taxation. Enraged again by the government's action, Winnipeg's advocates protested. The *Free Press* pointed out that the Speaker had not ruled other Council amendments concerning financial matters out of order and asked, why now, if not out of malice or sympathy for the Hudson's Bay Company. Others acted more directly, enticing Dr. Bird out of the House on the pretext of attending a dying patient, then dragging him from his carriage, and pouring hot tar over his head.[85]

During the same session, the legislature had been considering municipal legislation generally. Clarke lectured the Assembly on its merits:

> The people will begin to understand when a little bridge breaks down or
> a plank [is] misplaced, that instead of pitching into the government they
> will have to get the matter right themselves and if they neglect it and a
> horse breaks its leg and they are sued for damages the ratepayers will begin
> to understand the propriety of placing competent, careful men in office.[86]

The functioning of municipal government as a school in democracy was somewhat compromised by amending legislation later in the year which gave non-resident landowners the vote in municipal elections. One lesson to be learned was that property needed representation.[87] Although he claimed that it was modelled on Ontario, in one key feature it was not. It was voluntary. Any parish or township could request municipal incorporation when its population reached 30 households, but it did not have to.[88] In the absence of municipal institutions—whether county, township, village, town, or city, as in Ontario—a district or a parish remained under the jurisdiction of its Court of Session. The legislation thus perpetuated two systems of local governance, whereas Ontario had replaced one with another.

While some consideration was given to incorporating Winnipeg under the more general provincial legislation, many boosters considered that route insulting and inadequate in the powers they wanted for their city. By November 1873, chastened by the outrage expressed over the earlier bill and ever alert to possible new sources of political support, Clarke took up Winnipeg's cause and assured its proponents that the government would give them what they wished.[89] Rising in the Assembly on November 6, 1873, to introduce the bill, Clarke presented himself as the city's champion and found Joseph Royal just as eager to commend incorporation. Indeed, Royal even suggested that printing or reading the bill in French was unnecessary, since "all the members present understand English sufficiently well so as to know the provisions of the Bill." The next day the bill passed with little discussion.[90]

School legislation also provoked questions about the appropriate model, even as the systems in Ontario and Quebec were themselves being fundamentally changed at the time and did not offer clear precedents. The Manitoba legislation passed in May 1871 made a board of education that stood at arm's length from the government responsible for administering the system, as was the case in Ontario until 1876 when a ministry of education was established.[91] In this, Manitoba also had what ultramontane Catholic forces sought for Quebec: an autonomous board or council that gave separate responsibilities to Protestant and Catholic panels. Only in 1874 did Quebec abolish its department of education and achieve such an arrangement. In Manitoba, where the parish system conformed to religious and linguistic communities, a dual system reflected the will of residents who wanted their children educated in ways sympathetic to their own culture. Protestants and Catholics did not need to separate or dissent from the majority schools in their locales, as in the older provinces. From the outset a dual system existed with separate Protestant and Catholic sections of the board of education, an equal number of Protestant and Catholic school districts, which conformed to the old parishes, and an equally divided provincial financial grant. As in Ontario, the Manitoba legislation permitted school districts a variety of ways to raise revenue locally—by subscription, tuition, or property assessment.[92] Although Manitoba's school system was, as Joseph Royal argued, in many ways a hybrid suited to local conditions and informed by structures under debate elsewhere, to the English community it was one that responded to French and Catholic concerns rather than implementing the separation of church and state that they wanted. To them, the denominational system indicated the government's "antipathy to Ontario precedent."[93]

During the debate on the bill and over the next several years, Protestants interpreted a number of the system's features as giving unfair advantage to the Catholic section. In particular, the equal division of the provincial grant provoked concerns over the greater resources given to the smaller section. Instead, English opponents argued that the grant should be proportional to the number of students in each district.[95] Other problems in financing the system further discredited it with former Ontarians. The ability of local trustees to fund their schools was frustrated by their inability to compel local Clerks of the Peace, who were unelected officials of the Courts of Session and were responsible for assessing and collecting school taxes, to turn monies over to them. Nor did the provincial government, they were told, have authority to compel payment. In consequence, one public school, that in North St. Andrew's, had to close in 1872. As well, because school districts were unincorporated bodies, they could not borrow money on the security of their ability to tax. A final frustration to those familiar with school promotion in Ontario was the absence of compulsory school attendance, something which, they claimed, would not only advance the province's development, but would also help prevent crime.[95]

By 1873 both the principle and practice of a dual school system had provoked such dissatisfaction that the Act was amended. However, to the chagrin of the Canadian party, the government chose to set a maximum amount ($1,000) that trustees could raise through taxes in any year to build or repair schools. Such a measure might have offered some solace to Catholic parishes in which poor ratepayers feared the burden of taxes and also expected the Church to contribute funds, but to the English, who viewed themselves as much more progressive than the Métis, the limit hindered their ability to advance their communities. Similarly, they objected to the restrictions on school visiting that limited clergymen to informally inspecting only those schools in their denominational system; unspoken was their conviction that the Catholic system would be inefficient and reduced to an adjunct of the Church. [96] The amendments passed, but perhaps were more significant in revealing that from its beginning as a province, Manitoba had a school question that divided its citizens.

The property rights also became protected in a series of early acts. In the past the intimacy of a small community—in which people mostly knew one another and one another's business and often frequented the same places—had secured verbal contracts and commitments in the absence of any formal state mechanism. The anticipation of new people and new capital familiar with more formal property regimes demanded clearly documented transactions and claims. As Archibald confided to Howe, "The inhabitants [have] lived half a century under the defective arrangements of the past... . Many have nothing to show but possession." Moreover, the only system of registry remained in the Hudson's Bay Company's hands and were considered by the company to be its private property. Archibald lamented, "It did not seem proper that all evidence of title now existing in the Province should be in the hands of private persons."[97] Any system of private property rested on the assumption of the right of the knowledgeable and fully competent individual to contract obligations and to convey interests to others, but that ability required public access to reliable knowledge.

Among the legislation of the first legislature were acts concerning fraud, the sale of real estate to recover debts, the legal ability of married women to convey property held in their own name, the responsibilities of masters and servants, and the claims of heirs to intestate estates. And, of course, written rights of property required provision for the registration of instruments conveying and declaring interests in property: an act to establish registry offices and to prescribe appropriate forms of conveyance, resembling that of Ontario, was passed in the first session. A concern for the clarity of written contracts informed deliberations over registration. For example, by preferring the French proscription against interlineal and marginal notes on deeds to the English tolerance of initialled changes, the legislature hoped to prevent frauds and swindles.[98]

As well, state intervention endeavoured to protect transfers of real estate. A purchaser who wished to bar any liability of vendors secured by that property could appeal to the Court of Queen's Bench for ratification of title. Clear title could be obtained if no creditor appeared after legal written notice had been published in the official gazette for four weeks and after the notice had been read for two Sundays at the door of the parish church in which the property was located or at the most frequented place, if there was no church. The provision for verbal notice acknowledged the continuing significance of oral communication in the province, although the longer duration of published notice indicated preference again for written contracts. Published notice also facilitated the greater distance between purchasers, vendors, and creditors since the earlier provisions of the Laws of the Governor and Council of Assiniboia had required the posting of legal notices on the doors of all churches in the settlement, a much more complicated arrangement in a growing property market.[99]

The importance of securing property rights in the new province was also evidenced in the numerous acts of incorporation sought by private business corporations and more controversially by religious and educational institutions, in particular the Roman Catholic bishop of St. Boniface and the Anglican Diocese of Rupert's Land. The opposition in the assembly objected to the unlimited land holding permitted under the charters proposed for the Catholic and Anglican churches. Fearing that the churches might become landlords or at the very least impediments to settlement, Hay, Norquay, and Sutherland wanted to limit their ownership to 5,000 acres beyond their current holdings. In high moral indignation, Clarke asserted the personal integrity of the prelates heading the two churches and objected to the imputation that under the guise of holding land for charitable, religious, and educational purposes they intended to engross huge estates. Even were it so, he asserted the right of any corporation or individual to hold unlimited property and went so far as to defend the Canada Company of Upper Canada for its promotion of settlement. In fact, Clarke informed the House, the bishops had discussed such a restriction earlier, but with some confusion in collaboratively drafting their proposals it had been left out. The acts of incorporation passed with the 5,000-acre limit, which no doubt both bishops found acceptable.[100] The debate was significant, however, for the concerns it revealed about incorporated property rights.

One matter concerning property, perhaps the most critical, was beyond the limit of provincial competence: the location and distribution of Métis lands. A homeland for the Métis inhabitants had been the main objective of Riel's Provisional Government. The Dominion government, however, had rejected Riel's demand that the administration of Métis lands rest with the provincial legislature.[101] Whether the Dominion government discharged the responsibilities it claimed has been debated vigorously, but it remains beyond the purview of this essay. The provincial legislature could only express its disappointment over delays and urge action.[102]

Once distributed, however, Métis lands, like other forms of real property, came under provincial law and provincial politicians tried to contain the erosion of the homeland that they feared was resulting from the delay in the distribution of land, the intrusion of migrants from eastern Canada, and the activities of speculators who were rumoured to be buying up Métis rights. Archibald had reported in 1870 that French leaders, no doubt Taché in particular, had wanted Métis lands entailed for at least a generation in order to keep the community together. The Lieutenant-Governor had disagreed with any practice that would impede the "free use and transmission" of real property, which he believed should be conveyed as easily as personal property.[103] However, the idea of entail remained current.

Clarke and others who had defended the churches' unlimited land owning did have grave reservations about speculators accumulating huge interests in land, especially those who bought up land granted to Métis children under section 31 of the Manitoba Act. On February 25 he reminded the assembly that a Dominion order-in-council of the previous year had given the province competence to impose regulations once those eligible had received their grant: "If the children of Half-breeds are not protected in their rights it will not be the fault of the Dominion Government but of this house." And they needed protection, he contended, from swindlers paying only a fraction of what their land was worth.[104]

A few days later Girard introduced a bill to "aid vendors of real estate in certain cases." Inspired by Roman law, its provisions would have given vendors up to six months to appeal and regain their land, if they discovered that they had sold it for less than half its value. Without explicitly mentioning the Métis—although all knew to whom the bill applied—Girard explained that "its object is to protect the weak from the strong." Implicitly it rejected as pretence the assumption that all bargained freely and equally in the marketplace. Hay protested that he believed that "if a man is capable of holding land, he is capable of selling it." Moreover, he thought the cancellation of sales was unfair to the purchaser who in effect would have given a free loan of his money to the vendor for up to six months. The other English members defended the freedom of bargaining and in a split on national lines voted to give the bill a six-month hoist, a parliamentary procedure that in effect killed the bill by postponing its consideration.[105]

But sufficient support did exist in the assembly for some protection for the Métis, described by Donald Smith as intelligent as any other people, but "from custom" more "confiding." Picking on the weakest points in Hay's criticism of the earlier bill, Smith sponsored a Half-Breed Land Grant Protection Bill that narrowed the circumstances in which transactions could be cancelled to those involving unallocated land under the Métis grant. On Archibald's recommendation the Dominion government had decided to assign the lands promised to the Métis under the Manitoba Act by lotteries in townships reserved in the main for that purpose. However, before their lands were located many Métis, both adults on their own and on behalf of their minor children, sold their grants to speculators who gambled on picking up good lands cheaply. Since the location of the land at the time of sale was unknown and since many of the purchasers were, in Smith's words, "land sharks" and "neither honest nor just," the assumption of a knowledgeable vendor was untenable. His bill prevented the legal transfer of title before the issue of a patent, which of course awaited location, and gave Métis vendors the right to cancel the sale and return the purchase price. Were they unable to do so, they could still regain title, but the amount paid by the erstwhile purchaser would remain a lien against the property, at the rate of 7% interest, which, if unpaid after a year, would force the sale of the land at auction. Although Smith did not expand upon it, that encumbrance and substantial interest rate would hinder the subsequent sale of the land and encourage vendor and purchaser to renegotiate the sale. As a precedent for retroactive—or, perhaps, restorative—legislation, Smith offered the example of the Canadian government's decision not to redeem the 20-year notes issued in compensation for losses during the Lower Canadian Rebellion of 1837 at par value but for the price paid by third-party purchasers.

Although not a government bill, Smith's initiative drew support from Clarke. In justification for what some criticized as interference in free contracts, the Attorney General added that, unlike other land grants, such as the scrip given to the Ontario and Quebec militia volunteers who had served in Manitoba after the resistance, the Métis grant fell under provisions of the Manitoba Act that gave the province jurisdiction over its administration. Reflecting his Quebec legal training and practice, Clarke, like Girard, appealed to Roman legal principles of justice for the weak. The province had the responsibility, indeed the obligation, to afford protection. Those opposed offered essentially the same objections as they had to Girard's bill. Norquay, of mixed ancestry himself, considered the bill a personal insult for assuming an inability to manage his own property and asked, "What right have we to cancel the bargain of any man, and what right have we to set up a rate of interest for a man's money?"[106] These arguments proved less persuasive the second time and the bill passed.[107]

Anticipating legislation of this sort, Lieutenant-Governor Morris had sought instructions from Alexander Campbell, Dominion minister of the Interior. The latter would not countenance legislation that treated Métis property rights differently from those of any other citizen and which impaired the legal ability of individuals to convey their interests. Campbell told Morris to reserve any legislation of this sort.[108] Accordingly, Morris referred Smith's bill to Ottawa, not on the grounds that it defined differential property rights, but because its application was retroactive, its effect would stimulate nuisance litigation, and it failed to define procedures for the sales of land against which liens had been obtained. The Liberal government of Alexander Mackenzie replaced that of Macdonald in 1873 and its response was more sympathetic. The Dominion cabinet accepted the recommendation of A.A. Dorion, minister of Justice, that the legislation be approved since it protected vendors ignorant of their property rights and their value, while at the same time providing recourse to purchasers. The Half-Breed Land Grant Protection Act came into effect on February 28, 1874.[109]

The legislative record of Manitoba's first legislature was a substantial one, which introduced the basic institutions of the state and of property. Its accomplishments, however, were not without division. Issues concerning education, municipal incorporation, and Métis property rights, among others, revealed that Manitoba's politics from the province's birth were fraught with ethno-religious tensions.

Conclusion

Marc-Amable Girard's biographer has reported that he "is reputed to have said, 'I am the first French Premier of the Province, and it is my opinion I will be the last'."[110] He was correct. Girard's brief government completed Manitoba's transition to provincial status and responsible government. His implementation of electoral redistribution signaled the French Catholic community's acceptance of representation by population and the end of ethno-religious dualism grounded in the old parish system. Girard, like Archibald, knew that inevitably in time the English population of the province would far outnumber the French. The period for entrenching French and Catholic interests was very brief and contested.

The government's fall did not end Girard's political career. He remained active in provincial politics for almost another decade. His ability to defend French interests while working with English-speaking politicians allowed him to play a well-regarded role in the cabinet of John Norquay from 1879 to 1883. Provincial legislation prohibiting Senators from sitting in the legislature kept him from running again. Probably he was not greatly displeased. Being in Ottawa made it easier to visit his old home, to which he remained attached, and was much more appealing to his wife, who always favoured Montreal over St. Boniface. In the Senate, where he served until his death in 1892, Girard supported

Conservative railway policy and, to the end of his life, vigorously defended the French language in western Canada and the dual school system in Manitoba.[111]

Lieutenant-Governor Adams G. Archibald had hoped that Manitobans would let bygones be bygones. They would not and, therefore, Archibald did not proceed on his instructions to implement responsible government. Had he done so, it was possible that Louis Riel could have become Premier, a development that would have enraged English Protestants across the country. Managing provincial politics and the legislature proved an exhausting task for Archibald, especially when he lacked support from the Dominion. His successor, Alexander Morris, could not continue that approach to government. Astutely, he recognized that allowing the courts to resolve the question of guilt for Thomas Scott's death would remove the amnesty question from politics and allow Manitoba to embark upon responsible government. Giving Manitoba responsible government, and requiring the province to deal with the issues that exacerbated relations between its two ethno-religious communities, would also extricate the Dominion government from the unresolved questions concerning communal rights raised in the Manitoba Act.

Notes

1. Morris to R.W. Scott, Secretary of State, July 13, 1874, quoted in Frank A. Milligan, "The Lieutenant-Governorship in Manitoba, 1870–1882" (MA thesis, University of Manitoba, 1948), 179.

2. The issue of responsible government, inherent in the demands for provincial status and an elected legislature voiced by Louis Riel in November 1869, by no means enjoyed undivided support in the Red River Settlement. For Riel, provincial status and responsible government were essential tools to protect Métis lands and to secure their participation in opening the North-West. The convention of delegates elected from the English and French parishes debated the merits of different ways in which the North-West might enter Confederation—as a Crown Colony, a territory under Dominion jurisdiction, or a province. Concerns about the expense of provincial government, the underdeveloped transportation and institutional infrastructure, and political inexperience persuaded the English-speaking delegates and some Métis representatives to reject Riel's position and to seek provincial status only after an "exceptional" period as a territory. However, when the Provisional Government, of which Riel was president, drafted its list of rights to send to Ottawa, the demand for provincial status was reasserted. See "The Proceedings in the Convention, February 3 to February 5, 1870," in W.L. Morton (ed.), *Manitoba: The Birth of a Province* (Winnipeg: Manitoba Record Society, 1965), 5–24; George F.G. Stanley, *Louis Riel* (Toronto: McGraw-Hill Ryerson, 1985), 93–94.

3. Historians have generally commended Archibald for his conciliatory approach to the Métis and his successor Morris for astutely knowing when to hand over government. Morton, *Manitoba: A History* (Toronto: University of Toronto Press, 1967), 142–48; John T. Saywell, *The Office of Lieutenant-Governor: A Study in Canadian Government and Politics* (Toronto: University of Toronto Press, 1957),

63–66; Douglas N. Sprague, *Canada and the Métis, 1869–1885* (Waterloo: Wilfrid Laurier University Press, 1988), 1–27; N.E.A. Ronaghan, "The Archibald Administration in Manitoba, 1870–1872" (PhD dissertation, University of Manitoba, 1986).

4. Archibald to Lord Lisgar, April 19, 1872, quoted in Saywell, *The Office of Lieutenant-Governor*, 62.

5. A.I. Silver, *The French-Canadian Idea of Confederation, 1864–1900* (Toronto: University of Toronto Press, 1982), 78–87.

6. K.G. Pryke, "Archibald, Sir Adams George," *Dictionary of Canadian Biography, vol. XII: 1891 to 1900* (Toronto: University of Toronto Press, 1990), 30–33.

7. Macdonald had considered Donald A. Smith a candidate for Lieutenant-Governor, although Smith let his unwillingness be known before the matter progressed very far. Smith to Northcote, May 9, 1870, quoted in Beckles Willson, *The Life of Lord Strathcona and Mount Royal* (London: Cassell, 1915), 250–51; Saywell, *The Office of Lieutenant-Governor*, 62.

8. Saywell, *The Office of Lieutenant-Governor*, 62.

9. Canada, House of Commons, *Debates*, May 7, 1870. 1425–26.

10. Silver, *The French-Canadian Idea of Confederation*, 69–73.

11. "Memorandum Connected with the Fenian Invasion of Manitoba in October, 1871," November 10, 1871, in Canada, House of Commons, *Journals*, 1874, App. 6: "Report of the Select Committee on the Causes of the Difficulties in the North West in 1869 and 1870," 142.

12. *The New Nation*, July 1, 1870, quoted in Stanley, *Louis Riel*, 149. That same day Riel wrote to Taché, who was journeying east for clarification of the Dominion government's commitment to an amnesty for those engaged in the resistance: "My profoundest respects to Mr. Archibald, we much desire his coming." Riel to Taché, July 24, 1870, in "Report of the Select Committee on the Causes of the Difficulties in the North West in 1869 and 1870," 37.

13. Quoted in Stanley, *Louis Riel*, 149.

14. Riel to Joseph Dubuc, October 21, 1870, in George Stanley (ed.), *The Collected Writings of Louis Riel*, vol. 1 (Edmonton: University of Alberta Press, 1985), 120–21.

15. "At least in our favour, the Governor is, without a doubt, sympathetic to our cause." Joseph Dubuc to Louis Riel, September 6, 1870, quoted in Saywell, *The Office of Lieutenant-Governor*, 62.

16. Howe to Archibald, August 4, 1870, in Canada, *Sessional Papers*, 1871, no. 20, 4–5.

17. Archibald to Howe, January 20, 1872, in "Report of the Select Committee on the Causes of the Difficulties in the North West in 1869 and 1870," 152.

18. Emerging as a faction prior to the resistance of 1869, the "Canadian" party had called for the acquisition of the North-West by the Dominion of Canada and encouraged westward migration of others from Ontario. Hostile to Riel and prone to making derogatory remarks about the Métis, a number of these former Ontarians took up arms against the Provisional Government. Among those who were taken prisoner by Riel for their opposition was Thomas Scott, who was executed for insubordination towards his captors. After the birth of the province, the "Canadian" or "loyalist" party attracted a growing number of new settlers from Ontario, many of whom remained angry over Scott's death and the concessions won by the Métis, whom they considered traitors. Lovell Clark, "Schultz, John Christian," *Dictionary of Canadian Biography, vol. XII: 1891 to 1900*, 949–52.

19. "St. Andrew's," *The Manitoban*, November 19, 1870: 2.

20. "Testimony of Walter Robert Bown," in "Report of the Select Committee to Enquire into the Causes of the Difficulties in the North West in 1869 and 1870," 114. Cf. Stanley, *Louis Riel*, 150–3, 159–61.

21. Archibald to Macdonald, October 9, 1871, quoted in Stanley, *Louis Riel*, 160.

22. Ronaghan, "The Archibald Administration in Manitoba," 537.

23. Stanley, *Louis Riel*, 164.

24. For example, an inquest that Archibald struck in 1870 to investigate the death of the Métis Elzéar Goulet, who drowned trying to escape a stoning by three Ontarians, was inconclusive, even though the identities of the culprits were well known in the bars and streets of Winnipeg and among the Métis. Around the same time two other Riel supporters were killed, while several others were seriously injured in assaults. J.A. Jackson, "Goulet, Elzéar," *Dictionary of Canadian Biography, vol. X: 1861 to 1870* (Toronto: University of Toronto Press, 1975), 329–30.

25. In what was both an historical review and a mitigation of criticism against his administration, Archibald was both right and wrong. For example, a Supreme Court of Manitoba, renamed the Court of Queen's Bench in 1872, had been legislated in the Manitoba Act, but not until 1872 did the Dominion government appoint anyone to the bench. In the interim, the General Quarterly Court, which the Hudson's Bay Company had created in the 1830s, exercised transitional judicial authority, although not until October 1870 was Francis G. Johnson appointed to it. A judiciary did exist, but it was a transitional and understaffed one. On the establishment of Manitoba's judiciary, see Dale Brawn, *The Court of Queen's Bench of Manitoba, 1870–1950: A Biographical History* (Toronto: University of Toronto, Press, 2006), 15–18, 22–24.

26. [A.G. Archibald] "Manitoba, The History of a Year," *The Manitoban*, January 1, 1872.

27. Testimony of Adams G. Archibald, in "Report of the Select Committee to Enquire into the Causes of the Difficulties in the North West in 1869 and 1870," 138–39.

28. Milligan, "The Lieutenant-Governorship in Manitoba," 89.

29. John L. Finlay, "Boyd, Alfred," *Dictionary of Canadian Biography, vol. XIII: 1901–1910* (Toronto: University of Toronto Press, 1994), 104–05.

30. Archibald to Joseph Howe, September 17, 1870, quoted in Milligan, "The Lieutenant-Governorship in Manitoba," 89; Dubuc to Riel, March 20, 1871, quoted in Stanley, *Louis Riel*, 168; G.O. Rothney, "Girard, Marc-Amable," *Dictionary of Canadian Biography, vol. XII: 1891 to 1900*, 369–73.

31. Saywell, *The Office of Lieutenant-Governor*, 63.

32. Murray S. Donnelly, *The Government of Manitoba* (Toronto: University of Toronto Press, 1963), 17.

33. Milligan, "The Lieutenant-Governorship in Manitoba," 90; Stanley, *Louis Riel*, 165.

34. Macdonald to Archibald, November 1, 1870, quoted in Saywell, *The Office of Lieutenant-Governor*, 64.

35. Ronaghan, "The Archibald Administration in Manitoba," 534–43.

36. The Archdiocese of St. Boniface was established on September 22, 1871. Until then, Taché was Bishop. Jean Hamelin, "Taché, Alexandre-Antoine," *Dictionary of Canadian Biography, vol. XI: 1891 to 1900*, 1006.

37. Stanley, *Louis Riel*, 165.

38. Gerald Friesen, "Norquay, John," *Dictionary of Canadian Biography, vol. XI: 1881 to 1890* (Toronto: University of Toronto Press, 1982), 643.

39. Finlay, "Boyd, Alfred," 105.

40. Quoted in Rothney, "Girard, Marc-Amable," 370. Dubuc's opinion, quoted above, was a bit unfair. He did arrange to have Archibald meet Riel and he did join the others in urging Riel in 1873 to seek the Commons seat for Provencher opened with Cartier's death. As well, before the Commons committee investigating the amnesty in 1874, he gave testimony favourable to Riel. His cautious counsel that

Riel keep a low profile in Manitoba appreciated the real personal danger the Métis leader confronted. Conservative, Catholic, and nationalist, he nonetheless was moderate and not ultramontane in his approach to English-French relations. Throughout, Girard's position was consistent with that of Cartier.

41. A.I. Silver, "Royal, Joseph," *Dictionary of Canadian Biography, vol. XIII: 1890 to 1901*, 911.

42. Lovell Clark, "Clarke, Henry Joseph," *Dictionary of Canadian Biography, vol. XI: 1881 to 1890*, 192–93.

43. Quoted in Clark, "Clarke, Henry Joseph," 193.

44. Stanley, *Louis Riel*, 171.

45. Archibald to Ritchot, October 4, 1871, in "Report of the Select Committee to Enquire into the Causes of the Difficulties in the North West in 1869 and 1870," 90–91; Stanley, *Louis Riel*, 173–74.

46. Testimony of Marc-Amable Girard, in "Report of the Select Committee to Enquire into the Causes of the Difficulties in the North West in 1869 and 1870," 180.

47. Stanley, *Louis Riel*, 170–71.

48. Testimony of Adams G. Archibald in "Report of the Select Committee to Enquire into the Causes of the Difficulties in the North West in 1869 and 1870," 141–42.

49. Stanley, *Louis Riel*, 175, 183; Saywell, *The Office of Lieutenant-Governor*, 73.

50. Archibald to Macdonald, October 7, 1871, quoted in Saywell, *The Office of Lieutenant-Governor*, 68–69.

51. Archibald to Howe, January 20, 1872, in "Report of the Select Committee to Enquire into the Causes of the Difficulties in the North West in 1869 and 1870," 151.

52. Saywell, *The Office of Lieutenant-Governor*, 71–73.

53. Stanley, *Louis Riel*, 184.

54. Ruth Swan, "Unequal Justice: The Métis in O'Donoghue's Raid of 1871," *Manitoba History* 39 (2000): 24–38.

55. Milligan, "The Lieutenant-Governorship in Manitoba," 110.

56. Stanley, *Louis Riel*, 185–86.

57. Jean Friesen, "Morris, Alexander," *Dictionary of Canadian Biography, vol. XI: 1881 to 1890*, 608–11; Brawn, *The Court of Queen's Bench of Manitoba*, 24–46.

58. Milligan, "The Lieutenant-Governorship in Manitoba," 141, 150.

59. Ibid., 142–44; Sprague, *Canada and the Métis*, 82; Stanley, *Louis Riel*, 188.

60. Milligan, "The Lieutenant-Governorship in Manitoba," 149–50; Stanley, *Louis Riel*, 193.

61. Milligan, "The Lieutenant-Governorship in Manitoba," 167.

62. Ibid., 174.

63. Clark, "Clarke, Henry Joseph," 193.

64. J.L. Johnston, "Lord Gordon Gordon," Historical and Scientific Society of Manitoba, *Papers*, 3rd series, 7 (1952), 7–20.

65. Milligan, "The Lieutenant-Governorship in Manitoba," 175–76; "Le Secret d'un Ministre," *Le Métis*, 25 juillet 1874.

66. Milligan, "The Lieutenant-Governorship in Manitoba," 172; Saywell, *The Office of Lieutenant-Governor*, 74.

67. "Provincial Parliament," *The Manitoban*, February 12, 1872; "Political Ostracism," *Manitoba Free Press*, December 7, 1872; Stanley, *Louis Riel*, 187; Ruth Swan, "Frank Cornish—The Man," *Manitoba History* 9 (Spring 1985).

68. "The Parliament," *The Manitoban*, March 1, 8, 1873; "The Legislature," *Manitoba Free Press*, March 1, 1873.

69. "Provincial Parliament," *Manitoba Free Press*, November 15, 1873.

70. John A. Macdonald tendered his Conservative government's resignation on November 5, 1873 after a parliamentary inquiry had sustained Liberal charges that the prime minister had sought election funds from Montreal businessman Hugh Allan, who expected that the government would award him the contract to build the Canadian Pacific Railway. Alexander Mackenzie formed a new government, but immediately called an election for January. The Manitoba boundary necessarily had to wait.

71. "Provincial Parliament," *Manitoba Free Press*, November 15, 1873; "Speech from the Throne," *The Manitoban*, November 8, 1873. The newly elected Mackenzie government later declined to consider enlarging the province or to increase the provincial subsidy. "Bulletin Parliamentaire," *Le Métis*, 3 octobre 1874.

72. "Nouvelles divisions electorales," *Le Métis*, 8 novembre 1873; "La nouvelle loi sûr les divisions electorales," *Le Métis*, 15 novembre 1873; "Parliamentary: Legislative Assembly," *The Manitoban*, November 15, 1873.

73. "Responsabilité ministèrielle," *Le Métis*, 14 juillet 1874.

74. "Le Nouveau Cabinet," *Le Métis*, 8 juillet 1874.

75. "Bulletin Parliamentaire," *Le Métis*, 3 octobre 1874.

76. Ibid.

77. The bill was rejected in effect when a procedural amendment introduced by Royal was passed calling for the assembly to rise from the committee of the whole that was considering it. "Bulletin Parliamentaire," *Le Métis*, 10 octobre 1874.

78. Ibid.

79. "Grande Assemblée," *Le Métis*, 22 novembre 1874.

80. "Une Situation nouvelle," *Le Métis*, 5 decembre 1874. "Le dernier Cabinet," *Le Métis*, 12 decembre 1874.

81. "Provincial Parliament," *The Manitoban*, March 18, 1871. See Brawn, *The Court of Queen's Bench of Manitoba*.

82. "Legislative Assembly," *The Manitoban*, March 25, 1871; "Supreme Court Bill," *Manitoba News-Letter*, April 8, 1871.

83. "Close of the Session," *The Manitoban*, February 26, 1872; cf. "The Opening of Parliament," *The Manitoban*, January 15, 1872.

84. "The Legislature," *Manitoba Free Press*, March 8, 1873; "The Iron Heel," *Manitoba Free Press*, March 8, 1873.

85. "Incorporation: Injustice and Indignation," *Manitoba Free Press*, March 8, 1873; "A Word with Mr. Speaker," *Manitoba Free Press*, March 8, 1873.

86. "The Parliament," *The Manitoban*, February 22, 1873; "The Legislature," *Manitoba Free Press*, February 22, 1873.

87. "Provincial Parliament," *Manitoba Free Press*, November 15, 1873.

88. Alfred T. Phillips, "Development of Municipal Institutions in Manitoba to 1886" (MA thesis, University of Manitoba, 1948).

89. "Winnipeg Incorporation," *Manitoba Free Press*, November 1, 1873.

90. "Provincial Parliament," *Manitoba Free Press*, November 15, 1873.

91. "The New School Bill," Toronto *Globe and Mail*, January 5, 1871. See Charles E. Phillips, *The Development of Education in Canada* (Toronto: Gage, 1957), 236–37.

92. Keith Wilson and Alexander Gregor, *The Development of Education in Manitoba* (Dubuque, IA: Kendall/Hunt, 1984), 31.

93. "La Session," *Le Métis*, 8 mars 1873; "The School Act," *Manitoba Free Press*, January 18, 1873.

94. "Legislative Assembly," *The Manitoban*, May 6, 1871.

95. Ibid.; "Official School Correspondence," *Manitoba Free Press*, January 18, 1873; "The School Act," *Manitoba Free Press*, January 18, 1873; "Compulsory Education," *Manitoba Free Press*, May 24, 1873.

96. "The Legislature," *Manitoba Free Press*, March 8, 1873.

97. Archibald to Howe, April 9, 1871, RG 15, Records of the Department of Interior, vol. 229: 1437, Library and Archives Canada.

98. "The Parliament," *The Manitoban*, March 8, 1873; "The Legislature," *Manitoba Free Press*, March 1, 1873.

99. "The Parliament," *The Manitoban*, March 1, 1873.

100. "Legislative Assembly," *The Manitoban*, April 22, 29, 1871; "Legislative Proceedings," *Manitoba News-Letter*, April 19, 1873; "Incorporation of St. Boniface," *Manitoba News-Letter*, April 15, 1871.

101. Sprague, *Canada and the Métis*, 90; Thomas Flanagan, *Métis Lands in Manitoba* (Calgary: University of Calgary Press, 1991), 36–37.

102. See for example the Assembly's debate on drafting a communication to the Dominion government calling for action on Métis lands and on the grant of lands to the so-called "old settlers." "Provincial Parliament," *Manitoba Free Press*, November 15, 1873.

103. Archibald to Howe, December 27, 1870, quoted in Flanagan, *Metis Lands in Manitoba*, 66.

104. "The Parliament," *The Manitoban*, February 15, 1875. Cf. Flanagan, *Métis Lands in Manitoba*, 103–05.

105. "The Parliament," *The Manitoban*, March 1, 1873.

106. "The Parliament," *The Manitoban*, March 8, 15, 1873; "Legislature de Manitoba," *Le Métis*, 5 avril 1873.

107. Support for both bills was more evenly divided than the outcomes suggested. Smith's bill passed 14 votes to 8, whereas Girard's bill had been defeated 10 votes to 7. But four members, Breland, Clarke, Schmidt, and Smith, who supported the second bill had been absent for the division on the first and probably the first three at least would have voted in favour. (A fifth absentee, Cunningham, opposed Smith's bill.) The significant difference was the change of side taken by Boyd, Howard, and McTavish (two members, Bunn and Bird participated in neither division).

108. Flanagan, *Métis Lands in Manitoba*, 104.

109. Ibid., 105.

110. Rothney, "Girard, Marc Amable," 373.

111. Ibid.

Robert A. Davis 1874–1878

RUTH SWAN

Robert Atkinson Davis, 1874–1878

Robert Davis remains virtually unknown in the province which he served as its second Premier. There is no landmark in Manitoba or street name in Winnipeg to memorialize his contribution and only a posthumous portrait in the Hall of Premiers in the Legislative Building commemorates his administration. Yet his role in shaping the political and governmental system during the province's emergence from federal tutelage is a significant one and reveals a great deal about the conditions of Manitoban public life during the 1870s.

An Anglo-Quebecker in North America

Robert Atkinson Davis was born on March 9, 1841, near the village of Dudswell in the Eastern Townships of what was then Canada East. Robert and his twin brother, Thomas Priestley Davis, were the only sons of Thomas Davis, Sr. and his American-born wife, Anna Urania Chaffee. The first immigrant in this Davis line was Thomas Sr.'s father, Charles, a private in the British army's 103rd Regiment of Foot, whose regiment was settled in eastern Quebec after the defeat of Napoleon. He took up land on the St. Francis River near Richmond, Lower Canada. Anna Chafffee was from a group of non-Loyalist Americans who had moved north to farm.[1]

Most of the Eastern Townships were first settled not by the French but the British, who remained a majority until well after Confederation. The Davis family was Anglican in religion and Thomas Davis, Sr. participated in the organization of the municipal council and school board. He was appointed as the clerk of the Circuit Court for Wolfe County in 1855, his certificate being signed by Sir George E. Cartier.[2] The appointment indicates that Thomas Sr. had ties with the Liberal-Conservative Party, the dominant political alignment of mostly-moderate British and French supporters. Life close to the border with Vermont and New Hampshire resulted in considerable movement of settlers back and forth across the boundary, as was the case with Davis's mother's family. It was typical for individuals to look south for better opportunities, particularly after the mid-19th century, when thousands of Quebecers, both French and English, moved to the United States.

The twin brothers attended St. Francis College in Richmond, Quebec, where their grandparents lived, and in 1861 became schoolteachers in Dudswell. Robert Davis later claimed that he had attended law classes at McGill University in Montreal for a few months, but he did not complete a degree. After the Civil War, the brothers set out for the mining frontier of the American Rockies. Robert and Thomas had their photo taken in the railroad town of Sheyenne, Dakota Territory, but their correspondence shows that they lived in different states for most of this time. Robert was in the gold fields near Helena, Montana, while Thomas headed for the silver mines of Black Hawk, Colorado. They did not stake mining claims, but engaged in a more secure source of income than prospecting, that of freighting teams of horses for the prospectors. During his first stay in the United States, Robert wrote to his sister Adelaide: "I do not think very highly of Canada compared to this country." But he discouraged her from traveling across the west to visit them, citing fear of Native hostilities and attacks on American steamboats and railways.[3]

The brothers made the most of their opportunities. Robert returned home when he had saved the considerable sum of $5,000. In March of 1870, he married Susan Augusta True, an American living in the Eastern Townships, at Coaticook, Quebec.[4] Immediately after their marriage, they set out for the Canadian West. Thomas had also returned to the Townships, married a local woman, Helen Lebaron, and headed for Bismarck, North Dakota. It is not clear why the twin brothers followed such similar paths in heading for the northern plains, but chose frontier settlements that were on different sides of the international boundary. There is evidence that the brothers maintained amicable ties over the years. One of their sisters, Matilda Leavitt, left an abusive husband in Quebec and moved with her adult children to Jamestown, N.D. after Robert had moved to the United States as well.[5]

Settling Into Red River

For Canadians, Upper Fort Garry was extremely remote and difficult to visit before the railway's arrival in 1878. In November 1869, as the dispute between residents of Red River and the Canadian government about the terms of Red River's entry into Confederation was simmering, Riel and his Métis cavalry had taken military control of the region by establishing guards on the road system from La Barrière at St. Norbert, by the capture and occupation of Upper Fort Garry, and by the capture of some Canadians and mixed-blood people deemed agents of Canada in the winter of 1869–70. The Métis cavalry patrolled the trails south of Fort Garry and did not allow strangers to enter without the prescribed pass signed by the Secretary and later President of the Provisional Government, Louis Riel.[6]

It seems strange that Robert Davis decided to risk taking his wife to a zone of conflict. Canadians, especially Protestants from Ontario, had made themselves unpopular in the months preceding the arrival of the Lieutenant-Governor designate, William McDougall, through their assumption of superiority over the local residents. During the Resistance of 1869 and 1870, the Canadians and their allies learned that they could not take the annexation of Red River by Canada for granted. When Thomas Scott was executed by a Provisional Government firing squad on March 4, 1870, local chronicler Alexander Begg noted that "a deep gloom has settled over the settlement on account of this deed." Scott's execution would not be forgiven by Protestants in Ontario.[7]

Two months after Scott's execution, in May 1870, Begg laconically reported to his journal that "a gentleman and his wife by the name of Davis arrived to-day he says he hails from Sherbrooke, Canada East." Robert Davis's arrival is reputed to have been challenging. He had left his wife south of the settlement and drove up the east side of the Red towards St. Boniface. He unhitched his valuable horse from the wagon, took off his clothes and tied them to the harness, swimming his horse across the river—a cold swim in early May. It is possible that Davis took this bracing route to avoid being escorted to the Upper Fort by Louis Riel's excitable guards—it was, after all, dangerous to be a Canadian in Red River. He dressed, tied up his horse and approached the gate. When challenged, he replied in French, a language he was fluent in, and his presence did not alarm the guards who were suspicious of anyone speaking English. He was taken to see President Riel, whose office was in the Upper Fort. Davis is reputed to have had an amicable encounter with Riel, eased by Davis's fluency in French and candid explanation about his goals. Granted the crucial pass signed by Riel, Davis withdrew to the riverbank, retrieved his horse, and recrossed the river to his wagon on the St. Boniface side of the Red River. He drove back to his wife and they made their appearance in the settlement the next day as duly noted by Alexander Begg.[8]

On May 14, 1870, Begg reported that "the man Davis and his wife had left Emmerling's Hotel but it is not known where he has gone." By the following fall, after the arrival of the Wolseley Expedition, which brought the assurance of Canadian control over the colony, Davis had purchased Emmerling's Hotel from "Dutch George," a German-American annexationist who had given up on the plans of various Americans who hoped that the Red River Settlement would join the United States. Davis used his nest egg from Montana to run the renamed Davis House. He had capital and so was already a businessman of note in the rugged little village at the heart of the settlement when he was only 29 years old. Begg later concluded that the Davis House hotel "proved to be a Bonanza to its new proprietor, the house being crowded from morning to night with the many strangers visiting the town as well as the volunteers [disbanded from the Wolseley Expedition] stationed at Fort Garry."[9]

Dr. John O'Donnell, a political opponent who later disparaged Davis's talents as provincial Premier, allowed that he excelled as a saloonkeeper. Davis had "the countenance of an innocent abroad," claimed O'Donnell, who admitted that this characteristic was politically valuable. When men of different political views had an argument at the Davis House, in his well-appointed saloon, the proprietor "would invite them to share a little glass of port or perhaps some excellent whiskey sent to him by an old Scotchman in Montreal, which had been aging in his cellar for over thirty years, and on the way home they agreed that Mr. Davis was the prince of good fellows." Owning a hotel in frontier Winnipeg was an excellent political opportunity because only men could vote and many of the potential voters were recent immigrants who enjoyed the food and beverages provided by their genial host. Indeed, O'Donnell described Davis in terms that epitomize the North American frontier saloonkeeper of the time. [10]

Recovering from the Red River Resistance, Winnipeg quickly emerged as the commercial centre for the new Province, but it remained a divided settlement. The disbanded Wolseley volunteers and the young men from Canada, mostly Ontario, who were looking for land and new adventures resided on the west side of the Red and north of the Assiniboine River while the Métis stayed on the French or east side of the Red and south of the Assiniboine. There had been a pattern of Canadian-led violence against the Métis and they experienced difficulties in finding safety except on the east side of the Red. As historian W.L. Morton put it, "Order had to be maintained while the volunteers fought with half-breeds in the saloons of Winnipeg, and brawling that on at least one occasion ended in the unpunished killing of the *métis* Elzéar Goulet."[11]

Davis disregarded the divisions and the danger and reached out to the French community by advertising in the newspaper, *Le Métis*:

M.[onsieur] Davis a constament en vente les vins et liqueurs les plus choisis et de toutes sortes qu'il débite à meilleur marché que n'importe où dans Winnipeg.[12]

It is likely that many Winnipeg voters did not read the French language newspaper and therefore were unaware of Davis's attempts to market his business to the French quarter, but many of the older settlers and fur traders did speak French. A man like Davis who could appeal to voters on both sides of the Red River as a moderate was very welcome to those tired of ethnic and religious conflict, hostility and violence. Davis planned to upgrade his hotel and advertised in the Winnipeg papers his "commodious billiard hall" and new barber shop. He also erected the first street lamp in Winnipeg in front of Davis House.[13]

Entering Public Life

When Robert Davis began his public career, he emerged as a spokesman for and leader of Winnipeg's nascent business community. His main constituents were young, white males who were in a minority in 1870, but who would quickly gain strength as immigration brought in greater numbers of English-speaking immigrants from Ontario. Unlike Davis, they were not generally sympathetic to the concerns of the "older settlers" (the Métis and the English-speaking mixed-race employees of the HBC). The propagandists for the Thomas Scott affair in Ontario and Red River alike, most notably the influential Dr. John C. Schultz, a physician, businessman and speculator, had painted the Métis as violent and dangerous. But the Ontarians were equally prone to violence.

The new province was divided administratively as well as spatially between Catholic and Anglican parishes and so there was already distrust over religious differences, compounded by misunderstanding over language. The newcomers did not understand French or Cree, the two main components of the Michif language, or Bungee, which was mixed English and Cree. They were ignorant of local customs, which had favoured the traditions of the buffalo hunters and York boat voyageurs. Winnipeg evolved as an enclave of English-speaking newcomers while surrounded by the farms of Cree- or Bungee-speaking mixed-bloods (Red River British) to the north and west, Michif-speaking Métis and other French Canadians to the east, south and west.[14] Ethnocultural suspicions were compounded by the actions of the Métis during the resistance (taking prisoners, threatening to shoot several of them and killing Scott), so that anyone associated with the Provisional Government was in danger and leaders such as Riel, O'Donoghue and Lépine were forced to flee to the United States. Violent acts committed by the so-called Orangemen and volunteers, including a number of assaults and the deaths of Norbert Parisien and Elzear Goulet, remained unresolved.[15]

Duality and the Quebec Model

From 1870 to 1874, the federal government led by Sir John A. Macdonald maintained tight control over the provincial legislature by charging the Lieutenant-Governors with the total management of both the politics and government of the tiny province. The first Lieutenant-Governor, Adams Archibald, had the challenge when he arrived in 1870 of establishing political and administrative institutions in Manitoba. He recognized the religious and linguistic duality entrenched in the Manitoba Act by supporting the balance of French and English, Catholic and Protestant, as reflected in the even balance of the population in the 1870 census. Out of a total of 11,963 people in Manitoba, there were: 5,757 French Métis, 4,083 English mixed-bloods (Red River British), 1,565 whites, and 558 "Indians."[16] Archibald excluded extremists on both sides—Louis Riel and his close associates for the Métis side and John C. Schultz and the so-called "Canadian party" on the Canadian side. Archibald ignored the demands for one Protestant education system and provincial constituencies in the first election were based on the parish system. The 12 Catholic parishes voted for the French candidates (or English Catholic supporters like Henry Clarke) and the 12 Anglican parishes voted for the English (the old settlers including English mixed-race people) or the Canadians.[17]

Archibald was prohibited by the federal government from establishing the principle of "responsible government" in which the Premier picked his own cabinet; the new Lieutenant-Governor was expected to choose the cabinet himself.[18] Manitoba voters were denied local control over their provincial government as a result. Using the Lieutenant-Governor, the federal government maintained control over the disposition of all public land, which had been one of the main contentions behind the Resistance to Canadian occupation in 1869–70, and it was impossible for the provincial government to develop the economy or assure the Métis and other "old settlers" that their land rights would be protected when all decisions about land were made in Ottawa, despite the definition in the Manitoba Act of a 1.6 million-acre settlement reserve for pre-1870 residents. Manitoba was also circumscribed by small provincial boundaries which further limited the provincial tax base. In these ways, Prime Minister John A. Macdonald kept the political evolution of Manitoba in check until local agitation forced the second Lieutenant-Governor, Alexander Morris, to cede the choice of first minister and cabinet to the legislature in 1874. Although Macdonald argued that the local politicians were not capable of running a government, this decision to prevent cabinet government was colonialist and sowed the seeds of long-standing western alienation. While Macdonald wanted to ensure that the Métis would not continue to exercise political power in Manitoba until the French were swamped by English-speaking immigrants and that Louis Riel would never be Premier, he succeeded in alienating many Manitoba newcomers from Quebec and Ontario who were disillusioned with the control Ottawa exercised over economic development. Manitoba was still a colony, despite the illusion of provincial status and democratic institutions. This lack of local control led to financial instability and eventually a ministerial crisis.[19]

During his first two years in Manitoba, Davis had focused on personal concerns. He was running an ambitious business establishment which thrived on the efforts of its proprietor. On September 4, 1872, Le Métis announced that "Monsieur Davis" had been awarded the contract from the Dominion Government to build three public buildings, the Post Office, Customs, Land Office and the Receiver General. Since Robert Davis was reported visiting the East in the spring of 1872, he may have spent time in Ottawa lobbying for this lucrative contract. This successful patronage contract indicates that Davis, like his father, clearly had good ties with the Conservative Party. In November 1872, his wife, Susan, gave birth to a daughter, Della. But Susan died a few days later from an infection related to the birth and Davis was left with an infant daughter and no relatives nearby to help raise her. He decided to take Della to Paterson, New Jersey, to be raised by his late wife's sister.[20] Bereft of wife and child after just two years in Winnipeg, Davis plunged into the public issues that affected his own interests.

Running for Office

In 1872, Davis became active in local political matters, starting with the fight to incorporate the City of Winnipeg, which occupied him throughout 1873. He was drawn to politics in order to promote the agenda of people like himself who were interested in furthering civic business opportunities and administrative reform, which meant challenging the stifling economic and political influence of the Hudson's Bay Company (HBC). Robert Davis had contested his first election in 1872 when he challenged the HBC's powerful Commissioner, Donald A. Smith, who was simultaneously an MLA and MP during the early 1870s, for the presidency of the Provincial Agricultural Association. Davis lost, but continued his active role as civic leader when he became chairman of a committee to investigate the election riots in September 1872. Davis also became engaged in other local political activities such as election as a Protestant school trustee. But it was his activism supporting the incorporation of Winnipeg as a city in 1872 and 1873 which drew him into provincial politics.[21]

Newcomers like Davis resented Donald A. Smith and the HBC because they resented the political influence of the Company on land development in Winnipeg and its hostility to the incorporation of Winnipeg. They also suspected that the Company charged inflated freight rates on river streamers moving between Manitoba and Minnesota. Davis's political activity was further stimulated by a battle over the location of Dominion government buildings, specifically whether they should be centrally located in the business centre of town or near Upper Fort Garry, and properties owned by the HBC. In May 1872, local businessmen organized a public meeting at Davis House to petition the federal government to change the site of the Immigration sheds; there was also concern about the site of the Post Office. A committee made up of Robert Davis, Alexander Begg and A.G.B. Bannatyne was asked to draft a petition to Ottawa. This agitation had prompted demands for the incorporation of Winnipeg so that the town could raise its own taxes and control development.[22]

Davis was part of the group that organized a local Board of Trade in 1872 and promoted the cause of incorporating the City of Winnipeg during 1873. The Provincial Legislature vacillated and the bill before the house was rejected. The Speaker of the House, Dr. Bird, from an old HBC family, suffered the indignity of being physically attacked, including being tarred and feathered, as punishment for not calling a vote on the bill. Davis strongly criticized the provincial administration for its ineffectual handling of the incorporation issue which helped to bring him to prominence by leading a protest committee. When incorporation was finally achieved and civic elections held in January 1874, Davis was talked about as a candidate for civic office, but he did not win a seat on the new city council. He had already set his ambition on a seat in the provincial Legislature.[23]

In Ottawa, the fall of Macdonald's government over the CPR scandal led to a federal election in February 1874. In Manitoba, Riel won election in Provencher for the second time although he was not able to campaign; he was still influential with the Métis and French. Donald Smith beat A.G.B. Bannatyne in Selkirk, but the Winnipeg businessmen were goaded into action by Smith's political success. Smith had to resign his provincial seat in the electoral division of Winnipeg and Davis ran in the by-election. He drew upon the support of the business community, including a group of populists, the Patrons of Husbandry, often called Grangers, then organizing in Canada and the United States. Davis and Begg had organized a Manitoba chapter, the "British American Grangers of Manitoba" in 1874. The Manitoba Grange proclaimed its opposition to "corporations, companies, monopolies, or cliques," and specifically aimed at the HBC. Begg later claimed that the Grangers "marched to the polls in a body and secured his return as a member for Winnipeg before Alexander McMicken and his friends had time to realize the situation."[24] There was no secret ballot. McMicken, the son of Gilbert McMicken, Macdonald's appointee as head of the Winnipeg Land Office, was also literally an "agent" for the Dominion government. His family was highly unsympathetic to French or to Métis land rights. Davis was successful in forming a new alliance that included both French and English speakers and he won his seat as a spokesman for moderates who would not oppose French and Catholic rights. The hotelier and saloonkeeper became the new Member of the Legislative Assembly for Winnipeg. The Grangers fell into disarray after the election.

The Defeat of Attorney General Clarke

Once elected to the Legislative Assembly, Davis worked with the French Party to overthrow the domineering but increasingly unpopular Attorney General, Henry Clarke, and bring down the sitting government. Clarke was a bilingual, Quebec-trained lawyer who represented the French Catholic parish of St. Charles, on the Assiniboine. Clarke was also a bully who was verbally abusive in the House and intimidated members. His manoeuvres and political opportunism did not win him the premiership he craved, but cabinet members did not know how to get rid of him without themselves losing power.[25]

The French Party was frustrated with Clarke's duplicity as well as with the denial of responsible government. In the absence of a designated Premier between 1870 and 1874, Clarke repeatedly tried to claim the functions if not the title of Premier. But, as noted by Alexander Begg and others, Clarke's duplicity was exposed:

> while he was an out and out supporter of the French party, in fact their champion during the time we are now writing of, we will yet have to chronicle … his coquetry with the English, and the final abandonment of the French, which culminated in an avowed hostility.[26]

The French Party had expected Clarke to defend their interests in the cabinet, but the sectarian violence and hostility resulting from the "reign of terror," the trials of the Pembina Métis for supporting O'Donoghue and the Fenians, the harassment of Riel and Lépine and the later trials of Ambroise Lépine and André Nault for participating in Scott's execution, all disillusioned many of the French population about Clarke's loyalty. He had also annoyed the Canadian group in Winnipeg with his indecisiveness over civic incorporation, and his redistribution bill did not please any faction.

Lieutenant-Governor Morris, who had replaced Archibald, was also frustrated with the personal feuds and antagonisms within the cabinet by 1874 and wondered how he had kept them working together for so long. It was difficult to get rid of Clarke without splitting the French Party, an alliance of the French Métis and the bloc of French Quebecers, often designated the Quebec Party, recruited to Manitoba by the powerful Roman Catholic Archbishop, Joseph Taché. One of the French Quebecers, Joseph Dubuc, noted later in his memoirs that his colleague in the Quebec Party, Joseph Royal, who was in the cabinet, was also exasperated with Clarke's actions. Royal observed that a government without a responsible Premier was defective. When the new session of the legislature opened in July 1874, it was the newcomer, Robert Davis, who arranged a vote of non-confidence moved by an English MLA and seconded by a French MLA. This motion carried by a vote of 15 to 7 and forced Clarke's resignation.[27]

Begg reported that "the advent of the new member seemed to raise the courage of the House." Clarke accused his opponents of hatching the non-confidence "plot from the back room of a city tavern."[28] According to Dubuc, Clarke reacted with verbal threats and abuse but Davis was not intimidated. He knew that the Catholic clergy were offended by Clarke's political behaviour and by charges Clarke had abandoned his wife for another woman. When Clarke was shown to have left his wife, it caused considerable scandal in the settlement. Davis threatened to reveal other scandals that had tainted Clarke in Montreal before he moved to Winnipeg. Clarke in turn challenged Davis to a duel and Davis agreed. "Tell me the place and the time and I will be there," he recalled in a later newspaper interview. "But it will be a waste of time. I know your type." Davis recalled his triumph:

> The excitement at this time was uncontrollable. I told him he had
> undertaken to bluff the wrong man. It wouldn't work. But if he really
> wanted satisfaction, he could have it then or any other time…. From that
> time, Henry J. Clarke became a changed man … he was a whipped man
> and knew it. And he has never been in the House from that day to this.[29]

It was unusual for a businessman in Winnipeg to reach out to the beleaguered French community across the Red River. The persecution of the leaders of the Provisional Government by the federal government and its Manitoba sympathizers continued unabated without the promised amnesty for the events of 1870. Several of the leaders of 1869–70, such as Riel, had to flee the country or continually hide out with supporters. The political show trials of the three Métis who were charged with treason felony demonstrated that Canadian politicians would not be sympathetic to those who took up arms against the government. Even the moderate Lieutenant-Governor Archibald had lost his position for shaking hands with Riel.

Davis took a moderate approach and did not oppose French Catholic representation on principle; he may have lost votes in his own constituency for developing an alliance with the French Quebec lawyers like Dubuc and Royal and with Riel's supporters like Louis Schmidt. Davis was comfortable in following the model of bilingualism and biculturalism in the legislature and political system. That system had, after all, been the basis of politics in the old Province of Canada in which he himself had been raised. Of course after 1867, that system of French/English and Catholic/Protestant dualism had been abandoned with the move to Confederation and separate provincehood for Quebec and Ontario, but Davis had been out of Canada seeking his fortune when the old dualist system crumbled and was abandoned.[30]

Attacking the Deficit

Davis's success resulted from his appeal to disparate interests which transcended ethnic and religious politics. He appealed to the English Party (the Country-born or English mixed-race group) and Winnipeg businessmen (mostly Ontario Canadians) with the authority of a serious local businessman. He cemented his alliance with the broad French Party (both the Métis and French Quebecers) by speaking French and supporting French-language rights, as well as supporting the unresolved Métis land claims.

When Macdonald's government was defeated by the Liberals over the CPR scandal, there was further confusion over land development with the new administration led by Alexander Mackenzie. Provincial politicians quietly fumed as they had little power to deal with the frustrations plaguing Manitoba settlers, old and new. The tension over the Métis land question and the confusion resulting from Ottawa's handling of the issue continued to cause problems during Davis's tenure in the cabinet and as Premier. The major result was that provincial politicians realized they were powerless to control the economic development of the province when the Dominion Government maintained the power to decide how land ownership and development would proceed. Railway development was on the horizon and ambitious Winnipeg businessmen wanted to profit from the sale of Manitoba land which would quickly increase in value with the new transportation system bringing in immigrants and economic development. The provincial cabinet was frustrated by their weak political position. Having just achieved responsible government, they were powerless to pass legislation that would promote the economic prosperity of the "postage-stamp"-sized province and to solve problems plaguing their voters.

As Treasurer in 1874, Davis focused on the financial difficulties of the government, particularly the deficit. He established and chaired a Board of Audit that included James McKay, President of the appointed Legislative Council, and the Premier, Marc Girard. Davis was also authorized to examine the books of the Registrar of Winnipeg and to investigate provincial services used by the city.[31] These investigations helped him to get an understanding of the problems causing the cost overruns and to plan how to trim the deficit and increase revenue.

The main cause of the deficit was that the basic unavoidable costs of government simply outstripped the revenues available to the province. Manitoba depended on a federal subsidy instead of control over public lands for economic development. Since the boundaries of the province were small, they did not include population outside of the settlement belt along the Red and Assiniboine Rivers. Various delegations had gone to Ottawa to demand a higher subsidy without success and, since the cabinet was not able to cut expenses, the provincial debt grew every year. When Royal visited Ottawa in March 1874, before the fall of the administration piloted in the Legislature by Clarke, the Dominion government refused his request to expand provincial boundaries or to adjust the subsidy which was based on population. Mackenzie's government insisted that the only way to economize was to abolish the Upper House, or Legislative Council, composed of seven members appointed for life. The French Party appreciated the need for economy, but it was reluctant to vote out the appointed Council with its equal representation of French and English when their group faced overwhelming immigration of English-speakers, resulting in a loss of ethnic influence.

In the fall of 1874, Prime Minister Mackenzie sent the minister of the Interior, David Laird, to Red River to meet with the new provincial cabinet led by Premier Girard. Mackenzie then offered to increase the subsidy if the provincial government would reduce expenditures, especially with the Justice Department and government services. Mackenzie again advised them to abolish the Upper House which would save on salaries, government printing and the services provided to the Council. Davis and his cabinet colleagues had been successful in convincing the visiting minister that the financial crisis was real. Nevertheless, the political situation in Manitoba was unstable. Laird warned Morris that the promises of aid from Ottawa would not be carried out until the expected elections in December confirmed the new ministry.[32]

In the meantime, the trial of Ambroise Lépine for the murder of Thomas Scott once again inflamed the population into opposing camps and reminded everyone about the bad memories of the resistance in 1869–70, escalating into ethnic violence. Frank Cornish, a skilled debater and friend of the intolerant Dr. Schultz, was appointed prosecutor and Joseph Royal, editor of the French-language newspaper and supporter of Riel, defended the accused. On October 27, 1874, Morris wired the Prime Minister that the jury had found Lépine guilty and that he was sentenced to hang. The trial exacerbated hostility between the French Métis supporters and the anti-French faction in Winnipeg.[33]

This was bad timing for the Girard administration, which had to face the electorate in December, and the result was another ministerial crisis. Two English Protestant members of the cabinet, Hay and Ogletree, both strongly identified with the Ontario group in Manitoba and refused to go to the polls with a French-speaking Premier. Girard was forced to resign. The population was still divided over the Lépine trial and there were eruptions of public violence. Rumours surfaced that Riel would lead a gang of armed Métis to free Lépine while the Orangemen in Winnipeg planned to lynch him if he tried. Lieutenant-Governor Morris ordered the police to protect the prisoner. Archbishop Taché circulated a petition to free him. Many of Winnipeg's prominent citizens, including Davis, signed a petition for clemency.[34]

In January 1875, after the election, Governor-General Lord Dufferin granted Lépine an imperial pardon, reduced his sentence to two years and included time served. However, anti-French sentiments in the province had forced Girard and Dubuc to resign. In addition, the new province faced the strains of self-government amidst a period of major social and political upheaval during the decade. These were strains that Robert Davis was capable of managing for a time by maintaining an alliance among contending groups and by addressing the administrative and governmental needs of the new province.[35]

Davis's Premiership

Robert Davis agreed to serve as Premier and chose only two cabinet members, Joseph Royal and Colin Inkster. Royal was an influential MLA, representing the French and Métis interests, while Inkster was an unelected member of the Legislative Council, widely perceived as representing the Country-born in the Legislative Council. In writing about the change, Alexander Morris noted that:

> Davis stated ... he would act in a reconstruction to avoid the putting of the two races against each other, and to take away the cry that would be used in the elections... . I understand from Messrs. Girard and Dubuc that the new Government will have their support and, they believe that of their party while it ought to be acceptable to the English.[36]

In this way, Davis tried to forge a coalition of moderates who could work together. Meanwhile, violence occurred during the election meetings and the opposition candidates to Davis and his colleagues attacked French minority rights. At a town hall meeting, during "eight hours of speechifying," Davis publicly defended French rights in Manitoba, stating that he would not wish to be at the head of a government which would oppress the French. The writer for the *Standard* described speakers like Frank Cornish (first mayor of Winnipeg) and the editor of the *Winnipeg Free Press*, W.L. Luxton, another MLA, as "francophobic." The meeting broke up when a chair was aimed the heads of some of the audience.[37]

The election of December 1874 enabled Davis, who won his seat in Winnipeg, to form a government with the support of eight French members led by Joseph Royal; Norquay led the English Party with seven and Cornish led the Canadian opposition with eight. To offset the minority situation, Davis took his skeleton government to the legislature and formed a coalition in March 1875 by inviting Norquay and Nolin into the cabinet with Royal, Inkster and himself. Norquay had to abandon his demand to end French as an official language and Davis compromised by promising a redistribution bill to give the English more seats in recognition of their increase in population. Davis also added Charles Nolin to the cabinet as a French Métis representative, as Nolin objected to the Métis being represented by French Canadians. James McKay, partly Scottish and partly French Métis, had resigned with the Girard ministry. The Métis resented the elite position of the Quebec professional class. Davis took the precaution of securing resignation letters, addressed to both Royal and Davis, from the new ministers and so he controlled their appointments. In this and in other ways, including constant press reports, Davis continually made it clear that Joseph Royal was the second-most powerful person in cabinet and that it was a joint administration of moderate anglophones and francophones, the embodiment of the old practice of the Province of Canada which Royal and Davis, as former Canadians, would have known well.[38]

The secret of Davis's success was his creation of political stability. But more broadly, the Davis administration addressed a host of administrative and political matters ranging from the regularization of property transfers and business activities to continual adjustments to the administration of education and justice.[39] The popularity and relative activism of the Davis-Royal administration for the next three years kept them in power until 1878. Since Davis and Royal were the only Canadians in the cabinet and the others were of part-Aboriginal ancestry (Inkster, Norquay and Nolin), the new cabinet succeeded in recognizing the interests of the "old settlers" and gave them a stronger voice in Manitoba's second legislature than they had between 1870 and 1874. Compromise offset Norquay's and the English Party's objection to French as a official language. The moderates survived with the support of the English mixed-bloods who preferred Davis and Royal to the extremists from Ontario. The radicals were excluded, but the French lost power because their political leaders, Joseph Royal and Marc-Amable Girard, could not be Premier. Davis achieved the top position because he had an English name, was a Protestant who could speak French, and was able to work with people who were of different ethnic backgrounds and different religions. Leaders of the Ontario Canadian group like Hay and Cornish lost because they were intolerant of different languages, Roman Catholics and Aboriginal ancestry. Henry Clarke, who was supposed to support the French and Catholic cause, lost his position because of corruption. Davis's most powerful opponents, like Schultz and Donald A. Smith, preferred the federal arena to fight for Manitoba issues.

With the support of the French Party, led by lawyer and Attorney General Joseph Royal, Premier Davis pursued his financial agenda to end corruption and the deficit created by his predecessors. He continued as Provincial Treasurer and ensured that new auditing and accountability procedures eliminated graft in the Attorney General's office by, for example, ending Clarke's practice of serving as his own prosecutor and charging the province for each court case.

Davis also continued the attempts of the previous cabinet to lobby Ottawa for "better terms." They argued that the federal subsidy which substituted for the control of public lands was too small to cover the expenses of the new province. The Prime Minister had promised in November 1874, a month before the election, that Ottawa would increase the subsidy if the Manitoba cabinet could reduce expenditures, proposing the abolition of the Legislative Council. This body was the Manitoba upper house of seven members appointed for life. This issue reignited debates about ethnic duality as it was based on the Quebec model of a bicameral legislature. Ethnic representation was critical. Four members were Protestant and three (McKay, Hamelin and Dauphinais) were Catholic, but four had part-Aboriginal ancestry: the Catholics plus Colin Inkster, who represented the "old settlers." To induce the appointees to vote themselves out of office, most were offered other patronage positions: Inkster was made sheriff of Assiniboia, Ogletree, an Ontarian, became a magistrate, and McKay became President of the cabinet. The only member who did not receive an appointment was Dr. John O'Donnell which may explain O'Donnell's later negative assessment of the "Hotel Premier of Manitoba." The abolition of the relatively costly upper house paved the way for a considerable increase in the federal subsidy.

To pacify the English and Canadian parties, the Davis-Royal administration, as it was often called, agreed to a redistribution of constituencies which would result in more English seats. The French Party worried about their loss of power and the threat of the English groups to abolish French as an official language and separate Catholic schools, which was an important right that Archbishop Taché wanted protected.[95] Davis continued to support his French colleagues and said in a speech in 1876: "There would always be sufficient English-speaking members in this House who will insist upon giving their French fellow subjects their rights to protect them."[40]

Davis saw the railway as a means of encouraging immigration and economic development. Like all business and commercial people in Manitoba, including the HBC's Donald Smith, he wanted to be part of the opening of the Canadian West. Davis led the Winnipeg businessmen who lobbied to have the CPR cross the Red River at Winnipeg rather than Selkirk. Selkirk had higher banks that protected against Red River flooding, but Winnipeg landowners were more numerous and had already invested in property in anticipation of the big boom. One of the biggest landowners in Winnipeg was the HBC, and Upper Fort Garry was located on the Assiniboine River near the Forks. While Smith, western head of the HBC, focused on federal politics as a member of Parliament from Manitoba to pursue his interest in railways, Davis ensured that the province lobbied for Winnipeg interests. In February 1877, Alexander Begg reported on a mass meeting that was held in Winnipeg to press for the building of the Manitoba Western Railway. Premier Davis seconded a motion to pass a by-law to raise $200,000 to support the project. He was also a member of the standing committee which demanded the construction of a bridge crossing the Red River at the provincial capital and to support a grant of land for railway extension.[41]

As Premier, Davis became disillusioned with attempting to resolve matters with the federal government. The continued control by Ottawa over public lands, like the denial of responsible government for the first four years of provincehood, had made it difficult for the Manitoba government to have a strong impact on the provincial economy. Davis realized fully that the province did not have a strong position when he went to Ottawa to negotiate "better terms" in 1876. Prime Minister Mackenzie later complained to Lieutenant-Governor Morris that Davis had told "friends" in Toronto that "unless something effective were done, they would have to look to the States."[42] Although the Premier was successful in persuading Mackenzie to agree to extend the province's small boundaries after the next census was taken in 1881, Davis had by that time retired and moved south. He has not often been credited with this successful negotiation for better terms since the boundary extension occurred when John Norquay was Premier.

Like Louis Riel as head of the Provisional Government, Davis considered the option of an American alliance for Manitoba while trying to fight for Manitoba rights. Unlike Riel, he was not driven into exile for his political leadership, but he chose to move south, where he was drawn by better economic opportunities and personal circumstances. In 1876, he had met a young woman, Elizabeth McGonagil, on the train through Illinois on his way to Ottawa. Davis married her six months later. He moved out of Canada in 1878 to be united with his new wife, a decision taken at face value even by his erstwhile critics. The continuing difficulty in balancing the interests in a fractious legislature might also have made retirement attractive. The crisis for control of the provincial cabinet that occurred after his departure indicates the continuing problem of maintaining stable government and attests to Davis's skill in managing those difficulties. Upon his departure, Davis's allies remarked upon his roles in strengthening provincial finances and in preserving the political partnerships among French and English, and between Red River natives and Ontario and Quebec newcomers.[43]

Life After Politics

Robert Davis had many ties with the United States, including his adventures in the American Rockies after the Civil War and his two marriages to American nationals. After he moved in 1878 to join his wife, Elizabeth, they lived variously in Calona, Rock Island and South Chicago, Illinois. As a real estate developer, Davis sold town lots in the immigrant neighbourhoods close to the stockyards and steel mills of South Chicago, where he eventually made his home. He kept some of his Winnipeg real estate for some time, profiting from property sales while returning to visit on occasion. In 1881, he sent telegrams to Prime Minister Macdonald, bidding on the construction of the Canadian railway on behalf of an American syndicate headquartered in New York. He offered to underwrite the CPR for $20 million and 20 million acres of land. The Prime Minister did not answer these telegrams. Davis did not name his financiers, but hinted that they were among the "leading railways men in Chicago and New York." Davis later criticized Ottawa's acceptance of the CPR monopoly, believing that the northern prairies would have benefited from competing railway lines.[44]

In the mid-1890s, Davis's marriage broke up. He experienced the embarrassment and expense of defending a breach of promise suit dating from his days as Premier and soon after that was resolved he separated from his wife. Each accused the other of "infidelity." It appears that they never divorced. Davis pursued his prosperous real estate investments in Illinois and traveled extensively around the United States, but maintained ties with his relatives in Quebec and elsewhere. In 1903, Davis died in Phoenix, Arizona, after suffering for some time with Bright's Disease, a kidney affliction.[45]

Conclusion

Starting as a hotelkeeper, Robert Davis became a notable figure in Winnipeg's emergence as Manitoba's major centre and a key leader in the first decade of provincial politics. He was distinguished by his skills in overcoming ethnic tensions by supporting French minority rights and by creating an alliance of moderates to provide the first stable provincial government. He reorganized the finances as Provincial Treasurer and worked to limit provincial debt. Due to his sympathy with the French and Catholic interests as well as his Winnipeg business outlook, he was an effective broker between the interest groups that contested for political advantage in Manitoba. He was able to mediate between the various elements of Métis, Country-born, Ontario-Canadian and French-Canadian alike as well as the singular force of the HBC. Although he did not achieve lasting fame and indeed only lived in the province for eight years, his comprehension of the political and economic system created by the Manitoba Act allowed him to respect equal rights for, and the dual order of, French and English, and to provide a phase of political and administrative maturation and stability for the new province.

Notes

1. Archives of Manitoba (AM), R.A. Davis Papers, Robert Atkinson to Charles Davis, January 1, 1816; Copies of marriage and death certificates of Thomas Davis and Anna Davis. Ruth Swan, "research notes re visit to Davis Farm, Dudswell, Quebec, 1986."

2. AM, R.A. Davis Papers, Certificate of appointment of Thomas Davis; Province of Canada, 1861 Census, Wolfe County; generally on Davis's early life see Ruth Swan, "Robert Atkinson Davis," *Dictionary of Canadian Biography* XIII (Toronto, University of Toronto Press, 1994), 253–56. On the Townships and Dudswell, see C.P. de Volpi and P.H. Scowen (eds.), *The Eastern Townships: A Pictorial Record* (Montreal: Dev-Sco Publications, 1962), Plate 20, and Janice Tyrwhitt (ed.), *Bartlett's Canada: A Pre-Confederation Journey* (Toronto: McClelland & Stewart, 1968), 63.

3. Bishop's University Archives, Eastern Townships Collection, 1861 Census for Wolfe County; AM, R.A. Davis Papers, Robert Davis, Helena, Montana, to his family, miscellaneous letters September 9, 1866 to February 16, 1868, Robert Davis to Adelaide Davis, November 23, 1867; Thomas Davis, Black Hawk, Colorado, to his family, miscellaneous letters. Cf. *Winnipeg Free Press*, July 15, 1874.

4. AM, R.A. Davis Papers, copy of Marriage Certificate of Robert Davis and Susan True, March 9, 1870.

5. AM, R.A. Davis Papers, Thomas Davis, Bismarck, North Dakota, to William Wallace Davis, July 24, 1886, July 27, 1893; W.W. Leavitt, Milbank, South Dakota, to Mrs. C.A. Bishop, Dudswell Centre, June 4, 1903; *Manitoba Free Press*, May 13 and 27, 1876.

6. There is a lengthy literature. A contemporary account of travel is John O'Donnell, *Manitoba As I Saw It* (Winnipeg: Clarke, 1909), 10–12, 20–24, while a key account of Red River during the Resistance is found in W.L. Morton ed. *Alexander Begg's Red River Journal and Other Papers* (Toronto, Champlain Society, 1956), Introduction, 368–69; *The New Nation*, May 4, 1870; Details on the Métis control over access to Red River are documented in Ruth Swan & Janelle Reynolds, "Andre Nault" *Dictionary of Canadian Biography* XIV; *The New Nation*, May 13, 1870.

7. See D.N. Sprague, *Canada and the Métis, 1869–1885* (Waterloo: Wilfrid Laurier University Press); Frits Pannekoek, *A Snug Little Flock: the Social Origins of the Riel Resistance, 1869–1870* (Winnipeg: Watson & Dwyer, 1991); Morton, *Alexander Begg's Red River Journal*, Introduction.

8. Morton, *Alexander Begg's Red River Journal*, 369.

9. Ibid., *Alexander Begg's Red River Journal*, 371; Alexander Begg and Walter R. Nursey, *Ten Years in Winnipeg: A Narration of the Principal Events in the History of the City of Winnipeg* (Winnipeg: Times, 1879), 14; see also *Manitoba and Northwest Herald*, June 3, 1971.

10. John O'Donnell, *Manitoba As I Saw It*, xx. The frontier saloonkeeper is described in Richard Erdoes, *Saloons of the Old West* (New York: Knopf, 1979), Chapter 5.

11. W.L. Morton, *Manitoba: A History* (Toronto: University of Toronto Press, 1967), 145.

12. Translation: "Mr. Davis has always in stock the very best choice of wines and liquors of all sorts which he sells at the best prices in Winnipeg." *Le Métis*, le 21 septembre 1871. See also ad, "Hotel Davis Winnipeg," *Le Métis*, 15 May 1872.

13. *Winnipeg Free Press*, November 30, 1872; Begg and Nursey, *Ten Years in Winnipeg*, 79.

14. Peter Bakker, *A Language of its Own: the Genesis of Michif, the Mixed Cree-French Language of the Canadian Métis* (Oxford: Oxford University Press, Studies in Anthropological Linguistics, 1997); Eleanor M. Blain, "The Bungee Dialect of the Red River Settlement" (Master's thesis, University of Manitoba, 1989); Eleanor M. Blain, Speech of the Lower Red River Settlement," in W. Cowan (ed.), *Papers of the Eighteenth Algonquian Conference* (Ottawa: Carleton University, 1987), 7–16; David Pentland, "Metchif and Bungee: Languages of the Fur Trade" "Voices of Rupertsland Conference" (Winnipeg, 1986).

15. See D.N. Sprague, *Canada and the Métis*, passim. F. Shore, "The Canadians and the Métis, the Re-Creation of Red River, 1858–1872" (PhD dissertation, University of Manitoba, 1991).

16. W.L. Morton, *Manitoba*, 145.

17. Ibid., 145–49; Murray Donnelly, *The Government of Manitoba* (Toronto: University of Toronto Press, 1963), 14ff.

18. Murray Donnelly, *The Government of Manitoba*, 14–25. See David Burley, "Marc-Amable Girard" in this volume.

19. Morton, *Manitoba*, Sprague, *Canada and the Métis*.

20. *Manitoban*, May 4, 1872, *Le Métis*, le 4 septembre 1872, *Manitoba Free Press*, November 30, 1872; Ruth Swan, "Robert Atkinson Davis" *Dictionary of Canadian Biography*, XIII.

21. Begg and Nursey, *Ten Years in Winnipeg*, passim. See also Ruben Bellan, *Winnipeg First Century: An Economic History* (Winnipeg: Queenston House, 1978).

22. Begg and Nursey, *Ten Years in Winnipeg*, passim.

23. Ibid., passim.

24. Ibid., 96–97.

25. Lovell C. Clark, "Henry Joseph Clarke," *Dictionary of Canadian Biography*, XI.

26. Begg and Nursey, *Ten Years in Winnipeg*, 80.

27. AM, Dubuc Papers, B26, B26, p. 25, p. 27.

28. Begg and Nursey, *Ten Years in Winnipeg*, 99–100.

29. *Winnipeg Sun*, June 2, 1883.

30. On the dual system in mid-19th century Canada, see J.M.S. Careless, *The Union of the Canadas 1841–1857* (Toronto: McClelland & Stewart, 1967); on the decline of the system see W.L. Morton, *The Critical Years, Canada 1857–1873* (Toronto: McClelland & Stewart, 1964); generally on Quebec's emergence from the Union to Provincehood see Paul-André Linteau et al., *Quebec, A History 1867–1929* (Toronto: Lorimer, 1983).

31. AM, Alexander Morris Papers, B1, #1925, July 24, 1874; B1, #1827, Registrar of Winnipeg, #1829, Provincial Services.

32. AM, Alexander Morris Papers, B2, #134, Mackenzie to Morris; #133, Laird to Morris.

33. AM, Alexander Morris Papers, B2, TB1 #178, Morris to Mackenzie, #184, 181, #182, etc. #186.

34. AM, Alexander Morris Papers, B2, TB1, #186, Taché's petition to Governor-General Dufferin.

35. The issues are examined in Morton, *Manitoba*, Chapters 7 and 8, and the considerable upheavals of the decade convincingly plotted in G.A. Friesen, "Homeland to Hinterland: Political Transition in Manitoba, 1870 to 1879" *Historical Papers* (Canadian Historical Association, 1979), 33–47.

36. AM, Alexander Morris Papers, B2: 137.

37. AM, Alexander Morris Papers, B1, Board of Audit, #1825, 24 July 1874, B2, Morris telegrams, #133, 134, 137, 135; B1, #957-958, resignation letters; the election meeting is described in *The Standard*, December 19, 1874.

38. E.g., *Manitoba Free Press*, January 23, 1875, September 30, 1876.

39. See *Statutes of Manitoba*, annual volumes, 1st to 4th Sessions of the 2nd Parliament, 1874 to 1878 (Winnipeg: Queen's Printer, 1875 to 1879).

40. *Manitoba Free Press*, January 26, 1876; the *Free Press* had previously been very critical of the Davis-Royal administration.

41. Begg and Nursey, *Ten Years in Winnipeg* (n.p.: 1879), 154.

42. AM, Morris Papers, Ketchson Collection, 166, December 3, 1876

43. See Friesen, "Homeland to Hinterland," passim.; contemporary assessments are found in *Manitoba Free Press*, October 16, 1878; *Le Métis*, quoted in the *Sherbrooke Record*, January 14, 1903; Begg and Nursey, *Ten Years in Winnipeg*, 104.

44. E.g., *Le Métis*, le 30 juin 1881; *Winnipeg Sun*, June 2, 1883; Library and Archives Canada, John A. Macdonald Papers, R.A. Davis to J.A. Macdonald, January 15, 1881, January 17, 1881, mfm. reel 53048.

45. *Brandon Weekly Sun*, March 19, 1896; obituary *Sherbrooke Record*, January 14, 1903; Certificate of Death, State of Arizona, 1903. Ruth Swan, "Robert Atkinson Davis," *Dictionary of Canadian Biography*, XIII.

John Norquay

1878–1887

G.A. FRIESEN

John Norquay, 1878–1887

An eloquent speaker and shrewd leader, John Norquay was the most prominent citizen of mixed Aboriginal and European heritage in Manitoba during the 1870s and 1880s. In comparison, Louis Riel, who led a resistance movement there in 1869–70 and became more famous as a consequence of events in the North-West Territories in 1884–85, was an occasional and relatively minor presence. Norquay travelled among the leaders of provincial society in these decades and participated in a number of business investments, including land purchases, gold prospecting, and the development of a coal mine. He became a central figure in the legislature in the 1870s as a member of the opposition and a cabinet minister and, from late 1878 to late 1887, he dominated the government of which he was Premier. During these nine turbulent years, political parties of eastern Canadian origin were established in Manitoba, serious quarrels with the federal government erupted over a number of crucial matters of policy, and Confederation itself was called into question in almost every province of the new dominion. Norquay fell from power as a result of an extraordinary intervention into provincial affairs by Prime Minister Sir John A. Macdonald. He died shortly after, in July 1889. He should be remembered as one of the community's key leaders in the period when it navigated the transition from fur trade to agriculture.

The changes that Norquay witnessed in his relatively brief life constituted the Manitoba version of some of the greatest cultural changes in human history. Within a span of five decades, such economic institutions as property rights and labour relations shifted from Aboriginal and 17th-century mercantile conventions to those of an industrial capitalist system. The administration of public affairs moved from hunting camps and trading posts to elected legislatures. A revolution in local productive activities—from buffalo to wheat, from York boat to railway—completely altered prairie residents' ways of life. Print became a medium of communication and literacy a measure of power. Norquay adjusted smoothly to these extraordinary transformations.

Assessments of John Norquay's career have been contradictory. Donald Creighton fixed Norquay's reputation for a generation when he suggested that the Manitoba Premier "staggered on blindly and ineffectually for so many years."[1] Peter Waite reinforced this view with his slighting reference to "desperate financial expedients"[2] resorted to by Norquay's government in the 1880s. Local historical writing offered a very different opinion. James A. Jackson's provincial history asserted Norquay's "personal integrity" and argued that the Premier fell victim to "Canadian politics" because he was more concerned with the fortunes of his province than Macdonald's Conservative Party: "He was the victim of the party system, whose introduction into the province he had resisted. His loyalty to Manitoba always stood before his loyalty to party or faction."[3] W.L. Morton, in his influential history of Manitoba, depicted the fall of Norquay's government as a turning point marking the end of "old Red River." In place of French-English cooperation and orderly development based on river-lot society, Morton suggested, a new Protestant and English-speaking Manitoba was integrated into a rapidly expanding, trade-based civilization. As one of the peripheral zones in a national economy, Manitoba witnessed the sudden "triumph of Ontario democracy."[4] The Manitoba historians were kinder to Norquay than their eastern Canadian colleagues and, not surprisingly, more aware of the problems he faced.

This essay rejects the Creighton-Waite judgments and endorses the views of W.L. Morton and James A. Jackson. It argues, first, that John Norquay was a child of the old order and grew to maturity in a world governed by the buffalo hunt and the Hudson's Bay Company. Second, it suggests that during the 1870s he adjusted quickly to the drastic changes in community affairs and the development of local political factions without abandoning the principles he espoused when first elected. Third, it summarizes the story of his nine years as Premier and his fall from power. It expands on the sympathetic Manitoba interpretations by suggesting that, though his conflicts with Ottawa were partly of his own making, they should also be attributed to the power of international capital, the insistent demands of Sir John A. Macdonald and his allies, and betrayal by the Premier's erstwhile friends in Winnipeg. Because he died suddenly and tragically in 1889 at the age of 48, Norquay lost the opportunity to restore his reputation and, perhaps, to resume his remarkable political career. But his contributions during the province's first 20 years place this descendant of mixed Aboriginal and European families at the forefront of Manitoba's founders.

Red River, 1841–69

Born in 1841 in the English-speaking, mixed-heritage community of St. Andrew's parish, Red River Settlement, John Norquay was a grandchild of the fur trade. He grew up in a farm and hunt-based community descended mainly from women of Aboriginal or mixed heritage and the British men, mainly Orkney-origin labourers in the Hudson's Bay Company, whom they married "according to the custom of the country." Three of his four great-grandmothers were of Aboriginal or mixed heritage and all four of his great-grandfathers were English, Scot or Orcadian. John's parents, both children of fur-trade marriages, died when he was very young, his mother when he was two and his father five years later.[5]

John was looked after by his grandmother, Jean Norquay Spence, for the rest of his childhood years. While living with her, he attended the parish school. Because of his obvious strengths as a student, he was selected by Bishop Anderson to be an exhibitioner and then a scholar at the main Church of England educational institution in the settlement, St. John's College. Upon graduation, he taught in parish schools for about eight years. In 1862, when he was 21, he married Elizabeth Setter of Portage la Prairie, who was also descended from Orkney employees of the Hudson's Bay Company and their country wives. The Norquays farmed in the St. Andrew's and High Bluff districts in the 1860s and early 1870s, when seven of their eight children were born. He was not involved in politics during the decade, not even the famous events associated with Louis Riel's resistance movement in 1869–70, and no documents survive that might testify to his view of the episode.

Red River settlers relied on the farm and the buffalo hunt for survival during these decades. Their two central economic activities were administered by distinctive institutions that shaped Norquay's perceptions of public affairs. The buffalo hunt was managed by its male participants who met daily in council, usually in the centre of the ring of carts.

They would sit with legs crossed, arms folded, brows knit, eyes downcast and listen to a succession of brief speeches. The main speakers were the captain of the day and the chief of the hunt. Deference was always paid to age and experience. The most senior spoke last and their views constituted a decision. The assembly considered affairs of the hunt but also external relations or diplomacy. For Red River people in these decades, such questions often involved the Dakota (Sioux) and the maintenance of peace between the two communities. The 1860 hunt encountered a large Dakota band, many of whom wore paint and feathers and who sang as they rode near the Métis carts, and "never seemed to tire of gazing on us," as a writer commented.[6] When such encounters required, they would conduct elaborate ceremonies in which clear diplomatic conventions were obeyed. In 1860, by an exchange of presents, the meeting stipulated that there would be "no sly approaches to each other's camp by night, and that if any infringed the rule, those molested were at liberty to shoot the culprits."[7] This was government in the style of the buffalo hunt.

The farming district known as the Red River Settlement, organized as the District of Assiniboia within the Hudson's Bay Company territories, operated according to recognized rules of order, with motions and votes, minutes of meetings, and printed statutes. In this way it introduced a bounty on wolves, obliged residents to perform a measure of statute labour, and authorized the conduct of a limited court system. There were definite limits to its powers. In an 1849 legal case concerning the HBC monopoly on trade, for example, a "free trader," Guillaume Sayer, was found guilty but went unpunished because the court did not possess sufficient force to impose its judgement on the armed Métis who surrounded the courtroom.

As a child and young adult, Norquay learned the ins and outs of government through settlement gossip and the columns of the *Nor'Wester* newspaper, founded in 1859. Having received an excellent education, he would have been aware of local political talk and a smattering of international news but, after his marriage in 1862, he was probably consumed by the demands of his growing family. He seems to have spent little or no time on public affairs, given the absence of his name from the newspaper and public documents. He would have understood that both types of government, the council of the buffalo hunt and the Council of Assiniboia, depended on the consent of the governed. This consent was not easily won and had to be renewed, more or less in person, when questions arose. Community leaders lived within a few miles of those whom they led, their decisions were subject to careful review in daily conversations, and regulations or punishments had to be seen to be acceptable or would never take effect. Both types of government were rooted in a community that differed significantly from Britain and Canada in the same years. The Red River of the 1840s and 1850s was closer to the fur trade, to Aboriginal assumptions, and to the direct exercise of power by armed individuals and groups.[8]

John Norquay was accustomed to the rhythms of Red River, its assumptions about government, its distance from Europe and eastern North America. One of the few surviving testimonials to his family life in this era, his wife's discussion of life on Red River farms, recorded by W.J. Healy in the 1920s, illustrated their isolation and self-containment. She noted that they made all their own furniture, preserved berries by drying and pressing them in a cake, pounded choke cherries into pemmican "just as we use currant jelly with mutton," and ground wheat to make flour. The Norquays understood the rules of hay-cutting, the obligation to provide aid to neighbours in need, the centrality of church and Bible in settlement life, and the names and locations of roots and barks utilized by Aboriginal people to ward off scurvy or to make the least greasy pemmican.[9] Their world was linked to the events and letters of Europe by strong but slender ties. They knew dramatists of Elizabethan times, European monarchs and wars, industrialists' triumphs in Manchester and Birmingham. But all of these print-communicated matters were far removed from the farms on which the Norquays lived. The effective distance from Red River to London, read in emotional terms and in the language of the senses, was much greater in 1860 than it was a decade later, in 1870, after the trans-Atlantic telegraph cable was laid, after Canada became a relatively autonomous nation-state in 1867, and after the North-West was annexed by the Canadian state in July 1870.

Legislature and Cabinet, 1870–78

John Norquay took no active part in the troubles of 1869–70. His brother, Thomas, carried messages between the Canadians at Portage la Prairie and Riel's party at Fort Garry. His cousin, John Norquay Sr., was elected in March 1870 to represent St. Margaret's parish in Riel's provisional government. John Jr. apparently attended several meetings during these tense days. His signature appears on his cousin's certificate of election as one of the two representatives of St. Margaret's parish in the colony's provisional government in the winter of 1870.[10] Later that year, when the first provincial election approached, John's name was one of those mentioned as a possible member of the legislature. At the public meeting in High Bluff constituency, he and his cousin were both nominated. The elder stepped down and John Jr. was declared elected by acclamation.[11]

What made politics so unstable in the first half of the 1870s was the sudden addition of Ontarians to Manitoba society. Of the 12,000 residents before their arrival, half were French-speaking Roman Catholics (5,800) and one third (4,100) were English-speaking Protestants, described locally as Métis and Halfbreeds respectively, both of mixed Aboriginal and European ancestry. About one eighth (1,500) were European-origin Canadians (English and French-speaking) or British (including the Selkirk settler families), and about 1,000 were Aboriginal. Of this total, only 8% (fewer than 1,000 people) were born outside the Northwest.[12] The troops of Colonel Garnet Wolseley's expeditionary force who seized control of the Settlement in the name of Canada in July 1870, largely Ontario Protestant recruits, upset this relatively placid community by introducing their vengeful, anti-French, anti-Catholic and, especially, anti-Riel sentiments into local life.[13] They were reinforced by Ontario immigrants in succeeding years, perhaps 15,000 in the first half of the decade and another 20,000 in the second half. They changed Manitoba so drastically that, by 1880, the little province was unrecognizable—and unacceptable—to many of the pre-1870 residents, especially those whose first language was French. The 1881 census counted over 60,000 residents in the province. Such a rate of growth, nearly 20% annually, fuelled mainly by Ontarians (though Icelanders, Low German-speaking Mennonites, and some French

Canadians returning from the United States were part of the mix), and accompanied by Métis out-migration, illustrates how significant was the transition in this short span.

Norquay represented the electors of High Bluff from 1870 to 1874. West of the growing capital of Winnipeg, and just east of the village of Portage la Prairie, the High Bluff district changed in these years from an outpost of English-speaking and Protestant mixed-race people to an increasingly Ontarian community. The assertive newcomers put considerable pressure on their MLA. He resisted the pressure most of the time, finding a parliamentary home in a small group of English-speaking moderates, and winning a reputation as an effective speaker. The Canadian party, or self-styled "Loyalists," under the leadership of Schultz, had conducted a series of public meetings in 1871 which questioned the representative nature of the cabinet, especially the English side, and threatened to topple the government. Though the uproar was calculated simply to secure Schultz a position in the cabinet, it led to outbreaks of violence and, in particular, a dangerous raid by some Canadian hotheads on the home of Riel's mother. The English representatives in the cabinet, A.T. Boyd and Thomas Howard, were simply unable to stand up to Schultz at the stormy public forums. Lieutenant-Governor Archibald withstood the challenge (his English opponents called him "Smooth Archy"), by securing Boyd's resignation and replacing him with Norquay, his new minister of Public Works and Agriculture. As Archibald told Prime Minister Macdonald, Norquay was "a Halfbreed of fair education and good abilities ... the principal man in the exclusively English parishes of the Upper Assiniboine and ... the leader of the opposition during the last session."[14]

Norquay attended several gala entertainments during the Christmas season and then settled down to the steady routine of Executive Council meetings and departmental business. The Agriculture portfolio was small, requiring simply the allocation of grants to local agricultural societies and, in hard times, the distribution of seed grain. Public Works demanded more attention because it accounted for a large portion of the budget and came in for regular criticism. Ferries had to be licensed and their fee structures approved, public buildings such as court houses and jails had to be erected, and, as thaw, flood and freeze-up soon made evident, substantial bridges had to be built. Norquay's enthusiasm carried expenditures beyond the budget in 1872 but the appointment of a Public Accounts committee in the legislature and general sympathy for his position averted criticism of the informal business procedures in the department. His first term as minister was a success.

Politics demanded much more than competent administration and eloquent speeches. Norquay needed to have luck as well as skill in manoeuvring among the various factions in local politics. In 1873, he moved closer to the English-speaking factions in Manitoba politics as the province became ever more sharply divided between the French and English. The issues of half-breed lands, amnesty for Riel and his followers, and punishment for the "executioners" of Thomas Scott—all of them arising from the 1869–70 resistance—remained contentious. He won the affection of Ontarians in the spring session when he opposed a draft bill favouring Métis property-holders. The bill would have permitted Métis sellers of scrip—Métis only—to regain their land in future by repayment of the purchase price plus 7% interest. Supporters of the bill argued that speculators were discouraging

Métis who already distrusted officials because of the long-delayed distribution of land to pre-1870 settlers. In reply, Norquay and the Ontarian opponents of the bill asserted the sanctity of business contracts. As Norquay explained: "When I state my opinion I state it as a Half-breed myself, and when this House goes to the country, the verdict of the people will be that this Bill is an insult to the Half-breeds themselves."[15]

Norquay's new tack was evident again in the autumn session when he made common cause with cabinet members H.J.H. Clarke and Thomas Howard to undermine their cabinet colleague, Joseph Royal. At the urging of Ontarians, the three supported a hastily devised redistribution act which would give the English-speaking population more representatives than the French in the Assembly. Since the bill was to be reviewed at the next session, the cabinet split did not cause irreparable damage at the time but it did illustrate the pressures of a changing provincial population. Even the French-language weekly, Le Métis, joked about it, suggesting that to cast the Ontarian extremists as victors in a chess match, as its opponents at The Gazette had done, was inaccurate but, if the analogy was to be used, then Norquay, "le gros ministre de travaux publics devrait au moins représenter une tour," not a knight.[16] The joke derived from Norquay's size—he stood over six feet tall and weighed more than 300 pounds—but its bite came from the suggestion that a true knight would not have betrayed his principles, and that's why, as a chess piece, Norquay was merely a rook or castle.

The Clarke government fell in 1874, partly as a result of the French-English conflicts. The short-lived Girard administration then passed a number of bills, including another redistribution measure which, to Norquay's dismay, amalgamated districts of newcomers and old settlers in his High Bluff seat. He had long opposed this approach, arguing in the assembly that the "front settlers" along the river "who have their narrow elongated lots and who possess certain privileges should feel anxious to preserve their interests intact." They had "formed the bulwarks of struggling civilization in this Province," he told his colleagues, and had a right to elect a representative "activated by the same motives of local interest, as they are themselves."[17] His protests were to no avail; the act passed, and the House was dissolved for Manitoba's second election. Recognizing the political implications of the new act for High Bluff, Norquay moved to the constituency of St. Andrews South along the Red River, the area in which he had grown up and taught. There he cooperated with the Ontarian faction in order to defeat an incumbent member in the hotly contested election. He remained the representative of this English-speaking, Protestant, fur trade-descended community until his death.

Norquay's alliance with the Ontarians flourished for another few months. He became Leader of the Opposition, continuing his partnership with W.F. Luxton, editor of the Free Press, and F.E. Cornish, the most outspoken of the anti-French, anti-Catholic agitators. When the new Premier, R.A. Davis, sought to placate this increasingly important contingent, he invited Norquay to join the Cabinet. The arrangement between Norquay and his English-speaking group was maintained while the government sought increased federal aid in exchange for a promise to abolish Manitoba's upper chamber, the Legislative Council, a drastic step that required several legislative attempts before it passed the Council itself. During one of the debates that led to the Council's abolition, Norquay argued that the upper house had been necessary in the early 1870s because it guaranteed the rights of a certain minority (the French-speaking Métis). Appropriate legislation having been passed in the years since (presumably that dealing with protection of Métis lands), he stated "the reasonable demands of a majority" of Manitobans should now be accepted. The French language could not be dispensed with in the Assembly, he said, and the Ontarian agitation over its status should end: "No doubt the time will come when the privilege claimed by those speaking the French language will be waived, but he, for his part, would never like to see them deprived of the privilege of speaking their language on the floor of the House and in the Courts of Justice."[18] It was a generous sentiment, all the more important because it would provoke the anger of his erstwhile allies.

Norquay's faction disintegrated in 1875–76. He and his colleagues differed over the use of French as a language of instruction and then over the merits of the dual religious (Protestant-Roman Catholic) school system. The final straw was an Ontarian proposal to redistribute seats in the Assembly strictly according to the principle of representation by population. Such a measure would have given the English-speaking population 16 seats as opposed to eight for the French-speaking districts. Norquay refused to support the Ontarian position in these debates. As he told the legislature, his preferred reallocation would ensure eight seats for French-speaking districts, eight for "old settler" English-speaking districts, and eight for "new settlers," five of them in "outlying districts" which had been developed after 1870. He wished to give "just representation to every party" in the province—"that is, in regard to interests and elements." This was not precisely representation by population, he admitted, but it would ensure that "the old residents of the Province … the pioneers of the country," for whom he acted as spokesman, were fully represented. The original citizens had been fair to the newcomers in the early years, he said, and "now that the numbers and wealth of the newcomers would bring about a new era, this attitude of the old settlers would no doubt be remembered to their advantage (cheers)."[19]

In fact, Norquay had introduced an important new factor to provincial politics and made a fateful transition from one bloc to another. He had articulated the distinct interests of a mediating "third force" in local politics—the "old settlers"—many of whom were of mixed Aboriginal and European fur trade descent and others the descendants of Lord Selkirk's 1812 Settlement. This "old settler" faction, he argued, should be seen as a buffer between the irreconcilable "French Catholic" and "Ontario Protestant" groups. And he gave up leadership of the anti-French Ontarians who had been his erstwhile allies. In an age when local party organizations and federal party lines did not exist in Manitoba, this factionalism was as close as the province came to disciplined, principle-based groups.

The balancing of the factions worked for two years. By this time Norquay was viewed as the leading advocate of compromise between old and new. When he introduced legislation to establish new constituency boundaries in 1877, contemporary observers described him as the pre-eminent parliamentarian on the floor of the House. He was still identified with the English-speaking old settlers but his eloquence and his reputation for moderation had carried him beyond the role of leader of a faction. It carried the government through to the resignation of Premier Davis in 1878.

The election differed little from the two preceding contests. At a raucous meeting in St. Andrews parish, the lamps were extinguished and shots were fired but no one was brought to trial for excessive enthusiasm. Having observed the operation of the secret ballot in 1874 and found it wanting, Norquay introduced an optional system (open or secret ballot) that permitted monitors to determine if his government—or the opposition—had successfully bribed individual voters. Personalities mattered in these contests but, for the first time, economic development also entered public discussion. Another hot issue in English-speaking areas was the degree of accommodation to be shown by the English-speaking to the French. Norquay's coalition of French and old settler factions won the election easily. The opposition would number between 7 and 10 in a house of 24.

Like every other member of the Manitoba legislature, Norquay had adapted to the conventions of the British parliamentary system during the 1870s. The local version of parliamentary democracy was unstable and Norquay navigated erratically, securing allies and abandoning them—honourably, according to some observers, without scruple according to others—while he learned the ropes. He endured some difficult moments but he also won respect. The experienced Canadian politician and Lieutenant-Governor of Manitoba, Alexander Morris, writing to Sir John A. Macdonald in 1877, described him as "the best educated of the English half breeds and a capital speaker."[20] His articulation of a three-faction context in Manitoba politics and his personal command in tense public meetings stood him in good stead and ensured that he became the obvious candidate for the premiership.

To Govern is to Choose, 1879

In the spring of 1879 Norquay, accompanied by his experienced cabinet colleague, Joseph Royal, travelled to Ottawa to negotiate another installment of "better terms" for the rapidly growing province. He, Royal and two aides spent the entire month of March in Ottawa's Russell House, conducting talks with the new Macdonald Conservative government. The Manitoba agenda included enlarged boundaries, an increased federal subsidy, federal aid for land drainage and for construction of public buildings such as courthouses and land titles offices, and a change in the route of the transcontinental railway. The two Manitobans found a federal government willing to make a deal.

Macdonald had been returned to office on promises of national economic development. The West would be central to this project. On the matter of public buildings, Macdonald recalled Cartier's promise in 1870, during the negotiations leading to the Manitoba Act, that the federal government would pay for such construction and immediately handed the issue to civil servants who would arrange a timetable.[21] An enlargement of the province? Soon. Increased financial aid for the province? Yes, with qualifications. Location of the rail line? Though such details could not be settled finally because he had yet to find a syndicate to build the line, Macdonald seems to have made a secret commitment that the proposed transcontinental route would trace a line south of Lake Manitoba, rather than through the Interlake district and across the northern prairies as had been projected by the preceding administration. These were important concessions. They represented policies and relationships that diverged sharply from Manitoba's experience under the Liberal government of Alexander Mackenzie. It is not too much to say that Norquay's nine-year career as Premier was spent working out the implications of the month-long bargaining session.

What could Macdonald possibly have coveted that Manitoba might offer in exchange? The Prime Minister's chief preoccupation was to discover a variety of valuable inducements that might entice a private corporation to build a rail line from central Canada to the Pacific. He recognized that such capitalists would expect money and land grants—these were government's essential tools in the business of railway building—but they would also want some support against potential competitors. To achieve the most effective negotiating conditions possible, Macdonald was seeking a free hand in railway policy. He did not want a provincial government complicating matters. He must have thought that the concessions he made to Norquay were a small price to pay.

Though Norquay returned to Manitoba a hero, the popular acclaim was short-lived. Within a week, the few Métis in the House destroyed their political faction, the so-called "French party," and placed his government in jeopardy. That is, the French-speaking Métis split with their Quebec-origin, French-speaking colleagues, charging that the latter had done nothing to assist Métis communities in their time of need. The "Quebec French," led by Joseph Royal, pointed out to the Métis that, if the two French-speaking contingents in the Assembly remained united, they could dump Norquay, make an alliance with Sir John A. Macdonald's Conservatives in Manitoba, and take over the provincial government under Royal's premiership. This was a bold step, taken on the expectation that central Canadian party loyalties—which did not yet prevail in local elections—would suffice to hold this unlikely group together. It was the first attempt to establish federal parties in Manitoba local politics.

The quick demise of Royal's scheme demonstrated that local factional—as opposed to national party—loyalties remained a potent force.[22] Norquay abandoned the French. He turned for support in the legislature to the ultra-Protestant Ontarians, promising he would terminate the various concessions French Catholics had enjoyed during the preceding decade. He then dismissed Joseph Royal, his overly-ambitious French-Canadian colleague, from the cabinet, won several decisive votes in the House, introduced measures curtailing the number of official documents printed in French, and redistributed constituencies yet again to appease newly arrived Ontarians. Finally, he called an election in the late fall of 1879 and was easily returned to power.

After the election, Norquay reversed course again. He watched without apparent regret as the anti-French language measures were disallowed by the federal government. He reconstructed his cabinet and, eventually, included two new French representatives among the five, just as his 1878 administration had done.[23] The redistribution removed two or three seats (of eight or nine) from the control of French-language voters, reducing the power of their faction at the critical moment when English-speaking Ontarians were arriving in greater numbers in Manitoba. Despite his apparently erratic actions, Norquay maintained his hold on power while adjusting to the changing political realities of a rapidly growing population and, remarkably, while reconciling English- and French-speaking Manitobans.

The biggest losers in the ministerial changes of 1879 were the communities of mixed Aboriginal-European ancestry, whether French- or English-speaking. Henceforth, the "old settlers" in English-speaking districts relied mainly on the Premier himself to represent their interests. The Métis leaders, Charles Nolin and the Lépine brothers, who had been responsible for the initial protest in the Assembly, left the province upon the failure of their coup attempt. As wet weather in the spring and summer of 1879 destroyed their crops in the Red River Valley, other disaffected Métis followed them up the trails to Qu'Appelle, Montana and Saskatchewan. The Métis resistance in Manitoba was effectively ended. The community of mixed ancestry could no longer control events. The factionalism of the 1870s—the key characteristic of Manitoba parliamentary democracy in the decade—was in retreat. Henceforth, Norquay's government relied on the deals it could make with Sir John A. Macdonald and, not surprisingly, was soon opposed by newly arrived Manitobans who had grown up as Ontario Clear Grits, Reformers or, as they were increasingly known, Liberals.

The Premier and the Party System, 1879–87

The years from 1879 to 1887 may be described as the Norquay era in Manitoba. Railway matters succeeded land as the central public policy issue. Representatives of the provincial government made annual pilgrimages to Ottawa in quest of higher subsidies. Race, language, and religion were less prominent but only because the factional conflicts of the 1870s were replaced by an intermediate phase in party history, a slow crystallizing of a two-party system similar to that in central and eastern Canada. John Norquay managed to secure a majority for his administration in the elections of 1878, 1879, 1883 and 1886 but, in 1887, when he attacked the Canadian Pacific Railway once too often, he became expendable. The Manitoba Premier's fall from power represented a remarkable episode in Canadian history, one precipitated by Sir John A. Macdonald, who feared a loss of international investor confidence and damage to Conservative party fortunes.

By the close of 1879, Norquay had consolidated his position in provincial politics. The "French party," though split into three factions by the intrigues of Royal, Girard and the remaining Métis, was still held together by the powerful hand of Archbishop Taché. Given his willingness to work with the French representatives other than Royal, Norquay won Taché's approval and, henceforth, could count on the French group for support in the Assembly and for two Cabinet members. The English who professed Conservative loyalties in federal politics were divided into two camps, associated with Thomas Scott (a sometime mayor of Winnipeg and, obviously, not the man executed by Riel in 1870) and Norquay, but for the moment the Premier had the upper hand. The Reformers (or Liberals) continued to reject the idea of federal party lines in the local sphere and, by giving their support to Norquay, ensured that he would have a large majority.

Manitoba's population grew rapidly between 1879 and 1881. The province had regular rail service to the east via the St. Paul, Minneapolis & Manitoba as of December 1878, the first hundred miles of rail line west of Winnipeg were placed under contract in the summer of 1879, and federal legislation to incorporate the new Canadian Pacific Railway was passed in February 1881. Land prices, both urban and rural, were rising so quickly that ordinary folk were buying and selling with the professionals; one bank head office in Montreal felt obliged to issue a directive to its Winnipeg employees—clerks and manager alike—asking that the staff's private speculation in real estate end forthwith. But the boom ended in a spectacular crash in the spring of 1882.

John Norquay rode this wave of prosperity and emerged from the crash unscathed. His trips to Ottawa increased in regularity—one in 1879, two in 1880, another in 1881, and one more in 1882. He secured better financial terms, compensation for provincial work on land drainage and, best of all, in 1881, a definite enlargement of provincial boundaries, north to the 53rd parallel, west to the 102nd meridian and east to the as-yet-undefined Ontario border.[24] When, after the boundary expansion, he was fêted at a banquet in Winnipeg, his speech on the future of the province was cheered to the echo. He had won substantial concessions by dint of diplomatic pressure and sheer persistence.

The Premier lived in a modest farm home along the Red River north of Winnipeg during the 1870s and early 1880s. He served on the most important councils of the Anglican Church and was elected to the boards of St. John's College and St. John's Ladies School. Having travelled to the North-West in a number of parties, including those of A.W. Ogilvie of Montreal and W.B. Scarth of Toronto, he knew the land fairly well and recognized the possibilities for private gain. He joined small business syndicates, one that sought a railway charter, another that owned a coal deposit near Medicine Hat, though in neither case was the source of his funds apparent. He also joined two syndicates seeking to develop gold mines near Kenora. He was tying his fortunes to the future of the west, of course, but he was also building close relationships with a number of local investors. In these ventures, he was clearly allied with Dr. Benson, W.B. Scarth, and J.H. Ashdown of Winnipeg, J.E. Woodworth of Brandon, and E.P. Leacock of Birtle. These men were active in Conservative politics—Woodworth and Leacock sat in the provincial House and Scarth was later elected to the House of Commons—and keenly interested in resource-based investments. Because Norquay understood the region and possessed excellent political contacts, such investors would want to cultivate his friendship.

Norquay moved from the St. Andrews farm on the banks of the river, and the Aboriginal-European community surrounding it, into a new and comfortable, though not palatial, dwelling on a residential street in north Winnipeg in 1885. His investments, particularly the Saskatchewan Coal Mining and Transportation Company, became increasingly worrisome. And, as the struggles within his following threatened to push him from power, he turned again to thoughts of elevation to more secure and prestigious positions: a seat in the Senate and the offices of Lieutenant-Governor of the North-West Territories and minister of the Interior all were canvassed at various times between 1882 and 1886.

A variety of factors postponed Norquay's release from the uncertainties of the Manitoba Assembly. Thomas Greenway, a former Ontario member of Parliament, moulded a Liberal Party on the opposition benches in the local House in the early 1880s.[25] The old rift between the forces of Schultz and Scott, on the one hand, and Norquay and some Winnipeg business leaders, on the other, meant the Premier had to woo the Ontario-origin Conservatives on his backbenches. And throughout these years, railway policy was the cause of discontent.

When the terms of the proposed Dominion contract with the CPR were made public in December 1880, Winnipeg business leaders fiercely opposed its "monopoly clause." This clause promised that for a period of 20 years no line would be built south of the main line except southwest or west of southwest, and any branch running from the main CPR track must stop 15 miles from the American border.[26] When the Manitoba assembly went ahead and passed a charter for a branch railway that ignored these conditions, Macdonald disallowed the legislation. The federal announcement in early 1882 provoked more Winnipeg anger but Norquay could do nothing. Indeed, it is likely that he had accepted Macdonald's paramountcy in railway matters in 1879, a fact that tied his hands whenever he tried to appeal for a change in federal government policy.

Norquay's relations with the one-time Ontarians in the legislature grew more testy in the spring of 1882 when a bill for the incorporation of the Orange Lodge reached the floor of the House. The government did not prevent its passage, despite the concerns of its French supporters, but by some mystery the bill was never given royal assent. Some Orangemen fixed the blame upon Norquay and resolved to defeat him. These problems, taken in conjunction with the bursting of the Winnipeg economic bubble in 1882, the Premier's growing interest in business ventures, and his long-standing conflict with some Ontarian Conservatives weakened the government.[27] Then, in November 1882, Macdonald disallowed three more railway charters. While Norquay temporized on whether to re-enact the bills, his government ran the risk of falling between the increasingly formalized Liberal and Conservative parties.

By calling a snap election for January 1883, Norquay caught the Liberals before they could organize properly. More important, Sir John A. Macdonald came to his rescue. Even the Orangemen responded to Sir John's intervention: at his urging, their 10,000 leaflets critical of the Norquay administration were never distributed. The government did not win an overwhelming victory—about 52% to 48% of the popular vote and five ministerial acclamations—but it emerged with a 20–10 seat margin in the Assembly.

Though Norquay was again tempted to seek middle ground between Conservatives and Liberals, the threat of a Tory revolt during the 1883 Throne Speech debate forced him to declare publicly his affiliation to the Conservative Party. From this point, Manitoba politics adhered to the conventions of the eastern Canadian two-party system and its partisan loyalties. Such labels did nothing, however, to assure the survival of Norquay's administration. The province's finances were still so straitened that it could not meet citizens' increasingly insistent demands for services. Branch railway construction, their greatest need, depended upon Macdonald's perception of the national interest and, in particular, the threat posed by each charter to the CPR monopoly. And a combination of problems, from an early frost to freight rate increases and a drop in the price of grain drove farmers to organize a protest movement in self-defense. The divisions within the Conservative Party, temporarily forestalled by Macdonald's intervention in the 1883 election campaign, returned within a few months and the Liberals, now a real force in the Assembly, exploited Norquay's weaknesses at every opportunity.

Once again, Norquay turned to Macdonald. Negotiation for more funds to deal with pressing demands for infrastructure—dikes, schools, roads, bridges—was nothing new for the Manitoba Premier. However, his persistence in pressing for "better terms" so soon after the previous concessions did not please the Prime Minister. Because Norquay had finally declared his allegiance to the Conservative Party in provincial politics, Macdonald swallowed his impatience and responded favourably to the story of woe told by his "insatiable" colleague. In the spring of 1884, he approved a new and generous financial arrangement. The terms included a clause declaring that this would be a final settlement of Manitoba claims, a clause that would have to be passed in the local legislature. To the disgust of Macdonald and the chagrin of die-hard Manitoba Conservatives, Norquay was unable, or perhaps unwilling, to carry the deal through the Assembly. In late 1884, Norquay tried to smooth the troubled waters by carrying provincial congratulations to a great Toronto banquet marking the fortieth anniversary of Sir John's entry into public life. Four months later, a telegram from Macdonald and strong backing from Norquay's Winnipeg business allies saved a local by-election. Agreement on "better terms"—nearly identical to those of the 1884 arrangement, including the "finality clause"—was finally reached in early 1885. Though his personal relations with the Manitoba Premier had been strained, Sir John A. appreciated Norquay's position. And the Manitoba Premier's sympathy and assistance were even more welcome during the North-West uprising, which broke out in March. Their correspondence continued to be friendly throughout the year.

Rural economic problems and the legal challenge over the Manitoba-Ontario boundary were the other main issues in local politics in the mid-1880s. Despite losing a court battle over the location of Manitoba's eastern border (the Judicial Committee of the Privy Council chose the present line despite Manitoba's claim that it should be drawn much further eastward) and despite the agitation arising from the meetings of the new Farmers' Protective Union of Manitoba, Norquay did not worry about either issue. Rather, the most disturbing aspect of the 1885–86 session lay in the charge made by Thomas Greenway, Leader of the Opposition, that Norquay had cheated his own government for personal gain. Norquay established a one-person Royal Commission in 1886, led by Chief Justice Wallbridge, to investigate the so-called "coal steal" and "notorious asylum business." The asylum charge concerned land at Selkirk once owned by Norquay and some associates which the government had selected as the site of the provincial asylum. The "coal steal" originated in Norquay's presidency of the Saskatchewan Coal Mining and Transportation Company, a shaky operation that he had tried to rescue with a contract to supply the provincial government's coal needs. Wallbridge, as Royal Commissioner, absolved the Premier of all guilt. Nevertheless, Norquay's reputation for honesty had become sullied.

On March 20, 1886, the federal government announced the disallowance of two more railway charters. Once again, Norquay insisted that Manitoba had the right to pass legislation, including railway legislation, within areas of provincial competence. This policy alienated Conservative Party loyalists, however, while winning little support among hard-pressed farmers. And yet Macdonald's 1886 summer tour of western Canada on the newly completed Canadian Pacific, which included a short stay in Winnipeg, served to mend Tory fences once again.[28] Seemingly secure in the Conservative Party, Premier Norquay then called a provincial election for November 1886. His platform included, to the surprise of some, a promise to end the Canadian Pacific railway monopoly. In effect, he was pledging to fight Macdonald, his most important patron, and the man who had just come to his aid.

The 1886 campaign was the most demanding of Norquay's career. He stumped the entire province, speaking at two and three meetings per day (54 in total), travelling by horse (he claimed to have covered 1,000 miles by horse), as well as by rail. Despite these heroic efforts, Lieutenant-Governor James Aikins judged that only Macdonald's endorsement saved Norquay from defeat. A more generous judgement would also emphasize the role of a modest gerrymander and Norquay's personal popularity in Winnipeg and the old Red River ridings. His losses came in the areas settled in the 1880s and further from rail service. The popular vote was a dead heat but the seats divided 18 to 15 in favour of the government, with 2 Independents. It had been a close contest but Norquay's government had just barely survived.

Fall from Office, 1887

The new government was less stable than its predecessors. The newest members in the House represented new settlers, wanted action on branch lines, and were impatient in the face of delays. During the winter of 1886–87, Norquay and his cabinet undoubtedly thought they could bring pressure to bear upon Ottawa and the Canadian Pacific that would solve the rail problems. However, their reluctance to grant tax concessions to the Canadian Pacific alienated its vice-president, W.C. Van Horne, who declined to construct new branch lines. And yet another mission to Ottawa resulted in no new policy initiatives from Sir John A. Macdonald. The provincial government then raised the ante by promising two new rail lines, one to Hudson Bay and the other to the 49th parallel.

The collapse of Norquay's political fortunes occurred as a result of these decisions on branch railways. George Stephen, CPR president, claimed that a link between Winnipeg and a Minneapolis or Chicago-based competitor would "bust" his railway.[29] In a letter to the Prime Minister in May 1887 he offered to bribe Norquay to leave politics, if only for a year or two:

> [it would be] a patriotic act to persuade Norquay to resign... I fancy the chief obstacle in the way lies in the fact that he has not the means of living without an official salary. Looking at the position as it affects the country apart altogether from Party politics, I think I might be justified in saying to you that if you saw fit to urge "resignation" upon Norquay, I would take measures to enable you to say to him that you would see that he got his $2000 a year for say two years, in case he should be so long out of office.

Either that, Stephen warned, or the CPR line north of Lake Superior "will have to stop running, there will be no use for it."[30] Whether news of Stephen's offer ever reached Norquay is doubtful.

The Manitoba Premier spent most of his time during the next five months, June through October 1887, trying to build a rail line to the American border where it could hook up with the CPR's competitor, the Northern Pacific. His resistance was just one among a number of mutinous acts between 1885 and 1888 that made this period stand out in Canadian history. Riel's armed uprising in the North-West, the Nova Scotia legislature's secession resolution, Quebec's election of a nationalist Premier, Ontario's continuing contests over resource policy, and the convening of the first "interprovincial" or Premiers' conference in October 1887 constituted a crisis of confidence in Confederation itself. In this list, the two prairie challenges were the most important: the Red River Valley Railway defied the federal government, challenged the very existence of the CPR, and shook international investors' confidence in the country. The value of CPR stocks plummeted in London, losing $11 million from its total capitalization by early June and $20 million by September. George Stephen was writing to Macdonald often in these months, plotting a strategy to defeat the Norquay branch line project. The CPR prevented a Manitoba bond issue in London at the last moment, blackened the province's reputation in Chicago and New York, and told the Roman Catholic seminary's leaders in Montreal not to listen to Norquay's appeal for funds. In late October, Norquay's last expedient, a bond issue by the city of Winnipeg, failed. Provincial civil servants were not being paid and the government was out of money. The Merchants Bank, its banker, would not release funds without Ottawa's approval and Macdonald would not budge. But even this was not enough to topple a Premier. That required a financial scandal, one that Macdonald seems to have concocted.

The plot may have been arranged early in the year but the final shape only became evident in June when CPR vice-president Van Horne noted in a letter to president George Stephen that Macdonald seemed to have a "scheme to smash Norquay's railway."[31] At the end of June, Macdonald received a complete report on the situation from a Manitoba lieutenant. In this assessment, W.B. Scarth concluded that the government should fall:

> They are a bad lot & they are of no use but of great injury to Dominion Conservatism. Norquay has never been true…

Scarth suggested cryptically that

> LaRivière says he wired Norquay on the strength of a promise from you. If this is untrue, I do not think you should give them the land. The whole concern is rotten[,] cannot be trusted by the Conservatives or the country & will continue to deceive, & betray us and injure us in the future as in the past.[32]

The Prime Minister's plan was simple. Earlier in the year, Manitoba's treasurer, LaRivière, had arranged a transfer of land from Ottawa on the promise that Manitoba would use the revenue from the subsequent sale of these lands to construct a railway to Hudson Bay. LaRivière wired Norquay to say that Macdonald had approved the transfer of 256,000 acres of land. Norquay used this assurance to grant $256,000 in bonds to the railway company. Macdonald then denied that a deal had ever been struck. Just as Norquay had been kept in power by the Prime Minister, so he was removed by him. Macdonald told his Manitoba lieutenants that Canada faced potential civil war in 1887: "The issue now is an … attempt by the Manitoba Govt to break the Constitution & to act as the Southern States did—openly attempting to break up the Dominion."[33] These were extreme sentiments but they suggested the tenor of the debate and the depth of Macdonald's determination to be rid of

Norquay forever. George Stephen held similarly apocalyptic views, claiming that collapse of the CPR would end Canada's hopes as a nation.

The plan to dump Norquay was put into action in mid-September. Macdonald wrote Lieutenant-Governor Aikins, chiding him for not keeping a close watch on the Manitoba government. In suggesting that the Premier had been playing fast and loose with government funds, Macdonald levied two specific charges: that the government had used certain trust funds either for ordinary revenue or for election expenses; and that the Premier had granted a large sum in government bonds, about a quarter of a million dollars, to the Hudson Bay Railway before securing land from the federal government as security. Macdonald also warned his Conservative friends in Manitoba about the rumours concerning Norquay's financial dealings.

There is no doubt that Norquay understood the land grant and financial procedures and had not followed them to the letter as he should. It seems clear that he handed over the bonds in two installments, the first $128,000 in December 1886 without cabinet approval and the second in February 1887, on the strength of the telegrams from LaRivière in Ottawa. In September 1887, when he launched his attack on Norquay, Macdonald denied that he had approved such a transfer. LaRivière fulminated but could do nothing beyond asserting his honesty. E.P. Leacock, Conservative member of the Manitoba Assembly, made the charges public in late October and, when the Red River Valley Railway project collapsed in November, Norquay had run out of alternatives. The governing party fell apart. LaRivière tried to mend matters by visiting Macdonald in Ottawa but he was coldly rebuffed: "I had to tell LaRivière that he must have dreamt this story," the Prime Minister told Lieutenant-Governor Aikins.[34] It was a carefully phrased statement, one that was open to several interpretations. Norquay's ministry resigned on December 23, 1887 and was replaced by a cabinet led by D.H. Harrison. Within a month, it had lost two crucial by-elections. Thomas Greenway became the first Liberal Premier of the province in late January 1888. Macdonald's plan had worked and the CPR had survived another challenge.

Norquay was invited by his colleagues to become Leader of the Opposition. He was still the strongest man on the Conservative side, despite the scorn of Macdonald loyalists. To supplement his income, he was soon "behind a clerk's desk in the law office of F.S. Kennedy, learning the use of the cyclostyle."[35] His life in the Assembly was far from pleasant because the new government was determined to "blacken the black charges" against him. At one point, Greenway and Martin even "professed to have evidence that would warrant criminal proceedings against him."[36] They later backed away from these allegations but continued to make political capital out of the Norquay government's failings and to dismiss civil servants who had been its employees.

Norquay's end was quick and tragic. His party was decimated in the election of July 1888. He held his own seat by only two votes and was henceforth the leader of a small opposition group. He was seen by Macdonald's men as an obstacle to Conservative Party unity in the province. Scarth told Macdonald that the five Conservatives in the House

> are of no use to the Conservative party. Norquay himself is worse than useless because he is able and unstable and therefore dangerous. His four

followers are under him useless; under an able and stable leader they might be steady and mediocre Conservatives.[37]

As Macdonald told Stephen in disgust, "Until Norquay is finally squelched we can have no Conservative party in Manitoba. By and by the new settlers will take the control into their own hands."[38]

Conclusion

Norquay died suddenly during an apparent appendicitis attack in July 1889. He left a life insurance policy, one plot of land, and little else. Because his death was unexpected and came on the heels of unresolved debates within political circles, it unleashed a wave of criticism directed at Macdonald. The Prime Minister felt obliged to explain his case at length to his Manitoba supporters. He also wrote a letter to Mrs. Norquay, though he complained to his Winnipeg agent that he could not understand

> how our friends should feel annoyed at me in not going through the form of condolence, when I look back and consider how Norquay's Government was broken up by Conservatives leaving him on account of his breach of trust issuing the Bonds, and remember, as I and my colleagues do, his continual breach of promise to the Dominion Government, notwithstanding the repeated instances of our coming to his aid.[39]

It was a blunt defence, not fair to Norquay but a typically partisan statement of the Prime Minister's view of the world.

John Norquay began life as a relatively poor member of the fur trade's "old order." Despite these handicaps, he possessed several crucial advantages including his Aboriginal-European grandmother's literate household, an exceptional education, and unquestioned abilities. He learned the languages of the fur trade world, developed skills as a public speaker, and then became an administrator during his six years as a cabinet minister during the 1870s. He proved to be adept at manoeuvring among the Ontarian, "old settler," and French-speaking factions in an era when politics in Canada's first new province were dependent on local loyalties and prone to sudden shifts in alignment. He adapted pragmatically to the changing population balance in the community but was loyal to the communities of old Red River. He was not, despite what his opponents said in moments of disappointment, an anti-French zealot. Though he alienated some people, he chose his allies shrewdly and became a respected public servant.

Norquay maintained his hold on office for nine years, winning majorities in the House in no fewer than four elections. During this period, he exerted great pressure on the federal government to improve Manitoba's financial position within Confederation. Because the economic circumstances of a new and rapidly growing province differed so much from the older provinces, Prime Minister Macdonald recognized the merits of Norquay's arguments and regularly acquiesced to the Premier's pleas for support. Measures to sustain land drainage, extend the boundary, erect public buildings, and increase the federal subsidy all testified to Norquay's effectiveness as a negotiator and, of course, to his ability to get along with Sir John.

On the crucial matter of railway policy, Norquay was caught between local business interests seeking economic development, farm families crying out for improved transportation, the Canadian Pacific's investors fearing huge financial losses, and the Northern Pacific's James J. Hill anticipating competitive advantages. The federal Conservative Party was wedded to the Canadian Pacific and, willy-nilly, to the international investors who sustained it. Local Liberals, now part of the two-party system that structured parliamentary and governmental institutions, sought to destabilize the provincial government for partisan purposes. Norquay tried to be both a Conservative and an advocate of better terms. He maintained this ambiguity for as long as he could but, in 1887, he opposed the CPR and Sir John once too often. The Prime Minister then used the power of his office in an underhanded way—at least, that is how it appears—to force his resignation.

Despite the rigours of party politics, Norquay was recognized in Manitoba as a generous, personable, principled man. At his funeral, Anglican Bishop Robert Machray said, "Always there stood out the kind heart and amiable disposition, that endeared him wherever he was known." Citizens of the province contributed $1 gifts for the erection of a monument that stands over his grave in St. John's Cathedral cemetery. Though Louis Riel, another local citizen of mixed Aboriginal and European heritage, claimed to be the founder of the province, John Norquay was more important in shaping the crucial institutions of the state, including the modern party system, the provincial economy, and the physical infrastructure of roads, bridges, drainage systems, and public buildings. He served as mediator between the west and the nation at a pivotal moment, Confederation's fragile second decade, and, despite the crisis that toppled him, he served both Manitoba and Canada well. He can be described as a defender of provincial rights, of course, but also as Sir John A. Macdonald's reluctant, awkward ally. In ideological terms, he was a pragmatist, one who supported the development of the western economy and western entrepreneurs. He was a churchman, a family man, and a tolerant defender of the cultural mixing that has been Manitoba's hallmark ever since.

Notes

1. Donald Creighton, *John A. Macdonald: The Old Chieftain* (Toronto: Macmillan, 1955), 494.
2. Peter Waite, *Canada 1874–1896: Arduous Destiny* (Toronto: McClelland and Stewart, 1971), 197.
3. James A. Jackson, *Centennial History of Manitoba* (Toronto: Manitoba Historical Society in association with McClelland and Stewart Limited, 1970), 13.
4. W.L. Morton, *Manitoba: A History* (Toronto: University of Toronto Press 1957, 1967) 229, 232–33.
5. One of Norquay's grandfathers, Oman Norquay, arrived at York Factory in 1791, at the age of 18, and worked at posts along the Saskatchewan River for a quarter-century. He retired in 1818 to a small farm near the White Horse Plain, just west of present-day Winnipeg, and died there at the age of 47

in 1820. Norquay's other grandfather, Jacob Truthwaite, was the child of a Londoner and his country wife, and worked in the fur trade before retiring to Lockport in Red River, where he died at the age of 86 in 1873. Our John Norquay's father, also John, was born on the Saskatchewan about 1810, worked as a labourer at Norway House on a five-year contract (1833–38), and then farmed on a 100-acre river lot in St. Andrews parish, Red River Settlement. He married Isabella Truthwaite, also of Orkney-Aboriginal descent, in 1832, when she was 14, and they had six children during the next decade, the fifth of whom was the future Premier. Two years after John's birth, in 1843, Isabella died in a scarlet fever epidemic. John senior remarried but he, too, died suddenly and unexpectedly, in 1849 at the age of 39 years. See Ellen Cooke, *Fur Trade Profiles: Five Ancestors of Premier John Norquay* (Winnipeg: np, 1978, copyright Ellen Gillies Cooke).

6. *The Nor'Wester*, August 14, 1860 and August 28, 1860.

7. Ibid., July 14, 1860.

8. A longer discussion of these legal issues is contained in Gerald Friesen, A.C. Hamilton and Murray Sinclair "'Justice Systems' and Manitoba's Aboriginal People: An Historical Survey" in Gerald Friesen (ed.), *River Road: Essays on Manitoba and Prairie History* (Winnipeg: University of Manitoba Press 1996), an abridged version of Chapter 3 of the *Report of the Aboriginal Justice Inquiry* volume I (Winnipeg: Queen's Printer 1992).

9. W.J. Healy, *Women of Red River: Being a Book Written from the Recollections of Women Surviving from the Red River Era* (Winnipeg: Russell, Lang & Co, 1923), 145–56.

10. The Premier's cousin, two years older, was described as Sr. in several documents at the time. Archives of Manitoba (AM), T. Bunn Papers, Election Returns, March 1, 1870.

11. AM, Elections–Provincial 1870, High Bluff, December 27, 1870.

12. Gerhard J. Ens, *Homeland to Hinterland: The Changing Worlds of the Red River Metis in the Nineteenth Century* (Toronto: University of Toronto Press, 1996), 140.

13. Allen Ronaghan, "The Archibald Administration in Manitoba 1870–72" (PhD dissertation, University of Manitoba, 1987), and Frederick J. Shore "The Canadians and the Métis: The Re-creation of Manitoba, 1858–1872" (PhD dissertation, University of Manitoba, 1991).

14. Library and Archives Canada (LAC) John A. Macdonald Papers, Archibald to Macdonald, December 13 and 16, 1871; AM, Norquay Papers, "Oath of Office," December 14, 1871; on votes in this Legislature, see Ens, *Homeland*, 140–49.

15. *The Manitoban*, March 15, 1873, p. 1; *Le Métis*, April 5, 1873, p. 2.

16. *Le Métis*, November 29, 1873, p. 2, also November 15, p. 1; *The Manitoban*, November 8 and 15, 1873; AM, Lieutenant Governor Morris Papers, #1790; AM, Schultz Papers, Donald Gunn to Schultz, November 3, 1873

17. *Manitoba Free Press*, July 14, 1873, pp. 2–3 and July 18, p. 3.

18. Ibid., January 26, 1876, p. 3; Ruth Swan "Ethnicity and the Canadianization of Red River Politics" (MA thesis, University of Manitoba, 1991).

19. *Manitoba Free Press*, February 22,1877, p. 2. In 1870, the French- and English-speaking groups had 12 seats each; in 1874, the English had 14, the French 10; Norquay's compromise law would ensure eight seats to the "French element," eight to the "old settlers" in English-speaking areas, and eight to the "new English element," five of these in the "outlying districts" which had been settled after 1870; see John L. Holmes "Factors Affecting Politics in Manitoba: A Study of the Provincial Elections, 1870–1899" (MA thesis, University of Manitoba, 1939). Ruth Swan, in "Ethnicity and the Canadianization," reaches different conclusions.

20. AM, Morris Papers, Alexander Morris to John A. Macdonald, October 22, 1877.

21. AM, Norquay Papers, "1879 letterbook."

22. Gerald Friesen, "Homeland to Hinterland: Political Transition in Manitoba, 1870 to 1879." Pp. 33–47 in Canadian Historical Association, *Historical Papers / Communications historiques* (1979).

23. It would have been introduced before the next election in any case, one could argue, so it only hastened the inevitable.

24. J.A. Maxwell, "Financial Relations Between Manitoba and the Dominion, 1870–86," *Canadian Historical Review* 15 (1934): 376–89 and J.A. Maxwell, *Federal Subsidies to the Provincial Governments in Canada* (Cambridge: Harvard University Press, 1937).

25. D.J. Hall, *Clifford Sifton: Volume I, The Young Napoleon 1861–1900* (Vancouver: University of British Columbia Press, 1981), 18–33; Joseph A. Hilts, "The Political Career of Thomas Greenway" (PhD dissertation, University of Manitoba, 1974), 71–76.

26. W. Kaye Lamb, *History of the Canadian Pacific Railway* (New York: Macmillan 1977), 72–75.

27. It seems likely that the "better terms" negotiated between Ottawa and Winnipeg in the spring of 1882 constituted, as some have argued, part of a deal between the Manitoba premier and Sir John A. Macdonald which had as its main object an end to agitation over disallowance in the western provinces; John W. Dafoe, *Clifford Sifton in Relation to His Times* (Toronto: Macmillan, 1931).

28. Donald Creighton, *John A. Macdonald: The Old Chieftain* (Toronto: Macmillan 1955), 458–60.

29. LAC, Macdonald Papers, Stephen to Macdonald, May 15, 1887.

30. Ibid., May 17, 1887.

31. LAC, W.C. Van Horne Letterbook 21, Van Horne to Stephen, June 21, 1887.

32. LAC, Macdonald Papers, W.B. Scarth to Macdonald, June 25, 1887.

33. LAC, W.B. Scarth Papers, Macdonald to Scarth, October 11, 1887.

34. LAC, Macdonald Papers, Macdonald to J.C. Aikins, December 12, 1887.

35. AM, Schultz Papers, John Christian Schultz to Stewart Mulvey, February 5, 1888. By early 1889, Norquay had left the law office and was selling insurance from his home. He aided the CPR in a taxation dispute and was said to be anxious for a reconciliation with Macdonald but the Prime Minister was unyielding.

36. LAC, Macdonald Papers, J.C. Aikins to Macdonald, May 29, 1888.

37. Ibid., W.B. Scarth to Macdonald, August 8, 1888.

38. LAC, George Stephen Papers, Macdonald to Stephen, July 7, 1888.

39. LAC, H.H. Smith Papers, Macdonald to Smith, July 17, 1889. Norquay left no will but the Surrogate Court document concerning his estate listed his possessions as a life insurance policy valued at $2500 and a quarter section of land valued at $120; AM, Surrogate Court, Eastern Judicial District of Manitoba, re John Norquay, deceased, "Application for administration," October 5, 1889 signed by Thomas Norquay, his son, and supplemented May 20, 1892.

David H. Harrison

1887–1888

Karine Duhamel

David H. Harrison, 1887–1888

David Howard Harrison was born in London, Canada West, on June 1, 1843. He was the son of Milner Harrison, a business owner and active local politician in St. Mary's, the southwestern Ontario town located between Stratford and London. The Harrison family moved to St. Mary's in 1845 after emigrating from Yorkshire, England in 1820. Milner had established a thriving general store on St. Mary's main thoroughfare, Queen Street, during the town's emergence as an agricultural centre located on the Grand Trunk Railway.

According to local historian William Johnston, Milner Harrison was a very good businessman, and was able to retire with a "considerable fortune, the result of hard work and careful manipulation of his affairs." Milner Harrison served as the Reeve for St. Mary's in 1861 and 1862, and was later noted for his generous contribution of over $5,000 to the construction of the Knox Church, a branch of St. Mary's First Presbyterian Church. Milner laid the cornerstone for it in 1879, and a local historian of the area stated: "It is proper to say here that the marvellous progress displayed in re-building was largely due to efforts of the Harrison family."[1]

The Harrisons were prominent in St. Mary's and their house, which sat on grounds north of the Grand Trunk Railway, had a spectacular view of the valley below. While David Howard Harrison's father was of some repute as a businessman, he remained, according to the locals, a man who displayed "the most perfect contempt for the nambypambyism [sic] of those who affect what is called high society."[2]

While Milner Harrison had made his fortune largely on business acumen, he believed in education for his children. David attended St. Mary's, the local public school, and later Caradoc Academy and Galt Grammar School—which had, by this time, gained a reputation as one of the top schools in the Province of Canada. After completing grammar school, he enrolled in the Faculty of Arts at the University of Toronto. Harrison eventually sought his medical degree, and in 1864 graduated from McGill Medical College. He then established himself as a physician in his childhood home, and began his own family shortly thereafter. Harrison married Margaret Notman, who had their child in 1871. Margaret died two years later, and Harrison remarried in 1874, to Kate Stevenson of Sarnia.

Following in his father's footsteps, Harrison became politically active as town councillor in St. Mary's before moving to south-central Manitoba in 1882 to try his luck as a farmer and rancher. His father accompanied David on this venture, and they quickly acquired considerable tracts of land in the area of Newdale, west of Minnedosa on a CPR branch line. The new municipality formed one year later was named the municipality of Harrison.

A man of considerable experience and demonstrated ability by the 1880s, Harrison's political views were mostly conservative, and he quickly sought public office in the province of Manitoba aligned with other Conservatives like John Norquay. Harrison himself was described as a "straight Conservative" in an 1883 *Manitoba Free Press* article.[3] Although Norquay and his government were technically non-partisan, they were sympathetic to and patronized by the federal Conservative Party, and many were active members of it. Despite these party affiliations, W.L. Morton argues that the cornerstones of the Norquay administration were both his effort to bridge the gap between the French and English as well as his desire to present a united front to advance Manitoba's concerns. According to Morton, "Premier Norquay had been a representative provincial administration and not a party government."[4] This all began to change, according to Morton, as of 1882 when Greenway and other dissenters began to voice highly critical opinions of the government. In turn, Norquay was increasingly forced to defend the Macdonald government on several issues and finally "to assume the role of provincial Conservative administration." Even though the relationship between Norquay and Macdonald was at times close, they were hardly governing in conjunction, and Norquay pursued his own policy of trying to govern with a united provincial front despite increasing fractures in the Legislature.[5]

Soon after moving to Manitoba, Harrison demonstrated the depth of his ambitions for success in public office. In late 1882, Harrison wrote to Premier Norquay, introducing himself as the candidate for Minnedosa in the upcoming 1883 election. By the summer of 1883, Harrison and Norquay had developed a warm friendship based on their mutual love of hunting ducks and prairie chickens, and the proximity of the Premier's summer residence to Harrison's substantial land holdings.[6] Norquay's relationship with the Prime Minister, Sir John A. Macdonald, was something that Harrison admired, and Norquay cultivated his new member's fondness for the Prime Minister while also attending to Harrison's claims for patronage. In keeping with the political practice of the time, Norquay and other Premiers both made and broke deals with their national counterpart with varying degrees of secrecy and success. Norquay's relationship with Sir John A. Macdonald enjoyed highs and lows, most notably ending when Macdonald accused Norquay of theft in 1887 and put in motion a plan to "be rid of Norquay forever." Indeed, Friesen suggests that Macdonald both kept Norquay in power and assured his downfall.[7]

Harrison rose quickly within the Norquay administration, due to his ambition, as well as his well-developed oratorical and debating skills. He was a bit of an anomaly, a medical doctor-turned-politician among men mostly involved in commercial activity. In 1883, shortly after his election, Harrison was chosen to provide the government response to the Speech from the Throne. According to the *Manitoba Free Press*, "Dr. Harrison moved the address in a very able and well-delivered speech."[8] Harrison was reported to have expressed regret that the duty had not been delivered by someone with more experience or ability. He also lauded the values of progress, and noted the economic strides forward made by the province. At the same time, like other Manitoba politicians, Harrison was highly critical of Ottawa for its "parsimonious" treatment of the province, which laboured under fiscal dependency and constitutional subordination. Harrison's concerns, and those of his colleagues, were centred on three principal elements as described by W.L. Morton. These included the question of better terms for Confederation, the issue of the union or separation of provincial and federal political parties, and the issue of "provincial rights," which involved mainly the question of railway rights to charter provincial lines.[9] As he stated, "While we feel, and are ever willing to acknowledge our obligations as a Province of the Dominion—while regarding ourselves as one of the family—we also claim our right to be treated as such."[10]

Harrison was re-elected for the new constituency of West Minnedosa in 1886. By August of the same year, Harrison had been appointed as minister of Agriculture, Statistics, and Health, a significant portfolio in a growing province whose economy was largely based on agriculture. Although quiet on many issues, Harrison joined the debate most often in support of Norquay, indicating both his high regard for the Premier, as well as his desire to move ahead in government. This desire was also manifested in his relationship with Macdonald, and in 1886 the *Free Press* accused him of ignoring his constituency for the "Dominion's standpoint" on the railway question, and called him useless locally in representing the interests of the farmers in his area.[11]

Despite being known as an ally of Norquay, in May 1887 a minor scandal called Harrison's honesty into question and revealed his ambition. In a rather mundane debate regarding printing rates, Harrison accused William Luxton, owner of the *Free Press* and member of the Opposition, of charging exorbitant printing rates in its government contract. Harrison pointed out that the printing rates were higher than at any previous time in the province's short history.

Luxton fired back, accusing Harrison of being a turncoat and an opportunist who, only a few short years ago, had been against public printing. Even more explosively, though, Luxton announced that in 1883, he had received a note from Dr. Harrison through the Speaker of the House asking for a meeting, "the object of which was to throw the government over because of its extravagance."[12] The government to which Luxton was referring was Norquay's, to which Harrison had just been elected. Luxton then went on to reveal several meetings in 1884, including meetings with Opposition Leader Thomas Greenway, "resulting in Dr. Harrison proposed voting against what he was pleased to call a corrupt government, but the real object of which was to secure a position for himself in the government, no matter what the complexion of the government was."[13]

If Luxton's story had been uncorroborated, it would have been less damaging. But his account was supported by two other members, including Greenway, who said that "ever since the honourable gentleman had entered the House he had schemed to get a position in the government. If he could not get it from one side, he was bound to get it from the other."[14] Joseph Martin, the other Opposition member who corroborated the allegations, added that Harrison's only condition for his defection would be that Norquay, whom he referred to as "the old man," would be provided for through a patronage appointment.

Despite these damaging stories, Norquay seems to have given Harrison the benefit of the doubt, or perhaps he understood that his own position was so precarious that he needed to keep Harrison in the fray. Norquay was often seconded by Harrison during this session, especially in reference to resolutions regarding any possible disallowance of the legislation concerning the Red River Valley Railway (RRVR). The session ended June 6, 1887, and the *Free Press* announced that it had been one of the most memorable in the history of

Manitoba due to the stand taken to secure a railway to compete with the monopoly of the CPR.[15]

The railway question was at the forefront of Manitoba politics in this era. For some time, the Manitoba government had been proposing to build competing railway lines, and its legislation and planning had continually been disallowed by the federal government, which had to manage the considerable interests of the CPR as well as sticky boundary questions in its own political calculations. In May 1887, Harrison urged the house to authorize the expense of estimates in full so as not to delay the construction of the RRVR from Winnipeg to the United States border (and connection with the Northern Pacific) for the next session, fearing the disallowance of the Act in the interim. The House obliged, for federal disallowance was considered a particularly offensive practice by both government and opposition in the province. One member accused the Dominion government of sticking its finger in Manitoba's railway pie, and considered that Manitoba had been treated, in this area, as the "scullery maid to the other sisters of Confederation."[16]

As planned by Norquay, construction began on July 2, 1887. Work on the RRVR had been contracted to the firm of Ryan and Haney, and was scheduled to be completed by September 1. On the day of the ceremonial start of construction, a report from Ottawa announced the federal cabinet's decision to disallow the RRVR Act; this was confirmed by an Order-in-Council on July 16, 1887.[17]

Despite Norquay's subsequent attempts to press for building of the line, his efforts were thwarted by injunctions against the RRVR by the CPR via Mr. Browning, a gentleman from Montreal who had purchased two lots in the direct line of construction. This injunction was removed by October 1887, but by that point financial concerns had become the obstacles against which proponents of the RRVR struggled. Norquay had released bonds into the London market, which did not sell, partially due to the intervention of Sir John A. Macdonald.[18] Norquay subsequently released them to the public on October 11, 1887, but these too failed to sell. In fact, by October 21, the Morning Call reported that only $2,750 worth had been sold.[19]

According to Manitoba historian J.A. Jackson, however, it was the question of Hudson's Bay Railway bonds that proved to be the deciding factor in pushing Norquay out of office. Under the terms of the contract, the province was to pay the builders of the line $225,000 in provincial bonds upon completion of 40 miles of railway line. The subsidy was to be secured by way of a Dominion land grant to the railway, which A.A.C. LaRivière, Provincial Treasurer, confirmed in Ottawa with Sir John A. Macdonald before turning over the bonds. Upon receiving confirmation, Manitoba turned over the bonds, but Macdonald failed to grant the land transfer.[20]

Harrison and LaRivière were thus sent to Ottawa in December 1887 to attempt to rectify this problem, and to achieve the transfer. Macdonald denied the promise had ever been made. Macdonald, who had long doubted Norquay's dithering decision making and political reliability, seized upon the moment to offer the ambitious Harrison a compromise, and avail himself of a new political ally. Norquay's refusal to abide by his own promise to stop passing hostile railway legislation made him extremely unpopular with the Prime Minister. In addition, the press in Manitoba had vilified Norquay, suggesting his corruption and deliberate mismanagement of bonds. This charge was of course a product of Macdonald's own ruthless campaign against the beleaguered Premier. The *Free Press* announced a "robbery of the bonds,"[21] as well as printed headlines declaring "Norquay Must Go."[22]

Harrison's previous actions had demonstrated his ambition, as well as his limited sense of political loyalty. As such, Macdonald proposed a coalition government made up of "honest members" from both sides. In addition, Harrison was convinced by Macdonald to accept a compromise whereby Harrison would secure the agreement of both sides of the legislature to stop passing hostile provincial railway legislation. In return, Macdonald promised to end the monopoly of the CPR in Manitoba in 1891. The acceptance of the new plan in a legislature and in a province already enamoured with the concept of a competing railway was uncertain at best. Harrison returned to Manitoba to a party torn apart by Norquay's and LaRivière's uncertain handling of the railway situation, and both soon resigned in a special session requested by Conservative MLA E.P. Leacock, a member of the Conservative Anti-Disallowance Association, formed in March 1887.[23]

When Norquay was forced to resign in 1887, the unanimous choice by the "government party" was Harrison. He officially became Premier of the province of Manitoba on December 26, 1887. The ever-mischievous *Manitoba Free Press* reported that Harrison's seizure of the premiership had been fixed by a shady deal, all the more believable to those who doubted Harrison after the minor scandal earlier in the year. On December 27, 1887, the *Free Press* reported that Harrison's and LaRivière's trip to Ottawa had been a secret one, as both had claimed they were going elsewhere—Harrison to St. Mary's, to visit relatives, and LaRivière to Montreal, to see his sick son. The paper further claimed that both had taken secretive, circuitous routes to the capital. The result of the deal, according to private despatches cited by the paper, was that Harrison agreed to abandon the RRVR project and continue the monopoly in exchange for the premiership, and that both Norquay and LaRivière would be appointed to lucrative Dominion posts.[24]

Upon becoming Premier, Harrison retained his portfolio of Agriculture, Statistics and Health, and added Provincial Treasurer to his duties. He appointed Joseph Burke to the position of Provincial Secretary. Despite the "secret deal" with Macdonald, Harrison publicly pledged to secure early and successful completion of the RRVR, continuing where Norquay had left off, and securing the achievement that Norquay had been unable to deliver.[25] Harrison had promised Macdonald to discuss and push for the compromise negotiated in Ottawa earlier that month, but no evidence suggests he ever did so. Though he stated that both parties were opposed to the deal, many members claimed it had never been discussed.[26]

The reception of the "new" government in the press was mixed, with Norquay's traditional opponent, the *Manitoba Free Press*, disparaging the change. The newspaper argued that there was no difference between Norquay and Harrison, and that the shuffle was simply a perpetuation of the Norquay administration.[27] Despite his critics, Harrison was convinced he could govern. Before he could proceed with the business of governance or of railway completion, however, he had to deal with two key by-elections—contests that led directly to the fall of his brief administration. Joseph Burke's appointment was submitted to popular approval in one by-election in St. François-Xavier, while the other attempted to fill the seat of Assiniboia vacated recently by James Murray. Both elections were handled badly, and the campaigns marred even further by a lack of finances. In Assiniboia, the Independent Conservative candidate, Ness, was challenged by the Independent Duncan MacArthur. MacArthur was victorious in the contest, a "knock-out blow," according to the *Free Press*.[28] To make matters even worse, voters in St. François-Xavier also rejected Harrison's new Provincial Secretary, Joseph Burke, and elected Liberal F.H. Francis instead. Despite poor planning on the part of the Harrison government, the Liberals running in St. François-Xavier also assured its mostly Francophone population of voters that they would be treated by a new Liberal administration as they had been in the past. Thus, despite Burke actually being French as opposed to the Liberal candidate, the Liberals were able to win this crucial contest.

Harrison took the result of the St. François-Xavier election, in particular, as a vote of non-confidence in his administration.[29] When the legislature convened on January 12, the *Free Press* commented on Premier Harrison's demeanour. According to the newspaper account, Harrison "looked as though he carried the sorrows of the world on his broad shoulders. He looked worried and appeared to be very nervius [sic]."[30] The writer added, somewhat sarcastically, that Harrison probably felt that it was less fun to fill Norquay's shoes than he might have thought, illustrating the perceived continuing ambition Harrison harboured for bigger and better things.

On January 13, 1888, Harrison submitted his resignation as leader of the party to the Conservative caucus. On January 16, he announced it in the legislature. The *Free Press* reported a full gallery on this day, probably expecting, according to the reporter present, "to see an explosion or something of that sort which would blow Dr. Harrison all through the window and seat Mr. Greenway proudly in his seat."[31] Although there was no explosion, Harrison did announce his intention to resign for failing to hold the confidence of the House, and Norquay was restored, albeit as Leader of the Opposition rather than as Premier. As the *Free Press* trumpeted, "[Norquay] was in the saddle again; his rival was down in the dark!"[32]

After his devastating loss, Harrison abandoned active political life: there is no record of his further involvement in local or provincial politics. He became a banker in Neepawa, where he worked and continued to deal in farm land, until moving to British Columbia in 1900. There, Harrison returned to business, and had a "significant interest" in the International Ice and Cold Storage Co.[33] The 1901 census listed Harrison, along with wife Katherine and 35-year-old son, Thomas, as boarders in a house in downtown Vancouver.[34] Harrison died on September 8, 1905, in Vancouver after an unspecified "lingering illness."[35] He was survived by his widow and three children, W.M. Harrison of Winnipeg, George Harrison of Neepawa, and a daughter, Mrs. John Wemyss of Neepawa.

Harrison lived in a period of great change in Manitoba's political system, yet his impact on Manitoba politics was negligible. His superior oratorical skill, political maneouvring and entrepreneurial drive might have positioned him to have a bigger impact on provincial politics but he was unable to avoid the legacy of Norquay's government. Harrison's considerable ambitions, so clear in his efforts within the legislature and in the backrooms of nascent party politics, were thwarted by the lack of cohesion in the Conservative ranks. The loss of the two crucial by-elections demonstrated the limits of the Norquay party and Harrison's own impact. His political demise spelled the eclipse of provincial Conservative forces for more than a decade. Harrison's brief premiership demonstrates the mutability of political allegiances in the late 19th century and the way that politics was still a game played more in the corridors of power than in the court of public opinion.

Notes

1. William Johnston, *History of Perth County, 1825–1902* (Stratford: Beacon Harold Fine Printing Division, 1903, 1976).
2. Ibid.
3. *Manitoba Free Press*, June 26, 1883, p. 4.
4. W.L. Morton, *Manitoba: A History* (Toronto, University of Toronto Press, 1967), 219–20.
5. Ibid., 220–21.
6. Zenon Gawron, *Dictionary of Canadian Biography Online*, "David Howard Harrison," http://www.biographi.ca/009004-119.01-e.php?&id_nbr=6769&interval=25&&PHPSESSID=joo14deb6kmp7sarapp8n5uhh7 . Accessed July 27, 2008.
7. For more on this, see the chapter on John Norquay in this publication.
8. *Manitoba Free Press*, May 22, 1883.
9. See Morton, *Manitoba: A History*, 213–16.
10. *Manitoba Free Press*, May 22, 1883.
11. Ibid., April 2, 1886, p. 2.
12. *The Manitoba Sun*, May 27, 1887.
13. Ibid.
14. Ibid.
15. *Manitoba Free Press*, June 11, 1887.
16. *The Manitoba Sun*, April 27, 1887.
17. *Canada Gazette* 21, no. 3 (July 16, 1887): 98. Also cited in J.A. Jackson, "The Disallowance of Manitoba Railway Legislation in the 1880s: Railway Policy as a Factor in the Relations of Manitoba with the Dominion, 1878–1888" (MA thesis, University of Manitoba, Winnipeg, 1945), 89.
18. Private, Macdonald to John Rose, June 25, 1887. Cited in Jackson, "The Disallowance of Manitoba Railway Legislation," 94. Also cited in J.A. Hilts, "The Political Career of Thomas Greenway" (PhD dissertation, University of Manitoba, Winnipeg, 1974), 100.
19. "Built This Year," *Morning Call*, October 21, 1887, p. 1.
20. Jackson, "The Disallowance of Manitoba Railway Legislation," 101–02.
21. *Manitoba Free Press*, December 2, 1887.
22. "The Political Crisis," *Manitoba Free Press*, December 15, 1887, p. 1.

23. Hilts, "The Political Career of Thomas Greenway" 97.

24. "How It Was Fixed," *Manitoba Free Press*, December 27, 1887, p. 2.

25. *Morning Call*, December 23, 1887, p.1.

26. Zenon Gawron, *Dictionary of Canadian Biography Online*, "David Howard Harrison" http://www.biographi.ca/009004-119.01-e.php?&id_nbr=6769&interval=25&&PHPSESSID=joo14deb6kmp7sarapp8n5uhh7 . Accessed July 27, 2008.

27. "A Constitutional Question," *Manitoba Free Press*, January 3, 1888, p. 2.

28. *Manitoba Free Press*, January 11, 1888.

29. Jackson, "The Disallowance of Manitoba Railway Legislation," 105.

30. *Manitoba Free Press*, January 12, 1888.

31. Ibid., January 16, 1888.

32. Ibid.

33. "Former Manitoba Premier Dead," *Manitoba Free Press*, September 6, 1905, p. 1. See *Daily Nor-Wester*, October and November 1894

34. *Canadian Census* (online), 1901, "David Howard Harrison" http://www.automatedgenealogy.com/census/View.jsp?id=59848&highlight=12&desc=1901+Census+of+Canada+page+containing+David+H+Harrison . Accessed August 19, 2008.

35. *Manitoba Free Press*, September 6, 1905, p. 1.

Thomas Greenway

1888–1900

James Mochoruk

Thomas Greenway, 1888–1900

While his name has been enshrined in Canadian political history as one half of the "Laurier-Greenway Compromise of 1896" which settled the Manitoba Schools Question, Thomas Greenway, Manitoba's first Liberal Premier, has not been well regarded by historians. He has been variously described as "a shrewd mediocrity,"[1] possessed of a "certain plodding dullness,"[2] and ultimately as a man who could not even dominate his own administration, becoming completely overshadowed by Clifford Sifton, his youthful cabinet colleague.[3] Still, as a founder and leader of the provincial Liberal Party from 1883 to 1903 and as Premier from 1888 to 1900, the career of Thomas Greenway deserves careful attention. He was the individual most responsible for the birth of partisan politics in Manitoba. He was a key figure in developing the notion of "provincial rights" as a cornerstone of Manitoba's political discourse. More to the point, he presided over the final transition of Manitoba from a communally-based political entity, where power was shared between the province's ethnic, linguistic, and religious communities, into a "modern" political culture where partisanship, majoritarianism, and liberal capitalism determined political power.

Thomas Greenway Jr. was English-born, in Kilhampton, Cornwall, on March 25, 1838. He was the oldest child of Thomas and Elizabeth (Heard) Greenway. The family migrated to Canada West when Thomas was 6 years of age, eventually acquiring land in the frontier region of Stephen Township, Huron County. Greenway's youth was marked by neither ease nor luxury. The family lived the typically difficult life of frontier farmers. His father died when Greenway was only 11 years old and for the next few years the family was supported primarily by his mother's earnings as a school teacher. He was raised a Methodist and had no formal education beyond the grammar school level.[4] Yet, whatever his early disadvantages, he emerged as a young man of considerable ambition. By age 22 Greenway had married Annie Hincks with whom he had seven children, and he was moving into the business and political worlds of Canada West.

After working as a store clerk in the town of Bervie, Greenway commenced his business career as a general store owner in Devon, later renamed Centralia, and expanded his commercial interests by opening two more stores over the next 10 years. In 1865 he launched his public career, first as the appointed postmaster for Devon, then as the elected, non-partisan vice-reeve and finally as reeve of Stephen Township from 1867 to 1874. Despite this non-partisan label, however, by the late 1860s Greenway had clearly attached himself to the local wing of the Liberal-Conservative (Conservative) party via his connection to John and Isaac Carling, of brewing and political fame, from nearby London, Ontario.[5]

Greenway, however, did not seem to be much of a partisan politician at this point in his career. When he ran in the federal election of 1872 little in his speeches separated him from his Reform opponent, except for his support of the government then in power.[6] In short, he responded to the prevailing passions and opinions in ways which he thought best served his interests, an approach that would dominate his political career. Running as a Liberal-Conservative in the riding of South Huron, Greenway lost in the elections of 1872 and

1874 to the Reform (Liberal) candidate, Malcolm C. Cameron. In 1875, he finally reached Parliament, by acclamation, after Cameron unexpectedly withdrew during the campaign. Both the Liberal and Conservative press claimed victory, owing to Greenway's ambiguous political positions.[7] Once in Parliament he achieved considerable notoriety when he supported the low tariff policies of the Liberals in the federal budget of 1876. Ostracized by the Tories for this "betrayal," he increasingly aligned himself with the Liberal/Reform government.[8] When the next federal election was called in 1878, Greenway immediately declared his intention to run on behalf of the Reformers. But with just three weeks left before election day, he stepped aside to allow his old rival, Malcolm Cameron, to take the nomination. This sudden change of heart was the direct result of a business arrangement worked out between Greenway and Cameron: Cameron would provide the funding for a land speculation and settlement project in Manitoba, which Greenway would lead as the recruiter, salesman and "man on the spot," in return for approximately one-third of all profits arising from Cameron's investment.[9] This arrangement caused Greenway to leave Ontario and it changed his life as well as Manitoba politics.

The Manitoba to which Thomas Greenway linked his future in 1878 was an exciting place for an ambitious man. There was still no railway linking the province with central Canada, but Sir John A. Macdonald's recent election victory and commitment to a transcontinental railway promised to alter that situation in the near future. A man who entered on the ground floor of the western land boom could do very well indeed. And this was certainly Greenway's intention. At 40 years of age, having lost his first wife to smallpox three years earlier and having married Emma Essery, a woman 16 years his junior (which meant the likelihood of an even larger family to support), the former MP was looking for economic opportunities. Indeed, he was desperately in need of them.[10]

As early as 1879 Greenway's financial hopes were coming to fruition. He had led the first of several groups of settlers west, laid claims to a homestead in his own name, and was busy subdividing some of this land into town lots in Crystal City, an endeavour he believed would earn large returns once railway service was established. In the heady days of the land boom of 1879–83, Greenway profited both on the sale of his own lands and those he was handling for Cameron, and other Liberals like Sir Richard Cartwright. He was able to make enough from his one-third of Cameron and Cartwright's land deals and his own speculations to purchase over 1,600 acres of land in his own name and build a major farming and purebred stock-raising operation, Prairie Home Stock Farm, outside Crystal City in the 1880s and 1890s.

Greenway also found himself back in politics, easily winning the December 16, 1879 election in the new provincial constituency of Mountain. His non-partisan stance in this election campaign may well have been, as one historian noted, a "result of his desire to serve the interests of his constituents and his own land schemes,"[11] but it also meshed with Manitoba's brand of politics. Owing to the province's unique constitutional status within Confederation—a province in name, but without the financial resources or independence from Ottawa which provincial status usually carried[12]—relations between the province and the dominion were complex. In fiscal and political terms, Manitoba was a client of Ottawa.

Because of this relationship, overt partisan politics could be disastrous at the provincial level. Even a Conservative in federal matters such as Premier John Norquay identified himself as a representative of Manitoba and not any one party.[13]

Greenway had little trouble following suit during his first years in Manitoba politics. He quickly emerged as a man of ability and served Norquay's administration well. He authored new legislation on municipalities which helped to make Manitoba's Municipal Act of 1881 conform to Ontario standards of local governance. He secured provincial support for a number of improvements in his home riding, such as the construction of two bridges across the Pembina River. However, he failed in his efforts to secure a railway extension to the original site of Crystal City. In fact, after the CPR acquired control of the Manitoba and South Western Colonization Railway late in 1882—the line Greenway had hoped would run through his town lots—the extension from Manitou to Whitewater bypassed his lands entirely. This decision forced Crystal City, buildings and all, to be moved to a new location slightly over one mile north of Greenway's land in 1885, dashing his hopes for windfall profits on those lots.[14] Even before his personal disappointment about the railway's location, Greenway had emerged as a severe critic of the CPR, its "monopoly clause," and Premier Norquay's apparent acquiescence to the dictates of Prime Minister Macdonald on railways.

From 1879 to 1882, Greenway played a careful political game. The Conservative federal government wielded considerable influence over affairs in Manitoba. Provincial politics, including the control of local MLAs, were dominated more by the personal force of Premier Norquay than by party loyalty. During this period, Greenway downplayed his Liberal connections, quietly maintained his opposition to the tariff portion of the federal government's National Policy, supported Norquay's local improvement projects, and offered only mild criticisms of the Premier's early enunciation of a provincial rights platform— which included demands for increased federal payments, control over the province's natural resources or a sizeable grant in lieu of such control, and increases in the territory of the province.[15] Greenway decided not to confront Norquay directly until he believed that he had found the Premier's Achilles heel. But he was determined to challenge the Premier and the entire edifice of traditional politics in Manitoba at some point.

Greenway's opportunity began to emerge in 1882 when Norquay confronted a series of issues related to Manitoba's relationship with Ottawa. The Premier's problem stemmed from his need to get "better terms" for Manitoba from Ottawa. Unfortunately for Norquay, he could only accomplish this by "demanding" more from the Dominion, arguing that Manitoba had certain inherent "provincial rights" while simultaneously going along with some of Ottawa's more controversial policies. On one level, this strategy worked well, for Manitoba received a major boundary extension in 1881 and substantial increases in federal subsidy payments in 1882 and 1885. However, Norquay had to surrender some of what he himself had claimed to be Manitoba's rights in order to make these gains. On occasion the price was acceptance of the federal government's right to disallow provincial railway charters, while at others it was support for the much-hated tariffs of the National Policy or a grudging acknowledgement that Manitoba might never gain control over its public lands and would instead have to settle for an annual cash subsidy in lieu of such lands. In Manitoba these concessions could be portrayed as a "sellout" of the province's rights, a point often made by Greenway, while in Ottawa any reluctance Premier Norquay demonstrated in accepting such concessions was likely to raise the ire of Prime Minister Macdonald.[16]

The province was entering difficult economic times. The collapse of the Manitoba land boom in 1883 and a devastating early frost in the fall of that year crippled the provincial economy. Thousands of farmers were driven to the edge of bankruptcy or worse. What had been a smoldering sense of discontent with the monopolistic CPR, the federal Conservative government which allowed the CPR to "gouge" western farmers with its high freight rates, and Ottawa's "National Policy" of high tariffs, burst into a prairie fire of western resentment. Two new farm organizations sprang to life in southwestern Manitoba that fall and winter, the Farmer's Protective Union of Manitoba and Northwest Farmer's Union.[17] The second of these soon came under the domination of men who were decidedly Liberal, such as Charles Stewart, "and budding politicians like Clifford Sifton, … Joseph Martin and R.P. Roblin."[18] As a result, even as this farmers' organization emerged in 1883–84, based upon a critique of the protective tariff, federal disallowance of western railways, high freight rates, and the Dominion's retention of public lands, it became a branch of the Liberal Party.

Over the next few years Greenway and his allies successfully harnessed the growing political and economic discontent of Manitoba farmers to the cause of "provincial rights" and the Liberal Party. By 1885, "[l]eading Liberals, particularly Thomas Greenway, had become household names in rural Manitoba through their advocacy of the farmers' cause."[19] Despite their popularity in the rural parts of the province, Greenway and the Liberals would need to become better organized if they hoped to unseat Norquay, for the Premier had a powerful political machine. Starting early in 1885, a more permanent and effective Liberal organization was created in Manitoba. In February 1885, Winnipeg Liberals formed a local organization under the leadership of James Fisher, a lawyer, and F.C. Wade, a journalist and lawyer; in March, Brandon's Liberals, led by the mayor, James Smart, and the young lawyer, Clifford Sifton, formed a local Reform Association; and finally, a provincewide convention of Liberals was held in Winnipeg at the end of March, at which the Association of Manitoba Liberals was formed. To no one's surprise, Thomas Greenway was named the party leader.[20]

The timing of this convention was fortuitous for Greenway because it was held just days after Norquay accepted the most substantial package of "better terms" yet offered to Manitoba by the Dominion. In all, Manitoba's treasury stood to gain approximately $300,000 per year, a huge sum for the perpetually underfunded province.[21] The catch was the "finality clause" attached to the offer. In exchange for these better terms Norquay had to agree that they constituted the final settlement of all outstanding issues between Manitoba and Ottawa. Manitoba could no longer seek control over the province's natural resources, no longer ask for additional boundary extensions, and no longer charter southward-running railways.

Led by Greenway, the Liberals attending the party's convention adopted resolutions attacking the "final settlement" and establishing a Liberal platform focusing upon provincial rights.[22] Greenway and the Liberals would now claim that Norquay had sold out Manitoba's inherent rights for a few dollars and some swamp lands! Still, while sole possession of the provincial rights platform was valuable, there was still much work to be done on the party's organization. Local Liberal and/or Reform associations needed to be set up in every provincial riding and, perhaps even more importantly, differences between the Winnipeg and rural wings of the party had to be resolved. This split was serious enough that in early 1886 an attempt was made by James Fisher, W.F. Luxton of the *Free Press*, and other Winnipeg-based members of the party executive to have Greenway dumped in favour of Fisher.[23] Supported by the rural members and key figures from western Manitoba such as Clifford Sifton, Greenway easily survived this coup attempt and emerged from the party's June provincial convention in a strong position.

This strength, however, did not translate into victory in the provincial election of 1887. Greenway ran a campaign highly critical of the Norquay administration and which attacked the character of prominent Tories such as Norquay and his leading French lieutenant, A.A.C. Larivière.[24] Joseph Martin, the fiery Liberal from Portage la Prairie, also re-introduced an issue that would become a hallmark of Manitoba politics over the next decade—the expenditure of government funds (printing and translation costs) related to the official use of French in Manitoba and the "undue" influence of French-speaking politicians in a province that had become overwhelmingly English.[25] But it was all to no avail. Despite impressive Liberal gains and an almost even split of the popular vote, Norquay's Conservatives still held a slight majority in the Manitoba House.

As matters turned out, 1887 witnessed a remarkable set of political developments which pitted Premier Norquay against Prime Minister Macdonald. The resulting battle would see the Prime Minister drive Norquay from office. Although his personal papers do not record his thoughts on the events of 1887, Greenway must have been amazed to witness the destruction of his old foe Norquay at the hands of the Prime Minister. Macdonald's assault on Norquay was a remarkable piece of political skullduggery, culminating in a manufactured financial scandal, which forced the resignations of both Norquay and his Provincial Treasurer in December 1887.[26] Dr. D.H. Harrison of Minnedosa briefly attempted to shore-up the Conservative government, but failed. On January 16, 1888, the Lieutenant-Governor had no choice but to ask the leader of the opposition, the Honourable Thomas Greenway, to form a government. Largely as a result of the actions of a Conservative Prime Minister, Manitoba had its first Liberal Premier.

Just a few months shy of his 50th birthday Thomas Greenway embarked upon what would prove to be a 12-year career as Premier of Manitoba. Since he had more or less backed into power, he did not have a strong mandate to govern. Beyond this, without executive-level experience of his own or among his followers, cabinet construction would be difficult. He would also need to craft a cabinet which represented constituencies in which he had little support, notably the francophone community and the Winnipeg business fraternity. Finally, the issues that he had been pushing against while in opposition—federal disallowance of railway legislation, the federal government's high tariff policy, and Manitoba's second-class status within Confederation—all still confronted the province and seemed no nearer to a satisfactory resolution than while the Conservatives were in office.

Greenway immediately named Joseph Martin, the 36-year-old lawyer from Portage la Prairie, as his Attorney General and Commissioner of Railways. The Premier reserved the position of minister for agriculture (still referred to as "Commissioner of Agriculture, Statistics and Health") for himself and then turned to Lyman Jones, the 45-year-old mayor of Winnipeg, to serve as Provincial Treasurer. Jones had not run in the last election and a seat would have to be found for him, but Greenway needed a representative from the Winnipeg business community in his cabinet. James Smart, a 30-year-old hardware merchant and former mayor of Brandon, was brought in as minister of Public Works, underscoring the importance of southwestern Manitoba to this new government. All that was missing now was the appointment of a francophone. The most obvious choice for a French representative in his cabinet, the Quebec-born Alphonse Martin of Morris, declined for unspecified reasons.[27] This forced the new Premier to approach a former Norquay supporter, James Émile Prendergast, the member for La Véréndrye, to fill the "French slot" in cabinet. The appointment of this prominent francophone lawyer and member of the Catholic section of the School Board turned out well for Greenway, because Prendergast's decision led another francophone member, Thomas Gelley, to cross the floor and support the Liberals. Under the circumstances, every bit of support Greenway could muster in the House was essential.

The francophone support for Greenway from Prendergast, Gelley, and A.F. Martin seems odd in retrospect, given that his government would eventually distinguish itself by alienating the French and Roman Catholic minority in Manitoba with its school and language legislation. But Manitoba's French Catholic leaders had no reason to distrust the new administration in 1888. Joseph Martin and a few other Liberals had made comments about curtailing French language rights in Manitoba, but then again so had John Norquay back in 1878. More importantly, Prendergast and the cultural leader of Franco-Manitoba, Archbishop Taché of St. Boniface, believed that they had guarantees from the leaders of the provincial Liberals that French language and Catholic school rights would be protected. In January 1888, a by-election in the primarily French constituency of St. Francis-Xavier had resulted in a surprise victory for the Liberal candidate, F.H. Francis, over the French-speaking Conservative, Joseph Burke. Before accepting the Liberal nomination, Francis had insisted that the party promise "to respect the linguistic and educational rights of the French if it came to power. Francis received the desired assurances and Joseph Martin, one of the Liberal leaders, reiterated the promise to respect French rights in a 'powerful speech' during the hard fought campaign in St. Francis-Xavier."[28] Then in February Greenway visited Archbishop Taché's residence and, according to Taché's Vicar-General and another witness, reiterated these promises and guaranteed that his government would do nothing to alter any of the French electoral districts in Manitoba.[29]

Greenway's successful manoeuvering in the matter of French support was followed by a series of other successes. The disarray of the Conservative opposition allowed for easy by-election victories for his cabinet appointees, while two Conservative resignations from the Legislature provided Greenway with a comfortable working majority when the House reconvened. But most importantly, by February 1888 the CPR was ready to abandon its insistence upon exercising the monopoly clause in Manitoba, and Ottawa could now safely cease its practice of disallowing Manitoba's railway legislation. As a result, Premier Greenway was called to Ottawa to help negotiate a settlement between Manitoba and the Dominion that would put an end to all major disagreements between the two levels of government.[30]

Greenway adjourned the Provincial Assembly on March 1, so that he and Attorney General Martin could travel to Ottawa to meet with the federal cabinet. Once there Greenway realized to his chagrin that Macdonald was still negotiating with the CPR over just how much the abandonment of the monopoly clause would cost the Canadian government.[31] The newly elected Premier expected a speedy resolution of the disallowance question and was upset when it turned out that he had been summoned east only to sit and wait while the federal cabinet worked out details with the CPR. To show his distaste for such delays, he and Martin left Ottawa before any arrangements on disallowance were made. He did, however, stay in Ontario long enough for the Prime Minister to track him down and call him back to Ottawa with the promise of a speedy resolution. Although not all of the specifics were in place, by the time Greenway and Martin left for Winnipeg at the end of March, they had assurances that the practice of railway disallowance was a thing of the past.

Greenway could not have hoped for a more auspicious beginning to his tenure as Premier. He could claim to have accomplished in three months something that Norquay had failed to do in a decade. He had slain the dragon that was the CPR monopoly and forced the Dominion to concede Manitoba's constitutional right to charter, and even build, railways. Small wonder then that Greenway and Martin's trip home resembled a victory tour. Between Emerson and Winnipeg, the two made numerous speeches "proclaiming the end of disallowance and claiming credit for the accomplishment."[32] The new and undisputed champion of Manitoba's rights had triumphed.

Greenway used his newfound popularity that spring to push through a legislative agenda which included two new pieces of railway legislation, provincewide redistribution of electoral districts favouring the Liberal Party, and the introduction of universal manhood suffrage. He also reduced the size and cost of government by introducing a series of economy measures, including the dismissal of several public servants. Most importantly, Greenway engaged in a series of complex negotiations with the CPR, the Northern Pacific Railway, and the promoters of the Manitoba Central Railway.[33] These negotiations were motivated by Greenway's desire to secure more railway service and lower freight rates for Manitobans while gaining access to the deep pockets of the railway companies for political purposes, particularly those of Henry Villard and the Northern Pacific Railway.

Premier Greenway believed he was conducting these negotiations in a masterful fashion.[34] He used the local promoters of the Manitoba Central to help hasten the demise of the CPR monopoly even as he and Joseph Martin were making a deal with the Northern Pacific which would ultimately cut the Manitoba Central out of the picture entirely. At the same time the Premier was also allegedly receiving money from both the Manitoba Central and the Northern Pacific, charges which were never conclusively proven.[35] As clever as Greenway was in these manoeuvres, however, it became clear that his background as a small-town merchant and land speculator had not prepared him to play with the big boys of the railway business.

When Greenway and Martin returned from Chicago and New York in the summer of 1888 with a contract between Manitoba and the Northern Pacific (and allegedly $50,000 each as a bribe), they had an agreement which promised the rapid completion of the Red River Valley Railway (RRVR) by the Northern Pacific, which would transform it into the Northern Pacific and Manitoba Railway (NPM), and tie this line to the Northern Pacific's extensive American system. Additional lines from Morris to Brandon and from Winnipeg to Portage la Prairie were also to be built, and freight rates were to be decreased immediately for many Manitoba farmers. The problem, however, was that Greenway had made all of his calculations based upon Manitoba's requirements. As historian J.E. Rea observes,

> transcontinental railways seldom make decisions based on local conditions alone. The attraction for Villard was not the scattered traffic of Manitoba. The Northern Pacific was being challenged in the area of Seattle, Wash., by the CPR. It could not lower its rates to meet this incursion as American law required that it reduce them throughout its entire system. What Villard needed was a makeweight. If he could acquire control of the RRVR, which was beyond American law, he could threaten the CPR in Manitoba and force it to back off in the Pacific northwest.[36]

This was exactly what happened. Late in 1889 the Northern Pacific brought its Manitoba rates in line with those of the CPR and, in exchange, the Northern Pacific received control over freight traffic in the Puget Sound region. Everyone came away a winner, except Manitoba.

Still, the impact of this fiasco was in the future, and 1888 was a good year for Greenway. Even before he and Martin had completed their railway negotiations, the Premier decided to test his strength at the polls. With Norquay still hanging tenaciously to the leadership of the disintegrating Conservative Party, and aided by the redistribution of provincial ridings, Greenway and the Liberals won a massive victory in July. Of 38 seats in the newly enlarged Legislature, 33 were won by Greenway supporters. According to historian W.L. Morton, the old "communal" districts had been largely erased from the electoral map, completing "the triumph of Grit democracy in Manitoba."[37]

For Greenway, however, success was never unalloyed. Even as he was basking in the glow of these returns, including his own re-election by acclamation, he was aware there was a plot afoot to have him and Joseph Martin ousted as leaders of the provincial Liberals. This plot was hatched in the offices of the *Manitoba Free Press* with the aid of Greenway's erstwhile friend, businessman Hugh Sutherland. The motivating issue was railways, primarily dissatisfaction with the Northern Pacific contract, and Sutherland's desire to have the provincial government direct its energy towards his Hudson Bay Railway plan. Greenway was informed of this plot and rather neatly circumvented the schemers.[38] But his problems were just beginning. The *Free Press* launched an editorial campaign critical of the Northern Pacific contract. W.F. Luxton, the editor and proprietor of the *Free Press*, wanted the local promoters of the Manitoba Central to build and operate the RRVR. He also wanted that rail line, no matter who built or owned it, to be a common carrier for other railways. This policy, he believed, would prevent a new form of monopoly from developing in Manitoba's transportation industry.

Attacks from a Liberal paper were difficult enough for the government to endure, but nothing compared to what happened next. Just as the debate over the Northern Pacific contract was coming before the Legislature in September 1888, Luxton sold controlling interest in the *Free Press* to agents of the CPR. The single most influential paper in western Canada was now in the hands of Greenway's arch-rivals. When the Northern Pacific contract came up for ratification in the assembly, five Liberals joined the Conservatives in opposing the terms of the contract. Most significant among the defectors was Rodmond P. Roblin, who would eventually cross the floor and emerge as the Conservatives' most dynamic force.[39]

The worst, however, was still to come. On October 1, 1888 the *Free Press* charged that Greenway had accepted a bribe of $2,500 from the lawyer of the Manitoba Central prior to the provincial election, and had attempted to solicit another $10,000 in exchange for special consideration from the government. Greenway and Martin were also charged with having received $50,000 each from the Northern Pacific. Winnipeg's Conservative paper, *The Morning Call*, soon joined the attack. Joseph Martin filed libel suits against the editors of both papers, but a Grand Jury refused to let the suits proceed, an unsatisfactory decision in the view of Greenway and Martin. Greenway then called a Royal Commission to examine the charges of bribery. Both the *Free Press* and *The Morning Call* refused to take part in the proceedings, believing the Commission's terms of reference were too narrow and designed to exonerate Greenway and Martin. As a result, even though the question of payments from the Manitoba Central seemed clear-cut (and despite the existence of some later-revealed documentation in the account books of the Northern Pacific which showed that its Counsel had in fact paid $50,000 each to Greenway and Martin),[40] the Royal Commission found the charges against Greenway and Martin unsubstantiated.

Even as the two politicians were dodging this scandal, Martin in his role as Railway Commissioner was creating another public battle. In order to complete Northern Pacific Manitoba's extension to Portage la Prairie, it was necessary to cross the CPR mainline just south of Winnipeg. Martin, a director of the NPM as well as Attorney General and Railway Commissioner, did not bother to go through the proper legal procedures to procure crossing rights. The CPR, which had every right to expect that all such procedures would be followed, and whose leaders detested Martin, decided to block the crossing site at Fort Whyte until such time as all legal niceties were observed. What came next was comic opera. William Whyte, the CPR's regional manager, ordered CPR crews to dismantle the NPM crossing, to set a derailed locomotive engine at the crossing point, and to keep a CPR train in constant motion over the contested section of track. Incensed, Martin called for volunteers in Winnipeg and created a special police force in order to protect "Manitoba's rights." Violence was only narrowly avoided and this battle for Manitoba's rights against the supposedly high-handed CPR fizzled when the matter was passed to the courts.[41]

While the Greenway government was largely occupied with railway matters in 1888 and early 1889, there were other important issues brewing beneath the surface of Manitoba politics. For example, Greenway, who had himself come to Manitoba as a land speculator and settler, was deeply enmeshed in plans to encourage more immigration to Manitoba, both as a private individual and as minister of Agriculture. The promotion of immigration raised important questions, notably regarding the desirability of certain immigrant groups. Previous governments had encouraged block settlements of Mennonites and Icelanders, while the Roman Catholic Church had encouraged the repatriation of French Canadians from New England and direct settlement from Quebec. Yet Manitoba had been most successful in attracting settlers from rural, Protestant Ontario. Indeed, this group constituted the majority of post-1870 immigrants.

To most of those who had come to Manitoba over the preceding 20 years, the terms of the 1870 Manitoba Act, which guaranteed linguistic, educational, and representational rights for Manitoba's original "dual" majority, were outmoded, inefficient, and expensive. Earlier administrations had already whittled away at the core of the Act: Métis land rights were dismantled, the upper house of the Manitoba Legislature was abolished; and political and administrative institutions had been redesigned to more closely mirror Ontario's model. The new Greenway administration had already greatly increased the pace of Manitoba's political remaking with its moves to universal male suffrage, political redistribution, and representation by population. Yet there were still elements of the original political settlement in place, most notably the practice of printing all government documents in both French and English and maintaining public funding for "separate" parochial schools.

The emergence of the Manitoba Schools Question, in actuality a mixture of educational and language law "reform," was a logical extension of Greenway's approach to, and understanding of, politics.[42] Greenway's Liberals had campaigned in both 1886 and 1888 on a platform of reduced expenditure and efficiency, particularly in regards to education.[43] Moreover, the Premier and many other Manitoba Liberals were believers in the Ontario model of "national" or secular schools. Thus, while Greenway was not particularly biased against either Catholicism or Quebec, he preferred the Protestant and Ontario way of handling education. In addition, there was no denying the growing popularity among many English-speaking Canadians of the underlying message of D'Alton McCarthy, the Ontario Tory renegade, and his attacks upon Roman Catholic cultural and political influence. When joined with the Manitoba Liberals' notion of political majoritarianism, it was almost inevitable that Greenway's government would act in ways that attacked Manitoba's French language and Roman Catholic institutional status. It was, to be blunt, good politics.

The first warning of the major transformation to come surfaced in Brandon in May 1889. In an editorial entitled "Separate Schools," the *Brandon Sun* railed against the method of funding education in Manitoba and called for a moratorium on the public funding of all denominational schools, arguing that this practice gave Roman Catholics "a preference to which they have no right."[44] Encouraged by public reaction, the *Sun* lashed out again at the end of May and once more in June.[45] Because the *Brandon Sun* was so closely linked to Brandon's two most powerful Liberals, James Smart, the minister of Public Works and Clifford Sifton, it is almost certain that such ideas were in accord with their own.[46] The overwhelmingly positive response to the *Sun*'s editorials, however, seemed to raise the possibility of an even more radical approach to educational reform than the Liberals had originally thought possible.

The unexpected death of Conservative leader John Norquay in July 1889 opened up even more opportunities. While Norquay had been a voice for compromise between French and English, Catholic and Protestant, and Old Red River Settlers and "New Manitobans," others in his party believed that the time for compromise had ended. Only six days after Norquay's death, Charles Cliffe, vice-president of Manitoba's Conservative Party and editor of Brandon's Conservative newspaper, *The Brandon Mail*, opined that Manitoba should not only do away with dual schools but abolish the use of French as an official language, both as measures of economy.[47] In his next editorial, Cliffe advocated that the Conservatives adopt these positions as official policy at the upcoming leadership convention—before the Liberals did so![48]

Just as there had once been a race between the Liberals and Conservatives to be the champion of provincial rights, a new race was on to champion unilingualism. On August 1 a piece appeared in the pro-Liberal *Winnipeg Sun* indicating that the Liberals were indeed planning drastic changes regarding the official use of French and the denominational school system.[49] On the same day, Greenway and Smart were out on the picnic circuit in southwestern Manitoba, providing Smart, the Premier's point man on education, an opportunity to lay out some of the government's proposed changes.

Smart's speech made clear that Manitoba would finally have a formal Department of Education and that the schools would be made "national, at least so far as the qualification of the teachers and the secular course of instruction are concerned." From a Catholic perspective this was alarming, for although Smart did not state that the government would categorically rule out public funding for denominational schools or completely abolish the "separate school system," the use of the terms "national" and "secular" was a good indication of where the government was headed. Manitoba's dual school system was about to be changed beyond recognition.[50]

If Smart and Greenway's position on education was beginning to crystalize, it was not yet entirely clear what the Premier proposed to do on the related issue of the official use of French. The events of the next few days would, however, raise the question most forcefully. On August 5, 1889 Joseph Martin joined D'Alton McCarthy at a public meeting in Portage la Prairie. McCarthy gave his standard speech on the threat to national well-being posed by dual languages and separate schools, indeed with all "special rights" for the French and Roman Catholics which prevented Canada from being "a British country in fact as it is in name." The thunderous applause clearly inspired Martin. Taking up McCarthy's comments, Martin implied that the next session of the Manitoba legislature "would once for all settle these two great issues [dual language and separate schools]." While he held back from stating any official government policy, he left a strong impression that his views reflected the intentions of the government.[51]

Martin was well aware that he had overstepped his authority. In a letter to Greenway the day after his Portage la Prairie speech, Martin offered a half-hearted apology. While admitting that he had been "going it rather strong" on the platform and was ready to accept censure for his comments, Martin argued that the recently announced creation of a Department of Education and the subsequent abandonment of the separate "Boards of Education" would cost the government any French support it had. If that was so, "what possible object can we have in not meeting the strong demand for the abolition of the French language? The connection of the two seemed so clear last night that without realizing that I was going a little too far I spoke as if it were the settled policy of the Government to do both things."[52]

The Premier was now in an interesting situation. His government's *official* policy on the school question and the use of the French language had not been announced, yet two trial balloons had already been floated. Since there would be no legislative session until early in 1890, Greenway and his colleagues would have several months to judge public reaction to the statements made by Smart and Martin before having to put any policy before the Legislature.

There was some immediate fallout from the events of early August. Prendergast resigned from the cabinet, acting on a letter submitted several months earlier when he saw the direction his colleagues were moving. Archbishop Taché wrote polite but pointed letters to the editor of the *Free Press*, defending the concept of separate schools and the quality of instruction offered in Manitoba's Catholic schools, and questioning the accuracy of the financial claims made concerning their costs.[53] Greenway proceeded cautiously. On August 10 he repudiated Martin's position on the abolition of the official status of French.[54] Yet before the month was over, the government's official publication, the *Manitoba Gazette*, was printed in English only, a first in Manitoba's history. Lieutenant-Governor Schultz was perturbed by this action, but accepted Greenway's personal explanation to him that this was merely a question of cost.[55]

Manitoba's francophones, and Archbishop Taché in particular, were disturbed by these events. Taché, traveling to Ottawa, Montreal, and Quebec City to participate in a series of religious celebrations, used the opportunity to lobby on behalf of French and Catholic rights in Manitoba, but apparently to no avail. Later that fall, Taché encouraged the French community to organize public meetings in St. Boniface and in smaller French communities, all of which passed resolutions calling upon the government to protect the French and Catholic rights enshrined in the Manitoba Act of 1870.[56] Taché also met with Greenway to discuss these matters but the Premier, according to Taché, was remarkably silent about government plans for the upcoming session.[57]

Meanwhile, the political situation across Canada was becoming complex. A national furor had already arisen over Quebec's Jesuit Estates Act of 1888. Protestant-Catholic tensions were greatly intensified by Manitoba's legislation. The question of language rights, Catholic school funding, and minority rights in general were at the top of the national political agenda in 1889–90, threatening to tear apart Canada's two major parties. With a provincial Liberal administration seemingly poised to attack French language rights and the old separate school system, the new leader of the federal Liberal Party, the French-speaking, Roman Catholic, Wilfrid Laurier, was in a quandary. He could not afford to alienate the Church or Quebec, but neither could he afford to become estranged from the powerful Ontario wing of the Liberal party, which supported Greenway and "British" Manitoba. The Conservatives were in an even worse situation, if only because they were in power. Prime Minister Macdonald was well aware that D'Alton McCarthy and his Equal Rights Association were extremely popular within his party and amongst the Orange Lodges of Canada, which were major supporters of the Tories. But Macdonald had made a political career out of working closely with conservative French politicians and their clerical friends in Quebec, and he had no desire to put an end to that alliance. For these reasons, both Macdonald and Laurier desperately strove to avoid language and school reform.[58] However, neither federal party leader could stifle the Manitoba government's legislative agenda for 1890.

The assault upon both French and Catholic rights in Manitoba was launched with a bill designed to abolish the official use of French in the Assembly, the courts, the civil service, and government records. Attorney General Martin then introduced two additional measures. The first called for the creation of a provincial department of education while the second abolished Manitoba's denominational school system, replacing it with a nonsectarian, publicly funded system. As the debate on this legislation unfolded, it was clear that the definition of "nonsectarian" was murky. As he noted during debates on the second reading of the Bills, Martin personally wished that the government's legislation had kept all religious instruction out of Manitoba's public schools. But his remarks made clear that the influence of the province's leading Protestant clergymen had taken its toll; Manitoba's schools were not to be totally secular, or "Godless" as the critics would have it. Instead, nonsectarian, Christian religious instruction would be allowed, but only a prescribed type and amount.[59]

This triumvirate of legislation was to become Thomas Greenway's political legacy, and for the next six years it would shape not only Manitoba politics, but Canadian politics as well. All three bills were passed and then signed into law by Lieutenant-Governor Schultz in March 1890, despite protests by Archbishop Taché and the French and Catholic minority. John A. Macdonald's federal government did not instruct the Lieutenant-Governor to reserve the bills and refused to use its own power of disallowance in this matter. Macdonald decided that the place to settle this issue was in the courts.[60]

This federal decision was a major political victory for Greenway and the English-speaking Protestant majority he represented. It indicated that, despite the questionable constitutional propriety of the legislation, Macdonald feared taking action. Given the weak political position Greenway had occupied just months earlier, the turnabout was remarkable. While the issue worked its way through the courts, Greenway could proceed with his money-saving and politically popular "reforms." In political terms this meant he had an issue at his disposal which he could dress up in his favourite brand of political rhetoric: the defense of provincial rights.

As the legal test case, Barrett *vs* the City of Winnipeg, went forward, it provided much grist for the political mill. In Manitoba, Justice Killam ruled that Manitoba had been within its rights in passing the school legislation and, when appealed to the Manitoba Court of Queen's Bench, two of the three appellate judges concurred in this ruling against the Catholic minority. However, the Supreme Court of Canada ruled on appeal that Manitoba's 1890 public school legislation violated the intent of the Manitoba Act of 1870. But this was not the end of the matter; a further appeal could still be made by Manitoba to the Judicial Committee of the Privy Council in Great Britain.

Before this final appeal was launched, however, Greenway's government took another politically astute step, one designed by the newest member of Manitoba's cabinet. The Premier had long desired that Clifford Sifton join his cabinet and the temporary absence of Joseph Martin, who had resigned his portfolio to run in the federal election of 1891, gave Greenway his opportunity to convince Sifton to join the government as Attorney General.[61] Martin, with his propensity for law-suits, for public battles with the CPR and *Free Press*, and for intemperate comments, had become more of a liability than an asset. Sifton, meanwhile, brought a finely honed sense of both the law and politics and a much more positive set of relationships with the always-important CPR. In this regard Sifton was particularly important to Greenway, for the deal which the Premier and Martin had worked out with the Northern Pacific was not yielding the desired results of lower freight rates and rail line extensions. A rapprochement with the CPR was necessary if Greenway's aggressive plans for railway expansion were to be fulfilled, and Sifton seemed the most likely person to achieve this.[62]

But it was in the matter of the school question that Sifton would prove most valuable. Sifton decided that a diversionary tactic was in order and he arranged to have a Winnipeg Anglican, Alexander Logan, launch a court case seeking public funding for Anglican schools. As Sifton and Greenway expected, in light of the recent ruling of the Supreme Court of Canada, the Logan case sped through the Canadian courts and received a favourable judgement. Based on the precedent of the Barrett case, it was found that Manitoba's new public education system worked against the right to denominational schools enshrined in the Manitoba Act of 1870.[63] This case would also be appealed and Sifton, the architect of this strategy, believed that by having a second related matter before them, the Imperial Court would see that any successful challenge to Manitoba's policy of "national" schools would result in a fragmentation of educational funding and of education itself.[64]

While legal manoeuvring was going on, and Greenway was working to improve his relations with the CPR, he began to make preparations for the next provincial election. If the federal government had reserved or disallowed any of Manitoba's 1890 legislation, it is likely that Greenway would have called an election soon after, running a campaign on a platform of provincial rights and essentially against the federal government. Macdonald's response to the school question had been designed, at least partially, to avoid just such an event.[65] But the strategy of referring matters to the courts could only delay matters for so long. The Prime Minister himself had managed to conduct one last successful electoral campaign in 1891 during this hiatus, but it was clear that a Privy Council ruling would be made soon and, no matter which way it went, it would be a political bombshell.

Greenway and Sifton had no intention of being caught unprepared. Indeed, both men wanted a renewed mandate for their government before the Privy Council rendered its ruling. There was some concern that the Council might concur with the unanimous ruling of the Supreme Court and find in favour of the Catholic and Anglican appeals. So Greenway decided to run his campaign for re-election on the school question, that is, on the "principle" that no matter what the courts decided, the government would ensure the implementation of a national public school system for Manitoba in one form or another. Professional politician that he was, the Premier took every step possible to ensure victory. He personally supervised yet another significant gerrymander of Manitoba's constituencies,[66] while Sifton employed dubious methods to ensure the passage of a new Election Act which placed the government in a most enviable electoral position.[67] Greenway also played a key role in raising and distributing campaign funds. Meanwhile, Sifton became the government's most effective voice on the school issue, constantly discussing the matter on the stump and assuring his listeners that even if the courts decided against Manitoba's new school laws, there were other methods available to ensure that a "proper" system of national schools would be maintained.

The election of July 23, 1892 turned out to be a more closely contested race than most expected. A Liberal majority was re-elected, taking 26 of 40 seats, but by comparison to the results of 1888, it was not a sweeping a victory. In fact, two Liberal cabinet members were defeated and the Liberals took just slightly over 50% of the popular vote.[68] Victory it was nonetheless and one in which Greenway believed the school question had been the decisive issue.

Victory was made all the sweeter one week later when, on July 30, 1892, the Privy Council ruled on the Barrett and Logan cases, and overturned the Supreme Court of Canada's decisions. In effect, Manitoba's position against funding denominational schools was upheld.[69] Oddly enough, there was a potential political risk for Greenway. If the school question faded into obscurity, what would be his next great issue? His political career up to this point had been defined by his stand on volatile issues: free trade, railways, disallowance, provincial rights, and the school question. He had climbed to political prominence through his positions on these matters and had won important battles. But where would he turn now? As an economic slump set in there was little prospect for more railway construction or new immigration. In the previous federal election campaign, the Liberal position on unrestricted reciprocity had proven decidedly unpopular with Canadian voters, so this was not likely to be a useful issue for Greenway. With the school question apparently settled, Greenway faced the dull prospect of running a good and efficient administration and henceforth running on his record.

Fortunately for Greenway, the school question was far from settled. The Catholic minority had no intention of abandoning the fight and a series of new approaches were made to the federal government. Citing subsections of both Section 22 of the Manitoba Act and Section 93 of the British North America Act, representatives for Manitoba's Catholics petitioned the Dominion government for "remedial action," effectively demanding that the Dominion take legislative action to force Manitoba to restore the rights of the Catholic minority.[70]

The federal government, in general disarray following the death of Prime Minister Macdonald in June 1891, had moved cautiously on the school question. Sir John Thompson, who had become Prime Minister in December of 1892 after the John Abbott interregnum, was highly sensitive to the divisive nature of the school question. As a Methodist convert to Catholicism due to his marriage, Thompson knew that Protestants across Canada would look askance at any strong action by the federal government on behalf of the Catholic minority. Thompson decided to turn to the courts yet again, this time to get a legal ruling on whether or not the federal government had the power to intervene in this matter. In the "Brophy case," the Dominion formulated six questions for the Supreme Court of Canada to answer in regards to the matter. The government of Manitoba, although listed as a respondent, did not send counsel to the Court when arguments were made on October 17, 1893. Sifton went on record for the Manitoba government questioning the wisdom of raising the subject again.[71]

Meanwhile, the province had proved itself incapable of "reforming" the old Catholic schools of Manitoba out of existence. From 1890 until 1894 many of the separate schools had found ways around the Public School Act, especially in rural areas where the French Catholic population constituted a majority. Early in 1894, however, bowing to pressure from local Protestants and the Orange Order, the government introduced an amendment to the School Act which closed all loopholes that allowed government funds to go to separate schools.[72]

Until this time there had been some, including Lieutenant-Governor Schultz, who believed that Greenway was still open to compromise. But this hope was fading. Manitoba was mired in an economic depression, wheat prices were falling, no progress was being made on new railways, and a new farmers' organization cum political movement, "The Patrons of Industry," was emerging. The Premier could ill afford to lose any support on a popular issue, particularly one which he himself had created. Indeed, Lieutenant-Governor Schultz was now convinced that the Premier, even if he personally wanted to compromise, would not be allowed to do so by members of his own government, a sentiment echoed later by J.D. Cameron, Greenway's Provincial Secretary.[73]

Worse yet for the Catholic minority, only one week after the 1894 amendment to the School Act was brought before the legislature, the Supreme Court of Canada rendered a negative verdict on the Brophy case. The court majority found that the Privy Council ruling in the Barrett and Logan cases meant that the Catholic minority of Manitoba did not have the right to appeal to the federal government for remedial action. But still, the school question was not ended. It was inevitable that this decision would also be appealed to Britain, where the case could not be heard until December 1894.

The result of this last appeal was dramatic. In January 1895 the Privy Council reversed the decision of the Supreme Court and ruled that the Dominion government had the right, and indeed the duty, to deal with the question. As Morton noted, "the poisoned chalice of the dreaded obligation to deal with the Manitoba School Question" had again been passed back to the federal government."[74] The Catholic minority in Manitoba was pleased with the decision and immediately called for federal action to restore its rights. Complicating matters somewhat, however, was that a host of new participants were now involved. In June 1894 the long-time champion of French and Catholic rights in Manitoba, Archbishop Taché, passed away; in December of the same year Prime Minister Sir John Thompson died; and finally, in January 1895, Premier Greenway was laid low with erysipelas,[75] a skin infection that left him largely unable to work for four months. This meant that the key players now were the youthful Archbishop Langevin of St. Boniface, the ineffectual Prime Minister Mackenzie Bowell, and the acting Premier of Manitoba, Clifford Sifton. And one new player was added to the roster early in 1895. In February the Dominion cabinet announced that it would constitute itself as a tribunal in order to hear the case of the Catholic minority for remedial action. Sifton, without consulting Greenway, made the provocative decision to appoint D'Alton McCarthy to present Manitoba's case![76]

No matter who represented the province, the Manitoba government was likely to lose. Forced to accept legal and political responsibility for defending minority rights, the federal government could not do anything other than issue a remedial order. On March 21, 1895, the cabinet issued its order for Manitoba to alter the School Act in order to restore Roman Catholic school rights and to provide funding for those schools. As expected, this order elicited a storm of protest in Manitoba. But the fact was that a "remedial order" from the Dominion cabinet had little real legal impact. What did such an order actually mean? With Premier Greenway still incapacitated, Sifton adjourned the Manitoba legislature until May in order to give Manitoba time to consider its response.[77]

In the interim, Sifton headed to Ontario in April to campaign on behalf of an Equal Rights Association candidate who was running in a by-election in the federal constituency of Haldimand. The campaign stops gave Sifton access to the Ontario press in order to make Manitoba's case against the Dominion order on school legislation, and to raise his own national political profile.[78] For his part, a convalescing Greenway returned to the office and began crafting his own reply to the remedial order. He too was unwilling to give in or compromise, but he was willing to delay matters still further, hoping to stall until a federal election had to be called. When he was invited to Ottawa in May to discuss matters further he agreed. These talks yielded no compromise since Greenway, accompanied by Sifton, refused to meet with any members of the Dominion cabinet and spoke only with the Governor General, Lord Aberdeen. The only real result of this trip was a minor relapse in Greenway's now fragile health.[79] Back in Winnipeg in June 1895, Sifton drafted and Greenway read to the Legislature a "Memorial" to the Dominion government which flatly refused to implement the remedial order, indicating that Ottawa had not done enough to study the matter before issuing its order.[80] Prime Minister Mackenzie Bowell's government, itself badly divided on how to proceed, announced on July 6 that if Manitoba did not voluntarily restore minority rights within six months, the federal Parliament would force the province to do so via remedial legislation. However, Bowell made it clear that reaching a negotiated settlement during these six months was still possible.[81]

This new federal action put Manitoba in the driver's seat. Greenway and Sifton realized that they had six full months to prepare and that they were already in a strong position. The popular response in Manitoba and Ontario was behind them and the federal Conservatives were badly divided on the issue. In fact, if played carefully the school question could be parlayed into a campaign issue at both the provincial and federal levels. For these reasons, Greenway made no attempt to seek a compromise and instead rebuffed Bowell's overtures when the Prime Minister visited the west in September. Instead, Greenway's efforts were all focused upon preparing for a provincial election.

In September the voters' lists were updated and Winnipeg lawyer F.C. Wade prepared a summary of the government's position on the school question, packaged as a highly inflammatory pamphlet, which was distributed to party supporters and newspapers throughout the province.[82] For his part, Sifton headed to Montreal to confer with Wilfrid Laurier to coordinate the policies of the national and provincial parties. Although there is no record of this meeting, it has often been speculated that it was here that the outlines of the famous Laurier-Greenway compromise were first worked out.[83]

On December 20, 1895, just days after Sifton's return from Montreal, Manitoba's response to the federal government was issued and the writs were dropped for a provincial election to be held on January 15, 1896. The two events were clearly linked, for Manitoba's response to the Dominion made it clear that remedial legislation would be viewed as an attack upon "provincial autonomy." Indeed, "so drastic a proceeding as the coercion of a Province, in order to impose upon it a policy repugnant to the declared wishes of its people," declared the government statement on the threatened federal order, "can only be justified by clear and unmistakable proof of flagrant wrongdoing on the part of the Provincial authority."[84] This was wrongdoing which the province denied. The subsequent election call was made on one issue—and one issue alone—the school question. As Greenway put it, "The menacing attitude assumed by the Dominion Government with reference to the educational legislation of the province has made it necessary to take the sense of the electors upon the question thus forced upon them."[85] Thomas Greenway was back in his favourite pose as the champion of provincial rights. His health was a concern, but he was sure of his footing and in the brief campaign of 1895–96 he made short work of the opposition.

This election constituted a major victory for Greenway. The Liberals took nine seats by acclamation and 22 in open contests. Two "Patrons" and two "Independent Liberals" were also elected, but only five Conservatives won seats. This was a victory to savour; a victory which certainly sent a message to Ottawa. Greenway had good reason to claim in the press and his private correspondence that the federal government should have learned a lesson.[86]

Ottawa could not back down. Minority rights, especially Catholic rights, were far too important, especially for Quebec. Even as his ministry introduced remedial legislation to the House of Commons, Prime Minister Bowell sent emissaries to Winnipeg, first Donald Smith then a three-man commission, to try and reach a negotiated compromise that would make the legislation unnecessary. But to no avail. Premier Greenway became mysteriously ill just when the three commissioners arrived in Winnipeg and he left all negotiations to the most hard-line of his colleagues, J.D. Cameron and Clifford Sifton.[87] The strategy of both the Manitoba and federal Liberals had become "delay, delay, delay" until Bowell's administration ran out of time in the last parliamentary session of its tenure. In Ottawa, debate on the remedial bill dragged on and by April 16, 1896 all attempts to pass the legislation were abandoned. Within a week the House was prorogued and an election called. A federal election would be fought over Manitoba's schools.

Prime Minister Bowell resigned as leader of the Conservatives and Sir Charles Tupper succeeded him. The 75-year old Tupper conducted a strong campaign, and stood firm on the promise of remedial legislation. But Tupper temporized, insisting that federal legislation would allow Manitoba the right to maintain a "national" school system, but with reasonable protections for the Catholic minority.[88] Laurier campaigned on the vague promise of "sunny ways," implying that negotiation rather than legislation should be used by Ottawa to settle the issue. Meanwhile, he allowed his Quebec lieutenant, Israel Tarte, to make claims in that province indicating that a Liberal government would support minority rights in Manitoba, even as Laurier was promising Ontario voters that no coercion would be used.[89]

When election day arrived on June 23, 1896, the Liberals won nationally but not in Manitoba. In a bizarre twist, the school question, now a major issue across Canada, was viewed in Manitoba as a settled matter. The province had voted twice on the issue (1892 and 1896) and having provided strong mandates to their provincial politicians both times, Manitoba voters seemed quite certain that their leaders would prevent any attempt at federal coercion. Thus, in Manitoba's seven federal ridings the school question was but one of several issues which affected the outcome. Railway policy (Tupper had promised to build a railway to Hudson Bay) and the role played by the CPR on behalf of several Conservative candidates, as well as general economic questions such as the tariff, were all factors in Manitoba's constituencies. As a result, the Liberals did not win the sweeping victory in Manitoba that Greenway, Sifton, and other Liberals had hoped for. In fact, four of the seven ridings in Manitoba went to the Conservatives.

Still, Laurier and the Liberals had won office and all that was left to be done was for the "sunny ways" approach to be applied to the school question. But with Sifton's influence growing and Greenway's in decline, the Premier was left largely out of the loop on these federal-provincial negotiations. Sifton announced to the Premier that he was heading to Ottawa in August to negotiate with Laurier, although he politely invited Greenway to accompany him. The Premier was clearly upset by this, but his frustration was aimed not at Sifton, but at Laurier who had ignored him for the entire six weeks since the election. Greenway gave his assent first to Sifton's trip east and then later to the "Memorandum Re Settlement of School Question" which Sifton brought back with him. This assent was the sum total of his involvement in the negotiation of the Laurier-Greenway compromise.[90]

Historian J.E. Rea characterized this inappropriately named agreement as a "compromise between winners."[91] There was little in the agreement for the minority, as became apparent both when the text of the memorandum was made public in November 1896 and when the Manitoba Public Schools Act of 1897 was passed. Manitoba retained its system of national schools and school funding; religious instruction could be offered for a half hour after school had ended for the day; where a sizable grouping of one faith (Catholic or Protestant) existed within a school, a teacher of that denomination would be employed; and most famously of all was the question of bilingual schools. When 10 or more students in any school spoke any language other than English, instruction was to be "in French, or such other language, and English upon the bilingual system."[92] This last clause created considerable problems for Manitoba's educators in the ensuing two decades, as the floodgates of eastern and central European immigration were just about to be opened, ironically, by Clifford Sifton, who became federal minister of the Interior. This influx would lead to demands for bilingual education in a host of languages never anticipated by the framers of the legislation.

For Thomas Greenway it should have been the best of times. He had won a major election victory, his position on the school question was vindicated, and he could feel that he had played a key role in bringing the federal Liberal Party out of the political wilderness. Beyond this, Manitoba and Canada embarked upon an economic boom of unprecedented proportions: wheat prices were rising, businesses in Winnipeg and throughout the country were thriving, and William Mackenzie and Donald Mann were building their railway up into the northwestern frontier of Manitoba, a railway that would become the basis for their new transcontinental Canadian Northern line and in the process open up a whole new farming, lumbering, and fishing frontier for Manitoba. Still, while the years after 1896 were good for Manitoba, this was not the case for Greenway. His *de facto* co-Premier, Clifford Sifton, having settled the school question, took his reward and moved on to the federal cabinet. A powerful ally in the federal cabinet did not, as it turned out, do Greenway or Manitoba much good. Sifton soon proved that he was not about to do anything that did not serve his own interests or those of the federal Liberal Party. Greenway was also aware that many of his supporters were displeased with the compromise of 1896, claiming that the provisions relating to bilingual education had gone too far and were a form of kowtowing to Quebec. Greenway paid a price in the farming districts of Manitoba for the Laurier-Sifton acceptance of the National Policy of high tariffs once they settled into office. Federal immigration policy also hurt Greenway. Sifton's new immigration policy recruited thousands to Manitoba and the North-West, but they were not desirable settlers to Anglo-Protestant Manitoba. The eastern and central Europeans flooding through Winnipeg were met with considerable hostility, but Greenway, who himself preferred British, Canadian, and American settlers, reluctantly defended the new immigration policy.[93]

In the face of all this, Greenway knew that he needed another popular issue to rejuvenate the political fortunes of the provincial Liberals. And he believed he had found that issue in renewed railway development, particularly a plan to have a new line built linking Winnipeg to Duluth, Minnesota which would end the CPR's monopoly of the shipping route to the Great Lakes. His ultimate goal was to have this line reduce shipping costs on grain to 10¢ per hundredweight. The Premier had actually advocated such a line since 1892, but Sifton's influence and close ties to the CPR along with depressed economic conditions had prevented the project from moving forward. Now, however, both obstacles were gone and Greenway made an attempt at striking a railway deal early in 1897. But everywhere he turned, he was thwarted by the CPR. By the time of the next provincial election, Greenway's scheme, his only major policy initiative between 1896 and 1899, seemed nothing but a pipe dream.[94]

During Greenway's last term in office, he had little sense that his popularity with the electorate was dwindling. Greenway, the consummate politician, underestimated the appeal and political savvy of the Conservatives and their new leader, Hugh John Macdonald, the former Prime Minister's son, and one of the most popular figures in Winnipeg public life. Despite yet another gerrymander of a few key ridings, when Manitobans went to the polls on December 7, 1899, Greenway was shocked by the result. His Liberals barely won the popular vote, but after losing six ridings by narrow margins, they were defeated as a government. Macdonald's Tories had 22 seats, the Liberals 17, and one Independent was elected. As a result, on January 6, 1900 Thomas Greenway resigned as Premier.[95]

The remainder of Greenway's political career is hardly noteworthy. It was clear that the 61-year old desperately wanted to get out of politics. He wanted to step down as Liberal leader and secure a Senate appointment or some other federal sinecure that would provide an income equal to or better than his Premier's salary of $4,000 per year. Unfortunately for Greenway, while a Senate seat was offered to him, his colleagues in Manitoba were emphatic that he must stay on as leader to hold the party together. Greenway stayed.[96]

At first, the former Premier was an effective Leader of the Opposition. In the first session of the new Legislature, he defended his government's record, denied all charges of corruption, and pilloried the Conservatives for their overtly racist franchise legislation which sought to exclude eastern European immigrants. He also worked on behalf of the federal Liberals during the 1900 federal campaign. Shortly thereafter, time, health, and financial issues began catching up to Greenway. When the dynamic Rodmond P. Roblin replaced Macdonald as leader of the Conservatives and Premier in 1900, Greenway seemed less capable of running a strong opposition. His primary concern now seemed to be staving off personal bankruptcy and recovering from a series of illnesses. So mediocre and uninspiring was his leadership that he presided over the almost total annihilation of the provincial party he had helped to create in the 1880s; indeed, when Premier Roblin called the next provincial election in the summer of 1903, the Liberals were reduced to only eight seats, a staggering decline from the glory days of 1896.

Reeling from this loss, and now without any immediate hope of gaining a federal sinecure, in 1904 Greenway decided to run at the federal level in the riding of Lisgar. He won the seat but his return to the House of Commons after a 27-year absence was not triumphal. He spoke little and when the one matter which might have excited him arose—the Autonomy Bills of 1905 creating the new provinces of Saskatchewan and Alberta, which at first guaranteed government funding for separate schools in the two new provinces—he backed away, hoping again to receive a well-paying federal appointment. This strategy worked and in 1908 Greenway's wish was realized. In September Prime Minister Laurier appointed Greenway to the Board of Railway Commissioners, a position that came with a salary of $7,000 per year. But, as was so often the case in Thomas Greenway's public life, he was not be able to enjoy the victory. On October 30, just as he arrived in Ottawa to take up his new position, Greenway suffered a heart attack and died the same day.

Conclusion

Political issues always seemed to present themselves to Greenway not as ideological matters, but as opportunities. His genius lay in his ability to read the changes in the political landscape, and respond accordingly. He changed political allegiances when it made political sense. He disavowed promises made when it worked to his advantage. He could be cold and calculating when he abandoned political allies. Marked by charges of corruption and bribery, of ruthless gerrymandering, of broken promises and a lack of principle, Greenway's career is a study in political expediency.

Still, it must be said, Greenway's approach to politics served him well for many years. But as he aged, his lack of imagination and his propensity to react to trends rather than lead them, took their toll. By the time of the Manitoba Schools Question, Greenway was no longer the master of his own government. He abdicated that responsibility to Clifford Sifton, who emerged as the effective leader of the Greenway government by the mid-1890s. Much more of an ideologue and manager than Greenway, Sifton ran the Liberal Party in Manitoba and built ties with the federal party. Greenway made no efforts to prevent the loss of power. His biographer Joseph Hilts suggests that "Greenway believed that his relationship with Sifton was that of father and son." As a result, the Premier "attempted to assist the Attorney General in his political ambitions."[97] Greenway realized Sifton's talent, ambition, and influence. As the Liberal Party of Manitoba came to be more reliant upon urban support in Winnipeg, Brandon, and other growing towns, Sifton—the urban lawyer and businessman with one foot still in the farming community—seemed to be the man most capable of reconciling the interests of rural and urban areas. Whether he thought of Sifton as a son or not was immaterial: Greenway needed Sifton. It was Sifton who was so valuable in improving Manitoba's relations with the CPR; it was Sifton who took the lead in renewing railway construction in Manitoba by crafting a bold provincial railway financing scheme in 1895, paving the way for Mackenzie and Mann to begin their storied railway building career in Manitoba; and finally, it was Sifton who plotted Manitoba's response to Ottawa's school policy.[98]

By the late 1890s Greenway did not seem to have the energy to undertake these challenges on his own. His interest in political affairs was waning. His personal finances were a mess. He maintained his interest in land speculation, had a penchant for fine, large homes, and did everything in his power to expand his Prairie Home Stock Farm. He thought of himself as a shrewd operator who could afford a lavish lifestyle. But the reality was different. Constantly in debt to various creditors, he regularly refinanced loans and mortgages, and was usually only one step ahead of insolvency. Indeed, Greenway expended virtually all of his income as Premier on keeping his home and model farm going and was completely dependent upon his Premier's salary to keep his head above water. He could not afford to lose office. In desperate need of continuing political success in order to assure financial survival, Greenway was more than willing to offer power and authority to Sifton, the man he thought most capable of keeping him in office.

Greenway released the genie of anti-French, anti-Catholic sentiment, not so much out of conviction, but rather because of his well-developed talent for profiting from an emerging popular issue. As a result, he bears a considerable share of the responsibility for what the Manitoba Schools Question did to French-English and Catholic-Protestant relations not just in Manitoba but across Canada. Greenway's legacy is a mixed one. He helped Manitoba achieve more of its "provincial rights" and played a role in ending the practice of disallowance. He also made Manitoba's politics more transparent by ending the charade of non-partisan politics and implementing simple majoritarianism within the province. However, he accomplished this by means that discredited the party system, legislative process, and many of the policies that he helped to create.

Notes

1. W.L. Morton, *Manitoba: A History* (Toronto: University of Toronto Press, 1957), 278.
2. D.J. Hall, *Clifford Sifton: Volume I, The Young Napoleon, 1861–1900.* (Vancouver: University of British Columbia Press, 1981), 34–35.
3. Joseph A. Hilts, "The Political Career of Thomas Greenway" (PhD dissertation, University of Manitoba, 1974), 378–84. This political biography is an outstanding piece of scholarship and all students of Manitoba political history must turn to this work in order to understand Greenway.
4. Keith Wilson, *Canadian Biographical Series: Thomas Greenway* (Winnipeg: Faculty of Education, University of Manitoba, 1985), 1; and Hilts, "The Political Career of Thomas Greenway," 2.
5. John Carling was both the minister of Agriculture and Public Works in Sandfield Macdonald's provincial government and an MP in John A. Macdonald's federal administration. In effect, he was the lynch-pin between the Ontario and federal governments. His brother, Isaac, was a Conservative MPP who also supported Sandfield Macdonald's administration. As Greenway's biographer makes clear, it was the Carlings who became Greenway's political patrons and helped engineer his first foray into federal politics in 1872. See Peter E.P. Dembsky, "Carling, Sir John," *Dictionary of Canadian Biography: Vol. XIV*, on-line edition; and Hilts, "The Political Career of Thomas Greenway," 2–19.
6. Hilts, "The Political Career of Thomas Greenway," 8.
7. All of the newspaper reports are cited in Hilts, "The Political Career of Thomas Greenway," 22–23.
8. J.E. Rea, "Greenway, Thomas," *Dictionary of Canadian Biography: Vol. XIII*, 417.
9. Ibid., and Hilts, "The Political Career of Thomas Greenway," 32 and 41.
10. By 1878 his commercial career in Ontario had foundered and he no longer owned any stores. His only real asset was a sizeable home in Centralia, Ontario, and yet he had a young wife and now eight children to provide for, as he and Emma had already had the first of the seven children of his second family. Still, he was not without resources. Knowing something about Manitoba lands from his time on the parliamentary committee on immigration and colonization, and backed financially by Cameron and the former Liberal minister of Finance, Sir Richard Cartwright, Greenway had a reasonable expectation of recouping his fortunes in Manitoba.
11. Rea, "Greenway, Thomas," 417.
12. Manitoba's public lands had all been reserved "for purposes of the Dominion." This meant that all land sales, land grants, as well as the rental of grazing and timber lands and the assessment of stumpage fees for timbering and royalty fees for mineral extraction—fairly important sources of funding for the older provinces—were beyond the control of Manitoba's treasury. Beyond this, Manitoba had not really enjoyed the full benefits of "responsible government" until Norquay came to power, as the first Lieutenants-Governor of Manitoba had exercised far more power than their counterparts in the

other provinces for the first few years of Manitoba's existence. Thus, the Manitoba Greenway came to in 1878 was, in political terms, a true anomaly in constitutional terms: a province in name, but closer to a "territory" in terms of its actual status and therefore much more subject to the whims of the federal government in almost every regard. For a lengthier discussion of this status and how it was arrived at, see Jim Mochoruk, *Formidable Heritage: Manitoba's North and the Cost of Development, 1870–1930* (Winnipeg: University of Manitoba Press, 2004), 105–13.

13. Morton, *Manitoba*, 197.

14. Hilts, "The Political Career of Thomas Greenway," 50–56, 60, 74, 77 and 85–88.

15. Mochoruk, *Formidable Heritage*, 112–13.

16. For a more detailed discussion of these various negotiations, see ibid., 112–21.

17. Brian McCutcheon, "The Economic and Social Structure of Political Agrarianism in Manitoba, 1870–1900" (PhD dissertation, University of British Columbia, 1974), 98–115 and passim.

18. Morton, *Manitoba*, 211.

19. Hall, *Clifford Sifton, Vol, I*, 28.

20. Ibid.

21. The Dominion agreed to: increase provincial subsidies; aid branch-line railway construction in Manitoba; spend $100,000 investigating the feasibility of a railway to Hudson Bay; provide land grants to help pay for the construction of such a railway; and grant Manitoba ownership of all swamp lands within the province, which could then be improved and sold or rented by the province. The pot was further sweetened by a grant of 150,000 acres of land in order to endow a provincial university. See Mochoruk, *Formidable Heritage*, 115–17.

22. *Manitoba Free Press*, April 1, 1885.

23. Hall, *Clifford Sifton, Vol. I*, 28–30. Winnipeg's interests were quite different from those of the farmers. By 1885–86 the City Council, Winnipeg Board of Trade and several other civic organizations had fought for and received special freight rates for Winnipeg shippers, won the right to grade grain in Winnipeg and allied themselves with major figures in the grain trade, such as the Ogilvie family—all of which placed Winnipeg's economic interests at odds with representatives of rural Manitoba. See Ruben Bellan, *Winnipeg First Century: An Economic History* (Winnipeg: Queenston House, 1978), 48–52.

24. Hall, *Clifford Sifton, Vol. I*, 30; and Hilts, "The Political Career of Thomas Greenway," 94.

25. This was hardly a new issue in Manitoba politics. Norquay's cabinet colleague, C.P. Brown, had commenced his political career in Manitoba in 1874 by running as an independent Liberal in opposition to French language rights and the dual public school system. Meanwhile, Norquay's own rise to power as Premier had briefly pitted French against English. When Joseph Royal, the dominant French Canadian politician in Manitoba in the 1870s, had tried to maintain a strict dualism in Manitoba politics Norquay had responded by creating an all-English ministry in 1878 which was at least briefly committed to reducing French language rights and political representation in Manitoba. On Brown's views see Jim Mochoruk, "Corydon Partlow Brown," *Dictionary of Canadian Biography: Vol. XII*, 128–29; on Norquay see Gerald Friesen, "John Norquay," *Dictionary of Canadian Biography: Vol. XI*, online edition; on Martin see Larry Fisk, "Controversy on the Prairies: Issues in the General Provincial Elections of Manitoba, 1870–1969" (PhD dissertation, University of Alberta, 1975), 116–18.

26. T.D. Regehr, *The Canadian Northern Railway* (Toronto: The Macmillan Company of Canada, 1976), 8–12.

27. For Martin's polite—but frustratingly vague—refusal to serve in the cabinet, see Provincial Archives of Manitoba (PAM) Greenway Papers, GR 1662, G484, Box 1 #9 "AF Martin to Greenway, n.d."

28. Raymond Huel, *Archbishop A.-A. Taché of St. Boniface: The "Good Fight" and the Illusive Vision* (Edmonton: University of Alberta Press, 2003), 283.

29. Ibid. See also, A.-A. Taché, *A Page of the History of the Schools in Manitoba During Seventy-Five Years* (St. Boniface: n.p., 1893), 25–28.

30. Morton, *Manitoba*, 230–31.

31. The price turned out to be a loan guarantee covering bonds worth $15,000,000—a capital fund which the CPR intended to use to build and or acquire grain-handling facilities in the west and to buy two American railways. See Regehr, *The Canadian Northern Railway*, 13–14.

32. Hilts, "The Political Career of Thomas Greenway," 121.

33. The best way of following at least one portion of the twists and turns of these negotiations—particularly the way in which the MCR was cut out of the picture and the way in which Greenway used Joseph Martin as his scapegoat—is to read the printed correspondence file related to this matter. See PAM, Greenway Papers, GR 1662, G524, # 11938, "Correspondence Related to The Manitoba Central Railway"; see also, ibid., #11951, "Thomas Scoble (Managing Director of the MCR) to Thomas Greenway, Winnipeg, April 30, 1888."

34. Ibid. As these documents indicate, Greenway would say one thing to one group, something else to another, and then use his own Attorney General and Railway Commissioner as a scapegoat to explain why certain promises had not been kept.

35. Ibid., #11952, "Copy of a Report of a Committee of the Executive Council, November 10, 1888." (This document established the Royal Commission to investigate the allegations of bribery made against Greenway and Martin in the pages of *The Call* and the *Free Press*. It was vague on the amount of the bribes coming from the Northern Pacific, but specified that the MCR was alleged to have provided $12,500 for Liberal election purposes in exchange for Greenway and Martin's support on certain legislative matters.)

36. Rea, "Greenway, Thomas," 418. For even more detail, see Regehr, *The Canadian Northern Railway*, 15–17.

37. Morton, *Manitoba*, 232.

38. D.J. Hall gives most of the credit for this to Clifford Sifton, who was approached by the plotters to join them. Sifton instead notified Greenway, who immediately leaked the story to the press to flush his opponents out of the woodwork—and then denied that there was any such scheme afoot. See Hall, *Clifford Sifton, Vol. I*, 36; and Hilts, "The Political Career of Thomas Greenway," 143.

39. Roblin was himself involved with the promoters of the Manitoba Central Railway, thus his decision to abandon Greenway was not based entirely upon principle.

40. Hilts, "The Political Career of Thomas Greenway," 152.

41. For a short retelling of this story see Hall, *Clifford Sifton, Vol. I*, 37–38.

42. The historiography surrounding this issue is fairly simple. On the one hand, it has often been argued that the emergence of the Manitoba Schools Question was related to the Greenway government's desire to create a political issue which could deflect criticism over railways and the related charges of corruption. This charge was first made in the pages of the *Manitoba Free Press*. See the editorial dated September 12, 1889. See also R.E. Clague, "The Political Aspects of the Manitoba School Question" (MA thesis, University of Manitoba, 1939), 292. Another important interpretation is that the school question was largely the product of an impetuous speech by Joseph Martin, inspired by

the visit of D'Alton McCarthy to Manitoba. McCarthy, as president of the Equal Rights Association, was seeking to fan the flames of indignation over Quebec's Jesuit Estates Act of 1888 and the "unfair advantages" enjoyed by the French within Canada, and in this interpretation, he clearly inspired Martin to new heights. This view was held most strongly by Lovell Clark. See Lovell Clark (ed.), *The Manitoba School Question: Majority Rule or Minority Rights* (Toronto: Copp Clark Publishing, 1968), 4. Neither of these views is accepted in this essay, for these approaches reduce the Schools Question to a mere political distraction, to an offshoot of an Ontario issue or a sudden spontaneous development.

43. Hilts, "The Political Career of Thomas Greenway," 188–93.

44. *Brandon Sun*, May 16, 1889. (This was actually the follow-up to a more mildly written piece which had appeared on May 2.)

45. Ibid., May 30, 1889 and June 20, 1889.

46. On the *Sun's* connection to Sifton and Smart, see Hall, *Clifford Sifton, Vol. I*, 41. Greenway's biographer speculates that these editorials were part of the government's attempt "to gauge public reaction to proposed changes in the [provincial] education system." See Hilts, "The Political Career of Thomas Greenway," 201. It is clear that as early as March 1889 James Smart had, in fact, been assigned the task of introducing some reforms in Manitoba's education system. So change of some sort was clearly in the works long before the editorials appeared in the *Sun*. See *Manitoba Free Press*, March 2, 1889.

47. *The Brandon Mail*, July 11, 1889.

48. Ibid., July 18, 1889.

49. *The Winnipeg Sun*, August 1, 1889.

50. For a report of Smart's entire speech see *The Brandon Sun*, August 8, 1889.

51. The text of this report on the two speeches is reprinted in Clark, *The Manitoba School Question*, 36–38. Prior to this speech, it is not clear just exactly what the policy of the government was on the language question. Some have argued that with the exception of Prendergast (the lone French representative in the cabinet) there was already broad agreement to do away with the printing of government documents in French, primarily as an economy measure. This would be in accord with Martin's interpretation of where matters stood at the time.

52. PAM, Greenway Papers, GR 1662, G491, #2111, "Joseph Martin to Greenway, August 6, 1889, Portage la Prairie."

53. See *Two Letters of Archbishop Taché on the School Question* (St. Boniface, MB: n.p., 1889), brochure.

54. *Manitoba Daily Free Press*, August 10, 1889.

55. Hilts, "The Political Career of Thomas Greenway," 213–14.

56. Huel, *Archbishop A.-A. Taché of St. Boniface*, 286–87.

57. Ibid., 287.

58. See P.B. Waite, *Canada, 1874–1896: Arduous Destiny* (Toronto: McClelland and Stewart, 1971), , 213–17 and 254–55.

59. *Manitoba Free Press*, March 5, 6 and 8, 1890, "Extracts from the reports of the debates of the Legislative Assembly of Manitoba." Cited in Clark, *The Manitoba School Question*, 55–57.

60. Donald Creighton, *John A. Macdonald: The Old Chieftain* (Toronto: Macmillan, 1965), 543–44.

61. Hall, *Clifford Sifton, Vol. I*, 50–51.

62. See Hilts "The Political Career of Thomas Greenway," 160–67 and Hall, *Clifford Sifton, Vol. I*, 58–59.

63. Hall, *Clifford Sifton, Vol. I*, 54–56.

64. Ibid., 55–56.

65. Creighton, *John A. Macdonald*, 543–44.

66. Hilts, "The Political Career of Thomas Greenway," 225–26.

67. Hall, *Clifford Sifton, Vol. I*, 56–58.

68. Ibid., 61. Most notably James Smart, the original author of the school policy lost his seat.

69. For a brief description of the ruling see Waite, *Canada, 1874–1896*, 249.

70. Huel, *Archbishop A.-A. Taché of St. Boniface*, 299–300.

71. Hall, *Clifford Sifton, Vol. I*, 80–81.

72. Ibid., 83.

73. See Hilts, "The Political Career of Thomas Greenway," 229–30, and Waite, *Canada, 1874–1896*, 255.

74. Morton, *Manitoba*, 270.

75. This was a type of skin infection with serious side effects in a day and age before the development of anti-biotics. Greenway's case must have been serious as he was unable to attend to any official duties from January through to April of 1895.

76. Hall, *Clifford Sifton, Vol. I*, 93.

77. Ibid., 94.

78. Ibid., 94–97.

79. Hilts, "The Political Career of Thomas Greenway," 234–36.

80. "Extract from the Reply of the Government and Legislature of Manitoba, June 25, 1895," cited in Clark, *The Manitoba School Question*, 168–70.

81. Ibid., 171–72; Waite, *Canada, 1874–1896*, 258; and Paul Crunican, *Priests and Politicians: Manitoba Schools and the Election of 1896* (Toronto: University of Toronto Press, 1974), 110.

82. For an abridged version of this pamphlet, see Clark, *The Manitoba School Question*, 84–89.

83. Hall, *Clifford Sifton, Vol. I*, 98; and Hilts, "The Political Career of Thomas Greenway," 238–39.

84. "Extracts from the Final Rejoinder of the Government of Manitoba, December 20, 1895," cited in Clark, *The Manitoba School Question*, 174.

85. Cited in Hilts, "The Political Career of Thomas Greenway," 239.

86. Ibid., 241–42.

87. Ibid., 242–49.

88. Hall, *Clifford Sifton, Vol. I*, 109.

89. Hilts, "The Political Career of Thomas Greenway," 256.

90. Ibid., 260; and Hall, *Clifford Sifton, Vol. I*, 117–18.

91. Rea, "Greenway, Thomas," 421.

92. Legislative Library of Manitoba, *Manitoba Statutes*, 60 Vic, c. 26.

93. Hilts, "The Political Career of Thomas Greenway," chapter 6.

94. Ibid.

95. Ibid.

96. Ibid., 334–40.

97. Ibid., 379–80.

98. Ibid., 380.

Hugh John Macdonald

1900

RORY HENRY

Hugh John Macdonald, 1900

Hugh John Macdonald was perhaps the most prominent Manitoban to ever seek and hold the office of Premier. Yet Macdonald's tenure as Premier was brief, better measured in days, not years. Macdonald himself would have agreed that his time in office was a footnote in his own life, let alone in the history of the office itself. Yet his brief period in office remains important, as it demonstrates a significant shift in the approach of Premiers to their roles and responsibilities, as well as in the party system.

Education and Career

Macdonald was born on March 13, 1850 in Kingston, Canada, and was the only surviving son of Sir John A. Macdonald. He grew up in Kingston and completed a BA at the new University of Toronto in 1869. Like many socially prominent young men in post-Confederation Canada, he was an active member of the militia. He undertook duty in the summer of 1866 in a rifle battalion defending Cornwall, Ontario against the threat of a Fenian attack from the United States, traveled west in 1870 as an ensign in Colonel Wolseley's Expedition to assert Canadian authority over Manitoba, and later helped to organize and serviced in the 90th Winnipeg Regiment of Rifles in the 1885 North-West Resistance. After his first taste of life in western Canada, Macdonald returned to Toronto to finish studying law, and was called to the Ontario bar in 1872.[1]

Macdonald practiced law for a decade in Toronto and Kingston in several partnerships including his father. In 1876 he married Mary Jean King. They had one daughter, Daisy. His wife was a Roman Catholic, though Macdonald did not convert, and the "mixed" marriage was a source of controversy. She died in 1881 and in 1883 Macdonald remarried, to Agnes Gertrude Vankoughnet of Toronto, a daughter of a Tory ally of his father. They had one son, Hugh, who died in 1906 while a student of law. Daisy Macdonald married in Winnipeg and was a mainstay of local society throughout her long life.

In 1882, Macdonald decided to move west and settle in Winnipeg. Like many people at that time he was hoping to take advantage of the promise of booming Manitoba and also to strike a path away from the limelight of his famous father. Winnipeg in the 1880s and 1890s was a growing city and the key to the expansion of Canada and the development of the West. Macdonald built up a strong law practice in partnership, not coincidentally, with John Stewart Tupper, a son of Charles Tupper, a prominent Tory ally of Sir John A. The law office of two sons of Fathers of Confederation was a distinctive and useful one in Winnipeg and Canada.

Manitoba and Political Involvement in the 1890s

Macdonald acted in an unofficial role as his father's eyes on the ground in the West, but he avoided continuous pressure to seek office himself. Throughout his life he claimed to dislike politics and avoided comparisons with his famous father. In the 1891 federal election, he was finally compelled to run for a seat in the riding of Winnipeg. Macdonald won and his father proudly introduced him to the House of Commons to the applause of all parties. Unfortunately, Sir John A. died only weeks later. Without the pressure from his father to stay in Ottawa, Hugh John resigned his seat two years later to return to Winnipeg and his law practice. While he believed in the value of politics, he did not enjoy the practice of it, which at the time was highly competitive, with elections that were often if not always corrupt, and with an open understanding that to the winners would go the spoils of office. These practices meant a fierce round of battles over voters lists and ballots, the organization of supporters on election day by means both fair and foul, and frequent court challenges of the outcomes.[2] The battle for spoils also meant that all politicians, including backbenchers, were perpetually lobbied for jobs and contracts and were expected to recommend the firing of disloyal civil servants to make way for party loyalists and their kin. Macdonald gave every indication he did not like that part of politics. As he wrote to his uncle after his federal victory, "I may be obligated to sit for the whole parliament term but nothing will induce me to seek re-election for a political career is not one in which I would succeed and the life of a politician is distasteful and more than distasteful to me."[3] Resisting renewed pressure to run in 1896, he told Prime Minister Charles Tupper that he feared that his health would collapse if he had to endure a lengthy term in office and added that he only retained good health due to regular exercise and outdoor activity.[4]

Despite his dislike of public life, Macdonald was continually involved in politics. He was a compelling public figure and he was prepared to listen to the call of duty. An early historian of Manitoba and contemporary of Macdonald's, George Bryce, professor at Manitoba College and the president of the Manitoba Historical Society, wrote that Macdonald "possesse[d] to an eminent degree the magnetic personality of his talented father, and [was] personally one of the most popular men in Canada."[5] Prime Minister Mackenzie Bowell tried to drag him back into public life in 1894, but Macdonald refused. In 1896, he could not deny the request from Prime Minister Sir Charles Tupper. That spring, Macdonald was sworn into cabinet as Minister of the Interior and Superintendent General of Indian Affairs, a key ministry for western Canada. In the federal election held in June 1896, Macdonald won in Winnipeg but Tupper's Conservatives were turned out of office. Macdonald's return to federal politics was short-lived. The Liberal party managed to turn up positive evidence of wrongdoing by Macdonald's campaigners. While many of their allegations were likely spurious,[6] there was clear evidence that some supporters had broken the rules of the Elections Act by providing rides to the polls for electors. As this news was breaking, steps were already being taken to shift Macdonald into another political role to aid the Conservative party's return to national power.

In late March 1897, Hugh John was officially unseated by the Supreme Court of Canada. In the newspapers, he mused about moving to opportunities in provincial politics. A week later, once the provincial legislature prorogued, opposition Conservative MLAs gathered together and handed the leadership of the party to Macdonald. The previous leader (and future Premier), Rodmond P. Roblin, fully supported the change, recognising that with Macdonald as leader the party's chances of unseating the Liberal Greenway administration were significantly enhanced. Macdonald made it clear from the start that his immediate goal was to use his position as leader to heal rifts in the Conservative party and divisions in their voting base that had arisen during the Manitoba Schools Question.[7]

Macdonald agreed with the principle behind the Greenway government's determination to do away with denominational schooling, but not with the measures used. As he made clear in 1896, Macdonald was strongly sympathetic with Charles Tupper's decision as Prime Minister to enforce court rulings that Manitoba had acted unconstitutionally—requiring Ottawa to intervene and pass so-called remedial legislation. Macdonald warned Tupper, however, that he did not have any sympathy for returning to the previous era of separate religious-based Protestant and Catholic schooling. On the contrary, he favoured a "mild" reform that would allow some religious instruction where numbers warranted at the end of the school day. He warned Tupper that, except for the "French constituencies," Manitobans of all political views were so strongly in favour of "national" (i.e. non-denominational) schools that he feared political rebellion if the federal government acted too strongly. He added that there was a good curricular model to be found in the "Irish National Schools Series" that would meet both Catholic and Protestant sensibilities. Indeed, while he supported national schools, out of respect for the French population he opposed the use of the schools question as a political issue to drive voters from one party to the other.[8]

While the provincial Tories hoped to use Macdonald's stature and popularity to seize provincial power, the strategy for the federal Conservative party was equally clear. They hoped that taking power in the provinces would provide them with the base they needed to return to power federally. Their hope was that the same strategy would work for Macdonald personally, and after a stint as Premier, he would return to the federal arena.

Macdonald took his role seriously and spent the next two years rebuilding the party. He tirelessly spoke at public meetings and met with supporters, and he worked to develop a platform that would go beyond the usual concerns of settlement promotion and railway construction and the flip-flops of programs and loyalties that often occurred among leaders and voters alike.[9] Macdonald's platform was the first issued by Manitoba Conservatives. His predecessors in the office of the Premier had been focused primarily on the physical infrastructure of the province—settlement and railways. For the early Premiers, political interest in the social and cultural aspects of the state were primarily seen in terms of cultural accommodations between English, French, and initially the Métis. Historians generally argue that the political transition to a majoritarian, Anglo-Protestant culture began in Manitoba with the Greenway government and the events surrounding the schools question.[10] The social and cultural aspects of nation building increasingly became vote-determining issues, as the numbers of Anglo-Protestant voters increased, Eastern European immigrants began to appear in large numbers and the influence of the French-Canadian Catholics declined.

It was in this context of epochal change that Macdonald developed the Conservative party's first official platform. Recognising the concerns that people had with the changes that were occurring in Manitoba and the West, Macdonald and the party based their new platform in the common concern of how to improve and solidify society in the face of fears of the erosion of traditional society.

Concerns over the evolving identity and character of the citizenry were widespread from the 1890s onwards. Issues that seem commonplace now—industrialisation, immigration, urbanisation, and fundamental advances in science, technology and medicine—changed the way people viewed the world and their place in it. Observers were clear that the seemingly solid foundations of political, social and economic life were eroding as a result. Definitions of religion, family, and government were all changing, and social leaders were fearful that the erosions of those institutions would result in social decline, akin to the decline and fall of Rome. Manitobans were subject to these anxieties. The transition of Manitoba from a recently carved out colonial settlement to a bustling part of the modern world formed an essential part of Macdonald's life. He arrived in the West when Winnipeg was little more than a muddy village. A little over a decade later and it had taken on all the trappings of a city, and was giving every indication it would grow into a city to rival great North American centres like Chicago.[11]

Chief among Macdonald's goals was making Canada a vital part of the British Empire. Like many in the settler dominions of Canada, Australia and New Zealand, he turned to the British connection as a means of ensuring that Manitobans would have the right characteristics to allow them to thrive and survive in the modern age. Imperialists like Macdonald believed that the growth and establishment of the Empire and the dominions required British citizens to continual demonstrate self-control, self-discipline, and other elements of a strong character to rule over others. Macdonald was careful to distinguish his commitment to the imperial identity from nativism and anti-Catholicism by making it clear that his concerns had nothing to do with French Canadians, or even northern Europeans, but solely with the Slavic immigrants recruited by Sifton and the Liberals. Without a strong character and set of values, the Slavs (and by extension, Tories argued, the Liberals) would seek the easiest path and doom the nation to moral weakness and decline. Macdonald's imperial identifications were strong, and one his opponents knew they had to weaken. In October 1899 war broke out in the Transvaal. Hoping to discredit Macdonald, the federal Liberals offered him command of the Manitoba contingent that was being organized. Once Macdonald declined, the provincial Liberals sent out a flyer accusing him of disloyalty.[12]

To further address concerns about the disintegration of values and behaviour, Macdonald's platform included a commitment to prohibition. While he did not agree with the principle of prohibition, Macdonald argued that, since the public had twice voted for prohibition in 1889 and 1892, he would enact the strongest laws within the power of the province to bring it about. By restricting access to alcohol, prohibitionists argued, the risk of social decline due to criminal or deviant behaviour would be reduced. Less consumption of alcohol meant healthier, happier people, which would make for a stronger province and nation. The adoption of prohibition was also a way for the Conservatives to steal a policy from the traditionally "dry" Liberals.

Macdonald hoped to strengthen the traditional family in other, smaller ways, by addressing such issues as married women and property rights, and workers and workplace accident compensation. Additionally, Macdonald was not above more elementary populism, such as calling for a lowering of MLA pay and a reduction in the size of cabinet. Macdonald's platform also promised to address concerns more traditionally raised by politicians before (and after) him, such as improving railway policy, dealing with the provincial debt, improving relations with Ottawa, and dealing with electoral fraud by cleaning up the voting lists, which was also a way to limit voting by recent immigrants, which the Liberals were notorious for facilitating.

Electoral Victory and Premiership

On November 16, 1899 the writs for the election were dropped, and on December 7, 1899 the Macdonald government was elected with 23 seats to the Liberals' 15, with one independent. Macdonald campaigned on his name, his reputation and his party's platform. He was aided by the support of prominent federal Conservative donors and politicians such as Sir Charles Tupper. Perhaps more importantly he benefited from divisions in the Liberal ranks—support for Clifford Sifton at the time was far from unanimous.[13]

Macdonald set his cabinet, with himself as Premier and four others as ministers (two without portfolio, as a money-saving measure). As was the custom of the time they had to seek immediate re-election, and all five were returned through by-elections at the end of the month. By March 29, 1900 Macdonald was ready to open his first and only session of the legislature, complete with a Throne Speech, budget and an ambitious 82 pieces of legislation which were disposed of by session's end. The session was surprising to many observers—in large part because Macdonald's government moved immediately to do the things they had pledged to do in the campaign.

Macdonald's first and only Throne Speech began with a review of imperial unity and the events of the Boer War. In case anyone doubted the government's imperial loyalties, the Throne Speech intoned that the war in South Africa "has caused a wave of patriotic enthusiasm … and has furnished conclusive evidence to foreign states of the strength of the bond which binds all parts of the empire together."[14] The new Premier was committed to implement his election promises. Chief among them was the prohibition law, sometimes called the Macdonald Act despite his refusal to write it (he hired it out to lawyer J.A.M. Aikins) on the grounds he didn't believe in prohibition. The act attempted to ban liquor from all but private, medicinal, or religious use. While the bill was passed in Macdonald's legislature, dealing with its eventual proclamation and implementation was left to his successor R.P. Roblin, and dealing with it became a defining moment for his premiership.[15]

Another major legislative initiative Macdonald pushed through was reform of the election laws. In part it was an attempt to clean up the electoral rolls to allegedly ensure fairer elections. However, its main focus was on a revision of the franchise. Prior to the reforms, in order to vote a man had only to have lived in Manitoba for three years. With Macdonald's changes, men would have to reside in the province for at least seven years—or three years and be able to read the Manitoba Act in English, French, German, Swedish, or Icelandic. Macdonald admitted that his target was voting by "Galicians and Doukhobors" whose knowledge of the favoured languages was considered unlikely.[16] There was no consideration of female enfranchisement.

Macdonald's term was also notable for the first introduction of direct taxation on corporations and financial institutions to help address the government's deficit. For the same reason, municipalities would be required by law to pay a portion of the costs of administering justice. The government spent some time on the issue of Manitoba's fiscal history, calling a commission of inquiry into the province's fiscal practices. The report, which was tabled but never printed, was used by the government to show that the Greenway administration had been guilty of lax administrative procedures and excessive spending on matters ranging from trifles to railway grants. It argued that the previous Norquay government had not left the province with a large debt, as Greenway had charged throughout his time in office. The result was the entrenchment of the ritualistic mutual blame of Tories and Grits, which may have done little substantively but it did further reinforce through mutual antagonism the party identifications of each side in the legislature.[17]

With the session complete after a lengthy if leisurely pace, which lasted from March until July, Macdonald concluded admistrative matters and resigned as Premier on October 29, 1900, a move that likely did not surprise many. Greenway, for one, argued that the prohibition bill—and by extension the entire session—was all part of Macdonald's plan to bump off Sifton "The whole matter was an entire deception and was used merely for the purpose of supplying a foothold to defeat the minister of the Interior at the Brandon election." This was not far-fetched; even Macdonald's electoral triumph of December 1899 was announced in the Conservative press as a triumph in the war against the "Sifton" machine.[18]

As part of the Tory plan to return to power federally, Macdonald again ran for a federal seat, this time to unseat the main thorn in the Tory side, Brandon Liberal and minister of the Interior, Clifford Sifton. In the 1899 provincial election, the Tory support in the areas that comprised Sifton's Brandon seat had been very strong—strong enough that it was thought that with Macdonald as the candidate, Sifton could be eliminated. However, Sifton had learned from the 1899 provincial election, and worked his riding and retooled his electoral machine to crush Conservative hopes of an upset.[19]

Career after Politics

Macdonald returned to his law practice, likely quite happy to no longer be an elected politician. He did maintain his involvement in the party, serving behind the scenes and sometimes as president of the party. In 1911 Macdonald returned to his mission to reshape the citizens of the province, this time directly influencing the behavior of many Winnipeggers as Police Magistrate. In this post, Macdonald was able to deal directly with behaviour and character, sparing those he thought had the right stuff to turn their lives around and gain control of their actions, and throwing the book at those who did not. Most observers agreed that in this position he found his true calling.[20] In 1913, he was created a knight bachelor. This recognition was part of a decision by the Borden government in Ottawa to strengthen Canada's ties with Great Britain by once again accepting imperial honours. Nor was Macdonald completely finished with provincial politics. In 1915 he served on the commission investigating charges of financial irregularities in the construction of Manitoba's legislative buildings—finding Roblin and others guilty of conspiracy to defraud the province.

Macdonald died on March 29, 1929, and lay in state before the magnificent provincial legislature building whose construction he had investigated, before his burial in St. John's Anglican Cathedral cemetery.

Conclusion

The brief tenure of Hugh John Macdonald as Premier is a notable part of Manitoba's political transition. First, Macdonald's rule was focused almost entirely on using the state to develop and define the social and cultural aspects of the province. Previous Premiers had used factors such as character and identity as wedge issues designed to gain an electoral advantage for their political party. For Macdonald such issues were the actual purpose of politics. If Greenway marked the transition to modern politics among Premiers, Macdonald marked its arrival. Gone were the old non-partisan politics of development, replaced with a politics of class and identity that would culminate in the clashes of 1919 and the accommodations that followed. The second important aspect of Macdonald's election and premiership is that he healed fractures in the Conservative party, and built a renewed base of support that created a strong foundation for the Conservatives in the two-party system, one that would vie for government in Manitoba for the next 20 years and survive in weakened form for many more after.

Notes

1. Reliable details on Macdonald's life are found in Hal Guest, "Hugh John Macdonald," *Dictionary of Canadian Biography*, Volume XV; a more detailed study is found in Henry James Guest, "Reluctant Politician: A Biography of Sir Hugh John Macdonald" (MA thesis, University of Manitoba, 1973).
2. An excellent account is in John English, *The Decline of Politics: The Conservatives and the Party System* (Toronto: University of Toronto Press, 1993), Chapter 1.
3. Macdonald to James Williams quoted in Keith Wilson, *Hugh John Macdonald: Manitobans in Profile* (Winnipeg: Peguis Publishers, 1980), 29.
4. Library and Archives Canada, Tupper Papers, Macdonald to Tupper, January 17, 1896.
5. George Bryce, *A History of Manitoba: Its Resources and People* (Toronto: The Canada History Company, 1906), 357.
6. This matter is carefully investigated in Guest, "Reluctant Politician," 221–31.
7. Guest, "Reluctant Politician," 233; on the larger issues surrounding the Manitoba Schools Question see Peter B. Waite, *Canada 1874–1896, Arduous Destiny* (Toronto: McClelland & Stewart, 1971), and Ramsay Cook and R.C. Brown, *Canada 1896–1921: A Nation Transformed* (Toronto: McClelland & Stewart, 1974).

8. Library and Archives Canada, Tupper Papers, Macdonald to Charles Tupper, January 17, 1896, April 3, 1896; Wilson, *Hugh John Macdonald*, 31–34.

9. The flip-flops on issues were remarkable in the 1895/1896 federal and provincial elections in the province: see Roland Pajares, "The Federal Election of 1896 in Manitoba Revisited" (MA thesis, Department of History, University of Manitoba, 2008).

10. W.L. Morton, *Manitoba: A History* (rev. ed., Toronto: University of Toronto Press, 1965), Chapter 12.

11. See R. Rory Henry, "Making Modern Citizens: The Construction of Masculine Middle-Class Identity in the Canadian Prairies, 1890–1920," in Robert Wardhaugh (ed.), *Toward Defining the Prairies: Region, Culture and History* (Winnipeg: University of Manitoba Press, 2001); see also Robert Wardhaugh, "Gateway to Empire: Imperial Sentiment in Winnipeg, 1867–1917," in Colin Coates (ed.), *Imperial Canada 1867-1917* (Edinburgh: Centre for Canadian Studies, 1997), 206–19.

12. Guest, "Reluctant Politician," 265.

13. See D.J. Hall, *Clifford Sifton, Vol. I, The Young Napoleon* (Vancouver: University of British Columbia Press, 1981), Chapters 10 and 12.

14. Throne Speech, quoted in *Morning Telegram*, March 30, 1900, p. 1.

15. *Morning Telegram*, June 2 and 12, 1900; Roblin used a third plebiscite and a "local option" policy to severely reduce prohibition. See James Gray, *Booze: When Whiskey Ruled the West* (Calgary: Fifth House, 1995), 65–71; for a more general perspective see Craig Heron, *Booze: A Distilled History* (Toronto: Between the Lines, 2003).

16. *Morning Telegram*, June 8, 1900.

17. Guest, "Reluctant Politician," 296; *Morning Telegram*, May 11, 12 and 16, 1900, June 8, 1900.

18. *Morning Telegram*, June 2, 1902; *Morning Telegram,* December 8, 1899.

19. See Hall, *Clifford Sifton, Vol. I*, Chapter 12.

20. Roy St. George Stubbs, *Lawyers and Laymen of Western Canada*, (Toronto: Ryerson Press, 1939), 58.

Rodmond P. Roblin

James Blanchard

Rodmond Palen Roblin, 1900–1915

Rodmond Palen Roblin had the second-longest tenure of any of Manitoba's premiers. A remarkably successful politician, he was a member of the Manitoba Legislature for 23 years and served as premier from October 1900 until May 1915. The son of a comfortable but by no means wealthy Loyalist farm family in eastern Ontario, he also achieved considerable success in a variety of business ventures and he was a founding member of the Winnipeg Grain Exchange. He led the province during a period of enormous growth in both population and wealth and his government put in place many new institutions and legislation that responded to and encouraged that growth. Roblin was in many ways typical of the politicians of 19th- and early-20th-century Canada, fiercely partisan and a master of the use of patronage to build and maintain party loyalty. His aggressive style made him many enemies and it is their assessments that have survived, tending to focus attention on the ignominious end of his long career. A comprehensive biography may well be impossible because of the mysterious disappearance of almost all his personal papers and files. Although there are stories that they were burned in 1915 or 1916, when he was charged with conspiracy to defraud the Crown, it is not known what happened to them. Only one biography of Roblin exists, written by Conservative supporter Hugh Ross while the ex-premier was still alive.[1]

Rodmond Roblin was born February 15, 1853, in Prince Edward County, Ontario. He was the son of James Platt and Deborah Roblin and the grandson of Philip Roblin, who had come to the Bay of Quinte area in 1784, a United Empire Loyalist refugee from New York. Two of his uncles, John P. and David, had been members of the Upper Canadian Legislature. The older Roblins were Reformers and supporters of Robert Baldwin. As one historian has stated, "Reform zeal ran through the family."[2]

The family was Methodist and in his early years Rodmond was a lay preacher. His powerful speaking style undoubtedly owed much to the fiery sermons of the Methodist missionaries who travelled the back roads of Ontario. Roblin's parents sent him to a Methodist Church school, Albert College, in Belleville, where, enrolled in the Commercial Course, he studied bookkeeping, arithmetic, grammar and spelling. He wanted to study law, but his mother needed her oldest, strongest son to run the farm.

On September 13, 1875, Roblin married Adelaide Demill, also of Loyalist stock, born three days before him in the same township. The Roblins soon had a son, the first of four. They were Liberals and named the boy Wilfrid Laurier, after the up-and-coming young Liberal member of Parliament (MP). This choice of names must have caused some amusement later in Roblin's career when he and Laurier were political opponents.

The restless ambition that would drive him throughout his life inspired R.P. Roblin to look beyond the life of a farmer; he entered municipal politics, becoming the Treasurer of Sophiasburg Township, Prince Edward County. He started a cheese factory on the family property and became a buyer for a cheese exporter. He was about to establish himself as an exporter on his own account when he was badly injured in a buggy accident. While recuperating, he read a pamphlet about the Northwest and decided to emigrate.

Leaving his wife and young son safely at home in Ontario, Roblin headed west with the wave of Ontario homesteaders who, infected with "Manitoba fever," swept into the province in the late 1870s and early 1880s. Later in life, he would often describe sharing a Winnipeg lean-to with other young immigrants and working from dawn to dusk in a saw mill and on construction. While this was partly conscious mythmaking, there is no doubt that Roblin had to work hard to raise the capital needed to establish himself in the West.

At the suggestion of a Methodist missionary, F.W. Warnes, Roblin settled in the Carman area. He did not farm but traveled through the country as a peddler, selling from the back of his wagon and trading for furs. In 1879, he pooled his resources with his brother-in-law, M.E. Demill, and purchased, for $1,600, a quarter-section of land in present-day Carman at the point where they believed the proposed Manitoba and Southwestern Railway was going to cross the Boyne River. He built a general store, a grain warehouse and, in 1885, a comfortable frame home for his wife and sons. Roblin worked hard to secure a railroad connection, so essential for the growth of any western town. In 1889 the first train rolled into the town and the fortunes of Carman and of R.P. Roblin improved together. Roblin quickly added the roles of grain buyer and mortgage lender to that of general merchant. In 1884 Roblin acquired a quarter-section of land northeast of Carman, employing a manager to farm the land. By 1902 he owned a section and a half farmed by a manager using modern equipment and methods. In 1909 he signed over this farm to his son, Arthur, who worked it until 1948. Roblin, however, continued to spend part of most summers on the property.

It was as a grain merchant that Rodmond Roblin achieved his greatest business success. By the time the railroad arrived, he had built the first elevator in Carman and had become the district's most important grain buyer. In 1887 Roblin was one of the founders of the Winnipeg Grain and Produce Exchange, and by 1889 his expanding grain business moved to Winnipeg. He built a comfortable house at 211 Garry Street where he lived for the rest of his life. By 1894 R.P. Roblin and Company had offices in the Grain Exchange Building on Princess Street and he was a member of the Council of the Exchange and the Chair of the Board of Grain Examiners, an important grain industry administrative body. In 1893 Roblin and a number of other grain traders formed the Northern Elevator Company, which built a line of country elevators to compete with the more extensive networks of firms like Ogilvie Flour Mills and the Lake of the Woods Milling Company. Four years later he became President of the Dominion Elevator Company in which he was partners with fellow industry pioneers Daniel and W.W. McMillan, Robert Muir, Frederick Phillips, Samuel McGaw and Hugh Paterson.[3]

Roblin had participated in politics almost from the time of his arrival in Carman. In the 1880s he belonged to the Farmer's Protective Union of Manitoba, a protest movement that sought redress for farmers' grievances against the CPR, among other issues.[4] He was elected Warden of the County of North Dufferin and then Reeve of Dufferin Municipality. After two unsuccessful attempts, he was elected in a March 1888 by-election as the member of the Legislative Assembly (MLA) for North Dufferin. For 23 of the next 27 years he would be an MLA.

For his first speech in the Legislature on April 16, 1888, Roblin, who already had a reputation as an orator, was given the important task of moving the adoption of the speech from the throne. On Roblin's speaking style, Arthur Ford, a well-known Tory journalist and editor, later had this to say: "He was a hearty, robust individual and was a power on the stump in the days when tub thumping oratory was popular. No man could wrap himself in the Union Jack with more effect upon his audiences."[5] As well as being a powerful speaker, R.P. Roblin had qualities that set him apart from other politicians of the time. Historian W.L. Morton wrote that he was "possessed of a trenchant grasp of principle, [who] brought to his party a range of ability none of his predecessors in Manitoban politics had possessed with the sole exception of Clifford Sifton."[6] Yet Roblin's positive qualities were balanced by a fierce combativeness, aggravated by the exaggerated partisanship that characterized politics in his day. He could use his great oratorical skill to wound and humiliate his opponents and as a result, he made enemies. A typical example of Roblin's style is his attack, in 1904, on Liberal MLA Horace Chevrier, who had suggested that government members were improperly benefiting from the sale of public lands. Roblin, "in an aggressive reply characterized the speaker as a 'political coward' without knowledge, or experience, or qualities which would commend his vague assertions to the indulgence of the House."[7]

Roblin's belligerence was combined with what W.L. Morton described as "a certain pomposity of speech and manner, a self confidence which verged on arrogance," traits that certainly irritated his political enemies. A poem printed in the *Free Press* in 1912, shortly after Roblin received his knighthood, suggests the kind of animosity the Premier could inspire in his opponents:

> When I was a lad of low degree
> I always climbed the highest tree
> and have never lost my young ambition
> To sit aloft in high position…
> Of chivalry I have been cured
> By defeats I have endured;
> And I find a braggart rudeness
> More effective in its crudeness
> A noisy rough and tumble fight
> Inspires my people with delight
> So my knightly sword grows rusty
> While I swing my meat axe trusty.

In his personal life R.P. Roblin was unpretentious. He and his wife stayed in their house on Garry Street long after their upper-middle-class neighbours of the 1890s had moved to more fashionable districts. The Roblins were good neighbours. In January 1912, for example, when fire consumed the Excelsior Motor Works near his home, Premier Roblin invited the people who had lived above the Motor Works into his house for the night, arranging for them to keep their furniture in his garage.

His wife, Adelaide, seldom appeared in the society columns of the newspapers and she was not one of the leaders of the increasingly sophisticated and wealthy Winnipeg elite of her time. But she was well liked, worked hard for her church, Grace Methodist, and so great was the respect felt for her that when she died in January 1928, the Legislature was adjourned for the day so that all the members could attend her funeral.

The Roblins also avoided the high life of Ottawa. The journalist Arthur Ford tells us that Roblin had no

> side or no airs to him… I recall on one occasion there was a Provincial conference at Ottawa shortly after the return of the Borden Government. The Governor-General was entertaining the Provincial dignitaries at Rideau Hall. That evening I found Sir Rodmond in the lobby of the old Russell House dry-smoking a big cigar—he chewed cigars and seldom smoked them.
>
> "Why are you not up at Rideau Hall?" I asked.
>
> "Oh, I leave that to Bob," he replied, "he likes it."[8]

When Roblin first took his seat in the old Manitoba Legislature on Kennedy Street in the spring of 1888, the electoral map of the province was about to be drastically altered. The original 24 ridings, 12 English and 12 French, were replaced by 30 new ridings with boundaries based on population not language. The change reduced the number of seats in French-speaking areas to 5. Other changes were to follow, all designed to replace the accommodations granted to the French community in the Manitoba Act with partisan, majoritarian politics more to the taste of the now-dominant Ontario Protestant population. While Roblin was part of this new majority, he was to prove less enthusiastic about the changes than some of his colleagues.

Although he was elected as a Liberal, Roblin soon began to distance himself from Thomas Greenway's party. Their first disagreement was over railway policy. Greenway had been fortunate to come to power at the same time the CPR gave up its monopoly over railway construction in the West, a monopoly that his predecessor, John Norquay, had tried and failed to break. Greenway was thus free, in 1888, to make provision for railway service that would compete with the CPR and result in lower rates. He made an arrangement with the Northern Pacific Railway, the American transcontinental, to complete a new rail line up the west side of the Red River. The deal was controversial and there were charges that Greenway and Joseph Martin, his Attorney General, had been bribed by the Northern Pacific. The hoped-for reduction in freight rates never materialized due to a secret no-competition agreement between the CPR and the Northern Pacific.[9]

Roblin, who favoured an alternate plan, charged that the Premier had not made the best deal possible and voted against Greenway along with four other Liberals. Although the others eventually all returned to the party, Roblin did not. In fact the break became permanent when the Liberals proceeded to remove the special status of the French language guaranteed in the Manitoba Act, something Greenway had promised during the election campaign not to do. Roblin voted, in 1890, with his fellow disaffected Liberal, Thomas Prendergast, to censure the government for ceasing the publication of Legislative documents in French.[10] When the bill to abolish the Catholic and Protestant school boards came before the Legislature, Roblin was one of 11 members to oppose it and the only English Protestant to do so.

Roblin opposed making education a totally secular matter, administered by a government department under a minister of the Crown. During the debate on second reading he had stated that it was "desirable that politics and education should be divorced as far as possible" and that the schools were better left in the hands of a Board of Education made up of people who were experts.[11] As a graduate of a church school and a Methodist, he may have preferred, like Archbishop Robert Machray, some Protestant clergy, and the Roman Catholic church, to maintain the existing provincial School Board so that religion would still have a role in the school system.

Roblin's break with the Liberals may also have owed something to his own political ambitions which would have been difficult to achieve in a group dominated by Greenway, Joseph Martin and Clifford Sifton. Although he at first insisted that he was still a Liberal, it was not long before Roblin accepted the leadership of the Conservative Party in the Legislature and became Leader of the Opposition.

In the General Election of 1892 Roblin was forced to run in Morden constituency because his own riding of North Dufferin had been gerrymandered out of existence. The electors of Morden rejected him and for the next four years he focused all his energies on his business. In 1896 he ran again, this time in Woodlands, which was closer to Carman, and he was elected with a healthy majority of 339. He was again Leader of the Opposition until 1899 when he stepped aside so that Hugh John Macdonald, the son of Sir John A., and a more experienced and popular politician, could lead the Party in the general election of that year. The Conservatives won, increasing their numbers in the House from 6 members to 24, and Macdonald became Premier. Roblin again ran in Woodlands and was re-elected, although with a reduced majority of 156.

In the 1899 campaign the Conservatives proclaimed the first platform the party had ever placed before the voters. It included a number of progressive planks: government ownership of railways was promised "where practicable" and Macdonald said he wanted government control of freight rates on lines that had received financial support from the Province. There was to be a new act to ensure that workmen who were injured on the job would receive compensation, but perhaps the most important promise Macdonald had made was that he would ban the retail sale of liquor in Manitoba.

With this victory Hugh John Macdonald laid the foundation Rodmond Roblin would build on over the next decade and a half. Macdonald did not stay long in the Premier's office; he was convinced by the party to run in Brandon against Victor Sifton in the federal election of 1900. He was defeated and thereafter confined himself to the role of elder statesman.

Rodmond Roblin had declined the offer of a cabinet post in Macdonald's government, citing his business responsibilities. It is possible, however, that as in the days when he was part of Greenway's caucus, he was unwilling to play a supporting role. Once the way was open he again assumed the leadership and he became Premier, Railway Commissioner and minister of Agriculture in October 1900. In his first cabinet he retained two of Macdonald's ministers, David McFadden of Emerson, a prominent member of the Orange Lodge,[12] and John Davidson of Neepawa. He also appointed Colin Campbell as Attorney General and Robert Rogers as minister of Public Works, two men who were to be his closest collaborators for most of his years in power.

One of the most difficult issues facing the new Premier was Prohibition. The dire effects of drink were visible everywhere; men frequently died young from overconsumption of spirits that could contain just about anything, including sulphuric acid,[13] and women and children suffered when the family income was spent on drink. The temperance movement of the day, consisting of a loose coalition of many different organizations and led by influential clergy and community leaders, had enormous political influence. Few politicians would risk defeat at the polls by admitting to being against prohibition. Roblin, a wise politician and a good Methodist, always described himself as a "temperance man."

The Macdonald government had introduced a Prohibition Act in June 1900 which would have ended the retail trade in liquor and limited consumption to private homes and for medicinal and church use. The Act was to be proclaimed one year hence. Control of trade was a federal responsibility and the waiting period was intended to give the government an opportunity to test the law in the courts. Colin Campbell, the new Attorney General, managed the case and the appeal process all the way to the Judicial Committee of the Privy Council in London. Finally, in November 1901, the Judicial Committee declared that Manitoba did indeed have the power to control the liquor business and it only remained for Premier Roblin to have the Act proclaimed.

The way in which R.P. Roblin chose to handle the issue drove a permanent wedge between his government and a majority of the temperance movement. In January 1902, the Premier announced that he wanted to hold a referendum on the Act to ensure that it had the public support without which it would be impossible to enforce. Temperance supporters, expecting a timely proclamation of the Act, were outraged by this turn of events. The Dominion Alliance, one of the largest temperance groups, was meeting in Winnipeg at the time and passed a resolution calling for a boycott of the referendum. Some disagreed with the boycott strategy, arguing that it was self-defeating, but most stayed away from the polls.

The Referendum Act was introduced in the Legislature by Colin Campbell on February 19 and the vote was set for April 2. If a majority approved, the Act would come into force on June 1, 1902. There was a spirited campaign with meetings sponsored by both sides in the debate. The results were 15,000 in favour and 22,000 against proclaiming the Act. Having lost the vote, many temperance supporters repudiated the result. There were charges of unfairness in the conduct of the vote and Roblin was accused of playing into the hands of the liquor interests. The Reverend J.B. Silcox, a Baptist clergyman, expressed the decidedly un-Christian sentiment that the Premier's betrayal "should never be forgotten and never forgiven."[14]

Over the years Roblin would pursue a policy which stopped short of complete Prohibition. Instead his government used licensing to control the worst abuses of the liquor trade and left the decision on actual prohibition to each municipality—the so-called "local option." As Colin Campbell commented, the Roblin Tories belived that "It is better to have a lawful traffic properly controlled than an unlawful traffic uncontrolled." During the Roblin years the wide-open saloons of the old Winnipeg were gradually replaced with strictly regulated beer parlours. Saloons and wholesale liquor sales were abolished in rural districts and villages. Winnipeg hotels were required to have at least 50 rooms for rent before they could get a license, fees were increased and the number of licenses allowed in Winnipeg was reduced from one per 500 people to one per 1,200. The drinking age was raised from 16 to 18.

By the end of Roblin's regime, local option referenda had established prohibition in 80% of the province, including the entire district north of 53°. In 1913 he told a temperance group demanding a new provincial referendum that such a vote, should it fail, would jeopardize all the local option resolutions so laboriously passed over the previous decade. On the other hand, many districts, such as Winnipeg and St. Boniface, had rejected prohibition and Roblin reminded them that support for prohibition was far from unanimous and many men "object to being dictated to as to the things they shall have on their tables."[15]

Early in his first term Roblin made a breakthrough on the issue that had thwarted Manitoba politicians for decades—railway competition. In February 1901 he announced an agreement with the Northern Pacific to lease all their lines in Manitoba—354 miles of track—for 999 years. A short time later he told the public that the lines would in turn be leased to the Canadian Northern, at the time a small railway just setting out on a decade of stupendous expansion. The Canadian Northern gave the province control of freight rates in return for the lease and provincial guarantees of its construction bonds. Thus began a fruitful relationship that resulted in lower freight rates for Manitobans and the construction of close to 1,500 miles of new railway lines through the province's farming districts as well as an alternate route to the head of the lakes.[16]

The deal enjoyed general support in Manitoba and the West. Even some Liberals, such as Frank Oliver of Edmonton, admitted that Roblin had succeeded where many others had failed and that the whole North-West would benefit. Since the federal government was responsible for transportation, Roblin's bill had to be ratified by the Liberal-controlled Parliament. It was passed due to the support of Manitoba Liberal chieftain Clifford Sifton, who saw that the plan would benefit farmers.

In October 1901 Roblin announced that the Canadian Northern freight rate for carrying grain would be 10¢ a hundredweight between Winnipeg and the Lakehead, well below the prevailing CPR rate of 14¢. The Canadian Pacific was forced to lower its rates accordingly. The success of his railway policy was Roblin's major accomplishment during his first term and it was one of the things that cemented his control of a large part of the farm vote. Throughout his years in office he reminded farmers of the extra money his deal had put in their pockets.[17] Another measure popular with farmers was the imposition in 1901 of taxes on railways and other corporations. The taxes generated substantial sums of money for public works.

In March 1903, preparations for a general election had begun with the passage of a redistribution bill which, among other things, re-established Roblin's gerrymandered riding of Dufferin. Nominations took place in June and the Premier campaigned with characteristic energy, speaking at ten meetings in communities across Manitoba in two weeks. This was an impressive feat, considering the distances travelled, by train, and the strain of speaking, often for two or three hours, without the aid of a microphone.

The Liberals, under ex-Premier Greenway, tried to make corruption the election issue. The *Free Press* opened the attack on June 24, with a headline about irregularities to do with the drainage project in the Dufferin Marshes, a swampy region that extended from Carman almost to the Red River and for many miles north and south. The building of drains and ditches had begun under the Greenway government and would continue for decades. The *Free Press* charged that the contractor in charge of the project in 1900, G.H. Macdonell, had been told by minister of Public Works D.H. McFadden that if he wanted the government to pay his invoices, he would have to make a contribution of $5,000 to the Conservative Party. The contractor refused and had trouble collecting money owed him. In 1901 he sold his contract to R.F. Manning who was, incidentally, a Conservative Party worker. Manning, Roblin and McFadden denied there was any truth in the story and John Dafoe, editor of the *Free Press*, was charged with libel, arrested, and released on bail.

The contractor's charges were highly plausible under the conventions of contemporary political fund-raising. The accusations were answered by Roblin with an attack on the Liberals:

> When I took office I found that Mr. Whitehead had been overpaid by the Greenway Government no less than $45,000 ... for which he had never turned a shovel of earth. He did no work and the money had been paid to him.[18]

Roblin was making a clever and plausible counter-charge. Charles Whitehead was an active Liberal and an associate of Clifford Sifton; Manning was a supporter of the Conservatives and a worker and organizer for the party. Awarding government contracts to political supporters was common practice for both of Manitoba's political parties. Many if not most civil service jobs were awarded as patronage to party supporters. One of the first things Hugh John Macdonald and his colleagues did upon winning the 1899 election was to remove a large number of political appointees from government positions. For example, Clifford Sifton's father lost his job as Chief Clerk in the Department of Public Works.[19]

Patronage of this sort was well established in Canadian political life at the time, as were machine politics in general. S.J.R. Noel writes that "every province has experienced machine rule for some considerable period of its history. These machines were invariably identified with the powerful politicians who presided over them."[20] Roblin built a Conservative machine in Manitoba with the help of Robert Rogers who, as minister of Public Works, presided over the distribution of patronage and the closely related matter of organizing and winning election campaigns. Rogers' considerable talents as an organizer were also used by the federal Conservative party and he ran their western campaigns in 1904, 1908 and 1911.[21]

A party machine's main function was to win elections and to raise the money necessary to do so. Although it is impossible to prove, it can be assumed that the activities of the Conservative machine did win elections, especially in close seats where a few votes could tip the balance. We know a great deal about the inner workings of the Roblin organization because of the Royal Commissions that were active after his fall from power in 1915. One of these commissions, chaired by Judge George Paterson, inquired into all expenditures for road work during the 1914 election year. The testimony from Conservative Party workers in several constituencies, evidence we can assume was, for the most part, truthful, illustrates how money was raised for election expenses. The appropriation for road building in 1914 was under the control of the minister of Public Works, Dr. Montague. Conservative MLAs applied to Montague for a share of the money for their constituencies and arranged for the hiring of crews and foremen to do the work. The sitting government members thus had a substantial war chest with which to ensure party loyalty.

What is clear from the Paterson Commission is that much more road work was paid for than was ever completed. This was because the men listed in the pay sheets, and who received cheques and cash payments, were frequently not doing road construction at all; they were party workers who spent their time going to political meetings, driving voters to be registered or to vote and buying drinks and paying bribes. In Emerson Constituency John Probyzanski was hired in March by the local MLA, D.H. McFadden, to supervise road construction. Probyzanski's real job, however, was to drum up support for the Conservatives in the July 10 provincial election. He was instructed to go to every political meeting in the riding and try to convince "the boys" to vote Tory by buying them drinks and giving them money. He went to McFadden to ask for cash and he was told "you got all kinds of money there, all kinds of chances; what the hell else do you want." McFadden was referring to the road work pay sheets that Probyzanski controlled and it was clear that he expected the other man to finance his activities by submitting false claims for pay. Judge Paterson discovered similar activities in Roblin Constituency where the MLA, F.Y. Newton, was assisted in his campaign by Joseph Norquay, W.J. Williamson, W.J. Dunlop and Percy Field, all of whom were hired as road construction supervisors for 25 days at $4 a day but worked exclusively on Newton's campaign.[22]

These were standard electoral techniques employed by both parties in all parts of Canada at the provincial and federal levels. In May 1906, for example, the "thin red line scandal" was much in the news. An inquiry by the House of Commons Election Laws Committee was looking into allegations that, during the 1904 federal election, Liberal returning officers in Manitoba had rearranged the voting lists, assigning Liberal voters to polls where they were most needed. The lists were then, according to the charges, sent to R.E.A. Leach, a Liberal organizer in Winnipeg, and he proceeded to draw a red line through the names of some 9,300 Conservative voters. The red-lined names were not on the lists when they were printed and this resulted, according to Robert Rogers, in at least four lost seats for the Tories. There were charges and counter charges but, as usual, no real resolution of the issue.

In the 1903 election, in spite of the charges of corruption, the Conservatives were returned with a resounding victory, increasing their total seats to 31 as opposed to 9

Liberals. Roblin, running again in Dufferin, won with the largest margin—419 votes—of any candidate in the province. The Tories also won the popular vote—26,929 for the Tories, 23,740 for the Liberals and 2,563 for independents. Policies in tune with what the public wanted and an organization that could deliver the vote enabled Roblin to repeat his 1903 victory three more times over the next 11 years.

As the only leader of a Conservative government anywhere in the country, Roblin began to attract attention from outside Manitoba. He was profiled in the "Canadian Celebrities" feature of the *Canadian Magazine* and he was asked to write "A Western Canadian View of the Fiscal Question" for the *North American Review*, in which he argued in support of Joseph Chamberlain's plan for a preferential tariff for Dominion and colonial goods in Great Britain.[23] The article is also of interest for what it reveals of Roblin's social attitudes. He charges that the free trade policy Britain had pursued for over half a century was supported by politicians "whose education was more on classical than commercial lines." He continued that:

> It seems indeed to have been an accepted maxim of Political Economy in Great Britain, that no man was qualified to guide the destinies of British trade unless he is absolutely ignorant of the first principles of business.[24]

Roblin saw himself as one who did understand business principles and had succeeded in spite of not having had a classical education.

In September 1905 Manitoba was joined in Confederation by Saskatchewan and Alberta. These provinces were given territory extending from the American boundary north to the 60th parallel, while Manitoba was left with a northern border at 53°, where it had been since 1882. Laurier argued that he was prevented from extending Manitoba's northern boundary because of the conflicting claims of Ontario and Saskatchewan for territory along the shore of Hudson's Bay. Roblin wanted not only the same northern boundary as the new provinces but the same payments in lieu of control of Crown lands with their rich natural resources. The negotiations, frequently accompanied by rancour and political infighting, went on for seven years and the deadlock was not finally broken until the election of Robert Borden's Conservative government in 1911.

In January 1906 Roblin turned his attention to the inadequacy of the province's telephone system. Introducing the motion to establish a Select Committee of the Legislature to look into the matter, Colin Campbell said that telephones "have become such a part of our existence that it would be hard for us to get along without them…"[25] However, the service in Manitoba was uneven. The Bell Telephone Company provided service in the more populated areas, but would not build lines in the less profitable country districts; some towns had telephone systems that were not connected to one another, and most working people could not afford the high cost of having a telephone.

A few weeks later the Committee tabled its report, recommending, among other things, that the Telephone system be operated by the government as a public utility and that the Provincial Government construct a long-distance network to connect the local municipal telephone systems. It was not until the end of 1907 that Roblin sat down to negotiate the purchase of the Manitoba division of the Bell Telephone Company with the president of the company, C.F. Size. Size had opened with a price of $4 million, but Roblin announced on January 1, 1908, that he had been able to settle on $3.4 million, to be paid with 4% Manitoba Debentures. In answer to criticism from the Liberals and others over the cost of the system, R.P. Roblin asserted that he had made the best possible deal, adding that "whatever profit there is in its operation from this time on will belong to the people of Manitoba rather than a private company." The Premier undertook to extend the service to rural areas and to keep rates low.

Public ownership of utilities, embraced by Roblin and his government, is not a policy now usually associated with Conservatives. But in the first decades of the 20th century this key part of the Progressive program in the United States was embraced by many Canadian politicians. For example, the Conservative administration of James Whitney in Ontario had only recently established the publicly owned Ontario Hydro. Robert Borden was allying himself with businessmen like A.E. Kemp and J.W. Flavelle—Conservatives who saw a larger role for government in managing enterprises like railways and public utilities, using efficient business methods. This point of view was closely related to a desire to see an end to patronage and corruption in politics but men like Borden would have only partial success, so entrenched were the old political methods.

In the spring of 1906, the Liberals elected a new leader, Edward Brown, a wealthy businessman from Portage la Prairie who seemed to espouse these more progressive views. When Roblin attacked, calling him a "kindergarten politician," he said he was not a politician at all but merely a concerned citizen of the province "having a deep interest in its affairs." He said that what was needed was an experienced businessman like himself to properly manage the province's affairs, instead of men like Roblin whose experience was "in playing the political game." The machine politics practiced with such skill by men like Roblin would now increasingly come under attack.[26]

In September 1906 Rodmond Roblin demonstrated his political acumen when he announced a program that was to get him more national attention than almost anything else he did as Premier. In a speech to a meeting of young Conservatives, Roblin announced that he would amend the Public Schools Act to require all schools to fly a Union Jack during school hours or risk losing their provincial grants. He claimed that the influx of European and American immigrants into Manitoba had led in recent years to the flying of other flags, such as the Stars and Stripes on July 4. He said that people "born under foreign flags" who came to Canada and enjoyed all the benefits of British laws and institutions without honouring the British flag were "undesirable."[27]

Roblin's measure, a relatively mild one in an era when openly expressed nativist prejudice against immigrants could be quite ugly, was positively received by many Anglo-Canadians and he was widely praised in the Canadian Tory press. Back in Manitoba, not everyone was as enthusiastic about the measure. During the debate over the amendment in January 1907 the Liberals called the measure "Czar-like" and argued that it tried to ensure patriotism in people by fines when they were already perfectly patriotic. Liberal papers like the *Free Press* and *Winnipeg Tribune* criticized the measure for making something compulsory that should be a matter of choice. Mennonite school trustees were especially troubled by the rule, worrying that it represented an erosion of their right, guaranteed when they first came to Manitoba, to give their first allegiance not to the state but to their religion.

The debate over the flag policy revealed the deep divisions between Manitobans of British and non-British origin. Loyalty to the British Empire and devotion to British legal and the parliamentary systems were the sort of attitudes Anglo-Canadians hoped to encourage in non-British immigrants as part of the process of assimilation. The schools were seen as the melting pot in which immigrant children would be transformed into loyal, English-speaking Canadians.

Debates over school policies often provided a forum in which the larger issues of the place of immigrants in the predominantly Anglo-Canadian society of western Canada were discussed. The educational situation in Manitoba during Roblin's time in office reflected the growing complexity of the population. While Greenway had been successful in establishing a state-supported school system, the storm of controversy which resulted obliged him to make concessions to the French and Catholic citizens of Manitoba—the so-called Laurier-Greenway compromise of 1897. The system thus created employed Catholic teachers if there were at least 40 Catholic students in an urban school (10 in a rural school), and if the heads of 10 families requested it, religious instruction would be given to their children by a clergyman. Lastly, in schools where 10 pupils spoke French or any language other than English, they would be taught in English and their mother tongue "on the bilingual system."[28]

By 1915 there were 126 French bilingual schools, 61 German Mennonite bilingual schools and 111 schools where children were instructed in Polish and Ruthenian or Ukrainian as well as English. There were about 450 bilingual teachers in these schools teaching almost 17,000 students. A special Normal School had been established under Roblin to prepare Ukrainian-speaking teachers for the classroom and there were also training facilities for French- and German-speaking teachers.[29]

As the 1906 provincial election campaign opened, the Liberals re-introduced the education debate by campaigning on a promise to enact compulsory attendance legislation, compelling all students of school age to actually go to school. This provision had been specifically omitted from the changes to the Schools Act in the 1890s because of the recognized right of Catholic parents to support church schools, and their anxiety that such a clause would force them to send their children to public schools. Attendance, the Liberals argued, especially in rural districts, was only averaging about 60% to 70% of potential students and something had to be done.

Roblin countered that the current system of truancy officers was working well and took his usual position that opening up the Education Act to make this change would unleash another bitter and divisive debate over schools like the one in the 1890s. Roblin's fears seemed well founded when Archbishop Langevin, who campaigned for a return to the old Protestant and Catholic school system, was attacked by state school advocate J.W. Dafoe of the *Free Press* for intervening in politics. Langevin defended himself, stating that the Church had "the right and duty of guiding the conscience of the faithful during election time and on political matters."[30]

Langevin was not the only cleric to speak out during the 1906 election campaign. Protestant clergy involved in the temperance movement were also vocal in their criticism of what they considered to be the Roblin government's bad faith over the prohibition issue. Influential clergymen like Salem Bland, a Methodist, spoke out. He wrote to the *Free Press*, saying that the Conservatives' betrayal of the temperance movement made "every drop of British blood in me tingle."[31] Presbyterian C.W. Gordon worried that Manitoba faced "a moral Waterloo" if the Conservatives remained in office.

The Premier countered these attacks by having prominent Tory and temperance supporter J.A.M. Aikins recount in speech after speech the actions the Conservative government had taken to control the liquor business. Aikins often read directly from the statute, reminding people that the Roblin administration had made a long list of changes which severely restricted the liquor business.

When the 1906 election results were tallied the Roblin Tories were still firmly in the saddle although with a slightly reduced 28 seats against 13 for the Liberals. Rodmond Roblin again won his Dufferin seat by a healthy majority while Edward Brown was defeated in Portage la Prairie. In spite of sustained attacks from his opponents, Manitobans continued to support Roblin's policies.

Roblin's cabinet was restructured after the election, with two new ministers reflecting the government's expanding role in the life of the province. Brandon lawyer George Coldwell became the first minister of Education and J.H. Howden, a Neepawa lawyer, was appointed minister of Telephones and Telegraphs. Rogers and Campbell retained their key positions in the government.

In the decade and a half before World War I, politicians, both federal and provincial, vied for the support of the large and growing community of western farmers and of the powerful Grain Growers movement that was their principal political organization. Under skilful and passionate leaders like E.A. Partridge and W.R. Motherwell, the Grain Growers had enormous influence on policy at this time. The *Grain Growers Guide* newspaper, published by the organization, was read in farm homes across the prairies. In an attempt to respond to their various grievances and demands, governments established a number of Royal Commissions and investigations into the grain industry and enacted numerous pieces of legislation culminating in the 1912 Canada Grain Act, which established the Board of Grain Commissioners who had broad powers to regulate the industry and protect the interests of grain producers.

Roblin's electoral base was on the farms, and, as Arthur Ford says "[h]e never lost touch with the rural community and he knew half the farmers of the province by their first name. He was never happier than when chinning with his farmer constituents." During the 1907 election campaign Roblin had spoken at a Grain Growers event, promising to meet with them after the election to seek their advice.

The key issue the Grain Growers were struggling with in 1907 was membership in the Winnipeg Grain and Produce Exchange. The farmers' organization, under the leadership of E.A. Partridge, had organized a cooperative, the Grain Growers Grain Company, that had purchased a seat on the Exchange in order to fully participate in the grain trade. The Grain

Exchange had expelled the cooperative company on the grounds that paying dividends to Grain Growers members who were not company shareholders, a normal practice for cooperatives, was against the rules of the Exchange. The situation was exacerbated by the animosity that many of the private grain companies and traders felt toward the crusading Partridge, who over the years had accused them of fixing prices, tampering with scales and cheating hard-working grain producers out of the returns they deserved.

Soon after the 1906 election, the Grain Growers took their case to Robert Rogers, who was at the time Acting Premier. On April 2, Rogers sent an ultimatum to the Grain Exchange saying that the Grain Growers must be reinstated by April 15 or the government would call a special session "for the purpose of remedying this and other grievances by Legislative amendments" to the Charter of the Exchange. For their part the Grain Growers agreed to stop paying dividends to non-shareholders. On April 12, the Grain Growers Grain Company formally reapplied for admission, promising to abide by the rules of the Exchange. On April 15, the president of the Exchange wrote to Rogers and reported that the Exchange members at a general meeting agreed to readmit the Grain Growers.

It appeared that the crisis was resolved but the friction between the company and the Exchange was far from over. During the next year and a half the Grain Growers continued to push for major changes to the Charter of the Exchange. Although Roblin was one of its founders, he knew his government could not survive without the support of farmers. He responded with a bill to amend the Charter, passed into law in early 1908. Its passage produced a crisis in the grain industry. Trading on the Exchange was suspended and the value of seats fell from $2,500 to $1,000. For a while there was no way to establish a price for wheat in western Canada. The Exchange's massive new building at the corner of Rory and Lombard Avenue was nearing completion, and yet it seemed the Exchange might disappear.

By November 1908, however, the Exchange had changed its structure to that of a voluntary organization without a provincial charter. For the moment the crisis was over and trading resumed in the new building on Lombard Street. The *Grain Growers Guide* was, of course, not impressed with the change and a cartoon by Arch Dale showed the old exchange, depicted as a huge serpent, shedding its skin but retaining all its bad old characteristics.

The Grain Growers associations on the prairies were strong advocates of government ownership of grain elevators, at both the local stations and at the Lakehead where the large terminal elevators stood. The farmers believed that this would put an end to the alleged dishonest practices of the private grain companies and in 1909 they lobbied hard on the issue. Transportation, storage and grading of grain were a federal responsibility and Roblin along with the premiers of Saskatchewan and Alberta said they could not act until the federal government conferred these powers on the provinces. Early in the following year, however, Roblin established an Elevator Commission to operate a line of publicly owned elevators, choosing the members from a list provided by the Grain Growers. He may have been motivated in part by the Conservative defeat in a December by-election in which the elevator issue was a key factor.[32] The system was not financially successful and in 1912 the

Commission's massive losses convinced Premier Roblin that the best course would be to lease the elevators to the Grain Growers Grain Company.

In 1909, Tobias Norris replaced Edward Brown as Leader of the Opposition. Norris was a farmer and auctioneer who had been a member of the Legislature for two terms. Roblin tended to discount Norris, saying he would guarantee Conservative success. But Norris, faced with the difficult task of defeating a government which had complete control of patronage and a powerful party machine, sought to tip the balance by making alliances with groups outside the Liberal Party, the same strategy that Robert Borden used to bring down the federal Liberals in 1911. Norris slowly began to knit together a coalition of forces opposed to Roblin—the temperance movement, supporters of women's suffrage, those wanting an end to the bilingual education system, including the Orange Lodge, and the proponents of American Progressive ideas about the participation of the general public in the political process. Over the next five years this alliance of anti-Roblin groups would seriously weaken his hold on power.

The 1910 session of the Legislature opened in January and the Speech from the Throne introduced a Workmen's Compensation Act which would provide income for those injured on the job, something that had been promised by Macdonald a decade before. It was an improvement over the existing system under which the only recourse for an injured worker was to go to court and sue his employer for compensation. This legislation may have reflected the Tories' concern over the increase in political activity by labour groups.

On July 11, 1910, a general election gave Roblin and the Conservative Party a third majority. The strength of the parties was unchanged with 28 Conservatives and 13 Liberals. There was, however, a significant change in the composition of the Legislature, with a total of 10 seats changing their party allegiance. One of the more important was the defeat of the Conservative candidate by Liberal Solomon Hart Green in Winnipeg North. The young lawyer from New Brunswick would vigorously attack the government over the next four years, as would other Liberals like Thomas Johnson, Liberal member from Winnipeg West, another lawyer and a native of Iceland.

Although the *Canadian Annual Review* of 1909 had said of the Roblin government that "Its fighting leader, and Prime Minister, maintained his usual bold front to political foes … vigorously backed by Hon. Robert Rogers and Hon. Colin Campbell," the Conservative leadership was aging: Roblin was in his late 50s by 1910, Colin Campbell was 51 and Robert Rogers was 49. Many of the key Liberal members were younger men: both Norris and Johnson were in their early 40s, A.B. Hudson, who would be elected in 1914, was in his 30s and S.H. Green was 27.

In 1911, after having played a key role in the election of Robert Borden's Conservative government, Robert Rogers accepted a post in the federal cabinet; with his departure, Roblin appears to have begun to prepare for retirement. He resigned from the positions of minister of Agriculture, Railroad Commissioner and Commissioner of Public Lands and gave Colin Campbell the politically powerful position of minister of Public Works. There is little doubt that Roblin expected Campbell to succeed him. He would later write to Campbell that "No other member of the Government except myself ever pretended to have courage or knowledge to justify leadership." But Campbell became gravely ill in 1913 and retired from politics, passing away in the fall of 1914. Roblin would be obliged to continue as Premier.[33]

At the same time the Liberals attacked the government on a number of fronts, pressing their demands for change. In his first speech in the Legislature, Green called for the adoption of the practice of legislative initiative. A favourite concept of the American Progressives, the initiative proposal allowed a group of citizens to promote a piece of legislation, present it to the public and, if it was supported in a referendum, have it passed into law. The initiative proposal was formally supported by the Liberal Party, the Trades and Labour Council, and the United Grain Growers. It was also being promoted by the Direct Legislation League, under the presidency of prominent Liberal James H. Ashdown.

Although he was clearly influenced by the American Progressives in such areas as his support for public ownership, Roblin was strongly resistant to direct legislation. He spoke eloquently against the legislative initiative, saying it would make the Legislature an unthinking machine and government a farce. In 1913, when it was once more proposed by the Liberals, he said Canada had

> a perfect machinery of government... . Those who are pushing this propaganda have their eyes riveted on the Republican form of government; they look to Washington for inspiration. We Conservatives look to London ... we take our stand absolutely and unequivocally upon the British constitution and ideals of government...[34]

In 1912, with the Conservatives in power in Ottawa, the deadlock over the province's northern boundary was broken, and Manitoba's territory was extended to the 60th parallel. The 1912 legislative session saw the passage of the Building Trades Protection Act, which mandated amongst other things that scaffolding, ladders and machinery must be safe and that this was the responsibility of the employer. The introduction of the Act was triggered by the well publicized death of a young man killed while working on the Fort Garry Hotel site, and by 1915 the inspector appointed under the Act proudly reported that the number of fatalities on building sites had been reduced to only one for the year.

In 1912, Roblin and the Conservative Party took stock of his accomplishments. He was knighted at the time of the King's birthday in May and a number of events were held in his honour. On April 11, there was a political lunch at the Manitoba Club hosted by J.A.M. Aikins, the MP for Brandon, followed in the evening by a banquet attended by 1,500 people at the Royal Alexandra Hotel. There is little doubt that he would have retired at this time but for the illness and resignation of Colin Campbell. Roblin took Dr. W.H. Montague into his cabinet to replace Campbell as minister of Public Works in November 1913. Not in the best of health, Montague was not the man Roblin needed by his side as he prepared to face the onslaught of a renewed Liberal Party.

The province's schools were once more a central issue in 1912 and 1913. Controversy also raged over the Coldwell amendments to the Public Schools Act. In a speech in Minnedosa in November 1913 the Premier explained that the changes were meant to "assist the Winnipeg School Board in its effort to take over the Catholic Schools at Winnipeg and operate them under the Public School Act of this province." As a concession to Roman Catholic parents, members of religious orders would continue to teach in the schools.[35]

The Manitoba Liberals promised that if they were elected they would rescind the changes as well as ensure that children in Manitoba were taught only in English and that a compulsory attendance clause was in the Act. The Orange Lodge entered the fray with a manifesto telling Orangemen to support only candidates who would promise to vote for "the abolition of the bilingual school system, and for the enactment of a satisfactory compulsory school attendance clause."[36] Roblin countered by reminding the Liberals that the system they now wished to abandon had been put in place by the Laurier-Greenway compromise. He said his government was being attacked by the Liberals "because it will not penalize and attack, and punish the children of parents who speak a language other than English."

This, then, was the climate in which, as 1914 began, Roblin and his colleagues prepared for a general election in early July. As the campaign commenced, Roblin faced Norris's coalition of anti-government groups. The proponents of women's suffrage allied themselves with the Liberal Party. Nellie McClung ridiculed Roblin in the highly effective "Parliament of Women" that she and her colleagues staged at the Walker Theatre during the campaign. In spite of the fact that women who were property owners had been able to vote in municipal elections for many years, as well as vote and run in school board elections, he countered all demands for women's suffrage with arguments that politics was a dirty game not fit for women and that "a woman's place is in the home." He opposed this and other reforms, portraying change as radical and unnecessary in a province that was doing well as it was.

In spite of a determined and united opposition, when the election came on July 10, 1914, R.P. Roblin once again won a majority although it was the smallest he had ever had, 27 Conservatives to 22 Liberals. The Conservatives lost the popular vote, getting 71,000 to the Liberals' 62,000 and 15,000 for other parties.

Throughout the short fall session in September 1914 and the 1915 session which opened on February 10, the Liberals continued to question the government about school reform, prohibition, and votes for women. Outside the Legislature J.W. Dafoe trained all the guns of the *Free Press* on the Roblin government, even hiring a private detective to look for scandal. But it was when the Public Accounts Committee took up the consideration of the expenditures on the new legislative buildings on March 11, 1915, that the Liberal opposition began to realize that it had found a significant gap in the government's defences.

There had been warning signs that all was not well with the project during the fall session. Dr. Montague stated that the estimated cost of the Legislature had risen by $1.5 million over the original figure of $2.8 million. In February he received approval to spend this amount, over the protests of opposition members. The additional costs, Montague explained, resulted from various necessary changes in the original design of the building, such as a change from piles to reinforced concrete caissons as the footings under the structure. During the Public Accounts Committee review of the project, the Liberals, aggressively led by Winnipeg members A.B. Hudson and Thomas Johnson, demanded a detailed explanation of the extra costs. They estimated that the contractor, Thomas Kelly, had been overpaid by about $800,000. The Liberal members of the Committee had difficulty supporting their charges, however, because Kelly refused to turn over any documentation; it was later established that the architect, V.W. Horwood, had lied during his testimony, and the works inspector, William Salt, was in the United States, unavailable for questioning.

The Committee, with its Conservative majority, reported at the end of March that there were no irregularities. The Liberals moved an amendment to the report, subsequently printed in the *Free Press*, demanding a Royal Commission to enquire into the matter. Roblin fought back and there was a bitter and rancorous debate lasting until 1:20 on the morning of April 1, 1915. When the Legislature finally adjourned it was the Premier's intention to prorogue the house later that day after using his majority to vote down the Liberal amendment.

The following afternoon, however, Roblin announced in the House that a Royal Commission would indeed be appointed. What had caused this uncharacteristic capitulation on Roblin's part? During a morning meeting with the Lieutenant-Governor, Sir Douglas Cameron, it is thought that the Queen's representative had issued an ultimatum—if Roblin did not agree to a Royal Commission Cameron would dismiss him as Premier and call on the Liberals to form a government.[37]

Cameron had been approached by the Leader of the Opposition the previous evening and presented with a petition signed by all the Liberal members, asking for a Royal Commission. Cameron consulted with T.G. Mathers, Chief Justice of the Court of King's Bench and a prominent Liberal, as well as Isaac Campbell, a Liberal lawyer and sometime politician before his meeting with the Premier. The constitutionality of Cameron's actions was debated in the Winnipeg papers. While his actions in consulting with people other than Roblin may not have been strictly correct, they would prove to be justified by the revelations, during the course of the Royal Commission's work, that there had been massive corruption in the form of inflated payments made to Kelly and subsequent donations by him to the Tories.

The Royal Commission, consisting of Judges T.G. Mathers, D.A. Macdonald and Hugh John Macdonald, convened on April 27 and by May 7 witnesses had confirmed the charges of corruption made against Roblin's government. Roblin officially resigned as Premier on May 12 and the next day the Liberals under Tobias Norris took power. In its final report, issued on August 24, 1915, the Commission concluded that Kelly had been overpaid by at least $892,000 and in turn had donated a "large sum" to the Conservative Party. The province sued Thomas Kelly to recover the money and a year later he was sentenced to two and a half years in prison and ordered to repay a total of $1.2 million to the province. By 1941, when the debt was written off, only $30,000 had been collected.

In August 1915 R.P. Roblin, Dr. Montague, J.H. Howden and George Coldwell were all charged with conspiracy to defraud the Crown. The following July they stood trial but the jury was unable to agree on a verdict and the charges were finally dismissed in June 1917.

On September 16, 1915, a general election was held and the Conservative Party, under the leadership of J.A.M. Aikins, was all but wiped out, emerging from the struggle with only five members. It would be over 40 years before the party formed another government, under Roblin's grandson.

When he left politics in 1915, Roblin resumed his former position as president of the Dominion Elevator Company and remained in that post until 1928.[38] Roblin established the Consolidated Motor Company in 1916 with his son George, and his other sons, Charles and W.L. Roblin, joined the firm when they returned from World War I. The business was located on the corner of Portage and Main and Roblin was still keeping office hours there well into his 80s. He did participate in politics again, appearing at the first Conservative National Leadership Convention in Winnipeg in October 1927 as a Delegate at Large. In the Convention handbook he listed his recreation as "hard work."

Rodmond Roblin passed away on February 16, 1937, in Warm Springs, Arkansas, where he often went in the winter. He was 84 years old. He died a moderately wealthy man, leaving an estate valued at $60,000, not a great fortune but a considerable amount of money in the depths of the Depression. His main asset seems to have been the Adelaide Block, named for his first wife, which still stands on Osborne Street. The list of Roblin's assets, like those of many Winnipeggers of his class, included thousands of dollars worth of stocks in enterprises that had begun hopefully in the city's boom period before World War I and were later written off as worthless.

Rodmond Roblin was an unusually successful political leader who as Premier managed to win majorities through four elections and almost 15 years in office. He learned the art of politics in the Ontario of the 1870s, when he was a Liberal and the Liberal Party machine of Oliver Mowat was in control of the province. Through the 1880s and 1890s he participated in the political life of his adopted province and by the time he became Premier he was an accomplished professional politician. He proved to be a good leader for the province in the heady years before 1913, taking advantage of the steady growth and prosperity to build a solid foundation for the public institutions of Manitoba. His most visible legacies are the great public buildings that were built by his government and still serve us today. He was a strong supporter of the British connection. He wanted new immigrants to assimilate, but on issues like bilingual schools and the rights of Franco-Manitobans he was somewhat moderate and he took positions that cost him the support of groups like the Orange Lodge. He took a moderate approach to the control of the liquor trade as well, in spite of the resulting loss of support from the politically influential temperance movement.

He was a progressive in that he greatly expanded the role of the government in the economy of the province. His agreement with Canadian Northern, labour legislation like the Workmen's Compensation Act and the Building Trades Protection Act, at the time quite advanced and unknown in many jurisdictions, and public ownership of utilities like the Manitoba Telephone System are all examples of his progressive attitude. He was profoundly conservative in other areas, considering reforms like legislative initiatives that deviated from British parliamentary tradition to be dangerous innovations. In this he was out of step with the reforming mood of many Canadians at the time, who saw such changes as a way to end the old politics of patronage and backroom deals. His opposition to votes for women was also out of step with the views of a growing number of Canadians. It seems to have been based on a traditional view that the role of women was to raise children and provide a comfortable home for their families.

His greatest strength and in the end his greatest weakness was his mastery of party politics as they had been honed in Canada after Confederation. The use of patronage in the form of government positions and contracts to secure party loyalty and to provide money for donations to the party were common techniques, but by the 1910s there was a growing sense that this style of politics should be replaced with something better. The revelations in the spring of 1915 of kickbacks and misuse of public funds were particularly shocking to Manitobans whose sons were at that very moment sacrificing their lives for democracy in the second Battle of Ypres. As the war dragged on and the numbers of casualties mounted, old-style politicians like Roblin and Robert Rogers fell out of favour and men who called for clean efficient government took their places.

What are we to think of Rodmond Roblin, a man with so many accomplishments who ended his career in such an ignominious way? In the end, while we may agree with W.L. Morton, that "Sir Rodmond deserved a better fate" and that he was a man of "marked ability and fine achievements," we cannot ignore the fact that as the undisputed chief of his party he was responsible for the catastrophe which destroyed it.

Notes

1. N. McClung, *The Stream Runs Fast* (Toronto: Thomas Allen, 1945), 102–22; Margaret McWilliams, *Manitoba Milestones* (Toronto: J.M. Dent, 1928), 196–98; W.L. Morton, *Manitoba: A History* (Toronto: University of Toronto Press, 1957), 211; Hugh R. Ross, *Thirty-Five Years in the Limelight: Sir Rodmond P. Roblin and His Times* (Winnipeg: Farmer's Advocate, 1936).

2. James A. Eadie, "David Roblin," *Dictionary of Canadian Biography Online*, http://www.biographi.ca/EN/ShowBio.asp?BioId=38799, consulted October 2007.

3. Allan Levine, *The Exchange: 100 Years of Trading Grain in Winnipeg* (Winnipeg: Peguis, 1987), 53, 54.

4. Morton, *Manitoba: A History*, 211.

5. Arthur Ford, *As the World Wags On* (Toronto: Ryerson Press, 1950), 27.

6. Morton, *Manitoba: A History*, 281.

7. Michael Payne, "Rodmond Roblin" (unpublished paper, Winnipeg, Historic Resources Branch, n.d.), 32.

8. Ford, *The World Wags On*, 27–28. The "Bob" referred to is Robert Rogers.

9. T.D. Regehr, *The Canadian Northern Railway* (Toronto: Macmillan of Canada, 1976), 14–17.

10. Payne, "Rodmond Roblin," 24–25.

11. *Manitoba Daily Free Press*, March 6, 1890.

12. It was common at this time to include representatives of this powerful organization in Cabinet and all the Conservative Prime Ministers had done so, as would Sir Robert Borden when he came to power in 1911.

13. Peter C. Newman, *Bronfman Dynasty* (Toronto: McLelland and Stewart, 1978), 85. See Craig Heron, *Booze: A Distilled History* (Toronto: Between the Lines, 2003) for a history of the temperance movement.

14. *Canadian Annual Review* (1902): 375.

15. *Canadian Annual Review* (1913): 334.

16. See Regehr, *The Canadian Northern Railway*, 89–100 for a detailed account of the negotiations leading to this agreement.

17. *Canadian Annual Review* (1903): 18.

18. Ibid., 188.

19. F.H. Schofield, *Story of Manitoba,* vol. 2 (Winnipeg: S.J. Clarke Publishers, 1913), 100.

20. S.J.R. Noel, "Dividing the Spoils," *Journal of Canadian Studies* 22, no. 2 (1987): 79–80.

21. John English, *The Decline of Politics* (Toronto: University of Toronto Press, 1977), 15.

22. *Report of the Royal Commission on Expenditures for Road Work During the Year 1914* (Winnipeg: King's Printer, February 1917).

23. R.H. Macdonald, "Rodmond Palen Roblin," *The Canadian Magazine* 21 (1903): 426–28; R.P. Roblin, "A Western Canadian View of the Fiscal Question," *North American Review* 177, no. 5 (1903): 667–77.

24. Roblin, "A Western Canadian View," 668.

25. *Canadian Annual Review* (1906): 433.

26. Ibid., 448.

27. Quoted in "Record of the Roblin Administration, 1900–1909," Conservative Party, 1910, p. 38.

28. Morton, *Manitoba: A History*, 271.

29. Alexander Gregor, *The Development of Education in Manitoba* (Dubuque, IA: Kendall/Hunt Publishers, 1984), 71, 76–77.

30. *Canadian Annual Review* (1907): 585.

31. Ibid.

32. Morton, *Manitoba: A History*, 299; *Canadian Annual Review* (1910): 487–88.

33. Quoted in Leland Clark, "My Dear Campbell," *Manitoba Pageant* 19, no. 2 (1974): 4.

34. *Canadian Annual Review* (1913): 537.

35. Ibid., 564.

36. Ibid., 537.

37. Morton, *Manitoba: A History,* 342; and James A. Jackson, *The Centennial History of Manitoba* (Winnipeg: Manitoba Historical Society, 1970), 185.

38. Charles Anderson, *Grain: The Entrepreneurs* (Winnipeg: Watson and Dwyer, 1991), 23–26; Levine, *The Exchange*, 53 and 54.

Tobias C. Norris

1915–1922

MORRIS MOTT

T.C. Norris, 1915–1922

Introduction

T.C. Norris was Premier of Manitoba from 1915 to 1922. The Liberal government he led from 1915 to 1920 was one of the most active and important in the history of the province. It passed legislation that changed forever the gender relations, the education system, the working conditions, and many of the political, social, and economic practices of Manitobans. The Norris government's reforms were very popular. However, like all World War I governments, Norris's alienated significant groups of people, either by making controversial decisions itself or by taking sides on difficult federal government choices. Furthermore, at the end of the war many Manitobans were disillusioned with both the Liberal and Conservative parties and refused to support either of them. For these reasons, Norris and the Liberals were returned as only a minority government in 1920, then replaced in 1922 by a United Farmers of Manitoba government committed to economical, non-partisan administration.

Early Life and Early Political Career[1]

Tobias Crawford Norris was born in Peel County near Brampton, Ontario, on September 5, 1861 to Irish Methodist parents. His formal education stopped at some point in high school. Evidently Norris spent most of his teens and 20s as a farm and construction labourer. In the mid-1880s, he learned from fellow workers on a railway construction crew of the marvelous opportunities available for young men in the Canadian West. Norris moved to Manitoba, probably in the late 1880s rather than the early 1890s as is sometimes mentioned.[2] He soon purchased land near Griswold, a small agricultural service centre about 26 miles west of Brandon on the main line of the Canadian Pacific Railway (CPR).

By 1892 Norris was also operating a livery stable in the village. His partner in the business was a chap named Robert Lowe, and it may be that Norris was Lowe's employee before becoming his associate. In any case, it seems likely that it was while performing duties around the livery stable that Norris began to develop the skills and make the contacts that led to a political career.

In pioneer days, and indeed until after World War II when the year-round use of automobiles became common, the livery stable was one of the most important establishments in small prairie towns and villages. This was where farmers from the district left their horses and buggies (or sleighs) while conducting business or socializing. This was where traveling salesmen, loan collectors, and other representatives of urban commerce or industry rented horses, vehicles, and sometimes drivers after arriving in town on a train. There were people of all kinds around a livery stable, and individuals such as Norris who worked in these establishments had to be good with horses, willing to work long hours in different types of weather and, most important, capable of getting along with both the "respectable" and "rough" elements of the population.

While running the livery stable Norris became well known to the people of Griswold district and to more than a few from outside it. His contacts throughout the local area, the province of Manitoba, and the eastern prairies grew as a result of travels associated with another of his occupations—auctioneering. He may have begun to call sales shortly after arriving in Griswold, but certainly he was doing so by the mid-1890s and he continued to do so until the 1920s. Norris was one of the most popular Manitoba auctioneers of his time. He was knowledgeable about the going price of land, machinery, and especially livestock. He was able to "work" that price from members of his audience without offending them in the process. Then, after the sale was over, "Toby" or "Crawford" (as he was sometimes called) often mixed with people who had attended the sale. He would talk with them, laugh with them, perhaps share a social drink or two. He was an unusually amiable man, a very good storyteller with a wonderful sense of humour and the appealing capacity to make fun of himself.

Norris's political career began in 1895 when he gained a seat on the Council of the Rural Municipality of Sifton, in which Griswold was located. But "higher" office was both available and appealing to a man who, by the mid-1890s, was reasonably successful in both his farming and other businesses, who possessed some oratorical ability, and who had many friends and acquaintances in rural Manitoba. He had become a Liberal supporter shortly after moving to Manitoba. Before the provincial election of 1896 Norris sought the Liberal nomination for the Lansdowne constituency in which he resided. He received it, then won the seat as a supporter of the Thomas Greenway Liberal government and especially of the "national" (non-denominational) schools policy it had inaugurated in 1890 and which it was struggling to maintain in the face of some local and a great deal of national criticism.[3]

Over the next few years Norris rose to prominence in his party. He was re-elected as Lansdowne member of the Legislative Assembly (MLA) in 1899, though the Liberal party was defeated by the Conservatives who were to govern the province until 1915. In the election of 1903 he lost his seat by sixteen votes, but used the next four years to enhance his knowledge of provincial affairs and to extend his political contacts. In 1907 he regained the Lansdowne seat.[4] By this time he was a leading spokesman for the Liberals.

Unfortunately for Norris, his provincial Liberal party had already lost three straight elections and showed few signs that its fortunes would soon improve. For this lack of success at the polls, the Liberals of Manitoba could blame themselves to a large extent. In 1897 they had alienated most of their British Protestant supporters, but had gained very little gratitude from French Roman Catholics and other minorities by agreeing to the famous Laurier-Greenway Compromise, which anticipated adjustments to the School Act that allowed for half an hour of religious instruction at the end of each day and, if numbers warranted, for instruction on the "bilingual system" (whatever that meant) in English and any other language. Moreover, from 1899 to 1910 the leaders of the party were men who lacked energy or who were unable to articulate the ways in which their policies differed from those of the government.[5]

However, the Manitoba Liberals' failures were attributable to more than their own shortcomings. They were associated with a federal Liberal Party led by Wilfrid Laurier that had been in power in Ottawa since 1896, but which from the point of view of many Manitobans had reneged on promises regarding key issues. It had failed to make meaningful reductions in the protective tariff, and it had refused to extend Manitoba's boundaries or to transfer control over natural resources to the province. Furthermore, after 1900 the provincial Conservatives were led by Rodmond P. Roblin, and he and his minister of Public Works, Robert Rogers, were very skilled at dispensing government jobs, contracts, and licenses in order to reward and acquire friends. The Conservatives also provided efficient if not clean government. They were especially competent in building up the province's infrastructure of roads, railroads, and public buildings.[6]

In 1910, however, the provincial Liberals made some decisions that soon would have positive consequences. At their convention that year, they consciously reached out to reformers whom the Conservatives had ignored or ridiculed. Among these reformers were advocates of prohibition; proponents of women's suffrage, direct legislation, and other electoral or franchise reforms; believers in the usefulness and fairness of the "single tax" on unimproved land values; promoters of compulsory school attendance laws and of a school system in which adequate instruction in English would be given to all students; exponents of better enforcement of factory and workplace safety regulations; and supporters of mothers' allowances and other initiatives that would speak to the problems which were increasingly evident in the swelling city of Winnipeg (with some 42,000 people in 1901 but 163,000 in 1916).[7]

At the same 1910 convention the Liberals acclaimed T.C. Norris as their new leader. He replaced Ed Brown, who recently had moved to Winnipeg from Portage la Prairie and who had been leader since 1907, but had not been able to win a seat. The absence of leadership candidates other than Norris was an indication of an unhealthy party, but the delegates had good reasons to accept the Griswold bachelor. He was an impressive man physically, handsomely slender and well over six feet tall (unusual for men of the early 20th century). As Liberal House Leader in Brown's absence he had demonstrated ability in formal debate. He also had revealed, in speeches in skating rinks, schools, and community halls, that he could use his clear voice and his sense of humour to hold a crowd's attention. Moreover, many if not most of the delegates knew him personally. They had met him at auction sales or at the Liberal rallies around the province where Norris had been a popular attraction for several years.[8]

The Liberals failed to gain ground in the election held a few months after the convention of 1910, but over the next few years they became more aggressive and popular. After 1911 they were able effectively to criticize the Conservative government for the unexpected expense of its recently established government telephone system and for the failure of its provincially owned grain elevator network. The Liberals also scored points by noting that Conservatives were in power both provincially and federally when the "Laurier boom" collapsed in 1912–13. Meanwhile, Liberals gained more and more support from those who believed that the Conservative political machine was taking partisan politics to ridiculous lengths, and from reformers who knew they would never receive satisfaction from a Roblin administration. A Liberal resurgence was evident particularly in the general election of

1914 in which, if one includes among the Liberals F.J. Dixon (a Labour candidate who ran with Liberal support), the Norris-led party took 21 of 49 seats, a marked improvement over the 13 of 41 they had won four years earlier.[9]

This election took place on July 16, 1914, and less than three weeks later Manitobans and all Canadians were at war. In September an Emergency War Session of the provincial Legislative Assembly was called to give the Roblin government authority to make financial arrangements necessary to carry out responsibilities during the conflict. The matters dealt with were routine, but Dr. W.H. Montague, the minister of Public Works now that Robert Rogers was in the federal Cabinet, aroused interest from Liberal MLAs when he announced that the cost of the province's new legislative building, under construction since 1913, would surpass estimates by several hundred thousand dollars.

During the next session, which opened in February 1915, the Liberals pressed for details. They could sense a scandal, but their questions were parried by the Conservative majority in the Assembly and especially in its Public Accounts Committee. When the Liberals realized that the government was not going to grant their request for an enquiry, they petitioned Lieutenant-Governor Sir Douglas Cameron to refuse to prorogue the Legislature until a Royal Commission had examined "all matters pertaining to the construction" of the building. Cameron agreed to this request.[10] By early May a three-man Commission headed by Chief Justice T.G. Mathers had discovered evidence that the contractors had been overpaid and had "kicked back" large sums of money to the Conservative Party. On May 12 Roblin resigned and T.C. Norris was asked to form a government.[11]

Norris did so, and then quickly arranged to have an election in September. "Never in the history of Canadian politics" had a government appealed to the electorate on a shorter record, Norris quipped.[12] The issue, of course, was the record of the Conservative, not the Liberal, government. Norris's supporters, including three Labour-Liberal candidates, were elected in 42 of 49 constituencies.[13]

Premier of Manitoba

The Norris government that held office from 1915 to 1920 was composed of very competent individuals who were intellectually alert if they were not well-educated. Most were veteran Liberals. They were better informed on rural affairs and problems than on urban ones, and their strong belief in majoritarian democracy made them unresponsive to claims to "rights" made by minority groups. This said, Norris's ministers were as dedicated and capable as any group of individuals who ever administered the province.

Norris was Premier as well as Provincial Land Commissioner and Railways Commissioner. The Attorney-General until November 1917 was Winnipeg lawyer Albert B. Hudson, who later served as a member of Parliament in Ottawa and a judge on the Supreme Court of Canada. The man who succeeded Hudson as Attorney-General had been Norris's minister of Public Works. This was T.H. Johnson, a lawyer and the most prominent Icelandic-Canadian of his time. The new minister of Public Works, after Johnson became Attorney-General, was George Grierson of Minnedosa, a financial agent who had previously taught school for 16 years. The minister of Education was a highly respected Deloraine physician, Dr. Robert S.

Thornton. Another physician, this one from Gladstone, was Dr. J.W. Armstrong, provincial secretary and municipal commissioner. Ed Brown, the former leader of the Liberal Party, was now (since 1909) a Winnipeg financial broker and he was the provincial treasurer. Finally, the minister of Agriculture and Immigration was Valentine Winkler, a successful lumber merchant from Morden.[14]

By the time Norris became premier it was becoming obvious that World War I would require large numbers of men at the front and immense sacrifices from virtually all Canadians. Probably Manitoba had a higher proportion of enthusiastic supporters of the war than any other province,[15] and Norris agreed with the prevailing attitude among the people he governed. Britain, Canada, and all their allies were "fighting for ... principles which had been won at great cost in centuries past," he said. They were fighting for liberty, justice, freedom, and democracy.[16] At a recruiting meeting for Winnipeg's 90th Battalion held in November 1915, he told the young men who were present that "if you don't enlist you will be ashamed of it all the rest of your lives."[17] He expressed the same sentiment many times on other occasions.

Along with other Canadians who believed the war was a just and even a holy crusade, Norris was an early supporter of conscription and union government.[18] Like many Western Canadians, he did not feel that the Conservative Prime Minister, Robert Borden, should lead such a coalition government. However, over the summer of 1917 it became clear to Norris and others that the only pro-conscription union government that could be formed was one led by Borden.[19] Borden's union government was established in October and its main mandate was to enforce and administer the compulsory Military Service Act that had been passed earlier by the Conservatives. In the federal election held in December, Norris campaigned strenuously for the new Union government and its conscription policy.[20]

Not only was Norris one of many Canadians who believed that the war in Europe was being fought for justice, liberty, and democracy: he was also among those who felt it was "the duty of those who remained behind to see that these same things prevailed in Canada."[21] This helps explain the emphasis placed by Norris and the members of his governments on running clean, scandal-free administrations. It also helps explain his first administration's effort to preserve and extend "justice" and "democracy" by implementing what one historian called "a breathtaking" number of important political, economic, and social reforms.[22]

Norris was heavily influenced by what Paul F. Sharp once called the agrarian "prewar crusade for democracy."[23] He, along with most rural people, believed that governments were too controlled by small, powerful groups, especially bankers, tariff-protected manufacturers, railway investors, and speculators. These people made large amounts of money "not by fair and honest effort, but by means of special privileges...."[24] Norris and other farmers felt that institutions and practices should be adjusted so that the "producing classes," which meant essentially workers and small businessmen such as farmers, would have more influence. Norris referred to himself as a "democrat," and frequently he mentioned his confidence that the instincts and intelligence of normal people could be trusted. In fact, he proudly acknowledged that he was essentially an agent and spokesman for the people.[25]

If common people had more political clout they themselves would begin to enjoy the reasonable degree of prosperity they deserved for their hard work.[26] There would be another benefit as well: Christian principles would be more frequently and more thoroughly applied in everyday life. As Richard Allen has pointed out, the Social Gospel was the "religion of the agrarian revolt."[27] Norris was not a devout man, but he was a Methodist influenced by Social Gospel ideas and he placed a high priority on reducing poverty, ignorance, and other economic and social problems. Unlike many of the farmers and others who were committed to reform, however, Norris did not believe that all problems could be eliminated. He believed, for example, that giving women the vote would bring positive results but it was not a "panacea" as some people seemed to think.[28] He also recognized that certain reforms might be appropriate only at specific times. For example, his support for prohibition during the war was based on an assumption that the reform would enhance military and economic efficiency.[29] Actually, Norris enjoyed drinking and the conversation and laughter that usually accompanied it; in normal times he was more an advocate of moderation than of prohibition.[30]

Norris was, of course, the leader of a party that had committed itself before it took office to carrying out a number of reforms. He placed great emphasis on keeping his pledges, so he was determined to take action once he became premier. By 1915–16, moreover, the war had produced a general willingness to contribute to military victory by using the state to eliminate sin and inefficiency. The prevailing assumptions that only a morally worthy and economically vigorous nation would defeat the enemy meant that Norris and his supporters could implement their reforms with more confidence than they could have in 1910 or even 1914.[31]

The most important of the remarkable number of reform measures adopted between 1916 and 1920 can be summarized here.[32] They were reforms that spoke to problems that had emerged early in the 20th century in a rapidly growing, industrializing province, and which during the war a self-denying population was more ready to accept than would have been the case a few years earlier.

Many of the reforms benefited women. Norris was never married but, as one writer put it, he was "by no means a misogynist."[33] He was not a prominent champion of women's rights and privileges but he was sympathetic to their causes. The result was that in 1916 the females of Manitoba became the first in any province to receive the right to vote. By 1920 they had been made eligible for provincial and municipal offices. By the same year, widowed mothers with dependent children had become eligible for financial assistance; a Dower Act had been passed to ensure that a wife inherited portions of her husband's estate and that a married man could not transfer certain kinds of property without spousal consent; and a Minimum Wage Board had been established to fix, by industry and district, minimum wages for female employees.

The major political reform introduced by the Norris government was the Initiative and Referendum Act of 1916, which allowed for use of two types of direct legislation. The Act was declared *ultra vires* by the courts. According to W.L. Morton, if it had been necessary to do so "the constitution could have been adopted to the working of direct legislation."

But direct legislation appealed primarily "to those who had a special cause to advance," and since the Norris government established many specific reforms through normal legislative procedures, and since (non-binding) referenda were used by the Norris government to gauge public opinion on two different prohibition measures, no great pressure developed to get around the court decision.[34] Among other political reforms adopted the most important was the creation of a Civil Service Commission to make decisions on the hiring and promotion of government employees based on training rather than party allegiance. A system of preferential voting for Winnipeg MLAs was also adopted; the motivation for this measure was the desire to have opinions of different groups of voters reflected more accurately in the representatives elected.[35] Still with regard to political reforms, acts were passed to prevent election "saw-offs,"[36] to facilitate protests against "dirty tricks," to limit amounts of money that candidates could spend or parties hold, and to provide for public awareness of sources of campaign funds.

The Liberals had complained for many years about Roblin government policies in education, and initiatives of immense, permanent consequence were taken in this field.[37] School attendance became compulsory. English became the only language of instruction. (Legislation to ensure adequate instruction in English was a reform long overdue, from the point of view of Norris and his supporters, but, as will be noted, by disallowing bilingual education the Norris government created lasting enemies.) More money was spent building new classrooms or repairing old ones, accommodating more students, training new teachers and upgrading the qualifications of experienced ones, and introducing or improving medical and dental inspection programs. The University of Manitoba became more closely controlled and more liberally financed by the provincial government.

Among the many other progressive actions taken by Norris and his government, the 1916 prohibition of sale (except as prescribed for medical reasons) of all but low-percentage alcoholic beverages was likely the most significant. The prohibition legislation was passed after a referendum had indicated that a majority of Manitobans were in favour. Then, along the same lines, in 1920, again after a referendum had indicated Manitobans' views on the matter (and after the federal government had given provinces the power to do so), Norris's government banned the importation of alcoholic beverages from outside the province.

Several measures were designed to improve conditions for wage-earning men and women. Greater resources were put into factory inspections. Legislation was passed to limit hours of work for females and minors. The Workmen's Compensation Act, initially passed by the Roblin Conservatives, was improved. Provisions were made to ensure that fair wages were paid by employers who received government contracts. A Minimum Wage Board was established as mentioned to set minimum wages by industry and district for female employees. Finally, after the Winnipeg General Strike of 1919, a Permanent Joint Council of Industry was created to inquire into labour disputes, working conditions, and wages, and to recommend legislation.

Some other very significant reform initiatives should be mentioned. There were improvements to the province's public health system and, as part of this effort, better health care became available to rural Manitobans, especially through an act that facilitated cooperation among municipalities in the creation of hospitals. The provincial prison system was also reformed. There was an improved Game Protection Act. Municipalities received authority to tax unoccupied lands more heavily. Provisions were made to help cities and towns outside Winnipeg gain access to hydroelectric power, and major improvements were realized in the provincial road system.

The vast majority of these actions benefited farmers, and in fact they were supported, if not demanded, by spokesmen for the province's largest farm organization, the Manitoba Grain Growers' Association. A host of further Norris measures were adopted specifically in the interests of farmers. The Noxious Weeds Act was improved. Purchasers of farm machinery were protected from misrepresentation by salesmen. Formation of consumer co-operatives was facilitated. Funds were provided to enable farmers in less affluent districts to purchase animals (this was known as Val Winkler's "cow scheme"). Money was loaned to municipalities to enable them to supply seed grain. More important, through a Farm Loans Act and a Rural Credits Act, both passed in 1917, programs were designed to give farmers all over the province access to money at low rates of interest. Then, just after the war, when chartered banks decided that they would no longer support these initiatives, the Norris government established a Provincial Savings Bank through which loans were made to farmers at rates below those of the banks.

As W.L. Morton once wrote, the Norris government of 1915–20 not only "did much to redeem the public life of the province from the shame of ... scandals," it also passed an "enlightened and courageous programme of legislation."[38] Most Manitobans approved of the reforms introduced. However, in the later years of World War I, many Manitobans, like other Canadians, became resentful of sacrifices they were making, suspicious of others who did not seem to be pulling their weight, and angry at governments of all kinds. Through some specific initiatives the Norris government had alienated significant groups. Furthermore, by the end of the war many voters, especially rural ones, had become convinced that both of the traditional parties, the Liberals and Conservatives, were unsatisfactory. All of these things worked together to cause Norris's downfall.

In 1920 he called an election. He seemed confident of victory, and in the early weeks of the quiet campaign that ensued it appeared that confidence was justified. However, in the later stages of electioneering it became obvious that there was more opposition to the government than Norris had estimated.

Some of the opposition came from those who believed the government had been extravagant. Government expenditures had risen from about $6 million in 1914 to nearly $11 million in 1920, and the province's net debt had moved from about $27 million in the former year to approximately $32 million in the latter.[39] In order to raise money, the Liberals imposed new or increased taxes on land, amusements, and corporations. Despite the tax hikes, they ran deficits in three years out of the five. The Conservative Party made much of this, as did other organizations.[40]

The Norris government suffered somewhat from the charge of exorbitance, but probably it was harmed just as much by the criticism that it had not spent enough money on worthwhile measures, in particular measures designed to benefit veterans and families of those who had lost their lives in the war. Norris and his government had done the normal provincial things for servicemen and their dependents. Money to assist families had been raised through a Patriotic War Tax collected from municipalities. Soldiers and their families had been protected from suits for debt and from foreclosures on their property. Veterans' organizations had been granted exemptions from taxation. Returned men had been given preference when they applied for housing loans and when they applied for some government jobs; they had also been given interest-free loans to take Normal School classes.[41] This was not a bad record, but Winnipeg was home to some of the most vocal and best organized returned soldiers groups in the country, and they were not impressed. Many of the forty-two candidates who ran in 1920 as Independents did so partly because they wanted more assistance for those who had sacrificed most during the war. The votes they gained likely cost the Liberals one or two seats in Winnipeg, where the party took only four of the ten available.[42]

Certain ethnic minorities also opposed Norris. French-Canadians, Ukrainians, and Germans especially did so. They had good reasons. Norris and his Liberal Party had been inclined since the 1880s to act on the assumption that majorities had the democratic right to impose their will on minorities. During the war the ethnic minorities had not been as committed to the Allied cause as those of British ancestry. Norris, like the majority in his province, showed little sympathy for individuals and groups not totally committed to victory. "This fight must be won on behalf of democracy," he once said, and those who stood in the way of military success "should be put in jail or some other place."[43]

As mentioned, Norris's determination to help win the war had led him to support Borden's Union government. This government not only had implemented the previous Conservative government's policy of conscription, which was designed in part to force French-Canadians and other minorities to do their part. It had also benefited from the Conservatives' Wartime Elections Act which, for purposes of the federal election of 1917, disenfranchised conscientious objectors and individuals who had been born in enemy countries and not naturalized by 1902.[44] Moreover, in February 1919, when "foreigners" became associated by Norris and many citizens with growing labour radicalism, the Premier had established an Alien Investigation Board to identify aliens who had favoured the German cause and whom the federal government might want to deport.[45] Most important in terms of political impact, in 1916 Norris had made English the only accepted language of instruction in Manitoba's public schools.

Among British Protestant Manitobans this decision to repeal the bilingual clause of the Manitoba School Act may well have been the most popular the Norris government had ever made.[46] But it left Norris open to the charge that when Leader of the Opposition he had misled voters from minority groups. In the elections of 1914 and 1915 he and several other Liberals had made it clear that, once elected, they would ensure that English was adequately taught in every school. They had indicated at the same time that instruction in at least some other languages would continue. By 1916, however, Norris, along with Education Minister Dr. Robert Thornton and most Liberals, had concluded that adequate instruction in English and the bilingual clause were incompatible and that the latter had to go. An attempt made by Norris and a couple of other moderates to arrange for concessions to French-Canadians came to naught because no compromise was possible between some Cabinet ministers (especially Thornton) who were opposed to any compromises, and French MLAs who insisted on retention of all privileges.[47]

The adoption of unilingual education was followed in the next few years by the implementation of several measures designed to make schools more effective inculcators of "British" ideals and values.[48] Ukrainians, Germans, French-Canadians and other minorities resented these measures, as they did Norris's Alien Investigation Board and his support for conscription and the Wartime Elections Act. In the election of 1920 Norris paid a price for his majoritarianism and his ethnocentric streak. Five French-Canadian and two Ukrainian MLAs were elected to oppose his government.[49]

Related to the resentment of Norris that developed because of the treatment of ethnic minorities was that which appeared because, in the federal election of 1917, he had abandoned the national Liberal Party and its leader, Sir Wilfrid Laurier. His decision to support the Union government had been applauded and even demanded by most Manitoba Liberals. A significant minority, however, never forgave him for his disloyalty and naivety, as they saw it, and for the next several years an organization of "diehard" Laurier Liberals existed in the province. Their criticisms of "betrayers" such as Norris had an impact as the Union government became increasingly unpopular between 1918 and 1920.[50] In the provincial election of 1920, an unknown but significant number of these "diehard" Liberals supported labour, farmer, and three Laurier Liberal candidates.[51]

Norris's actions during the Winnipeg General Strike of May–June 1919 also antagonized a significant section of the population. Both the background to and the history of this event are well known.[52] It is enough to say here that in the late war years rapid inflation and increasing government interference in labour relations caused many workers to become anxious and resentful, and that in the spring of 1919 about 30,000 Winnipeg labourers joined in a general strike to indicate sympathy for specific grievances of building trades and metal trades employees. Norris adopted a "neutral" attitude towards this strike.[53] However, he dismissed provincial employees who joined the walk-out, and insisted that no negotiations for legislation to recognize the right to collective bargaining would occur until after the strike was called off.[54] Thereafter labourers saw him as just another politician who identified with employers and capitalists. He and the members of his government actually possessed a progressive record on labour matters, but by 1920 they were referred to by the *Western Labour News* as "tools" of a federal government that had "resorted to the most autocratic and oppressive measures known in history" to defeat the strikers.[55] As a result, in 1920 eighteen candidates sponsored by labour parties, along with several independents, ran in opposition to the "oppressive" Norris government.

On the other hand, it must be noted that many rural voters were disturbed by radical labour and believed that if Norris had erred it was by being too soft on the strikers. So did Winnipeggers who identified strongly with returned soldiers, who were very suspicious of "foreigners" and who blamed foreign agitators for labour unrest. One individual elected as a Liberal MLA in 1915, J.W. Wilton, ran as an opponent of Norris in 1920 because, in his estimation, the premier had failed to act decisively in the face of an attempted "revolution."[56]

Norris could have withstood a challenger who had understandable complaints against specific policies or positions. He could not, however, withstand one that came from these groups plus others who had no major criticisms to offer of his performance, but who felt that parties either were undesirable or had been too powerful. They wanted to assert their political independence.

There always had been a number of Manitobans who prided themselves on their complete freedom from party allegiances. There had been more who viewed themselves as Liberals or Conservatives when it came to federal elections but believed that the administration of provincial affairs was not something on which men of "common sense" could differ seriously.[57] The overwhelming Liberal victory of 1915 resulted partly from the fact that both these groups had voted Liberal in order to penalize the disgraced Conservatives.[58] But in 1920 even voters who possessed no important reason and no great desire to defeat the Norris administration refused to vote for it. In Manitoba as elsewhere in Canada, between about 1919 and 1922 political independence was more in fashion than it ever had been before.[59]

In Manitoba in 1920 there were certainly a large number of independent candidates. Some were former Conservatives who could see that independence was popular; others ran because they wanted a more effective opposition.[60] They might have strange policies or appeal to peculiar constituencies. One man ran on the word of God![61] A woman was a "children's candidate" who promoted the "interests ... of the mother and child."[62] Candidates were nominated by many organizations, including a Winnipeg community club.[63] However, most of the candidates who were not nominated by a political party were either selected or endorsed by local chapters of the United Farmers of Manitoba (UFM), which was the name recently adopted by the Manitoba Grain Growers' Association. Except for those who ran in districts where ethnic minorities were numerous, these farm candidates had no major criticisms of the Norris government. They ran against it because at least in name it was a party government. In the early 1920s, this was enough to make it suspect.[64]

The farmers were among those who had felt for some time that in provincial (as opposed to federal) politics parties were superfluous. By the end of the first decade of the 20th century, many of them also felt that even at the federal level, where legitimate ideological differences might come into play, parties had a negative influence. They stifled both the voice and the will of the people. Their existence meant that ordinary elected members of legislative bodies could not represent their constituents adequately on specific issues, because party leaders enforced discipline and everyone had to articulate the party "line." Furthermore, by gaining access to these same party leaders, privileged groups in society acquired wealth and power.[65]

The beliefs that parties frustrated real democracy and were unnecessary had become common among Manitoba farmers by World War I. These beliefs had been confirmed thereafter by the formation of the Union government and by the use of referenda on two prohibition measures. By 1920 the farmers were suspicious of anyone who attached himself to a party.[66] As would become clear in 1921, many of them also believed in "group government," the cause championed most enthusiastically by Henry Wise Wood, leader of the United Farmers of Alberta. Like Wood, they hoped that governments could be formed not by leaders of parties but by representatives of the different "groups" of MLAs who happened to emerge from an election.[67]

Norris agreed with some of this. He knew that party leaders often abused power. As Premier he had taken steps to reduce the number of politically motivated appointments. In fact, one of the problems that the Laurier Liberals had with him was that he had been too pure on patronage.[68] He did not insist that Liberal backbenchers support his government on specific issues. The "primary responsibility of the individual member is to his constituency," he said.[69] Of course this was an easy thing to say for a Premier with an overwhelming majority, but Norris believed in this principle and he had acted on it.[70]

However, Norris's thinking differed from that of the farmers in two respects. First, he felt that parties and caucuses were useful and even indispensable. They fostered stability because they allowed elected representatives with similar views to get things done. Second, he believed that government by groups, which in practice meant occupational groups, would be unworkable. In his view, coherent priorities for managing public affairs could be devised and implemented only when a lieutenant-governor relied on advice from one group of men who had consulted with a caucus and therefore could expect their advice to be supported.[71]

In 1920 the farmers of Manitoba knew that no provincial administration could have done more for them than Norris's. They recognized he had governed in a non-partisan fashion. They knew that he and his ministers had fulfilled election promises "more completely than any other government on record," to quote the *Grain Growers' Guide*.[72] Still, Norris led a party and he believed in parties. If farmers simply elected party candidates, their capacity to influence legislation and public affairs would be diminished. Many of them believed that farmers were particularly well-suited—some of them felt that they were chosen by God—to establish the "new era" of Canadian history that so many people talked about at the end of the war.[73] Although the leaders of the UFM did not encourage them to do so, the rank and file of the organization backed twenty-six independent candidates through the UFM locals.[74]

A few days before the polling Norris expressed surprise that Manitobans, and especially Manitoban farmers, might "disown the worker" while at the same time "applauding the work" he had done.[75] His anxiety was justified. When the returns came in, they showed that the Liberals had won 21 seats, farm candidates had won 12, labour candidates 11, Conservatives 7, and other Independents 4. Traditional parties had been abandoned. The Liberals' portion of the popular vote had dropped from 54% in 1915 to 36% in 1920, but the Conservatives' share had gone down from 33% to under 17%. Independent or third party (essentially labour party) candidates had received nearly half the votes cast in 1920; in 1915 they had gained 13%. The election of 1920 revealed above all else the degree to which Manitobans had become dissatisfied with normal party politics.[76]

The Second Term and Electoral Defeat

After the election, Norris was still the leader of the largest group in the Assembly, so he was asked to form another government. He did so with no guarantee of support from non-Liberal MLAs. His minority government lasted two years and was not successful. It managed to increase aid to hospitals, to improve Manitoba's Child Welfare Act, and to make some extensions to benefits available to veterans and their families. But it did nothing dramatic.

One minor reason for this was that his second Cabinet was not quite as competent as the first. Val Winkler died in 1920. He was replaced as minister of Agriculture and Immigration by the capable G.H. Malcolm of Birtle. George A. Grierson gave way in Public Works to the popular Colonel Charles D. McPherson of Portage, a prominent Liberal who had been overseas during the war. The main problem with the individuals in government was not that the new ministers were weak but that veteran ministers such as Johnson, Armstrong, and Thornton were starting to show their age. The first two left politics before the next election, which was held in 1922, and Thornton became ill while the campaign was underway. Norris himself was not strong and vigorous in the early 1920s, and it appears that at some point in 1922 or 1923 he suffered a mild stroke.[77]

However, the government's failures were caused mainly by the resistance or expected resistance of combinations of opposing "groups." Manitobans, like most Canadians, believed by the early 1920s that no truly important reform had been neglected.[78] Priorities could not be agreed upon. In the legislative sessions of 1921 and 1922 a total of 379 bills were introduced, but only 132 were passed.[79] In these years Manitobans lacked a stable government. They did not, however, come to the conclusion that stronger political parties were desirable. They had had enough of strong, disciplined parties back in the pre-war years.

As far as Norris and his supporters were concerned, it was not only impossible to inaugurate significant new programs but, due to the post-war depression that had set in, it was also difficult to maintain and justify those that had been instituted by 1920. In order to increase revenues the government introduced a net profits tax on non-professional businesses, and tried unsuccessfully to bring in personal income and gasoline taxes.[80] However, deficits in both 1921 and 1922 were between $600,000 and $2 million, depending upon who was doing the counting.[81] In the early 1920s it seemed reasonable to conclude that since 1915 the Liberals had instituted measures which the province could not now afford. Moreover, because in these difficult years several farmers were forced to go into arrears on payments for their provincial government loans, the Norris administration was susceptible to charges of poor management.

In the election of 1922, which was called after Norris interpreted a motion of unsure from the assembly as an expression of lack of confidence, the perceived extravagance of his governments was an important issue. Ironically, so was Norris's alleged responsibility for the legislative "stagnation" of 1920–22.[82] But perhaps even more damaging was the fact that in the spring of 1922 Norris and his followers became more closely identified with the federal Liberal Party than they had been. Especially among rural Manitobans, the federal Liberals had become unpalatable, and by extension so were their provincial associates.

The failings of the Laurier Liberal governments of the 1896–1911 years have been mentioned. By about 1910 it had become clear to Manitoba's farmers that the Liberals were not only just as corrupt and cliquish as the Conservatives, but also nearly as unlikely to implement truly progressive measures, especially a downward revision of the tariff. Then, in 1911, the party regained esteem when it championed free trade and negotiated a reciprocity agreement with the United States. But the Liberals were defeated in the federal election of 1911, and one main reason was that urban and especially Eastern Canadian Liberals turned against their own leaders. Thereafter, the Liberal Party seemed just as dominated by Eastern "interests" as the Conservative Party. "The history of the Liberal Party from 1896 to 1916," wrote an observer in the *Grain Growers' Guide* early in 1917, "does not warrant any hope that … it will ever stir a finger to curb the governing class."[83]

The election of 1917 and the maintenance of high tariffs by a Union government after the war, despite promises to reduce them and replace the revenue through effective income tax provisions, indicated further that no real differences between the two federal parties existed. So did developments at the Liberal leadership convention of August 1919, called due to the death in February of Sir Wilfrid Laurier. There, a low tariff plank was included in the platform, but clear opposition to it was expressed by many delegates, and the new leader, William Lyon Mackenzie King of Ontario, refrained from committing himself to lower tariffs in his acceptance speech.[84] By 1920, Manitobans had concluded that the Liberal Party was indecisive and hypocritical.

In large part because the Liberals seemed untrustworthy, in the federal election of 1921 the farmers of Manitoba for the most part supported independent candidates committed to a Farmers' Platform issued earlier by the Canadian Council of Agriculture. In Manitoba, as in Ontario, Saskatchewan, and Alberta, these independent candidates did "astonishingly well."[85] Twelve "Progressives," as they were called, ran in the keystone province, and all twelve were elected. The Conservatives were shut out completely. The Liberals won only one seat, and that was taken by A.B. Hudson, Norris's former Attorney-General and a declared supporter of most Progressive principles.[86]

In the provincial election of 1920 Norris and his provincial followers had been punished for being advocates of the party system, but they had not been identified closely with the federal Liberals. This was because there had been open disagreement between federal and provincial wings of the party over the 1916 school legislation and the formation of the Union government, among other things, and also because at the federal convention of August 1919, Norris and his provincial followers ostentatiously had made it a point to see what policies were adopted before deciding if they would support them.[87]

In 1922, however, Norris and the provincial Liberals became more closely tied to the federal party, and they were punished for being so. The key developments occurred in April. By then the Norris minority government had been defeated in the legislature, and it was clear that an election would take place later in the summer. By then, as well, the United Farmers of Manitoba had decided to take political action at the provincial level and, unlike in 1920, to do so through the provincial organization.[88] The farmers were excited about the successes of agrarian candidates in both the recent federal election and earlier provincial elections in Ontario and Alberta. It seemed that through independent political action their aspirations to simultaneously purify politics and further their own interests might be realized.

Early in the month Norris and most of his Cabinet ministers were not disposed to confront the farmers. But Ed Brown, the former leader, and A.E. Hill, chief officer of the Dominion Liberal Party in Manitoba and a Griswold-Hartney merchant who was close to Norris, believed that the UFM was going to fight with the Liberals whether the Liberals entered the ring or stayed in their corner. The only chance for victory, Norris was advised, was to gain the support of every man or woman in the province who had voted or might vote Liberal.[89]

Norris acquiesced as Hill arranged for a convention of Manitoba Liberals to be held in Winnipeg on April 25–26, 1922. For a short time it appeared that the plan of advertising the provincial party's association with the federal wing might bring positive results. This was because in mid-April, Norris and two Cabinet ministers went to Ottawa and, through discussions with representatives of the federal Liberal government, made a significant breakthrough in negotiations for transfer of control over Manitoba's natural resources to the province.[90] An announcement that notable progress had been made towards answering the old and very important questions of just how and on what terms the transfer should take place came just a few days before Hill's convention. During that event, much was made of the benefits of cooperation between provincial and federal Liberals, and a resolution congratulating King and his government on its enlightened attitude towards the West was passed unanimously.[91]

However, as it turned out, the late spring and early summer of 1922 proved a bad time for provincial Liberals to be associated closely with their federal counterparts. Between the end of April and July 18, the date of the provincial election, a number of events transpired that reminded rural Manitobans of how untrustworthy and how partisan the federal party could be. It became clear that federal Liberals were not committed to regulations that would force politicians to distance themselves from corporations[92]; that they were not eager to restore the Crow's Nest Pass freight rates, so favourable to farmers, which had been established in 1897 but temporarily suspended in both 1918 and 1919[93]; that they might "tinker" with the protective tariffs but never "made adjustments that amount to anything."[94] These developments as well as others[95] reminded farmers that they could trust only their own farmer candidates, and should avoid helping federal Liberals. In the circumstances that prevailed after the April 25–26 convention this meant defeating Norris and the provincial party.[96]

By early in July Norris seems to have realized that Hill's strategy had backfired. He tried to put distance between himself and the King government by emphasizing his unpopularity since 1916 among federal Liberals.[97] He also pointed out that UFM policies differed little from Liberal ones, and said that the UFM offered no substantial criticism of what his governments had done.[98] He noted that the prominent Winnipeg citizens who had formed a Progressive party at the provincial level to run city candidates in support of the UFM platform were, in many cases, the same people who had criticized the amounts of money he had spent on rural schools and roads, who had opposed his farm loans and rural credit schemes, and who had fought both his business profits tax and his proposed income tax which were designed in part to relieve farmers' tax burden.[99] He reiterated his opinion that group government could not work, and he reminded voters that the deplorable practices often associated with parties had not occurred while he had been premier.[100]

All of these propositions seemed to fall on deaf ears. A few days after the election Norris wrote to King and mentioned the "stoic demeanor" of so many voters. It had been "impossible to reach them by argument," Norris observed.[101] This suggests that from the start of the campaign Norris had little chance of winning. But the well-informed John W. Dafoe, editor of the *Free Press*, believed that Norris had made an important blunder when he allowed himself to become identified closely with federal Liberals. He said that this had furnished "just the pretext" that farmers needed to reject the premier.[102] In 1922 Norris was no more popular among labourers or ethnic minorities than he had been in 1920, so the collapse of farm support meant disaster. The results of the election showed that 28 UFM and Progressive candidates had been returned compared to 8 Liberals, 7 Conservatives, 6 labour candidates, and 6 Independents.[103]

Later Career

Norris led the provincial Liberals for another four and a half years following the election of 1922. By the mid 1920s he had regained his health somewhat. He was more like the witty, gregarious man he had been in the 1910s. Sometimes he revealed his feelings that Manitobans and especially rural Manitobans had treated him thanklessly. But Norris was a democrat if he was anything, and he accepted the verdict of 1922 even though he remained hurt by it.

In these years of opposition Norris was not, as has been argued, a "bitter opponent of co-operation" with the new UFM or "Progressive" government as it came to be known, and he worked with, not against, Mackenzie King in the latter's efforts to entice federal Progressive MPs and their supporters "back" to Liberalism.[104] Norris regarded John Bracken, the former Principal of the Manitoba Agricultural College who became leader of the provincial Progressives and therefore Premier after the 1922 election, as a "thorough gentleman," and he was on very good personal terms with most of Bracken's followers in the Legislative Assembly.[105] He knew that the UFM government could not be activist in the economic circumstances of the early to mid-1920s. Like many Liberals he feared that a farmers' government might legislate in the interest of only one "class" (occupational group), but he agreed with much of what the first (1922–27) Bracken administration was doing, and his disparaging remarks usually came after someone had made uncomplimentary references to the governments he had led.[106] Furthermore, by his actions during the federal election of 1925 he earned the praise and gratitude of Mackenzie King by refusing to cause a divide of the "progressive" vote in one part of Manitoba and helping to unite it in another. He refused to run as a Liberal or "fusion" Liberal/Conservative candidate in Brandon constituency against the federal Progressive leader Robert Forke, and accepted instead the Grit nomination in South Winnipeg, where he ran unsuccessfully against Robert Rogers, the old Tory "Minister of Elections" of the Roblin years, a man disliked not only by Liberals but also by others who placed a priority on clean politics.[107] (Norris resigned his provincial seat to do this, but regained it later through a by-election.)

It is true, however, that as leader of the Manitoba Liberals Norris represented an obstacle to the reconciliation between provincial Liberals and Progressives that his departure in 1926 was supposed to facilitate (but which as it turned out was not completed until 1932).[108] Many Franco-Manitobans simply would not vote for a party or a government of which Norris was a prominent member, and in his first years in power Bracken could not afford to alienate his French supporters by pursuing an alliance with the man who had repealed the bilingual clause and supported Union government.[109] In fact, so strong was the animosity among French Canadians in Manitoba and across the Dominion that it probably cost Norris a post in the federal Cabinet. Mackenzie King offered him such a position at the beginning of the campaigning in the federal election of 1925. As the days went by, however, King dropped the matter because he became aware of the intense opposition among French supporters in Quebec as elsewhere to the appointment of Norris. In the end, the problem went away when Norris did not win against Rogers in the South Winnipeg seat.[110]

In the spring of 1926, in part because he realized that he was as much a liability as an asset to his party, Norris announced his intention to resign as Liberal leader. Virtually all the active Manitoba Liberals—even (quietly) some French Canadian ones—agreed that "Crawford" should receive a federal government appointment. He might have been chosen the lieutenant-governor of the province later in 1926 when that position became available, but lieutenant-governors were more or less expected to be wealthy and married and Norris was neither. He was passed over in favour of longtime Liberal T.A. Burrows. Other positions that opened up had prior claimants. Finally, in 1928, shortly after a 1927 provincial election in which Norris, no longer the leader, had won the Lansdowne seat for the tenth time, and after several Liberals had begun to express disappointment in the way in which he was being ignored, he was appointed to the Board of Railway Commissioners.[111]

Norris remained on the Board until he reached the age of 75 in September 1936. He died one month later in Toronto. He was buried in that city, not far from where he had been born and raised, and near three sisters and a brother who were still alive.[112]

Conclusion

T.C. Norris became premier of Manitoba just as Canadians were beginning to realize that World War I was the most serious conflict in their history. He believed the war was a just one and he did everything he could as a provincial leader to boost the military effort and to defend and extend at home the ideals for which he believed Canadians were fighting in Europe. The war atmosphere intensified the commitment he felt already to democracy, justice, and freedom, and it motivated him and members of his 1915–20 government to pass reform legislation that was truly remarkable in scope and impact.

In the process of doing these things he ignored rights and privileges of ethnic groups who were not as committed to a British and Canadian victory as he was, or who seemed to advocate principles that were "foreign." He also alienated some Liberals who were not as convinced as he was by 1917 that for the time being loyalty to party must be relinquished. As a result certain ethnic groups, many labourers, and some diehard Grits refused to vote for him after the war.

Norris was not surprised by this reaction. He was certainly surprised, however, that shortly after the war the majority of British Protestant farmers deserted him. Norris was a rural man familiar with rural problems. He knew that rural people appreciated his unpretentiousness, his eye for the absurd and the comical, his straightforwardness. He was confident he had served rural people well as Premier. He had led the kind of clean and essentially non-partisan government they wanted. The reforms he had passed were reforms which many of them had long demanded and which during the war more of them would condone. Yet these farmers joined with other groups to deny him a majority in 1920 and then to defeat him in 1922.

They did this because he was the leader of a party and, by 1922, an openly Liberal Party. At the end of the war farmers were even more convinced than they usually were that their legitimate interests coincided with those of all Canadians.[113] They were also certain that their vision and voice would be silenced if they supported traditional political parties. Even old friends like T.C. Norris had to be sacrificed. He was replaced as Premier by John Bracken, a man interested in public affairs but not in politics. He was non-partisan in the extreme—exactly the kind of person the farmers believed was best suited to the job.

Notes

The author acknowledges the assistance received from John H. Thompson, Gerald Friesen, the late Ed Rea, John Kendle, Terry Cook, and the editors of this volume. He also acknowledges financial support provided by the St. Paul's College–SSHRC Research Grants Program, The Brandon University Research Fund, and the John S. Ewart Memorial Fund.

1. This account of Norris's early life and early political involvment is based upon the following: *Brandon Sun*, October 29, 1936; *Manitoba Free Press* (hereafter *FP*), February 7, 1896, August 17, 1935, October 30, 1936; *Toronto Globe*, October 30, 1936; *Winnipeg Tribune* (hereafter *Tribune*), October 29, 1936; *Griswold Ledger*, February 22, 1899, June 18, 1903, August 18, 1904, March 9, 1905; Provincial Library of Manitoba (hereafter PLM), *Biographical Scrapbooks*, B6, pp. 110–12; Public Archives of Manitoba (hereafter PAM), T.C. Norris Papers, MG 13 H1, item 1514, J. Maclean memo on Norris; *Henderson's Gazetteer and Directory of Manitoba and the Northwest Territories, 1886–1904*; n.a., *Bridging the Years, 1867–1967*, Griswold Centennial Booklet (Griswold: Griswold United Church Women, ca. 1967), 51; Robert Harvey, *Pioneers of Manitoba* (Winnipeg: The Prairie Publishing Company, 1970), 47; interview with Mr. D.L. Campbell, Winnipeg, August 5, 1983; interview with Mr. and Mrs. Les Speers, Griswold, August 21, 1983; J.H. Evans, "The Norris Government As I Saw It" (unpublished manuscript in possession of Ms. Rosemary Malaher, Winnipeg), 5–6.

2. See *Bridging the Years*, 51; Ken Coates and Fred McGuinness, *Manitoba: The Province and the People* (Edmonton: Hurtig Publishers, 1987), 93; PLM, *Biographical Scrapbooks*, B6, p. 112.

3. *Bridging the Years*, 51; *Brandon Sun*, January 2, 1896; FP, August 17, 1935.

4. FP, October 30, 1936.

5. See Jon Gerrard with Gary Gerrard, *Battling for a Better Manitoba: A History of the Provincial Liberal Party* (Winnipeg: Heartland Associates Inc., 2006), 47–48.

6. W.L. Morton, *Manitoba: A History*, 2nd edition (Toronto: University of Toronto Press, 1967), chapters 12 and 13, passim; Alexander I. Inglis, "Some Political Factors in the Demise of the Roblin Government: 1915" (MA thesis, University of Manitoba, 1968), chapter 1; Lionel Orlikow, "A Survey of the Reform Movement in Manitoba, 1910 to 1920" (MA thesis, University of Manitoba, 1955), 18–22.

7. Orlikow, "Survey of the Reform Movement," 21–22; *Canadian Annual Review*, 1910: 491–92. Population figures for Winnipeg are from Alan Artibise, *Winnipeg: An Illustrated History* (Toronto, James Lorimer and Company and National Museums of Canada, 1977), 202.

8. FP, June 30, 1903, April 6, 1910, April 7, 1910; *Canadian Annual Review*, 1909: 495, 508; Campbell interview; Evans, "The Norris Government As I Saw It," 5–6.

9. Inglis, "Demise of the Roblin Government," chapter 2; especially p. 14; Orlikow, "Survey of the Reform Movement," chapter 2; Larry John Fisk, "Controversy on the Prairies: Issues in the General Provincial Elections of Manitoba 1870–1969" (PhD dissertation, University of Alberta, 1975), 242, 265.

10. Inglis, "Demise of the Roblin Government," 18–53, 70–82. In chapter 4 of his thesis, Inglis has some interesting observations on the constitutionality of Cameron's actions in this affair. The whole story of the construction of the Legislative Building and the scandal associated with it is told in Marilyn Baker, *Symbol in Stone: The Art and Politics of a Public Building* (Winnipeg: Hyperion Press, 1986).

11. *Canadian Annual Review*, 1915: 622–26.

12. FP, July 27, 1915.

13. Fisk, "Controversy on the Prairies," 285.

14. This comes from J.M. Bumsted, *Dictionary of Manitoba Biography* (Winnipeg: University of Manitoba Press, 1999); Evans, "The Norris Government As I Saw It," 6–11; *Canadian Parliamentary Guide*, "Manitoba" sections, 1915 to 1920.

15. For some voluntary enlistment statistics that support this statement, see C.A. Sharpe, "Enlistment in the Canadian Expeditionary Force 1914–1918: A Regional Analysis," *Journal of Canadian Studies* 18 (Winter 1983–84): 15–20. See also Margaret McWilliams, *Manitoba Milestones* (Toronto: J.M. Dent & Sons Ltd., 1928), 190–95. In the federal election of 1917, the win-the-war Union government received a much higher percentage of the popular vote in Manitoba than in any other province. Sir J. Murray Beck, *Pendulum of Power: Canada's Federal Elections* (Scarborough, ON: Prentice-Hall of Canada, Ltd., 1968), 148.

16. FP, September 19, 1914, February 26, 1915, November 15, 1915; *Grain Growers' Guide* (hereafter GGG), January 10, 1917.

17. FP, November 6, 1915.

18. Morton, *Manitoba*, 358; FP, January 17, 1917, March 9, 1917, August 10, 1917.

19. This became clear especially after the famous Western Liberal convention of August 7–8, 1917 which had a disappointing result for Norris and other pro-conscription Liberals. See D.J. Hall, *Clifford*

Sifton: vol. II, A Lonely Eminence, 1901–1929 (Vancouver: University of British Columbia Press, 1985), 283–86; Robert A. Wardhaugh, *Mackenzie King and the Prairie West* (Toronto: University of Toronto Press, 2000), 25–26; W.L. Morton, *The Progressive Party in Canada* (Toronto: University of Toronto Press, 1950), 54; *FP*, August 8–23, 1917.

20. PLM, *Political Scrapbooks*, entries for January 17, 1917, November 17, 1917, December 8, 1917; *Canadian Annual Review*, 1917: 613. On the developments that led to the Union government and on the election of 1917, see Robert Craig Brown, *Robert Laird Borden, A. Biography, vol. II: 1914–1937* (Toronto: MacMillan of Canada, 1980) chapters 8–10, and John English, *The Decline of Politics: The Conservatives and the Party System, 1901–1920* (Toronto: University of Toronto Press, 1993), chapters 7–10.

21. John Herd Thompson, *The Harvests of War* (Toronto: McClelland and Stewart Ltd., 1978), 97. See also the comments by Norris reported in *FP*, February 26, 1915.

22. Lionel Orlikow, "The Reform Movement in Manitoba, 1910–1915," in Donald Swainson (ed.), *Historical Essays on the Prairie Provinces* (Toronto: McClelland and Stewart Ltd., 1970), 228.

23. Paul F. Sharp, *The Agrarian Revolt in Western Canada: A Survey Showing American Parallels* (Minneapolis: University of Minnesota Press, 1948), chapter 4.

24. GGG, June 28, 1911. The comment was made in reference to manufacturers, but the same general accusation was made of all the "interests." See ibid., November 2, 1910, April 5, 1911, March 21, 1917; Nellie McClung, *The Stream Runs Fast, My Own Story* (Toronto: Thomas Allen Ltd., 1945), 71–72.

25. PLM, *Biography Scrapbooks*, B6, p. 110; *FP*, March 8, 1912, 2 January 21, 1914, March 28, 1914, January 5, 1920; *Brandon Daily News*, January 29, 1913.

26. See *The Farmers' Advocate and Home Journal* (hereafter *Advocate*), July 11, 1906, July 10, 1907, April 2, 1913.

27. Richard Allen, "The Social Gospel as the Religion of the Agrarian Revolt," in Carl Berger and Ramsay Cook (eds.), *The West and the Nation: Essays in Honour of W.L. Morton* (Toronto: McClelland and Stewart Ltd., 1976), 174–86.

28. *FP*, February 4, 1914, March 28, 1914.

29. Ibid., February 19, 1915, January 17, 1917.

30. Norris Papers, J. Maclean memo on Norris; Campbell interview.

31. The association between the War and the advancement of reform in Manitoba and across the prairies is made in Thompson, *Harvests of War*, chapter 5.

32. These measures are identified in the "Manitoba" sections of the *Canadian Annual Review*, 1916–1920. See also Orlikow, "The Reform Movement in Manitoba," 228, and James A. Jackson, *The Centennial History of Manitoba* (Winnipeg: Manitoba Historical Society, 1970), 189–93.

33. PLM, *Biographical Scrapbooks*, B6, p. 110. There is a very interesting comment on Norris and women of "low morals" in PAM, Howard Winkler Papers, MG14 B44, Box 1, file 1, Mrs. Winkler to Howard Winkler, February 18, 1913. (Thanks to Dr. Gerhard Ens for bringing this source to my attention.) In his interview with me, D.L. Campbell mentioned that Norris "had a lot of lady friends." He let the subject drop there, but the implication was that some of his lady friends would not be considered "ladies" by everyone.

34. W.L. Morton, "Direct Legislation and the Origins of the Progressive Movement," *Canadian Historical Review* 25 (September 1944): especially 288, 284.

35. Sharp, *Agrarian Revolt*, 73; GGG, October 24, 1917; *FP*, March 24, 1920.

36. Sometimes parties made mutual agreements not to challenge questionable results in particular constituencies. This happened, of course, when one party benefited from the questionable results in one place, the other party from the questionable results in another. The practice was known as "sawing off" election challenges.

37. These initiatives are identified in Alexander Gregor and Keith Wilson, *The Development of Education in Manitoba* (Dubuque, IA: Kendall/Hunt Publishing Company, 1984), chapter 6, and in Keith Wilson, "The Development of Education in Manitoba" (PhD dissertation, Michigan State University, 1967), chapter 7.

38. Morton, *Manitoba*, 356.

39. *Canadian Annual Review*, 1915: 617, 1920: 735; Government of Manitoba, *Public Accounts of the Province of Manitoba for the year ending November 30, 1915*, 9, and *for the year ending, November 30, 1920*, 20–21.

40. *Canadian Annual Review*, 1920: 749; *Western Labour News*, April 16, 1920; *Winnipeg Telegram* (hereafter *Telegram*), June 10, 1920; Fisk, "Controversy on the Prairies," 297.

41. *Canadian Annual Review*, "Manitoba" sections, 1916–1920.

42. See Desmond Morton and Glenn Wright, *Winning the Second Battle: Canadian Veterans and the Return to Civilian Life, 1915–1930* (Toronto: University of Toronto Press, 1987), especially chapters 4–6; Fisk, "Controversy on the Prairies," 311–15; PLM, *Political Scrapbooks*, entries for May 1, 1919, November 17, 1919, November 20, 1919; *FP*, January 30, 1919, February 3, 1920, June 24, 1920.

43. GGG, January 10, 1917.

44. Thompson, *Harvests of War*, 80.

45. Morris Mott, "The Foreign Peril: Nativism in Winnipeg, 1916–1923" (MA thesis, University of Manitoba, 1970), 25; Donald Avery, "The Radical Alien and the Winnipeg General Strike of 1919," in Berger and Cook (eds.), *The West and the Nation*, 219.

46. See GGG, March 15, 1916, March 29, 1916; Morton, *Progressive Party*, 227; *Gladstone Age*, July 13, 1922.

47. W.L. Morton, "Manitoba Schools and Canadian Nationality, 1890–1923," in Ramsay Cook, Craig Brown, and Carl Berger (eds.), *Minorities, Schools, and Politics* (Toronto: University of Toronto Press, 1969), 15–17; *FP*, April 6, 1910, March 25, 1914, January 12, 1916, February 19, 1916, February 24, 1916, February 25, 1916, March 1, 1916, March 9, 1916; *Brandon Daily News*, April 24, 1913; Wilfred Laurier Papers (microfilm), p. 19096, Laurier to Norris, February 22, 1916, p. 191398, Norris to Laurier, March 16, 1916, p. 191399, Laurier to Norris, March 20, 1916, p. 191437, Norris to Laurier, March 24, 1916.

48. Mott, "Foreign Peril," 82–91.

49. *Canadian Annual Review*, 1921: 739.

50. For reasons the popularity of the Union government fell, see Thompson, *Harvests of War*, chapter 7.

51. PLM, *Political Scrapbooks*, entries for October 18, 1917, December 14, 1918, December 19, 1918, April 28, 1920, May 7, 1920, June 11, 1920, and especially May 22, 1920; *Neepawa Press*, May 7, 1920, November 4, 1921. On Liberal Party divisions in Manitoba at this time, see Wardhaugh, *Mackenzie King and the Prairie West*, 45–46, 52–54, and Laurier Papers, pp. 202331–202338, J.E. Adamson to C.M Goddard, January 6, 1919.

52. For solid summaries, see Kenneth McNaught and David J. Bercuson, *The Winnipeg Strike: 1919* (Don

Mills: Longman Canada Ltd., 1974), and D.C. Masters, *The Winnipeg General Strike* (1950; Toronto: University of Toronto Press, 1973).

53. Morton, *Manitoba*, 368.

54. Ibid.; McNaught and Bercuson, *The Winnipeg General Strike*, 67–68.

55. *Western Labour News*, April 16, 1920.

56. PLM, *Political Scrapbooks*, entries for May 1, 1919, May 2, 1919, November 17, 1919; FP, February 3, 1920; Thomas Peterson, "Manitoba: Ethnic and Class Politics," in Martin Robin (ed.), *Canadian Provincial Politics: The Party Systems of the Ten Provinces*, 2nd edition (Scarborough, ON: Prentice-Hall of Canada Ltd., 1978), 75.

57. See *Brandon Mail*, November 18, 1886.

58. Morton, *Manitoba*, 348.

59. For the national context, see John Herd Thompson and Allen Seager, *Canada 1922–1939: Decades of Discord* (Toronto: McClelland and Stewart Limited, 1988), especially 14–18. Some important observations on "The Curse of Partyism" can be found in David Laycock, *Populism and Democratic Thought in the Canadian Prairies, 1910 to 1945* (Toronto: University of Toronto Press, 1990), 46–51.

60. FP, June 17, 1920; Fisk, "Controversy on the Prairies," 300–03.

61. Morton, *Manitoba*, 375.

62. FP, June 21, 1920.

63. FP, June 16, 1920.

64. See *Melita New Era*, June 3, 1920.

65. GGG, August 10, 1910.

66. See *Gladstone Age*, May 20, 1920.

67. See FP, April 13, 1921.

68. See King Papers (microfilm), pp. 67955–67958, H.A. Robson to King, June 30, 1922; Laurier Papers, pp. 202331–202332, J.E. Adamson to C.M. Goddard, January 6, 1919; FP, February 16, 1918.

69. FP, February 10, 1920. See also FP, March 1, 1916.

70. See FP, February 5, 1919, February 4, 1920.

71. FP, March 1, 1916, February 5, 1919, February 4, 1920, February 10, 1920, February 20, 1920; *Tribune*, April 13, 1921.

72. GGG, July 14, 1920. See also ibid., January 14, 1920; *Deloraine Times*, June 24, 1920; *Gladstone Age*, July 1, 1920.

73. See especially "The Divinely Ordained Occupation of Farming" by the Winnipeg social gospel clergyman Salem G. Bland in GGG, November 20, 1918. See also ibid., March 18, 1914, March 31, 1915, June 30, 1915.

74. Sharp, *Agrarian Revolt*, 168; Morton, *Progressive Party*, 98.

75. FP, June 26, 1920.

76. GGG, July 7, 1920; Fisk, "Controversy on the Prairies," 285–311.

77. Elizabeth Dafoe Library. University of Manitoba Archives, MS S3, John W. Dafoe Papers, box 9 folder 1, A.B. Hudson to Dafoe, April 18, 1922, A.B. Hudson to Dafoe, April 24, 1922; Campbell interview; PLM, *Political Scrapbooks*, entry for March 16, 1923.

78. See the informative chapter entitled "An End to Idealism," in Thomson and Seager, *Canada, 1922–1939*.

79. *Canadian Annual Review*, 1921: 766, 1922: 767.

80. Ibid., 1921: 754, 1922: 760–61.

81. Ibid., 1921: 752–53, 1922: 760–61.

82. *Birtle Eye-Witness*, July 11, 1922; GGG, June 21, 1922, July 5, 1922; *Tribune*, May 31, 1922.

83. GGG, January 10, 1917. See also Morton, *Progressive Party*, 9, 16–17; GGG, August 10, 1910, November 2, 1910, August 30, 1916, July 11, 1917.

84. Morton, *Progressive Party*, 80–82.

85. Ibid., 128.

86. Beck, *Pendulum of Power*, 160–61.

87. *Telegram*, August 2, 1919, August 6, 1919; Morton, *Progressive Party*, 79–80; R. MacGregor Dawson, *William Lyon Mackenzie King: A Political Biography* (Toronto: University of Toronto Press, 1958), 299.

88. *Canadian Annual Review*, 1922: 771.

89. For all of this see King Papers, p. 63140, A.E. Hill to A. Haydon, April 10, 1922; Dafoe Papers, box 3, folder 1, Dafoe to A.B. Hudson, March 30, 1922, box 4, folder 3, Dafoe to Clifford Sifton, April 10, 1922, box 9, folder 1, A.B. Hudson to Dafoe, April 18, 1922, A.B. Hudson to Dafoe, April 24, 1922; FP, April 28, 1922. Information on A.E. Hill has been gained from *Bridging the Years*, 72, Speers interview, and *Canadian Annual Review*, 1921: 750.

90. FP, April 22, 1922; John Ingram, "Manitoba and the 'Natural Resources Question,' 1870–1930: A History" (unpublished University of Manitoba research paper, 1974), 12–14; Jim Mochoruk, *Formidable Heritage: Manitoba's North and the Cost of Development, 1870 to 1930* (Winnipeg: University of Manitoba Press, 2004), 238–41.

91. King Papers, pp. 631159-63160, A.E. Hill to A. Haydon, May 3, 1922, p. 66921, Norris to King, April 28, 1922; FP, April 26, 1922, April 27, 1922, June 15, 1922.

92. See Wardhaugh, *Mackenzie King and the West*, 73–74; *Canadian Annual Review*, 1922: 235; GGG, May 3, 1922; *Virden Empire-Advance*, June 9, 1922.

93. See Dawson, *King*, 393–97; Wardhaugh, *Mackenzie King and the West*, 79–81; GGG, June 28, 1922, July 5, 1922; *Virden Empire-Advance*, June 6, 1922.

94. The quotation is from GGG, June 14, 1922. See also FP, June 8, 1922, June 17, 1922; Dawson, *King*, 391–93; Wardhaugh, *Mackenzie King and the West*, 78–79.

95. See *Minnedosa Tribune*, May 11, 1922; *Gladstone Age*, July 13, 1922; Dafoe Papers, box 4, folder 3, Dafoe to Clifford Sifton, May 6, 1922; FP, April 26, 1922, April 28, 1922, June 28, 1922.

96. GGG, June 28, 1922.

97. Dafoe Papers, box 4, folder 3, Dafoe to Sifton, July 7, 1922; FP, July 7, 1922, July 8, 1922.

98. FP, May 12, 1922, May 26, 1922, June 15, 1922, July 14, 1922.

99. Ibid., July 4, 1922, July 5, 1922, July 15, 1922; *Tribune*, May 31, 1922.

100. FP, May 8, 1922, May 26, 1922, July 14, 1922.

101. King Papers, p. 66924, Norris to King, July 21, 1922.

102. Dafoe Papers, box 4, folder 3, Dafoe to Sifton, May 6, 1922. See also Sharp, *Agrarian Revolt*, 169; *Gladstone Age*, July 20, 1922.

103. Fisk, "Controversy on the Prairies," 335.

104. An erroneous impression of Norris's attitude and actions will be gained from H. Blair Neatby, *William Lyon Mackenzie King, vol. II, 1924–1932: The Lonely Heights* (Toronto: University of Toronto Press, 1963), especially 252, and from a particular way of reading both Wardhaugh, *Mackenzie King and the*

West, especially 140, and John Kendle, *John Bracken; A Political Biography* (Toronto: University of Toronto Press, 1979), especially 40, 63–64.

105. Meighen papers (microfilm), pp. 81256-81257, F.G. Taylor to Meighen, March 25, 1922; King Papers, p. 66931, Norris to King, August 8, 1922; *FP*, March 26, 1926, October 30, 1936; Campbell interview.

106. *Tribune*, January 23, 1923; *FP*, July 26, 1923, July 31, 1925, March 29, 1927, April 31, 1927, July 14, 1927; Campbell interview.

107. *Tribune*, May 30, 1925; Meighen Papers, p. 046119, clipping from *London Free Press*, July 21, 1925; King Papers, p. 99394, L.C. Moyer to E. Lapointe, September 30, 1925, pp. 103244–103246, King to Norris, November 23, 1925, p. 111037, William J. Donovan to King, January 9, 1926; Ramsay Cook (ed.), *The Dafoe-Sifton Correspondence 1919–1927* (Altona, MB: Manitoba Record Society, 1966), 213, Dafoe to Sifton, April 3, 1925.

108. See Kendle, Bracken, 63–65; Wardhaugh, *Mackenzie King and the West*, 132–34,144–47. The man who replaced Norris as Leader was H.A. Robson, and he proved surprisingly reluctant to join with the Progressives.

109. Kendle, *Bracken*, 63; King Papers, p. 63299, A.E. Hill to King, November 24, 1922, pp. 119178–119179, L.C. Moyer to King, January 23, 1926.

110. King Papers, p. 98358, L.C. Moyer to A. Haydon, August 25, 1925, p. 98359, A. Haydon to L.C. Moyer, August 26, 1925, p. 99393, L.C. Moyer to E. Lapointe, September 30, 1925, p. 99394, E. Lapointe to L.C. Moyer, September 30, 1925, p. 97179, King to C.A Dunning, September 14, 1925, pp. 99998–99999, Union St. Joseph du Canada to King, October 24, 1925, p. 107040, King to C.A. Stewart, September 14, 1925, p. 107612, Ligue D'Action Francaise to King, October 26, 1925, p. 107613, L.C. Moyer to Anatole Vanier, October 27, 1925, pp. 98076–98078, Société St. Jean-Baptiste to King, October 28, 1925, pp. 129737–129741, King to J.G. Gardiner, March 3, 1928; *FP*, October 1, 1925, October 6, 1925, October 12, 1925.

111. King Papers, pp. 112589–112591, A.B. Hudson to King, March 20, 1926, and King to Hudson, March 31, 1926, pp. 109492–109495, T.A. Burrows to King, May 29, 1926 and June 5, 1926, pp. 112140–112141, F.C. Hamilton to King, February 12, 1926, pp. 112159–112160, Hamilton to King, September 16, 1926, p. 112142, King to Hamilton, February 15, 1926, pp. 125586–125587, H.A. Robson to King, December 2, 1927, pp. 84458–84464, "Report of Thomas Taylor" on Liberal Party in Manitoba, December 15, 1927, pp. 129730–129735, J.G. Gardiner to King, January 17, 1928; *FP*, April 11, 1928; Deborah Anne Welch, "T. A. Burrows, 1857–1929: A Case Study of a Manitoba Businessman and Politician" (MA thesis, University of Manitoba, 1983), 130–31; PAM, Ralph Maybank Papers, MG14 B35, file 88, "Political Memo of 1926–27," 88–89, and memo of March 29, 1927.

112. *FP*, October 29, 1936, October 30, 1936, November 2, 1936; *Brandon Sun*, October 29, 1936.

113. See especially the previously mentioned column by Salem G. Bland, "The Divinely Ordained Occupation of Farming," GGG, November 20, 1918.

John Bracken

1922–1943

<small>ROBERT WARDHAUGH AND
JASON THISTLEWAITE</small>

John Bracken, 1922–1943

John Bracken first came to Manitoba in 1906 as a hard-working agronomist. After years of professional agricultural work, including a return to Winnipeg as principal of the Agricultural College in 1920, with no political experience he was chosen leader and therefore Premier of the United Farmers' government in 1922. By the time he resigned the premiership 20 years later, Bracken had transformed Manitoba politics into a peculiar brand of non-partisanship and coalition government—"Brackenism"—that changed the structure of politics in the province. He also led governments during the acquisition of jurisdiction over, and first serious exploitation of, its non-agricultural natural resources, managed the province through the catastrophic economic crisis of the Great Depression, and became the champion of both the province of Manitoba and the Prairie region in the quest for a new fiscal arrangement and a renewed federalism.

Early Life and Career

John Bracken was born on July 22, 1883 in Ellisville, in eastern Ontario's Leeds County. His parents, Ephraim and Alberta, named their first-born child after his pioneering Scottish great-grandfather who had immigrated to Canada shortly after the War of 1812. The family, of Scottish, Irish, and English origins, had one more son and three daughters in the following five years. In 1889 Ephraim moved the family to Seeley's Bay where he purchased a dairy farm. One of John's childhood memories was of a trip to nearby Kingston to attend the funeral of Prime Minister John A. Macdonald. Although Ephraim was a lifelong Conservative, his political beliefs and loyalties were never impressed upon his son. Instead, hard work and perseverance were, and John embraced responsibility at a young age and worked tirelessly for his family on the farm. Alberta Bracken, meanwhile, took pride in the quality and temperament of her children. She was a Methodist and believed they should grow up in an environment that instilled principles of temperance, respect, duty, and reliability. John was an impressive athlete and enjoyed playing many sports, but his greatest love was cycling, the sporting rage of the 1890s. His sisters remember being awakened long before first light to John sneaking down the stairs to race his bike along local roads, only to come back for a short nap before his chores started at 5:00 a.m.[1]

Alberta and Ephraim knew that their son had a good mind and they realized the value of education. Seeley's Bay had no high school but John was fortunate that his parents could afford to send him to Brockville Collegiate in September 1897. During his first term, however, the lure of team sports and the experience of being away from home took a toll on his grades. After some stern talk from his parents during the Christmas break, John refocused and prioritized his schooling. He realized that he needed to pass the tough Ontario matriculation exam in order to continue toward his grammar school studies and proceed to university. John felt confident heading into his exams that spring. A month later, he nervously searched for his name in the Brockville newspaper; he looked down the list but his name was not there. He had failed his exams. John was crushed but he showed few signs of disappointment upon his arrival home in September 1898. His parents did not question his test results; they knew their son was a determined and hard worker, and that ultimately he would prove successful, even if he had to learn some difficult lessons along the way.[2]

Meanwhile, John found that he enjoyed running the farm and he asked his father if he could manage the daily operations by himself. He wanted to make the Bracken farm the best in Leeds County and he became intrigued by the techniques and machinery of the new doctrines of scientific agriculture. He also learned of a two-year course offered at the Ontario Agricultural College (OAC) in Guelph. On September 13, 1902, at the age of 19, John enrolled in the program.[3]

John excelled and placed first in the Christmas exams. Following his second year, he wished to retake the matriculation exam in order to finish his final two years and earn a degree in Agriculture. He went back to Brockville Collegiate where, to his surprise, the headmaster informed him that he had in fact passed the exams. The newspaper had made a printing error. For six years John had internalized that failing grade. After two more years at OAC, he graduated in 1906 with an impeccable record.[4] Years later, Bracken reminisced about the valuable experience gained at OAC and the lessons he would later incorporate into his particular brand of politics: "It was there we learned how to take defeat like men and congratulate our more efficient competitor. It was there that organization was power."[5]

With a degree in agriculture, it did not take Bracken long to find employment. He was offered a job at the Seed Branch of the Department of Agriculture in Ottawa for $75 a month. Bracken would not stay in Ontario for long. He was offered a position with the Branch in Winnipeg, and in May 1906 he left for the West. Bracken was in charge of organizing wheat competitions and seed fairs. As his biographer, John Kendle, points out, "it was his baptism in administrative work and he soon found that he not only liked it but was good at it." Bracken quickly gained the respect of the Manitoba farming community. He was intelligent, conscientious, forthright, and frank.[6] Early in 1907 he was recruited by W.R. Motherwell, the minister of Agriculture in Saskatchewan, to become the new superintendent of fairs and institutes and secretary of the Saskatchewan Stock Breeders' Association. In pursuit of a "sound and stable agriculture," Bracken toured Saskatchewan for two years, educating farmers on better methods. "The land will produce forty bushels to the acre or it will produce ten; the difference in the production is you," he told his audiences.[7] The work demonstrated Bracken's methodical and well-organized approach to solving problems. He "attended to the smallest detail. His letters were businesslike and to the point. There were no flattering remarks or rhetorical flourishes. If anything, he was perhaps a little too austere. He was willing to be firm and decisive even if the news he conveyed was unpalatable." Bracken became a known commodity in his field. He was at ease talking with Prairie farmers and "his strongest asset was that he did not talk down to his farm audience."[8] In 1909 Bracken accepted a position with the new College of Agriculture at the University of Saskatchewan in Saskatoon. As professor of Field Husbandry, Bracken spent the next 10 years organizing the academic program, experimenting, writing, and lecturing. He became an expert on dry-land farming.

During his years at OAC, John had met Alice Bruce, who worked at the College as a typist. While employed by the Saskatchewan government, he returned to Guelph to marry Alice and the couple moved to Regina and then Saskatoon in 1910. The couple had four sons: John (1911), Doug (1913), Gordon (1916), and George (1918).

John Bracken may have been an expert on dry-land farming but he soon realized that agriculture on the Prairies presented difficulties that could not be solved simply through growing techniques. Farming was a business and a business had to be profitable.[9] Farmers were saddled with the results of the National Policy, including high tariffs, freight rates, and production costs. Nonetheless, he still held to his belief that responsibility for crop failure ultimately lay with the individual farmer. John Bracken formed few close friendships while in Saskatoon. "He was polite and friendly," Kendle notes, "but never gave the impression that he wished people to get too close. He kept his own counsel and generally went his own way. He was firm in his opinions, with a natural air of authority, and did not like to be challenged."[10]

In 1920 Bracken's expertise and experience earned him the position of principal of the Manitoba Agricultural College. He and Alice moved their family to Winnipeg, which had grown considerably since he had first come west in 1906. Established in 1905, the Agricultural College was an important institution in Manitoba thanks to its active extension work as well as regular programs, though it did suffer retrenchment during the post-war period. For Bracken, this would be the most readily fulfilling period of his working life. During his two years there, Bracken undertook a major agricultural survey of the province. He wrote two books: *Crop Production in Western Canada* (1920) and *Dry Farming in Western Canada* (1921).

The Move to Politics

Manitoba was in political and economic turmoil when the Brackens arrived in 1920. For the next two years the Liberals under Premier T.C. Norris struggled to hold office with a minority government and only 21 members in a 55-seat legislature. In July 1922 the Norris government resigned amid allegations of corruption and fraud. It was a difficult time to be in government. The nation was in the grip of a nasty recession following World War I and Manitoba shared in the suffering. Agricultural prices were abysmal and labour protest and urban problems, shown by the six-week General Strike in Winnipeg in 1919, were widespread. The provincial government was facing serious challenges.

Manitoba farmers were particularly dissatisfied with the provincial Liberal program that seemed to exclude their concerns. After the defeat of reciprocity in the federal election of 1911, farmers were increasingly dissatisfied with both the federal and provincial responses to their plight. They became disgruntled with the traditional party system and decided it was time to mobilize the growing momentum of the "agrarian revolt" into political action. In 1916 the Canadian Council of Agriculture published the Farmer's Platform. By 1919 the Farmer's Platform was heralded as a New National Policy. In Ottawa, Manitoban T.A. Crerar, the federal minister of Agriculture, resigned from the Borden Union government and formed a group of western progressives. This move opened the door for political candidates who rejected the party system and supported the New National Policy to run for federal office. Consequently, the Manitoba Grain Grower's Association, Saskatchewan Grain Growers, and the United Farmers of Alberta pledged support for any candidates willing to fight for the Farmers' Platform. In Manitoba the prospect of federal participation raised the question of farmers also entering provincial politics. The election victory of the United Farmers of Ontario in 1919 provided further incentive. By 1920 the Manitoba Grain Growers responded to their expanding membership and calls for action by changing the organization's name to the United Farmers of Manitoba (usually dubbed the UFM) and selecting candidates for the provincial election of that year.[11] The UFM rejected partisan politics and instead sought group, co-operative, and efficient government. The new party advocated the populist trinity of initiative, referendum, and recall. Each constituency was left to decide if it would run a UFM candidate and the party functioned with no overall leader. Premier Norris, who headed an activist and pro-agrarian government, did not regard the UFM as a serious threat and paid the political price. When the votes were tallied, the shape of Manitoba politics was altered dramatically. The Liberals won 21 seats, the Conservatives 7, the Labour party 11, and the Independents 4. To the surprise of the mainstream political parties, the UFM won 12 constituencies.[12]

For the next two years, the UFM refused to take on the role of official opposition, claiming that they represented the interests of their constituents and not a partisan party. When the Liberals lost a motion of censure, Norris was forced to call an election for July 29, 1922. By this point the UFM had become a formidable political force. While they were still without a leader, the Farmers had developed a progressive agrarian platform and an impressive grassroots organization. They were also successful at gaining support from the Winnipeg business community, which hoped a UFM government would be fiscally conservative.[13] The alliance between the Farmers and Winnipeg business proved a formidable political challenge for the other parties and on election night, the UFM won office with 24 seats. The Liberals won 7, the Conservatives 6, Labour 6, and Independents 8.[14] The 1922 election represented a political divide in the history of Manitoba. It abruptly put an end to an era dominated by party politics and commenced one that was "non-partisan, experimental, and pragmatic."[15]

When the telephone rang just after midnight on Friday, July 21, 1922, John and Alice Bracken had no idea how dramatically their life was about to change. On the line was W.R. Clubb, a newly elected member of the provincial legislature who represented new governing group—the United Farmers of Manitoba. Clubb asked Bracken to meet with the UFM Council about leading the Farmers in the legislature and, therefore, accept the mantle of Premier. The UFM also asked T.A. Crerer and Robert Hoey to consider interviewing for the premiership. A shocked Bracken reluctantly agreed to ponder the offer and then discuss it with the party at a meeting at the Odd Fellows Hall on Kennedy Street in Winnipeg at 10:00 a.m. the following day. While he did not plan to accept the offer, Bracken figured he should at least hear what the Farmers had to say. As president of the Manitoba Agricultural College, he could offer advice.

Crerar had only recently stepped down as leader of the National Progressive Party. He met the United Farmers at 9:00 a.m. on July 22, listened to their proposals, but declined. Hoey, the UFM secretary, also turned down the offer, leaving John Bracken as the last candidate for the job. Bracken's informal demeanour immediately appealed to the Farmers who were seeking a grassroots-type leader. Bracken talked with the 24 members of the party and listened to their platform. He then proceeded to outline the problems and challenges facing agriculture in Manitoba. To the assembled Farmers, Bracken spoke a language they could understand; it was not laden with political rhetoric, but instead offered a logical, step-by-step analysis of the task ahead for the new but inexperienced government. While sympathetic to the Farmers' movement, Bracken indicated that he did not believe he was the right man for the job.[16]

The UFM were impressed and agreed unanimously that Bracken was their man. After three more meetings, Bracken reluctantly agreed to accept the position. He was so non-partisan that he had never even cast a vote in Manitoba and yet he was being asked to lead a newly elected, inexperienced party, not to mention a province facing serious economic challenges. But Bracken was impressed by the Farmers. Their progressive nature represented the type of politics he could embrace. John Bracken was non-partisan and had no political experience, but at age 37 he was ambitious and he enjoyed new challenges. He did not want to see the UFM fail or their unique opportunity squandered. On July 21, at 5:20 p.m., John Bracken became leader of the United Farmers of Manitoba and the Premier of the province.[17]

Despite his lack of experience, Bracken's selection was generally well received in Manitoba. "Professor Bracken is confronted with a business task, calling for powers of organization, foresight, acumen and sagacity—the qualities of the administration and businessman," J.W. Dafoe commented in the *Manitoba Free Press*. "A highly competent agricultural expert has been placed at the head of affairs in a province which is in its wealth-producing activities, primarily agricultural."[18]

Premier Bracken

As the new Premier of Manitoba, John Bracken had three immediate priorities: appoint a cabinet, find himself a seat in the legislature, and develop a legislative agenda. For his cabinet, Bracken wanted a group of like-minded men who possessed a keen sense of businesslike organization. He chose Winnipeger Richard Craig as Attorney General, Duncan McLeod from Deloraine as Provincial Secretary, Neil Cameron from Minnedosa as Agriculture minister, W.R. Clubb, of Morris, as minister of Public Works, and F.M. Black, representing Rupertsland, as Provincial Treasurer. He took the Education portfolio for himself.[19] The old French-English/Catholic-Protestant feud, which had manifested itself in the School Question and then plagued politics in Manitoba for decades, temporarily disappeared with the selection of P.A. Talbot, the MLA for La Vérendrye, as Speaker.[20] Three northern constituencies had their elections deferred and Bracken chose to run in one of them—The Pas. Bracken promised an efficient administration that would reduce expenses, eliminate inefficient and wasteful services, focus on the development of natural resources, and "re-establish the faith of the people in public life and public officials."[21] While wheat was Manitoba's major export, the economy had to diversify and expand its mining base in particular. The by-election was held on October 5 and Bracken won handily.

Back in Winnipeg, the UFM had a bare majority with 28 seats. Bracken immediately set about restructuring the province's finances to alleviate the deficit, which at the time was costing the province $3,500 a day. The new session opened with a Speech from the Throne that referred to a new non-partisan era in Manitoban politics: "We are not here to play politics or to represent a single class but to get down to the serious business of giving this province an efficient government, and in that task we will welcome all the co-operation offered to us from the opposite side of the House."[22] This opening line remained Bracken's credo for the duration of his career. He immediately streamlined the civil service. His initiatives included a 2% income tax, new automobile license fees, a new gasoline tax, and a sinking fund for the gradual remission of the provincial debt. His tough reforms proved successful and Manitoba managed to produce a small surplus of over $133,000 in 1924, although higher international wheat prices helped relieve much of the debt.[23]

The public could admire the Bracken government's businesslike approach as well as its squeaky-clean image, free from partisan taint, but the lack of experience hurt. The rejection of party discipline and the emphasis on individual constituency representation were admirable traits but it was difficult to translate that idealism into a workable government. Bracken emphasized "team" but his team was filled with players who had rarely seen action. The Premier had to be patient in handling his caucus. While the government may have lacked experience, the opposition parties did not. Political veterans, such as Conservatives Fawcett Taylor, Sanford Evans, and John Haig, and Labourites such as John Queen, Fred Dixon, and William Ivens, were not about to give a group of political neophytes, who had somehow stumbled into government, an easy ride. If Bracken misstepped, his critics were ready to pounce.

Aside from the general state of the economy, three issues faced the new Bracken government: education, the Wheat Board, and the liquor referendum. Since prohibition had been introduced in 1919, illegal liquor production had overwhelmed provincial police. Bracken maintained that the issue should be free of partisan politics and approved a proposal by the Moderation League to hold a referendum on the introduction of government regulation of liquor sales. Although he personally supported prohibition, in 1923 a majority of voters supported the reintroduction of liquor sales under government control. The Liquor Control Act established a Government Liquor Commission to administer and sell alcohol. Profits from the sale of liquor materialized into a steady stream of revenue for the province in years to come. But the Act proved difficult to enforce and by 1927 views on drinking were becoming more liberal. Another referendum supported the sale of beer by the glass in public establishments as well as the sale of alcohol for home consumption. As the minister of Education, Bracken's next priority was the shaky financial base of Manitoba's sprawling locally-run school system. He appointed a Royal Commission under President Walter Murray of the University of Saskatchewan which recommended special grants in low-assessment districts, a minimum income for teachers, and consolidating school units from the more than 3,000 that had been created. In 1924 Bracken introduced legislation to prohibit the closure of any more schools.[24]

The possible revival of the Canadian Wheat Board posed the greatest test for Bracken during his first term. With the elimination of the board at the end of the war, Bracken was aware that national wheat marketing was a popular issue among western farmers. He was also aware, however, that the three Prairie provinces did not hold the same position on the issue. Manitoba relied less on wheat than Saskatchewan and Alberta, both of which favoured the scheme, and the Wheat Board was unpopular with the influential Grain Exchange crowd. The Premier had to be careful to avoid dividing his party's support between Winnipeg business interests, which opposed the bill, and southern Manitoban farmers, who were in favour. In 1922 the federal Liberal government of Mackenzie King passed legislation to create a new board, contingent upon the co-operation and granting of concurrent enabling powers by the Prairie provinces. Alberta and Saskatchewan granted the necessary powers. Bracken personally favoured a co-operative selling agency but he decided to allow a free vote in the legislature. The bill was defeated with six of Bracken's members voting against it.[25] With the failure of the Wheat Board, the farmers' organizations reverted to the novel idea of provincial wheat pools.

While the "free" vote in the legislature reflected Bracken's non-partisan approach, it also demonstrated that he was learning politics. The caucus was bitterly divided on the issue and a free vote allowed him to avoid the result being interpreted as a vote of non-confidence. This tactic, his biographer notes, revealed his "ingenuity for marrying his principles and his personal goals. It was a tactic that over the years many in Manitoba were to find both frustrating and infuriating."[26] According to Manitoba historian W.L. Morton, "popular-democratic rhetoric" of the UFM provided Bracken with the incentive for experimentation with parliamentary procedure and he took full advantage of it. Morton claims the result was "to reduce the legislature to an office of record of constituency opinion, and to divide the power hitherto vested in the Crown and the legislature between the Executive Council and the electoral districts of rural Manitoba."[27]

Bracken also addressed stagnated efforts to develop an effective provincial road system. In 1925 the government put major arterial highways under provincial jurisdiction, south from Selkirk to the border and west from Winnipeg to Brandon and Saskatoon. To compliment the government's work on roads, the Premier introduced legislation to complete the Hudson's Bay Railway to Flin Flon. By its completion in 1928, the line populated and firmly established Flin Flon as a model for economic development on the northern frontier.[28]

By 1925 the UFM government was in control of the legislature and the province's affairs. But the workload was straining the Premier. Bracken's doctors advised him to slow down but it was too late and "for the rest of his political days he was subject to bouts of exhaustion and discomfort." While Bracken had a firmer grip on his party, he maintained control through a quiet authoritarianism. He spoke surprisingly little in the legislature and when he did, his speeches were "dry and fact laden." Commentators noted that Bracken treated the legislature as if it were a schoolroom and he the schoolmaster: "It was a quietly arrogant, patronizing stance but not offensively so."[29]

The opposition parties were coming to realize that Bracken's stewardship was difficult to oppose. Some members of the provincial Liberal Party suggested a coalition with the UFM in order to unite the political centre and isolate the Conservatives. To Bracken, coalition was a practical means of ensuring effective and co-operative government while avoiding the pitfalls of partisanship. The old guard of the Liberal Party objected, however, and accused its younger members of collusion with the UFM. Liberal leader T.C. Norris was staunchly opposed unless he would become Premier. This "diehard" faction had the support of Premier Jimmy Gardiner's Liberal "machine" in Saskatchewan. Gardiner used his influence "to interfere in the Manitoba situation and create obstacles to any proposed fusion."[30] But a provincial coalition suited Liberal Prime Minister Mackenzie King's desires for co-operation between the Farmers and the Liberals in order to build support for the federal Liberal Party in Manitoba. If the Farmers were absorbed provincially, King believed he was assuring long-term support in the Prairies.[31] The Prime Minister pressured the provincial Liberal Party to co-operate with Bracken.

Bracken saw two particular benefits from such a coalition. He could fight the Conservatives through a united front and he could fill a crucial position in his cabinet. The Premier knew that his trusted advisor and ally, Richard Craig, was contemplating retirement and he believed that an influential Liberal replacement would lay the foundation for an alliance between the two groups. Bracken's plan, however, suffered from poor timing. He tried to convince Hugh Amos Robson, prominent Winnipeg lawyer and author of the Royal Commission that had inquired into the 1919 General Strike, to enter the government and take a cabinet position as Attorney General. Gardiner learned of this arrangement and convinced Robson that he should run for Liberal leader, which he successfully did in March 1927. Robson's victory temporarily bridged the division between the provincial Liberals.[32] Robson and Gardiner believed that the Bracken government was vulnerable and that the Liberals had an opportunity to reunite and gain office without losing their identity in a coalition.[33]

Premier Bracken announced a provincial election for June 28, 1927. A UFM election pamphlet boasted about "what may be accomplished when politics is divorced from the business affairs of the government." As one Liberal commented, "Bracken is going to be re-elected. They have given reasonably decent government. You can't say much against them." When the results were in, the UFM, by now usually dubbed Progressives, won the election, gaining one riding to pad their slim majority. The Conservatives rebounded with 15 seats, the Liberals 7, Labour 3, and Independents 1. Bracken won the contest on the message that the Farmers had paid off the debt and put Manitoba back on a "pay-as-you-go" system. The UFM had also successfully won the support of the Winnipeg business community which had come to respect and trust efficient and cautious administration, then labelled "Brackenism."[34] But the election also demonstrated that with the return of economic stability, some Manitoba voters were gradually drifting back to partisan groups.

Developing and Controlling Natural Resources

Bracken's second term as Premier before and after the onset of the Great Depression was dominated by economic issues. Despite his commitment to agriculture, the Premier was concerned with Manitoba's dependence on the wheat economy. He realized that for the province to diversify, it needed control over its natural resources. Since Manitoba entered Confederation in 1870, the federal government had maintained control over the province's resources to allow Ottawa to foster and develop a settlement policy. When Saskatchewan and Alberta joined Confederation in 1905, their resources were also withheld on the same basis. As time passed, however, the issue joined the tariff and freight rates in becoming a regional grievance. By 1911 negotiations between Ottawa and the Prairie provinces commenced over the inevitable transfer of resource control. The discussions became bogged down over the issue of a compensation package for the resources already used.

Bracken knew that Liberal Prime Minister Mackenzie King was sympathetic to the provincial position and accepted the "moral" basis of the West's grievance. During his first term the Premier negotiated with Ottawa but obtaining an acceptable agreement proved difficult.[35] As the province moved to open its northern frontier and confronted issues with pulpwood concessions, mineral development, water power, and rail accessibility, the lack of progress on the resource issue became increasingly embarrassing for Bracken.[36] The Premier grew frustrated with the negotiations with King and saw "no hope of settling anything" through further discussion.[37] Both Saskatchewan and Alberta were also frustrated by Ottawa's failure to reach a transfer agreement.

In the meantime, Bracken was involved in negotiations with the Winnipeg Electric Company (WEC) over a proposed site at Seven Sisters rapids on the Winnipeg River for a new hydroelectric plant. There were several complications in the development of the plant. The most problematic issue was that the property belonged to the federal government and could only be developed by the WEC if the site was transferred to the Manitoba government. In addition, in January 1928 the Bracken government committed itself to a policy of public ownership. But as the debate continued, it became clear to the Premier that public ownership would be unprofitable and inefficient. As a result, Bracken sought to gain provincial control over the site at Seven Sisters and then find a way to permit private development without facing political reprisals from opposition parties in the legislature.[38]

Dr. T.H. Hogg, chief hydraulic engineer of the Ontario Hydro-Electric Power Commission, was hired to advise Manitoba on the issue. Hogg issued his report on March 5, 1928, concluding that the government should pursue private development of the land with the Winnipeg Electricity Company while trying to secure a deal on electricity rates. Instead of immediately approaching the WEC and disclosing the results of Hogg's report, Bracken contacted Andrew McLimont, the president of the WEC, and asked how much it would cost to acquire the site and at what rate the WEC would offer electricity to the province. Although Bracken had already come to the conclusion that a hydroelectric plant should be privately developed by the WEC, he gave the impression that the province was still considering public ownership in order to improve his bargaining stance. The Premier's posturing paid off and the government was able to negotiate the lowest electric rates of any province in the country.

The stress of the negotiations took a toll on Bracken's health. He was seriously ill throughout the discussions, conducting some of them from his sick bed. The Premier suffered stomach problems later diagnosed as pernicious anaemia.[39] On March 20, 1928, following medical advice, Bracken left for a holiday in California. Upon returning, the Premier was faced with a crisis. Both Labour and Conservative MLAs accused him of mismanaging the Seven Sisters negotiations and of breaking his promises to implement public ownership of the site. Conservative leader Fawcett Taylor alleged that Bracken had flouted the decision of the House to uphold public ownership. He accused the government of abandoning its own commitment to public ownership and of selling out to private interests.[40] Most emphatically, Bracken was accused of deliberately avoiding a debate on the issue in the legislature.

The commotion in Manitoba led the federal government to delay the transfer of the site to the province and the WEC. Although Bracken was dismayed by the delay, he recognized that his party and the provincial Liberals shared common ground on the Seven Sisters transfer. Liberal leader Hugh Robson wrote to Prime Minister King that the Seven Sisters controversy, along with the delays in transferring Manitoba's natural resources, was a "great impediment to liberalism" in the province.[41] Bracken's argument to King underlined the Premier's strategy regarding group government. Delay, he claimed, "only adds to the prestige of the Labour Party ... it contributes to the disintegration of the Liberals, creates discontent among the progressives, encourages friction between Liberals and Progressives, and tends indirectly to the advantage of the Conservatives."[42] The Prime Minister desired a Liberal-Progressive coalition in Manitoba and realized that the sooner the natural resource issue was resolved, the sooner the coalition could become reality.

The possibility of a rejuvenated Liberal front in Manitoba was an important enough incentive for the Prime Minister to finally end Ottawa's "continuous procrastination" over the resource issue.[43] King knew that "national parties are federal in structure" and "local disputes would affect federal fortunes in Manitoba."[44] By 1928 the successful transfer of the natural resources, along with the site at Seven Sisters, was inextricably tied to fusion between the Manitoba Liberals and Bracken's Progressives. King's strategy included the appointment of former Premier T.C. Norris to the Board of the Railway Commission, thus removing a Liberal stalwart opposed to coalition.[45] King also told Saskatchewan Premier Jimmy Gardiner to stop interfering with Robson and the Manitoba Liberals. This paved the way for an agreement and by the spring of 1928 Robson agreed to work with Bracken. The goodwill between Liberals and Progressives also paved the way for successful negotiations regarding the transfer of the natural resources later that summer. In July Bracken convinced King to appoint a Royal Commission to examine the contentious subsidy issue which had long hampered resource negotiations. These efforts also resulted in the decision that the Liberals and Progressives would run a joint candidate, David McKenzie, in a by-election in the rural riding of Lansdowne to oust Norris, now the lone dissenter to a coalition. McKenzie would join Bracken's cabinet as minister of Natural Resources.[46]

Unfortunately for Bracken, his success with the Liberals was overshadowed by a scandal over the secretive nature of the negotiations between the government and the WEC. During the by-election, Conservative leader Fawcett Taylor alleged that in exchange for the Seven Sister's contract, the WEC had made financial contributions to the UFM. He went further, however. Amidst the attacks on the Bracken government for not allowing a debate and selling out to private interests, Taylor alleged that Bracken had been bought off. Taylor was convinced that at least $50,000 had exchanged hands and that high-profile members of the government were connected to the WEC. Taylor's accusation did not affect the outcome of the by-election, which the government won,[47] but the scandal took its toll on the Premier's fragile health. Bracken was in bed much of the time and at the end of November 1928, he checked into a sanatorium in Michigan where he spent the next two months recovering.[48] Bracken returned to a political storm. A Royal Commission was announced on January 29, 1929 to investigate the Conservative charges.[49]

Throughout February Bracken faced intense pressure to either resign or call an election. He did neither but the Premier did accept the resignations of W.R. Clubb and W.J. Major to relieve the pressure. The two cabinet ministers had approached Bracken and told him that they had purchased shares in the WEC during the negotiations. The scandal dominated the political scene in Manitoba, receiving extensive daily coverage in the press: "The Manitoba public sat enthralled, although somewhat bemused, with the goings-on in Winnipeg. Nothing as exciting or as full of fury, pomposity, rhetoric, and high comedy had happened in Manitoba since the days of the Roblin government." The Premier testified in front of the inquiry that the actions of his cabinet members were unwise but they in no way interfered with the negotiations or ensuing contract. In the end the inquiry concluded that "Bracken and his cabinet were completely exonerated of any corruption or dishonesty in connection with the Seven Sisters power agreement, and all the assertions that Taylor has made proved unfounded."[50] Finally, on May 16, the legislature ratified the bill to lease the Seven Sisters to the WEC. Bracken even managed to bring Clubb and Major back into cabinet following the confessions from a Conservative and the Speaker of the House that they had also bought stock in WEC.[51] Despite 18 months of political hell, the Bracken government laid the foundations for the Manitoba power system while also taking important steps towards diversifying the economy.

The Seven Sisters scandal also convinced Bracken that fusion with the Liberals was now necessary even though Robson was highly critical of Bracken throughout the affair. When Clubb and Major resigned, the Premier commenced negotiations with Robson to enter the cabinet as Attorney General. With pressure mounting from Prime Minister King, the Manitoba Liberals held a convention on March 19 to consider coalition. At the convention, Robson opposed coalition but the Liberal Party did appoint a negotiating committee. The Liberals would support the government in the legislature.

Meanwhile, Manitoba's economy did relatively well from 1925 to 1930. In 1929 the Hudson's Bay Railway reached the port of Churchill and within months the first bushels of Manitoba No. 1 wheat were crossing the Atlantic.[52] The mining industry in the north was vastly expanded, creating 1,500 full time jobs in the new mining towns of Flin Flon,

Sherridon, Bissett, and Wadhope, which also created an additional 6,000 to 7,000 service and retail jobs. Moreover, efforts to improve Manitoba's hydroelectricity industry paid dividends, employing another 1,200 workers at the newsprint paper mill in Pine Falls. In total it is estimated that 35,000 jobs were created during Bracken's second term.[53] The Premier's diversification policies were so successful "that the value of industrial production exceeded that of agricultural production."[54]

In June 1929 Bracken travelled to Ottawa to attend the final proceedings of the Turgeon Commission on the natural resource transfer. The successful transfer served as the crowning achievement of Bracken's second term. On December 14, 1929 the agreement was signed and the resources were formally transferred to Manitoba. The province also secured a compensation package worth $4.7 million. Immediately following the Commission in June, Bracken left Canada for a five-month European vacation: "The province was in sound financial shape, there was no important legislation pending, and all the major issues of the previous seven years had been resolved."[55] If he was fatigued, however, the onset of the Great Depression would only place further strain on the Premier.

Governing in Economic Depression

The Great Depression crippled the Prairie West. Low prices, collapsed markets, drought, crop disease, and insects destroyed the wheat economy. Long lines of destitute, unemployed workers crowded the streets of the cities and demanded government aid. John Bracken held to his belief that regardless of the circumstances, individual hard work and perseverance were the keys to success and prosperity. While his faith in the work ethic was not shaken during the years of the Depression, his views of the state's role in the economy and society were. Bracken's frustrating and humiliating confrontations with R.B. Bennett's Conservative government in Ottawa convinced him that the Canadian federal structure created at the time of Confederation in 1867 was proving unworkable in the midst of Depression.

As Premier and Provincial Treasurer, Bracken was responsible for Manitoba's economic strategy during the difficult years of the Depression. The plight of agriculture was of most concern in the early years of the crisis. The Premier believed that increasing tariff levels imposed by Ottawa along with the decreased international demand for wheat would only compound the situation for Manitoba farmers. The old National Policy of John A. Macdonald had imposed high tariff levels to the detriment of agriculture and the Prairies. "The West does not ask for sympathy," Bracken claimed, "only for understanding and a frank and thorough examination of the facts. It asks only for an equally frank and equally thorough and truly National Policy—one aimed to cope with the Western situation in the best interests of Canada as a whole."[56] The solution was to find markets for wheat but this could only be accomplished with the aid of the federal government. In July 1930, the Tories came to power in Ottawa and Bracken realized that manufacturing Ontario was the base of Conservative support. Federal economic policy, therefore, would likely discriminate against Prairie farmers in favour of eastern industrialists. Manitoba's relationship with Ottawa was likely to become strained. Bracken repeatedly demanded a compensation package from Ottawa that reflected the discriminatory effect higher international tariffs had on farmers.

Although he requested federal intervention, he maintained faith in the market and told provincial creditors that regardless of aid from Ottawa, Manitobans would "roll up their sleeves. Tighten our belts. Loosen our coats. Make ourselves more efficient [and] outside the question of markets we shall have to save ourselves."[57] Hard work and co-operation, however, were not enough to save the wheat pools. In February 1930 the pools could no longer guarantee their wheat prices. In order to prevent the banks from forcing the pools to sell their grain, the governments of the three Prairie provinces agreed to guarantee the pool prices. No one expected prices to keep falling. By 1932 the main market price fell to 34¢ a bushel, the lowest in 300 years. As Kendle explains, "the pools were dead and the western provinces had to meet their obligations."[58]

Manitoba also needed to address the growing problem of urban unemployment. Indeed, Bracken would come to lead the provinces in pushing the federal government for aid. Bracken realized that the local municipalities had no capacity to deal with the issue of unemployment relief. By September 1930 over 4,000 single men needed daily meal and bed tickets, and over 2,000 families required relief in Winnipeg. The federal government responded with the Unemployment Relief Act that pledged $20 million, of which Manitoba received less than $2 million.[59] Bracken believed that Ottawa shared in the costs of unemployment because federal immigration policies were at the root of much of the problem. Bennett's relief policies were contingent on the municipalities matching and even doubling Ottawa's contribution. Bracken realized the result would be massive debt. Under constant pressure from Bracken, the Prime Minister retreated and agreed to reduce the rural municipalities' commitment. The federal government grudgingly increased its responsibility to relief through the funding of public works projects, such as bridges in Winnipeg and rural roads. But Bracken realized that matching dollar for dollar with Ottawa would not get the province out of debt or depression.

By 1932 the financial situation in Manitoba was dire. The wheat pools were bankrupt and the province was forced to pay out over $3 million to cover the losses to farmers. The problems increased as Manitoba's credit dried up and federal relief was devoted to debt payments. Bracken urged loan and credit institutions to co-operate with farmers and demonstrate an appreciation of the desperate situation.[60] The Premier's response to Manitoba's financial distress focussed on the maintenance of essential services through manipulation of the tax regime. He repealed the child welfare tax and soldier's relief tax, and introduced new taxes on liquor, cigarettes, cigars, and tobacco. His most radical policy initiative was to increase personal income taxes. This move included uniform reductions in tax exemptions for all tax brackets and a universal income tax increase of 0.5%. Bracken explained that "the conditions demand rational treatment, the courage to make unpopular decisions, a sacrifice on the part of many, and tolerance on the part of all."[61] The Premier's response was consistent with his personal beliefs. It was restrained and conservative even if it pushed for intervention.[62]

But Manitoba's economic plight only worsened. The province was having difficulty floating loans both in Canada and abroad. The British decision to abandon the gold standard and Ottawa's decision to maintain the Canadian dollar against depreciation made it impossible for Manitoba to meet its maturing obligations. Again, Bracken had to turn to Prime Minister Bennett for aid. The Premier also had to request more money to cover relief expenditures. The situation was desperate. The province was $683,000 short of meeting its relief commitments and required $3.5 million in overdraft privileges. Maturing obligations from the major banks were falling due early in 1932. Bracken believed that Bennett was playing politics and delaying helping the province in order to bolster the provincial Tories.[63]

John Bracken decided that his party needed a new mandate if it was to deal with the challenges of the Depression. The emergency, he argued, necessitated group government. It was no time for the petty squabbles of partisan politics. He called for a union with Conservatives, Liberals, and Labourites. Bracken realized that the Conservative and Labour parties would balk. With Robson gone to the Manitoba Court of Appeal, the path to fusion with the Liberals was clear. He received some help from T.A. Crerar, who sent a letter to Liberal Leader Murdoch Mackay requesting coalition. At the Liberal convention held on January 12, 1932, delegates overwhelmingly accepted coalition with Bracken. The Premier now had the strongest slate of candidates under his leadership since first entering politics. It also left the provincial Liberal party in shambles with "diehards" running separate candidates in some ridings.[64] In May, Liberals J.S. McDiarmid, Ewen McPherson, and Murdoch Mackay entered Bracken's cabinet.[65]

Throughout the election campaign in the summer of 1932 Bracken gave some of his most impressive speeches. He argued that the Depression was not a time to debate the nuances of financial policy or such issues as public versus private ownership. Rather it was a time when the leaders of Manitoba had to commit all their energy and resources to combat the economic crisis. "The only political platform I have," Bracken claimed, "is whatever is best for Manitoba, not just for farmers, not just for city people, but all people without respect of class or creed."[66] The Liberal-Progressive strategy, however, was to attack Bennett's Conservatives in Ottawa. And these attacks successfully disarmed Bracken's major political opponents in Manitoba—the provincial Tories. While the Premier claimed to be opposing "petty party politics, his criticism of the federal Conservatives, and by extension the provincial party, proved highly effective."[67] In the election of June 16, 1932, voters gave Bracken's coalition 38 seats, a strong majority. The Conservatives won 20, the Labour Party 5, and the Independents 2.[68] At a time when provincial governments were being decimated across Canada as a result of the Depression, Bracken manipulated the popular vision of a non-partisan coalition to hold his government together and to make it even stronger.

Coalition Government

Emboldened by a majority, Premier Bracken continued to look for ways to cut spending and improve the province's financial situation. This would prove difficult as Manitoba suffered six consecutive crop failures in which its net value of production was little more than half of what it had been in the late 1920s. In addition, the city of Winnipeg led the municipalities in bearing the heaviest relief burden and by 1936 it had borrowed $3.5 million from the province. While the Bennett government lectured Bracken on fiscal restraint, the Premier could simply throw up his hands in frustration. Immediately after the election, Bracken further slashed cabinet and civil service salaries. But Ottawa ceased lending money to the western provinces to cover direct relief costs. Bracken indicated repeatedly that the result would be provincial bankruptcy. It was becoming nearly impossible for Manitoba to borrow money. The province had maturities worth over $12 million scheduled to fall due in late 1932 and 1933.[69]

Bracken's relationship with Bennett deteriorated even further in 1933. The Prime Minister warned that if the province did not adjust its financial management and find new sources of capital, a financial controller under federal jurisdiction would be appointed. This letter shook Bracken. In response, he summoned the opposition Conservative Party for consultations on the budget and rumours circulated about another coalition. The budget of 1933 included a reduction in government expenditures by $650,000 and a 2% income tax on all salaries and earnings, which at the time was the highest in North America. The objective was to reduce the deficit from $2.65 million to $500,000. Despite the uproar in the legislature, Bracken's tough approach proved successful. By 1935 not only was the Manitoba budget balanced, but the federal government was so impressed that it decided to help Manitoba negotiate with the banks over the maturing obligations of provincial loans.[70] John Bracken's government had not only survived the Depression, it had actually strengthened its position.

The Depression challenged Bracken's views of government, order, and civil society but his faith in the market economy and in political stability never wavered.[71] Despite the desperation of the Depression, Bracken did not believe the crisis led naturally to disorder. He assumed and expected people to maintain the same balanced and orderly approach as himself. He expected them to control their responses, analyze the source of the problems, work to solve them, be patient with the solutions, and sacrifice to achieve positive results. Bracken was uncomfortable with confrontation and believed that rarely did it prove productive or effective. As a result, "his record, on occasions when he had to face a challenge from those of different ideological persuasion, was not a happy one." When over 500 farmers organized by the Farmers' Unity League marched on Winnipeg in 1932, Bracken was unsympathetic and accused them of being communist pawns. The Flin Flon Strike of 1934 demonstrated that Bracken, as with most members of the governing elite, "too quickly assumed that all criticism and questioning were the work of agitators or communists." Bracken was relieved in July 1935 when Bennett halted the relief camp workers' On-to-Ottawa Trek in Regina, rather than allowing it to reach Winnipeg. Perhaps not surprisingly, in 1936 the Premier was burned in effigy by a procession of the urban unemployed.[72]

Manitoba emerged in surprisingly good fiscal condition from the worst ravages of the Depression. But according to Kendle, "the drastic cuts in capital and current expenditures severely limited the programme of the government, and even more than usual the legislature became a glorified municipal council concerned with good housekeeping and administrative measures."[73] Bracken surprised the electorate, the opposition parties, and even his own members when he called a snap election in the summer of 1936. The Premier prepared a 400-page manifesto that explained the difficulties his government faced in maintaining legitimacy while trying to implement a "Manitoban new deal." He held his traditional line that hard work, perseverance, and businesslike administration would prevail.[74] As the *Winnipeg Tribune* noted, it was based on Bracken's proven technique of "plodding good sense."[75]

The political situation in 1936 was different from any Bracken had previously faced. The emergence of the Social Credit Party and the Co-operative Commonwealth Federation (CCF) posed new threats to divide the progressive vote in Manitoba. Bracken's government had been in power for 14 years and was perceived as representing the status quo. The winds of change inevitably threaten governments in power for long periods of time. The choice of the election date was also bewildering. It was held on July 27, when the harvest and holiday seasons were in full swing. The results of the election reflected these factors—the government was reduced to 23 seats. The Conservatives, now under Errick Willis, increased their seat total to 16, the united CCF and Independent Labour Party (ILP) won 8, and the Social Credit party picked up 5. Faced with a minority government, a shocked Bracken now attempted to form a coalition with the Conservatives. He promised that he would resign in two years, allowing Willis take over the reigns of government. The Conservative leader was willing to consider the proposal but his party was opposed. The Social Credit group, however, announced that they would support the Bracken government in return for an economic survey of the province.[76] Amongst the new cabinet were two future Premiers— Stuart Garson and Douglas Campbell. Bracken was holding on to office but his grip had never been so tenuous.

Remaking Federalism

In 1937 Bracken's agenda was dominated by negotiations with the federal government (again led by the Liberals under Mackenzie King) over debt restructuring. At a meeting of the National Finance Committee, Bracken made a speech detailing a plan for the dominion and provinces to unite and agree on a "secure adjustment of interest rates" for provincial and municipal bonds. Interest payments had plagued the efforts of Manitoba to locate financing for its bonds. By late 1936 both Manitoba and Saskatchewan were close to default on several maturing bank loans and Alberta had already declared bankruptcy. Bracken's argument convinced Prime Minister King to ask the newly created Bank of Canada to review Manitoba's finances.[77] The review was completed by February 11, 1937. It concluded that although Manitoba and Saskatchewan failed to use the windfall from high wheat prices between 1926 and 1929 to diversify their economies, "the Manitoba government has made strong and commendable efforts to keep its budget and avoid unnecessary increases in debt, by imposing taxation on a scale at least as high as that of any other province in Canada, and of restricting expenditures as far as it was possible to go without curtailing services to an extent which would not have been in the public interest."[78]

The Bank's report pleased Bracken but more importantly it emphasized the depths to which Manitobans had suffered during the Depression. There was no room for additional taxes; relief expenses continued to cripple the provincial treasury; debt refunding proposals were unrealistic; revenues were not adequate or insufficiently elastic "to enable the province to bear the burdens which modern practices of government and the force of depression have placed upon it."[79] The federal cabinet met for less than an hour before deciding it was necessary to appoint a Royal Commission to re-evaluate the entire federal-provincial relationship in Canada.[80] On August 14, 1937 Prime Minister King announced that the Royal Commission on Dominion-Provincial Relations would commence hearings in Winnipeg on November 29, 1937. Meanwhile, Manitoba would receive $750,000 in temporary aid from Ottawa.

Bracken was convinced that the Royal Commission was essential to review the entire dominion-provincial relationship. He argued as early as 1929 that the federal arrangement unfairly burdened the provinces with the fiscal load of the municipalities, and from his experience during the Depression, he realized that this burden could bankrupt Manitoba. Bracken rejected a provincial or regional solution and repeatedly emphasized that the problem was "a result of the Dominion-Provincial relationship determined at Confederation."[81] The Rowell-Sirois Commission would ultimately "re-examine the economic and financial basis of Confederation and of the distribution of legislative powers in the light of the economic and social developments of the last seventy years." The scope of inquiry was immense, including over 427 briefs, 10,702 pages of evidence and hearings in 10 cities across the country during 1937 and 1938. Accordingly, Bracken immediately set about putting together Manitoba's economic case since 1870 and announced an economic survey of the province. The problems were clear: "One-tenth of the province was unemployed, wealth production had been halved, young people were without employment opportunities, and agriculture had been bankrupted by economic and climatic forces." As such, Bracken argued, it was now time for a "new deal." The most compelling argument for restructured dominion subsidies for Manitoba was the remarkable reduction in federal support to the province—from 88% of total revenue in 1875 to 12% in 1936. Stuart Garson, one of Bracken's cabinet ministers and the Manitoba representative at the commission hearings, argued that it was necessary for a "national solution by national instruments upon a national scale."[82]

Throughout 1938 Bracken campaigned across the Prairies to build support for the Royal Commission. He echoed Garson's call for a national solution and a "new deal" for Canada. He called for a compensation package to be offered to the West in return for carrying the burden of Confederation.[83] The present distribution of taxation fields had proven inadequate. Premier Mitchell Hepburn of Ontario was not impressed. He argued that the West's economic difficulty was not a national problem but rather local in origin.[84] Premier Hepburn and Premier Maurice Duplessis of Quebec withdrew from further proceedings in the summer of 1938. Moreover, Alberta under Social Credit Premier William Aberhart broke regional solidarity by refusing to appear before the Commission. As a consequence the concluding sessions in the fall of 1938 were dominated by the other "have-not" provinces. Nonetheless, Bracken found opportunity to defend the western position and respond to Hepburn's comments. He employed a team strategy that included speeches from Garson as well as University of Chicago economist Jacob Viner, hired by the Manitoba government as a consultant for the Commission. Both men stripped away Hepburn's political rhetoric, revealing an empty criticism, void of statistical analysis and ignorant of the tariff's economic discrimination towards the West. Viner's analysis of the impact of the tariff was a coherent and analytical demonstration that the Prairie provinces had suffered unduly relative to the rest of the nation.[85]

John Bracken concluded Manitoba's case with a critique of Hepburn's argument that the fiscal problems of the West were local in origin. Despite Bracken's often dry and fact-laden oratory, he engaged Hepburn with a lively response that challenged anyone to prove that the wheat problem had originated in the Prairies. Bracken "agreed with Hepburn that governments should live within their incomes. And western Canada could do that if, having sold its products in the competitive market of the world, it could buy in the same markets. But that, unfortunately, was not the case. It sold in a low market and bought in a protected market to the advantage of Ontario." As Kendle correctly notes, "Manitoba's brief turned out to be the most comprehensive and best argued of all those submitted."[86] The Rowell-Sirois Commission, with *Winnipeg Free Press* editor J.W. Dafoe as one of the commissioners, resulted in a remarkably astute assessment of the major challenges facing Canadian federalism. Unfortunately, the recommendations were to be lost amid the upheavals of World War II.

The Commission hearings elevated Bracken's national status. While a defender of his province and region, he declared himself a strong federalist.[87] As the *Tribune* observed, "on its face the record shows that Bracken is beginning to emerge from the cocoon of political provincialism into the larger statesmanship of the national field."[88] The issue of the Wheat Board, re-established in 1935, and the larger issue of wheat marketing provided Bracken a regional and national audience in the late 1930s. He urged national action to save the agricultural industry. In particular he called for major tariff reductions and assured minimum prices.[89] Bracken's new status, and favourable impression on Prime Minister King, helped secure a compromise price for wheat at 70¢ a bushel in 1939.

While deliberations over the Rowell-Sirois Commission continued, the world's attention turned towards Europe. Germany invaded Poland on September 1, 1939 and two days later, Great Britain and France declared war. A week later, Canada declared war on Germany. Bracken's government, meanwhile, continued to serve as the loudest voice urging implementation of the Rowell-Sirois Report. When it was released in May 1940, it called for Ottawa to assume provincial debts and relief costs in return for control over the provinces' personal income, corporation, and succession taxes. Most importantly for Bracken it called for a national adjustment grant to compensate the provinces. The Premier was convinced that the Report vindicated his province and all it had suffered. He pushed for a conference to move toward implementation but Mackenzie King responded that consideration of Rowell-Sirois would have to wait until the end of the war.[90] Bracken was disappointed and frustrated. He was briefly optimistic when a dominion-provincial conference to discuss the recommendations was called in January 1941. Implementation was scuttled, however, when Premiers Mitch Hepburn of Ontario, William Aberhart of Alberta, and Duff Pattullo of British Columbia condemned the Report as a tool of the federal government. Bracken realized that the dominion would likely invade provincial tax fields to support the war effort without offering compensation. As anticipated, in 1942 the tax-rental agreements stipulated that the provinces surrender certain tax fields for one year beyond the end of the war. Manitoba would remain one of the few voices calling for a return to Rowell-Sirois and its proposed system of unconditional grants to the provinces. The post-war era, however, would take Canadian federalism in a different direction and the momentum of the Commission was lost. Bracken, along with Garson, never stopped believing that a genuine opportunity to fix the problems and bring balance to Canadian federalism had been dissipated.

A Wartime Government

By late 1940 Bracken believed that if there was ever a time when stable, efficient, and group government was needed, it was during wartime. With no consultation with his cabinet or caucus, Bracken initiated talks with the other parties. He planned on replacing members of his cabinet with representatives of the other parties. The scheme would only go forward if all the parties agreed to co-operate.[91] The Premier wrote to the party leaders, reminding them that he "had never looked upon party politics in provincial affairs with any favour."[92] In the Manitoba legislature all three parties agreed to form a coalition with Bracken's government, in return for two Conservatives and one CCF-ILP member entering cabinet. Two other members would be brought in as ministers without portfolio. S.J. Farmer of the CCF-ILP became minister of Labour, James McLenaghen of the Conservatives became minister of Health and Public Welfare, while Conservative Alex Welch and Social Credit Norman Turnbull became ministers without portfolio. The cabinet increased in size to 12 members. Bracken realized that for the parties to reject his offer of a non-partisan coalition during wartime was to court political suicide. "Bracken may have been an idealist," Kendle notes, "but he was also an astute political realist. He had boxed his political opponents."[93]

Bracken's new coalition government faced the electorate on April 22, 1941. Not surprisingly, with no opposition parties and partisanship effectively muzzled, it was the most low-key election in Manitoba's history, "unmatched for brevity and serenity."[94] Only 18 constituency contests out of 55 took place and Bracken spoke a mere eight times. His platform consisted of the implementation of Rowell-Sirois, the need for post-war planning, and a fair deal for agriculture. The coalition easily maintained power by winning 50 seats.[95] He had now been Premier for almost 19 years, longer than any politician in the British Commonwealth.

John Bracken had focused on dominion-provincial relations for six long years. The failure of Rowell-Sirois to resolve long-standing problems facing the Canadian federal structure was exceedingly frustrating. Kendle argues that this frustration, combined with his elevated status as champion of the Prairie West, led Bracken to become restless with the arena of provincial politics and to consider entering the federal realm. While true to an extent, this interpretation is exaggerated in order to explain his future decisions. As Kendle admits, "Bracken harboured no federal political ambitions" and was not considering federal politics until he was suddenly faced with a very surprising offer.[96]

A National Party Leader

On November 3, 1941 former Conservative Prime Minister, and now Senator, Arthur Meighen travelled to Winnipeg and met Bracken at the legislative buildings. Meighen's arrival surprised the Premier but the reason for his trip was cause for even greater shock. Meighen asked Bracken whether he would consider letting his name stand for the leadership of the federal Conservative Party. As a progressive and a long-time opponent of the provincial Tories, not to mention the federal government of R.B. Bennett, John Bracken was not an obvious choice. Meighen believed, however, that with the growing popularity of the CCF in the cities, the rural vote was fertile ground for the Conservatives. Realizing that Bracken was recognized as a spokesman for western Canada and increasingly a critic of the King government, Meighen believed Bracken was a suitable candidate.[97] There was little time to waste because nominations had to be submitted at the general party meeting by November 7, only four days hence.

Bracken was surprised by the offer and, while he did not immediately turn it down, he was not enthusiastic. He told Meighen that he was a poor public speaker and would be a disappointment in the federal arena. After meeting again with Meighen and discussing the issue only with Garson, Bracken was left to ponder his decision. Meighen departed for Ottawa to attend the nomination meeting. He realized that despite the Premier's decision, Bracken's nomination would not be an easy sell to party stalwarts. Facing a groundswell in favour of his own candidacy, Meighen phoned Bracken a couple of days into the convention and told him that his nomination would not be accepted regardless.[98] Bracken was relieved but the offer had piqued his curiosity and ambition. Under considerable pressure from the party, Arthur Meighen accepted the leadership of the federal Conservative Party. His tenure, however, would be short-lived.

By 1942 the Liberal government in Ottawa was plunged into heated debate over conscription. Japan's entry into the war prompted the Manitoba government, led by Bracken, to call for conscription.[99] When the King government responded with its 1942 plebiscite, Bracken called it the "crowning indignity."[100] Increasingly, the Manitoba Premier found himself infuriated by Mackenzie King's vacillating brand of politics. But the Prime Minister's plebiscite outmanoeuvred the Conservatives. When Meighen lost a critical by-election in York South and therefore the opportunity to enter Parliament, his hold on the Conservative leadership slipped.[101] The defeat reflected the difficulties faced by a party in desperate need of remaking itself. Not only did the issue of Conservative leadership need to be addressed but the party's entire platform needed serious reform.

On August 19 Meighen wrote to Bracken and advised him that the Conservatives were holding a policy conference at Port Hope, Ontario, later that month. He hoped the Manitoba Premier would consider the leadership of the party. Bracken took two weeks to reply. He indicated that he would meet with Meighen but that he had no desire to leave Manitoba or to enter federal politics "for any party."[102] While Bracken did not attend the Port Hope conference in September, he called the new Conservative platform "more modern and progressive than any previously associated with the party."[103] The conference called for conscription, a new agricultural policy, collective bargaining, low-cost housing, and improved unemployment insurance and old-age pension schemes. A leadership convention was set for December 9–11 in Winnipeg. Those in the party who favoured the Port Hope proposals now set their sights on John Bracken. Meighen, meanwhile, focused on tweaking the Manitoba Premier's well-known sense of duty and responsibility. When Bracken took the national spotlight in November by criticizing the federal Liberal policy on conscription, the choice seemed logical. Even Bennett now agreed that his old nemesis would be a good choice to coalesce the anti-King forces, the rural and agricultural vote, and the anti-CCF forces.[104]

If John Bracken was going to abandon his secure position as Premier of Manitoba, accept a partisan job that he had not wanted, and take over the leadership of a troubled party, it would be on his own terms. Bracken needed assurances that at the leadership convention, the party would be presented as changing its platform rather than himself presented as a convert to Conservatism. In particular, he wanted the name of the party changed to reflect its modernization. In a letter to Meighen, Bracken suggested a new name—the Progressive Conservative Party. On December 9 at the convention in Winnipeg, Bracken's proposal was read to the delegates and met with immediate furor. The motion for a vote on the name change caused such an uproar that it was postponed until a new leader was chosen.

The candidates' speeches took place that evening. The Manitoba Premier was now thoroughly befuddled. If he was going to contest the leadership, it would have to be without his desired preconditions. Just as when he first entered politics in 1922, Bracken withheld his decision until the very last minute. The deadline was 8:00 p.m. but by five minutes to the hour the delegates still did not know whether Bracken would contest the leadership. Tension mounted as the deadline loomed. When Bracken finally appeared with only seconds to spare and began moving towards the stage, the crowd jumped to its feet.[105] Voting took place the next day and Bracken won on the second ballot, defeating such rival candidates as H.H. Stevens, Howard Green, and John Diefenbaker. After his acceptance speech, the delegates endorsed the name change to the Progressive Conservative Party.

Stuart Garson, Bracken's Provincial Treasurer, took over as Premier of Manitoba on January 8, 1943. While Bracken's decision was generally supported, many wondered whether the marriage of the non-partisan Premier to the federal Conservative Party could succeed. Mackenzie King had come to respect Bracken as Premier of Manitoba, and appreciated his logical and practical mind. The Prime Minister knew, however, that Bracken was now entering a very different political situation. "Were I wishing to see the Conservative party thrown into utter confusion," King commented, "and the worst possible choice made, and one that would give me the least possible trouble, I would hope that Bracken might be chosen."[106] King did not believe that Bracken was truly a Conservative nor did he buy the attempt to modernize the party through a name change.[107]

Bracken had a difficult task ahead of him: his party was divided and without direction. With only 40 seats to the Liberals 184, the Conservative Party was in its weakest state ever. The federal organization was near collapse and there was not one Conservative provincial government holding office in the nation. He himself had never experienced the role of opposing a government. The "Port Hope Conservatives" who supported Bracken's style of progressivism believed it was time to move the party toward the new social order that was proving so successful to the CCF and soon the Liberals. The "Torontonian old guard," including influential Ontario Premier George Drew, wanted to maintain the status quo and defend Canada's position within the Commonwealth while favouring low taxes and decreased state intervention.[108] The "old guard" also rejected Bracken's western populist and grassroots brand of politics. Yet the main reason he was chosen to lead the party was based on the hope that he would rekindle Tory fortunes in the West. In the 1940 federal election, the Conservatives won only four seats in British Columbia, two in Saskatchewan, one in Manitoba, and none in Alberta. The region was disgruntled with the Liberals and the time seemed opportune. It was here that Bracken would have to deliver in order to silence his critics.

Bracken decided not to seek a by-election seat in Parliament, to the surprise of his party and the delight of the Liberals. The party would remain handicapped as long as the leader was not present in the House. Instead he followed his populist instincts and travelled the country in an attempt to gain a national perspective and profile. He focused on attacking King's handling of the war, particularly the conscription issue. The task often proved difficult because King continually pointed to Bracken's absence from Parliament. After the CCF's electoral victory in Saskatchewan in 1944, and the party's success in the first national opinion polls, the King Liberals effectively undercut socially-progressive policy initiatives by embracing a series of proposals including family allowances and old age pensions. This manoeuvre also took the wind out of Bracken's sails. It is usually argued that the Liberal Green Book proposals stole the CCF thunder; in fact it also stole the thunder of Bracken's Progressive Conservatives. Bracken also alienated party fortunes in Quebec with his strong stance in favour of conscription and by suggesting that the province had "borne a lesser burden in human sacrifices of the war."[109] Bracken was strongly convinced about the ineffectiveness of Liberal military policies, particularly after a trip in late 1944 to inspect Canadian troops in Europe.[110] But by taking such a strong stance on the issue of military conscription, Bracken firmly aligned his party with the Tory "old guard," making it difficult to make inroads into either the West or Quebec. Bracken was not building new political territory for the Conservatives as planned.

And the 1945 federal election results reflected this reality, representing the first real failure in the political career of John Bracken. The Liberals won 127 seats, the Progressive Conservatives won 68, the CCF won 29, and the Social Credit won 13. Even though the PCs gained 28 seats, including Bracken's election in Manitoba's Neepawa riding, expectations were much higher.[111] It was becoming clear that Bracken was better suited to the non-partisan tradition he had created in Manitoba. Most of the party hierarchy considered Bracken's selection a mistake: "He gave no real lead in policy formation, he was ineffectual as a party broker, he was an atrocious public speaker, and he seemed politically naïve on the larger stage of national politics." The stress caught up with Bracken and he again developed symptoms of pernicious anaemia.[112]

Following the election and the war, Bracken's role as Progressive Conservative leader drew increasing criticism from within the party. He had been chosen leader, he was given his chance to prove his mettle in an election, and he had failed. In 1947, following Tory defeats in two federal by-elections, Bracken was accused of not holding the confidence of the party. Indeed, he had come to a similar conclusion himself. He announced his resignation on July 19, 1948.[113]

Conclusion

In retirement John and Alice Bracken purchased and moved to a farm at Manotick on the Rideau River near Ottawa. The area reminded John of his childhood home at Seeley's Bay. He spent most of his time working on the farm and his new herd of Jersey cattle. He grew alfalfa and built up a sizeable herd of prize palamino horses. He gradually recovered his health. Bracken was called upon twice by the Manitoba government and he served as chair on two commissions—one on liquor laws and the other on the box car distribution problem. John Bracken died on March 18, 1969 at his farm. He was buried at Rideauvale cemetery at Kars, near his boyhood home.

John Bracken's pragmatic and efficiency-driven view of the world provided him with a sense of calm rationality that pervaded most of his life and often dulled a surprising or unsettling political problem into a simple matter of logic and strategy. Nevertheless, for a man with absolutely no political experience to take up the reigns of leadership of a non-partisan group of farmers, and lead a province through its most difficult period for over 20 years, remains a remarkable accomplishment for any politician. He was the longest-serving Premier in Manitoba history. Bracken's non-partisan style clearly had vast appeal. He was the epitome of a populist leader but he differed from most populists in Canada in one essential way: he was successful. The popularity of coalition government, however, should not be all that surprising. Partisanship is generally distasteful to the electorate. Particularly during times of crisis, such as the Depression or war, the notion of a union government holds popular sway. John Bracken was able to make coalition government work by remaining consistent to his principles of non-partisanship, co-operation, and efficiency. It was a panacea that was difficult to combat and frustrating for political opponents to oppose. As the *Tribune* observed in 1931, "the best brains we have should be in a position of responsibility, and we have no time for party warfare. Men and women of vision and understanding in Manitoba regardless of party affiliations will support the union government proposal because it is in the public interest. The party leaders will do well to give this situation most careful consideration."[114]

As Premier, John Bracken produced results for Manitoba. He led the province through its most difficult years of Depression while serving to stabilize and diversify the economy and open the north to capital development. He represented Manitoba well in its relationship with the federal government and he led the provinces in the campaign to revise and renew Canadian federalism.

Notes

1. John Kendle, *John Bracken: A Political Biography* (Toronto: University of Toronto Press, 1979). 3–5.
2. Ibid., 7–8.
3. Ibid., 9.
4. Ibid.,12.
5. John Bracken, "Retrospectus," *The OAC Review* (February 1907): 213–18.
6. Kendle, *John Bracken*, 16–17.
7. As quoted in Kendle, *John Bracken*, 18.
8. Kendle, *John Bracken*, 18.
9. Jeffery Taylor, *Fashioning Farmers: Ideology, Agricultural Knowledge and the Manitoba Farm Movement, 1890–1925* (Regina: Canadian Plains Research Center, 1994), 36–41.
10. Kendle, *John Bracken*, 23.
11. W.L. Morton, *Manitoba: A History* (Toronto: University of Toronto Press, 1967), 362.
12. Ibid., 375.
13. Ibid, 379.
14. It appeared likely that the Progressive Association would elect one in Winnipeg and three contests were deferred until autumn in The Pas, Rupertsland, and Ethelbert. Kendle, *John Bracken*, 28.
15. Morton, *Manitoba: A History*, 380.
16. Kendle, *John Bracken*, 28.
17. Morton, *Manitoba: A History*, 53; 31.
18. *Manitoba Free Press*, July 21, 1922.
19. Kendle, *John Bracken*, 32.
20. "The farmers' movement offered the French representatives a haven from the party divisions and personal antagonisms of 1916 and gave them a means of joining in the government of their province without loss of their identity." Morton, *Manitoba: A History*, 384.
21. *The Pas Herald and Mining News*, October 6, 1922; *Free Press*, October 2, 1922.
22. As quoted in Morton, *Manitoba: A History*, 384.
23. Kendle, *John Bracken*, 37-39.
24. Ibid., 43.
25. *Free Press*, April 13, 1923.
26. Kendle, *John Bracken*, 45.
27. Morton, *Manitoba: A History*, 385.
28. Ibid., 401.
29. Kendle, *John Bracken*, 48–49.
30. Ibid., 132.
31. Robert Wardhaugh, *Mackenzie King and the Prairie West* (Toronto: University of Toronto Press, 2000) 131.
32. Ibid., 132.
33. Kendle, *John Bracken*, 60.
34. Ibid., 65–66.
35. Wardhaugh, *Mackenzie King*, 15; 75.

36. See Jim Mochoruk, *Formidable Heritage: Manitoba's North and the Cost of Development 1870 to 1930* (Winnipeg: University of Manitoba Press, 2004), 217–89

37. As quoted by Wardhaugh, *Mackenzie King*, 96.

38. Kendle, *John Bracken*, 70-1.

39. Ibid., 72, 77, 48.

40. Ibid., 86.

41. As quoted in Kendle, *John Bracken*, 80.

42. As quoted in Kendle, *John Bracken*, 81.

43. As quoted in Kendle, *John Bracken*, 82.

44. As quoted in Wardhaugh, *Mackenzie King*, 140.

45. Wardhaugh, *Mackenzie King*, 141.

46. Ibid., 144; Kendle, *John Bracken*, 85.

47. Kendle, *John Bracken*, 86.

48. For much of his life, Bracken was particularly susceptible to colds and viral affections. Since the mid-1920s he had suffered from severe stomach pains, constipation, and a general weariness and fatigue. The problems were likely the result of anemia and extreme nervous tension. Kendle, *John Bracken*, 87–88.

49. Kendle, *John Bracken*, 89.

50. Ibid., 90, 100.

51. John Haig, Taylor's principal lieutenant, and P.A. Talbot, speaker of the House, along with Labour MLA John Queen, bought shares. Kendle, *John Bracken*, 93.

52. Morton, *Manitoba: A History*, 407.

53. Mochoruk, *Formidable Heritage*, 295–96.

54. Morton, *Manitoba: A History*, 402.

55. Kendle, *John Bracken*, 107.

56. As quoted in Kendle, 107, *John Bracken*.

57. As quoted in Kendle, *John Bracken*, 110.

58. Kendle, *John Bracken*, 108.

59. Ibid., 112-13.

60. Ibid., 108-9.

61. *Tribune* and *Free Press*, March 22, 1932.

62. Kendle, *John Bracken*, 110.

63. Ibid., 118, 119.

64. Wardhaugh, *Mackenzie King*, 172.

65. Kendle, *John Bracken*, 125.

66. *Free Press*, May 28, 1932.

67. Kendle, *John Bracken*, 125.

68. Ibid., 126.

69. Ibid., 127–28.

70. Ibid., 130–32.

71. Ibid., 133–34.

72. Ibid., 135, 140.

73. Ibid., 140.

74. *Tribune*, July 4, 1936.

75. Kendle, *John Bracken*, 141.

76. Lyle Dick, "The 1936 Provincial Election in Manitoba: An Analysis" (Graduate Research Paper, University of Manitoba, 1975), 8.

77. Wardhaugh, *Mackenzie King*, 214.

78. Kendle, *John Bracken*, 153.

79. Ibid., 153–54.

80. *Tribune*, February 17, 1937.

81. Barry Ferguson and Robert Wardhaugh. "Impossible Conditions of Inequality: John W. Dafoe, the Rowell-Sirois Royal Commission, and the Interpretation of Canadian Federalism," *Canadian Historical Review* (December 2003): 559.

82. Kendle, *John Bracken*, 155, 159.

83. Ibid., 157.

84. *Free Press*, May 3, 1938.

85. Provincial Archives of Manitoba, Bracken Papers, Jacob Viner, "Manitoba's Argument with Respect to the Burden on the Prairie Provinces as a Result of Dominion Tariff Policy: A Supplementary Statement," November 1938.

86. Kendle, *John Bracken*, 161–63.

87. Ibid., 161.

88. As quoted in Kendle, *John Bracken*, 161.

89. Kendle, *John Bracken*, 165.

90. Ferguson and Wardhaugh, "Impossible Conditions," 573.

91. Kendle, *John Bracken*, 174.

92. As quoted in Kendle, *John Bracken*, 175.

93. Kendle, *John Bracken*, 176–78.

94. As quoted in Kendle, *John Bracken*, 181.

95. Kendle, *John Bracken*, 181.

96. Ibid., 182–83.

97. Roger Graham, *Arthur Meighen* (Toronto: Clarke, Irwin and Company, 1965), 98

98. Kendle, *John Bracken*, 184.

99. Ibid., 185.

100. As quoted in J.L. Granatstein, *The Politics of Survival: The Conservative Party of Canada, 1939–1945* (Toronto: University of Toronto Press, 1967), 138.

101. Granatstein, *The Politics of Survival*, 106.

102. Kendle, *John Bracken*, 186.

103. As quoted in Kendle, *John Bracken*, 187.

104. Kendle, *John Bracken*, 187.

105. Ibid., 188–91.

106. As quoted in Kendle, *John Bracken*, 195.

107. Wardhaugh, *Mackenzie King*, 240.

108. Kendle, *John Bracken*, 195, Granatstein, *The Politics of Survival*, 152.

109. *Globe and Mail*, October 16, 1944.

110. Kendle, *John Bracken*, 218.

111. Granatstein, *The Politics of Survival*, 188.
112. Kendle, *John Bracken*, 206, 225.
113. Ibid., 236.
114. *Tribune*, October 7, 1931.

Stuart S. Garson

1943–1948

RAYMOND BLAKE

Stuart S. Garson, 1943–1948

Stuart Sinclair Garson was first elected to the Manitoba legislature as a Liberal-Progressive in 1927. Premier John Bracken made him the Provincial Treasurer in 1936 at the height of the Great Depression, and Garson soon demonstrated that he was a capable politician and administrator. There can be little doubt that Manitoba's experience during the Great Depression made him cautious in all matters of public finance. At the Treasury, he soon realized that the only long-term solution to Manitoba's precarious financial position was a new fiscal arrangement between the provinces and Ottawa, and the federal government had to recognize the plight of the "have-not" provinces. One prominent historian noted almost 40 years ago that Stuart Garson became so intensely involved in federal-provincial relations that "it became almost an obsession" and he was almost bloody-minded in the pursuit of a fiscal arrangement that recognized the inequities of Confederation.[1] None of this changed when he became premier of Manitoba on January 8, 1943, when Bracken accepted the leadership of the Conservative Party of Canada. Garson was clearly a committed federalist, and like many of the political leaders of his generation, he realized also that the state would have to assume a greater role after the end of World War II, especially in the provision of social security. Even so, Garson's postwar progressive agenda remained rooted in caution and the art of the practical, but he sought to make Confederation work for all of Canada's provinces.

W.L. Morton, the noted Manitoba historian, wrote that Garson was a typical Manitoban: "Ontario-born and Manitoba-bred, intense and dry-minded."[2] His family moved from St. Catharine's, Ontario, to Winnipeg, three years after young Stuart was born in 1898. His father had been a member of the Ontario legislature and supporter of Premier Oliver Mowat, who Stuart Garson himself later described as "that great defender of Ontario's provincial rights against their invasion by Sir John A. Macdonald's Dominion Government."[3] In Manitoba, Stuart's father became a successful businessman and a member of the local Liberal elite. After his father's premature death, Stuart worked to support the family, but he managed to graduate in 1918 from the University of Manitoba and the Manitoba Law School. He had been unable to enlist during World War I because he had a slight disability from polio that he had contracted when he was 13, and he moved to Ashern in the Interlake Region to practice law. He was drawn to politics on the urgings of Premier John Bracken, and became the Liberal-Progressive member for Fairford, but he continued to practice law with the firm of Johnston, Garson, Forrester and Davison.[4] In Winnipeg, he met Emily Topper, the daughter of a successful grain elevator owner. Like Garson, she had attended the University of Manitoba, where she received the gold medal in French. She completed a graduate degree at the Sorbonne in Paris. They were married in 1933 and had two daughters.

When he moved to the front rows of Bracken's government as Provincial Treasurer in 1936, he was the youngest member of the provincial cabinet.[5] Many of the issues that were important to Garson as premier had their origins in the period he served as Provincial Treasurer. When Premier Bracken appointed Garson to the Treasury post, he let it be known that even with a new Provincial Treasurer, the government had no intention of undertaking any "major experiments of an untried or unproven or unsound character,"[6] clearly a reference to Bracken's views on some of the new political ideologies that were emerging in the western provinces. There was little worry of Garson being overly zealous or adventuresome as he was cautious by nature, and Manitoba was essentially broke. By 1932, the province was in danger of bankruptcy when it spent nearly $8 million on relief, and the federal government had to guarantee all loans for the province and its municipalities. Still, by 1936, interest payments on the public debt took 42% of the total provincial expenditure largely because of the cost of relief during the Depression, and at one point in 1937 the government did not have enough money to pay its civil servants.[7] The Depression hit Manitoba particularly hard, and it did not take Garson long to figure out that Manitoba's financial crisis could be solved only with a new fiscal arrangement between the provinces and the federal government.

As Manitoba wrestled with providing relief for the unemployed during the height of the Great Depression, Garson never missed an opportunity to remind Ottawa of Manitoba's struggle with financial collapse. In 1936, he told Ottawa that Manitoba's problems stemmed in large measures from the lack of fiscal equity between the provinces. Indeed, the fiscal arrangements existing in the Confederation agreements did not provide Manitoba and many of the other provinces with an adequate financial capacity to deal with the social problems created by the Depression. The federal government simply had to provide greater financial resources to the province to allow it to meet its social service needs. Moreover, Garson also believed that the financial demands placed on Manitoba for relief payments during the 1930s was essentially a national problem and he insisted that the issue of provincial relief could only be addressed efficiently and equitably by the national government.[8] It was Manitoba's precarious financial position that led in no small part to an examination of the federal-provincial fiscal and taxation requirements in the Royal Commission on Dominion-Provincial Relations (Rowell-Sirois Commission) in 1937.[9] Garson quickly established himself as an expert on federal-provincial relations and oversaw Manitoba's submission to the Royal Commission.[10] He felt vindicated in his harsh criticism of the fiscal terms of Confederation in 1940 when the Commission recommended a readjustment of federal-provincial finances, but was extremely disappointed that the Commission's recommendations were not implemented at the Dominion-Provincial Conference held in January 1941 because of the opposition of the Premiers of Alberta, British Columbia, and Ontario.[11] Bracken and Garson returned to Winnipeg disillusioned with the outcome in Ottawa, but convinced that they had to continue to push for the adoption of the Rowell-Sirois report.

Garson and Bracken also held a general belief that the problems facing Manitoba could not be solved in the atmosphere of party politics; the only hope was a united coalition where all interests in the province could be represented.[12] It was the repudiation of the recommendations contained in the Rowell-Sirois report and the outbreak of war in 1939 that prompted Bracken to convince all four parties in the Manitoba legislature to join a coalition government. The political parties all wanted a fair deal for Manitoba in Confederation and, at the same time, they believed a concerted effort was crucial for winning the war. In Garson's view, the political arguments of the various parties in the two decades before the coalition government in 1940 had all been meaningless because the parties were arguing essentially over how to spend monies the province simply did not have.[13] The most critical question facing the province was how to achieve the financial capacity to survive on the revenues earned within the province and those provided by the existing fiscal arrangement under the British North America Act. On the resolution to this question rested the ability of the province to survive and maintain a level of services that would sustain its current population.[14] This was the theme that permeated Garson's term as Premier.

When Bracken agreed to contest the leadership of the Conservative Party of Canada after considerable lobbying by Arthur Meighen and other stalwarts within the party, the Liberal-Progressive coalition government unanimously selected Garson as the party leader and Premier. By the time that Bracken entered federal politics in 1942, Garson had clearly become the most powerful minister in the administration. Bracken had discussed the Conservative leadership with Garson but it is not clear what Garson advised. He did suggest to him at one point, however, that he should have "no further dealings with the Conservatives if they would not consider changing their name [to the Progressive Conservatives]."[15] Garson remained committed to the coalition government in Manitoba, and insisted as premier that all of his ministers remain neutral in federal politics, but there was no doubt that Garson threw his support behind the Liberals. J.W. Pickersgill, then at the Prime Minister's office in Ottawa, claims that it was through Garson's efforts that King won 10 of the 12 seats in Manitoba.[16] Garson would follow Bracken's path and jump to the federal arena, but he chose the Liberal party.[17]

When he moved into the Premier's office on January 15, 1943, Garson refused to relinquish any control over the matters that were important to him, such as the province's financial state and its relationship with Ottawa. He continued as Provincial Treasurer, minister of Dominion-Provincial Relations, minister of Telephones, and minister in charge of the Manitoba Power Commission. For Garson, this was all perfectly logical: he told the legislature in his 1944 Budget Speech that he remained Provincial Treasurer as well as Premier because government policy in all departments

> in the discernible future will be so closely connected with and so vitally dependent upon Treasury policy that, as Premier, I shall have to keep very closely in touch with [the] main items of Treasury policy—indeed, so closely in touch that the carrying of actual Treasury portfolio will not present any significantly additional duties beyond those which I should have been required to assume as Premier, in any event.[18]

He might also have said the same about intergovernmental relations. This meant, of course, that there would be no radical changes in policy or approach to government when he replaced Bracken as premier in 1943. In fact, the two had worked closely together, and John W. Dafoe, the editor of the *Winnipeg Free Press*, assured his readers that Garson had already put his stamp on the province:

[H]e and Mr. Bracken have operated as a team for several years past. Both know and understand probably more fully than any other provincial ministers both the implication and necessities of [the Rowell-Sirois report]… The masterly advocacy of the Manitoba case, which won kudos everywhere, was due as much to Mr. Garson as his premier.[19]

But Garson could only manage such a heavy load as premier with the assistance of managers in the civil service upon whom he could rely. Like Bracken before him, Garson was committed to a permanent executive that had superior administrative talent. In 1945, Garson appointed an executive assistant and secretary to the cabinet but the position was abolished after he left the Premier's office.[20] Garson also relied on experts outside government to provide policy analysis.

This was evident as Garson prepared for the postwar period. He was one of many enlightened political leaders throughout the war who believed that his province—and the whole of Canada—had to be better prepared for the postwar period than it had been in the aftermath of the Great War. He believed that both Ottawa and Winnipeg needed to have a well-developed plan for postwar reconstruction. To that end, he appointed an Advisory Committee on Coordination of Post-War Planning in late 1944,[21] and he was the first premier to appear before the House of Commons Committee on Reconstruction and Re-establishment. In keeping with his view of Canada, Garson saw Manitoba's postwar planning as a part of the national effort to create employment opportunities for those who could work and adequate social security for those who were unable to provide for themselves. To him, a national plan and nine separate plans were woefully inadequate; a nation like Canada needed a single coherent postwar plan that had the provinces and Ottawa working together towards a common purpose.[22] Moreover, Garson realized that postwar planning could not only be the preserve of governments; he wanted the public to play a role. Of course, this was in keeping with the non-partisan nature of his provincial government. He also looked to the social scientists in the universities. He joined with the government of Minnesota to have its state university work with the province's university to prepare a study on postwar planning which resulted in a report, "The Mid-continent and the Peace."[23]

Garson was also committed to the maintenance and efficacy of private ownership in the economy and was determined that his province not follow the model advocated by the Co-operative Commonwealth Federation (CCF) in neighbouring Saskatchewan. In many of his speeches he stressed the importance of the provinces and Ottawa working together to solve the problems within the free enterprise system. For instance, at the Dominion-Provincial Conference of 1945–46 he called on all the Premiers and the Prime Minister to "co-operate in creating an environment in which free enterprise can provide for full employment." Only if free enterprise failed to achieve what was expected of it should the state intervene.[24]

Garson's liberalism in Manitoba was a combination of the business liberalism of C.D. Howe and the social liberalism of Paul Martin. He was committed to providing the proper environment for free enterprise to flourish. Chief among these conditions was the necessity of maintaining the purchasing power of Canadians to keep industrial capacity growing. He supported the federal Liberals' plan to implement a universal family allowance as one way to maintain purchasing power. After all, it was imperative that the state help maintain full employment to ensure the strength of the current purchasing power, and that could be achieved through social programs and a fair system of taxation. That could not be achieved, however, if the province had to tax too heavily to provide the level of services that citizens demanded. Garson advocated an elimination of all regressive features in the tax system in favour of taxation that was "progressive in character," so that it would leave "the largest amount of purchasing power in the hands most likely to spend it, and thereby create the widest possible market for our productive powers and in so doing create employment."[25] He desired a tax policy that would lead to full employment which, he maintained, was essential for postwar reconstruction. He also believed that free-enterprisers knew full well that it had to be "progressive in its attitude towards welfare measures and to improvements in the living standards of the people."[26] Yet, Garson realised that the province's finances had to be managed prudently and the debt problems of the 1930s had to be avoided.

Still, Garson believed that provincial governments had a role to play in postwar reconstruction. His reconstruction philosophy was premised on three assumptions. First, the financial resources of the provinces had to be adequate to carry out a postwar plan, and Garson maintained that this could be achieved in Manitoba only through the implementation of the substance of the Rowell-Sirois Report. Second, free enterprise would be responsible for providing a high level of employment and the public sector would only serve to fill any gaps. It was also understood that the state would create the environment and furnish the infrastructure to allow free enterprise to triumph. The third assumption was that the combined efforts of free enterprise and the public sector working together could create full employment.[27]

Beyond those assumptions Garson realized that the state should initiate a series of projects that were intrinsically important to raising the living standard of the province's residents, but even he realized many of these initiatives would contribute to creating employment. The first of these projects was a rural electrification scheme. The province had taken over the hydro-electric system when it went bankrupt during the Depression, and under Garson it had been restored to "excellent and sound" management in his view.[28] In 1942 Bracken appointed the Manitoba Farm Electrification Enquiry Commission to explore the best way to extend the hydroelectric system throughout the province. Garson outlined the plan for a farm electrification program for Manitoba when he tabled the report of the commission on February 6, 1943. He proposed that 1,000 farms be provided with electricity in the first year after the war.[29]

Garson was also committed to a program of social services. "The consequences of not having it [social security] would be so disastrous that no government, whatever its political stripe, would dare not introduce such a program," he said.[30] In fact, in the February 1943 budget, Garson proposed an increase of $1.25 per month in old age and blind pensions with the expectation that the federal government would contribute an additional $3.75.[31] The federal government did not follow suit. He appointed a Royal Commission on Adult

Education in 1945 to assess how rural Manitoba might adjust to the changing situation in the postwar period. According to Gerald Friesen, while the appointment of the Commission was innovative and progressive, Garson "did nothing" to implement even the modest recommendations contained in the report.[32]

However, Garson demonstrated a more progressive side when he introduced the Manitoba Health Plan in the legislature in 1944.[33] Garson described his health plan as being "carefully considered" and on a "very economic basis." This was clearly in keeping with the cabinet's insistence on fiscal prudence, or economy as M.S. Donnelly described their approach.[34] Two basic goals underlay the proposals: first, the prevention of disease, and second, the provision of a variety of services—including curative medical services, hospitalization, dental care, and nursing services—to all residents of Manitoba. The plan proposed the provision of full-time public health service at a cost the population could afford. The plan also included the provision of diagnostic facilities, such as X-ray and laboratory services, without cost to patients. A third basic principle of the Health Service Plan was to provide a family doctor for all Manitobans. Yet, Garson believed that the plan would not be complete without the provision of hospital facilities in rural communities. And he maintained that the program could not be delivered unless the federal government provided much of the funding. As Garson told the Dominion-Provincial Conference in 1945–46, "The first and most important grants that should be made by the Federal Government are those having to do with Public Health and Preventive Medicine, and of these the most urgent is a grant to assist the provinces to establish throughout their rural areas proper preventive services."[35] After all, Manitoba had been relatively innovative in the health field, having been the first provincial government to establish a department of health and public welfare as well as a number of other innovations, including the first public health nursing service in Canada.[36] Garson's government was both fiscally and socially conservative, yet, at the same time, it was committed to "socialized" medicine as the only means to meet its obligations to the Manitoba citizenry. In essence, the origins of Canada's present health care system can be found in the politically conservative 1940s in Manitoba.[37]

In addition to rural electrification and health, Garson had several other priorities for the postwar period. These included capital projects and education needed to sustain the agricultural economy; the construction of highways, drainage systems, and the general expansion of infrastructure projects and other public works, such as sewer and water for small towns; the construction of schools and other buildings required for educational purposes, especially in rural Manitoba; and a variety of projects and services relating to the conservation and development of natural resources. Yet, Garson was quick to point out that these projects should generate wealth in the province and be "self-liquidating"; above all, he insisted that fiscal prudence must be the order of the day. In fact, the government had set aside after 1943 a postwar fund of $600,000 to finance the rural electrification plan and other projects.[38]

For Garson, however, the question revolved around who should shoulder the costs for postwar reconstruction and rehabilitation. Even though there was general agreement that reconstruction was a broadly based program—much of which fell under provincial jurisdiction—he had warned in his first speech to the legislature as Premier on February 12, 1943, that the "honeymoon of million dollar surpluses is over ... and the province is entering an era in which the cost of the war will come home to us."[39] He acknowledged that the postwar costs would potentially be far greater than those for either the Depression or the war, and he told Manitobans time and time again that his government could not hope to do what was expected without "having a decent system of public finance in this country."[40] Manitoba could not provide the financial resources under the current fiscal arrangement with Ottawa; this fact was known for quite some time, and it had been at the forefront of the demand for change. The province had pressed for the Rowell-Sirois Commission, and had been extremely disappointed at the 1941 Dominion-Provincial Conference and with the premiers of Alberta, British Columbia and Ontario. They were content with the existing intergovernmental tax arrangement and had prevented the other provinces from finding a solution to the crisis.[41] As Garson never tired of telling those who would listen, it was such opposition that had led, in part, to the formation of his coalition government:

> We thought the best way of showing unity was by bringing the political parties in our Legislature together in one united front. We felt that until we could get through the war, until we could get our financial relationship with the other provinces and Canada reformed so that we could have a decent postwar program, that we did not have much need for party politics in Manitoba.[42]

He told the Canadian Club on March 29, 1943, that the "elaborate projects of post-war reconstruction could not be proceeded with until there had been a revision of the British North America Act and a new and modernized alignment of powers and responsibilities between the Dominion and provinces."[43]

Garson believed that Canada was a single financial community, and that the tax burdens of the country had to be divided as fairly as possible between the provinces, and in accordance with their ability to pay. He reminded the Edmonton Chamber of Commerce on October 6, 1944, that the financial capacity of the provinces varied immensely. The current system whereby the provinces had only the power to impose direct taxation upon taxable resources within their provincial boundaries failed to recognize the national nature of the Canadian economy. Only Ontario and Quebec, with their financial and industrial centres, had "the power to draw into their taxing jurisdiction wealth and income which originate in other provinces." The profits of Manitoba branches, he pointed out, were taken to the head offices of these provinces in the normal course of business, and these head offices and well-to-do shareholders of these organizations were located in Ontario and Quebec, and were taxed there. Yet, Manitoba had to shoulder the burden of the social costs of creating that income through its education and public health expenditures.[44] He did not need to point out that such an arrangement did not serve the interests of the western provinces.

In 1946, the Dominion-Provincial Tax Suspension Agreements of 1942 (that were used to finance the war) were coming to an end. This emergency measure had given the provinces a substantial annual grant from the Dominion treasury in exchange for their surrendering of certain tax fields to Ottawa, but Garson was obviously worried that some of the provinces, particularly Ontario and Quebec, would prevent any renewal or extension of the 1942 agreements. Garson, however, was delighted when Prime Minister Mackenzie King invited the Premiers to Ottawa in 1945 to discuss dominion-provincial relations. Perhaps more than any other Premier, Garson understood the financial parameters of federal-provincial relations, and he realized that Manitoba had benefited greatly from the wartime arrangement.[45] He came to Ottawa for the Dominion-Provincial Conference with high expectations and definite views on the need for a strong central government. He reminded the first plenary session at the conference that it was the financial predicament of the Manitoba treasury that had led to the appointment of the Rowell-Sirois Commission. He was hopeful of a new arrangement with Ottawa that incorporated the letter and the spirit of the British North America Act, and he attempted to impress upon his colleagues the importance of their job at the conference:

> The work of this Conference is the foundation upon which everything that we can hope to achieve now and after the war must be built. Perhaps it is more critical for us [Manitoba] than it is for most of the other provinces, but I think it is true also to say that there is no part of Canada, no province of Canada, no government of Canada, and no Canadian citizen but who should regard this Conference and the work it is doing as of equal importance to this country as was the San Francisco Conference [that established the United Nations] to the whole world.[46]

But he went on to say, "if this conference achieves no satisfactory results, our position will be that of having purchased the precarious prosperity which we are enjoying under the [wartime] agreement at the cost of a serious financial difficulty when it expires."[47] There was no time for delay, Garson warned, as the demands upon government in the postwar period would be enormous, and the provinces would have to be able to respond. Just as the temporary agreement permitted an orderly management of the war, so would a "sound and just tax structure" provide for a prosperous postwar Canada.[48]

At the beginning of the conference, which lasted intermittently for about a year, Ottawa proposed that the provinces agree not to impose taxes on corporations, incomes, and inheritances. In return, the federal government offered to pay statutory subsidies and to make additional payments so that the total transfers to the provinces would never be less than $181 million in any fiscal year. Ottawa eventually raised its subsidy to $15 per person. Moreover, the transfers would increase in proportion to a rise in population and national income. Ottawa promised to assume the cost of old age pensions for those 70 and older, and half the cost of pensions for those between 65 and 69, as well as a health insurance scheme. Ottawa was willing to assume responsibility for the unemployed employables, and contribute to a federal-provincial scheme of public works directed primarily at resource development.[49]

Garson was the strongest provincial supporter of the federal proposals at the 1945 federal-provincial conference. According to Doug Owram, he "seem[ed] to have held no partisan or ideological grudges against the Dominion planners." He had commented before the conference that "partisanship therefore is and will be a luxury which we should abandon during this critical period."[50] He argued throughout the Conference that Canada was a single economic and political unit:

> The only possible policy which can be of greatest service to all of the citizens of a country such as Canada is one which takes cognizance of the inter-dependence of all of its parts and renders equal justice to Canadians in whatever parts of Canada they may reside.[51]

Without continuing the wartime pact in some form, he knew that the capacity of his province to meet the demands of the public in the postwar period was in jeopardy. He reminded the conference that much of the income and employment since the Depression resulted from wartime spending, and it was critical to maintain much of the spending by governments, businesses and citizens to keep the economy buoyant in the postwar period. Moreover, much of the expenditure from government would be directed towards education, health and public welfare, natural resources development, road building and provincial public works—and all of these areas fell within provincial jurisdiction. Of course, he pointed out, without adequate funding for the provinces, these areas would all suffer and impact adversely on the Canadian standard of living and the level of national income with the result that there would be greater difficulty in maintaining adequate employment.[52] Clearly, the provinces had a role to play in fostering postwar economic growth, but they needed the financial resources to be able to satisfactorily participate.

Garson argued that Canada had changed significantly since 1867. At the time, the Fathers of Confederation devised a fiscal arrangement that supported the provinces with limited responsibilities. They had not anticipated the very large expenditures that the provinces would have to make for the huge increases in public health, public welfare, and educational expenses that Manitoba, for instance, planned as part of its postwar reconstruction plan. The grants from Ottawa were "ridiculously inadequate" if the provinces hoped to meet their obligations in the areas of social spending, Garson argued, though it was the intention of the Fathers of Confederation that the provinces would have sufficient revenues to provide for their citizens even if the provinces were engaged in an array of public expenditure never contemplated in 1867. The notion that the federal government would have policies to reduce provincial disparities in income revenues remained very much a principle of Confederation, but Garson maintained that the fiscal transfers from Ottawa had not kept pace with provincial needs: "To increase the grant [per capita subsidy] is merely to give effect to the clear intent of the Canadian constitution which was that this grant should be a major source of the revenue required by the provinces to meet their responsibilities."[53] That principle had been violated during the Depression when the federal government refused to assume "full fiscal responsibility for unemployment," and provinces like Manitoba had to borrow heavily to secure the funds necessary to provide for their populations. Garson—and all the premiers for that matter—accepted the importance of providing social services and, as Owram states, "the necessity of using modern techniques of economic management to reduce the impact of downturns in the business cycle."[54] Now, the smaller and less developed provinces needed the financial resources to provide for their citizens.

Garson argued that a new fiscal arrangement was possible between the provinces and Ottawa without constitutional change: "What we need to do is not to depart from the constitution, but, on the contrary, to apply the language, the principles and the spirit of the constitution to the circumstances of 1945."[55] The Fathers of Confederation, he maintained, calculated that the grants decided upon in 1867 were adequate for provincial needs if the provinces budgeted "in an economical manner." The provincial revenues would have been adequate, Garson suggested, if the philosophy and expectations of government had remained constant after Confederation. But they had not, since the role of government had changed immensely, and governments had to provide services that were never contemplated at the time of union. Garson believed that the troubled dominion-provincial relationship had resulted because the federal government had abandoned the principles of Confederation as they were understood in 1867.[56]

When the conference turned into a squabble between the two wealthiest provinces (Quebec and Ontario) and the federal government, Garson did not try and hide his disappointment with Premiers George Drew and Maurice Duplessis. When the conference resumed in April 1946, the Manitoba Premier told the other First Ministers that he had come to Ottawa as a Canadian who wanted to do the best for the country, free of partisanship and selfish interests. Not surprisingly, he dismissed the fears of Drew and Duplessis that a new fiscal agreement between the provinces and Ottawa would diminish the powers of the provinces or jeopardise provincial rights or create a unitary state in Canada, as they had suggested.[57] He saw them as provincialists rather than nationalists, and he reminded them that the "power to tax is not synonymous with revenues." It was the plight of provinces, like Manitoba, that "lack adequate taxable resources" that had to be addressed. "The real problem is to decide whether in the interests of Canada and its citizens, the fields of income, corporation and inheritance taxes should be returned to the Provinces. For our part, their return to us is no solution."[58] He went on to say that the prewar taxation system was "unjust," as Canadians in various provinces enjoyed various different standards of living.[59] "This inefficient, unjust, and calamitous pre-war tax system was the result of a misconception of history, of law and of economics, which is still with us," Garson claimed. He reminded those gathered in Ottawa that before the war, the "wealthy provinces because they were wealthy could keep their income tax rates low." That could not work for Manitoba.[60] Garson was always quick to make a case for strengthening the fabric of the nation, and never afraid to ask his colleagues and the prime minister "Are we building a nation, or the Balkan states of North America?"[61]

At the May 1946 sessions, Garson was extremely angry that George Drew would suggest at the eleventh hour that Ontario needed $27 per capita as payment for surrendering taxing powers (rather than the $15 that Ottawa had offered). He told the conference that "the sudden announcement … in the closing hours of the conference is as effective a method as could be devised to destroy any possibility of agreement being reached between all the provinces and the Dominion."[62] Garson warned that the "less well-to-do provinces will be the first and the chief victims of the failure of the larger provinces and the Dominion government to reach an agreement."[63] Garson realized that it was the federal-provincial agreements in the early 1940s that had allowed Manitoba to stabilize and strengthen its financial position, and he realized that without a new agreement his province faced considerable financial uncertainty. For the prudent administrator whose primary concern was fiscal stability, Garson could not hide his genuine disappointment at the likely failure and he clearly blamed the Central Canadians. In fact, there was considerable animosity between Drew and Garson throughout the conference, and the Ontario premier did not take kindly to many of Garson's comments. He subsequently dismissed Garson's concerns as that of a Liberal partisan and "special pleading now ... on behalf of the Dominion government," to which Garson countered with an insult of his own: Drew simply did not understand the complexity of the Canadian situation. Garson went further, and reminded Drew that while he might regard Ontario as the "wheel horse of the Confederation," it was Manitoba and the West that provided the sustenance for the animal: "the lifeblood of his [Drew's] wheel horses is the wheat exporters' dollar, and without that lifeblood the wheel horses would be useless."[64] It was no surprise that the conference ended on an acrimonious note. King must have been pleased with Garson, nonetheless, as he had written earlier in his dairy: "I find Garson's views and my own almost identical."[65]

Drew would also have disliked Garson's position on a number of other issues, particularly those surrounding the orderly management of international economy, especially for agricultural products. Garson was interested in the grain trade because the stability of farm income was critical to Manitoba. And on this issue, once again, Garson demonstrated that he was more than willing to cooperate with Ottawa. He believed that it was critical for the federal government to have the assurances of the provinces that they were willing to "co-operate in the solution of jurisdictional problems which the Dominion government encounters when dealing with international matters and marketing control." Garson knew only too well how the international economy had failed during the 1930s, and he believed that a new international order could be best achieved if all provinces of Canada "co-operate[d] to give the Dominion government the power to implement its treaties and international agreements, which it does not now possess." Moreover, he told his colleagues, "We should therefore be prepared to clothe the Dominion government, as far as it lies within our power to do so, with all of the powers that it must have to build up a large multilateral trade within the sort of economic environment which it will face after the war."[66] He believed that the stabilization of farm income was only possible through multilateral trade, but his pronouncements at Ottawa angered Drew in particular, who saw himself as a defender of provincial rights against the incursions from a centralizing administration in Ottawa.

As Garson later announced, "we cannot see why the interests of the people of Manitoba should suffer" because of the decision of Ontario and Quebec not to accept the Dominion proposals. The federal budget subsequently authorized Ottawa to enter into separate agreements with the provinces, and Garson negotiated a deal with Ottawa that allowed his government "to protect our financial position ... until a general settlement" could be reached. In November 1946, Premier Garson signed a five-year tax agreement with Ottawa that was revised in January 1947, whereby Manitoba surrendered its right to levy income and corporation taxes and succession duties for a minimum annual payment of $13,512,000. An escalator clause was built into the agreement to reflect increases in population and a rise in the national income.[67] With the breakdown of negotiations in 1946, the Dominion proposals for social security and public investment were dropped, though Prime Minister Mackenzie King had written George Drew, one of the dissenting participants at the conference, that "once satisfactory financial relationships have been agreed upon, the Dominion Government will be prepared to resume in a general conference the working out of generally satisfactory arrangements relating to public investment and social welfare."[68]

While Garson was disappointed that the conference did not agree on a new framework for a national vision for the country or provide additional monies for health and other social programs, he had secured from Ottawa a five-year agreement that provided Manitoba with the financial resources to meet most of its commitments. Later, Ottawa also agreed to cancel one half of the province's debt for relief still owed to the federal government from the 1930s—Garson finally succeeding in convincing Ottawa that Manitoba was saddled with the debt because the federal fiscal arrangement failed to recognize that relief for the unemployed in the 1930s had been a national issue rather than a provincial and municipal one.[69] With a reduction in its debt and the new fiscal arrangement with Ottawa, according to W.L. Morton, "it was clear that the Garson government had won a measure of success for its long battle for a tolerable financial position for Manitoba in Confederation. The premature province of 1870," he surmised, "might at last be able to support the dignity of provincehood."[70] With the new funding agreement in place, Garson immediately turned his attention to providing new monies to municipalities and school boards to assist with the costs of education and social services to bring a measure of equality to rural Manitoba. Perhaps in typical Garson fashion, the relatively wealthy school districts received comparatively smaller grants than the poor districts. It also allowed Garson to proceed with his hospitalization scheme throughout the province, and embark on the first steps in the creation of a welfare state in Manitoba. Yet, also in typical Garson fashion, the government never lost sight of the importance of retiring its debt and spending within its means.[71]

Garson's coalition government held together in Manitoba during the 1945 election, when he insisted that a united effort was important for the upcoming negotiations with Ottawa over reconstruction and a new tax-rental agreement. The CCF, fearing that its continued participation in the coalition would harm both the provincial and the national fortunes of the party, withdrew in 1942 and went into opposition. In the following election the CCF remained an urban party, based in Winnipeg, and even though it captured 35% of the vote the coalition coasted to an easy victory with 40 seats; the members of the coalition frequently did not field candidates against each other, and many seats were won through acclamation. According to W.L. Morton, the coalition remained a "rural-based and rural-oriented government."[72] After the 1945 election, the word "coalition" was dropped and the cabinet was officially described as non-partisan. This extended to federal politics as well.[73] It might be a tad surprising, however, that Garson never once said that he represented a coalition government when he presented Manitoba's position at the federal-provincial conference.

It has been suggested that the coalition and non-partisan government of Garson (and Bracken) severely damaged political institutions in Manitoba as

> debate in the legislature almost ceased and the cabinet became a kind of regulatory board, a shadow of what such a body ought to be. The theory, held so strongly by Bracken, Garson, and Campbell, that political parties were unnecessary, shows how little they understood the parliamentary system, which, of course, is based on party government. Indeed, they very nearly succeeded in destroying it.[74]

It has also been argued that compromise and inaction were the major outcome as little new legislation was introduced in the legislature. In the 1945 session, for instance, 90% of the legislation introduced consisted of minor changes to existing laws and no new legislation of any consequence was introduced.[75]

During the time that he was Premier, there was little doubt that Garson was a Liberal and that he saw the importance of the party on the national political scene. One commentator has noted that Garson regarded "Liberalism as the only sound alternative to the doctrinaire view of conservatives and socialists,"[76] and the coalition government was one way of keeping the Liberal-Progressives in power. His commitment to the Manitoba coalition was one important reason that he remained in provincial politics as long as he did. As early as March 1943, Liberal Prime Minister Mackenzie King talked about bringing Garson into his cabinet. In 1946, when King and Garson again discussed the latter's move to Ottawa, King noted in his diary that Garson was worried that his coalition government would "go to pieces without him."[77] Garson believed that the coalition was absolutely necessary to provide Manitoba with the policies that he and Bracken had pursued, but federally there was no doubt that he was strongly committed to the Liberal Party and Mackenzie King. Garson was even nominated for the leadership of the federal Liberal Party when King resigned, but he chose instead to nominate Louis St. Laurent, who eventually won the leadership. He clearly held distinct views on "party politics" but that view changed completely when he moved from the provincial to the national political arena.

By the fall of 1947, Garson was clearly identifying himself as a Liberal, and he traveled extensively to speak about the virtues of Liberalism. The Saskatchewan Liberal Association, for instance, had him deliver a radio speech in the summer provincial election in 1948. By this time, it was clear that Garson was ready to return to the Liberal Party. It is likely that he was particularly interested in participating in Saskatchewan because T.C. Douglas, the leader of the CCF government, had actively campaigned for the Manitoba wing of the CCF against Garson in the previous Manitoba election. In his radio broadcast, Garson took great pains to show that Manitoba was one of the most progressive provinces in Canada and that despite the CCF claims, the Liberal Party was not "the unprogressive and reactionary tool of certain mysterious big interests whom they [the CCF] never take the trouble to name." This speech is also revealing for what it says about Garson and his political philosophy. He was proud of his record of public ownership, noting that "No province has more public ownership than Manitoba." He listed several radio stations, the Manitoba Co-operative Honey Producers, the Manitoba Sugar Company, various utilities, including the Manitoba Telephone System and Manitoba Hydro Commission, the Manitoba Rural Credit System, and the Liquor Control Commission. Garson was particularly proud of the Hydro Commission, explaining that it was responsible for the electrification of rural Manitoba throughout 1946 and 1947. Yet, Garson knew where to draw the line between what he called "proper and improper public ownership... Proper public ownership and public enterprise is that which, while it may or may not interfere with private enterprise, creates new and larger opportunities for free enterprise to expand and therefore helps rather than destroys private enterprise." The government, he said, should not participate in the commercial field in competition with its own taxpayers.[78]

Garson resigned as Premier on November 13, 1948, to become the minister of Justice in the Liberal government of Louis St. Laurent. When Garson was nominated in the Marquette constituency he described himself to the voters as a Liberal Progressive. He told his nominating convention that his positions as Premier and as the federal minister from Manitoba were really part of the same role. When he recapped his accomplishments as Provincial Treasurer and Premier, he focused only on how he had fought to establish a workable and effective federal arrangement for Canada—one in which Manitoba and the other provinces could thrive. For him, of course, it began with the fiscal crisis facing Manitoba in the 1930s and the appointment of the Rowell-Sirois Commission.[79] He described the commission's report as the Magna Carta of the "have-not" provinces and the "have-not" citizens of Canada. He rallied against Ontario and Quebec for being obstructionist and for standing in the path of modernizing dominion-provincial relations. With his agreement with Ottawa in 1947, he said that he had done what he could for Manitoba working in Winnipeg. Yet, the fiscal arrangement for an effective Canada was far from complete, but that, he told the Convention, could not be achieved from Winnipeg—it had to be decided in the federal field, and "in the settlement of this issue... . I want to do my part on the side of angels." He also said that he felt obligated to help the Dominion Government after it had helped to solve Manitoba's fiscal problems, but more than anything else he was a good Canadian "seeking to promote the welfare of the whole of Canada."[80] A few weeks later, Garson took his seat at the federal cabinet table, hoping to build a more sustainable federation from Ottawa, a role he could not fulfill as premier of Manitoba. After several years of courting by the federal Liberals, perhaps Garson had come to believe as Prime Minister King had once told him: "the province is a small affair ... [and] what Canada needs are the best man she could get from all parts [of the country]."[81]

Garson was re-elected in his Manitoba constituency in 1949 and again in 1953. He continued to serve in the government of Louis St. Laurent as minister of Justice until he was defeated in the Tory resurgence in 1957. In Ottawa he earned a reputation as an able administrator, but his friend J.W. Pickersgill has noted that Garson's propensity for detail and lengthy presentations prevented him from securing a more senior position in the cabinet. He might also have been hurt politically by allegations that he had delayed the release of a report from the federal combines commissioner into an alleged combine in flour-milling because of pressure from C.D. Howe, the minister of Industry, who had close ties with the sector. As it was, he chaired the first plenary session of a federal-provincial constitutional conference in 1950, after an amendment to the British North America Act in 1949 to make the Supreme Court of Canada the body of final judicial appeal in Canada, and he chaired the Canadian delegation to the Sixth General Assembly of the United Nations in Paris in 1952. After his defeat in 1957, he turned to practicing law in Winnipeg with the firm of Johnston, Garson, Forrester, Davison, and Taylor, where he remained until he retired in 1965. In 1971, he was made a Companion of the Order of Canada.

Conclusion

When Stuart Garson died in Winnipeg in 1977, his long-time friend and colleague, J.W. Pickersgill noted that the former Premier had died "almost forgotten." Out of politics for 20 years, Garson had faded from the public memory. Yet, he was—and remains—one of Manitoba's important political leaders and one of a handful from the province who played an important role on the national stage while he was Premier. The fiscal difficulty that he experienced first-hand during the Great Depression made him a committed federalist; he devoted much of his energy as Premier to negotiating a fiscal arrangement between the provinces and Ottawa that would allow the government of Manitoba to provide a level of services and programs to its people that met what he considered a national, or Canadian, standard. While Garson was clearly interested in pursuing a progressive agenda in health care and pensions, for instance, his Depression-era experience forced him to be cautious and prudent. While he provided sound management to Manitoba, his caution and fiscal conservatism prevented him from being a truly progressive Premier.

Notes

1. W.L. Morton, *Manitoba: A History* (Toronto: University of Toronto Press, 1967), 450.
2. Ibid.
3. Archives of Manitoba, P4960, file 6 "Remarks of Premier Stuart Garson at Evening Meeting of the Liberal Club of the University of Toronto," October 7, 1947.
4. See John Kendle, *John Bracken: A Political Biography* (Toronto: University of Toronto Press, 1979), 156–57, and Jon Gerrard, *Battling for a Better Manitoba: A History of the Provincial Liberal Party* (Winnipeg: Heartland Associates, Inc., 2006), 82–83.
5. Mark E. Vajcner, "Stuart Garson and the Manitoba Progressive Coalition," *Manitoba History* 26 (Autumn 1993): 29–30. This is one of the few published essays on Garson.
6. Quoted in Vajcner, "Stuart Garson and the Manitoba Progressive Coalition," 30.
7. M.S. Donnelly, *The Government of Manitoba* (Toronto: University of Toronto Press, 1963), 162–64.
8. *Manitoba's Case. A Submission to the Royal Commission on Dominion-Provincial Relations by the Government of Manitoba* (Winnipeg: n.p., 1937), 69–73.
9. For a discussion of the events leading to the creation of the Royal Commission, see Doug Owram, *The Government Generation: Canadian Intellectuals and the State, 1900–1945* (Toronto: University of Toronto Press, 1986), 236–42.

10. Barry Ferguson and Robert Wardhaugh, "'Impossible Conditions of Inequality': John W. Dafoe, the Rowell-Sirois Royal Commission, and the Interpretation of Canadian Federalism," *Canadian Historical Review* 84, no. 4 (December 2003): 565.

11. Owram, *The Government Generation*, 277–78.

12. See Kendle, *John Bracken*, 173–77, and Archives of Manitoba, Garson Family Collection (P4960), file 2, "The Stand of the Manitoba Non-Partisan Government in the Next Dominion Election and other Matters," March 14, 1945.

13. Ibid.

14. Morton, *Manitoba: A History*, 449.

15. Kendle, *John Bracken*, 286, note 30.

16. J.W. Pickersgill, *Seeing Canada Whole: A Memoir* (Toronto: Fitzhenry & Whiteside, 1994), 808.

17. Kendle, *John Bracken*, 189, and Pickersgill, *Seeing Canada Whole*, 228.

18. Archives of Manitoba, GR 43, G89 file 15–Budget Speech, 1944.

19. Quoted in P. James Giffen, *Rural Life. Portraits of the Prairie Town, 1946*, edited with an Afterword by Gerald Friesen (Winnipeg: University of Manitoba Press, 2004), 213.

20. M.S. Donnelly, *The Government of Manitoba* (Toronto: University of Toronto Press, 1963), 100 and 103–04.

21. Giffen, *Rural Life*, 215–16.

22. Archives of Manitoba, Garson Family Collection (P4960), file 2, "Summary of Remarks of Premier Stuart Garson at the First Meeting of the Advisory Committee on Co-ordination of Postwar Planning," September 19, 1944.

23. Archives of Manitoba, Garson Family Collection (P4960), file 1, Portage la Prairie Nominating Convention Remarks, October 18, 1943.

24. Dominion-Provincial Conference (1945), *Dominion and Provincial Submissions and Plenary Conference Discussions* (Ottawa: King's Printer, 1946), 132–33.

25. Ibid., 142

26. Archives of Manitoba, GR 3151, Attorney General's Department, Deputy Minister's Office, Box N-14-5-18, Remarks of Hon. Stuart Garson at Dominion-Provincial Conference, 1945.

27. Archives of Manitoba, Garson Family Collection (P4960), "Remarks of Premier Stuart Garson at Dinner Meeting, Manitoba Associated Boards of Trade," December 6, 1944.

28. Archives of Manitoba, Garson Family Collection (P4960), file 1, Portage la Prairie Nominating Convention Remarks, October 18, 1943.

29. *Winnipeg Free Press*, February 6, 1943.

30. Archives of Manitoba, Garson Family Collection (P4960), file 1, Portage la Prairie Nominating Convention Remarks, October 18, 1943.

31. *Winnipeg Free Press*, February 12, 1943. The Co-operative Commonwealth Federation had proposed in each of the several by-elections held in 1943 that Manitoba immediately adopt a social security system along the New Zealand model that had established universal pension and a system of medical and health benefits. Garson and his government attacked the CCF plan as simply too costly: the level of taxation required for such a plan in Manitoba, Garson maintained, could only be implemented at the "risk of driving business to more favourably situated provinces, in which the rates of taxation were lower." Moreover, Garson claimed that Manitoba had neither the financial resources nor the constitutional powers to introduce an extensive social security system. Vajcner, "Stuart Garson and the Manitoba Progressive Coalition," 32.

32. Giffen, *Rural Life*, 239.

33. Archives of Manitoba, GR 3151, Attorney General's Department, Deputy Minister's Office, Box N-14-5-18, Dominon-Provincial Conference, April 1946.

34. Donnelly, *The Government of Manitoba*, 106.

35. Dominion-Provincial Conference, *Dominion and Provincial Submissions and Plenary Conference Discussions*, 157–58.

36. Archives of Manitoba, P4960, file 4, "Remarks of Premier Stuart Garson to Liberal Nominating Convention," Winnipeg, September 18, 1945.

37. It was Scott MacNeil who first alerted me to Garson's health proposals.

38. Archives of Manitoba, file 4, "Remarks of Premier Stuart Garson Introducing the Government's Program to meet the exigencies of the immediate post-war period," September 7, 1945.

39. *Winnipeg Free Press*, February 12, 1943.

40. Archives of Manitoba, Garson Family Collection (P4960), file 1, Portage la Prairie Nominating Convention Remarks, October 18, 1943.

41. Ibid.

42. Ibid.

43. *Winnipeg Free Press*, March 30, 1943.

44. Archives of Manitoba, Garson Family Collection (P4960), file 2, Garson Address to Edmonton Chamber of Commerce, October 6, 1944.

45. Robert Bothwell, Ian Drummond, and John English, *Canada Since 1945* (Toronto: University of Toronto Press, 1989), 75, and see Kendle, *John Bracken*, 156–57.

46. Dominion-Provincial Conference, *Dominion and Provincial Submissions and Plenary Conference Discussions*, 30.

47. Ibid., 146.

48. Ibid., 148.

49. Ibid., 427. The second series of meetings was held in January 1946. See also Morton, *Manitoba: A History*, 460–61.

50. Quoted in Owram, *The Government Generation*, 324. Records of the Department of Finance, 3563, file G-OOA contains Mackintosh-Garson correspondence. Whitton Papers, vol. 4, Garson to Whitton, March 29, 1945.

51. Dominion-Provincial Conference, *Dominion and Provincial Submissions and Plenary Conference Discussions*, 139.

52. Dominion-Provincial Conference, "Plenary Session," January 26, 1946, 324–25.

53. Dominion-Provincial Conference, *Dominion and Provincial Submissions and Plenary Conference Discussions*, 160.

54. Dominion-Provincial Conference, Session of April 5, 1946, and Owram, *The Government Generation*, 325.

55. Archives of Manitoba, GR 3151, Attorney General's Department, Deputy Minister's Office, Box N-14-5-18, Remarks of Hon. Stuart Garson at Dominion-Provincial Conference, 1945; and Dominion-Provincial Conference, *Dominion and Provincial Submissions and Plenary Conference Discussions*, 158.

56. Dominion-Provincial Conference, *Dominion and Provincial Submissions and Plenary Conference Discussions*, 163.

57. Archives of Manitoba, P4960, file 6, "Remarks of Premier Stuart Garson at Evening Meetings of the Liberal Club of the University of Toronto," October 7, 1947.

58. Dominion-Provincial Conference, *Dominion and Provincial Submissions and Plenary Conference Discussions*, 441–45.

59. Ibid., 445.

60. Ibid., 446–47.

61. Archives of Manitoba, P4960. file 1, An address by Honourable Stuart Garson to the Canadian Newspapers Association, Winnipeg, August 17, 1944.

62. Dominion-Provincial Conference, *Dominion and Provincial Submissions and Plenary Conference Discussions*, 607.

63. Ibid., 606.

64. Ibid., 610.

65. Library and Archives Canada, Diaries of Prime Minister W.L.M. King (hereafter King Diaries), February 2, 1946.

66. Dominion-Provincial Conference, *Dominion and Provincial Submissions and Plenary Conference Discussions*, 154.

67. Morton, *Manitoba: A History*, 461, and Archives of Manitoba, P4960, file 6, "Remarks of Premier Stuart Garson at Annual Meeting of the Steinbach Board of Trade," January 29, 1947.

68. Archives of Manitoba, P4960, file 6, "Remarks of Premier Stuart Garson at Evening Meetings of the Liberal Club of the University of Toronto," October 7, 1947.

69. Dominion-Provincial Conference, *Dominion and Provincial Submissions and Plenary Conference Discussions*, 158.

70. Morton, *Manitoba: A History*, 461–62.

71. Ibid., 462.

72. Ibid., 450.

73. Donnelly, *Government of Manitoba*, 104.

74. Ibid., 67, and Vajcner, "Stuart Garson and the Manitoba Progressive Coalition,"31.

75. Donnelly, *Government of Manitoba*, 104.

76. Gregg Shilliday (ed.), *Manitoba 125: A History*, Volume 3 (Winnipeg: Great Plains Publications, 1995), 39.

77. King Diaries, March 15, 1943, December 9, 1944, February 2, 1946, and December 16, 1946.

78. Archives of Manitoba, "Text of Broadcast by Premier Stuart Garson for Use in Saskatchewan Election Campaign," June 1948.

79. See Archives of Manitoba, GR 3151, Attorney General's Department, Deputy Minister's Office, Box N-14-5-17, file "Re: Dominion Provincial Relations #230 Corresp./Misc Agreements 1930–40."

80. Archives of Manitoba, file 6, "Remarks of Hon. Stuart Garson to Marquette Liberal Progressive Association Nominating Convention, Shoal Lake, Manitoba, November 17, 1948."

81. King Diaries, December 16, 1946.

Douglas L. Campbell

JAMES MUIR

Douglas Lloyd Campbell, 1948–1958

Manitoba in 1948 was a rural province. It was governed by a farmer-led coalition that had, in varying guises, held power since 1922. The most important government program of the year was a massive attempt at rural electrification, begun during the war. In 1941, 51% of Manitoba's population was still rural and in 1946 there were only 19 towns and cities of more than 1,000 people. Rural Manitoba dominated the legislature as well. The division of seats favoured smaller-population rural ridings versus the large-population, multi-seat Winnipeg ridings that significantly under-represented Winnipeg in the legislature.

By 1958, Manitoba had changed: coalition government had been replaced by party government; government had entered or had been dragged into a wide range of other activities; and reorganization of electoral boundaries had thrust greater power into the hands of Winnipeg's voters. If nothing else, the great flood of 1950 clearly demonstrated once and for all the signal importance of Winnipeg to the province. In the years that followed the flood the city began to assert itself more in the politics and economy of the province. Urbanization and suburbanization marked the 1950s across Canada, but in the prairie provinces' biggest city and smallest province the effect of post-war urbanization was felt first and strongest. As of 1951 the rural population was down to 43%, and in 1961 it had declined even further to only 36% of Manitoba's population. In 1956 the number of towns and cities had risen to 27, and Winnipeg alone accounted for half of the province's people. In 1958 Manitoba was, in many ways, no longer the rural province it had been 10 years earlier.[1]

This transition occurred during the premiership of Douglas Lloyd Campbell: first elected in the sweep of 1922, appointed to cabinet by Bracken in the 1930s, and minister responsible for rural electrification under Stuart Garson. A farmer himself, if only in spirit while he was Premier, Campbell shepherded the transition but could not reap its benefits. In 1948 he had been the perfect match for the premiership: a populist farmer, an experienced politician, antagonistic to party politics, and fiscally conservative. Campbell changed little over the 10 years of his premiership, but the province changed around him. Those traits that made him ideal in 1948 characterized him by 1958 as out-of-touch with the needs and desires of the majority of Manitobans.

Doug Campbell was born in Portage la Prairie, 50 miles west of Winnipeg, in 1895. His parents came west from Ontario in 1880, his father Howard leaving a position as a junior partner at the Kent Mills in Chatham so that he and his wife could take up farming. According to Doug, his father "found [milling] to be increasingly hazardous" as grain dust collected in his lungs, and began looking for a new profession.

Campbell's mother Mary[2] had an aunt and uncle in Manitoba. The uncle, Francis Ogletree, one-time member of Manitoba's legislative council, arranged for a quarter section north of Portage near Flee Island. The land had first been homesteaded by a Vincent Vary, but while Vary had paid the $10 fee and built a house, he had neither met his residency requirement nor broken the land. Assured by Ogletree and Ogletree's lawyer that he would be able to get legal possession of the land, Campbell set out to homestead in 1880, travelling through Duluth and into Manitoba by boat, then by train west to Portage and north to his section. The farm cost the novice farmer $1,200—an incredible sum for farm land not broken, especially when there were still $10 homesteads available in the prairies. The property had some advantages, however: Howard could get possession immediately, rather than going through the homesteading process; the land was close to the railway; and Howard could work for wages while preparing his farm.

His neighbour to the south, William Davis, gave Campbell work on his own land and lent him a team of horses and a plough. When not working for Davis, Howard Campbell slowly began breaking the sod around his new house, cutting through 30 acres in the first summer—as much in one year as new homesteaders were required to clear in three.[3]

Doug's father was raised a Presbyterian, his mother as a Disciple of Christ. The Disciples had many adherents in Portage and she became deeply involved in the church, while Howard stopped regularly attending any church. In his later life, Doug Campbell remembered the services stretching on long past those of the Anglican church across the street. After the service Mrs. Campbell and her children remained behind to visit with other church members. As a child Doug attended with his mother, but as he grew into adulthood he followed his father's lead and stopped attending without ever having been baptized or taking the sacrament. Upon his marriage, Doug joined his wife Gladys' Methodist church, and they stayed within it, and then the United Church, the rest of their lives. They were not frequent churchgoers, but in later years Doug maintained positive feelings for Christianity generally, and for the Church of Christ in particular.[4]

Campbell was one of five children, three girls and two boys: Tena, May, Maude and Howard Wells (Wellie). As a boy, Doug attended the little Flee Island school, but for grades 11 and 12 he moved into Portage la Prairie. His maternal grandparents had followed his parents to Manitoba and, like his sisters, Doug stayed with them while studying. Fourteen miles separated Flee Island from Portage—too long for a daily commute alone by horse.

Upon finishing high school in 1913, Doug left Portage for Brandon College. His intention was to go forward from college into a professional career such as law, but his rural schooling left him ill-prepared for the expected language skills. While at Brandon he had hoped to pick up and improve in French and Latin. The two years he spent there frustrated him, and the chance to farm kept calling him back to the Portage area.

World War I, the influenza outbreak, labour unrest, and depression in manufactured goods and agricultural produce spurred on many new social movements. One of the most effective politically was led by farmers, federally in the Progressive Party and provincially in farmer organizations and parties. Farmer groups won the Alberta election, formed a coalition government with the labour party in Ontario, and helped propel many progressives to power federally in the years immediately following the war. In 1922, in Manitoba's second post-war election, the United Farmers of Manitoba (UFM) bested the older parties. It was this election that first swept the then 27-year-old Campbell into government as member of the Legislative Assembly (MLA) for Lakeside, the rural riding around Portage la Prairie.

In the years leading up to 1922, Lakeside had been a Liberal riding represented by

Colonel C.D. McPherson. In the 1920 general election, and in a 1921 by-election after he was appointed to cabinet, McPherson ran against and bested E.H. Muir, a local farmer, former reeve and resident of High Bluff. A Conservative, in 1921 Muir had run as a "Farmer," but by 1922 he was once again the Conservative candidate. McPherson sought re-election once more as a Liberal.

The UFM did not have a candidate at first. Several local men were considered, and how young Campbell came to the UFM and to be their candidate is unclear. In his unpublished memoir he was self-effacing in his telling of it: working one day with another farmer, Bill Fisher, the question of UFM candidates came up. After listing off several potential nominees, Campbell reports Fisher as saying: "I hear some of [the local UFM] talking about you." Campbell denied this as rumour, to which Fisher replied "Oh, you might as well try it. The rest of them are no damn good either!"

Campbell proved capable of the tough work a rural campaign required, going from farm to farm and encouraging both the men and the recently enfranchised women of every house to cast their vote for him. Lakeside was dotted with several one- and two-street hamlets, including High Bluff, which both Muir and Campbell called home. The Conservative and UFM candidates held meetings together in many of these little towns, each making speeches and working for the vote. Although Muir was officially the Conservative candidate and Campbell the UFM one, Muir challenged Campbell on his true colours, accusing him, as a supporter of McPherson in the 1920 election, of really being a "Liberal," while Muir was the "Farmer" candidate himself, despite holding the Conservative nomination. Campbell denied the connections at the time, and later maintained that he had held no party affiliation prior to 1922, or, keeping faith with UFM and Progressive ideals, really until the 1940s when the Bracken-Garson-Campbell coalition governments started to dissolve into clear parties. Despite these claims, Doug was raised in a very Liberal household, even though his father had voted Tory once in the 1910s. It is likely that many in Lakeside knew his family's party predilections.[5]

Campbell won the seat in part due to his extensive campaigning but also as part of the provincewide fervour for the UFM. Campbell remained Lakeside's MLA for 47 years (1922–69). When he finally stepped down he was the longest-serving elected representative in the Commonwealth.

Campbell sat in the backbenches for his first 14 years as an MLA. In 1936 Bracken appointed him minister of Agriculture and Immigration, a portfolio he held until 1948. In 1942 he was given the added role of minister in charge of the Manitoba Power Commission. It was from this shared role that his plan for rural electrification was born. It would be the most important aspect of his political career.

Coming to Power

Almost as soon as Louis St. Laurent was selected to be the new Liberal Prime Minister in 1948, gossip about the future of Manitoba's Premier, Stuart Garson, began circulating in Ottawa and Winnipeg. In early October, the *Winnipeg Free Press* reported that Manitoba politics were due for a shake-up: George Drew's selection as new leader of the federal

Progressive Conservatives would lead to demands that provincial parties drop out of coalitions, while Garson was being courted for St. Laurent's cabinet. Nevertheless, Garson denied any intention to leave the province.[6]

St. Laurent was to be sworn in on November 15, and by the beginning of that month tensions began building in the province. Hugh Boyd reported on Wednesday, November 3, that no one in Ottawa was denying rumours of Garson's move.[7] The next day the *Free Press* had moved on to considering who would replace Garson and how. MLAs from Springfield and St. Clemens were calling for a convention, but "informal sources" reported to the *Free Press* that, as in 1942 when Garson became Premier, the decision would be made in the coalition caucus. The paper listed five men as likely candidates: Campbell; Charles Rhodes Smith, minister of Labour; J.S. McDiarmid, minister of Mines and Resources; Bill Morton, minister responsible for the Telephones; and W.J. Parker, president of the Manitoba Wheat Pool. Despite the range of candidates, the paper already predicted that "Mr. Campbell is expected to make a strong bid for the premiership. Mr. Campbell, popular on the whole with farmers, is believed likely to find considerable support from the faction which wants a rural man to head the provincial government."[8]

On Friday, Garson held a caucus meeting and announced his intention to leave for the federal cabinet. He then left the caucus and legislature. The meeting broke up and the various coalition partners met on their own (at this point the coalition contained Liberal Progressives, Progressive Conservatives, Social Credit MLAs, and some independents; the CCF, some Conservatives, and the Communists had left or never entered the coalition). The coalition caucus met again for two hours late in the afternoon, then broke up for dinner and a second round of separate partner meetings. Garson's departure prompted several questions: Was the coalition worth continuing? Would the leader be picked by caucus or at a convention? If the caucus picked a leader would he only be *pro tem* pending a convention? What role would the Conservatives, in particular, play in the coalition? On Saturday the *Free Press* reported that the meetings ended at 11:23 Saturday morning, to resume at 3:00 that afternoon. Campbell seemed to be the leading choice as a caucus-chosen leader, with rural support that outweighed fellow Liberal Progressive Rhodes Smith's urban support. Working against Campbell was an apparent threat by the coalition Conservatives to pull out if he was selected.[9]

The Tories demanded four cabinet seats and, if necessary, the post of Deputy Premier, to remain in the coalition. The Liberals (and others) agreed at 11:35 p.m. on Saturday. At midnight a vote in caucus was held over whether Campbell or Errick Willis, Conservative leader, would be premier. At 12:35 an announcement was made:

> At a coalition caucus this evening as a result of a ballot taken, Hon. Douglas L. Campbell was chosen premier-elect over Hon. Errick F. Willis. Arrangements were made that Hon. Errick F. Willis will hereafter be designated deputy premier, and it was agreed that a cabinet would be formed composed of eight Liberal Progressives and four Progressive Conservatives.

The *Free Press* quoted one senior Tory:

> We thought for a while the whole thing was over and the coalition would break up.... But we've won and we got what we were after.

Campbell was sworn in as Premier the following Saturday morning.[10]

Campbell as Premier

Campbell had particular charms as a politician. He prided himself on plain talk, often without notes. He was particularly good with people: often recognising them after only a single meeting, he would greet them by recalling something significant about their lives that would draw out a personal bond. Many people from within the province and outside would write him, and with several he maintained a years-long correspondence about both affairs of state and their personal needs. He was almost always generous in this correspondence and when meeting people on the street or at events. Yet, he was also keenly aware of the lures of corruption, and generally refused to use his position to help people work the system. Campbell was very conscientious of running government fairly and efficiently as he saw it. At a policy level it was reflected in limiting debt and restricting the role of government to those places where it could provide support without regulating too greatly. At a personal level, it meant refraining from abusing public office through graft, patronage, or the personal use of power.

At first Campbell's government policy differed little from that of Garson. Under Campbell, the government continued to invest a great deal in rural electrification. In the years that followed, however, the government began investing in other large-scale projects, including hydro production, flood prevention and health care. To do some of this, particularly the electrical projects, the government needed to take on extensive new loans. Many of the debts accrued during the Depression remained to be paid. To regain and maintain its credit rating, the province started paying off its old debts and in 1947 it inaugurated an extensive debt repayment plan. In the lead-up to the presentation of the 1955 budget, Ronald D. Turner, the provincial treasurer, explained the debt retirement program followed throughout Campbell's tenure. First, he differentiated between government debt in general and "dead-weight debt," "borrowing for buildings, relief costs, and other non-revenue producing items." The principle of the program was to pay off this debt while allowing for some new debts, but only for those things that, in the government's view at least, would result in wealth production and thus pay for themselves over time. Turner noted that, in 1933–34, 31% of the province's revenues went towards the paying of interest on this "dead-weight" debt ($4.5 million of the $14-million budget). In 1940–41 the interest payments remained roughly the same. By 1955–56, however, the interest payments were more than halved to only $2 million, and the projection was to bring these interest payments down to $400,000 ten years later. The total "dead-weight" debt in 1947 was $67 million; this too had halved by 1955 to $34.5 million. The plan called for the outstanding Depression-era debt to be paid off by 1963, except for the money owed the federal government in treasury bills. This repayment plan did not mean the Garson and Campbell governments did not borrow money: between the war and 1955, Manitoba had borrowed $25 million a year. The repayment plan had cut the cost of this borrowing, however, from 1941 bond issues where interest rates had to be 2% higher than Ontario bonds, to September 1954 when Manitoba offered only 3.32% interest on its bonds, compared to the provincially guaranteed Ontario Hydro bonds at 3.57% issued the same year.[11]

Between coming to power in 1948 and 1955, the government introduced neither new taxes nor tax increases. Government was expected to live within its means, and those means were relatively restricted. For much of Campbell's term the province's economy grew, and government revenues increased, but in 1955 the government reported its first decline in revenue in six years.[12] By 1957, although personal income in Manitoba was fifth highest in the country, the provincial government's revenues were the lowest per capita and only 40% of British Columbia's per capita revenue.[13] Debt repayment and "stand-pat" budgets reflected Campbell's overall fiscal conservatism, shared with his predecessors and rooted in both his farming background and the experience of the 1930s. Nonetheless, by prioritizing spending, Campbell's government did take part in province-building akin to Manitoba's prairie neighbours.[14]

Rural Electrification

Campbell's lasting legacy is the reorganization and expansion of electricity production and distribution in Manitoba. He later claimed to have championed rural electrification as a social and economic policy right from the start of his political career.[15]

When Campbell first arrived in the legislature in 1922, electricity service was a patchwork of private, provincial and municipal organization. Winnipeg, for example, was serviced by the private Winnipeg Electric Company and the city-owned Winnipeg City Hydro, both of which produced power from dams along the Winnipeg River system and sold power throughout Winnipeg.[16] In 1919, municipalities could seek help from the provincial Ministry of Public Works in generating, purchasing and transmitting power. The system as a whole was uncoordinated and poorly planned. Electricity was produced by private or municipal firms, transmitted on private, municipal and provincial power lines, and sold to local customers by private or municipal companies. When Portage la Prairie first received hydro power in 1920, it was purchased from Winnipeg City Hydro, transmitted west on lines operated by the provincial government, and sold by the municipality.

During the Depression the Manitoba Power Commission (MPC), responsible for the transmission lines and for helping municipalities establish systems, began to restrict municipalities to buying power for street lighting and like utilities and started selling power directly to individual consumers. With more control over sales and expansion of local lines, the MPC could plan grid and production expansion on a provincewide basis. Despite the provincial consolidation of power transmission, sales, and to some degree production outside of the city of Winnipeg, little was done during the 1930s and early 1940s to actually expand the network—depression and war forestalling the investment required. Much of the province remained off-line.

In 1944, Campbell was appointed minister in charge of the MPC, and it was under his watch as both minister and Premier that Manitoba's major rural electrification project was run. This project in turn led to a general rethinking of electric power provision in the province, and the creation of a government power-generation, transmission and sales monopoly. To Campbell, modernization through electrification was of great significance for all on the farm, most particularly women:

> In our home, Gladys, my wife, had things very little better or different from what her mother and my mother had had... . But the minute farm electrification came to the area, the farm women of Manitoba (although the farm men certainly benefitted as well) stepped up in one fell swoop and became a different class of citizen to what they had been before. Not only did it provide them with refrigeration, stoves, washing machines, and many other appliances that were labour-savers and food-savers, but it also made other things [like indoor plumbing] so much more feasible than they had been before... . [W]hen electrification went in, it made possible all these modern conveniences whose lack had been a major drawback to life on the farm.[17]

As Joy Parr has pointed out, modernizing the home or farm after World War II "was not only about change, but about making change supportable." Modernization would be costly, and a significant financial risk for farmers still scarred by the Depression.[18] Campbell needed a policy that protected farm families from the full costs of electrification and secured their individual private investments in the project.

Rural electrification, as Campbell set it up, was a partnership between the provincial government, the MPC, and consumers. Electrification of a town or area began with a public meeting led by an MPC salesman and attended by local farmers and townspeople. If 10 or more people signed contracts, electricity would come. The province paid for the transmission lines and guaranteed the rates. The consumers, to sign up, undertook to wire their houses for electricity and to stock their house (and farm) with a minimum number of electrical appliances. These could be purchased from the MPC and paid for over time along with the electricity. The household had to have or purchase at least five small appliances from a list including irons, toasters, radios, waffle irons, sandwich toasters, electric engines and water heaters. In addition, the household had to have at least one large appliance, be it a vacuum cleaner, washing machine or refrigerator for the home or a milking machine or grain crusher for the barn (some heavy appliances, like a cream separator or water pump could serve both home and barn).[19] Failure to keep up one's payments could result in losing both hook-up and appliances. Customers who made prompt payment would receive a 10% discount on their bill. The demand that the *house* be wired and the pride of place given to household appliances underlined the importance of "women's" work to the electrification and modernization goal.

To sell electrification the MPC followed Winnipeg Hydro's lead and hired a home economist, Elizabeth Goulding. In columns published in MPC programs and at field days held at energized farms throughout the province, Goulding and her home economists stressed to farm women the utility of electricity and electric appliances in cooking, cleaning, and other tasks.[20] It was the home economists' appeal to rural women that created the demand for appliances and electrification.

The program was very popular with farmers, and there was a strong desire to be hooked up. The province made an effort to include as many people as possible, despite the set policies. Campbell often wrote letters of support to the MPC on behalf of farmers who had missed their opportunity to electrify under the program. In one case, Campbell wrote to the farmer as well:

> I was glad to know that the Manitoba Power Commission will probably
> be able to look after your requirements because, being a farmer myself, I
> know what a great boon electricity is to the farming community.[21]

Campbell was less sympathetic to critics of his program. A.E. Grassby, president of Winnipeg Piano, wrote Premier Campbell in 1949, complaining about the MPC underselling private appliance dealers. Campbell denied this, claiming the MPC did "not supply them below the cost of the goods and distribution."[22] Despite Campbell's claims, the program did compete with, and even undersell, private appliance dealers. For example, the MPC sold GE ovens and ranges on their own, while private appliance dealers had to sell the same with an accompanying "free" kitchen suite for $75 more than the MPC.[23] Such government interference in the market to support farmers as individual producers was acceptable.

Campbell was even less sympathetic to organized labour's concerns with rural electrification. In 1949 The International Electrical Workers' Union and the Trades and Labour Congress complained to Campbell that the MPC-organized, two-week training courses for "farmers and their sons" to learn how to wire their houses conflicted with the National Electrical Code endorsed by the provincial government. The union believed wiring should be left to licensed electricians, and the province should not encourage "incompetent and inefficient" work to be done by farmers. Campbell replied that the courses would prevent the very problems the union warned against. The union's concern in protecting the skills of its members was lost on Campbell, while his faith in the capacity of farmers assured him that there would be no safety problems created by letting loose hundreds of amateur electricians. The independent farmer, working for himself and his family, was the centre of Campbell's philosophy and policy.[24]

The Flood of 1950

Two years into his term came Campbell's first great test as Premier: the Red River flood of 1950. The flood affected many people in the province: farmers, small-town dwellers and Winnipeggers. In preparing for and responding to the flood, Campbell had to confront his own belief in small government and attempt to deal with the competing demands of rural and urban people on provincial policy and resources. Although flood reconstruction was successful, Campbell's reaction to the disaster propelled his alienation from Winnipeggers that would lead to his ultimate loss of the Premier's chair.

The flood was an odd natural disaster: it could be seen coming and plans could be made to prevent harm, and yet it did significant damage throughout the Red River Valley. The winter of 1949–50 stretched well into spring with late, heavy snowfalls. By mid-April flooding had already forced many from their homes in North Dakota and Minnesota. Watching the water coming, people along the Red River built sandbag dikes to protect their homes and towns or neighbourhoods. On April 20, the town of Emerson was flooded, followed on April 27 by Morris, both forcing complete evacuations. The first major Greater Winnipeg breach was in Wildwood in Fort Garry on May 6. By Thursday, May 11, 40,000 people from Emerson to Winnipeg had evacuated to escape the water. By the end of the weekend, on May 14, 80,000 people had left Winnipeg.[25] When the river crested in Winnipeg on May 12, one tenth of the city was under water, while other neighbourhoods below water level only remained dry because of vigilant guarding of the hastily built sandbag dikes.

Campbell delayed doing things during the flood or after that would result in a significant short- or long-term financial commitment for the government. The government encouraged the work of dike-building and evacuations, although they did not offer significant coordination. Much of the response was locally organized: towns and neighbourhoods organized dike-building and flood watches. Non-governmental organizations, most importantly the Red Cross, but also the Salvation Army, the Boy Scouts, and others coordinated on-the-spot relief and the Red Cross directed much of the organized evacuations, securing help from the railways, the airlines, and any people with vehicles. The evacuees often moved in with people on higher ground: family, friends, even willing strangers—most did not have to rely on the Red Cross or expect the province to find them space.

As the flood waters spread across the Red River Valley, moving north towards Winnipeg, Campbell remained reluctant to seek to have the flood proclaimed a national emergency, which in the past had been a signal of the fiscal pledge by both federal and provincial governments toward reconstruction. He appears to have trusted that, as in the past, the flood and its damage could be handled locally; a national emergency both meant that the province could not care for its own, and committed the provincial government to offering relief. He was reluctant to allow either. Until the federal government had assured him that it would take up a significant share of the costs, Campbell did not want to make any financial committment. It was not until the day after the breach of the sandbag walls in Wildwood that Campbell wrote to Prime Minister Louis St. Laurent asking for the declaration of a national emergency.

The water finally crested in Winnipeg 30.3 feet above normal winter ice level, and 23 feet above normal summer flow levels.[26] In the days that followed, as the flood waters slowly began to recede, Campbell began to turn more actively toward provincial direction of relief and reconstruction. On May 17 the Premier's office announced a joint federal-provincial commission to evaluate the size of loss and thus the federal government's share in reconstruction costs. While the commission met, the province would offer funds to people who demonstrated a particular need (a plan opposed by Conservative Duff Roblin who saw any need-based funding as unfair). On May 19 the province organized a meeting with the Red Cross to determine who would be responsible for what in the short- and long-term rehabilitation effort. Campbell began laying out a policy based upon rehabilitation and aid if necessary, not full compensation for all losses.[27]

As J.M. Bumsted has pointed out, the provincial government was spared significant expense because of the very sort of disaster the flood was. In an era when most visuals in the news were either still pictures in newspapers or newsreels at the cinema, the Red River flood was a perfect disaster. Unlike earthquakes, the Red River flood could be seen coming. News agencies could ensure that they had crews in place to pick up the story from preparation through breach of the dikes and crest of the water to receding and reconstruction: a full narrative arc in pictures and over several weeks. This allowed the Red Cross and other private agencies to organize effective relief drives across North America, in England, and beyond. The Red Cross alone raised half a million dollars from the rest of Canada and the United States. The province also established the Manitoba Flood Relief Fund to collect and administer funds for flood relief. By 1951, when it wound down, the fund had received $9 million, much in cash donations from abroad; it spent $7 million on rehabilitation.[28]

Thanks in large part to private donations, Campbell was able to limit the financial exposure of the provincial government in reconstruction. The core government agency was the Red River Valley Board, jointly funded by the provincial and federal governments. Created on May 31, the board was responsible for restoring buildings to their *pre-flood* conditions. The fund was not to be used to make improvements or changes to affected homes, farms and businesses. Through the board and in response to the immediate crisis, Campbell's government spent $22 million, $14.5 million of which was eventually reimbursed by the federal government.[29]

Despite its scale, clean-up was mainly complete by the beginning of winter in 1950. If, during the flood, Campbell had been reluctant to get involved and quick to limit the province's indemnity, then after the flood he was even more cautious. He would not compensate property owners who would in future be outside new permanent dykes created to control future floods in Winnipeg unless the federal government took up 75% of the cost. In 1953, federal government engineers suggested building a 25-mile dyke wall at Ste. Agathe, digging a channel at Portage la Prairie to drain excess water from the Assiniboine River into Lake Manitoba, and digging a floodway around the city of Winnipeg to divert excess water. Arriving just as the very expensive arrangement to buy out Winnipeg Electric was being discussed, Campbell was unprepared to spend the $47–$104 million total the scheme would cost. Having failed to secure federal co-payment, but faced with another, smaller flood in 1956, Campbell appointed a Royal Commission to investigate the costs and benefits of the scheme. Nonetheless, he remained open to attacks in the Winnipeg press and from his opponents in the legislature for failing to fully respond to the needs of Winnipeggers. Even in 1958, Roblin was able to run his Winnipeg campaign against Campbell's response to the flood and continued "failure" to prevent future floods.[30]

However successful the reconstruction, during the flood Campbell was seen as slow to act and uncaring about the plight of Winnipeggers. Campbell's response to the flood was the first of several times when he failed to properly understand Winnipeg and its needs. A self-described farmer and with political passions driven by his vision of rural life, the growth and demands of Manitoba's major city were often alien to him. Most Winnipeg MLAs— Conservative, CCF, or Labour Progressive Party (i.e. Communist)—remained outside of the coalition as well, limiting the urban experience of even his cabinet or caucus (even though Charles Rhodes Smith was a Winnipeg MLA and an important member of the coalition cabinet). The electoral map prior to 1958 disproportionately favoured rural areas, Campbell's heartland. He thus had limited capacity and little need to understand the city or respond to its concerns.

Hydroelectric Development

Despite his inclination toward individual self-sufficiency with limited government assistance, Campbell did recognize the need for a larger provincial role in some areas. This was most clear in the second half of his electricity program: building a provincially owned monopoly electricity producer, distributor and marketer. His failure to sympathize with the interests of Winnipeggers meant that this program was in the end less successful than rural electrification. By 1947, it had become clear that the imminent future demands on electricity in Manitoba would exceed the capacity of the Winnipeg River so that production on other rivers, most likely those in the far north of the province, had to be considered. Campbell, as minister in charge of the MPC, asked Dr. T.H. Hogg of the Ontario Hydro-Electric Power Commission to review the options before the province in providing more power.

Hogg issued his *Report on Supply of Electrical Energy in the Province of Manitoba* in March 1948. He identified four river systems that offered particularly good power potential: the already-dammed Winnipeg River and the Churchill, Nelson, and Saskatchewan-Dauphin rivers. In Ontario and New Brunswick electricity was being rationed. While such rationing was not yet required in Manitoba, the increase of electricity requirements both in the rural regions and in the growing and industrializing city of Winnipeg would put strains on the existing system. More development along the Winnipeg River was necessary, as was development on the northern rivers. Producing power in the north and transmitting it south would be expensive, however.

Hogg offered three plans for developing more hydro production. Under Option A, the present organization of power production and distribution would remain the same, but all new power generation development would be by the province. Option B would leave development of the north to private firms, or at least out of the province's responsibility (Winnipeg Electric and City Hydro were the obvious developers). Option C, Hogg's favoured recommendation, called for the consolidation of all production, transmission and sale of electricity in the province under a provincial government-owned monopoly. The province would purchase, absorb or expropriate all of the private and municipal power companies. Production costs in the north could then be offset by profits from southern dams.[31] The government decided to follow Hogg's advice and Campbell and his ministers set out to implement Option C.

In much of the province the MPC already looked after distribution and production. Over the next 10 years (and more) the MPC took over or purchased the local distribution systems from the public or private owners in towns like Selkirk or regions like the Swan River Valley, a process it had begun even prior to Hogg's report (for instance, taking over

Neepawa's distribution network in 1944). But Winnipeg posed a bigger problem. To bring about Option C, the province would have to take over the generators and distribution networks of both a public and a private company. In 1951 Campbell's government began to try to reorganize the Winnipeg production facilities.

The government passed legislation to expropriate Winnipeg Electric if necessary and convinced Winnipeg's mayor and a majority of city council to support Option C and turn over City Hydro to the province. Not everyone was convinced, however, and the *Winnipeg Free Press* launched a campaign against the imposition of Option C (a public monopoly that smacked of socialism) upon Winnipeg. The *Free Press* instead celebrated "Plan D," that let the province take over the rest of Manitoba but left the Winnipeg companies in place as both producers and local distributors and allowed for private producers to develop dams as long as all of the power was sold to a provincial pool that sold it back to the local distributors.

Plan D maintained the patina of a free market, but really only served to siphon a portion of the profits into private hands rather than into lower rates or new production capacity. Allied with the *Free Press* on this issue were a number of the city's business classes, who opposed any growth of the state into areas of private enterprise. The other important Winnipeg daily, the *Tribune*, although a Tory paper, sided with the Campbell government, as did many in the municipal government, including, much to the *Free Press*'s consternation, Joe Zuken and other Winnipeg Communists.[32]

The province opposed Plan D for a number of reasons. Most importantly, management of transmission and distribution from several different producers would be more costly and less efficient. Second, the various producers and distributors would all be responsible to different bodies: Winnipeg Electric to its shareholders, City Hydro to the city, and the MPC to the province and to all of its rural customers. Neither Winnipeg Electric nor City Hydro, for instance, would willingly sell their hydro to the pool at a low rate, only to have to buy it back at a much higher rate that would subsidize other developments. On the contrary, their interests would be against pooling and the province would have to compel it.

Campbell was no socialist, and he was genuinely opposed to the growth of the state, but he was also a firm believer in efficiency and keeping costs as low as possible. Convinced that Option C would be much more cost effective for all in the province, he and his government stood by their position, championing it in the legislature, on the radio, and in speeches both in and outside of Winnipeg.[33] In a February 1951 legislative address, Campbell laid out his vision for hydroelectricity in the province:

> The broad objectives of the Government's policy are to bring about conditions under which the power requirements of the main industrial and agricultural areas of this province will be assured. It will also be a fundamental objective that these power supplies be made available to the power consumer at the lowest cost and with the maximum stability of rate structure which can be achieved within the limitations of sound policy and sound management.

Campbell acknowledged, however, that Option C was unacceptable to many in Winnipeg. He proposed a modified version, whereby City Hydro would keep its generation facilities—both the dams on the Winnipeg River and the steam plant in the city—but all power produced would be pooled.[34]

Faced with the concerted opposition of the *Free Press* and parts of the local business class, the city council decided to put its support to a referendum in the spring of 1951. Campbell and several ministers tried to drum up support for the province's position. In the end they failed, and Plan D prevailed in the referendum.

Losing the referendum did not end Option C. Rather, the province entered into new negotiations with all of the parties. By 1953 it bought out the electricity production and distribution network of the private Winnipeg Electric for $55 million (the CCF attempted to legislate a buyout of Winnipeg Electric's gas system at the same time, but they were defeated on this measure).[35] The city-owned Winnipeg Hydro remained independent. It was given some of the former Winnipeg Electric's property and customers, but gave up all of its distribution network and customers outside of the city.

The Introduction of Hospital Insurance

Saskatchewan first introduced government-supported hospital insurance in 1947; British Columbia and Alberta, in their own ways, followed suit soon after. But in Manitoba neither Garson nor Campbell made hospital insurance a core of their programs. This did not mean that those who could not afford care all went without: a municipal scheme for providing hospital care to the indigent had been established much earlier. Provision for medical care was not bad in Manitoba: it had more hospital beds per capita than all provinces but British Columbia, and was roughly in the middle of the provinces respecting the number of hospital workers, physicians and dentists. Nonetheless, it was a private system, and people relied on private insurance, their own money or limited charity for services. And limited the charity was: in 1952 the combined health-services spending by the provincial and municipal governments was the second least of all of the provinces, $13.73 per person and only 61% of the national average. Four years later, spending was up to $17.99 per person per year, but this was now the least amount spent per person in Canada, and it remained only 66% of the national average.[36]

The Campbell government's lack of interest in provincial investment in health care was first tested in 1955. Much of the hospital care for indigents in Winnipeg and southern Manitoba fell to the Winnipeg General Hospital (WGH). Municipalities were charged per person per night for care. In late spring the hospital's board of trustees issued a statement to the government demanding it either subsidize indigent care or take it over entirely. Campbell offered instead a conference involving the provincial government, the municipalities and the hospitals, conceding that more assistance was necessary. After a meeting of the WGH board on April 1, municipalities were given seven days' notice of a 63% hike in fees for rural municipalities and a 52% increase for Winnipeg. Following two conferences between the province, the municipalities and hospitals through the month of April, an agreement was reached. The rate hikes would go forward, but the municipalities would pay 60% of indigent costs and the province would cover the balance.[37]

The slowness to act on hospital insurance, despite the western models of Saskatchewan, British Columbia and Alberta, rested in Campbell's notion of federal and provincial responsibility. While health care was a provincial responsibility under the British North America Act, Campbell and his predecessors had been willing to cede some of it to the federal government. In the immediate post-war period, Garson supported the federal position on taxation and King's 1945 proposals that included federal support for health insurance and hospitals.[38] At a federal-provincial meeting just days after the announcement of the indigent hospital stay support, Campbell reiterated Manitoba's position that the federal government had undertaken responsibility for significant health and hospital funding. Prime Minister St. Laurent, in his opening statement, had asserted that "We believe the proposals of 1945 are no longer suitable for 1955." Campbell, along with other Premiers, balked at this and demanded discussion of federal support for health insurance.[39]

Although the April 1955 meeting (or the October 1955 tax-rental federal-provincial meeting) did not produce a clear plan for federal action, in 1956 federal Health minister Paul Martin introduced a plan to provide federal funding toward hospital care once a majority of provinces had introduced, and a majority of the Canadian population was covered by, a provincial hospital plan with universal application.[40]

Campbell's government did not move quickly on the federal plan. When the Diefenbaker government came to power in 1957, Manitoba had still not introduced a universal hospital insurance plan. Rather, at Diefenbaker's first federal-provincial conference in November, Campbell demanded to hear the new government's plans for hospital insurance, for "until we know what action the federal government proposes to take … we cannot further develop our plans with any degree of certainty." The federal government did make changes, most importantly reducing the number of provinces necessary for the program to begin from six to five. Saskatchewan, British Columbia, Alberta and Newfoundland had provincial programs that were eligible for federal funding.[41] Campbell resolved Manitoba would be next.

By 1958, Campbell was into the fifth year of his third government and an election had to be called before June. Late in the final legislative session a hospital insurance plan was finally introduced. All Manitobans' hospital stays would be covered by the province as of July 1, 1958. Private hospital insurance contracts could continue until December 31, 1958. Any surplus premiums held by insurers would be either returned to the policy-holder or rolled over toward supplementary health insurance. Each individual was required to pay a monthly premium to the government of $2.05, or $4.10 for a family.

The insurance bill was rushed through the legislature. For example, the legislative committee heard only two witnesses, one from the Trades and Labour Congress and one from Christian Scientists, who wanted to be exempt from the premiums as they would not use the hospitals. The legislation was supported by Campbell's Liberal-Progressives, the Conservatives and the CCF. The *Winnipeg Free Press* asserted that the decision to introduce some plan was made, not by Campbell, but by the federal government in passing its legislation in 1957. Second, the paper explained the quick passage of the bill because no party wanted to go into the imminent election opposed to hospital insurance, and neither opposition party wanted to give the government space or time to celebrate the legislation in debate.[42]

Despite having the lowest health funding of the provinces in 1956, on July 1, 1958, when federal funding began, Manitoba was one of only five provinces to have eligible programs in place and was the first province to enact a plan following the federal government's announcement. Campbell's position on hospital insurance, like his response to the 1950 flood, reflected his views both of Manitoba's own wealth and the federal government's role. Manitoba was not a rich province, and prudence was necessary in planning programs. He seems to have recognized the need for flood relief in 1950, and generally for hospital insurance, but in both cases he felt responsibility had to be shared by the federal government simply to make any program viable in Manitoba.

Democratic Reform

In the election of 1953, the city of Winnipeg had three large ridings, represented by four members each. Electors would vote by ranking candidates and the four who ranked highest overall won for the riding. Registered voters in the province as of 1952 were almost evenly divided between 228,280 in urban areas and 224,083 in rural areas. Yet urban voters returned only 17 members to the legislature, while rural voters were divided into 40 one-member ridings; thus there was one member for every 13,428 urban voters and one member for every 5,602 rural voters. The disparity had to be resolved.

In 1953 the legislature established a select committee to re-evaluate the drawing of electoral boundaries. It reported in 1955, and Campbell's government responded by putting two pieces of legislation before the house. All three leaders supported some or all of the redistribution plans, to the point that provincial treasurer Ron Turner described the proponent of redistribution as "Camblinson," an amalgamation of all three party leaders' names: Campbell, Roblin, and Stinson. Under the first bill, the multiple-member seats in Winnipeg were to be abolished, replaced by smaller, one-MLA seats. The CCF opposed this measure, asserting that proportional representation through multi-member seats better reflected the true desires of the voters. The second bill established an independent electoral boundary commission to determine boundaries. The commission would be composed of the Chief Justice of the province, the president of the University of Manitoba, and the Chief Electoral Officer. The bill identified the boundaries of the urban areas of the province, and then established a four- to seven-seat division between urban and rural areas: 21 to 36. The ridings were to be determined by a number of criteria, according to one commentator to include "the community or diversity of interests in the population, the means of communication between the various parts, the physical features, and 'all other similar and relevant factors'." Although the less populated rural part of the province was still over-represented, the disparity was not quite as great as it had been. Here the CCF again differed, urging less disparity between rural and urban areas, although supporting the independent commission and the principles for determining riding areas.[43] The *Winnipeg Free Press* supported Campbell's reforms too. In an editorial at the end of the 1955 spring session, the newspaper complimented Campbell's government for introducing reforms that would significantly improve the quality of elections in the province. Foreshadowing 1958, the editorial continued, "As the Government depends for its support largely on the country constituencies it cannot be denied that … there is a considerable degree of selflessness on the part of the Government in making this change; even if it does less than complete justice to city voters." The paper did, however, bemoan the demise of ranking candidates.[44]

In 1958 Campbell attempted to initiate a second important reform: a permanent Speaker for the legislature. Campbell secured the passage of two pieces of legislation committing the legislature to the principle. The Speaker, selected by and with the real support of the whole assembly, would hold a continuing position, even if the government changed. A special riding, limited perhaps to the legislature's grounds, would be set aside for the Speaker, so that there would be no need for the Speaker to do constituency work, or seek election or re-election based on the changing political tides in the province. Campbell believed this would de-politicize the Speaker and thus lead to a more democratic house. In proposing the bills, Campbell sought the support of the opposition, having Duff Roblin, leader of the Conservatives, second one and Lloyd Stinson, leader of the CCF, second the other. Securing all-party support underscored Campbell's belief in this as a democratic move, showing the apolitical, good-government nature of the changes while also committing all parties to following the principles in the legislation. Roblin was willing to second the motion; however, he did not firmly commit to the principles.[45] The idea of a permanent speaker reflected Campbell's old prairie populist and progressive roots, which remained present if less vital in government policy by his last term.

End of an Era: The 1958 Election

Campbell waited until May 1, 1958, five years and 10 days into his mandate, to call his third election for the middle of June. Thanks to the reforms of 1955, Campbell was already at a disadvantage because the strength of rural votes was diminished. He also faced a much sharper opposition than ever before. The coalition was no more, so he and his government represented just one party, and could only rely on votes for that party to secure victory. The CCF were much the same as they had been in 1953, and did not challenge for government, but they could be spoilers. The Progressive Conservatives were a very different party, now under Duff Roblin, who was grandson of the last Conservative Premier in Manitoba, young (40 years old to Campbell's 63) and urban (he would run for, and win, the downtown Wolseley riding). The Manitoba election also followed both the 1957 and 1958 federal elections: the first resulting in the prairie-based Progressive Conservative John Diefenbaker's minority victory over the long-serving Liberals, the second in his landslide election-victory. In Manitoba the federal Liberals had been routed. The parallels between federal and provincial politics were obvious. Campbell's party had been the government for 36 years, as the federal Liberals had been for 22 years. Campbell had come to power as premier following Louis St. Laurent's rise to the prime ministership. Diefenbaker and Roblin were both relatively new leaders in their parties, and both seemed to have led significant regenerations of the Progressive Conservative party.

Reporting on the campaign and the leaders returned attention to Campbell's style. In describing a leaders' debate in rural Manitoba, Peter Desbarats in the *Winnipeg Tribune* wrote, "Mr. Campbell relies, literally, on the folksy approach … and it sounds quite natural the way he says things like 'I do try to tell the truth, in a simple way'." He continued, stressing Campbell's connection to his audience, "The premier is the most effective [of the three leaders] when it comes to narrating stock platform jokes… . Where hand-shaking ability is concerned, Mr. Campbell is the old master … and his memory for faces is astounding." Campbell would attend these meetings dressed formally in a well-pressed suit, looking the part of the serious farmer-in-politics, complementing the simple, common sense and populist approach of his speeches and personal meetings with Manitobans.[46] It was a style that served Campbell well in his own constituency and on the hustings in 1949 and 1953. It worked no longer. He now faced organized opposition parties with strong, locally popular candidates throughout the province. He faced parties with out-of-province, young, energetic and experienced workers organizing support—like Dalton Camp for the Progressive Conservatives and Stephen Lewis for the CCF.

The press moved against him. Tom Kent of the *Free Press* saw more liberal policies in Roblin's proposals than in the conservative, cautious governing style of Campbell's Liberal-Progressives.[47] Roblin's clearly pro-Winnipeg positions also set him apart from Campbell and appealed to the paper's reporters and editors.

Campbell lost support from both working people and the business classes. He had worked hard for rural electrification and the nationalization of hydroelectricity, but his reponse to the flood and to health care were perhaps more typical of his time in office. His general wariness of government action, and especially of government expenditure, did wonders for the province's balance sheet. But his government was slow to invest in infrastructure, be it public works like roads or the floodway, or public activity like education. Both the Progressive Conservatives and the CCF would offer not simply a change in government but a significant change in the style of government more in keeping with governments in much of the rest of Canada.

Roblin won the election, capturing as much of the popular vote as Campbell had in 1953—41%. But while in 1953 Campbell secured a sizable majority of the seats, the disparity in riding size between rural and urban Manitoba limited Roblin's take. In 1953 the Liberal-Progressives had won 35 of the Legislature's 57 seats; in 1958 Roblin won only 26. Campbell's party lost significantly, however, down from 35 to 19. Nor was his loss solely at the hands of Roblin and the Conservatives. The CCF increased their share of the popular vote from 17% to 20% and more than doubled their seats from 5 to 11, capitalizing on the new redistribution of urban ridings from which most of their members were elected. The combination of more urban seats, a growing boredom, frustration, even distaste for a government in power since 1922, and the provincial and federal regeneration of and excitement over the Progressive Conservatives defeated Campbell and the Liberal-Progressives.

The Conservatives' plurality of seats did not guarantee them the government. The morning after the election, Campbell met with his caucus to discuss what to do. At home for lunch, he met with Lloyd Stinson of the CCF to discuss their options. Both Stinson and Campbell were afraid that another election soon would result in a Roblin victory at the expense of both of their parties. In his own memoirs, Stinson recalls that "Campbell said he thought a coalition would be the most desirable solution for both parties.... He suggested two cabinet positions and possibly the Speakership for the CCF.... I insisted we would not consider coalition." Meetings continued between Campbell and Stinson, then with other negotiators, and several alternatives were considered, but no agreement was reached.[48]

Even though he was now in opposition, Campbell hoped his last attempt at democratic reform would go forward, and urged Roblin to institute the permanent speaker. When Roblin refused, Campbell tried to convince Stinson to join him in forcing Roblin to do so. In his memoirs, this incident still bothered Campbell, and he described Stinson as weakly unwilling to agree, quoting him:

> Well, it's a good thought but Doug I'd be afraid of it. If we did this to him and forced our man on him, that little bugger (his exact words) would call an election right away on that question.

To this, Campbell replied:

> Well, let him. That would be a great thing to go to the country on. He's going to call an election soon anyway now that he's in office.... What better than to take the reins in our own hands in the meantime and show that we mean it about a permanent Speaker.[49]

Campbell was upset at Roblin's rejection of the permanent Speaker. When Stinson chose not to support him, Campbell set out against Roblin, Stinson, and Roblin's eventual Speaker nominee, Abraham Harrison, a long-serving rural Conservative. After Roblin introduced his nominee, Campbell had first opportunity to respond. He asserted, according to Stinson, that while the Liberal-Progressives did not oppose Harrison personally, they opposed the method of his selection as nominee by Roblin and the governing party alone. Campbell knew this was a lost fight before he began, and probably counted on the CCF supporting the government. If they did not, Roblin might have been able to go to the polls immediately and cast both Campbell and Stinson as villains standing in the way of government. Nevertheless, Campbell fought the nominee. Stinson quotes Campbell as asserting in his speech,

> I tried to convince my honourable friend, the Leader of the CCF, that he himself would make an excellent Speaker. With my usual modesty, I admitted in private that I would make an excellent Speaker. But, I'm too old, and my honourable friend is too busy, and he is too ambitious.

The debate over the speaker continued for four hours, ending with the CCF supporting the Conservatives and the Liberals opposing.[50]

For the whole of Roblin's first, one-year government, Campbell and the Liberal-Progressives kept to this pattern of attacking the government head-on, but reserving some venom for the CCF as well. At the 1959 budget debate the Liberals were finally successful. Campbell proposed an amendment to the budget that would severely restrict the government's capacity to act without prior approval of the other parties. Roblin announced that he would treat the successful passing of such a motion as a vote of non-confidence. The CCF decided it was time to defeat the government, supported the Liberals over the Conservatives, and an election was called.

After Government

The 1959 election resulted in a further slipping of the Liberals at the polls, both in their percentage of the popular vote and in their seats. A decline in 5% of the popular vote, down to 30%, resulted in a total of only 11 seats, eight fewer than the year before, and only one more than the CCF. Roblin's Conservatives picked up most of the voters falling away from the Liberals. Although perhaps still the party of the Bracken government, the Progressive-UFM support had dissipated. The Conservatives had always had a rural presence, and under Roblin and his successors it grew, while after Campbell resigned the leadership to Gildas Molgat, the Liberals, at first slowly, then rapidly, disappeared from the rural Manitoban political landscape. In 1969 the party selected Robert (Bobby) Bend to replace Molgat as leader. Bend was one of Campbell's cabinet ministers and remained a Campbell Liberal: fiscally conservative and rural-minded. He was unsuccessful in gaining back rural votes for the party and lost urban votes as well. Campbell himself retired from the legislature in 1969, after serving 47 years. In the provincial election of that year the Liberals lost badly and lost the possibility of governing again in the 20th century.

Campbell's exit from public life in Manitoba was at first short-lived. In the early months of the Schreyer government, the new NDP Premier asked Campbell to take on the role of Ombudsman for Manitoba. Campbell refused, for while he thought the new position important, he had no desire to continue working. Schreyer then offered him a position on the Hydro Board. In later reminiscences, Campbell reported that he at first declined the appointment, saying:

> Look, Eddie, first and foremost, I still don't want the job or the amount of work it would entail. Also, for your own good, you shouldn't be offering me this position. Your group [NDP supporters] knows that I'm not a supporter of the government and you'd get a certain amount of criticism for appointing someone with another point of view to the socialistic one.

Campbell also added that, at 75, he was 10 years older than the mandatory retirement age for the civil service (although the board wasn't strictly covered by the act). Schreyer persisted and Campbell eventually agreed.[51]

Campbell's reticence may have been sincere, but as he also noted, Schreyer had given him "the opportunity to serve on the Board and a chance to get back into an area that I had always been intensely interested in and glad to be associated with." While he was minister in charge of hydro and Premier, Campbell's main concerns had been with distribution; in the early 1970s, however, Manitoba Hydro's greatest concern was in keeping up supply to meet demands. Under Premiers Roblin and Weir a plan to divert the Churchill River to the

Nelson had been studied. The NDP appointed David Cass-Beggs, a former Engineering professor from the University of Toronto and head of SaskPower during the Tommy Douglas era, as the new chair of the Hydro Board. Cass-Beggs favoured a different plan, relying on regulating the outflow from Lake Winnipeg. Campbell disagreed with Cass-Beggs's plan and found him most disagreeable as a person. After twice trying to convince Schreyer that the Hydro chairman was going in the wrong direction, Campbell resigned from the board

Over the next 20 years Campbell played a minor role in Manitoban public life, taking up with conservative, provincial-rights-oriented causes and parties. During the bilingualism debates of the mid-1980s Campbell publicly sided with Russell Doern against any expanded bilingual services. He took part in a handful of public meetings, but was not a driving force behind the movement. Following the failure of Doern's campaign, Campbell lent public support to the Confederation of Regions Party, which had no electoral success in Manitoba. Likewise in 1987 he was present at, but not instrumental in, the founding of the right-wing populist Reform Party in Winnipeg, again giving the movement his support. By the 1980s, however, he was an old man, and not willing to do serious political work.

Campbell's presence at the founding of the Reform Party was not some aberration or a sign of a hardening of attitude from his early Progressive and Liberal-Progressive leanings. Campbell was a conservative farmer in heart and mind. He was an active player in the Liberal Party while in power or in the legislature, and a sometime supporter of it after. But, like so many of the "farmer" candidates of 1922, he only reluctantly accepted a party label, and understood politics based on his prairie populist ideology rather than on political affiliation. What mattered most to him was the promotion of farmers, fiscal restraint, and government involvement where necessary, but limited to what he believed was possible and useful. Much as Manitoba changed away from him in the 1950s, so the Liberal Party did in the 1970s and 1980s. He created important legacies for the province in the 1950s, but like fellow Liberal Premiers of the era, his was a conservative provincial liberalism.[52]

Gladys Campbell died in May 1987. Doug lived another nine years, dying on April 23, 1995, at the age of 99. His funeral was held in Winnipeg.

Notes

1. Population figures from Peter J. Smith, "Urban Development Trends in the Prairie Provinces," in A.W. Rasporich, *The Making of the Modern West: Western Canada Since 1945* (Calgary: University of Calgary Press, 1984), 136, 141; Gerald Friesen, *The Canadian Prairies: A History* (Toronto: University of Toronto Press, 1987), 514–15.

2. The High Bluff history and the earlier *Trail of Pioneers* both list her as Mary Campbell, but I am uncertain if this reflects her maiden name or only her married name.

3. Douglas Campbell, "My Three Rs" (unpublished manuscript, held at the University of Manitoba), 132–34.

4. Ibid., 130–31, 146–47.

5. Ibid., 13–15, 146.

6. "Garson Denies Intention to Move to Ottawa," *Winnipeg Free Press* (October 4, 1948): 1.

7. "Ottawa Certain Garson to Join Federal Cabinet," *Winnipeg Free Press* (November 3, 1948): 1.

8. "After Garson? Coalition Parley Sought," *Winnipeg Free Press* (November 4, 1948): 1, 8.

9. "Coalition Government Hangs in Balance," *Winnipeg Free Press* (November 6, 1948): 1, 11.

10. "Campbell is New Premier," *Winnipeg Free Press* (November 8, 1948): 1.

11. Provincial Archives of Manitoba (PAM), P5579, R.D. Turner, "Post War Finance," provincial affairs broadcast, January 25, 1955.

12. Gordon Sinclair and John Sifton, "Government Errors Set Course for Rough Legislative Session," *Winnipeg Free Press* (April 2, 1955): 3.

13. "Manitoba Per Capita Revenue Lowest of all Provinces," *Winnipeg Free Press* (September 1, 1957): 5.

14. On Saskatchewan and Alberta in this period, see John Richards and Larry Pratt, *Prairie Capitalism: Power and Influence in the New West* (Toronto: McClelland and Stewart, 1979), 71–176.

15. Campbell, "My Three Rs," 55.

16. W.L. Morton, *Manitoba: A History* (Toronto: University of Toronto Press, 1967), 307–08.

17. Campbell, "My Three Rs," 59.

18. Joy Parr, *Domestic Goods: The Material, the Moral, and the Economic in the Postwar Years* (Toronto: University of Toronto Press, 1999), 33–34, 164, 234–37.

19. PAM, GR 43 G156, Manitoba Power Commission, Interim Sales Agreement, 1948.

20. Jenara Franklin, "Revelation Hydro Kitchen: My New Electric Range Reveals the Secret of Successful Meals," *Manitoba History* 48 (Autumn/Winter, 2004–05): 25–28.

21. PAM, EC 0016 GR 43 G 170, Gordon Douglas to DLC, January 24, 1949; W.D. Fallis to Douglas, January 27, 1949; DLC to Douglas, January 29, 1949.

22. PAM, EC 0016 GR 43 G 170, A.E. Grassby to DLC, March 24, 1949; DLC to Grassby, March 29, 1949; Grassby to DLC, April 14, 1949; DLC to Grassby, April 19, 1949.

23. PAM, MH 0035 GR 2375 I 9 5 17, W.D. Fallis to R.C. Smellie, August 12, 1953.

24. PAM, EC 0016 GR 43 G 170, Anderson to DLC, December 12, 1949; DLC to Anderson, December 20, 1949.

25. J.M. Bumsted, *The Manitoba Flood of 1950: An Illustrated History* (Winnipeg: Watson and Dwyer Publishers, 1993), 55, 67.

26. "Winnipeg.ca Guide Page: City Life; James Avenue Datum," <http://winnipeg.ca/Services/CityLife/HistoryOfWinnipeg/Flood/james_ave_datum.stm>, accessed by author January 28, 2008.

27. J.M. Bumsted, "Developing a Canadian Disaster Relief Policy: The 1950 Manitoba Flood," *Canadian Historical Review* 68, no. 3 (1987): 358–60.

28. Ibid., 356–57; Bumsted, *The Manitoba Flood of 1950*, 85, 97; Robert J. Sharpe and Kent Roach, *Brian Dickson: A Judge's Journey* (Toronto: Osgoode Society, 2003), 68–71.

29. Bumsted, "Developing a Canadian Disaster Relief Policy," 366, 371.

30. Ibid., 372; Bumsted, *The Manitoba Flood of 1950*, 99–103.

31. PAM, MH0035 GR2375 I 9 5 17, Dr. T.H. Hogg, Commissioner, *Report of the Manitoba Water Power Commission*, 1948.

32. Doug Smith, *Joe Zuken: Citizen and Socialist* (Toronto: James Lorimer and Co., 1990), 145.

33. See, for example, D.L. Campbell in the Manitoba Legislative Assembly, February 7, 1951; D.W. Stephens, "Manitoba's Power Possibilities and Problems," address to Prairie Roadbuilders' Convention held in Winnipeg, January 14, 1952; J.W. Sanger, "Manitoba's Power Problem," radio address on CBC, February 28, 1952; Stephens, address to Manitoba Electrical Association, March 6, 1952, all at PAM, MH0035 GR 1418 G 1 7 13.

34. PAM, MH0035 GR 1418 G 1 7 13, D.L. Campbell in the Manitoba Legislative Assembly, February 7, 1951, quotation from page 7.

35. Lloyd Stinson, *Political Warriors: Recollections of a Social Democrat* (Winnipeg: Queenston House Publishing, Inc., 1975), 113–14.

36. Malcolm G. Taylor, *Health Insurance and Canadian Public Policy: The Seven Decisions that Created the Canadian Health Insurance System and Their Outcomes*, 2nd ed. (Montreal: McGill-Queens University Press, 1987), 177–79.

37. *Winnipeg Free Press* (April 1, 1955): 1, 5; ibid. (April 2): 1; ibid. (April 8): 1; ibid. (April 22): 1.

38. Taylor, *Health Insurance and Canadian Public Policy*, 1–3; R.M. Burns, *The Acceptable Mean: The Tax Rental Agreements, 1941–1962* (Toronto: Canadian Tax Foundation, 1980), 66–69.

39. Taylor, *Health Insurance and Canadian Public Policy*, 207–11.

40. Ibid., 217–30.

41. Ibid., 231–33.

42. "Hospital Plan Hurts Religious Freedom–Christian Scientists," *Winnipeg Free Press* (April 8, 1958): 1; "Health Care Program Covers All Manitobans From July 1," *Winnipeg Free Press* (April 9): 3; "Racing and Floundering," *Winnipeg Free Press* (April 9).

43. Stinson, *Political Warriors*, 160–61; M.S. Donnelly, *The Government of Manitoba* (Toronto: University of Toronto Press, 1963), 78–80.

44. "Where Credit is Due," *Winnipeg Free Press* (April 1, 1955): 27.

45. Campbell, "My Three Rs," 151–53.

46. Desbarts, *Winnipeg Tribune* (June 2, 1958), as quoted in Stinson, *Political Warriors*, 166–67.

47. Duff Roblin, *Speaking For Myself* (Winnipeg: Great Plains Publications, 1999), 86.

48. Stinson, *Political Warriors*, 172–73.

49. Campbell, "My Three Rs," 148–51; quotations 149 [Coalition] and 151 [Speaker].

50. Stinson, *Political Warriors*, 178–79; Roblin, *Speaking for Myself*, 93–94. Stinson concluded, "in defeat, Doug Campbell was surprisingly bitter" (Stinson, *Political Warriors*, 173).

51. Campbell, "My Three Rs," 70–71.

52. A fruitful comparison may be found in Nova Scotia's Angus L. Macdonald. See Stephen Henderson, *Angus L. Macdonald: A Provincial Liberal* (Toronto: University of Toronto Press, 2007).

Duff Roblin

1958–1967

W.F.W. Neville

Duff Roblin, 1958–1967

In the early summer of 1954, the Progressive Conservative Party of Manitoba met in convention to choose a new leader. The party had been out of office since 1915, except for 10 years as the junior partner in a coalition dominated by the Liberal-Progressives. The chief leadership candidates were Errick F. Willis, who had led the party for 18 years, including 10 years as the senior Conservative in the coalition cabinets, and Duff Roblin, who had been elected to the legislature in 1949 running as a Progressive Conservative opposed to the coalition. Roblin won decisively on the second ballot. Though his victory was a harbinger of change, it may be doubted that many of those present could foresee the extent to which Roblin himself would prove the agent of that change. Roblin's goals were to revivify the Conservative Party, to re-establish the legislature as a forum for debate on alternative views on the future of Manitoba and, thereby, to establish the basis upon which a new government might be elected to provide new direction to the province. This he achieved, and more. During the ensuing 13 years, Roblin was to be the great modernizer: he reinvented his party, transformed the scope and operations of Manitoba government, and so reoriented public discourse and policy that, for the next forty years, his agenda affected those of his successors and made the Conservatives the dominant party in the province.

Duff Roblin was born in Winnipeg on June 17, 1917, the eldest of four children of Charles Dufferin Roblin and Sophia May Murdoch. He was also the grandson of a former premier, Sir Rodmond Roblin. He attended Winnipeg public schools and St. John's College School. Both Roblin's father and grandfather discouraged notions of his attending university, believing that he would benefit more from an early entry into the world of business. Notwithstanding, he spent a year in the Faculty of Arts at the University of Manitoba, a year in the business school at the University of Chicago, and a further year in the Agriculture Diploma program at the University of Manitoba. He then worked as a salesman for Blue Cross until the outbreak of war in 1939. He enlisted, ultimately attained the rank of Wing Commander in the RCAF, and was heavily involved in the logistics of the Normandy invasion. On demobilization, he and a partner assumed responsibility for a manufacturing business first established by his father, in which he was active until he became Leader of the Opposition. He married Mary MacKay in August 1958, shortly after becoming Premier.

Given his family history, Duff Roblin might have gravitated to politics under any circumstances, but the catalyst lay in the particular circumstances facing the province after the end of World War II. He felt strongly that the province had languished under the long dominance of the Progressives. The all-encompassing coalitions had stifled debate, discouraged discussion of public questions and over a long period had a stultifying effect on the progress of the province.[1] He argued that Manitoba, with its considerable human and other resources, was falling far short of its potential. It was, in consequence, disadvantaging its citizens and making it easier for them to seek greater opportunities elsewhere; this contributed to Manitoba falling even further behind other parts of the country. He was convinced that it was possible to establish in Manitoba a community that was vital, progressive, and productive—one which would provide opportunities for its people to flourish. In this, he saw the possibilities of the provincial state being not merely neutral and passive, but rather being a proactive agent in bringing about major and positive change.

In Opposition

Roblin acknowledged the searing effect of the Depression on the minds of those governing in Manitoba in the immediate postwar years. Indeed, he characterized it as a "debt depression complex." Yet elsewhere, with each passing year the evidence suggested that the massive investments made to meet the needs of wartime were paying rich dividends in the post-war economy. In this environment, the arguments advanced by J.M. Keynes—that public spending could be used to regulate the business cycle, stimulate the economy and create new jobs—had gained wide and growing acceptance. In the new prosperity, however, Manitoba was not fully a participant. Population growth was sluggish. Economic activity had increased, but did so at rates considerably below those being achieved nationally. There was a sense that Manitoba's falling behind was a function of its being directed by yesterday's men and yesterday's measures.

Roblin's appeal, on the other hand, was the appeal of modernization. He believed that public spending in areas like education, training, health, welfare, and economic development would contribute to greater and more diverse economic activity, leading, in turn, to greater prosperity. Public spending, in short, was to be seen as a form of investment. What he envisaged was the antithesis of the pay-as-you-go approach of the Coalition predicated on low taxes and spending no more than taxation brought in, to meet current needs.

Amongst the conditions necessary to effect these changes, Roblin believed it essential to re-establish political discourse as central to identifying needs, determining objectives and pursuing the means by which change could be effected. As one journalist observed later:

> The young Roblin was a rebel and, in a very real sense, a rebel who accomplished a revolution. The revolution was simply the restoration of the parliamentary system in Manitoba's political life… Whatever its original high ideals, the Coalition by 1949 had turned into a cozy arrangement to protect the political establishment from the rigours of politics.[2]

Essentially, Roblin argued for the necessity of putting politics back into politics. This meant re-establishing the parliamentary system and restoring competitive party politics as an essential part of the democratic process.

A Conservative—albeit a progressive Conservative—by inheritance and inclination, Roblin was convinced by the late 1940s that the province needed a new government and that his party represented the most promising vehicle to achieve this. The first task, however, was to get the Conservatives out of the Coalition. Challenged by friends to go from analysis to action, he became a candidate in the 1949 provincial election. Effectively, he ran as an Independent, that is, as a Progressive Conservative opposed to the Coalition, a stance which also put him in opposition to the party leadership and the overwhelming majority of the party's candidates. He won narrowly, as the fourth member in a four-member Winnipeg constituency.

A number of Liberals and Conservatives also ran against the Coalition in 1949 and six of them were elected. During the campaign and subsequently they succeeded in generating some public discussion over the need for new policies and for an effective opposition that could hold the government to account. In the spring of 1950, nature provided unexpected assistance. The 1950 flood caught the province and the government unprepared. Within the government, disagreements emerged publicly as to the seriousness of the threat posed by the rising waters. In August 1950, Errick Willis resigned from the cabinet and led most of the Conservatives out of the Coalition.

Roblin, now at one with his party, became its spokesman in the next budget debate and in the ensuing years proved an active and vocal member of the caucus. Simultaneously, he immersed himself in an ongoing review and assessment of what was taking place in government in Manitoba and elsewhere. Nonetheless, the party's overall policies remained largely indistinguishable from those of the government of which it had recently been part. In the 1953 general election, therefore, Roblin faced, and later acknowledged, an obvious but serious problem: "I had great difficulty addressing the electorate in any convincing fashion because basically our main platform was simply that we were not the government."[3] On election night the Conservatives made but slight gains. Early in 1954 a newly elected MLA from rural Manitoba, Arthur Ross, raised the question of leadership and proposed to force the issue. Willis, to stave off a divisive public row, agreed to a leadership convention. Ross, Willis and Roblin were all candidates. Somewhat counter-intuitively, Roblin was elected largely by the support of rural delegates and became the first urban leader of the party.

The party Roblin took over was essentially a shell. It had no policies of any significance or depth. Indeed, it stood for nothing that differentiated it from its rivals. Long years of coalition and uncontested elections meant that in many constituencies, there was no party organization and no real experience of mounting an election campaign. Not surprisingly, the party had no money. It had not experienced real electoral success for nearly 40 years and its base was narrow. Over the next four years Roblin worked ceaselessly to address these difficulties, seeing the challenge as less one of reviving an old party than of creating a new one.

He pursued policy development through research and wide consultations with individuals and groups whose advice he thought could be valuable. He drew heavily on the resources of the legislative library and archives in seeking an understanding of all the departments and agencies of the provincial government. Having identified what he regarded as the major topics he needed to address, he established a series of task forces whose membership typically included technical experts, political people and private citizens. Ralph Hedlin, a friend and later a well-known policy consultant, helped organize these groups.[4] These consultations embraced a wide swath within the community including, somewhat unusually for the time, members of the academic community. W.L. Morton, the province's premier historian, was consulted on historical questions; and Dr. J.C. Gilson, an agricultural economist at the University of Manitoba, later played a key role in devising a crop insurance program which became a model for other provinces.

He appointed fundraisers. He found, in Campbell MacLean, a prominent Winnipeg lawyer, a man who would serve as president of the party and take responsibility for keeping the party machinery in good shape. Roblin travelled extensively throughout the province, seeking opportunities and creating occasions that would bring him into contact with as many electors as possible. In some instances he turned weaknesses into strengths: unencumbered by the existence of local organizations and their sensibilities, he was free to meet and, indeed, to recruit leaders—not necessarily Conservatives—in various communities to assist him in the business of developing what they increasingly recognized was an essentially new party.

Some of these recruits not only supported his efforts but ultimately ran as Progressive Conservative candidates. Gurney Evans, a former chair of the Civil Service Commission, was recruited by Roblin in the 1954 election; he became minister of Industry in the Roblin cabinet. Dr. George Johnson, a respected medical doctor in Gimli, was recruited in the 1958 election—he subsequently served as minister of Health and later minister of Education, was a candidate for the party leadership when Roblin retired, and still later served as Lieutenant-Governor. Stewart McLean, a lawyer in Dauphin, was recruited, elected, and became minister of Education. Sterling Lyon, a young Crown attorney in the Attorney General's office, was recruited, elected and became Roblin's Attorney General before holding a number of other portfolios. He was an unsuccessful candidate to succeed Roblin in 1967 but was chosen leader in 1975 and subsequently served as Premier. Marcel Boulic, a Franco-Manitoban and a municipal reeve, was recruited, elected and became Provincial Secretary. George Hutton, a professional agronomist and practising farmer was recruited prior to the 1959 election, became minister of Agriculture and the point man on the floodway project. Viewed by Roblin as his "natural successor,"[5] Hutton subsequently left politics to work for the Food and Agricultural Organization of the United Nations. Later on, Roblin recruited a prominent businessman, Maitland Steinkopf, to enter politics and the cabinet where he oversaw planning for the 1970 Manitoba Centennial celebrations. Another lawyer and businessman, Sidney Spivak, was recruited in 1966: he proved an energetic minister of Industry and Commerce and later succeeded Walter Weir as leader of the party.

Of this period one Manitoba historian subsequently wrote:

> From the moment of his election ... in 1949, Roblin had been the party sparkplug. He worked long and hard to master the intricacies of government. He was assiduous in doing his homework and put new life into a moribund party. He recruited scores of like-minded, forward-looking people who might otherwise have scorned to be called Conservatives.[6]

It was not enough, obviously, for Roblin to create an organization, raise money and recruit candidates. The object was to create a party which, once in office, understood what it wanted to achieve and how to achieve it. In the process of identifying issues and developing strategies and policies, Roblin repositioned the Conservative Party into a party of the centre. Indeed, according to Nelson Wiseman, "After gaining the leadership in 1954 [Roblin] moved the Conservatives to the left, undercutting the CCF's position. In 1955, for example, he supported virtually every CCF resolution introduced in the legislature."[7]

Though employing somewhat different language, Roblin's own assessment was similar: "The Conservative Party is a party of empiricists. We're not here for the benefit of any clique or group or to serve a handful of people in Bay Street—even though we may catch hell from some people who think otherwise. We're a party of the middle."[8] If Roblin's approach, both in opposition and government, undercut the CCF, it was more damaging to the Liberals. Almost by default they criticized Roblin by advancing and defending a largely rural and conservative point of view which seemed increasingly on the margins of mainstream political opinion.

From 1949 to 1958 Roblin proved a dedicated student of Manitoba government in all its facets. Possessing great intellectual capacity and original ideas, in office he proved highly skilled in translating those ideas into effective programs. This phenomenon drove the transformative process which gradually recreated the party into something very much resembling its creator; this in turn, coupled with the electoral success that followed, ensured him a commanding role—much more than first among equals—in shaping the direction of his future governments.

Roblin's efforts to refashion the provincial Progressive Conservatives were overtaken by unanticipated developments affecting the federal party. In the late summer of 1956 the national leader, George Drew, resigned suddenly for health reasons. At a national convention in December, John Diefenbaker was elected leader. Initially, Diefenbaker raised only modest expectations of success but he soon demonstrated great skill in exploiting the vulnerability of a Liberal government grown tired and arrogant from long years in office. On June 10, 1957, the Conservatives under Diefenbaker elected enough members to form a minority government, thereby ending 22 years of continuous Liberal rule. In that upset, the Tories won 8 of Manitoba's 14 seats in the House of Commons. In a further election, on March 31, 1958, Diefenbaker led his party to the largest majority ever won in a federal election. In Manitoba, the federal party won all 14 seats.

These results suggested that a great many electors had abandoned the voting habits of a lifetime. And though no one could assume that the federal Tories' success would be directly transferred to their provincial *confrères*, the results were not auspicious for the rather aged Liberal-Progressive government of Manitoba. However, the legislature was approaching the end of its term and the Premier, D.L. Campbell, called a general election for June 16, 1958. Roblin was on the hustings very quickly and waged a vigorous campaign personally and through the media.

Roblin's 1958 campaign reflected the case he had been building and arguing for some time—that whatever good the incumbent government had done, both its instincts and policies had become burdensome to a province with great potential:

> We have, I'll admit, seen growth and development in this province and we're proud of it—we don't sell it short. But Manitoba is not an island— we live in the great Canadian nation. Looking at the rising Manitoba figures along with the rest, we find that Manitoba was 11 percent behind

the rest of the country in growth and development in 1949—now it is 30 percent behind.[9]

The election coverage of the two major Winnipeg newspapers of the time, the *Free Press* and the *Tribune*, conveys the sense that Roblin had taken charge of the campaign from the outset and had the government on the defensive for much of it.

What W.L. Morton had seen in Roblin's conduct as Leader of the Opposition was equally evident in the campaign and, subsequently, in his approach as Premier:

> Brisk, assertive, commanding, he revived boldness, decisiveness and trenchant criticism… He restored to public affairs a sense that issues mattered, a sense long dulled by the former government's belief that the whole of government was administration.[10]

On election night, the Conservatives won 26 seats, the Liberal-Progressives 19, the CCF 11, with one Independent. Roblin fell short of an outright majority or, as the *Free Press* observed in its front-page lead headline the next day: "Duff does Dief—'57 Style."[11] The Liberal-Progressives, coalition-makers to the end, quickly entered into discussions with the CCF with an eye on retaining office. Fearing, perhaps, that if Roblin became Premier he might soon "do Dief—'58 style," both Premier D.L. Campbell and the CCF leader, Lloyd Stinson, wanted badly to keep the Tories out[12] but, a week after the election, Campbell announced their failure to agree on acceptable terms; he would, accordingly, resign. The Lieutenant Governor called on Roblin, who became Premier on June 30, 1958.

Government

By August, the government was already announcing plans for reorganization in a number of departments. The legislature was called into special session in October to allow the government to act on a number of campaign promises requiring legislative approval. A short Throne Speech proposed substantial increases in education spending, "a vigorous industrial and tourist development program," including the creation of a development fund, extra funds for construction and reconstruction of roads and highways, new and adequate credit facilities for those engaged in agriculture, and enabling legislation to allow the province to participate in federal winter work relief projects. In November, in a major speech in the legislature, Roblin elaborated on the government's intentions for a very broad legislative program which included, among other things, increasing university facilities over five years; construction of a rehabilitation and convalescent hospital; new additions to the Portage and Selkirk hospitals for mental diseases; expanding prisoner probation services; a "fully reformed" Mothers' Allowance Act; aid for needy old age pensioners; possible change in the fair wage and workmen's compensation act; changes in child adoption laws; and the establishment of conservation, farm management, and statistics divisions in the Department of Agriculture.[13]

Though acrimonious, the minority government's first legislative session ended in late November with the government undefeated in the House. This was hardly surprising: neither opposition party wanted an election and the government's program had, in any case, many things that appealed to the CCF:

Many of [Roblin's] programmes, some dealing with labour, social welfare and economic development, were similar to the CCF platform. The Conservatives, for example, introduced a hospital insurance scheme, reorganized and centralized the public school system, and restructured the Winnipeg area municipal governments into a metropolitan system. These were all policies the CCF favoured. The Conservatives also adopted a CCF resolution on old age pensions that had been voted down for seventeen consecutive years.[14]

Having survived its first legislative test, the government proceeded with new proposals and activity on several fronts: a multimillion-dollar proposal for renewal of the oldest part of downtown Winnipeg was one of the most dramatic, but even more far-reaching was its decision to move quickly to implement some of the recommendations of the MacFarlane Royal Commission on Education.[15] By the end of February it had conducted a province-wide vote on a proposed amalgamation of school districts: the government's proposal was endorsed by nearly 70% of the voters and carried in 32 of the 36 school districts.[16]

Within days of these successful results, the legislature was back in session with a Throne Speech, described by one journalist as "the biggest legislative program in the province's history."[17] The highlights of the Speech, which encompassed both an immediate and longer-term agenda, included an announcement of the government's intention to proceed with a multimillion dollar diversion of the Red and Assiniboine Rivers to provide ongoing flood protection for the city of Winnipeg; the introduction of crop insurance for farmers; relieving municipalities of the responsibility for public welfare and the task of collecting hospital premiums; improved workers' compensation benefits; new scholarships and bursaries for university students and increased capital and operating grants to the University of Manitoba; and, for northern Manitoba, a package that included the establishment of an economic development authority, measures to introduce local self-government for organized territories, new northern nursing services, negotiations to reduce northern freight rates and a government scheme for northern TV. All, it was promised, could be achieved without raising taxes.

With a major legislative program underway and an even more substantial longer-term program in the offing, Roblin had laid the groundwork for an early return to the polls. In late March, he chose to treat a defeat on a procedural motion as a motion of non-confidence. He obtained a dissolution of the legislature and called an election for May 14, 1959. This election campaign bore many similarities to the previous one: the Liberal-Progressives, still led by D.L. Campbell, claimed to see in Roblin's programs a vindication of their earlier concern that a Roblin government would be financially ruinous and could only save itself through deficit spending or higher taxes. The CCF, which had supported most of the Roblin program, found itself having to argue that, although the Progressive Conservatives were more progressive than the Liberal-Progressives, neither were doing enough to address the issues directly affecting the disadvantaged or marginalized in Manitoba society. Roblin gave no quarter on either front and was now able to claim that the pledges made between 1954 and 1958 were in the process of being honoured. The tenor of the campaign thus provided a further demonstration of Roblin's repositioning his party in the centre of the political spectrum with the Liberal-Progressives now largely on the right and the CCF on the left. The election gave Roblin the majority he had sought: with over 45% of the popular vote, the Conservatives won 36 seats, the Liberal-Progressives 11 and the CCF 10.

Education

Roblin's highest priority was education: it was the matter on which, more than any other, he wished ultimately to be judged. It reflected his personal philosophy and his belief in the value of social investment. In practical terms, these convictions were reinforced by two further considerations. The first was the so-called "baby boom" of the late 1950s and 1960s which was placing unprecedented demands on the educational system. The second involved calculations as to the ultimate material and economic benefits of an increasingly educated population for the province as a whole. This latter consideration was of some political significance for a population, a considerable part of which was conditioned to low taxes and modest public spending. Almost annually, in his capacity as Provincial Treasurer, he married the philosophical case for improved education from primary to post-secondary levels with the practical case for the improved economic well-being of the province:

> Who can say what the monetary cost is of *not* building a road, a school, or a hospital? Must we assume that investment for growth can only be justified when it can be supported by a statement of profit and loss? … Successful economic development depends upon the full utilization of all resources including people. Much of our Budget has, therefore, been allocated to the support of human resources as the only foundation upon which our material progress can be lastingly built.[18]

The report of the MacFarlane Royal Commission had awaited the Roblin government on taking office. The Report's recommendations were wide-ranging and several were particularly notable. They argued for the raising of standards throughout the system generally and of the teaching profession in particular; for the reduction of the number of local school boards and the creation of larger school districts; and for aid to private and parochial schools. The Report also revisited the issue of French-language instruction in the schools and argued that French should be encouraged both as a language of instruction and as a subject of study.

The new government proceeded quickly to address the issue of standards but rather more cautiously with respect to the other more controversial recommendations. The creation of larger consolidated school districts for secondary education was provided for in law but made subject to local plebiscites, not all of which produced the hoped-for results in the first instance. The resort to plebiscites did not sit comfortably with everyone who expected more decisive and direct action by the government and the legislature. "The delicacy of the subject, its impact on custom, religious beliefs and prejudices, the native conservatism of the Minister of Education," W.L. Morton wrote, "all combined to produce an approach that invited obstruction by its timidity."[19] Roblin's view was that this somewhat unusual exercise in direct democracy could occasionally be justified in circumstances when "the issue is one of high local sensitivity where broad policies may conflict with legitimate local concerns."[20] "Legitimate local concerns" were presumably the reason that primary education was not included in the reorganization. Though acknowledging the rationale for this exception, Morton described it as "a fundamental error."[21]

The MacFarlane recommendations on private and parochial schools and on French language instruction precipitated public discussions which suggested that the issues surrounding the Manitoba Schools Question were by no means permanently laid to rest. Indeed, the recommendations aroused the passions of both those who felt vindicated by them and those who felt betrayed by them. Opposition to the proposals found voice, once again, in the editorial pages of the *Winnipeg Free Press,* but the reservations and divisions within the community were real. They were reflected inside the Conservative caucus in the legislature and, not least, in the views of the minister of Education, Stewart McLean. There was no quick or easy resolution. After considerable consultation, Roblin was to propose the concept of "shared services" and, ultimately, the wider use of French both as a language of instruction and as a subject of study. This proposal provided an opportunity for the two separate systems to draw upon common services—whether buses or textbooks— which government would provide to both. As is the nature of many compromises, the proposal opened a window of hope while largely failing to satisfy the most strenuous advocates on both sides. Roblin's own sympathies were very clear. In writing of these events more than 30 years later, he commented that

> the plan had, in my eyes, substantial merit. It would bring the separate
> school question back on the public agenda in a practical manner. It would
> break the hard crust of prejudice which had precluded consideration of
> this subject up to then, and it would open the door to other options when
> public opinion permitted. In any case, from a political point of view, we were
> pressed against the limits of our power. Even so, within the government
> this proposition was not a done deal. Caucus was distinctly uneasy, if not
> hostile, to the proposal. The debate in caucus reflected public opinion. It
> was very difficult, indeed. There are strongly held opinions in Manitoba
> which can only be described as unenlightened in matters of language and
> religion and the constitutional framework of the province.[22]

Notwithstanding his personal sympathies and understanding of the historical significance of the issue, Roblin clearly was pressed to the limits of his personal power. In the end, carrying the shared services proposal required Roblin to shuffle his cabinet and appoint as Education minister Dr. George Johnson who, unlike McLean, was philosophically and politically supportive of the proposal.[23]

These controversial educational reforms illustrate both the nature of Roblin's views and at least one measure of the constraints that operated even on him as a progressive operating in a political milieu which, on certain matters, remained conservative. Yet, overall, his government's record in education was substantial. During his tenure, three vocational colleges were established: Red River College in Winnipeg, Assiniboine College in Brandon and Keewatin College in The Pas. The two affiliated colleges of the University of Manitoba,

United College and Brandon College, became universities in their own right: the University of Winnipeg and Brandon University. Major public investment, in both programs and new construction, transformed the University of Manitoba, the province's largest and most diverse post-secondary institution.

In 1958–59, provincial spending on education was approximately $22.9 million; in 1967–68, which encompassed part of Roblin's last year as Premier, provincial spending on education was approximately $137.9 million; spending on education, which represented 21% of all provincial expenditure in 1958–59, represented 36% in 1967–68.[24] Expressed another way, over the same 11-year period (of which 9.5 years were under Roblin), provincial spending on health and social welfare increased by 367%; education by 591%; and natural resources and primary industry by 302%.[25]

For most of his premiership, Roblin was his own Provincial Treasurer. Occupying the two most important offices of the government, he ensured that public policy and public spending overall would bear his personal imprint and reflect the values and objectives in which he believed. From 1959 onwards his budget speeches struck consistent notes about the social responsibilities of the society to itself and to its least well-off members. In them, beyond the numbers and the technical information, there were echoes of the kind of reformist Toryism associated with Wilberforce, Shaftesbury and Disraeli in Britain and John A. Macdonald in Canada. There were also echoes of the famed Report of Sir William Beveridge, presented to the British government in 1942, which had argued for a comprehensive program of social security to address major social ills like poverty, unemployment, ignorance, squalor and disease; the Report provided the philosophical underpinnings of the British welfare state after World War II.[26]

Similar philosophical underpinnings were reflected, year after year, in his budget addresses to the legislature. Tabling the budget in 1959, Roblin said:

> Mr Speaker, no society can afford to do less—within its capacity—than is needed in the way of social security measures… By providing sustenance and shelter from economic storms to those of our citizens who cannot fully provide this sort of security for themselves—for whatever reason—we shall do our duty to our neighbours in a fuller and more acceptable way.[27]

His view of the role of government was clearly the very antithesis of laissez-faire.

This Tory—or perhaps, more accurately, "Red Tory"—approach could be defended on utilitarian grounds: investment in education and health would indeed make for better, happier, healthier lives but it would also confer economic benefits and thus repay, in whole or in part, the public investment required. This was a compelling argument but it seems likely that this practical justification also served a useful political purpose. Though Roblin, the progressive, was clearly the driving force in the government, the inescapable fact was that some of his colleagues in caucus and cabinet were more cautious, reflecting something of the political outlook of the previous era. By emphasizing long-term benefits, he was often able to lead them in rather unexpected directions. An interesting example is provided by Roblin's initiative through which Manitoba contributed modestly to the Colombo

Plan by sending Manitoba teachers to train teachers in Malaysia, an enlightened if not necessarily a politically popular gesture. Some members of the Liberal opposition opposed the contribution on the grounds that charity began at home.

Metro Government

By the late 1950s greater Winnipeg had come to represent half the total population of the province—but greater Winnipeg included the city of Winnipeg and a dozen or more smaller cities and towns of differing sizes and greatly differing wealth and resources. People, proximity and commerce made these communities highly interdependent but the relations between them were complicated and often contentious: the city of Winnipeg saw the suburban municipalities as benefiting freely from the range of amenities and services provided by the city even as allure of lower suburban taxes eroded the city's tax base.

Some of the smaller municipalities chafed at their inability to raise taxes comparable to those of Winnipeg and their inability to provide comparable services. They complained of the inadequacy of public transit—but were unwilling to bear a share of transit's chronic deficits. Where certain services were provided by individual municipalities, their scope and quality varied greatly with their size and wealth: Tuxedo and Brooklands, for example, though both very small, represented the wealthiest and the poorest communities within greater Winnipeg, a fact very much reflected in the level and quality of their municipal services.

Despite exhortations from within and without, the municipalities seemed incapable of effective collaboration on those many issues—traffic, transit, sewage and streets among them—which cut across their boundaries. It was in this environment that the Roblin government decided to act. In 1960, it legislated into existence the Metropolitan Corporation of Greater Winnipeg, thus creating a new intermediate level of government between the province and twelve greater Winnipeg municipalities. Vested in this corporation was the responsibility for dealing with the various "cross-boundary" issues that the municipalities had been unable to address themselves.

The new Metro government began early on to articulate and pursue a comprehensive approach to development and had some success in rationalizing and providing a number of common services. The Metro concept, however, never earned full acceptance by the smaller municipalities which resented the diminution of their authority, nor from Stephen Juba, the shrewd, populist mayor of Winnipeg, who sought one big amalgamated city. These difficulties, along with Metro's undoubted successes, combined to lead the Schreyer government to legislate the unification of all greater Winnipeg governments a decade later.

The Floodway

In 1950, Winnipeg and southern Manitoba experienced one of the greatest floods on record. If the Coalition government was insufficiently attuned to the need for preparedness, it also proved insensitive to the flood's potential as a political issue. Roblin, newly elected to the legislature, was both visible and vocal on the issue. The vulnerability of the government to Roblin's criticisms doubtless assisted his campaign to get the Conservatives out of the Coalition. Thereafter, flood control became part of his political agenda and, following his election as party leader, an ongoing concern.

Following the flood, the federal government, through the Prairie Farm Rehabilitation Administration (PFRA), agreed to undertake an extensive review of the history of flooding in southern Manitoba and to advise on feasible means of flood protection. The PFRA concluded that, based on past flooding, future serious floods were inevitable. Having canvassed numerous alternatives, it concluded that the best approach lay in building some sort of floodway which would divert potential flood waters around Winnipeg. Faced with a specific proposal, the Campbell government temporized. Fearful both of the substantial financial commitments required and the political risks of a major undertaking which could be perceived as benefiting only one part of the province, the government took no position on the proposal pending a cost-benefit analysis. Roblin, however, adopted the floodway proposal and made it his own. It was one of his major promises in the 1958 election.

In 1959 the cost-benefit study was released. It was highly favourable but pegged the cost at $63 million. Under the PFRA federal-provincial cost sharing formula then in place, the federal government would normally have contributed up to about one-third of the costs. Roblin wanted more—something, indeed, approaching 60%. The possibility that the federal government might be induced to provide more than usual failed to mollify many of the critics, including initially a few of the government's backbenchers and most of the Liberal-Progressive opposition. Both questioned the likelihood of future floods of such magnitude as to warrant so large an undertaking. On the matter of the actual cost, there was no doubt: the opposition was certain that the project was far too expensive and certainly beyond the means of a small province. Some in the opposition claimed that a floodway would not work. As Roblin notes, the opposition asserted that the interest-carrying charges on the project would be so high as to sink the project: they labelled it "Roblin's Folly."[28] Roblin, on the other hand, was so certain of the long-term benefits of the floodway, that he was prepared to go it alone, if it became necessary, without a federal contribution.

After prolonged and difficult negotiations, Prime Minister Diefenbaker finally proposed a federal share of 55%, and a deal was reached. This still left Manitoba with the responsibility for $26 million, an amount that the opposition continued to regard as excessive and beyond Manitoba's capacity. The opposition was not confined to the political realm. Roblin records that a small group of leading Winnipeg businessmen called on him, advised him that the floodway was not needed and, in any case, was unaffordable.[29] To avoid the costs of borrowing, the government chose to finance it out of current revenue by spreading the construction over a period of years, beginning in 1962 through to its completion in 1968.

The Red River Floodway proved to be a massive engineering project, by far the largest excavation project in Canada to that date, involving less excavation than the Panama Canal but exceeding slightly that of the Suez Canal.[30] Its subsequent impact transformed it into the single most visible and successful achievement of the Roblin years, an achievement no doubt made sweeter by the sense of vindication that accompanied it. The Floodway was used frequently in the 40 years that followed. In 1997, it saved Winnipeg from the ravages of "the flood of the century" and the billions of dollars of property damage and other losses which would otherwise have engulfed the city.

Roblin later received international recognition and honours for the scope and impact of the project. In 2002, the Floodway itself was designated by the federal government as a National Historic Site in recognition of its standing as a great Canadian engineering achievement with profound impacts on the region it served. The citation noted that, on the basis of the efficacy of its design and its capacity to handle flood waters in excess of its flood design function, the system had and would continue indefinitely to have a socio-economic impact of both provincial and national significance; and cited it as being of exceptional symbolic importance to Canadians, as an example of human success in controlling the forces of nature and of the challenges in doing so. In 2003 Roblin himself participated in the ceremony at The Forks at which the commemorative plaque was unveiled: it was a highly unusual occasion to have someone so intimately connected to a National Historic Site alive, well and participating in its commemoration.

Economic Development and Churchill Forest Industries

In the 1958 election campaign, Roblin argued that years of public inactivity and the relative unattractiveness of the province for investment meant that many needs had gone unmet and potential opportunities had gone untested. Much of what followed the change of government was directed to areas like education and social policy on the one side and to issues like flood control on the other. Roblin believed, however, that the policy of inaction had consequences that went beyond the development of human resources. Indeed, he argued that Manitobans could fall short of achieving their human potential if the province itself did not grasp and realize its economic potential. In his budget speech in 1961 the theme was reiterated:

> We have consistently maintained that inadequate capital investment in recent years has handicapped the growth of the Province. Not only is the government now faced with the present day needs for capital investments, it is also faced with a formidable accumulation of unfulfilled capital needs, inherited from a period of governmental inactivity and stringency. With statesmanlike foresight these capital charges could have been met at very much lower costs. Parsimony is rarely true economy. When such parsimony operates to inhibit normal growth, it can become the very opposite of true economy.[31]

When he called an election in 1962, Roblin announced that he would run on a program of economic development. Like other provincial governments of the era, the Roblin government saw the provincial state itself as a potential engine of development. Apart from agriculture and manufacturing, which were the pillars of provincial economic life, Roblin and his colleagues were particularly focussed on the potential of the north for a major forestry-products industry and on the north's vast hydroelectric potential. To that end, and to facilitate economic development generally, the government launched an active program of highway construction. By the time the Conservatives left office in 1969, most of the province, including many remote Aboriginal communities, had been linked by the construction of new roads. The government also embarked upon a major expansion of hydroelectric power, notably on the Saskatchewan and Nelson rivers, supported by large commitments of public spending. Indeed, the monies thus committed accounted for more than one-third of all the new investment in Manitoba during the period.[32]

One of the government's early acts was the creation of a development agency, the Manitoba Development Fund (MDF). Its mandate was to promote industrial and regional development "on sound business lines."[33] It was also empowered to be a lender of last resort. To put it at arm's length from the government, the MDF had an independent board, composed of businessmen familiar with issues in corporate investment, and a chairman, Rex Grose, the deputy minister of Industry and Commerce. The loans it made were to come, in the main, not from the Treasury but through bonds and debentures authorized by the board and guaranteed by the government. A number of developments were thereby funded, without financial losses, leading to the creation of several thousand jobs.

In the early 1960s, the MDF began searching for a company to undertake development of a paper industry based on the northern forest. The response of known businesses in the field was cautious and limited, partly because of the projected transportation costs of bringing paper products out of northern Manitoba and partly because the prevailing prices for the product were, as yet, too low to make the project viable without generous government financial support.[34] By the mid-1960s, the most promising expression of interest came from a Swiss-owned company, Monoca A.G. and a little-known American-based engineering firm, Technopulp, which proposed to undertake the project under the name Churchill Forest Industries (CFI).

The MDF entered into an agreement with CFI which—consistent with earlier and successful projects—provided that the MDF would retain full control of disbursements to the company under conditions that required proof of value received. Though several credible third parties[35] had vouched for CFI's owners, their assessments proved seriously wrong. From the start, the opposition in the legislature was sceptical about the *bona fides* of these off-shore companies and grew more so as time passed. Roblin records that in 1967, before he left office, Gildas Molgat, the Leader of the Opposition, "tabled an extensive list of well-framed and cogent questions concerning the Manitoba Development Fund, CFI and Alexander Kasser [the head of CFI]. The answers to those questions were prepared by Grose as MDF Chairman. Grose's position was that although flaws had been revealed by this series of questions, they were not fatal and the project could proceed." Roblin observed that the answers, "when they were presented ... did not satisfy the opposition. They should not have satisfied me."[36]

It appears, moreover, that the controls were substantially altered by Grose after Walter Weir succeeded Roblin as Premier in November 1967. The breakdown of control might have proven less consequential had the principals of CFI proven to be honest but it seems clear that neither the Roblin government at the outset, nor those of Walter Weir and Ed Schreyer which followed, knew nearly enough about the European promoters and owners of the project. Though relatively little money was disbursed before Roblin left office, disbursements accelerated rapidly thereafter. In the end, it appeared that tens of millions had been advanced to CFI not, as originally intended, for work completed, but through invoices for future goods and services not all of which were delivered. Sidney Green, who was minister of Mines in the early years of the Schreyer government, recounts that Grose acknowledged this change in practice during a meeting with the cabinet. It appeared to Green that "Grose ... did not trust the government to keep its commitments. The advancement of funds apparently was devised to make sure that the monies that had been promised would be forthcoming and that no steps would be taken by the government to discontinue funding."[37]

Faced with accumulating indications of malfeasance, the Schreyer government ultimately put CFI into receivership and appointed a Commission of Inquiry. Roblin and two former colleagues, including a future Premier, Sterling Lyon, testified before the Commission. Roblin, though acknowledging that the enterprise entailed risks, argued that the financial malfeasance would have been impossible had the original controls been kept in place. Nonetheless, the Commission report of 1974 was highly critical of the Roblin and Weir governments, accusing them of having done insufficient research on the men and companies they were dealing with, and with having established inadequate financial controls.[38] Though he believed that the breakdown in controls after he left office was the key to the CFI debacle, and that the Commission's conclusions lacked balance, he wrote, "Nonetheless, as leader of the government until 1967, I affirm my commitment to the original The Pas forestry development policy, and I accept the responsibility of office."[39]

Government, Politics and Elections

The 1962 Throne Speech extended undertakings and commitments of the preceding years such as a commitment to eliminate hospital premiums for post-secondary students, and increased funding for schools and the University of Manitoba. It also reflected other aspects of Roblin's impact on public policy in Manitoba—an interest in issues of broader significance than Manitoba alone: it signaled an intention to have the legislature examine and consider the possible impact of the European Common Market on Manitoba; the repatriation of the Constitution; a national contributory pension plan; and the province's position on a national medical plan.

That year had also seen a federal election which reduced the Diefenbaker government to minority status. With the ensuing political uncertainty came expectations that another election might occur in 1963. This may have explained Roblin's calling of a snap election on December 14, 1962, thus avoiding a possible federal election competing with an anticipated provincial election in 1963. Though the Conservatives lost one seat in the election, the results overall amounted to a substantial endorsement of the government. Following deferred elections in the north and recounts in several close contests, the Conservatives' results replicated those of 1959 with 36 seats. On the opposition side, however, the Liberals (as they now were) gained ground, winning 13 seats, and the CCF lost ground, winning 7. One Social Credit member was also elected. More notable, perhaps, was the change in popular vote: the Progressive Conservatives went from 46% in 1959 to 44% in 1962, while the Liberals, under a new leader, Gildas Molgat, rose from 30% to 38% and the CCF declined from 22% to 15%. The Liberals continued to offer the primary challenge to Roblin, suggesting that the forces of conservatism were by no means extinguished.

The central preoccupations of the government in the early stages continued into its middle and last years. In 1964, for example, the Throne Speech emphasized social issues and the links between education and employment: it proposed a variety of measures dealing with the elderly, the infirm, the physically disabled, rural workers and the deaf. The Liberals and the NDP both accused and congratulated the government for having stolen from their respective policy proposals—a charge repeated the following year as well. The Liberals also criticized what they characterized as the government's uncontrolled spending, a charge rooted in the legislature approving, at the end of the spring session, the largest current spending estimates in history, and capital borrowing of more than $220 million.

By 1966 the subjects mentioned in the Throne Speech impinged on every department of government with the emphasis yet again on education and social policy: there were 19 proposals related to education with, as previously, heavy emphasis on manpower development; and 25 references to hospital or hospital-related projects. The Speech also confirmed the government's readiness to proceed with development of the Nelson River's vast hydroelectric potential, described as the largest single development in Manitoba's history.

With a program which seemed to offer something for almost everyone, an election was widely predicted; one was called for June 23, 1966. For the government, the campaign proved more difficult than the previous two. After eight years in office, the Conservatives could no longer run solely on the basis of their goals, but found themselves having to defend an existing record. Though much in that record was positive, it was not "roses, roses" all the way. Despite a remarkably swift modernization of government and an equally remarkable transformation of its place and role in society, not all the government's hopes had been realized: population growth, for example, had remained sufficiently slow that Manitoba's share of the national population remained static or in slow decline. Though the province was enjoying unprecedented prosperity, that phenomenon was general across the country; and though much had been invested in education and social policy, the returns on the investment were insufficient to avoid deficit spending or higher taxes. The government's defenders, not surprisingly, argued that after nearly 40 years of being far behind the rest of the country, what had been achieved in eight years largely involved catching up to the rest of Canada. If, in 1962, the Liberals had criticized Roblin for going too far, too fast (and too expensively), in 1966 the NDP attacked the government for not going far or fast enough.

The election results demonstrated a significant erosion of support. The Progressive Conservatives won 31 seats, down five; the Liberals won 14 seats, up one; the NDP won 11 seats, up four; and, again, there was a solitary Social Crediter. Though the Liberals remained the official opposition, astute observers would note that, unlike 1962 when the Liberals, on the right, were the beneficiaries of whatever anti-Tory vote was out there, in 1966 the beneficiaries were on the left, with the NDP gaining significantly in both seats and popular vote.

The Throne Speech of 1966 opened the first session of the new Legislature and what proved to be Roblin's last year as Premier. Unusually, the Speech foretold increased taxes (with some tax relief promised for farmers) and some reduced services. It indicated an intention to have the province take over a larger share of the costs of education, and increased financial assistance to the University of Manitoba.

However, the most notable developments of the ensuing session—neither having much appeal to Conservatives—were the introduction of legislation to allow for the use of French as the language of instruction in schools where certain conditions were met, and the introduction, after years of avoiding it, of a 5% sales tax. Though the Liberals and the *Winnipeg Free Press* had been predicting a sales tax for at least four years, they were no less vigorous in denouncing it and its authors when it finally occurred. Roblin argued that financial incentives to promote further school consolidation made the sales tax unavoidable, particularly when—as he argued—he had been unable to wring a better deal from Ottawa in federal-provincial financial agreements. Whatever might have been the force of these arguments, the sales tax was highly unpopular, especially since it appeared to contradict the government's long-standing claim that it could be used to create a modern and progressive province without raising taxes.

The government was still dealing with these matters and their aftermath when, in the summer of 1967, the campaign for the leadership of the federal Conservatives began to gain momentum. Increasingly, attention focussed on Roblin and the likelihood of his candidacy. Roblin initially hesitated but eventually entered the race. John Dafoe offered a thoughtful rumination on that apparent hesitation, especially since there had been signs that Roblin had begun "bridge burning much earlier, in the program which Roblin presented to last spring's session of the Legislature. It had included some actions that Roblin had long wanted to take, but which were not designed to endear him to a large section of rural Manitoba Conservative opinion."[40] Dafoe cited the French language legislation, new legislation to encourage the consolidation of elementary school districts (legislation strongly resisted in Conservative rural Manitoba), and the introduction of the sales tax. These, he added, "produced rumblings of revolt within the Manitoba Conservative caucus. Little ... bubbled to the surface, and Roblin had the power to crush any rebellion which did break out. But by doing what he thought was right, rather than what many thought was politic, Roblin gave fuel to speculation that he would soon be leaving politics."[41]

National Politics

Roblin's decision to seek his party's national leadership had, indeed, long seemed inevitable. In the early 1960s he had become increasingly vocal and visible on the dominating political question of the period, the national and constitutional implications of the political and social transformation flowing from Quebec's "Quiet Revolution." To Roblin it became clear early on that this transformation was being accompanied by gradually escalating pressures from Quebec for a rethinking of Canadian federalism: its thrust was in the direction of enhancing the power and jurisdiction of the province. In 1962 and 1963, Roblin gave two important speeches in Quebec, in French, encouraging greater bilingualism across the country and arguing that Canadians, inside and outside Quebec, had together achieved great things and that, together, they could achieve still more. Both speeches were widely reported and commented on in Quebec and across the country.

An election in 1963 had produced a Liberal minority government under Lester Pearson. Diefenbaker, now in opposition, gave voice—even more than when Prime Minister—to his unhappiness with what he saw as the Liberals giving way to Quebec. Roblin found himself, along with other moderate Conservatives, concerned that Diefenbaker's not be the only Conservative voice being heard. He was increasingly seen as a Premier with a national rather than a provincial point of view. With Quebec an increasingly sensitive issue on the national agenda, Roblin and John Robarts, the Premier of Ontario, emerged as two powerful and constructive Conservative voices in discussions which increasingly involved the Prime Minister and the provincial Premiers. By the mid 1960s, Roblin's qualifications for national leadership were frequently noted: he was relatively youthful, bilingual, electorally successful, and a thoughtful and articulate commentator on the dominating issues of the time.

In 1965, Pearson called a federal election in search of a majority. Perhaps sensing that the 1965 election might be his last chance of returning to power, Diefenbaker made some attempts to recruit prominent new candidates: Roblin was one of them. The overtures carried with them a hint that Diefenbaker would promote Roblin as heir apparent if he ran and won. Nothing came of it. Much later, Diefenbaker, in his memoirs, claimed that he had met with Roblin, promised him a cabinet post if the Tories won, and alluded to Roblin's prospects to lead the party in the future.[42] Roblin said that, although the meeting took place, Diefenbaker made no mention of a Roblin candidacy in the election.[43]

The 1965 election results left Pearson's Liberals still short of a majority; Diefenbaker continued to lead a large caucus of Tories, in which Western Canadian MPs constituted a large part. Having now lost two successive elections, he nonetheless showed every intention of leading the party in the next election as well. As a consequence, in 1966 Dalton Camp announced that he would seek re-election as president of the Progressive Conservative Party on a platform of instituting a review of the party leadership. Camp was one of the country's brightest political strategists and analysts. In the 1950s he had played important roles in the successful campaigns of Diefenbaker, Roblin, and Nova Scotia Premier Robert Stanfield. Camp's victory cleared the way for a leadership convention in the fall of 1967.

Though long touted as a candidate, Roblin did not immediately declare himself. Camp, determined that a new generation of Tories succeed Diefenbaker, sought out both Roblin and Stanfield. Both were regarded as potentially strong candidates, not least because neither was directly involved in the bloodletting over Diefenbaker's leadership. Camp, with his formidable skills and network within the party, was prepared to go all out for whichever could be persuaded to run.

Roblin faced a dilemma: if Diefenbaker was not a candidate, Roblin had the potential to pick up much of Diefenbaker's western support. That support, however, could melt away if he appeared to be Camp's candidate. Mistakenly believing that Stanfield was not going to run, Roblin felt that he "had plenty of time for tactical delay in making [his] own announcement."[44] Stanfield, however, did declare and beat Roblin to it. Camp had tried to persuade either or both men to run and, succeeding with Stanfield, he committed himself to Stanfield believing—also mistakenly—that Roblin would not run. Later, Camp somewhat ruefully concluded that "Duff was waiting till all the presents were under the tree."[45] On the first ballot, in a field of nine candidates Stanfield led with Roblin second. On the final ballot their positions remained the same.

Resignation and After

Early in his career, Roblin had suggested that 10 years was probably the optimal period for a person to serve as premier. In announcing his candidacy for the federal leadership he also announced that, whatever the outcome, he would resign as Premier.[46] The convention over, he did so on November 27, 1967 and resigned his seat in the Legislature in May 1968.

Having run for the federal leadership, Roblin felt some obligation to answer the call to run in the next federal election, which occurred in 1968. There, he experienced the most visible manifestation of public displeasure a successful and prominent politician can suffer: defeat at the hands of a political neophyte. Though he ran in Winnipeg South Centre, a constituency which encompassed his old provincial riding, he was by this time running against Trudeaumania and public anger over the provincial sales tax. He lost decisively.

In 1974, he was invited by local Conservatives in Peterborough, Ontario to contest the riding on their behalf, running against a popular Liberal who was also a minister in the Trudeau cabinet. Roblin later described the decision as "foolhardy" and "disastrous."[47] Any independent assessment would have concluded similarly: his status as a parachute candidate, the injection of the CFI issue into the campaign by the local newspaper, and the national trend to the Liberals all contributed to another defeat. It was his final electoral campaign.

After the election, Roblin returned to Manitoba and to the world of business as the owner of a security company. In 1978 he was appointed to the Senate by Prime Minister Pierre Trudeau, on the recommendation of Joe Clark, then Leader of the Opposition in the House of Commons. There he was a passionate advocate for Senate reform and, in particular, the notion of electing Senators. With Brian Mulroney's victory in 1984, Roblin entered the cabinet as Leader of the Government in the Senate. He served in this capacity until 1986. He retired from the Senate in 1992, having reached statutory age of retirement for Senators.

In retirement, Roblin chaired a Manitoba commission on post-secondary education appointed by the government of Gary Filmon. He also endowed the Duff Roblin Professorship in Canadian Government at the University of Manitoba, a gift which was substantially matched by friends who raised funds privately to endow two substantial graduate fellowships in Roblin's name. In 1999 he published a memoir, *Speaking for Myself: Politics and Other Pursuits.* Over time he received a number of local and national honours including the Order of Canada and the Order of Manitoba and, in 2004, an invitation by both the Canadian and Manitoba governments to represent veterans at the 60th anniversary commemoration of the Normandy landings. There, on May 6, he delivered, briefly, a speech both elegant and eloquent.

Significance

Having offered a generally positive view of the Roblin years in the final chapter of the last edition of his history of Manitoba, W.L. Morton added an epilogue in which he observed that, "The historian can say nothing more weighty about the day before yesterday than any other thoughtful man or woman."[48] With that disclaimer Morton then offered an arresting observation:

> The Roblin government, as thoroughly as it tried to embody the will and aspiration of a new and dynamic society, was in fact a *tour de force*, attempted by one lonely and devoted man. He never succeeded in securing the support of … powerful elements in the province which should either have given the leadership he attempted, or at least have given support worthy of the leadership. One [of these elements] was the wealthy business community of Winnipeg. Partly because so much of it was branch office personnel, partly because so much of its wealth was controlled by widows who, not unnaturally, were cautious, but mostly because it was canny, reactionary, untravelled, fearful of ideas and imagination, it not only failed to support the government but became a dead weight on its efforts, neither aiding nor opposing, but deadening.[49]

A less harsh but not fundamentally different view was offered 20 years later by a Manitoba economist, Cy Gonick, in the context of an analysis of Manitoba's post-war political economy:

> The 1960s were a period of rapid growth and development for Manitoba, for which the Roblin government could take some credit. But measured in terms of its yardstick, it came up short... First, Manitoba remained relatively unattractive to investors. [Among other things] Roblin was restricted by the political instrument at his disposal—the Progressive Conservative Party of Manitoba. When he took over in the mid-1950s it still reflected the old political economy. However much he remade the party over the next five years, he still had to drag along a reluctant, doubting, hesitant association of small businessmen, farmers and senior citizens... . And when the government had to pay the price—a sudden rise in taxes—of a modernization program that had not yet yielded large economic returns, many … withdrew their support.[50]

There were, of course, setbacks, disappointments and blots on the record: the tangled fortunes of CFI; the perception in later years of high spending and high taxing, and hatred of the sales tax in particular; and, to be sure, the failure to stop Manitoba's decline relative to the rest of the country—the failure of what Gonick referred to as the "experiment" in using the state as an instrument of economic development.

Over time, it seems likely that these shortcomings were dwarfed by the magnitude of what was achieved. A long period of conservative government by Progressives was certainly replaced by progressive government by Conservatives but that should not obscure two important points. The first is that the instinctively progressive element in the

Roblin government was to a large degree personal: that is, driven by Roblin himself and a relatively small group of people—ministers, MLAs, bureaucrats and senior advisers, largely recruited by him and sharing his vision; and that the successes of the government were to a significant degree personal as well, owing much to his powers of persuasion which were strongly reinforced by the prerogatives that went with being leader of the party, leader of the government and, not least, electorally successful.

The second is that Roblin's success did largely mask the instinctive caution of a large part of the political and business classes. Many in his caucus reflected the same values and orientations of the former government: in truth, many of them represented precisely the same constituencies. Their support was achieved by Roblin's considerable powers of persuasion, and by the prospects of the enterprise proving successful. Yet, in situations where the going was rough, their instincts were highly conservative. Indeed, the election of Walter Weir as Roblin's successor embodied a return to the conservative, rural orientations of the Conservative Party of the past. And when Sidney Spivak, Weir's successor as party leader, spoke positively of the Roblin years, he was pointedly reminded by some senior members of his caucus that "these aren't the Roblin years anymore."[51]

The official opposition during Roblin's premiership, moreover, was, for the most part, unchanged: predominantly rural and largely conservative, it continued to decry the expansion of government, the rise in public spending and the concomitant increases in taxation. When, prior to the 1969 election, the Liberals elected a new leader, they reached back into the D.L. Campbell cabinet to find one. And finally, there was the milieu in which leader, party and government had to function: whether the business and other elites were as monolithic or as thoroughly resistant to change as Morton and Gonick suggest is open to argument; nonetheless they were—largely—cautious, conservative, and certainly unaccustomed to the kind of boldness and single-mindedness that Roblin offered.

Roblin, for his part, did not see the record as Morton, Gonick and other observers did. His own view was that the years of constrained and narrow views of the role of government, though they left a great void to be confronted, also presented a kind of *tabula rasa* on which it was possible to work creatively across a wide field of issues. Having spent years analysing policy and developing policy options, he approached office with the advantage of well-thought-out plans and, in his view, he found overwhelmingly that the people he needed to persuade and carry along were susceptible to well-reasoned arguments. It also helped, no doubt, that he was very tough, strong-minded, and very much in control of the government. Accordingly, though there was a range of philosophical views to be found in his caucus (including a few recalcitrants) and in his cabinet, he had reason generally to feel well-supported by colleagues and party. Only on the language issue did he feel that opinion within the caucus—which was reflective of a considerable body of opinion in the province—required him to stop short of where he felt true justice would have led him.[52]

Whether or not Roblin actually felt limited by the constraints described by Morton and Gonick, their assessments do say something about the environment out of which Roblin emerged and which, in no small measure, he altered. The fundamental dimensions of Roblin's impact seem to be widely agreed upon: that he recreated a competitive party system and thereby restored parliamentary government to Manitoba; that he largely transformed the conduct of government, redefined and enlarged its scope, and modernized its operations; that his government was, on a wide range of issues, progressive, enlightened and liberal; that in the tumultuous 1960s he brought a reasoned and reasoning voice to public discourse; that on many important fronts—education, health and the Floodway being notable examples—his policies had an enduring impact; and that all of these things contributed, in the late 1960s, to a fundamental and enduring political realignment in Manitoba. His legacy included the establishment of the Progressive Conservatives as the "natural governing party" until, arguably, the arrival of the Doer government at the end of the century. And, to the extent Roblin played a key role in establishing the positive state in Manitoba, he transformed the party system by helping to legitimize the NDP as the primary alternative to the Conservatives.

In November 1999, a so-called "Premiers' Symposium" at the University of Manitoba brought together Roblin and three of his successors, Ed Schreyer, Sterling Lyon and Howard Pawley, for a day of reflections and discussion of their times. In the course of their remarks, all three of Roblin's successors commented on the extent to which Roblin's government had shaped and affected politics and government in the years that followed. Schreyer, in particular, noted that, though he had sat in opposition to Roblin, he could not recall any significant government measure against which he had voted. Moreover, he commented that his own government's program was affected by the fact that many issues he would have addressed had already been substantially dealt with by the Roblin government. This would seem to reflect a wider agreement, in short, that Roblin brought Manitoba, its government and its politics into the modern era and was seminal in events and developments that followed. Beyond all this, moreover, Roblin became, by virtue of his convictions and conduct, a national figure who might well have become Prime Minister of Canada.

By any measure, the achievement, if not all-encompassing and absolute, was remarkable in its breadth and depth. Recalling the state of the province and its politics and political culture in 1958, the transformation and the legacy together make the case for Roblin having been the most significant Manitoba Premier of the 20th century. Roblin died in Winnipeg on May 30, 2010.

Notes

The author wishes to acknowledge and thank Dr Paul Thomas, Duff Roblin Professor of Government at the University of Manitoba, for his most helpful comments on an earlier draft of this paper.

1. According to Duff Roblin, "Most of the MLAs were resting quietly in a self-induced lethargy arising from the fact that a hoary coalition was governing the province." Duff Roblin, *Speaking for Myself: Politics and Other Pursuits* (Winnipeg: Great Plains Publications, 1999), 51.

2. John Dafoe, *The Globe Magazine*, September 2, 1967.

3. Roblin, *Speaking for Myself*, 58.

4. Ibid., 76.

5. Conversation with the author, August 28, 2007.

6. James A. Jackson, *The Centennial History of Manitoba* (Toronto: Manitoba Historical Society/ McClelland and Stewart, 1970), 247.

7. Nelson Wiseman, *Social Democracy in Manitoba: A History of the CCF–NDP* (Winnipeg: University of Manitoba Press, 1983), 69.

8. Quoted by Warner Troyer, *Saturday Night*, December 24, 1960.

9. *Winnipeg Tribune*, June 13, 1958.

10. W.L. Morton, *Manitoba: A History* (Toronto: University of Toronto Press, 1967), 483. If the public persona was much as Morton describes, the private Roblin was, indeed, private and reserved.

11. *Winnipeg Free Press*, June 17, 1958.

12. Lloyd Stinson, *Political Warriors: Recollections of a Social Democrat* (Winnipeg: Queenston House, 1975), 172.

13. *Winnipeg Free Press*, November 7, 1958.

14. Wiseman, *Social Democracy in Manitoba*, 71.

15. Dr. Robert MacFarlane was a former deputy minister of Education.

16. *Winnipeg Tribune*, February 28, 1959.

17. *Winnipeg Free Press*, March 11, 1959.

18. Manitoba, *Manitoba Budget and Economic Review* (Winnipeg: Department of Finance, 1960).

19. Morton, *Manitoba: A History*, 486.

20. Roblin, *Speaking for Myself*, 115.

21. Morton, *Manitoba: A History*, 486.

22. Roblin, *Speaking for Myself*, 117–18.

23. Ibid., 118–19.

24. Manitoba, *Manitoba Budget and Economic Review* (Winnipeg: Department of Finance, 1968).

25. Dominion Bureau of Statistics, cited in Cy Gonick, "The Manitoba Economy Since World War II," in J. Silver and J. Hull (eds.), *The Political Economy of Manitoba* (Regina: Canadian Plains Research Center, 1990).

26. Conversation with the author, August 28, 2007.

27. Manitoba, *Manitoba Budget and Economic Review* (Winnipeg: Department of Finance, 1959).

28. Roblin, *Speaking for Myself*, 171.

29. Ibid., 172.

30. Historic Sites and Monuments Board of Canada, *Submission Report*, 2000.

31. Manitoba, *Manitoba Budget and Economic Review* (Winnipeg: Department of Finance, 1961).

32. Gonick, "The Manitoba Economy Since World War II," 30.

33. Philip Mathias, *Forced Growth: Five Studies of Government Involvement in the Development of Canada* (Toronto: J. Lewis and Samuel, 1971), 127.

34. Ibid., 128. Also see Roblin, *Speaking for Myself*, 136.

35. Dun & Bradstreet was one of these. Cf. Roblin, *Speaking for Myself*, 136.

36. Roblin, *Speaking for Myself*, 137.

37. Sidney Green, *Rise and Fall of a Political Animal: A Memoir* (Winnipeg: Great Plains Publications, 2003), 130.

38. Cf. Roblin, *Speaking for Myself*, 140–44, for the essential points of his testimony and his overall conclusions.
39. Ibid.
40. John Dafoe, *The Globe Magazine*, September 2, 1967.
41. Ibid.
42. John G. Diefenbaker, *One Canada: Memoirs of the Right Honourable John G. Diefenbaker*, vol. 3, *The Tumultuous Years 1962–1967* (Toronto: Macmillan of Canada, 1977), 261–62.
43. Cf. Roblin, *Speaking for Myself*, 174–75.
44. Ibid., 175.
45. Conversation with the author, Trent University, December 1968.
46. *Winnipeg Free Press*, August 3, 1967.
47. Roblin, *Speaking for Myself*, 182.
48. Morton, *Manitoba: A History*, 501.
49. Ibid., 501–02.
50. Gonick, "The Manitoba Economy Since World War II," 31. Gonick taught at the Department of Economics, University of Manitoba. He was also an NDP member of the Manitoba Legislative Assembly from 1969 to 1973.
51. Warner Jorgensen, Progressive Conservative House Leader during Spivak's tenure as Leader of the Opposition, in conversation with the author, ca. May 1975.
52. Interview, October 9, 2004; also, Roblin, *Speaking for Myself*, 118.

Walter Weir

1967–1969

SCOTT MACNEIL

Walter Weir, 1967–1969

Perhaps no Manitoba Premier in the 20th century suffered more from the vagaries of changing public expectations and his own political miscalculations than Walter Weir. An "instinctive conservative" obsessed with fiscal priorities, Weir was chosen by his party in 1967 to replace Duff Roblin and curtail activist government.[1] Weir's brand of fiscal conservatism may have won over the Progressive Conservative rural wing at the 1967 leadership convention, but his emphasis on consolidation over growth was uninspiring. Caught between the dynamic personalities of Duff Roblin and Ed Schreyer, Walter Weir has received scant attention from historians. Regarded as a footnote if at all, he has been viewed almost solely through the prism of his 1969 electoral defeat.[2] Weir took power after his predecessor Duff Roblin had spent a decade raising the public's expectations of what the Manitoba government could, should, and would do for its citizenry and disciplining the Progressive Conservative Party to support his program. Weir then had to contend with a new confidence in activist government once Ed Schreyer became leader of the provincial New Democratic Party. His leadership did little to energize his cabinet, revitalize his party, or capture the imagination of Manitobans and Weir suffered political defeat a mere 19 months after taking office.

Birth, Schooling, Profession, and Marriage

A child of the Great Depression, Walter Cox-Smith Weir was born in central Manitoba on January 7, 1929. With parents Maude and James Dixon Weir, brother Bill and sister Enid, Walter's early years were spent in the hamlet of High Bluff, Manitoba, located 11 kilometres northeast of Portage la Prairie. When his father, a longtime United Grain Growers employee, was transferred down the road to Portage, Walter enrolled in the Portage Collegiate Institute, the same high school attended by two other Manitoba Premiers, Douglas Campbell and Sterling Lyon. Separated by only two years, Lyon and Weir knew each other during their teenage years.

Pursuing a career as an undertaker after graduation, Weir moved from Portage to Regina. In Saskatchewan he went on a blind date with a young nurse named Harriet ("Tommie") Thompson. They hit it off and were married in Davidson, Saskatchewan on November 3, 1951. Two years later they moved to the small town of Minnedosa, Manitoba where, at age 24, Walter purchased his own funeral home business.[3] Soon after arriving in Minnedosa, Walter and Tommie became parents for the first time with the birth of their daughter, Leslie, followed by three sons, John, Patrick and Cameron.

A Man of Substance

In the 1950s Weir's business and fraternal ties in the local community provided him with a solid reputation and a strong network. He soon became immersed in the local political scene. After a two-year stint as Chair of the local District Hospital Board he was elected to the municipal council. By 1958 he was both Deputy Mayor and the Chair of the Town Planning Commission.[4]

The late 1950s were a tumultuous period in Manitoba politics. Long in the tooth and short on ideas, and due to face the voters in 1958, the Liberal government led by Douglas Campbell was squeezed from all sides to take a stance on Ottawa's scheme to insure hospital and diagnostic services.[5] The Left, in the tradition of its Saskatchewan brethren, wanted Manitoba to join the federal cost-sharing program sooner rather than later. Meanwhile, voices on the right were decrying the "pell-mell march to socialism."[6] Progressive Conservative leader, Duff Roblin, fully aware that many in his party objected to both the cost and compulsory nature of the federal scheme, opposed the legislation.[7] As a fiscal conservative, Weir's sensibilities were offended by the notion that the state would assume the increased fiscal obligations attached to hospital insurance while barring private insurers from the field. Hoping to capitalize on the fact that a majority of Manitobans favoured of the plan, the provincial Liberals passed the Hospital Services and Diagnostics Act just before the 1958 election writ was dropped, but lost the subsequent election to the PCs, who won a workable minority. In the ensuing 11 months Roblin made few mistakes and, after engineering his own defeat on a procedural motion, he was confident a majority was in the offing when he called an election for May 14, 1959.[8]

In 1959, Minnedosa Conservatives were optimistic about their electoral chances. A year earlier the riding's Liberal incumbent, minister of Agriculture Charles Shuttleworth, had bested his Conservative rival, Sid Paler, by only 134 votes. Many Tories believed they could have won the seat had they run a better known candidate with rural ties. Believing Weir's town council experience and his business and social connections made him a strong candidate, local members convinced him to try his luck. Insisting he was only running "because pressure had been brought to bear," Weir won the nomination.[9] When the votes were counted in the 1959 election, Roblin got his majority. His caucus grew from 26 to 36, and sitting among the freshmen was Walter Weir, who had defeated Shuttleworth by an impressive 357 votes.

Caucus to Cabinet: A Conservative in a Progressive Cabinet

Weir joined a buoyant and upbeat group. Roblin's victory relegated the opposition to the status of minor players for a decade. Weir began his provincial career as part of a government of promise and action and he used his early opportunities to advertise his political skills. He quickly gained a reputation as a man with "an inborn ability to size up the 'politics' of a situation."[10] Weir was taken into cabinet as minister of Municipal Affairs in October 1961.

Weir's entry into the cabinet coincided with Roblin's push to get on with the "work of developing Manitoba."[11] Progress equaled change and in some cases it meant municipal feathers were going to be ruffled when it came to traditional responsibilities over schools, roads, and water. As such, Weir's new post was "loaded with the prospect of [his] running into irate municipal representatives."[12] With his rural roots and business and local political experience, it was a task for which Weir was ideally suited.

Just before Roblin's second majority was won in December of 1962, Weir was given another portfolio—Public Works, but the additional workload proved unmanageable. Weir was still running his Minnedosa funeral business, an arrangement that may have been feasible for a backbencher, but not for a cabinet minister. By the winter of 1963, trips to and from his home and business took a toll. After a late afternoon meeting with Weir to discuss highways, Armour MacKay, the Chair of the Eastern Manitoba Development Board, wrote to Premier Roblin, apprising him of Weir's condition and urging him to relieve Weir of one of his portfolios. Roblin removed Weir from Municipal Affairs and advised him to divest himself of his business and move to Winnipeg. However, Weir's workload remained heavy, since the Premier had big plans for his minister, including a massive mega-project that would add 6,400 kilometres of municipal roads to the provincial system.[13] Weir worked hard to bring the project to fruition. Asked in the late 1970s to identify his most important contribution to Manitoba, Weir reflected that the highways project was his greatest achievement.[14]

Weir's duties changed again after Roblin won a third consecutive majority in June 1966. Retaining Highways, his Public Works post was replaced by the Water Control and Conservation Branch. In cabinet, Weir became one of the main voices speaking for rural Manitoba. He believed that Winnipeg received too much prominence and that the government should reconcile its policies with its political base. But as Roblin observed, Weir's attachment to the rural population left him with "little feel for urban affairs, particularly for urban politics."[15] Regardless, by 1967 Weir's credibility with rural folk was established.

The Conservatives won the 1966 election but the loss of five seats, accompanied by a 5% drop in the Tory popular vote, signaled that Roblin's "regime was beginning to falter."[16] Frustrated by the unwillingness of voters to bear the costs of his mega-project agenda, Roblin belatedly entered the contest for the federal PC leadership in July 1967 but offered a sub-par performance at the convention where he lost to Robert Stanfield. Worse yet, when he ran as a federal Progressive Conservative candidate in Winnipeg South in the 1968 federal election, he suffered a "massive rejection."[17]

The Progressive Conservative Leadership

A low-key "family affair," the 1967 PC leadership race in Manitoba demonstrated that although Roblin may have succeeded "in making over the province," he "made no such impression upon his own party."[18] On social issues hard-line conservatives had never embraced the way he had "out-liberalled" the Liberals,[19] nor had they concurred with the logic of his fiscal policies. Intent on asserting its primacy within the party, the PC right wing sought a candidate committed to curtailing government spending. Roblin's departure allowed the Progressive Conservative Party of Manitoba to become, for the first time in a generation, truly conservative again.

The first declared candidate was the 40-year-old Attorney General, Sterling Lyon, from Fort Garry, but Walter Weir, 38 years old, was next. In the end the field consisted of a cozy group of four PC cabinet colleagues: Weir, Lyon, and cabinet veterans, the MLA for Dauphin, Stewart E. McLean, 54, and Assiniboia MLA, Dr. George Johnson, 47. To Weir it was an amiable race among his "best friends."[20] As sitting ministers, all four were wary of proposing anything that might be seen as conflicting with existing Roblin policy. As a result, the early campaign was bereft of major policy statements and became "a contest between the personalities—and not the policies—of the four contenders."[21]

Neither the progressive George Johnson nor the conservative Stewart McLean were serious contenders for the leadership. Weir's main competition came from Sterling Lyon. The 40-year old Lyon was regarded as the obvious choice to replace Roblin.[22] He had intellectual ability, portfolio experience, and a grasp of the pressing issues of federal-provincial relations.[23] The *Winnipeg Free Press* went so far as to dub him the "heir apparent."[24] Lyon also had the best-financed campaign. He claimed to be running to defeat the notion that Manitobans were prairie "have-nots" and instead to imbue the populace with a sense of "go-go" optimism.[25] But the optimism failed to resonate because it seemed to be a program predicated on ideas rather than proposals.

PC delegates assembled at Winnipeg's Marlborough Hotel on Thursday, November 23, 1967, and voting began after lunch at the Civic Auditorium on Saturday, November 25, 1967.[26] It was the first political convention in Manitoba to be aired before a live TV audience. However, if the victor was in doubt at the outset, the suspense was all but over after the first ballot. With 470 eligible delegates, the magic number was 236. Securing only 71 votes on the first ballot, Johnson was the first to be taken off the slate. McLean fared little better with 87 votes. With 141 votes, Lyon was "visibly shaken" by the realization that his showing did not augur well for success against the first place Weir, who had netted 167 votes.[27] Lyon's only hope to beat Weir was to get Johnson and his supporters onside, but the doctor demurred claiming his supporters were all over 21 and could "make up their own minds."[28] On the second ballot McLean lost support to Weir, finished a distant third, and dropped out. Lyon was left to suffer through an anti-climactic third and final ballot.[29] Tension drained from the auditorium and delegates were leaving before the final results were tallied. In the end, Weir won with 280 delegates to Lyon's 183.

In a characteristically brief and succinct address, Walter Weir promised to deliver "hold-the-line policies with a 'realistic balance sheet' in government spending."[30] The *Free Press* noted that it was "a refreshing change to have a premier who is intent on keeping taxes down rather than looking for new ways in which to empty the public purse."[31] The Weir victory exemplified the rural obsession with fiscal retrenchment and signaled a PC move to the right. But the shift temporarily left the centre unoccupied, thereby allowing the NDP to capitalize on the situation by claiming that significant segments of its social agenda were in fact centrist.[32]

New Job—Inherited Troubles

The pressures of the Premier's office exacted a high price from Walter Weir as he tried to reconcile his simple and succinct mandate with the difficult and often messy details of governance. Unlike most leaders who enjoy a grace period after victory, the new Premier was given no time to reflect upon the situation bequeathed to him by his predecessor. During Roblin's quest for the national PC leadership, many of Manitoba's policy positions had been placed on the backburner. Now, owing to a host of local and federal developments, many were based on dated scenarios.[33]

Sworn into office less than 41 hours after the convention, Weir shuffled the existing cabinet by rewarding his campaign manager, MLA Donald Craik, with the Mines portfolio. He entrusted the minister of Agriculture, his good friend, Harry Enns, with the vacant Highways portfolio.[34] Weir refrained from putting his stamp on the rest of the cabinet he inherited from Roblin. The cabinet contained three defeated leadership candidates nurturing ambitions and "divided loyalties."[35] Despite the pundits' observations that Weir was inheriting a united party,[36] ministers found the adjustment extremely difficult and the "team building" exercise suffered accordingly.[37]

The Roblin legacy haunted Weir. The new Premier hoped to command Roblin's level of respect and confidence from the cabinet. Younger than his rivals, low-key in style, less experienced in governmental administration, he could not match Roblin for control over cabinet and caucus. Whether it was hydro development, Medicare, auto insurance, bilingualism or constitutional reform, the inherited issues limited Weir from moving with his own agenda. Moreover, his tactic of accommodating the entrenched personalities in the cabinet, rather than replacing them, gave Weir with an unhappy team to work with. Rumours of internal strife became commonplace.[38]

Premier Weir's maiden speech in the legislature signalled his determination to broaden the tax base through economic expansion. To facilitate his approach, Weir hoped a province-wide spending review, first conceived under Roblin and dubbed "Operation Productivity," would allow a reduction in government expenditures.[39] A mainstay of Weir's plan involved inviting Manitoba's business community to assist the government in spurring economic development.[40] Manitoba business was among the most cautious and conservative of all the entrepreneurial classes in Canada,[41] and Weir misjudged the willingness of Manitoba's movers and shakers to mobilize and expend their capital to get the province moving.

Weir's other major pronouncement on his first day concerned the messiest of all the files inherited from Roblin—Medicare. Weir reiterated his own deep-seated opposition to the federal scheme by publicly urging Ottawa to postpone its implementation.[42] Knowing full well that Liberal Prime Minister Lester Pearson was on the record as saying there would be no amendments to the existing legislation, Weir nevertheless tried to change Ottawa's mind.[43] The reasons for Weir's determination to confront Ottawa on the issue are not hard to discern. He had always harboured a bias against government interference in the health sector and he opposed cost-sharing programs that might increase the draw on the provincial treasury. Weir would later tell Pearson that while "voluntary medical insurance should be made available to all citizens of Canada regardless of their income," the fact remained that the federal formula was too costly and went too far.[44] Weir was opposed to the plan's universal provisions and believed Manitoba's health obligation should be limited solely to assisting those who needed help in meeting the premium payments. In the coming months Weir lobbied, threatened, and pleaded with the federal government to reconsider its terms, all to no avail.

On only his second day in office, Weir went to Toronto to meet his fellow Premiers and observe the "Confederation of Tomorrow" conference then underway. Chaired by Ontario Premier John P. Robarts, the forum was designed to allow Canada's Premiers to address the national unity question, examine the federal-provincial relationship and consider Premier Daniel Johnson's "special status" plea for Quebec. Weir reported that the most important part of the conference had been the discussions surrounding a "new machinery for regional development" that would see the "have" provinces assist the "have-nots" in leveling the economic playing field.[45]

Upon accepting the leadership, Walter Weir claimed that "the magnitude of the responsibility" did not escape him yet, within weeks if not days, circumstances caused him to reassess his claim.[46] Weir's first weeks in office coincided with a period in Canadian politics that saw the Medicare rhetoric heat up, the debate over Quebec's "special status" become front and centre, and a tired Prime Minister announce his pending retirement.[47] According to Weir's personal secretary, Georgina Buddick, the transition period turned into a stressful time for both Weir and his staff.[48]

Weir was already feeling the strains on his health. The new Premier confessed to former MLA George Hutton that he was worried that the "hectic pace" would leave him with little time for his family.[49] Weir admitted privately that excessive hours of work and his heavy drinking[50] were causing his wife considerable worry. Weir was not alone in the 1960s in trying to navigate the pitfalls of a political and business culture that expected "serious men" to hold meetings over cigars and drinks. Weir, however, indulged more than most.

As a couple, Walter and Tommie had always been outgoing and sociable. Tommie, however, soon found that her husband's new position changed their relationship with the outside world.[51] The protocols of office created social isolation for the family which Tommie did not enjoy; it was contrasted by demands that mandated Walter's attendance at an unending series of social functions. For the family it meant Walter was often absent and now had little private life. With family time precious, Weir tried to compensate by bringing his children to work whenever circumstances permitted.[52] Within weeks of taking power, Weir confessed that "there are now days when I wish I was 'just one of the boys'."[53]

To make matters worse, Roblin was gone but his ghost was everywhere. Nowhere did this prove truer than in the person of Roblin's most influential advisor, the clerk of executive council, Derek Bedson.[54] An administrative and protocol master, Bedson had no equal in the government service and he was to leave his mark on Weir's premiership in more ways than one. Bedson moved to streamline the cabinet structure by overseeing the implementation of an entirely new executive council configuration.[55] The Treasury Board was replaced in the fall of 1968 by the more influential Management Committee of Cabinet (MCC). The politically contentious Manitoba Development Authority was renamed the Planning and Priorities Committee of Cabinet (PPCC).[56]

Weir was confident that in Bedson he had inherited an efficient professional who knew how to organize cabinet but he did not realize that he had also inherited a "holy terror" with a drive for absolute control over the operations of the Premier's office.[57] Bedson was determined to control access to the Premier and a confrontation between Bedson and Weir's Executive Assistant and trusted ally, Gordon Bradley, led to the latter's resignation. Bedson won complete control of the office and Weir was left isolated. When asked why the Premier allowed Bedson to triumph, Harry Enns attributes it to Weir's "lack of security."

Bedson's domineering personality not only alienated staffers but also damaged the efficiency of the Premier's office in 1968–69. [58]

1968 Vanishing Acts: Promises, Hopes and the Man

Before beginning the 1968 legislative session, Weir sought an approach to Medicare that would force Ottawa to alter the scheme's fiscal terms. Yet in the face of constant press inquiries, he admitted that his government was still in "limbo" over the appropriate course of action. An in-house assessment of the province's options was commissioned and a strategic plan adopted.[59] On February 2, 1968, Weir sent a letter to Prime Minister Pearson informing Ottawa that Manitoba would be deferring its entry into the Medicare scheme for at least one year.[60] In the meantime, he stated that Manitoba would use the time to "make every effort to bring about those changes in the federal plan which we consider to be desirable."[61]

By mid-winter many in Weir's cabinet were aware that his weak communication style and poor office administration left much to be desired. They were troubled when, three days before the session began, the government lost a by-election in a traditional Tory riding that Weir trumpeted as a "major test."[62] When the session began on March 7, 1968, the throne speech was devoid of enthusiasm. Weir confirmed that he had "No Go-Go Plans for Manitoba" and there would be no new major undertakings in the coming year.[63] Characterizing the speech as "strictly in the pop-gun category," the *Free Press* opined that the whole exercise amounted to nothing more than "five—well spaced—pages of legislative balloon juice and whiffle dust."[64]

While the government focused on fiscal restraint, economic expansion, and a promise to fix the education system, it could not ignore other issues. The draw on the provincial purse had to be controlled and to this end the province lobbied Ottawa for a more favourable deal on the federal-provincial tax-rental agreements due to expire on December 31, 1968.[65] Weir's goal was simple—Ottawa should allow Manitoba a 50% rebate on the taxes it collected in place of the existing 33% formula.[66] Further, the Manitoba Medical Services Insurance Act needed revision to facilitate Weir's decision to stay out of Medicare.

But caucus began quietly criticizing Weir's leadership. Questions were raised about the Premier's inability to control caucus. Weir's reputation was further damaged when a protest by "five hundred angry farmers" against the government's flaccid agricultural policies prompted a disgruntled PC MLA to threaten resignation unless the Premier committed to take the issues seriously and appoint a full-time agricultural minister.[67] For a man who owed his premiership to a rural base, the criticism was damaging and embarrassing. The situation only worsened when Weir's rural backbenchers led the charge against his plan to fix the educational funding deficit.[68] The resignation of northern Conservative MLA, Gordon Beard, in protest over Weir's failure to take northern issues seriously caused even more damage.

Weir's "slender legislative program," personal insecurities, divided cabinet, weak oratory skills, and recalcitrant caucus demonstrated that the 1968 "anything-but-bold approach of Premier Walter Weir" was an illusion.[69] The NDP wasted no time in portraying Weir's regime as an ideologically backward and socially heartless assortment of fiscally-obsessed right-wing conservatives. The NDP was well aware that Weir was going to have trouble explaining why his government was reversing itself on the enabling legislation for Medicare passed a year earlier by a vote of 44-2.[70]

Next to Medicare, the Manitoba Development Fund (MDF) was the year's most volatile issue. Wholly a Roblin construct, the MDF was a provincially-run corporation that extended loans to expanding industries in Manitoba, yet all details about lending were shielded from public scrutiny. Roblin managed to duck the issue of "secret loans" in 1967 as well as the furor. Initially Weir tried to argue, as had Roblin, that it was proper to bar any public access to the details of MDF investments to keep the process removed from political interference.[71] In the face of mounting criticism, however, Industry minister Sidney Spivak announced that the MDF would be required to issue quarterly progress reports and, if the opposition had queries about a specific loan, then MDF would be required to furnish a special report detailing particulars. There was, however, a caveat: all the new quarterly reports were to remain confidential. The negative reaction from the press and opposition was predictable, but Weir absolutely refused to appoint a provincial auditor-general to oversee the MDF loans.[72]

But the Medicare issue ruled supreme. Liberal leader Gil Molgat charged that Weir's decision to keep Manitoba out of the plan meant that taxpayers would be subsidizing the health care of Canadians in other provinces.[73] Roblin had argued that this was precisely why he had been forced to pass Manitoba's Medical Insurance Act in the spring of 1967.[74] NDP MLA Saul Cherniak accused Weir of being ignorant of Ottawa's Medicare Act and of using faulty math to generate doomsday financial scenarios. Weir's strategy, he said, was pinned on nothing more than a faint hope that the forthcoming federal Liberal convention would result in a leader opposed to the existing scheme.[75] That was indeed Weir's deferral strategy, hoping that Pearson's successor would repudiate the existing policy and adopt a voluntary plan.[76]

The last thing he wanted was a new federal leader who worshiped at the altar of universality. He was hoping for a miracle; instead he got Pierre Trudeau. After Trudeau's victory, Liberal Larry Desjardins asked Weir how he could still think that "deferring" Manitoba's entry into the Plan was going to pay off. The new Prime Minister was already on the record as saying Ottawa would go ahead with Medicare on July 1, 1968 regardless of opposition.[77] Trudeau dealt with Weir's threat to sue Ottawa to recoup Manitoba's share of any federal taxes by introducing a dedicated 2% "Medicare tax" in the 1968 federal budget.[78] By designating it a federal "social" surtax, Trudeau prevented the provinces "from sharing in its proceeds,"[79] thereby making any provincial legal action an exercise in futility. The problem with Weir's strategy was that he had prepared no fallback position.[80]

Another development that spring that further polarized the debate over Weir's Medicare position was his decision to raise the Manitoba Hospital Insurance Plan premiums by 80%. Although the increase may have been necessary to deal with chronic under-funding, it provoked a public furor.[81] While hospital insurance was still, strictly speaking, separate from Medicare, it was a distinction lost on the public. Instead the rate increase was another reflection of Weir's indifference to health-care access and affordability. Weir had to face 622,000 angry premium payers incensed over the news that the Manitoba Medical Association had increased its fee schedule by 23%, on top of a 12.5% increase in 1967.[82] Coming only four days after the news of the 80% hospital premium increase, the MMA announcement included a declaration that doctors would be reserving the right to "extra-bill" patients.[83] Together the two events conspired to amplify the outcry against Weir's Medicare stance, and it quickly coalesced into a petition of 50,000 signatures against his deferral strategy.[84] Unable to weather the storm, Weir was forced to capitulate, reverse his position, and confirm just one day after Trudeau's federal election victory that "on second thought, Manitoba would be joining the scheme after all."[85] Far from accenting Weir's resolve to get a better deal from Ottawa, his policy did little more than infuriate voters.

By the spring of 1968, Weir was finding it near impossible to get favourable media coverage. *The Winnipeg Free Press,* in particular, was unrelenting in its attacks on him. [86] To a large extent, the "War on Weir" was a result of his inability to step into Roblin's shoes. Columnist Chris Dafoe seized on Weir's odd behaviour and unexplained absences in the House by asking: "Does Walter Weir exist or is he simply a figment of the collective imagination of the Conservative party?"[87] Even the Tory *Tribune* was forced to admit that many party members were fearful that "the form of government being practiced by Mr. Weir is giving him a fuzzy and indecisive image."[88] Manitobans could be forgiven for thinking that Weir's most practical act had been to approve the sale of canned beer.[89] Yet, to be fair, Weir's inability to deliver on his agenda owed much to Ottawa's unwillingness to alter the conditions associated with a myriad of interlocking federal-provincial agreements.

Trudeau's victory, the Medicare reversal, the MDF quagmire, and an almost daily dose of news stories disparaging his performance led Weir to attempt to refurbish his public image in late September with a cabinet shuffle. The opposition, however, claimed the shuffle was nothing more than a shallow feat of "musical chairs."[90] Weir attempted to lay out his policies for the upcoming 1969 constitutional conference. He was opposed to Quebec's claim to "special status" and he believed linguistic rights were a secondary concern.[91] By year's end these pronouncements, coupled with Weir's increasing rhetoric over Ottawa's failure to address provincial needs, left no doubt he held a markedly different vision of Canada than his federal counterpart.

On the economic front, Weir resurrected an old project conceived under Roblin that included construction of a $1.5 million sawmill located in The Pas to be run by Churchill Forest Industries (CFI). Purportedly a project destined to be worth $100 million, subsequent events would see it gain infamy as a debacle that left Manitoba taxpayers on the hook for $137 million.[92]

1969 "No time left for …" Guess Who?

The year began well for Walter Weir. At the First Ministers' conference in Ottawa that February, Weir's star seemed to be on the rise.[93] Intended to codify the constitutional reform process, the gathering was an opportunity for the provinces to air their views on such federal issues as the Official Languages Act. The only agenda item of any interest to Weir, however, was the constitutionality of taxation and spending powers.[94] Neither Alberta Premier Harry Strom nor Saskatchewan Premier Ross Thatcher had much impact on the conference and it fell to Manitoba's Premier to speak for the Prairie region. Weir was alarmed by Trudeau's opening statement, realizing the fiscal equity issue was going to be sidelined in favour of "the long view of confederation."[95] Slated to speak the next day, Weir revised his entire address to highlight Ottawa's lack of fiscal fairness.[96] In the end, despite Weir's objections, the conference communiqué confirmed that a constitutional review would proceed. Committees were to deal with official languages, fundamental rights, the Senate and the Judiciary. While recognizing that a study of taxing powers was a "priority," it failed to gain committee status.[97]

Although Weir did not get what he wanted from the conference, his performance gained attention. He was praised for his anti-Quebec, pro-prairie, and anti-Trudeau stances.[98] Watching Weir's performance from Winnipeg, two of his cabinet ministers, Harry Enns and Donald Craik, were so impressed that they flew to Ottawa hoping to convince him to call a snap provincial election. Reasoning that Weir's newfound political capital should not go to waste, they tried to talk him into canceling the four pending provincial by-elections in favour of a general election. After much discussion, however, Weir chose to reject the advice, preferring instead to see how the by-elections played out.[99]

As Weir's national profile increased, so too did his confidence. On February 20, the party won three of the four by-elections. Weir was convinced that he was finally on the right track when the new legislative session began on February 27. Seeking to build on this momentum, the throne speech included a call for "proper constitutional practice in Canada" and an indictment of "federal extravagance."[100] Another portent of improving PC fortunes was the weakness of both opposition parties.

By 1969 the cost cutting associated with "Operation Productivity" was also reaping fiscal fruit. Under the program Weir's Finance minister, Gurney Evans, was able to slash more than $121 million from the government expense sheet that allowed him to table a budget with projections of a healthy surplus.[101] Manitoba, Evans boasted, was "the *only* senior government in Canada which has balanced its budget without increasing taxes in both of the last two years."[102] For the *Winnipeg Tribune* this was proof that Weir was finally "hitting his stride."

But if Medicare had been Weir's undoing in 1968, it was to be no less kind in 1969. That April he was publicly vilified for both the "onerous" premiums and for allowing the doctors who had opted out of the plan to employ the "cruel, vicious club" of "extra-billing." If patients could not pay on the spot, they were billed the full amount of the new MMA fee schedule: 15% more than the Medicare rates.[103] With over half of all Manitoba doctors "opting out" of the scheme, and with all the doctors in Brandon and Thompson staying outside the plan, many patients were outraged.

The Medicare hullabaloo was not the only issue Weir faced in 1969. A Manitoba Hydro application to dam South Indian Lake and flood an area of 2,000 square miles had become mired in controversy, not only because of the threat it posed to a hitherto ignored northern First Nations community, but also owing to questions it raised about the lack of government transparency. At a Public Utility Board (PUB) hearing in early January it became clear that both Native peoples and conservationists were strongly opposed to the proposed flooding. University engineers claimed that cheaper alternatives had not been examined. Resources minister Harry Enns vowed that the project would be going ahead and that no further cross-examination of government officials would be permitted. Amid accusations from Aboriginal groups that the welfare of the impacted community was being disregarded, two secret reports confirming that the dam would result in heavy losses for the local economy were leaked. The government reversed its position and claimed the project would not be approved until the hearings were complete and critics had been able to question officials. At the next hearing in late January, such a large crowd turned out that the proceedings had to be moved to the Winnipeg Auditorium. By the time the session was underway the government had changed its tune yet again, this time claiming that it would grant no license until both the hearings were complete and it had received an approving legislative committee report.[104]

By late May the situation was untenable and on May 22, just as the Liberals were rising in the house to demand the resignation of Harry Enns, Weir abruptly dissolved the legislature and called an election. Sensing the mood, NDP leader Russ Paulley bellowed across the chamber: "Well—you were premier for a little while anyway, Walter."[105]

Defeat in the Making—June 1969

The election call may have caught the other parties flat-footed but the Progressive Conservatives were no better prepared. The party had yet to reorganize its local associations to fit the new riding map created by the 1969 Electoral Divisions Act that had reduced the number of rural seats in the legislature by seven and added them to Winnipeg's electoral clout.[106] Moreover, since 1967 the PC party had done nothing to shore up its base, its membership rolls had been allowed to lapse, and its youth wing was almost non-existent. The exodus of three popular cabinet ministers, Sterling Lyon, Thelma Forbes, and George Johnson, did not help.[107] But most damaging was Weir's lackluster performance.

Instead of talking about provincial matters during the low-key campaign, Weir seemed anxious to make a platform out of federal issues, particularly those relating to the constitution.[108] Two weeks into the campaign the Premier was off to a follow-up conference to February's constitutional gathering. This time around, however, Weir was unable to elevate his profile because Trudeau had insisted on keeping both the conference agenda and its proceedings confidential. The conference actually damaged Weir's campaign. The Premier's four-day absence from the hustings allowed the NDP the opportunity to introduce a dynamic new leader, Ed Schreyer, just 34 years of age, to the Manitoba voter.[109] In addition, Weir blundered at the conference by suggesting it might be "wise" for Manitoba and Saskatchewan to consider testing the validity of Ottawa's proposed Official Languages Bill in the courts. He reversed his position 24 hours later. Bragging that he was "running on the free enterprise system" and would not stoop to offering the voters a shopping list or engage in a social auction to win votes, Weir gave voters little to look forward to.

The NDP, meanwhile, had recovered from the suddenness of the election call. The new leader, Ed Schreyer, quickly improved party fortunes and the convention provided an ideal opportunity for the NDP to gain the public spotlight. Not only had Schreyer's leadership win been decisive, but the NDP had emerged from the exercise united and energized. More importantly, it had adopted a socio-economic platform ideally suited to capturing the votes of erstwhile Liberals and drifting progressives.[110]

Weir's campaign was devoid of enthusiasm. His repeated boasting of consecutive balanced budgets produced little campaign excitement or energy. As one newspaper later noted, Weir was not the right type of politician for the time. By campaign's end Weir was clearly not the same man who had come to power in 1967. He had put on weight and appeared chronically fatigued. In an era when the news media culture regularly exposed voters to dynamic politicians elsewhere who imbued their constituents with hope, Weir's case for four more years of hold-the-line policies failed to resonate.

On election night, June 25, three things were confirmed. With 39% of the popular vote and 28 seats, Schreyer won; with 22 seats and 35% of the popular vote, Weir lost; and with 5 seats the Liberals were destroyed. One seat shy of a majority, Schreyer waited for Weir to concede. But avowing that it was his right "to question the judgment" of the voters, Weir called their choice to elect so many "socialists" a "mistake." He intimated that some sort of coalition might be possible to stop the socialist takeover. For two days Weir refused to concede.[111] Finally, it fell to another undertaker, Liberal Larry Desjardins, to bury the Weir government once and for all with his announcement that he would be sitting as a Liberal-Democrat on the NDP side of the house.[112]

When the PCs returned to the house that August in opposition, Weir warned Manitobans to be on the lookout for any "Marxist Communist economic opinions" amongst the new NDP government.[113] It was clear, however, that his days as leader were numbered. With Lyon out of the picture, the party looked over its electoral survivors to find a prospective leader. In short order, a willing contender was found in Winnipeg lawyer Sidney Spivak. Over the next 15 months Weir realized that he was being shut out and marginalized by the party apparatus. After surviving one call for a leadership review in November 1969, by late 1970 he could avoid it no longer and rather than suffer a preordained defeat, he gave notice that he would be stepping down. At age 41 Walter Weir's political career was over.

Following his departure from the public scene, "Gentleman Wally" moved to Toronto for a few years to work for a national funeral business. Soon, however, he was back in Minnedosa, where he worked on his estate planning and investment business.[114] Having "toiled in the limelight only briefly," Walter Weir died of a heart attack in his Minnedosa home on April 17, 1985 at the age of 56.[115]

Conclusion

Weir inherited a party that for a decade had been ruled with an iron fist by Duff Roblin. Unable to command the same level of control as his predecessor, Weir's style and one-dimensional approach to policy were a poor fit for a dynamic era. He failed to unite his caucus. Further, while recognized as a hard worker, his inability to implement the short-term steps needed to realize long-term goals led many to believe he had a poor understanding of what needed to be done. In most respects, the harsh conventional wisdom about Weir's tenure is true. Weir would discover too late that his economic playbook could not overcome the economic development project debt and Medicare mess bequeathed him by the departing Roblin.

In 1969 Walter Weir's fiscally-conservative style of governance and his instinctive political philosophy were insufficient to satisfy the voters. A new sense of individualism was emerging; "visions and values" were changing and the political beliefs of the generation forged by depression and war were giving way to a new kind of politics. In an era when the electorate increasingly expected their politicians to offer optimism and promise, policies wrapped in fiscal retrenchment that abandoned the political middle ground were doomed to failure.

Success in Manitoba politics usually rests on capturing the centre while playing to particular bases of support. While Weir had no trouble playing to his base, he failed to realize that he needed to reach out to the centre. Looking back, both Harry Enns and Sid Green claimed that Weir had a negligible impact upon the ideological underpinnings of the Manitoba PC party.[116] Both were of the opinion that his time was simply too brief to have any lasting impact. Yet Lyon's successful run in 1977 indicates that at least one Tory had learned the lesson of 1969: political polarization that keeps the base happy will pay greater dividends if it keeps the centre engaged.

When Walter Weir died, all too young, the words of opponent and foe alike were charitable and heartfelt. In the end the most accurate political epitaph for Walter Weir comes from an admiring opponent: "He was a perfect gentleman. [But] he was miscast for the role of premier."[117]

Notes

1. See Charles Taylor, *Radical Tories: The Conservative Tradition in Canada* (Toronto: House of Anansi Press Ltd., 1982), 74–75. In Taylor's book W.L. Morton makes the distinction between his reflective "conservatism" and the "instinctive conservatism" represented by Donald Creighton "who was never concerned to be a philosophic conservative." Like Creighton, Weir had little interest in the 'philosophic' aspect of conservatism.
2. Nelson Wiseman, *Social Democracy in Manitoba: A History of the CCF–NDP* (Winnipeg: University of Manitoba Press, 1983), 122.
3. Manitoba Government, *News Release*, March 10, 1978.
4. See "Men in the News: The Cabinet Shuffle," *Winnipeg Tribune*, November 2, 1961; Manitoba Government, *News Release*, March 10, 1978; Manitoba Government, *News Release*, November 28, 1967; and Premier Weir's obituary in the *Minnedosa Tribune*, April 25, 1985; *The Canadian Parliamentary Guide—1969*, 551.

5. "Private Insurance for Medicare: Policy History and Trajectory in the Four Western Provinces," Gregory P. Marchildon—Final Draft, September 18, 2005-Conference on Access to Care: Access to Justice The Legal Debate over Private Health Insurance in Canada Faculty of Law, University of Toronto September 16, 2005.

6. "'Go Slow' on Health Plan," *Winnipeg Tribune*, March 16, 1956. See also *Tribune* editorial, "No State Medicine Here," March 24, 1954.

7. Provincial Archives of Manitoba (PAM), Roblin to Bedson, February 2, 1957. Derek Bedson Papers, GR 0024, file P6441/3. "Duff Roblin, n.d., 1956–1963."

8. Wiseman, *Social Democracy in Manitoba*, 72.

9. "Walter Weir Gets Tory Nomination," *Minnedosa Tribune*, April 9, 1959.

10. "Men in the News: The Cabinet Shuffle," *Winnipeg Tribune*, November 2, 1961.

11. PAM, Executive Council Papers, File # 312, "Executive Council of Manitoba—Ministers of the Crown, Meetings, etc.," Roblin to Weir, May 15, 1959.

12. "Men in the News: The Cabinet Shuffle", *Winnipeg Tribune*, November 2, 1961.

13. Duff Roblin, *Speaking for Myself* (Winnipeg: Great Plains Publications, 1999), 155.

14. Weir-Warren radio interview, January 29, 1978. University of Manitoba, Elizabeth Dafoe Archives and Special Collections, Peter Warren Fonds, A97-79 TC 62, Box 1, Item 1.

15. Duff Roblin, *Speaking for Myself* (Winnipeg: Great Plains Publications, 1999), p 181.

16. Government of Manitoba, *Statement of Votes* (Winnipeg: Queen's Printer, 1977), 149–53. See Summary of Results of the 27th and 28th Manitoba General Elections. See also Wiseman, *Social Democracy in Manitoba*, 108–10.

17. Lloyd Stinson, *Political Warriors: Recollections of a Social Democrat* (Winnipeg: Queenston House Publishing, 1975), 205–06; "Roblin Loss," *Winnipeg Tribune*, June 29, 1968. See also, "Warning for Mr. Weir," *Winnipeg Free Press*, July 2, 1968. "It seems the most telling factor in Mr. Roblin's downfall was the backlash of public opinion against higher provincial taxes…"

18. D. McCormick, *"The Dissolution of the Coalition: Roblin's Rise to Leadership, 1949–54"* (36 pps., unpublished, c. 1970), 36. Discovered in the Gurney Evans files, MG 14, B 27, box 48, file "Govt" [*sic*]. McCormick's interpretation is directly at odds with that offered by the *Winnipeg Tribune* (see "Proud Roblin Ends Decade of Power," *Winnipeg Tribune*, November 25, 1967) on the day of the convention that asserted: " Mr. Roblin has left his unique stamp on Manitoba politics and, more particularly, on the Conservative party." In the opinion of this author, the *Tribune's* assessment was proved wrong within 24 hours of its printing.

19. "Proud Roblin Ends Decade of Power."

20. "Leadership Hopeful W.C. Weir Addresses…," *Minnedosa Tribune*, November 9, 1967.

21. "Image a Factor in Race", *Winnipeg Free Press*, October 17, 1967.

22. Interview with Sidney Green, October 18, 2007. Interview with Harry Enns, November 21, 2007. Mr. Green as a sitting NDP MLA in 1967 believed Lyon was the favourite going into the campaign. Mr. Enns, then Minister of Agriculture and close confidant of Weir was well aware at the time that Lyon was seen by many as the "heir apparent."

23. Interview with Harry Enns, November 21, 2007. As with many who either worked with or for Mr. Lyon, Mr. Enns acknowledges that the widespread belief that Lyon possessed an intellectual capacity second to none was well founded; See also, "Lyon: Make the Future With All We've Got," *Winnipeg Tribune*, November 21, 1967.

24. "Leadership Hopefuls At A Candid Glance: Winner's Aura and It Shows," *Winnipeg Free Press*, November 18, 1967.

25. "Lyon: Make the Future With All We've Got."

26. "First Tears, Then Cheers After the Vote," *Winnipeg Tribune*, November 29, 1967.

27. "Weir's Win: 'Just-Plain-Folks' Appeal and an Unbeatable Machine," *Winnipeg Free Press*, November 27, 1967.

28. "Weir Announces Cabinet Change," *Winnipeg Tribune*, November 27, 1967.

29. "Weir's Win: 'Just-Plain-Folks'.Appeal and an Unbeatable Machine."

30. "Weir Sworn Into Office as Fifth PC Premier," *Winnipeg Free Press*, November 29, 1967.

31. Editorial, "Mr. Weir's Difficult Task," *Winnipeg Free Press*, November 27, 1967.

32. Wiseman, *Social Democracy in Manitoba*, 120.

33. On many pressing and perennial issues, such as Unicity, the Roblin government had been less than decisive. Other policies were reactive in nature and driven by damage control (Northern Hydro and MDA) while federal-provincial issues were victims of either policy reversals (i.e. Medicare), or poorly conceived bargaining positions (i.e. tax-rental). As such, Weir inherited a number of nightmare files to which there may have been an identifiably Manitoba end game but to which there was no workable solution on the horizon.

34. "Dual Cabinet Change Likely," *Winnipeg Free Press*, November 27, 1967. See also "Weir Announces Cabinet Change," *Winnipeg Tribune*, November 27, 1967.

35. Interview with Harry Enns.

36. Editorial, "Premier Walter Weir," *Winnipeg Tribune*, November 27, 1967. The *Tribune* averred that as Weir assumed his duties, he could "be heartened in his task by the knowledge that he has a united and well-organized Progressive Conservative party behind him in Manitoba."

37. Interview with Harry Enns.

38. Ibid.

39. Weir to Mr. Gordon Lawson (acting chair, Manitoba Economic Consultative Board), March 3, 1968, PAM, Executive Council Papers, file: "Walter Weir—Replies to Letters Dec 67 to July 29, 1968"; see also Ian Wilson, "Derek Bedson: Clerk of the Executive Council of Manitoba, 1958 to 1981" (MA thesis: University of Manitoba, 2001), 75.

40. "Weir Aims to Aid Growth of Industry, Commerce," *Winnipeg Free Press*, November 28, 1967.

41. Tom Peterson, "Manitoba," *Canadian Annual Review of Politics and Public Affairs* (1968) (University of Toronto Press: Toronto, 1969), 172.

42. "MMS Talks Await Federal Move: Roblin," *Winnipeg Tribune*, November 20, 1967. A week before the leadership convention Roblin had publicly requested that Ottawa restrict the Medicare formula to cover only those citizens who could otherwise not afford premiums. Further, although he had confirmed on October 12, 1967 that he was very unhappy about the federal conditions surrounding the plan he had nevertheless confirmed: "Manitoba will go along with the national medical care program" (see "Federal Plan or Nothing, Says Roblin," *Winnipeg Tribune*, October 12, 1967.) By November 1967 he was openly questioning whether Manitoba would ever enter the program; "Weir Aims To Aid Growth of Industry, Commerce." See also "Weir Plans Economic Expansion," *Winnipeg Tribune*, November 28, 1967.

43. "Provinces Expected to Ask Ottawa to Back Medicare Delay," *Winnipeg Tribune*, November 16, 1967.

44. PAM, Walter Weir to Lester Pearson, February 2, 1968, Executive Council Papers, unnumbered File, "Walter Weir—replies to letters Dec 67 to July 29, 1968." See also, "Weir Plans Economic Expansion."

45. "Weir Confident Quebec can be Accommodated," *Winnipeg Free Press*, December 1, 1967; "Weir Promises Open Mind on Constitution," *Winnipeg Tribune*, December 1, 1967.

46. "Weir Sworn Into Office as Fifth PC Premier."

47. Richard Gwyn, *The Northern Magus* (PaperJacks Edition: Toronto, 1981), 64.

48. Interview with Georgina Buddick, October 15, 2007.

49. PAM, Weir to George Hutton, December 19, 1967, Executive Council Papers, unnumbered File, "Walter Weir–Replies to Letters Dec 67 to July 29, 1968."

50. PAM, Weir to Mr. G.N. Ripley [divisional manager, Canada Packers] December 21, 1967, Executive Council Papers, unnumbered File, "Walter Weir—Replies to Letters Dec 67 to July 29, 1968." In a warm letter to Ripley, Weir spoke of how he was eternally grateful for all the love and support he had received from his parents: "I feel very fortunate to have a father like him and a mother like his better half." But, when it came to his propensity to "party" he confessed he came by the talent naturally as he said, in this regard he was "a chip off the old block."

51. Interview with Georgina Buddick.

52. Ibid., October 15, 2007. Forty years later, Ms. Buddick clearly remembers the pride and affection exhibited by Weir towards his children during those days when they came to the office to "work" with "Dad."

53. PAM, Walter Weir to V.I. Leatherdale, December 22, 1967, Executive Council Papers, unnumbered File, "Walter Weir–Replies to Letters Dec 67 to July 29, 1968."

54. Lloyd Stinson, *Political Warriors*, 196.

55. The author is indebted to Professor Gregory Marchildon for drawing his attention to the important role played by Derek Bedson in the administration of the Manitoba Executive Council in the 1960s.

56. Christopher Dunn, *The Institutionalized Cabinet: Governing the Western Provinces* (Montreal: McGill Press, 1995), 113–14.

57. Interview with Georgina Buddick. Ms. Buddick went out of her way to note that Mr. Bedson was very adept at managing the protocol and affairs of the cabinet.

58. Interview with Harry Enns and interview with Georgina Buddick. It should be noted that Derek Bedson went on to serve as the Clerk under both Premiers Schreyer and Lyon. His ability to thrive in these administrations points to his parliamentary knowledge and cabinet efficiency. The explanation for the fiasco during Weir's tenure must be, in the opinion of the author, due to the fact that Weir was a more malleable figure than either Schreyer and Lyon and that the "political pressure-cooker" facing Weir never gave him a chance to address Bedson's relative power and its impact on the other staffers.

59. Tom Peterson, "Manitoba," in *Canadian Annual Review of Politics and Public Affairs* (1968), 164; see PAM, Memo, D.A. Young to Weir, January 15, 1968, Executive Council Papers, Office of the Premier, GR 1363, box Q-024246, file "Memo's, Correspondence for Mr. Weir's Signature."

60. PAM, Walter Weir to Lester Pearson, February 2, 1968, Executive Council Papers, unnumbered File, "Walter Weir–Replies to Letters Dec 67 to July 29, 1968." Peterson calls it a telegram in the *Canadian Annual Review for 1968,*" 164. However, in Weir's Executive Council Papers the only copy discovered so far is in a letter format.

61. Ibid.

62. Peterson, "Manitoba," 166.

63. "No Go-Go Plans for Manitoba, Weir Indicates," *Winnipeg Free Press*, March 7, 1967.

64. "Under the Dome," *Winnipeg Free Press*, March 8, 1968. The columnist, Ellen Simmons opined "it wasn't much" of a Throne speech, although she allowed that it did elicit "considerable comment (of the unquotable and unattributable kind) [sic] in the corridors after adjournment." Tom Peterson also remarked on the strangeness of their inclusion in his annual synopsis of events in Manitoba. See Peterson, "Manitoba," 164–65.

65. "No Go-Go Plans for Manitoba, Weir Indicates."

66. See "Evans Predicts Sound Economic Growth" and "Federal Fiscal Policies Lambasted," *Winnipeg Free Press*, April 9, 1968.

67. The day before their protest a report by the Royal Commission into Consumer Problems and Inflation had been released that said "that Manitoba's agriculture was likely to experience a 'further decline'." See Peterson, "Manitoba," 166, 172. The PC MLA who threatened to quit was Earl McKeller.

68. See "PC Asks School $ Cutback", Winnipeg Free Press, March 6, 1968; "School tax is Going Up But Policy's the Same: Weir", Winnipeg Free Press, March 20, 1968; "Govt. Levy Hike 'One Big Hoax'," Winnipeg Free Press, March 21, 1968.

69. "Under the Dome."

70. Ibid.; Peterson, "Manitoba," 164.

71. Stinson, *Political Warriors*, 200. See also "Under the Dome."

72. "People Betrayed…," *Winnipeg Free Press*, March 28, 1968. Also see Legislature highlights in *Free Press*, April 1, 1968.

73. "Govt. Priorities Lacking: Molgat," *Winnipeg Free Press,* March 13, 1968.

74. PAM, Telegram, Roblin to Pearson, November 15, 1967, Executive Council Papers, Office of the Premier, GR 1363, Box Q-024246, file #640.4, "Medicare." Roblin wrote: "To do otherwise would be to permit the people of this province to be taxed by your Government for a service they could not receive."

75. "Weir Stand Hit," *Winnipeg Free Press*, March 20, 1968.

76. Editorial, "Inviting Medicare," *Winnipeg Tribune*, May 8, 1967. The paper noted that: "Since he took office, Premier Weir has been desperately trying to buy time and to persuade Ottawa to change the terms of the national medicare plan. His goal has been to achieve a voluntary plan." See also "Weir Stand Hit."

77. "Desjardins Raps Govt. on Medicare Gamble," *Winnipeg Free Press*, April 10, 1968.

78. PAM, Walter Weir to Lester Pearson, February 2, 1968, Executive Council Papers, unnumbered File, "Walter Weir–Replies to Letters Dec 67 to July 29, 1968." See also "Weir May Take Ottawa to Court: Medicare Tax Without Consultation Seen as Unconstitutional," *Winnipeg Free Press*, March 19, 1968.

79. Malcolm Taylor, *Health Insurance and Canadian Public Policy* (McGill-Queen's University Press: Montreal, 1978), 391.

80. Weir did threaten to implement Manitoba's own voluntary plan "with or without federal help." See "Province Studies Plan for Voluntary Medicare," *Winnipeg Tribune*, April 26, 1968. Like most of Weir's attempts/threats to forestall the federal plan—a go-it-alone voluntary plan was too unrealistic for anyone to take seriously.

81. See "No Tax Hike Pledge 'a Lie'," *Winnipeg Free Press*, May 2, 1968. The Liberals accused the Weir government of breaking its Throne Speech promise of no new tax hikes, calling the 80% premium increase for the Manitoba Hospital Insurance Plan nothing more than a new provincial tax. See also "Hospital Costs Blamed: Premiums Going Up 80 Per Cent," *Winnipeg Free Press*, May 2, 1968. Whitney had good reason to bring forth the increase because under Roblin the program had remained under funded for years: "when the hospital services plan went into effect in 1959, premiums covered 40 per cent of operating costs. Now [1968] they covered only 20 per cent."

82. See "Doctors Endorse Plans to Up MMS rates 23%," *Winnipeg Tribune*, May 6, 1968; "Citizens' Group on the March for Medicare Backing," *Winnipeg Tribune*, June 1, 1968; "MDs' Fee Demand Termed 'Fantastic'," *Winnipeg Free Press*, April 26, 1968; and Peterson, "Manitoba," 165.

83. See "MDs' Fee Demand Termed 'Fantastic'" and Peterson, "Manitoba," 165.

84. The largest and most important organization to do battle with Weir over the issue, aside from the Manitoba Labour Federation, was the Citizens Committee on Medical Costs in Manitoba. An umbrella organization with academics, labour, and social activists, it was relentless from late May onwards in attacking the government's refusal to sign on to Ottawa's plan and was instrumental in collecting over 50,000 signatures for a pro-medicare petition. See "Citizens' Group on the March for Medicare Backing" *and* "Citizens to March For Names," *Winnipeg Tribune*, June 1, 1968.

85. Peterson, "Manitoba," 165.

86. Editorial, "The Reasons Why," *Winnipeg Tribune*, June 26, 1967.

87. "Under the Dome."

88. Peterson, "Manitoba," 167.

89. "Canned Beer June 10," *Winnipeg Free Press*, May 23, 1968.

90. Peterson, "Manitoba," 165–66.

91. Ibid., 167.

92. Wiseman, *Social Democracy in Manitoba*, 129.

93. "Ex-premier Walter Weir Dies," *Winnipeg Free Press*, April 18, 1985.

94. Library and Archives Canada (LAC), Weir opening statement, February 11, 1969, p. 99; LAC, Dominion-Provincial Conferences: Constitutional, 1969, RG 47, vol. 83, file "Verbatim Reports, February 10–12, 1969" (unrevised copy).

95. See LAC, Dominion-Provincial Conferences: Constitutional, 1969, RG 47, vol. 83, file "Verbatim Reports, February 10–12, 1969" pp. 93–106 (unrevised copy).

96. Interview with Georgina Buddick.

97. See *The Constitutional Review 1968–1971, Secretary's Report* (Ottawa: Canadian Intergovernmental Conference Secretariat, 1974).

98. Peterson, "Manitoba," 125; interview with Georgina Buddick.

99. Interview with Harry Enns.

100. Peterson, "Manitoba," 126.

101. See PAM, "Budget Policy" section, "1969—PC Election Handbook" (Black Binder), p. 1, Evans Papers, MG 14, B 27-1, box 4; Weir to Mr. Gordon Lawson (acting chair, Manitoba Economic Consultative Board), March 3, 1968, Executive Council Papers, file: "Walter Weir—Replies to Letters Dec 67 to July 29, 1968"; see also Wilson, "Derek Bedson: Clerk of the Executive Council of Manitoba, 1958 to 1981," 75.

102. PAM, "Budget Policy" section, "1969, PC Election Handbook" (Black Binder), p. 1., Evans Papers, MG 14, B 27-1, box 4.

103. See Sidney Green, *Rise and Fall of a Political Animal: A Memoir* (Winnipeg: Great Plains Publications, 2003), 60; Peterson, "Manitoba," 126;"Extra-Billing Used as Club: Hanuschak," *Winnipeg Free Press,* April 10, 1969.

104. Peterson, "Manitoba," 126–27.

105. "Quips, Caustic Comments Mark House Dissolution," *Winnipeg Free Press,* May 23, 1969; "Under the Dome."

106. Peterson, "Manitoba," 168.

107. Ibid., 129.

108. "Campaigns End," *Winnipeg Free Press,* June 24, 1969.

109. "Schreyer Crusades for Head-on Confrontation with Weir," *Winnipeg Tribune,* June 10, 1969.

110. Wiseman, *Social Democracy in Manitoba,* 120.

111. "Weir Feels Manitobans Will Correct 'Mistake'," *Winnipeg Free Press,* June 26, 1969; "Weir Must Go: Schreyer," *Winnipeg Tribune,* June 27, 1969.

112. Peterson, "Manitoba," 130.

113. "What's Left Out Important to Weir," *Winnipeg Free Press,* August 15, 1969.

114. "Weir is Dead," *Winnipeg Sun,* April 19, 1985.

115. Ibid.

116. Interview with Harry Enns and interview with Sidney Green, October 18, 2007. Enns holds the opinion that Walter Weir's influence over the future policy direction of the Manitoba PC party was minimal because his time at the helm was "simply too short." Green stated that Weirism had no impact "whatsoever" on the political dynamics of the province.

117. NDP MLA Ben Hanuschak quoted in "Weir is Dead."

Edward Schreyer

GREGORY MARCHILDON
AND KEN RASMUSSEN

1969–1977

Edward Richard Schreyer, 1969–1977

Edward Schreyer's election as Premier of Manitoba in 1969 was a watershed moment in both Canadian and Manitoba politics. On a symbolic level, Schreyer's successful bid for power signaled a willingness on the part of voters to not only accept a leader whose distinct ethnic background reflected neither of Canada's two dominant cultures, but also allowed other ethnic minorities to see in him a validation of their own place in this new and multicultural Canada.[1] As Gerald Friesen notes, Ed Schreyer "embodied the party's links with the 'little people'—Roman Catholics, non-British ethnic groups, and the working class."[2]

Schreyer's victory also reflected a loss of faith in the "old-line" Conservative Party, the steady postwar decline of the Liberal Party and the rise of the New Democratic Party (NDP) as a dominant force in Manitoba.[3] In this, his administration laid the groundwork for future NDP administrations under Howard Pawley and Gary Doer, and marked the beginning of the spread of social democratic governments beyond Saskatchewan. Indeed, Schreyer's election victory was the first for the NDP following its merger with the labour movement and abandonment of the Co-operative Commonwealth Federation (CCF) name in 1961.

Finally, Ed Schreyer was 33 years of age when he assumed office and, even more than Prime Minister Trudeau, was seen as a member of a new generation, sympathetic to the cultural shift of the 1960s. With the shift came a desire for governments to work actively towards a more "just society." One manifestation of this sea-change could be found in the anti-Vietnam war movement which animated many young activists on the left and which openly challenged the nature of Canada's relationship with the United States. Another was the focus on individual leaders as Trudeaumania illustrated. Like Trudeau, Schreyer was popular with the hip generation during his first years in office even if the political styles of the two leaders differed. As described by *Maclean's* magazine in 1969, "the mainstream of Canadian public opinion" was "flowing somewhere between Ed Schreyer's pragmatic populism and Pierre Elliott Trudeau's pragmatic elitism."[4]

Like earlier social democratic leaders next door in Saskatchewan, Schreyer found electoral popularity by offering a moderate brand of social democracy associated with the centre-left and making his party seem "safe" to a plurality of both urban and rural Manitobans. Through a combination of natural charisma and professional political skills, he was able to appeal to a broad spectrum of the public well beyond the members of his own political party, a feat that was impossible for his Conservative opponent Walter Weir. And Schreyer was able to take advantage of his personal appeal to initiate a number of major changes including public automobile insurance, pharmacare, municipal reform, improved French language services, and a new emphasis on Aboriginal and northern development. These changes led to real improvements in the lives of Manitobans, particularly the most disadvantaged and marginalized residents of the province.

The Making of a Reformer

Edward Richard Schreyer was born on December 21, 1935. His father, John, was a second-generation farmer of German descent who was born and raised in the ethnically diverse farming area around Beauséjour, about 50 kilometres northeast of Winnipeg. Schreyer's mother was born Elizabeth Gottried and, like her husband, was of German-Austrian and Roman Catholic background. While the largest group of farmers who settled in the Beauséjour area were German-speaking immigrants, they shared the region with Polish and Ukrainian settlers and a few French-Canadians. In short supply were families of British origin, most of whom farmed in the more prosperous parts of the province to the south.[5]

John and Elizabeth Schreyer were staunch supporters of the Canadian Wheat Board—their trust in the open market was shaken by their experiences in the Great Depression. While not unqualified supporters of government intervention in general, they did believe that the state should step in where it could improve upon market outcomes. And while they may not have been active members of the CCF, they voted for the CCF more often than other political parties. Influenced by his family, Ed Schreyer would go a step further by taking out membership in the CCF at 18 years of age.[6]

Following his education in a one-room schoolhouse and the regional high school in Beauséjour, Schreyer chose to leave the farm and go to university, first at United College (now the University of Winnipeg), and then the University of Manitoba, where he would receive degrees in Arts, Education and Pedagogy. Returning to Beauséjour as a schoolteacher, he began to devote almost all of his spare time to politics, largely due to the influence of farmer and CCF activist Jake Schulz.[7] Schreyer joined the Manitoba Farmers Union (MFU), an ambitious new farm lobby that represented a large number of the "ethnic" farmers who lived in the more northerly, less prosperous parts of the province. Schulz was the moving force behind the MFU. He had created the organization in the late 1940s as a more activist and left-wing alternative to the Manitoba Federation of Agriculture (MFA).[8] To many like Schreyer, the MFA represented the richer, Anglo-Saxon farmers of southern Manitoba who identified with the status quo and the old-line parties, particularly the Liberals.[9]

Recognizing the young man's talent, Jake Schulz convinced Schreyer to become his campaign manager when he ran for the CCF in the 1957 federal election. The 21-year-old's strategic acumen won the election for both Schulz and the CCF. Schreyer's connection to Jake Schulz went beyond politics. He was also romantically interested in Schulz's daughter, Lillian, or Lily as she was called. In 1960, Lily and Ed Schreyer married. They would raise three children together and Schreyer would hire Lily's brother—Herb Schulz—to be one of his executive assistants after he became Premier.[10]

In 1958, Schreyer decided to throw his own hat into Manitoba's political ring. Naturally, he ran in a riding—Brokenhead—that included his hometown. Trading on the skills he had gained in running Schulz's campaign and calling upon his MFU friends who were spreading the word on his behalf from farm to hamlet, village and town, Schreyer ran his campaign like a seasoned veteran. He won despite the fact that the election came in the immediate aftermath of the federal Diefenbaker landslide and the popularity of the provincial Progressive Conservatives under the vibrant leadership of Duff Roblin.[11]

At 22 years of age, Schreyer was the youngest member ever to enter the Manitoba Legislative Assembly where he would remain until he moved to federal politics and a seat in the House of Commons in 1965. His string of election victories marked him out as a dependable winner. As a member of an 11-person CCF caucus, Schreyer soon gained a reputation for not toeing the party line, especially on rural issues. Others saw him as more conservative than older CCF stalwarts; he viewed himself as more pragmatic than some of his CCF colleagues who habitually took what he perceived as inflexible stands on the pressing issues of the day. In turn, the old guard thought he was too much of a "fence sitter" on some issues and questioned his "socialist" commitment. This conflict with the left of the party would follow him throughout his career, but Schreyer's ability to reach out beyond the CCF's original base to win elections deflected much of the criticism.

These tendencies were in full view when the CCF debated the formation of the NDP. The idea of the party forging a direct link with organized labour through affiliation with the Canadian Labour Congress had created a split within the Manitoba CCF by 1959. While Schreyer agreed that the CCF needed to be transformed in order to obtain greater electoral traction, he remained uneasy about the greater power that might be given organized labour within the new party.[12] At the same time, he maintained good relations with individuals on both sides of the debate. The pro-NDP forces chose Schreyer as their candidate for chair of the Manitoba party because of the neutrality he displayed during the debate.[13]

While continuing to push issues concerning agriculture and rural life as an opposition critic, Schreyer gradually spent more of his time in Winnipeg. His position as MLA was secure, and in 1962, having recently obtained an MA degree in Political Science from the University of Manitoba, Schreyer was hired as a professor of International Relations at St. Paul's College, the English-language, Roman Catholic college of the University of Manitoba.

By 1965, Schreyer had spent almost seven years in the legislature as an opposition member. Restless and looking for new challenges, he decided to run in the upcoming federal election under the newly created NDP, then under the leadership of social-democratic icon Tommy Douglas. Again, he was successful, and this time in a riding that was predominantly urban, adding to his already considerable reputation as a political winner. But victory meant Schreyer had to move his young family from Manitoba to Ottawa, a move he found difficult. Initially, he was uncomfortable in his new environment. Despite his time in Winnipeg and his experience as a university professor, Schreyer was essentially a small-town boy who wanted to stay in close touch with his roots. His commitment to agricultural life and policy continued to show through. In a speech to the National Farmers Union after he became Premier, he spoke passionately of the centrality of rural communities and the family farm to the future of the country.[14] Warning that the threat of rural depopulation was "leading to a whole new set of complex urban problems," he argued for a durable farm policy that would deliver adequate, stable and predictable farm income and commodity price support to keep people in rural Canada. He then reflected on the alternative of urban life, drawing a negative portrait that he had formulated while living in both Ottawa and Winnipeg:

> It has been suggested, that in 20 years, 80% of the population of Canada will be packed into four or five cities. If we think we have problems now, we will be shocked by the rising rates of crime and social distress that derives from packing millions of human beings into the sprawling de-personalized megalopolis.[15]

But while the trend to greater urbanization was, from Schreyer's point of view, a problem, an important part of his eventual legacy as Premier would be to make Winnipeg a more effective and efficient city and thus a magnet to a growing number of young, rural Manitobans.

Rise to Power

By 1968, a number of NDP party activists were asking Schreyer to leave the federal scene and return home to take over the leadership of the provincial NDP. It was becoming evident that the decade-old Conservative government was running out of steam under the lackluster leadership of Walter Weir.[16] More importantly, rank-and-file members of the NDP were becoming increasingly dissatisfied with party leader Russ Paulley. Initially, Schreyer was torn about the decision. On one level, he wanted to come home and transform the Manitoba NDP from a third-rank party into a government; yet, he had little appetite for personally forcing Paulley out of office in a coup d'état.

Sid Green, a Winnipeg labour lawyer and local NDP caucus member who also had leadership aspirations, was more anxious than most to see Paulley go. He arranged a lunch meeting with the provincial NDP leader and Schreyer where he offered to support Schreyer rather than run himself if Paulley would agree to resign immediately and also support Schreyer. Paulley agreed in principle but not to the timing, and Schreyer quickly distanced himself from Green's proposal. Green then forced a leadership review with the support of some rank-and-file members but without the assistance of any of his fellow caucus members. Instead, the elected members supported Paulley during the leadership review on the understanding that he would step down as leader the following year making way for Schreyer, thereby explicitly supporting a man who had not yet agreed to run for leader. In their formal statement, caucus members baldly stated that Schreyer had "the best attributes for leadership with the Party and in the eyes of the electorate" and were confident that he would be "sufficiently responsive" to their "Draft Schreyer campaign for 1969."[17]

In the meantime, however, Green's actions forced a leadership vote between himself and Paulley. In reality, it was a choice between having Green as a leader immediately or the possibility of getting Schreyer a year later. Green lost and Paulley resigned the following year. Undaunted over his initial loss at the leadership review, Green immediately announced his candidacy, knowing full well that most of the caucus had spent months trying to lure Schreyer back to Manitoba. Realizing that the time was now right, Schreyer finally accepted the draft, and put his name forward for party leader to be decided in early June 1969. At the same time, the Conservatives under Weir tried to take advantage of the situation by calling a snap election five days before the scheduled end of the legislative session, and before the

NDP had a chance to anoint their new leader. The tactic backfired in part because Weir's timing was so transparently opportunistic. The *Winnipeg Free Press* even suggested that Manitobans might now be "as witless and gullible as Mr. Weir seems to think…"[18] In reality, the Conservatives had given Schreyer and the NDP a public relations gift—intense media coverage of the party convention a mere 17 days before the election.[19]

During the NDP leadership convention, Green appeared to be the more rigid and ideological of the two, and Schreyer was more than happy to position himself as the voice of social-democratic moderation. While both candidates subsequently argued that their ideological differences were minor even if their styles were quite different, differences in ideology nonetheless remained the working assumption of organized labour which solidly backed Green. The outcome, however, was never really in doubt. With the support of most of caucus along with a large number of party members attracted to his personal style, including a majority of the youth delegates, Schreyer defeated Green decisively.

With hardly a moment to catch his breath, Schreyer had to focus his party's attention on the election campaign. At dissolution, the NDP held only 12 of the 53 seats in the legislature. As everyone soon discovered, the caucus's faith in Schreyer was not misplaced and its laborious efforts to recruit him paid huge dividends. Before the convention, NDP support had been largely limited to north Winnipeg. Now the NDP had a 33-year-old telegenic leader at the helm who could simultaneously reach out to the farmers and small business owners of rural Manitoba as easily as university students and the highly educated urban professionals in the more prosperous parts of Winnipeg. Schreyer's appeal was enhanced by the fact that his ethnic origin was neither British nor Protestant, and he appealed to large sections of the Manitoba population with different ethnic origins and religious affiliations. Nelson Wiseman, one of the earliest chroniclers of the CCF–NDP in Manitoba, concluded that "the NDP could not have won with anyone but Ed Schreyer" in 1969.[20]

Schreyer's centre-left political philosophy appealed to many Manitobans who had never before voted NDP. In public, Schreyer called himself a social democrat, preferring to avoid the term socialist, a tag nonetheless applied to him by the Progressive Conservative Party as well as the major media in Manitoba. Indeed, his opponent, Walter Weir, went further, calling the NDP "Marxists" and "Communists"—precisely the kind of accusations that Schreyer's public persona effortlessly deflected.[21]

While Schreyer stressed the important role of governments—what he always referred to as the "instrumentality of government"—he only endorsed state intervention when and where the private sector was demonstrably not serving the public interest. In an interview shortly after the 1969 election, Schreyer explained that "a social democrat is one who endorses the notion that government is an instrument to be used by society to achieve certain ends, to bring about certain objectives, [and] initiate certain programs in order to protect people against exploitation in the market place…" But while social democrats were not philosophically "opposed to the use of the government ownership of a particular industry or service," neither should they "be pushing for it as a matter of doctrinaire philosophy," in his view.[22] In his reticence to intervene directly in the business life of the province, he seemed a reluctant social democrat to many on the left.

The second element of Schreyer's social democracy was his desire to seek greater equality of outcome in the human condition and the need to achieve this through redistributive social programs and progressive taxation. Thus, while he was reluctant to intervene in the economy except where clearly justified, he believed that the market, as a matter of course, generated inequalities that could only be countervailed by the state. In this, he was in agreement with socialists, left-wing social democrats, and even some left liberals. As Premier, and even later as Governor General and Ambassador, he always prominently displayed behind his desk a quotation from Franklin Delano Roosevelt which he considered the essence of social democracy: "The real test of our progress as a nation and society is not whether we add to the abundance of those who already have much, but whether we manage to add to the lives of those who have little."[23]

During his years as an opposition member in the legislature, Schreyer perceived his party as a loose coalition of reform-oriented farmers in the progressive or populist tradition, along with small "l" liberals, trade unionists and democratic socialists. Together, they forged what Schreyer believed was a unique, Canadian-style social democracy. Of these influences, Schreyer had a tendency to emphasize the liberal roots of social democracy. And throughout his life, he generously peppered his speeches with quotations from famous American liberals such as John F. Kennedy and most often, Franklin D. Roosevelt. In a speech to an American audience in 1971, he explained the nature of his political creed: "Like most small "l" liberals, I believe fervently in the Aristotlian maxim of the desirability of moderation in all things. And I think if one would ask for a check list of problems that needs solving, the social democrat and the small "l" liberal would produce the same list."[24] These and similar pronouncements made it easier for those who normally did not vote NDP to take a chance on election night. For his part, Schreyer knew that the NDP required Liberal voters to switch allegiance if it was to gain and maintain government in Manitoba. In this vein, Schreyer was greatly aided by the fact that the Conservative government and its relatively new leader, Walter Weir, had given up some of the middle ground once occupied by Duff Roblin and retreated to a more ideologically old-style conservative position. Centrist voters were looking for an alternative and since the provincial Liberals in 1969 were suffering from Trudeau's unpopular agricultural policies and internal party squabbles, they looked to Schreyer to fill the gap.

On election night, June 25, 1969, Schreyer made history by leading his party to power for the first time in Manitoba—the first social-democratic triumph outside of Saskatchewan. Victory may have been sweet, it may have been unexpected, but the margin was definitely thin. With 28 seats out of 57, Schreyer's new government was one seat short of a workable majority, a problem that was solved when Larry Desjardins, a disenchanted Liberal member who was comfortable with Schreyer's political philosophy and working style, agreed to sit with the NDP caucus as a "Liberal Democrat."

The NDP victory was based on a breakthrough in the northern part of Manitoba combined with continued growth of electoral support in rural Manitoba and Winnipeg. Schreyer had taken a personal interest in the north and he was able to translate this interest, together with the changing nature of the northern economy, into some substantial and durable gains

Table 1: Manitoba Provincial Elections during the Schreyer Era						
	1969 Election		1973 Election		1977 Election	
Party	Seats	% of Vote	Seats	% of Vote	Seats	% of Vote
New Democratic Party	28	39	31	42	23	39
Progressive Conservative	22	35	21	37	33	49
Liberal	5	24	5	19	1	12
Other	2	2	0	2	0	—
Total	57	100	57	100	57	100

for the party. The other factor which helps explain the 1969 victory was the redistribution of seats in the Manitoba electoral system which created more seats in Winnipeg and the vicinity around Winnipeg, which had been a much better source of NDP strength than the rural areas in the prosperous south which were solidly Progressive Conservative.[25]

Schreyer knew that the business community would not support the NDP in the election but he was prepared to go to great lengths to assuage their fears, and mediate their concerns. Confronting the shock and fear that was palpable following his election, he did everything he could to calm the waters and reassure key business leaders that he and his new government had no intention of driving the private sector out of the province. As such, the new Premier decided it would be best if he personally assumed the portfolio of Industry and Commerce to reinforce the message that his government would encourage and provide opportunities for business to invest in the province. Assurance was the key, moderation was the means. As he explained, his ambitions in terms of achieving a more equitable—or "just"—society and a vibrant business community were linked: "Our goals and programs for social justice and an enhanced quality of life for the people of Manitoba depend on a flourishing business community developing the economy of the province."[26]

Schreyer as Premier: Translating Platform into Policy

Because of the mere 17 days between the leadership convention and the election, Schreyer was forced to keep the NDP election platform short, simple, and straightforward. The first plank of the platform involved improving access to public health care; the second was the creation of a public automobile insurance company; the third was municipal reform, in particular the unification of Winnipeg into a single municipality (the "Unicity" concept); and the fourth was to review Walter Weir's decision to pursue a hydroelectric project that threatened to displace an entire Aboriginal community on South Indian Lake. All four promises, implemented early in the first term, would pave the way to the Schreyer government's re-election for a second term.

Initially, Schreyer felt ill-prepared for government—and with good reason. The press jumped on the inexperience of the new government. On the opening day of the first session, the regular legislative column in the *Winnipeg Free Press* observed that "almost the entire" government side of the house "was populated by strange faces ... struggling to achieve the right note of seriousness" while actually looking "like very happy tourists." Even NDP veterans conveyed "the impression that they were concentrating furiously on breathing silently and remaining motionless. Probably lest someone cough and wake them all out of a lovely dream."[27]

With no caucus experience in actually running a government, Schreyer knew how much he needed expert advice in how to go about implementing his government's ambitious policy agenda. For this, he at first relied upon the council of some key members of the "Saskatchewan Mafia," senior advisors who had worked for Tommy Douglas during his time as Premier of Saskatchewan and who were now variously employed as academics and public servants in other jurisdictions.[28] Through private interviews with Schreyer and members of his cabinet as well as lengthy memorandums, individuals such as George Cadbury, Tommy McLeod and Meyer Brownstone provided their advice on how Schreyer could manage cabinet so that it could quickly implement an innovative policy agenda.[29] Drawing on his experience as chair of Douglas's key cabinet committee, Cadbury told Schreyer that it was essential to create a

> Cabinet personality above individual ministers who, while running their Departments, will be asked as Cabinet Ministers to create an overall entity with a view above individual departmental needs. Such an entity can both override and protect individual ministers when necessary. This will be especially necessary when new Ministers [either] from inexperience or over enthusiasm make inevitable mistakes.[30]

Such advice led Schreyer to create a Planning and Priorities Committee of Cabinet and, along with it, a planning secretariat which attracted a sizeable number of bright young policy analysts. Schreyer wanted this cabinet committee, along with the planning secretariat, to push through his government's reform agenda and ensure that his political priorities would not be undermined by an expert bureaucracy taking advantage of inexperienced ministers with limited knowledge of their portfolios.[31] Howard Pawley, a Schreyer minister and the individual who would carry the Schreyer legacy into the 1980s as Premier of Manitoba, explained the new cabinet committee was Schreyer's way of making "it clear to the line departments, as well as the public, that an activist, policy-oriented government was in charge."[32]

At the same time, however, Schreyer made remarkably few changes to the senior bureaucracy. Derek Bedson, the Clerk of the Executive Council under the two previous Conservative administrations, was kept in his job. Bedson attended all the meetings of the Schreyer cabinet and later performed the same function for Sterling Lyon. Likewise, few changes were made in the line ministries and finance department, prompting one left-wing critic to complain that the entire secretariat of the Management Committee of Cabinet "remained unchanged and served as a highly conservative force within the government throughout the NDP regime."[33] From Schreyer's own perspective, however, he had found the right balance between respecting and maintaining a non-partisan and neutral public service, and bringing in new blood in key areas to guarantee policy momentum for his ambitious reform agenda.[34]

Upon taking power, Schreyer moved immediately on his election promise to improve access to public health care by reducing medicare premiums.[35] Weir's Conservative administration had been opposed to Liberal Prime Minister Lester Pearson's plan of national medicare, but when his own electorate plus the promise of federal cash finally pushed Weir to implement medicare, he set high premiums and even allowed doctors to opt out of the plan.[36] To rectify this, Schreyer named the NDP's most effective critic of Weir's medicare policy, Sid Green, as the government's new health minister. On November 1, 1969, premiums for medical care insurance were reduced by 88%, and the revenue loss was replaced with an income tax increase as promised in the election.[37]

While this reduction in premiums was largely uncontroversial, the same was not true for public automobile insurance. Originally conceived by the Douglas government of Saskatchewan, public auto insurance was a key plank in Manitoba CCF/NDP election platforms through the 1950s and 1960s. From 1966 until 1969, the Manitoba NDP annually introduced an amendment, calling for public automobile insurance, to the Conservative government's Throne Speech.[38] Once in power, the Schreyer government put forward Bill 56, which served as enabling legislation to establish a Crown corporation to administer compulsory automobile insurance coverage. This legislation put Schreyer in a direct confrontation with the insurance industry, small-town insurance brokers and the business community in general. While Schreyer hoped that this opposition would eventually learn to live with the change, he soon realized that his calculation was dead wrong.[39] Among those most opposed were the insurance corporations, which stood to lose $35 million in insurance premiums, and the 1,200 private insurance brokers, who saw their livelihoods threatened. The lobby they forged against public auto insurance—or Autopac as it was known—received hundreds of thousands of dollars from Toronto, the headquarters of many of the largest insurance companies in the country. Even if their Manitoba client base was small, these companies were panicked by the notion that any successful public auto insurance scheme initiated by Schreyer would have a ripple effect across the country.

During the ensuing Autopac crisis, Schreyer displayed his skills as a politician as well as his underlying political philosophy. Unlike many in his party, Schreyer was personally convinced that the insurance agents had a legitimate grievance, in contrast to the insurance companies. He also recognized that unless the government came up with a plan to involve the existing insurance agents he could not count on the support of Larry Desjardins, who was opposed to government ownership in the insurance industry—a critical consideration given his minority position in the legislature.[40]

To buy a little time and to ensure effective implementation, Schreyer appointed one of the lawyers in his cabinet, Howard Pawley, to manage the file. Pawley in turn appointed R.D. Blackburn, formerly chief executive of the Saskatchewan Government Insurance Office, to head up an implementation committee. By April the following year, the new Autopac bill received first reading in the legislature. Defending the program on the basis that it would reduce automobile insurance premiums by 20–30%, Schreyer began to build broader public support for the change among voters in Manitoba. He also ensured that auto insurance agents were placated by offering to compensate them for the loss of this part of their business and allowing them to sell basic government auto insurance as well as private supplementary coverage. These concessions served to dampen some of the opposition being mobilized by the Insurance Bureau of Canada and generated more public support.[41]

On second reading of the Autopac bill, the vote was evenly split and the Speaker had to vote with the government to allow the bill to move to committee. By third reading, it was obvious that Larry Desjardins' continued opposition to the bill would prevent it passing during the session and Schreyer took additional action to get his support. Desjardins was finally won over with a promise that would allow half the private insurance agents to sell government auto policies, and provide better compensation for the rest who would be forced out of the industry. Schreyer also agreed to establish a committee "to deal with any problems that might arise after the legislation was passed."[42] Desjardins finally voted with the government on the bill allowing the NDP to get 29 votes in favour compared to the 27 votes against Autopac. After the vote, the "house prorogued, ending the most exciting political session Manitoba has known since Louis Riel's provincial government of Red River."[43]

Schreyer's willingness to find compromise on Autopac demonstrated that while he was committed to the policy objective, he was never rigid on the means of implementation. But the battle over Autopac, and what he viewed as the overly hostile reaction of the business community, disappointed Schreyer. From his first day in office, he had worked assiduously to convince business leaders that he understood their needs. In fact, in his first Throne Speech, he had outlined a plan intended to alleviate their fears when he announced his appointment of two MLAs as parliamentary assistants, one of whom was Larry Desjardins, to aid him in "the area of economic development."[44] In his capacity as minister of Industry and Commerce, he joined a Chamber of Commerce promotion tour of Japan and appeared before the Toronto Board of Trade to tout investment opportunities in Manitoba during his first year in office. He continually repeated his mantra "that the goals of the Manitoba government and the business community are identical" and that his government would continue to recognize that "a high quality of life" for Manitobans "cannot be achieved without active co-operation between the province and the entrepreneurs of the private sector."[45] Despite all this, he found that the business community continued its policy of hostility to his government throughout the Autopac debate.

At the same time that Schreyer was implementing public auto insurance, his major blueprint for health reform—entitled the White Paper on Health—was also being opposed by an array of institutional groups including physicians and hospital boards.[46] Although only publicly released in 1972, Schreyer's most senior policy advisors as well as his Cabinet Committee on Health, Education and Social Policy had been quietly working on the plan for months if not years. One of the most ambitious provincial efforts to reshape the health care system, the White Paper proposed that the government redirect its resources from acute care in hospitals to home care, long-term care and illness prevention. It recommended a major overhaul of physician remuneration by the province, in particular advocating retrenchment through fee-for-service payment. It proposed public coverage for a range of prescription drugs. It also recommended a major structural change, one in which new regional health authorities would manage a number of services across the health continuum. The reforms recommended in the White Paper were predicated on two principles. The first was to improve economic efficiency and save public money by reducing the number of hospitals and hospital beds, redirecting resources to home care, long-term care, illness prevention and health promotion. The second was to offer patients more appropriate, more effective or more humane alternatives to hospital and physician care.[47]

Physicians in particular were opposed to both the sweeping recommendations in the White Paper as well as its guiding philosophy. It was also opposed by the physician members of the Manitoba Health Services Commission (MHSC). One sent Schreyer a 10-page memorandum decrying the White Paper and defending the existing fee-for-service system. In his view, the White Paper spent considerable "effort in indicating the medical profession's responsibility in controlling costs" but "none whatsoever" in indicating the patient's responsibility.[48] In a brief from another doctor, it was stated that the government "authors of the White Paper show signs of being in the advanced stages of a well recognized step-like [sic] confusion of the intellect…"[49]

Despite this opposition, Schreyer committed his government to significant health reforms. In 1974, his government proceeded with the country's first public home-care system, allowing those with chronic or age-related illnesses to receive appropriate medical and support services in the comfort of their homes.[50] For Schreyer, home care was a compassionate social policy which made sound fiscal policy in that it was designed to save the province millions of dollars in hospital care.[51] Decades later, the public home-care programs and services established by the Schreyer government are still considered the best in the country. In July 1973, the Schreyer government introduced Pharmacare for the elderly with the provincial government paying 80% of the cost of covered prescription drugs in excess of a $50 deductible; 18 months later this categorical program was converted into a universal Pharmacare plan, available to all Manitoba residents.[52] Schreyer also spearheaded the introduction of new neighbourhood health clinics but stopped short of reorganizing the entire system into geographically based health regions as suggested in the far-sighted White Paper.[53]

Another issue Schreyer hoped to resolve in his first mandate involved the unification of greater Winnipeg, which constituted roughly one half of the province's total population. Long a contentious issue, in the 1960s an umbrella Metro government had actually been superimposed upon the 13 greater Winnipeg municipalities—each with its own mayor, council and service administrations, including separate police forces and fire departments. The umbrella government was made responsible for certain common services, including sewer, water and transportation, but the municipalities were reluctant to work together, much less cooperate with the new Metro administration. The end result was a tenuous, at times dysfunctional, compromise between decentralism and centralism. Although the NDP had campaigned on the promise of unifying greater Winnipeg, Schreyer and his Urban Affairs minister, Saul Cherniak, had to toil long and hard to find a workable solution that would be tolerable to all stakeholders. But the initial effort, a White Paper, only served to complicate the issue further by proposing a centralizing financial system with a decentralized administration with direct input from community committees and resident advisory groups.[54] After much negotiating, a compromise was reached and, in 1971, a new city of Winnipeg was created under a single elected mayor and council which eventually led to a much more coherent and effective governance structure. While the "new council faced an almost insurmountable task in melding thirteen municipalities into one cohesive unit," in the end the Unicity framework introduced by the Schreyer government endured and became the foundation for a revitalized Winnipeg.[55]

Although Autopac is generally regarded as the Schreyer government's single most important achievement, Schreyer himself always saw the Nelson River hydro project as his government's most important long-term legacy.[56] Beginning as a Conservative initiative to develop a major hydroelectric power project on the Nelson River in northern Manitoba, it was the hot-button political issue in the dying days of the Weir administration. There was little concern about the project until it reached the phase of constructing a dam to divert water from the Churchill River to the Nelson River at South Indian Lake. However, a problem emerged when it became evident that raising the water levels at South Indian Lake involved forcibly relocating an existing Aboriginal community of approximately 600 First Nations and Métis people.[57] For this, the NDP (and the Liberals) criticized the Conservatives, calling for the resignation of the minister responsible.

During the election, Schreyer promised to initiate a major review of the water diversion project in an effort to avoid flooding the community, and once in office, he hired David Cass-Beggs, former President of the Saskatchewan Power Commission, to head up the review. Cass-Beggs ultimately recommended an alternative approach: a low-level diversion that would increase the water level by 16 feet rather than 32 feet, thereby not flooding the South Indian Lake settlement. The government implemented Cass-Begg's recommendation and built the diversion, although the knock-on effects of the project, including a major dispute between Winnipeg and Ottawa concerning the impact of the dam on other connected waterways as well as a judicial inquiry, would outlive Schreyer's term in office.[58] The controversy would also trigger suspicion and mistrust of successive provincial administrations by the Cree communities negatively affected by the project.[59]

Beyond his big platform promises, Schreyer introduced a human rights commission, a law reform commission, an ombudsman, a new landlord and tenant act as well as an office of the rentalsman to negotiate disputes over rent, and the extension of legal aid. In his view, these reforms not only improved the quality of life for the majority, they also provided tangible benefits to the least advantaged, and the most marginalized, of Manitobans.[60] In the same vein, he tried to restore French as a language of instruction but was personally defeated on the issue of extending public support to separate schools in a free vote in the legislature.[61]

Beyond the anticipated obstacles facing his government, Schreyer also found himself face to face with a series of unexpected challenges during his first term. In particular, he was criticized extensively for bad investments made by the Manitoba Development Corporation (MDC) which had ill-advisedly used public funds to prop up some ailing provincial businesses. One of the biggest MDC headaches—Churchill Forest Industries—although inherited from the Conservatives, was exacerbated by the fact that the Schreyer government extended even more public funding.[62] Then in 1971, realizing that the company had possibly acted in a fraudulent manner, Schreyer and his ministers took public control of Churchill Forest Industries. Yet throughout the whole fiasco, the government managed to convince most interested observers that the problems had originated with the Conservatives and were able to avoid a great deal of political damage even in the face of a $92-million loss.

While issues such as Churchill Forest caused some problems for his government in the first term, Schreyer appeared to suffer no personal loss of popularity; indeed, he received very favourable press, both in Winnipeg and on the national stage. One article commenting on his performance at the annual Premiers' conference noted that

> With his sideburns, stylish haircut, and soft green suit Mr. Schreyer steered clear of the other Premiers' traditional reluctance to discuss the value of the conference and their apparent reluctance to enjoy the obvious delights of Quebec City … with a wife glamorous enough to be a movie star, he is perhaps better equipped to savor the happening which is Quebec City this time of year.[63]

The 1973 Election

After four years in office, Schreyer felt confident to call an election on June 28, 1973. Having demonstrated political skills while implementing longstanding NDP promises, all the while retaining his personal popularity, it seemed relatively easy for him to campaign on his government's impressive record of achievement. As the campaign started, Schreyer confidently predicted that the NDP had permanently "left third party status behind."[64] He was largely correct. Aside from the 1988 election when it temporarily slid back to third-party status, the NDP has kept its first- and second-party status until the present.

After four years in office, it was relatively easy for the government to feel confident about the upcoming election. It had a successful agenda to campaign on, even though Schreyer admitted that during their first four years his administration had passed so much legislation, that it was in danger of outrunning the government's administrative capacity. He now wanted to consolidate his gains from the first term. And while he did make some new promises in the 1973 campaign, he also noted that the coming election would not involve "promising a whole series of new programs that are going to cost a lot of money, but rather asking for a mandate to carry on with new programs that have been initiated in the past three years."[65] Of these new promises, the most notable was a universal children's dental care program.

Just prior to the 1973 election, Schreyer ended the legislative session the way he began it, this time by eliminating all remaining medicare premiums, and making no apologies for the fact that his government was willing to use general tax revenues to eliminate what he viewed as a highly regressive form of taxation.[66] Schreyer believed that his ability to run an efficient tax regime justified the changes to medicare, and often noted that overall taxes in Manitoba were lower now than they had been when the Conservatives were in power.[67] Defending investments made by the MDC as well as his takeover of Churchill Forest Industries, he argued there was "room for both private and public enterprise in our economy," and that he was simply seeking to avoid "the kind of mongrel enterprise of the late 1960s where the public put up all the money and took the risk, while a few individuals were given ownership of all the profits."[68] "Government," he said, "is an instrument of the people—a useful tool to get things done," but argued it should be viewed as little more than a means to the end of creating a more equitable, more prosperous and freer society.[69] In this respect, Schreyer found himself somewhere in between the traditional liberal's emphasis on "equality of opportunity" and the socialist's emphasis on "equality of outcome."

During his first term, Schreyer had taken a strong interest in northern and Aboriginal development, and had created a Department of Northern Manitoba that would focus more heavily on servicing the north. For the first time in Manitoba, he encouraged regular meetings with an Aboriginal leadership—many of whom were from isolated northern reserves—that was just then emerging.[70] In the election campaign, he vowed to continue these policies, promising mortgage assistance for northern homeowners and a consumer monitoring board to keep retail prices lower in the north. Schreyer's emphasis on economic development was balanced with his environmental concerns about the north, and his approach was vocally supported by conservationists such as Farley Mowat.[71] Outside of Winnipeg, he was helped by the fact that both Liberal Leader Izzy Asper and Conservative leader Sidney Spivak were urban lawyers without a strong connection to, or understanding of, the issues facing rural Manitobans.

Schreyer's confidence in his record was vindicated, at least to a degree, in the 1973 election results (see Table 1). With a clear majority of 31 NDP seats, compared to 21 Conservative seats and 5 Liberal seats, his government now had an unambiguous majority.[72] Nonetheless, it was far less than the NDP's predicted sweep of 42 seats, the kind of overwhelming endorsement Schreyer hoped for. While three seats were gained, two of Schreyer's cabinet ministers—one of whom was Larry Desjardins—went down to defeat.

Second-Term Doldrums and Election Defeat

During the election campaign, Schreyer promised to continue his reform agenda but was vague about his vision and direction for the future. In part, he was simply pulling in his horns as he was wary of mounting criticism of his government's public investments. To consolidate his policy and program gains, he felt he needed to make substantive overtures to the business establishment, and to prove to them that there were no large interventionist plans on the drawing board. At the same time, Schreyer very much trusted that a Keynesian economic policy of careful pump-priming by the provincial government would increase private investment as well as employment. Unfortunately for his administration, the OPEC oil crisis and the appearance of stagflation—high unemployment combined with high inflation—were beginning to unravel the assumptions upon which this Keynesian orthodoxy was based.[73] In summing up this period, one observer gloomily noted that by "the time the 1977 election was called it appeared that the Keynesian party was over," and along with it "the excitement of reform and the uniqueness of Manitoba's own 'quiet revolution'."[74]

By the mid-1970s, inflation and high interest rates were causing economic havoc throughout Canada. When Prime Minister Trudeau introduced wage-and-price controls to deal with the problem, organized labour and the federal NDP fought the federal government on the logic that it would be much easier to control wages than prices, and that workers rather than business would ultimately pay the price of the new policy. Most Premiers also disagreed with the new policy.[75] Ed Schreyer was the one notable exception. In the face of significant opposition within his own NDP ranks, he argued controls on both wages and prices were "the only way to deal with the energy and commodity shortages looming in the future," and made "no apology for sounding like Pierre Trudeau," despite the growing unpopularity of the Prime Minister in Western Canada.[76]

Though accused of betraying organized labour and the NDP for his support of wage-and-price controls, Schreyer continued to push forward social policies and programs with the objective of making Manitoba a more equitable society. The public drug benefit plan was extended to all provincial residents and more funding was allocated to home care and emergency ambulance services. French-language services were increased and the first French-language teachers' training program was established. Income support and bankruptcy protection targeted small and medium-sized farmers and was intended to keep agricultural producers on the land, thereby slowing down the rate of rural depopulation. Probably the most significant new policy initiative was the package of family law reforms introduced by Schreyer's Justice minister, Howard Pawley, in 1977. The Marital Property Act was the first in Canada to provide for an equal division of all married persons' property in the event of divorce.[77]

The 1977 Election Defeat

Despite this record, the agenda nonetheless paled in comparison with the big ticket items of the first term, particularly Autopac. Thus, it was hardly surprising that by the time of the 1977 election, Schreyer was simultaneously being criticized by the left for his caution and the right for his uncompromising statism. His Conservative opponent, Sterling Lyon, pleaded with Manitobans to "throw out the socialists who follow alien doctrine laid down in Europe in the 19th century."[78] In contrast, Lyon offered the electorate a major retrenchment of government, promising to cut taxes and reduce public investment in the economy. In reality, however, the Conservatives' policy platform was less radical than Lyon's rhetoric, and the tenuous coalition of voters that Schreyer had managed to cobble together in 1969 began to break apart, particularly in Winnipeg and southwest Manitoba.[79]

Drawing upon past successes, NDP candidates emphasized Schreyer's leadership more than their policy platform. The main campaign slogan became: "Leadership you can trust." Admittedly, there were times on the campaign trail when Schreyer "was greeted almost as a figure of royalty," but he could not generate the excitement associated with 1969 nor the quiet confidence of 1973.[80] More disturbing, Schreyer was held personally responsible for highly unpopular wage-and-price controls. He was also held accountable for the government's alleged lack of business acumen. The MDC had moved from a financing agent to an outright owner of many failing companies and the government began to wear some of these failures, such as the Saunders Aircraft company, which racked up debts of some $32 million before it was closed down by the government. The government public housing agency was caught up in a land speculation deal that was driving up the price of land in Winnipeg, eventually forcing a shakeup of management. There were also charges of nepotism among senior managers in the tourism department.

The end result was a crushing defeat in the 1977 election. The NDP received the same popular 39% of the vote as it had in 1969, but ended up with only 23 seats, while the collapse of the Liberal vote resulted in a 39-seat majority for Sterling Lyon's Progressive Conservative Party and a greater percentage of the popular vote (49%) than the NDP had ever received. As with any two-term government, the Schreyer administration had accumulated considerable baggage. In addition, the strategy of relying so exclusively on Schreyer's leadership in the campaign may have been flawed for a couple of reasons. The approach fed the widely held perception that, while Schreyer was strong, the ministers making up his cabinet were weak. Indeed, Schreyer had probably tried to run too much in his government, thereby spreading himself too thin.[81] In addition, after eight years of office, Schreyer was tiring of the responsibilities of Premier. From 1973 on, the business of governing had become increasingly difficult owing to stagflation and the growing unhappiness of the electorate, particularly those who had been hurt the most because of rising inflation, unemployment and the application of wage-and-price controls—a demographic that had always been a dependable base of support for the NDP.[82]

Life after Premiership

Following this defeat, Schreyer became the leader of the official opposition, a position he stuck with for one year. During this time, he found little to enjoy in the job, and much to dislike, particularly when he found he could do little to stop Sterling Lyon from undoing or even reversing some of his earlier reforms and programs. Few could see much of a future for the NDP in Manitoba without Schreyer as leader. For this reason alone, his resignation in December 1978 seemed sudden and unexpected, shocking some of his closest colleagues.[83]

To the surprise of many Manitobans, Schreyer had agreed to become Canada's new Governor General when asked by Prime Minister Trudeau. Schreyer grabbed the opportunity. When asked why he took the job he simply responded, "How could I not accept it?"[84] Over the next five years, he would carry out his responsibilities with aplomb, heavily assisted by his wife Lily, whose outgoing personality was perfectly suited to the new role.

In 1984, Ed Schreyer stepped down as Governor General and was then appointed Canadian High Commissioner to Australia, Papua New Guinea, Soloman Islands and Ambassador to Vanuatu. After his term as High Commissioner ended, Schreyer returned to Winnipeg to become a visiting professor at the University of Winnipeg. Always interested in questions of energy and the environment after his experience with the Nelson River project, his post was in Energy and Resource Geography. In 1991, he became a visiting professor in Canadian natural resources and public administration at the University of Victoria, and from 1992 until 1994, a distinguished fellow at the same university's Institute of Integrated Energy Systems. After this, he took on a series of successive guest lectures and professorships in other Canadian universities as well as four German universities. In 2002, he was appointed chancellor of Brandon University.[85]

At the same time that he was writing and delivering lectures, Schreyer worked on various energy and environmental projects. As early as 1984, he had been appointed Chair of the Canadian Shield Foundation which provided grants for environmental research into the Precambrian Shield, a position he continues to occupy. He was also active as a director in various environmental organizations and energy companies including: Saskatchewan Energy Conservation and Development Authority (1993–96); Alternative Fueled Systems Inc (1994–99); International Institute of Sustainable Development (2000–present); Lake Winnipeg Stewardship Board (2003–present); Celaphon Oil & Gas Corporation (1994–96); and Alturas Oil and Gas Resources Ltd. (1997–2000). His concern about the energy future of the globe remained his major preoccupation.[86]

In 2006, just as he was turning 70, Schreyer was pulled back into politics when he ran for the NDP in his old federal seat of Selkirk-Interlake, which had been in the hands of right-leaning politicians since the election of a Reform Party MP in 1997. He did so because of his concern about the future of the family farm and his hope for a major breakthrough for the NDP in an election in which Liberals and Conservatives appeared deadlocked. Given his previous role as Governor-General, he knew that he would be censured—even ridiculed—for letting his name stand. Indeed, some columnists felt that Schreyer had stepped beyond the bounds of "good taste and common sense," while the Monarchist League of Canada declared that he had put the impartiality of Canada's highest office at risk.[87] He lost, unable to stop a major Conservative victory in the province and a minority government in the country.[88] The failed bid said much about the extent to which Schreyer's idealism and desire for a more equitable society ranked ahead of his desire for the respect and stature which attaches to elder statesmen who eschew all forms of direct political involvement.

Conclusion: The Schreyer Legacy

Ed Schreyer's legacy as Premier is twofold. One is the leadership style that he imprinted on the Manitoba NDP, facilitating its rise as one of two government parties in the province. The second is his policy legacy, much of which remains in place despite the changes of administration and government parties which followed. The two were connected by Schreyer's considerable charisma and his ability to relate to Manitobans from all regions of the province as well as all ethnicities, religions, and walks of life.

In terms of the leadership styles described by James McGregor Burns, Ed Schreyer as Premier of Manitoba occupied a mid-position between the charismatic leader and the transactional leader.[89] He transmitted his vision of a more equitable and cohesive society to Manitobans, and he translated it into a program of reform that was accepted by most by appealing to the common values and interests of all Manitobans. At the same time, he was very effective in recognizing the political reality of the province by bargaining for votes, seeking accommodation among elites while satisfying voters' more immediate needs and desires.

In many respects, Schreyer reflected a classic Manitoba style of non-partisan, pragmatic leadership, but in his case from the centre-left. He took, on occasion, controversial positions which were opposed by many within his own party, but every time he emerged victorious and stronger in the eyes of non-affiliated voters of Manitoba. Whether it was the issue of government funding of separate schools, which he favoured over opposition from within his party, or his support of the federal Liberals' wage-and-price controls, which was bitterly opposed by labour and the supporters of the labour movement in his own party, or his support for the War Measures Act in 1970, opposed by NDP leader Tommy Douglas, Schreyer always prevailed. Such issues showed his uncanny ability to lead in a way that has characterized many of the province's most effective Premiers who were viewed as being non-partisan and pragmatic. Thus, even though he was controversial within his own party, no one would, or could, challenge Schreyer's leadership. He had an ability to implement controversial policies and programs—from public auto insurance to substantive health-care reform—that were part of the legacy of his party, but to do so in a way that ensured the NDP remained a viable option for the moderate middle, many of whom had never considered voting for the NDP before Schreyer's leadership.

In these respects, Ed Schreyer was as popular outside of his party as within it. It was his popularity that made the difference in gaining office in 1969 and keeping office in 1973. While he well understood the cleavages in the province, he knew how to appeal to the ideals and objectives that united Manitobans. He conveyed identical political vision to members of his own party, refusing to reshape the message to suit the audience. Through example, Schreyer passed on at least some of these leadership skills to Howard Pawley and Gary Doer—his NDP successors as Premier.[90]

At the time, many on the left criticized Schreyer and his government for its "extreme incrementalism," and a set of social reform policies and programs which "were almost always within bounds that threatened no one."[91] However, they were wrong to conclude that his "legislative program … was no more extensive than that produced by preceding, more conservative governments."[92] Finally, while socialists within the NDP may have been ideologically uneasy with Schreyer, they were also more than willing to ride on the coattails of his popular appeal in order to gain office.

Schreyer saw himself as a modern social democrat with a philosophy that could trace its origins to both socialism and liberalism, but had gone beyond either to produce a political approach that was more adaptable to contemporary Canadian society and more consistent with the values of a majority of Manitobans. His programs and policies reflected his desire not only to improve equality of opportunity but to alter outcomes through redistributive programs and a stronger provincial economy. As Premier of Manitoba, Edward Schreyer succeeded at both.

Notes

The authors would like to acknowledge Scott MacNeil for his expert research assistance; Robert Wardhaugh and Barry Ferguson for their thoughtful comments; Paul Thomas for his detailed review; and the Honourable Edward Schreyer for consenting to an interview. Any remaining errors or omissions remain the responsibility of the authors. The authors are both professors in the Johnson-Shoyama Graduate School of Public Policy at the University of Regina.

1. Thomas Peterson, "Manitoba: Ethnic and Class Politics," in Martin Robin (ed.), *Canadian Provincial Politics: The Party Systems of the Ten Provinces* (Scarborough: Prentice-Hall Canada, 1978). It should be noted that John Norquay, Premier of Manitoba from 1878 until 1886, was of "mixed blood" (English-Aboriginal) origins: J.M. Bumsted, *Dictionary of Manitoba Biography* (Winnipeg: University of Manitoba Press, 1999), 188.

2. Gerald Friesen: *The Canadian Prairies: A History* (Toronto: University of Toronto Press, 1987), 421.

3. *Winnipeg Free Press*, column "Under The Dome," August 16, 1969. See "Canada 70 Team" editorial group from the *Toronto Telegram* and their booklet entitled *The Prairies: Alienation and Anger* (Toronto: Toronto Telegram, 1970), 56–57.

4. Douglas Marshall, "How Manitoba Turned 100 by Standing on Its Head," *Maclean's* (December 1970): 32.

5. Paul Beaulieu (ed.), *Ed Schreyer: A Social Democrat in Power* (Winnipeg: Queenston House, 1977), introduction by Paul Beaulieu.

6. G.P. Marchildon interview with the Honourable Edward Schreyer (hereafter referred to as Schreyer interview), Winnipeg, August 24, 2006.

7. Nelson Wiseman, *Social Democracy in Manitoba: A History of the CCF–NDP* (Winnipeg: University of Manitoba Press, 1983), 92. Also see Jacob Schulz, *The Rise and Fall of Canadian Farm Organizations* (Winnipeg: privately published, 1955).

8. The MFA was the successor organization to the once powerful United Farmers of Manitoba.

9. Wiseman, *Social Democracy in Manitoba*, 149.

10. Herb Schulz, *A View from the Ledge: An Insider's Look at the Schreyer Years* (Winnipeg: Heartland Associates, 2005).

11. Schreyer interview. Duff Roblin, *Speaking for Myself: Politics and Other Pursuits* (Winnipeg: Great Plains Publications, 1999).

12. Schreyer interview. In Schreyer's view, there was so much momentum behind the New Party that something "had to be done about it" but "in retrospect," he felt that the transformation has done little to improve the Party's electoral prospects since 1961.

13. Wiseman, *Social Democracy in Manitoba*, 98–99.

14. Address by Edward R. Schreyer to National Farmers Union, Winnipeg, December 8, 1971, reproduced in Beaulieu (ed.), *Ed Schreyer*, 15–22.

15. Beaulieu (ed.), *Ed Schreyer*, 18–19.

16. Edward R. Schreyer interview, July 5, 1969, quoted in Beaulieu (ed.), *Ed Schreyer*, 187.

17. Sidney Green, *Rise and Fall of a Political Animal: A Memoir* (Winnipeg: Great Plains Publications, 2003), 50–51.

18. *Winnipeg Free Press*, column "Under The Dome," August 16, 1969.

19. Rand Dyck, *Provincial Politics in Canada: Towards the Turn of the Century* (Scarborough: Prentice-Hall Canada, 1996), 407. Green, *Rise and Fall of a Political Animal*, 65–66.

20. Wiseman, *Social Democracy in Manitoba*, 152.

21. *Winnipeg Free Press*, August 15, 1969; and "Under The Dome" column, August 19, 1969.

22. *Winnipeg Tribune* interview with E.R. Schreyer, July 5, 1969, reproduced in Beaulieu (ed.), *Ed Schreyer*, 192.

23. Schreyer interview.

24. Edward R. Schreyer speech at Macalester College, St. Paul, Minnesota, January 23, 1971, reproduced in Beaulieu (ed.), *Ed Schreyer*, 3–7.

25. James McAllister, *The Government of Edward Schreyer: Democratic Socialism in Manitoba* (Kingston: McGill-Queen's University Press, 1984), 116.

26. "Schreyer talks to East with investment slant," *The Financial Post* (October 23, 1970): 3.

27. *Winnipeg Free Press*, column "Under The Dome," August 16, 1969.

28. Interview, Michael Decter, January 4, 2005.

29. Howard Pawley and C. Lloyd Brown-John, "Transitions: The New Democrats in Manitoba," in Donald Savoie (ed.), *Taking Power: Managing Government Transitions* (Ottawa: Canadian Centre for Management Development, 1993), 163–86.

30. Pawley and Brown-John, "Transitions," 166.

31. On the Schreyer cabinet and cabinet committees, see chapter 7 in Christopher Dunn, *The Institutionalized Cabinet: Governing the Western Provinces* (Montreal and Kingston: McGill-Queen's University Press, 1995).

32. Howard Pawley, "Governing Manitoba: Reflections of a Premier," in Maureen Mancuso et al. (eds.), *Leaders and Leadership in Canada* (Toronto: Oxford University Press, 1994), 127.

33. McAllister, *The Government of Edward Schreyer*, 27.

34. Ken Rasmussen, "The Manitoba Civil Service: A Quiet Tradition in Transition" in Evert Lindquist (ed.), *Government Restructuring and Career Public Services* (Toronto: Institute for Public Administration in Canada, 2000). Whether this "balance" worked in practice or not is open to debate, however. It appears that there was considerable tension between the new civil servants in the policy secretariat and the veteran civil servants in the rest of government, and that the constructive coexistence that existed between Douglas's bright, young planners and line department personnel was never achieved in the Schreyer government. Interview, James Eldridge, December 22, 2004. In *A View from the Ledge*, Herb Schulz contends that the bureaucracy played a largely negative role in the Schreyer government, alleging that some in the civil service actively worked undermining the government's policies.

35. Green, *Rise and Fall of a Political Animal*, 84.

36. Dyck, *Provincial Politics in Canada*, 406.

37. Public Archives of Manitoba (hereafter PAM), EC 0016, Q21740, Department of Health and Social Development: Comprehensive Eight-Year Review, 1969–1977: monthly medical (physician) care premiums for families fell from $9.80 to $1.10 while those for single individuals fell from $4.90 a month to 55¢. Monthly hospital premiums remained in force: $7.20 for families; and $3.60 for individuals (Dyck, *Provincial Politics in Canada*, 408). Green (*Rise and Fall of a Political Animal*, 84) has an unsatisfactory explanation for why Schreyer kept a small premium in place: "Schreyer believed that totally eliminating the premiums would in some way affect the manner in which they would be

collected if they were re-imposed in the future. This did not appear to be a real fear since there was no intention of imposing the premiums again" (Dyck, *Provincial Politics in Canada*, 408).

38. Green, *Rise and Fall of a Political Animal*, 101.

39. Douglas Marshall, "How Manitoba Turned 100 By Standing on Its Head," 36.

40. Schreyer interview.

41. McAllister, *The Government of Edward Schreyer*, 64–67.

42. Green, *Rise and Fall of a Political Animal*, 104–05.

43. Marshall, "How Manitoba Turned 100 By Standing on Its Head," 37.

44. *Winnipeg Free Press*, August 19, 1969.

45. "Schreyer Plans Trip to Japan," *Winnipeg Press Press* (August 1, 1969): 1.

46. Government of Manitoba, *White Paper on Health* (Winnipeg: Government of Manitoba, 1972).

47. *White Paper on Health*, 1–3. PAM, EC 0016, Q27674, 640.1, memorandum, Ted Tulchinsky, Assistant Deputy Minister of Health, to Marc Eliesen, Planning Secretary, December 6, 1972.

48. PAM EC 0016, Q27674, 640.1, memorandum, Dr. Doyle to Schreyer, August 17, 1972.

49. Ibid., brief prepared by Dr. M. Bruser (Obstetrics, Mall Medical Group), December 8, 1972.

50. Ibid., memorandum, Tulchinsky to Eliesen, December 6, 1972.

51. Edward Schreyer's presentation, DVD recording of Premier's Symposium (unedited), University of Manitoba, November 13, 1999 (hereafter referred to as Schreyer presentation).

52. PAM, EC 0016, Q21740, Department of Health and Social Development: Comprehensive Eight-Year Review, 1969–1977.

53. Dyck, *Provincial Politics in Canada*, 408. Schreyer interview.

54. The idea was the brainchild of Meyer Browstone, a political science professor at the University of Toronto who had once been a senior civil servant in the Douglas government in Saskatchewan. See Green, *Rise and Fall of a Political Animal*, 124–27.

55. Lloyd Stinson, *Political Warriors: Recollections of a Social Democrat* (Winnipeg: Queenston House, 1975), 337; for a complete discussion of the history, partisan political strife and impact of the Unicity compromise, see pp. 327–41.

56. Schreyer interview.

57. According to Dyck, *Provincial Politics in Canada*, 406–07, Manitoba Hydro agreed to pay a total of $60,000 for relocation.

58. Green, *Rise and Fall of a Political Animal*, 147–54. As time wore on in the dispute, Schreyer became increasingly bitter over the political opposition to the hydro project—particularly the Manitoba Liberal Party's position on the issue. Schreyer presentation, November 13, 1999.

59. For this complex story, see James B. Waldram, *As Long as the Rivers Run: Hydroelectric Development and Native Communities in Western Canada* (Winnipeg: University of Manitoba Press, 1988); Frank Quinn, "As Long as the Rivers Run: The Impacts of Corporate Water Development on Native Communities in Canada," *Canadian Journal of Native Studies* 9, no. 1 (1991): 137–54; and Fisheries and Oceans Canada, *Toward Assessing the Effects of Lake Winnipeg Regulation and Churchill River Diversion on Resource Harvesting in Native Communities in Northern Manitoba* (Winnipeg: Canadian Technical Report of Fisheries and Aquatic Sciences, Report 1974).

60. *Winnipeg Free Press* (May 30, 1973): 3.

61. Dyck, *Provincial Politics in Canada*, 408.

62. Schreyer interview.

63. "Schreyer Makes Quite A Splash," *Winnipeg Free Press* (August 5, 1969), 5.

64. Ron Campbell, "Election June 28," *Winnipeg Free Press* (May 25, 1973): 2.

65. Egon Frech, "Ask Mandate to Carry on—Schreyer" *Winnipeg Free Press* (June 23, 1973): 5.

66. The effective date for the elimination of all medicare premiums was June 1, 1973. PAM, EC 0016, Q21740, Department of Health and Social Development: Comprehensive Eight-Year Review, 1969–1977.

67. Ibid.

68. Egon Frech, "Ask Mandate to Carry on—Schreyer," 5.

69. "City Transit Plans backed by Schreyer," *Winnipeg Free Press* (May 30, 1973): 4–5.

70. Schreyer interview.

71. "Schreyer Unique: Mowat," *Winnipeg Free Press* (June 25 1973): 8.

72. Peterson, "Manitoba: Ethnic and Class Politics," 407.

73. Alex Netherton, "Paradigm and Shift: A Sketch of Manitoba Politics" in K. Brownsey and M. Howlett (eds.), *The Provincial State in Canada: Politics in the Provinces and Territories* (Toronto: Broadview Press, 2001).

74. Ibid., 220.

75. McAllister, *The Government of Edward Schreyer*, 71.

76. Susan Hoeschen, "It's Been Called Making It," *The Financial Post* (June 3, 1973): 1.

77. Peterson, "Manitoba: Ethnic and Class Politics," 411. Interview with Howard Pawley conducted by Gregory P. Marchildon, Winnipeg, August 24, 2006.

78. Quoted in, Wiseman, *Social Democracy in Manitoba*, 128.

79. Glen MacKenzie, "PCs and Liberals Closer to the Teachers Thinking than the NDP," *Winnipeg Free Press* (October 5, 1977).

80. *Winnipeg Free Press* (October 4, 1977).

81. This is Pawley's assessment at any rate. See Pawley, "Governing Manitoba," 123–24.

82. Schreyer interview.

83. Pawley interview.

84. Judith Timson, "From the Cabbage Patch to Rideau Hall," *Maclean's* (December 18, 1978): 21.

85. These included the University of British Columbia (1995), the University College of Cape Breton (1996), the University of Kiel (1997), the University of Trier (1998), the University of Marburg (1999), and the University of Dresden/Leipzig (1999). Entry for Edward Richard Schreyer in *Canadian Who's Who* (Toronto: University of Toronto Press, 2006), 1173.

86. Schreyer interview.

87. "Comes a Time to Just Let Go," *Calgary Herald* (December 30, 2005): A22; "Monarchists Critical of Schreyer's Election Bid: Say It Risks Impugning Office of Gov. Gen." *Edmonton Journal* (December 28, 2005): A3.

88. Schreyer interview. "NDP Icon Fails to Unseat Conservative Incumbent," *National Post* (January 24, 2006): C6.

89. James McGregor Burns, *Leadership* (New York: Basic Books, 1985).

90. Friesen, *The Canadian Prairies*, 421.

91. As quoted by John Loxley, "Economic Planning Under Social Democracy," in Jim Silver and Jeremy Hull (eds.), *The Political Economy of Manitoba* (Regina: Canadian Plains Research Center, 1990), 324.

92. McAllister, *The Government of Edward Schreyer*, 166.

Sterling R. Lyon

1977–1981

DAVID STEWART AND JARED WESLEY

Sterling Lyon, 1977–1981

Sterling Lyon, the province's 19th Premier, is widely considered one of Manitoba's most polarizing figures of the 20th century. Lyon's Conservative roots ran deep, and as a youth in the Tory heartland of Portage La Prairie, he was exposed to prominent federal Conservatives such as Arthur Meighen, John Bracken, and John Diefenbaker. Lyon is the only Manitoba Premier to be defeated after only one full term in office, a tumultuous period that saw him deal with major challenges such as the national conflict surrounding the patriation of the Constitution, fiscal woes brought on by a global recession, and disputes over Manitoba's status as a bilingual province.

Lyon's vision of smaller government based on traditions of parliamentary democracy was strongly expressed and controversial. His unapologetic dedication to such principles has subsequently inspired a measure of respect. Although he could not secure re-election, Lyon's one-term government should be seen in the context of subsequent Conservative (or conservative Republican) leaders such as Margaret Thatcher, Ronald Reagan, Brian Mulroney, Ralph Klein and Mike Harris. Lyon may well have been a Conservative ahead of his time.

From Dufferin Avenue to Broadway

The Lyon brand of politics that emerged in the late 1970s was a lifetime in the making. From his childhood in Portage la Prairie, to his educational and professional upbringing in Winnipeg, the future Premier's early life and career experiences helped shape his tenacious style and right-wing philosophy.

Lyon's roots were relatively modest. His mother, Ella Mae Cuthbert, separated from his father, David Rufus Lyon, shortly after Sterling's birth on January 30, 1927. Mother and child moved from Windsor, Ontario, back to the Cuthbert homestead in Portage. Forced to take in boarders to make ends meet, life in the Protestant (United Church) Cuthbert home taught the family the value of hard work and self-reliance.[1] These were lessons that stayed with Lyon as he worked his way through Central Public Elementary and Portage Collegiate. Earning the Governor General's Medal and an Isbister Scholarship, his attitude secured his reputation as "a red-headed bantam who scrapped his way through school."[2] These two sides of Lyon's personality—of intellect and intensity—proved permanent fixtures of his character.

Portage la Prairie was a veritable political hotbed during Lyon's childhood. A long-time stronghold for the Conservative Party, the area had become the mainspring of a growing number of prominent politicians. The list would eventually include two of Manitoba's most conservative Premiers, Douglas Campbell and Walter Weir, Lyon's high school classmate and future political colleague and rival. Raised during the era of R.B. Bennett in Ottawa and the laissez-faire Liberal-Progressive coalition in Winnipeg, Lyon's first-hand experience with politics could only reinforce his Conservative roots. And his grandfather, Sterling Rufus

Cuthbert, did not have to travel far to nurture these early-childhood experiences. Lyon's personal hero, Arthur Meighen, had grown up just five houses down from the Cuthbert home; Fawcett Taylor, Conservative Leader of the Official Opposition in the Manitoba legislature, often welcomed the young Lyon and his grandfather as visitors into his home; and Cal Miller, a Conservative member of Parliament and future Chief Justice of Manitoba, was a neighbour and an early mentor.[3] Thus, his Dufferin Avenue upbringing introduced Lyon to the world of Manitoba politics, and to life in the Conservative Party, in particular.

To finance his education, Lyon worked as a summer chainman and rodman for the highways department, and in 1945 he entered university with designs on a degree in commerce. Plans changed, and three years later, at the age of 21, he graduated from United College with a bachelor's degree in political science and history, and considerable time spent with the school's Conservative Party. That same year, Lyon travelled to Ottawa to participate in the federal Conservative leadership convention, where he supported John Diefenbaker in his unsuccessful campaign against George Drew. After one year as a police reporter with the *Winnipeg Free Press*, Lyon saved enough money to return to the University of Manitoba for law school, where he met fellow-classmate, and future NDP cabinet minister, Sidney Green. Shortly after qualifying for his bachelor of laws in 1953, Sterling Lyon married Barbara Jean Mayers, with whom he would raise five children.

Following university, Lyon opted to article with the Attorney-General's office from 1949 to 1953, requiring him to cease partisan activity. The experience, which he shared with future Liberal leader Charles Huband, not only prepared him for his four years as a Crown attorney (1953–57); it also allowed Lyon a crucial early glimpse into the inner workings of Manitoba's justice system, a preview that would serve him well as both Attorney-General and Appeals Court Judge. Indeed, his subsequent partnership in Boles, Christie & Lyon (1957–58) proved only a brief respite from his role with the Crown, as Lyon prepared to enter public life amid drastic changes to the Manitoba political climate.

The Loyal Tory "Hatchet Man"

Despite their popularity in Portage la Prairie, the Manitoba Conservatives occupied the opposition benches throughout much of Sterling Lyon's early life. Although they had governed from 1900 to 1915, the party was turned out of office in the 1920 election, seven years before Lyon's birth. The ensuing government—a fusion of Liberal-Progressives held together by a common allegiance to non-partisanship and a laissez-faire style of government—would hold power for the much of the next three decades.

Decades later, from his own seat in the legislature, the success of this early Liberal-Progressive strategy and philosophy would strike a chord with Lyon, as he called for a nostalgic return to "limited government" in Manitoba.

Amid the decline of the Liberal-Progressive coalition, Sterling Lyon made his political debut in the 1958 general election.[4] Hand-picked by Duff Roblin, the young Portage native won a hotly contested nomination and ran in the Winnipeg riding of Fort Garry-Charleswood, defeating Liberal-Progressive incumbent, and former mayor of Fort Garry,

Raymond Fennell, by 1,323 votes. At 31 years old, Lyon became one of the youngest members of the Manitoba legislature, second only to a 22-year-old CCF member from Brokenhead, Edward Schreyer.

For the next nine years, with Lyon by his side, Duff Roblin led his Conservative government with an interventionist program, emphasizing the progressive elements of the party's platform. The Premier moved beyond balanced budgets, risking an increase in public debt in favour of economic development. He rebuffed the small government claims of the Liberal-Progressives, calling instead for an increase in the scope of the civil service. All the while, Roblin promoted tax hikes as a means of paying for these and other new public expenditures and undertaking a massive program of province-building. In time, Lyon would come to repudiate many of these Keynesian pillars as part of his own leadership and election platforms. For the time being, however, he was a key, loyal member of the Tory cabinet.

Valued by Roblin for his "ability to keep his cool" and his "refusal to sit on the fence,"[5] Lyon served as the Premier's chief lieutenant throughout Roblin's term in office.[6] Whether as Attorney-General (1958–63; 1966–69), minister of Public Utilities (1961–63), minister of Tourism and Recreation (1966–67), minister of Mines and Natural Resources (1963–66), or Government House Leader (1966–69), Lyon was viewed with respect as "the party's hatchet man, sent to knock down persistent critics."[7] The wide variety of roles exposed him to a number of key portfolios, not the least important of which surrounded the mega-projects of Public Utilities and the controversies of Mines and Natural Resources. His second term as Attorney-General would also bring him into close contact and conflict with the young federal Justice minister, Pierre Elliot Trudeau.[8] In short, the political future looked bright for Lyon. As Roblin prepared for a much-anticipated jump to federal politics in 1967, his protégé was well-positioned to contend for the party leadership.

The ensuing 1967 provincial PC leadership race was a classic contest between the party's rural, populist element, and its less conservative urban wing. Walter Weir, a junior minister in Roblin's cabinet, spoke for the party's conservative grassroots, which he claimed had been marginalized during Roblin's term as leader. Lyon was branded as being closer to the political centre, whether due to his close connection to Roblin, his urban constituency and promises of urban development, or simply by default.[9] Alongside two other candidates, the two former Portage Collegiate schoolmates fought a rather low-key campaign, particularly when compared to subsequent Manitoba PC leadership contests. In the end, the party's aim to shore up its rural base and place a brake on state intervention resulted in a Weir victory on the third ballot.[10] While attracting the support of fellow cabinet ministers like Sidney Spivak, Lyon's reputation as a political "hatchet man" also played a role in his defeat, with many party members viewing Weir as the more popular and conciliatory of the two candidates.[11] After returning for two more years in cabinet—as Attorney-General and Government House Leader—the former heir apparent left public life for the first time in a decade. From the sidelines, Lyon watched as the Conservative Party went down to defeat in the 1969 election, victim of the public's disapproval of Weir's retrenchment policies.

His departure from politics was not to be permanent, however, and his loss to Weir would not be without its lessons. As Ed Schreyer became Manitoba's first NDP Premier, and as Prime Minister Pierre Trudeau ushered in the first of many rounds of constitutional negotiations, Lyon was turning down offers from law firms in Toronto and New York, and beginning his five-year term as corporate counsel for Winnipeg-based General Distributors. If his years of articling in the Attorney-General's office prepared him for the first phase in his political career, the move to the private sector proved just as influential to his return. Moreover, the 1967 leadership race taught Lyon much about the Manitoba Conservative Party: its followers, not unlike Manitoba voters in the decades to come, were prone to shifting between periods of progressivism and conservatism. With Weir's retirement in 1971, and his replacement by the more moderate Sidney Spivak as PC leader, the opportunity for a swing back to the political right soon presented itself. In the meantime, Lyon was gaining valuable experience and contacts within the Manitoba corporate community—assets that would prove crucial in his subsequent leadership bid. Business leaders and party insiders later suggested that it was this five-year hiatus that proved the turning point in the public life of Sterling Lyon.[12]

"And the Right Arm Slashed the Left"

The second stage in Lyon's political career opened, interestingly, with the 1974 federal election. In what would be the first of many showdowns with the Liberal Prime Minister, Lyon contested the Winnipeg South seat held by Pierre Trudeau's Minister of Defence, James Richardson. Lyon's loss, by just 1,400 votes, made him one of the few western Canadian Conservatives to lose to a Liberal in the campaign. Yet, his strong showing only served to whet Lyon's appetite for a return to full-time politics, and to renew interest in him among provincial party insiders.

Lyon's return was timely, in this sense; just months earlier, the Conservatives had picked up only a single new seat in the 1973 provincial election, and new leader Sidney Spivak's performance was in question. Behind closed doors, key Conservatives were attacking Spivak for his perceived softness on the NDP's "socialist" program. Suddenly, what had been a weakness in 1967 had become one of Lyon's greatest strengths. Fresh off the federal campaign trail, he and his supporters began preparing for a second bid to lead the Manitoba Conservative Party.

If Lyon were to become leader, Spivak would have to be convinced to step down or be forced out through a leadership review. The former route closed quickly as caucus failed in a traditional attempt to force the leader's resignation. Despite opposition from a growing number of Conservative MLAs, Spivak refused to step down, claiming that he retained the backing of the party's grassroots. This support was challenged and, following an unsuccessful bid to retain power at the party's March 1975 convention, Spivak joined Lyon in one of the longest and most divisive leadership races in the party's history.

The battle dragged on for almost six months, culminating in a vote by convention delegates on December 6. In an effort to maintain party unity, both candidates downplayed the ideological differences between them. Yet the divisions were stark: the party's progressive and youth wings formed ranks behind Spivak, while Lyon drew support from the party's right-wing establishment, caucus, and business elements. For his part, Spivak ran a defensive campaign, a style that did little to combat criticisms of his performance as leader. In addition to allegations of rigging delegate nomination meetings in Lac du Bonnet and the University of Winnipeg, as well as questions about Lyon's anonymously funded $3,600 monthly allowance during the leadership campaign, Spivak's team accused his opponents of launching an anti-Semitic "whisper campaign" against his character. While never substantiated or disconfirmed, these allegations marked the low point of a very ugly, personalized campaign.[13] Journalist Ted Allen captured the mood of the final convention:

> The knives were as surely drawn, the incisions made, sutures tied and swabbing up accomplished amid vinyl oak furnishings, maroon wall-to-wall and upholstered leatherette without unseemly displays of emotion. In fact, the right arm of the Conservative party ritually slashed the left arm, while the left replied in kind. And everyone smiled at the sterility of it all. Smiled and clapped each other's backs and was dreadfully careful not to reveal the rancor, anger and bitterness against which the operation was played out. It was a curious even spurious act of self-abuse.[14]

When the final votes were cast, Lyon emerged with a 57-vote edge (264 to 207), confirming his earlier predictions of a 50-delegate victory. He owed much of this majority to the support of 19 of 23 Conservative caucus members and eight of nine Manitoba Conservative MPs, whose support he gained despite lacking a seat in the legislature. The future Premier's strategy was fitting, in this sense, considering his traditional support for the concept of parliamentary sovereignty and responsible government.[15] Lyon had turned his 1967 liabilities—his aggressiveness and urban connections—into assets. In the process, regardless of the source of the intra-party rifts, he had convinced the majority of delegates that he was the candidate with the greatest ability to unite the Conservative Party and lead the Tories back to power in the next provincial election.

Restraining the "Socialist Supermen"

Within months, the new Tory leader re-entered the legislature, winning the rural riding of Souris-Killarney in a by-election on November 2, 1976. His easy victory, polling more than four times as many votes as his nearest challenger, would be a far cry from the challenges ahead. The Lyon brand of politics—"solitary, combative, and self-assured, derived from a lifetime of self-reliance"—was ready for its first foray into the province-wide market.[16]

Lyon's selection as leader marked a true turning point in Manitoba party politics, setting the stage for the emergence of neo-conservatism and social democracy as "the key themes of party competition and political debate."[17] Having travelled to British Columbia in 1976 to study campaign strategy under Social Credit Premiers W.A.C. and Bill Bennett, Lyon returned to Manitoba with plans to polarize the party system against the NDP.[18] Indeed, in an era that saw many political commentators decrying the lack of choice facing voters at the ballot box,[19] the Tories' sudden shift to the right set up one of the clearest choices ever offered to the Manitoba electorate. Media polls in the summer and fall of 1977 found the proportion of undecided voters as high as 40%; the number of independent candidates dropped precipitously, from 18 in 1973 to only one in 1977; and there was a sense that the ongoing polarization could push the centrist Liberal Party off the political landscape entirely.

The 1977 election was preceded by one of the longest election campaigns in Manitoba history. The official contest took place between September 6 and October 11, but all three major parties had been prepared months ahead of time, expecting the writs to be dropped in June. Lyon commissioned his own polls earlier in the year, and they projected a healthy Conservative majority, with as many as 35 of 57 seats. These numbers dwindled over the summer, as the harvest-time election drew near. The 1977 campaign was building toward what political scientist Alex Netherton calls a "paradigm shift" in the province's politics, and was a "critical election" by any definition of the term.[20]

For his part, Lyon's early approach had been to keep policy statements to a minimum and allow the New Democrats to defeat themselves.[21] At the same time, Lyon's rhetoric grew increasingly confrontational. The Tory leader pledged to "free" Manitoba from the "shackles" of social democracy and restore "normalcy" to the province's economy.[22] His speeches began referring to the NDP as "the handmaidens of communism"[23] and "socialist supermen,"[24] drawing parallels between New Democratic policies and those of Karl Marx and the Soviet politburo. Addressing the challenges facing Manitoba Hydro, for instance, Lyon suggested that, if Premier Schreyer were invited to be an energy consultant, "pray God, he will go to the Government of Russia."[25] On another occasion, Lyon once told a columnist: "My strongest political belief is anti-communism, anti-Marxism, because I think it is the anti-Christ in every sense of the anti-Christ... The only difference between a communist and a socialist [is that] they are both bears, but one has its claws retracted."[26] His anti-socialist zeal would only escalate over the next four years, culminating in the highly charged atmosphere of the 1977 and 1981 elections.

With these principles in mind, the Tory leader spent much of the campaign pinning the failings of Keynesian economics, including the province's recession, on the poor management of Schreyer and the New Democrats.[27] In an ironic reversal, Lyon had become the harshest critic of the political program he helped build through Roblin's reforms in the 1960s. Progressive tendencies were once again sidelined in the party, as Lyon helped polarize Manitoban politics and escape the policy convergence that had characterized much of the early Schreyer-Spivak period.

Lyon's promises were kept purposefully vague, and he offered few specifics when it came to the main pillars of the PC platform. Ambiguity should not be confused with ambivalence, however; the Tory leader had major changes in mind for Manitoba, under the campaign slogan, "Make it Happen." Lyon officially labelled his plans "a program of acute and protracted restraint," urging Manitobans "not to expect much" from a Conservative government in terms of new spending promises. The provincial government could not continue growing at the pace of the 1960s, Lyon argued, noting that the Manitoba economy was already showing critical signs of strain. In place of new programs and commitments, the platform suggested "that the mood of the people and the facts of the situation call for a more sober and thoughtful approach... No one is going to be fooled by promises of heaven on earth."[28]

This new approach promised a review of virtually all of the programs and Crown corporations introduced by the Schreyer government. Lyon repeatedly criticized the New Democrats for subsidizing failing businesses—like Flyer Buses, Saunders Aircraft, and Morden Fine Foods—through the Manitoba Development Corporation, and questioned Schreyer's decision to invest $300 million in new hydro development projects. The latter decision prompted Lyon to promise an official inquiry into the management practices at Manitoba Hydro, authorizing a commission to issue subpoenas to civil servants and New Democratic MLAs accused of political interference. The Tory leader also promised to pull Manitoba out of the mining business, and transfer state ownership of all 200,000 acres of land purchased through the Agricultural Credit Corporation to private hands. In the process, Lyon proposed a "drastic" reduction in the size of Manitoba's 14,000-member civil service, although no exact figures were discussed during the campaign. Special assurances were made guaranteeing the continuation of "vital" public services, like Medicare, Pharmacare and Autopac, but the Tories' overall message was clear: "We can establish services only as quickly as our economy is able to pay for them or as quickly as government is able to redirect resources from other programs. Government must live within its means."[29]

Those "means" were to be limited by the second major pillar of the PC platform: comprehensive tax relief. Included in this plan were tax cuts on personal and corporate income, and the abolition of "nuisance taxes," like succession duties, gift taxes and mineral acreage taxes. Again, Lyon remained silent on precise details, a tactic that drew Liberal leader Charles Huband away from his strengths in social policy and into a Tory-framed debate over taxes. Further Tory campaign promises included the party's intention to seek alternative energy sources; to address unemployment in the North; to develop a new Charter for the City of Winnipeg, emphasizing local decision-making; to develop incentive programs encouraging young people to stay in the province; to improve access to home ownership among the young and the elderly; to pursue the provision of alternative health care facilities, including home care; and to invest in university research. These pledges aside, three themes stood out as the core of Lyon's plans for "acute, protracted restraint": privatization, the reduction of the scope of the civil service, and tax relief. The triad would become a familiar rallying cry for neo-conservatives beyond Manitoba, with the Thatcher, Reagan, and Mulroney governments all adopting similar principles in the not-too-distant future.

The Conservative campaign showed considerable discipline throughout much of the 1977 contest, demonstrating the precision that had guided Lyon to the leadership two years earlier. Aside from well-scripted campaign stops in the heart of "Lyon Country," the new Tory leader kept a low profile compared to Huband and Schreyer. He did very little mainstreeting or townhalling in comparison to his opponents. He committed himself to being as "accessible as possible ... within reason" when it came to the press, conducting one-on-one media interviews amid private meetings with campaign organizers.[30] The backroom approach endeared Lyon to journalists and editors at the province's largest newspaper, the *Winnipeg Free Press*, who offered ringing endorsements of the Conservative campaign.

Lyon and his advisors reinforced their reputation for preparation and resolve as well. When he did make public appearances, the Tory leader consistently spoke before larger crowds than his opponents, with independent accounts estimating some audiences of over 1,500 people.[31] Tory organizers had smoothed over Lyon's image through newspaper advertisements emphasizing his role as a devoted father (pheasant hunting with his son during the campaign), son (campaigning with his mother), and husband (posing for promotional photos with his wife). Nonetheless, Lyon's presence on the campaign trail marked a noticeable departure from the more moderate approach of his predecessor, Sid Spivak.

In the end, the NDP and PC strategies proved to be polar opposites. The New Democratic campaign was billed as a one-man show, with Schreyer running on his record and reputation, and promising to weather the recession through continued social spending. His cabinet ministers remained remarkably silent during the campaign. The Attorney-General, and future Premier, Howard Pawley, refused to get involved in the key aspects of the campaign, earning the chastisement of Schreyer himself. The Mines minister, and Lyon's former law school classmate, Sidney Green, was quick to admit his role in the campaign's failure to resonate with voters,[32] while the minister of Public Works, Russell Doern, was critical of the Premier's decision to downplay the role of his cabinet during the campaign.[33] Lyon, conversely, emphasized the strengths of his Conservative "team," frequently using prominent members of caucus as spokespeople and "hatchet men" for the party. The Tory leader fought hard to persuade voters of the economic crisis at hand, and promoted himself as the only leader with real plans to change the status quo. He put the sitting Premier on the defensive, engaging him on the Conservative's agenda—the economy—before attacking Schreyer on his own campaign theme of "Leadership You Can Trust." It was a bold strategy, but one that was to be expected from a man who would "rather be right than be Premier."[34] In this sense, the 1977 campaign merely broadened Lyon's reputation as "a spellbinding speaker, cocky and abrasive," and a man who "relished the role of a fighter."[35]

By the third week of the campaign, Lyon was boasting of an imminent Conservative majority, and began openly musing about a possible list of cabinet ministers. Just as in 1975, this early confidence proved warranted. There are competing explanations of the results of the 1977 Manitoba election.[36] Some claim that Lyon's conservative rhetoric proved appealing to the electorate, while others suggest the outcome was less about ideology and more about simply removing the incumbent NDP government. Whatever the reason, voters placed unprecedented faith in Lyon's Conservatives. The Tories not only increased their presence in the legislature—up 10 seats, to 33, but also boosted the party's share of the popular vote by over 14 percentage points. Indeed, with the support of more than 49%

of voters—and a turnout of 77%—Lyon's Conservatives recorded the highest popular vote total of any single party in the history of Manitoba. The New Democrats were relegated to the Opposition benches for the first time in eight years, on the strength of just 23 seats and 39% of the popular vote. Most strikingly, three cabinet ministers were among the eight NDP incumbents to lose their seats to Tories.[37] The Liberal Party fared even worse, retaining only the single seat held by future federal cabinet minister Lloyd Axworthy. Even leader Charles Huband lost his bid to enter the legislature. Perhaps most satisfying to Lyon, one of the two Liberal seats lost to the Tories was in his hometown of Portage la Prairie.[38]

Former Prime Minister John Diefenbaker and future Prime Minister Joe Clark were among the first to call and congratulate the new Premier on his victory. Later, at a carefully orchestrated post-election event, former leader Sidney Spivak introduced Lyon to a crowd of cheering supporters, former Premier Duff Roblin among them. True to his backroom style, after one of the briefest victory addresses in the province's history, Lyon retired to his private quarters to celebrate with his family and close advisors. Within hours, Lyon would convene his first caucus meeting, and his programme of "acute, protracted restraint" would begin post-haste.

The Lyon Era

Sterling Lyon's term as Premier can perhaps best be described as "conservative." His bold fiscal policy earned him the reputation as the first of Canada's "neo-conservative" Premiers. More traditionally conservative was his opposition to the federal government's attempts to patriate the Constitution and entrench a Charter of Rights, based on his insistence on parliamentary supremacy. Journalists Sheppard and Valpy in their account of the 1981 Constitutional deal refer to Lyon as "the stubby, irascible Praetorian guardian of a vanishing British Canada."[39] Finally, his organization of government bespoke a preference for an older administrative model. As political scientist Chris Dunn puts it, "Lyon was obviously nostalgic for the days of the unaided cabinet."[40]

The massive victory in the 1977 election brought Lyon into office with a comfortable majority and, some argue, a mandate. The Premier wasted little time putting his stamp on the government and quickly dismissed a number of those who served as deputy ministers under Ed Schreyer.[41] He reduced the size of cabinet, appointing 14 ministers, a decline of two from the Schreyer era. The cabinet was closely balanced between Winnipeg and rural Manitoba with seven ministers from Winnipeg, one from northern Manitoba, and the rest from the mainly rural southern parts of the province.

The extent to which the 1977 election provided Lyon with an electoral endorsement for his attempts to reduce the size and scope of government is controversial. There is no question that the Conservatives in the election campaign "mounted a steady attack on the administration playing on alleged 'mismangement' and 'arrogance'."[42] As discussed, the party's critique of the government focused on high taxes, an out-of-control deficit and a bloated bureaucracy. In some ways the 1977 Manitoba campaign could be seen as a precursor of the 1984 federal campaign in which the Mulroney Tories spoke of handing civil servants "pink slips and running shoes." Nonetheless, the degree to which their campaign sought support for a more conservative path is somewhat contestable considering its concerted lack of detail. Moreover, as Lyon himself noted, "as a general rule, people vote governments out," rather than endorsing their successors.[43] However, as Netherton explains, Lyon "completely distanced the party from Roblin. Lyon promised to rid Manitoba of the 'Socialist' (read Keynesian) influence and to implement his own form of neo-conservatism. His 1977 victory gave him the mandate to do so."[44]

Unaided Cabinet?

The movement away from the party's progressive roots was to a certain extent a personal shift since Lyon served effectively as a cabinet minister throughout the entire Roblin era. Roblin's government had started Manitoba's administration on the road to institutionalization, a process generally associated with creating strong central agencies and reducing the autonomy of individual ministers. Lyon's approach to this kind of organization, which had continued apace under Premier Schreyer, indicated some dissatisfaction with this trend. One wonders whether those, like Lyon, who served many years in cabinet before becoming first minister, have a preference for organizational structures that provide more authority to individual cabinet ministers. Certainly, as Dunn's research demonstrates, Lyon had a "fondness for traditional unaided decision making modes."[45]

In keeping with this preference, Lyon "abolished most of the Schreyer-era cabinet committees, as well as the central agencies for planning and management. He made do with the minimum number possible, two standing committees."[46] As well, the Executive Council was downsized and its role reduced. To get advice on administrative restructuring, Lyon appointed a Task Force on Government Reorganization and Economy, co-chaired by Sidney Spivak, his predecessor as Conservative leader, and George Riley from Great West Life. Lyon saw this as a committee representing all sectors of the economy, while Dunn described it as "a committee of private sector oriented individuals who were preoccupied with a management perspective."[47] The report of the Task Force in 1978 critiqued the spending and management of the Schreyer government and offered support for the less institutionalized administrative structure favoured by Lyon. The most important cabinet structure under Lyon was the Treasury Board committee, which included a handful of line ministers and was initially chaired by Lyon himself.

Lyon's personal style, described variously as "pugnacious," "aggressive," "cocky" and "arrogant," might raise questions about the degree to which his approach to an unaided cabinet actually translated into autonomous ministers. However, insiders suggest that Lyon was willing to listen and devolve real authority to his ministers. Don Craik, his Finance minister for the bulk of the term, indicates that cabinet ministers "were to take full responsibility, not only for policy, but also for all administration."[48] Political scientist Graham White's interviews with various insiders similarly reveal a Premier open to discussion and persuasion. As White reports,

> One of Lyon's ministers noted that he "had a very high regard for cabinet
> as an institution" and consequently didn't impose his will on cabinet;
> because he didn't want ministers to proceed with policy without having

cleared it through cabinet, he applied this principle to himself. Other ministers described Lyon's acceptance of cabinet decisions in very similar terms.[49]

During the latter part of Lyon's term, there were some changes and the size of cabinet grew from 15 to 18, a number slightly higher than the last NDP administration. Lyon carefully maintained the balance between city and country, with those from the Conservatives' rural base outnumbering the Winnipeg ministers. The government also moved to a more developed cabinet committee system, adding a committee on Community Service and Economic Development and a sub-committee on Federal-Provincial Financial Arrangements. As Dunn argues, Lyon's "government accommodated a few tardily installed cabinet committees as well as the tentative introduction of planning considerations into the budget process."[50]

These changes were implemented in part to help manage a growing emphasis on mega-projects and in part because the Treasury Board, the only real standing cabinet committee for the first two years, had a very heavy agenda leading to policy delays. Finance minister Craik was a strong advocate of a more structured committee process.

Throughout the Lyon administration the Department of Finance exercised a good deal of authority and took on some of the functions performed under the Schreyer administration by the Planning and Management Committee. In summary, the Lyon government was marked by a strong and dominant Department of Finance, relative autonomy for cabinet ministers and departments, and a somewhat underdeveloped cabinet committee structure.

Fiscal Conservatism

The policy priorities of the Lyon government were clear. Before deficits and debts were perceived as problematic by most politicians, Lyon identified them as an issue requiring attention. As former NDP MLA Cy Gonick explains, Lyon "claimed spending was out of control and promised a policy of 'acute, protracted restraint.' It was a policy rooted in the belief that government has a limited place in business... and should have a different, sometimes smaller role in other activities as well."[51] The new Premier's background as corporate counsel may well have been influential in this regard, and his government hit the ground running on this agenda.[52] Lyon summoned the legislature for a quick fall session in which the government froze spending, repealed succession and gift taxes and delayed changes in family law.[53]

Netherton indicates that the government's "stated objectives were to balance the budget and to attain 'economy and efficiency' in the administration of government. It was to be five years of acute protracted restraint of public sector activities intended to curb the excesses of welfare state dependence and to put the private sector back in full control of provincial economic development."[54] Lyon essentially confirms this emphasis, indicating that he saw two priorities for his government—one economic, focusing on expenditure control, and the other on modernizing social programs. In his words, his government wanted to "combat dependency."[55] In a short time, these priorities would be widely interpreted as neo-conservative.

In an introduction to a speech at the Empire Club in Toronto in 1978, Lyon was described as a

> vocal politician who says what he thinks. He has said "the public sector is on trial." He has said that the federal government is "spending like drunken sailors." He criticizes socialists for their "ideological silliness." He is pitiless in his attempts to reduce what he terms "the maw; the animal"—in short the government bureaucracy... He not only utters words, he backs them up with action.[56]

In its 1979 Throne Speech, the government indicated its underlying ideology by noting that economic growth was needed for funding and expanding social programs. In pursuit of this agenda, the Progressive Conservative government lowered personal and corporate tax rates and royalties on mining companies. The growth of spending was reduced in the areas of social and health services, day care fees were raised, and tuition fees were allowed to rise. In addition, the government laid off 1,300 civil servants, and ended the rent control instituted by the New Democrats. Other government initiatives included an abolition of the Milk Marketing Board and a freeze on hydroelectric rates.

These changes were controversial. Gonick explains that the "Lyon government found itself embroiled in a series of confrontations with groups affected by spending cuts. Strike activity reached a new postwar high... the poor mobilized against real cuts in welfare benefits... Single mothers, day-care workers, hospital workers, civil servants, university students and faculty demonstrated against the declining level of day care, health and education services."[57] British Columbia Social Credit Premier Bill Bennett would face comparable public criticism as he tried to implement a similar neo-conservative program in 1983. Like Bennett, Lyon himself concedes that the government's program was not well explained.[58]

The Canadian economic situation was not conducive to helping the Lyon government meet its goals. High inflation and interest rates presented the government with difficult challenges, and compound interest made it virtually impossible for the Conservatives to balance their budget. As well, in the latter period of the administration the controls on public spending were somewhat loosened. Indeed, in 1981 provincial expenditures grew by almost 16%.[59] Finally, as the government approached the end of its term, its program focused not on restraint, but on mega-projects. These projects included public involvement in building an aluminum smelter and in potash development. As well, the government was eager to develop a western power grid that would allow it to sell electricity to its prairie neighbours. These projects were the government's priorities in its final year and formed the key element in its re-election campaign.[60]

The Lyon government did not launch a full-scale attack on NDP accomplishments. For instance, despite the recommendation of the aforementioned task force, the government supported the public automobile insurance system. Indeed, Lyon described the program as "a very good initiative in the public interest."[61] Other Conservative accomplishments included the provision of funding to separate schools and public funding of parties and elections. These initiatives indicate that the government cannot be fully viewed through a neo-conservative lens. As Wiseman summarizes

> the Lyon government failed miserably at living up to the standards set by its own rhetoric… it generated the largest deficit recorded in provincial history. And although it alienated the civil service and dismissed some bureaucrats… the size of the civil service did not shrink, but actually grew. Furthermore, the promise of economic prosperity based on less government involvement in the economy did not bear fruit.[62]

In his autobiography, Duff Roblin also questions the apparent disconnect between Lyon's rhetoric and performance. "In my day," Roblin argues, "Sterling was an active supporter of the progressive measures that we proposed from time to time… It's perfectly true that sometimes Sterling talked the right-wing talk, but he didn't always walk the walk, even as Premier. I think he should be credited with being far more open-minded than some would be later inclined to suggest."[63] Regardless of the extent to which his bite equalled his bark, however, the strength of Lyon's conservative rhetoric and the boldness of his program of restraint define his political career as staunchly conservative.

In the end, not unlike Premiers Douglas Campbell and Walter Weir before him, Lyon's brand of conservatism failed to strike a chord among voters. The Tories' campaign slogan, "Don't Stop Us Now," proved poignant, as the party managed to hold just 23 seats, and was confined to its traditional strongholds in south Winnipeg and southern rural areas. Several factors contributed to the Tories' loss of power in 1981. Lyon's absence from the campaign trail during the patriation negotiations was certainly detrimental to the Tory cause at home. So, too, was his inability to focus undivided attention on the Manitoba economy amid constitutional talks. Legislative reapportionment in 1981, which resulted in more Winnipeg seats than rural seats for the first time in the history of the Manitoba legislature, also played a role in the Conservatives' defeat. The redistribution cut into the Tories' main support base, and gave a boost to the more urban-centred New Democrats and Liberals. More than any other factor, however, Lyon attributes his party's loss to its failure to adequately explain the program of restraint. The long-term, principled nature of its goals was not conducive to short-term electoral gains, according to Lyon, and he freely admits that he had focused too heavily on fulfilling promises, as opposed to gaining re-election. For this, as usual, he makes no apologies and accepts full responsibility: "You cannot… be all things to all people and still be a person of principle. If that means you cannot win a succession of elections… that does not bother me."[64] Wiseman indicates the depth of public opposition to the Lyon government, noting that "In 1969 the NDP could not have won with anyone but Ed Schreyer. In 1981 it could have won with anyone. Everyone, including Howard Pawley, knew this."[65]

Charter Sceptic

Economic climate aside, the Lyon government served during a turbulent period in Canadian political history. The Parti Québécois won its first election in 1976 and held a referendum on sovereignty-association in 1980. The PQ lost that referendum, in part because the federal government committed to reform the Canadian Constitution. In pursuit of this goal the Trudeau Liberals placed a major emphasis on constitutional reform and convened numerous federal-provincial meetings on the subject. Indeed, more First Ministers Conferences were held in that period that at any previous time in Canadian history.

By happenstance, based on Manitoba's position in the 10-year rotation, Lyon was chair of the Council of Premiers from the summer of 1980 until the summer of 1981. The position gave him a platform from which to espouse his views about Canadian democracy.

With attempts to secure provincial agreement on patriation unsuccessful, the federal Liberals decided to proceed with a unilateral package that included a Charter of Rights. Lyon was an implacable opponent of Trudeau's proposal, and Sheppard and Valpy in their analysis of the constitutional negotiations describe him as "the Premier most ideologically opposed to an entrenched charter of rights."[66] Lyon referred to the Charter as "an alien and unnecessary United States-style innovation that is incompatible with our traditions of parliamentary sovereignty,"[67] in which the rights of individual citizens are protected through responsible government and legislative supremacy. Richard Sigurdson notes Lyon's opposition to this change and explains, "Premier Lyon expressed concerns that the Charter would undermine the role of the monarchy in Canada and that it would dictate the behaviour of provincial governments in relation to their religious, ethnic and ideological minorities."[68] It was this stance that "left him labelled as a dogmatic right-winger opposed to rights for minority language groups, women, aboriginals and just about anyone else who felt disaffected."[69]

Lyon, and seven other dissenting Premiers known as the Gang of Eight, attempted to prevent unilateral federal action. The Gang of Eight placed reference cases before the provincial courts of appeal in Manitoba, Newfoundland and Quebec. The Premiers, minus Bill Davis of Ontario and Richard Hatfield of New Brunswick, questioned the legality of amending the Constitution without provincial approval. In addition, the Gang of Eight put together its own constitutional package, with an amending formula preserving provincial sovereignty by providing financial compensation for provinces that opted out of amendments reducing their powers. Consistent with Lyon's convictions, this package did not contain a Charter of Rights.

Lyon has considered the failure to secure federal agreement to this package as his greatest regret as Premier. He notes that Quebec was a willing participant in this deal and wonders whether this might have made Meech Lake and the Charlottetown rounds of constitutional negotiation redundant by pre-empting the perception that Quebec was betrayed by the rest of Canada.[70]

The constitutionality of the federal government's unilateral package was eventually assessed by the Supreme Court of Canada, which concluded that patriation required the approval of a "significant number of provinces." This decision brought all first ministers to a final conference in Ottawa in 1981. Fortuitously, the final constitutional discussions coincided with the 1981 Manitoba election, a contest that Lyon knew would be difficult. As a result, he was forced to curtail his participation in the conference and return to campaign in Manitoba. Alberta Premier Peter Lougheed reported to Lyon that a package had been negotiated that was not quite what the Gang of Eight wanted, but was the best they could do. Lyon regretted that Quebec did not go along with the package but realized that his continued opposition would put him alone on the side of Quebec separatists in the midst of a provincial election. More importantly, given the Supreme Court's decision on the *Patriation* reference, Manitoba's lone opposition would not be sufficient to derail the package.[71] Lyon acquiesced to the deal under these terms, calling it "a victory for the country."[72]

Lyon's views about the Charter had not changed, but in the end a compromise was reached that essentially combined (with important modifications such as a Notwithstanding Clause and the loss of fiscal compensation) the federal Charter and the Gang of Eight's amending formula. Sheppard and Valpy note that Lyon had battled Trudeau over a Charter since the 1960s, when both served as Attorneys General, and that he "was a fierce duelist with Trudeau, giving no quarter and asking none; he might have played a stronger role at the finish but an election campaign took him to other fields of conflict."[73] In a gesture extended to all Premiers of the time, Lyon was appointed to the Privy Council of Canada in 1982, but his regrets over the process remain. He laments the immense time spent in constitutional discussions, not simply because it complicated his re-election, but because he felt it diverted attention from important issues such as interest rates, inflation and the economy more generally.[74]

Lyon's opposition to the Charter did not disappear. Years later, in a dissenting opinion as part of a judgement releasing a prisoner who had confessed his guilt, Lyon wrote:

> It has been said that the purpose of criminal justice should be the conviction of the guilty and the acquittal of the innocent. How this purpose can be served by allowing this guilty man to go free is the vexed problem which bedevils the courts as we begin to interpret and apply the provisions of the Charter to our traditional system of criminal justice.[75]

Lyon's concerns about the impact of the Charter on legislatures can in some ways be seen as prophetic. Reflecting on the shift in the nature of politics wrought by the Charter, Morton and Knopff lament that these changes are "deeply and fundamentally undemocratic, not just in the simple and obvious sense of being anti-majoritarian, but also in the more serious sense of eroding the habits and temperament of representative democracy."[76] There can be no doubt that the Charter has empowered and emboldened the judiciary, and that the fears Lyon voiced in the early 1980s have, to some degree, come to pass.

A Bilingual Manitoba?

During his time as Premier, Lyon was forced to address a third fundamental Canadian issue, the rights of linguistic minorities and more specifically the status of the French language in Manitoba. In 1890, the Manitoba legislature had ended the province's bilingual status and made English its only official language. Almost a century later, Manitoba francophone Georges Forest, after receiving a traffic ticket only in English, launched a legal challenge raising questions about whether the English-only legislation was constitutional. Lyon's government vociferously defended the legislation's constitutionality but, as Russell, Knopff and Morton explain, "the Supreme Court ruled that Manitoba's Official Language Act... which made English the official language of the province violated the constitutional requirement in section 23 of the Manitoba Act, 1870 [the Act creating Manitoba] that the province's laws be enacted in English and French."[77] It fell to the provincial government to respond to this, and as Dyck puts it, "Lyon complied with the ruling; albeit unenthusiastically."[78] He interpreted the Supreme Court ruling literally, offering simultaneous audio translation in the legislature and a gradual translation of provincial statutes over an extended period of time. These measures reflected Lyon's belief that services in French "were a simple courtesy and impossible to legislate."[79] St. Boniface College political scientist Raymond Hébert puts it more evocatively: "the Lyon government wanted to be as miserly as legally possible in the recognition of French-language rights in Manitoba."[80]

This was not the end of the bilingualism conflict and, in his subsequent period as opposition leader and ordinary opposition MLA, Lyon played an important part in resisting the expansion of francophone rights in Manitoba. Indeed, political scientist Geoffrey Lambert, in discussing Manitoba politics in 1983, suggests that Lyon's "forceful personality and unyielding opposition to the French language legislation dominated the political life of the province during 1983."[81] Political commentator Frances Russell, in her book on Manitoba language politics, indicates that to federal cabinet minister Lloyd Axworthy "Former Premier Lyon posed as much a threat to national unity as Quebec Premier René Levesque."[82] Finally, Raymond Hébert, in his analysis of the debate on the issue, maintains that Lyon's "Conservatives were willing to go to any lengths to defeat the Pawley government's constitutional amendment."[83] The issue of the status of the French language is without doubt one of the most controversial aspects of Lyon's political career.

Following the *Forest* decision some provincial statutes had been translated, but progress was slow and indeed some new legislation was approved in English alone. Another challenge was launched over a traffic ticket, and the Manitoba Court of Appeal indicated that these laws must be enforced. The federal Liberal and provincial NDP governments sought to provide a 10-year grace period for the translation of legislation, but, at the same time, make French an official language of the province. The strategy was hugely unpopular with the population—a number of municipal plebiscites recorded opposition to official bilingualism by as much as "3 to 1 in Winnipeg, and 16 to 1 in some rural areas"[84]—and strongly opposed by the Conservatives in the legislature. Russell credits Lyon for inflaming public opinion on this issue. As she explains, "Lyon's oratory set loose the politically explosive spectre of linguistic fears and loathing, of the French language being forced down Manitobans' throats by constitutional 'dictats' won by 'linguistic zealots'."[85] Hébert concurs, suggesting "Sterling Lyon himself set the tone."[86] As the authors of *Manitoba 125: A History* recall, "The language debate exposed emotions and inflamed passions. Death threats were directed to members of the Société Franco-Manitobaine. Police patrols became commonplace around cabinet ministers' homes."[87] Hébert concludes his impressive analysis of these events by noting that "The French-language crisis is a sorry part of Manitoba's history and it cannot be expunged from it, as some Tory MLAs would have liked to do."[88]

Lyon's opposition was not merely verbal. He led the Tories in a series of classic parliamentary delaying tactics, refusing to attend votes in the legislature. As Anstett and Thomas explain, "The Manitoba Legislative Assembly experienced a series of bell-ringing days during the debates on the Pawley government's French language proposals of 1983–84."[89] The ferocious Conservative opposition, based as it was in the strong feelings of many Manitobans, essentially brought the legislature to a standstill and convinced the Pawley government to relent and withdraw its linguistic legislation. Lyon's leadership (even after Filmon became leader) accomplished one of the rarest of parliamentary feats, forcing a majority government to withdraw a piece of legislation it saw as important.

Lyon maintains that the public disapproved of his government's actions in implementing the Supreme Court's *Forest* judgement, and that the Pawley government went far beyond anything the courts required. He warned that debate over the legislation would "divide Manitoba in a way that it hasn't been divided in a long time"[90] and, in the end, played a role in making that prophesy come true.

The Tories' actions during the 1983–84 legislative session reveal that electoral defeat had not mellowed Lyon. Political scientist Geoff Lambert suggests that Lyon "appeared to revel in his role as scrappy leader of the opposition."[91] Indeed, Lyon and the Manitoba Conservatives were not only opposing the provincial New Democrats, but running afoul of the federal Tories as well. Brian Mulroney's federal Conservatives joined the federal Liberals in passing a resolution in support of the Pawley legislation. Russell notes that Lyon regretted the actions of the federal Conservatives and stated with characteristic bluntness: "We think it is wrong. We will not be swayed by wrongheadedness whether it comes from the left, the right or the centre."[92]

Lyon resigned as leader in December 1983, making way for his one-time Consumer Affairs minister, Gary Filmon. Lyon continued to play a major role in the linguistic debates and remained a force in the legislature until the next election. To some observers his stature and continued presence in the legislature diminished Filmon. As Adams illustrates, "In one embarrassing incident in the legislature, Lyon shouted at his successor to sit down when Filmon appeared to be on the verge of making a tactical blunder."[93] Lyon did not contest the 1986 election and, in a fashion that contrasted with his forceful entry into the leadership, slipped out of the legislature and back into a role with the courts.

The Lyon Legacy

Although Lyon is the only Manitoba Premier never to be re-elected, he and his supporters seem content with his legacy. Lyon reflects that his emphasis on fiscal responsibility became the norm for governments over the next two decades, and suggests that this "might seem to indicate that this policy was sensible in the long run."[94] Lyon's perception has considerable merit, judging by the policies of subsequent Manitoba Conservative and New Democratic governments alike. As Wesley describes, "By the 1999 election, the NDP had abandoned the Keynesian values of the Schreyer and Pawley governments, replacing them with a liberal acceptance of efficiency, prudence and transparency in the public sector." This included "full acceptance of the Tories' 1995 balanced budget legislation" and "wide-scale tax relief."[95]

Indeed, Lyon turned out to be the first in a long line of neo-conservative governments in Canada, showing the way for leaders such as Brian Mulroney in Ottawa, Ralph Klein in Alberta, and Mike Harris in Ontario. In addition, his concerns over the new Constitution appear to be well founded, and conservative critics remain concerned about the diminished role the Charter has left for legislatures. In a very real sense, while drawing on political principles from days gone by, Lyon was a conservative ahead of his time.

Lyon was a polarizing figure in Manitoba politics, an impact for which he makes no apologies. The 1981 election that removed his government from office was also the first in Manitoba in which only two parties secured legislative representation. Indeed, despite descriptions of his government as "disastrous,"[96] it won 44% of the vote in 1981. This level of support was higher than that won by the New Democrats in 1969 and 1973, and by the victorious Conservatives in 1988 and 1995. His personal style was combative and his rhetoric was stark. Manitobans developed strong views about Lyon, but he was widely respected for his politics of conviction. In their discussion of the constitutional deal of 1981, Sheppard and Valpy indicate that some of the other Premiers were uncomfortable with the strength of Lyon's opposition. Bill Bennett of British Columbia felt that Lyon's rigid antagonism to Trudeau had hurt the Gang of Eight, and Allan Blakeney of Saskatchewan told his staff "that while he had heard lots of right wingers preaching their economic dogma when the occasion demanded, Lyon was the first one he had met who actually believed what he was spouting."[97]

In an era when Canadians believe that politicians will do or say anything to get elected, one can almost feel nostalgic for the Lyon approach. As the *Ottawa Citizen* wrote at the time of his appointment to the Manitoba Court of Appeal in 1986, "while he made enemies during his political career, the old-world manner he showed in person and his unflinching adherence to his principles—even when they proved unpopular—earned him many loyal friends and supporters."[98] Lyon's lasting ability to stir controversy was evident in the commentary on his appointment. Liberal critic Sheila Copps noted that Lyon "had opposed entrenching equality for women in the 1982 Charter of Rights and Freedoms" while New Democrat Svend Robinson called him an "arch enemy of equality."[99]

As a Justice, Lyon's ability to discuss political issues was restrained and, aside from the critique of the Charter for allowing the guilty to go free, he largely escaped public attention. There is nonetheless some irony in the fact that one of the leading critics of the Charter of Rights ended his public career as one of its interpreters.

Lyon served on the Manitoba Court of Appeals until his mandatory retirement in 2002. He has lived quietly in Winnipeg and returned to public attention only after almost losing his life in an automobile accident in 2002. His politics of conviction and his forceful personality made him an icon on the political right. Political reporter Clair Hoy, reflecting on a political biography he wrote on former Ontario Premier Bill Davis, captures this admiration. In his words, "I admire politicians who stand for something beyond getting elected. Most people do. I'd rather go with Sterling Lyon. You know where he stands."[100] This seems a fitting epitaph to the Lyon era.

Notes

1. Christopher Dunn, *The Institutionalized Cabinet: Governing the Western Provinces* (Montreal: McGill-Queen's University Press, 1995), 164.

2. Reginald W. Lewis, an introduction to Sterling Lyon's speech entitled "A Time for Fiscal Responsibility," in *The Empire Club of Canada Speeches, 1978–1979* (Toronto: The Empire Club Foundation, 1979), 106.

3. Sterling Lyon, *Manitoba Premiers' Symposium Address*, University of Manitoba, November 13, 1999.

4. For more on the development of the Manitoba party system, see Jared Wesley, "Spanning the Spectrum: Political Party Attitudes in Manitoba" (Master's thesis, University of Manitoba, 2004).

5. Duff Roblin, quoted in David Lee, "Tory Triumph Celebrated in Harmony," *Winnipeg Free Press*, October 12, 1977, p. 4.

6. Dunn, *Institutionalized Cabinet*, 164.

7. Murray Donnelly, "Manitoba," *Canadian Annual Review of Politics and Public Affairs* (1975): 179.

8. Robert Sheppard and Michael Valpy, *The National Deal* (Scarborough: Fleet, 1982), 183.

9. Russell Doern, *Wednesdays are Cabinet Days* (Winnipeg: Queenston House, 1981), 33.

10. Rand Dyck, *Provincial Politics in Canada: Towards the Turn of the Century* (Scarborough: Prentice-Hall Canada, 1996), 406.

11. Dunn, *Institutionalized Cabinet*, 164.

12. Wally Dennison, "Business Community Sees Better Climate Here," *Winnipeg Free Press*, October 14, 1977, p. 29.

13. Donnelly, "Manitoba," 178–79.

14. Ted Allan, "PC's on the Left Slash PC's on the Right," *Winnipeg Free Press*, December 6, 1975, p. 1.

15. As part of his acceptance speech, Lyon argued, "In our parliamentary system, the support of the caucus of the leader is paramount." "Nervous Moments in Victory: Sterling Lyon Promises New Leadership Approach," *Winnipeg Free Press*, December 8, 1975, p. 1.

16. Dunn, *Institutionalized Cabinet*, 163.

17. Harold Chorney and Phillip Hansen, "Neo-Conservatism, Social Democracy and 'Province Building': The Experience of Manitoba," Canadian Review of Sociology and Anthropology 22 (1985): 9.

18. Tom Peterson, "Ethnic and Class Politics in Manitoba," in Robert Martin (ed.), *Canadian Provincial Politics: The Party Systems of the Ten Provinces* (Scarborough: Prentice Hall, 1978), 104; Roger Gibbins, *Prairie Politics and Society: Regionalism in Decline* (Scarborough: Butterworth, 1980), 126.

19. See Janine Brodie and Jane Jenson, *Crisis, Challenge and Change: Party and Class in Canada* (Toronto: Methuen, 1980).

20. The concept of a "critical election" is drawn largely from American political science. Among students of electoral realignment, including David Mahew, each critical election consists of a common set of elements, including: a noticeable build-up of socio-economic tension within the electorate; a high level of voter interest and turnout; the emergence of a new, highly ideological vein of political debate; a shift from local issues to issues of a broader (i.e., provincial or national) character; and proposals for widespread institutional and political change. See David R. Mahew, *Electoral Realignments: A Critique of an American Genre* (London: Yale University Press, 2002).

21. Murray Donnelly, "Manitoba," *Canadian Annual Review of Politics and Public Affairs* (1976): 238.

22. Chorney and Hansen, "Neo-Conservatism," 10.

23. Dunn, *Institutionalized Cabinet*, 164.

24. Jim Haggarty, "PC Leader Hits NDP Spending," *Winnipeg Free Press*, September 22, 1977, p. 9.

25. "Schreyer Labelled Unfit for Any Kind of Work in Energy," *Winnipeg Free Press*, September 26, 1977, p. 8.

26. J.M. Bumsted, "The Socialist Experiment," in Gregg Shilliday (ed.), *Manitoba 125: A History* (Winnipeg: Great Plains Publications, 1995), 131.

27. Chorney and Hansen, "Neo-Conservatism," 9.

28. The remainder of the Tory platform was tempered by moderate rhetoric including the promotion of political, economic, cultural, and social choice; the respect for human dignity; the encouragement of voluntarism; government transparency; and increased emphasis on decision-making at the local level.

29. Lee, "Election Manifesto Calls for Acute Restraint," *Winnipeg Free Press*, September 21, p. A9.30. Roblin quoted in Arlene Billinkoff, "What's in Store for Manitoba," *Winnipeg Free Press*, October 14, 1977, p. 57.

31. Debbie Sproat, "About 1,500 PCs Attend Bash in Lyon 'Country'," *Winnipeg Free Press*, October 8, 1977, p. 11.

32. Debbie Sproat, "Green Promises Firm Opposition," *Winnipeg Free Press*, October 12, 1977, p. 16.

33. Doern, *Wednesdays*, 197.

34. Geoffrey Lambert, Introduction to Sterling Lyon's *Manitoba Premiers' Symposium Address*, November 13, 1999.

35. Dyck, *Provincial Politics*, 386.

36. Gibbins, *Prairie Politics*, 126.

37. The New Democrats lost Emerson, Thompson, St. Matthews, Gimli, Radisson, Osborne, Dauphin, and Springfield to the Conservatives. Ian Turnbull (Education), René Toupin (Consumer Affairs), and Peter Burtniak (Highways) were the three cabinet ministers unseated.

38. The Liberals also lost Assiniboine to the Conservatives.

39. Sheppard and Valpy, *The National Deal*, 10, 11.

40. Dunn, *Institutionalized Cabinet*, 108.

41. Doern, *Wednesdays*, 106.

42. Ibid., 195.

43. Lyon, *Manitoba Premiers' Symposium Address*.

44. Alex Netherton, "Paradigm and Shift: A Sketch of Manitoba Politics." In Keith Brownsey and Michael Howlett (eds.), *The Provincial State in Canada: Politics in the Provinces and Territories* (Peterborough, ON: Broadview, 2001), 220.

45. Dunn, *Institutionalized Cabinet*, 163.

46. Ibid.

47. Ibid., 166.

48. Ibid., 170.

49. Graham White, *Cabinets and First Ministers* (Vancouver: UBC Press, 2005), 88.

50. Dunn, *Institutionalized Cabinet*, 169.

51. Cy Gonick, "The Manitoba Economy Since World War II" in Jim Silver and Jeremy Hull (eds.), *The Political Economy of Manitoba* (Regina: Canada Plains Research Center, 1990), 36.

52. Dennison, "Business Community."

53. Lyon, *Manitoba Premiers' Symposium Address*.

54. Netherton, "Paradigm and Shift," 220.

55. Lyon, *Manitoba Premiers' Symposium Address.*

56. Lewis, introduction to Sterling Lyon's speech entitled "A Time for Fiscal Responsibility," 106.

57. Gonick, "The Manitoba Economy Since World War II," 37.

58. Lyon, *Manitoba Premiers' Symposium Address.*

59. Geoffrey Lambert, "Manitoba," *Canadian Annual Review of Politics and Public Affairs* (1981): 396.

60. Dyck, *Provincial Politics,* 398; Chorney and Hansen, "Neo-Conservatism," 11.

61. Lyon, *Manitoba Premiers' Symposium Address.*

62. Nelson Wiseman, *Social Democracy in Manitoba* (Winnipeg: University of Manitoba Press, 1983), 151.

63. Duff Roblin, *Speaking for Myself: Politics and Other Pursuits* (Winnipeg: Great Plains Publications, 1999), 102.

64. Bumsted, "The Socialist Experiment," 145.

65. Wiseman, *Social Democracy in Manitoba,* 152.

66. Sheppard and Valpy, *The National Deal,* 268.

67. Kent Roach, *The Supreme Court on Trial: Judicial Activism or Democratic Dialogue* (Toronto: Irwin Law, 2001), 86.

68. Richard Sigurdson, "Left- and Right-Wing Charterphobia in Canada: A Critique of the Critics," in *International Journal of Canadian Studies* (Spring–Fall 1993): 101.

69. Bumsted, "The Socialist Experiment," 145.

70. Lyon, *Manitoba Premiers' Symposium Address.*

71. Ibid.

72. Bumsted, "The Socialist Experiment," 147.

73. Sheppard and Valpy, *The National Deal,* 183 and 11.

74. Lyon, *Manitoba Premiers' Symposium Address.*

75. "Manitoba Judge Claims Charter is Letting Guilty Thugs Go Free," *Toronto Star,* February 21, 1988, A6.

76. F.L. Morton and Rainer Knopff, *The Charter Revolution and the Court Party* (Peterborough: Broadview, 2000), 149.

77. Peter H. Russell, Rainer Knopff and F.L. Morton, *Federalism and the Charter* (Ottawa: Carleton University Press, 1989), 627.

78. Dyck, *Provincial Politics,* 397.

79. As quoted in Ingebor Boyens, "A Decade of Discontent" in *Manitoba 125: A History,* Volume 3 (Winnipeg: Great Plains Publications, 1995), 152.

80. Raymond Hébert, *Manitoba's French-Language Crisis: A Cautionary Tale* (Montreal: McGill-Queen's University Press, 2005), 32, 33.

81. Geoffrey Lambert, "Manitoba," *Canadian Annual Review of Politics and Public Affairs* (1983): 268.

82. Frances Russell, *The Canadian Crucible* (Winnipeg: Heartland Associates, 2003), 433.

83. Hébert, *Manitoba's French-Language Crisis,* 218.

84. Boyens "A Decade of Discontent," 155.

85. Russell, *The Canadian Crucible,* 26.

86. Hébert, *Manitoba's French-Language Crisis,* 217

87. Boyens, "A Decade of Discontent," 155.

88. Hébert, *Manitoba's French-Language Crisis,* 221.

89. Andy Anstett and Paul G. Thomas, "Manitoba: The Role of the Legislature in a Polarized Political System" in Gary Levy and Graham White (eds.), *Provincial and Territorial Legislatures in Canada* (Toronto: University of Toronto Press, 1989), 103.

90. Lyon, *Manitoba Premiers' Symposium Address*.

91. Geoffrey Lambert, "Manitoba," *Canadian Annual Review of Politics and Public Affairs* (1982): 263.

92. As quoted in Russell, *The Canadian Crucible*, 388.

93. Paul Adams, "Manitoba," *Canadian Annual Review of Politics and Public Affairs* (1984): 261.

94. Lyon, *Manitoba Premiers' Symposium Address*.

95. Jared J. Wesley, "Spanning the Spectrum: Political Party Attitudes in Manitoba" (Master of Arts thesis, University of Manitoba), 66, 116–17.

96. Gonick, "The Manitoba Economy Since World War II," 47.

97. Sheppard and Valpy, *The National Deal,* 247 and 192.

98. "Some Manitoba Hackles Raised When Ex-Premier Appointed to Bench," *Ottawa Citizen*, December 26, 1986, F20.

99 "Hnatyshyn Under Fire Over Lyon Judgeship," *Toronto Star*, February 5, 1987, H12.

100. *Kingston Whig Standard Magazine*, May 25, 1985, p. 1.

Howard Pawley

1981–1988

GREGORY MARCHILDON

Howard Russell Pawley, 1981–1988

Howard Pawley's greatest feat as a politician and Premier was to reconstruct the New Democratic Party of Manitoba after the fall of the Schreyer government in 1977. His political acumen and his considerable organizational talents were directly responsible for leading the party back to power within one term of the NDP defeat. In addition, his ability to focus on this political task allowed him to achieve a second term of government despite the exigencies of an economic recession and a language controversy that seared the soul of the province. In addition to entrenching some of the social democratic policies and programs originating in the Schreyer administration, Pawley's major contribution as Manitoba's nineteenth premier was to jump-start the Manitoba economy in a major recession and initiate his own egalitarian agenda in terms of human rights, language rights, women's rights and access to information.[1]

Howard Pawley may have lacked Ed Schreyer's charisma, but he made up for it with perseverance. His ability to reach out to the warring factions within his party not only kept his government in power but also ensured that the NDP would remain a viable government party in the future. Underestimated by opponents as well as rivals within his own party, Pawley continually took advantage of this perception to get the upper hand in political struggles—with opposition leaders and with key figures in his own party.

Early Political Activism

Howard Pawley was born in Brampton, Ontario, on November 21, 1934. His parents were politically active in the Co-operative Commonwealth Federation (CCF) and, in part because of their religious backgrounds, deeply influenced by the social gospel movement. Strict Methodists, his parents did not allow drinking or smoking in the house and they frowned upon dancing.[2] Pawley was deeply influenced by his parents' religious convictions and while still a youngster considered becoming a Unitarian minister. While he eventually rejected certain aspects of organized religion, and the more prudish aspects of his upbringing, Pawley's demeanour occasionally earned him the nickname "Preacher Pawley" in later life.

Unlike drinking and dancing, politics was more than fair game in the Pawley household. Daily discussions often focused on CCF policies and leaders such as J.S. Woodsworth and Tommy Douglas.[3] A farmer in the Brampton area, Pawley's father ran as a CCF candidate for Peel County in the provincial election of 1937. Though defeated, he had much more success in the 1943 election, coming very close to defeating the local Conservative candidate. While Howard Pawley was only nine years of age at the time, he always remembered the excitement of that election. Similarly, a year later, he eagerly joined in his family's celebration of the CCF's first major victory in Canada when it was elected to form a government in Saskatchewan.[4]

Pawley attended Brampton High School where history was his favourite subject. In 1952, his life changed unexpectedly when his father became a sales manager for the Cockshutt Plough Company, sold the farm, and moved 17-year-old Howard and the rest of his family to Winnipeg. Pawley was heartsick at leaving the farm but adjusted quickly to living in what was then one of Canada's largest cities. Here, he would soon come to know CCF politics Manitoba-style, joining the party and getting to meet such luminaries as Stanley Knowles. In 1955, after finishing high school, he attended the Manitoba Normal School in order to acquire a teaching certificate. Following this, he spent one very unhappy term teaching in a one-room rural school just outside of Winnipeg. He enrolled at United College (now the University of Winnipeg) in order to prepare himself for eventual entry into law school at the University of Manitoba.[5]

At United College, Pawley became the leader of the CCF Club.[6] Though the CCF had very limited electoral success, Pawley was convinced that it would one day form a government in the province and country if it was organized and mobilized more effectively. Like many others in his party, he sought to improve the party's provincial fortunes by imitating the example of Tommy Douglas, who had been running a CCF government in Saskatchewan since 1944 based upon a vigorous party organization.[7]

As with most CCFers of the time, Pawley drew little distinction between the federal and provincial wings of the party. Often he worked simultaneously for both. His great energy and enthusiasm for the organizational side of politics served him well from the beginning, and he ended up with important party responsibilities at a very young age. He also agreed to run as a sacrificial candidate in two federal elections simply to give the CCF some presence. In 1958, even though he was only 24 years old and still studying law, Pawley became chair of the Manitoba CCF.[8]

By the late 1950s, Pawley was fully engaged in the passionate debate over the future of the CCF. Two competing visions were seeking to direct the electoral agenda. One faction, led by Pawley and Al Mackling, argued that the CCF should continue solely on the basis of individual memberships, rather than permit affiliate memberships, to trade unions, and thereby adhere more closely to its farmer-populist roots.[9] The New Party faction wanted a more direct linkage with organized labour through affiliate memberships, hoping to increase its appeal to workers in Canada's industrialized heartland. Arguing the need for the party to rebrand itself as a *new* social democratic party, the New Party faction was heavily supported by organized labour in Winnipeg.[10]

While time would eventually moderate his political beliefs, in the 1950s Pawley saw himself as a committed socialist. Wary of what he viewed as the innate conservatism of mainstream unionists, he was convinced that the structural changes being proposed would give organized labour too powerful a voice within the party and pull it away from its socialist origins and towards the centre of the political spectrum.[11] New Party supporters firmly believed a more pragmatic and modern approach was necessary to capture the hearts and minds of a growing middle class, including increasingly affluent workers in unionized jobs in the private sector. In a debate concerning the costs and benefits of large-scale public ownership, Pawley argued that a socialist party should be prepared to "lead public thought" on this issue and other ideas, even if it happened to "be unpopular" at the time.[12]

Pawley's position on the New Party diverged significantly from that of another young and rising star within the party, Ed Schreyer. Whereas Schreyer was torn between remaining true to the left-wing farmers' movement that had historically formed one base of CCF support, or abandoning it in favour of the electoral benefits that might accrue from appealing more directly to urban workers, Pawley displayed no such ambivalence. Pawley's most important objection to the New Party was organizational, however. He felt that the union affiliates in the New Party would deliver power to organized labour without a corresponding responsibility to recruit and retain new members, and he believed this would result in a weaker membership base. In the end, however, the New Party faction won out, and the New Democratic Party (NDP) emerged out of the old CCF. Disappointed but not bitter, Pawley pragmatically accepted the decision and worked as hard for the NDP as he had for the CCF.[13]

Despite his initial difference with Schreyer over the New Party, the two men were destined to be linked—by both politics and family. In 1960, Pawley married Ed Schreyer's cousin, Adele Schreyer. He had been articling as a lawyer when he met Adele in a Winnipeg drugstore. Initially, they made their home in the town of Stonewall, just outside of Winnipeg, where they established a law firm that Adele managed. When Ed Schreyer entered federal politics, he used extra space in Pawley's law office as a constituency office. In 1967, after being offered the job of town solicitor, Pawley moved his law office to Selkirk, less than 20 kilometres north of Winnipeg.[14]

These were invigorating years for both Howard and Adele Pawley. Their growing law practice became increasingly lucrative. They thoroughly enjoyed the business of running a small law firm together while raising their two children, Christopher and Charysse.[15] Howard Pawley, however, was lured back into politics, once temporarily, and later more permanently. In 1965, he agreed to run in the federal election as the NDP candidate in the Selkirk-Interlake constituency. Unlike his earlier efforts, he was convinced he had a chance to win but he came in second to the Conservative incumbent.[16] Though disappointed, he held out hope of eventually becoming a member of Parliament; instead, in a strange twist of fate, he would end up running for provincial office.

Howard Pawley was part of the "draft Schreyer" movement that convinced Ed Schreyer to leave federal politics in order to become provincial leader of the NDP. The draft finally succeeded, but the party found itself deciding the leadership and running a provincial campaign at the same time in 1969. In May of that year, Pawley was hospitalized with an injured back after a serious car accident. Schreyer went directly to the hospital and asked Pawley to allow his name to be put on the ballot for the Selkirk riding, explaining that his efforts to recruit other candidates had failed. Pawley objected on the grounds that his back injury would hinder campaigning. Schreyer agreed, and said that while he did not think Pawley was likely to win the riding from the popular Conservative incumbent, it was nonetheless important for the NDP to have a candidate in every riding, and that the election would at least give Pawley public visibility which he could use to his advantage the next time he ran in federal politics. Pawley assented and, after a rapid nomination process attended by only eight individuals from the riding, his wife Adele immediately went from door to door, campaigning on his behalf.[17]

Released from hospital only 10 days before the election on June 25, Pawley nonetheless won the riding as part of the Schreyer breakthrough for the NDP. After almost two decades of late-night meetings and knocking on doors, Pawley would finally see the provincial wing of his party have the opportunity to translate its principles into action. As someone who had never sat in the legislature, however, Pawley could hardly expect to get a cabinet post immediately. Not only was he prepared to sit as a backbencher for some time, he was looking forward to returning to his legal work. As desirable as it might be to play an important role in the new government, a cabinet post would force him to leave his rewarding law practice.[18]

Cabinet Minister in the Schreyer Government

Despite his status as a parliamentary rookie, Pawley became the thirteenth and last minister to be picked for cabinet by the new Premier.[19] Pawley would have been easy to overlook. Quietly unassuming and uncharismatic—indeed the most common description was "dull and grey"—Pawley was the opposite of Schreyer in outward demeanour. As a consequence, he was often underestimated by those around him, something which he understood and used to his advantage whenever possible. In reality, the political Pawley was tough and calculating. In the words of Russell Doern, an NDP political veteran and fellow minister in the Schreyer government, under Pawley's "gentle exterior" hid an "experienced professional politician," a "boxer" who knew how to "go the distance" with the best in the business.[20]

As minister of both Municipal Affairs and Government Services, Pawley's portfolios were initially viewed as minor positions in the new government. The opposite would soon prove true. One of the key platforms in the election was the NDP's promise to introduce comprehensive automobile insurance through a government-run agency. It was to be modeled on the Saskatchewan Government Insurance Office introduced by Tommy Douglas's provincial government in 1948. Naturally, the insurance industry and its allies in the business community, as well as the Conservatives and Liberals, were strongly opposed. The job of managing the public auto insurance file fell to Pawley, including the task of piloting the new bill through the legislature in the face of vitriolic criticism from hundreds of local insurance agents as well as the large insurance companies and the business community.[21]

Eager to succeed, Pawley was not above taking unorthodox steps to get a successful result. He "discreetly encouraged the establishment of an organization called Manitobans for Public Auto Insurance" in an effort to "counteract the insurance industry's campaign" against the government.[22] He then pushed the "Autopac" bill through the various readings as quickly as possible so that the new program could deliver tangible benefits to Manitobans early enough that he could help turn a polarized issue into a political benefit before the end of the first term of government. By 1970, Pawley's task was complete, and the Manitoba Public Insurance Corporation was up and running.

Pawley performed so well that in 1973 Schreyer appointed him Attorney-General and also kept him as minister of Municipal Affairs because of the skilful way he had managed the government's relationship with the generally conservative municipal politicians since

1969. His legal background coupled with a lifelong commitment to legal and social reform led Pawley to push for an agenda in his new portfolio that reflected many of his interests. Among other changes, he introduced what were at that time the most advanced family law reforms in the country. It was at this juncture that Pawley, at least privately, began to consider the possibility of taking on the leadership of the party and government, but only after Ed Schreyer had stepped aside.[23] At the same time, however, Pawley was also aware of rumours that Schreyer might abandon both the NDP and provincial politics in favour of a federal appointment as a senior cabinet minister in the Trudeau government.[24]

The rumours turned out to be false. Schreyer had, however, begun to lose some of his interest in the premiership by this time.[25] Criticism of the Schreyer government's management of public enterprises was mounting, the single most important factor leading to its defeat in the election of 1977. For the next year Schreyer continued as leader of the official opposition but his heart was not in the job, and in December 1978, he suddenly announced he was resigning and accepting Prime Minister Trudeau's offer to become Canada's next Governor General. The news stunned Canadians in general and the members of the Manitoba NDP in particular. For weeks afterwards, it was as if many party members simply could not accept the loss. As they gradually recovered from the shock, however, a number of MLAs approached Pawley to convince him to step in as the new leader, at least on an interim basis.[26] Their reasoning was simple. There were deep divisions within the party and they felt that Pawley was in the best position to bring peace. The factionalism centred largely on one individual—Sid Green. Green's supporters felt he should be the leader while his opponents—and there were many—believed that he was too divisive, too individualistic and too egotistical to make a good leader.[27]

Building the Party: One Member at a Time

Howard Pawley was not Ed Schreyer's natural heir. At the same time, however, the ex-Premier had chosen not to anoint a successor. While many in the party wasted time bemoaning the fact that there was no one in the Manitoba NDP with "Schreyeresque" qualities to fill the void, Pawley moved quickly to declare his own interest in the job. While lacking Schreyer's charisma and worldly confidence, Pawley concluded that the party needed a different kind of leader if it was going to grow to the size and strength necessary to take government again. Fully aware that some in the party saw him as weak—lacking the requisite "royal jelly" of leadership—he also knew that his more conciliatory approach was much more acceptable to the party than Green's confrontational and at times arrogant demeanour.[28]

When it came time to pick a new leader in the new year the party caucus was divided. Sid Green and his supporters wanted to settle the issue immediately or, at a minimum, allow potential candidates to be interim leader. The anti-Green forces wanted an interim leader, a mere caretaker, until a new permanent leader could be selected at the annual convention in the fall of 1979, giving them time to find a Schreyer-type saviour. This faction was led by Saul Cherniak, one of the provincial NDP's longest-serving MLAs. Pawley threw his hat in the ring as the candidate of the middle, keeping the option open to run but making it clear that the final decision rested with the party, not the caucus, in its fall convention. Pawley's shrewd calculation paid off. He received 10 votes, two more than Sid Green and seven more than Cherniak. Pawley had picked up most of the anti-Green vote without having to attack Green directly.[29] While his caucus support was far from the picture of unanimity that the party conveyed to the media, it gave Pawley what he wanted: an organizational base from which he could lay the groundwork for his leadership campaign. In his press comments afterwards, Pawley tried to assure the party establishment and voters in Manitoba of his intention to "carry on with the direction, policies and approach of the last eight or nine years" and that he would avoid "doctrinaire or extreme" positions. In contrast to the late 1950s, Howard Pawley was now perceived as a moderate social democrat.[30]

Over the next 10 months, Pawley took full advantage of his interim-leader position and his organizational skills to get a lock on the leadership. To enhance his odds of winning, and to give his party a fighting chance in the next election, Pawley began a momentous rebuilding effort. At the time of Schreyer's departure the party apparatus was close to broken. Moreover, it had never exhibited the same degree of internal democracy, flexibility and dynamism that was the hallmark of its Saskatchewan conterpart under Tommy Douglas. The lack of proper tending to the party's grassroots had been one of the reasons for the 1977 defeat. By the time of the election call, the number of core party supporters had shrunk to the point that there were simply too few to do a proper job; moreover, they were too disorganized to fight an effective campaign.[31] Pawley wanted to reinvigorate the party so that it was a permanent part of Manitoba's political landscape, not simply a machine that came to life at election time.[32] To have any chance of toppling Sterling Lyon and his Progressive Conservative government from power, Pawley needed to reconstruct the party itself.

One of Pawley's first steps was to set up an extensive consultation with party members throughout the province in an effort to generate new policies. He received some valuable advice from Tommy Douglas, who told him to "form policy committees with caucus members and prospective candidates, blitz the province and build the organization at the rank and file level, as you would tend a garden."[33] As a result, the task forces set up by Pawley travelled throughout the province, consulting and discussing until new position papers on policy issues were developed. He strove to increase party membership, focussing specifically on younger people.

These activities also helped Pawley in his leadership campaign. By convention time in November of 1979, Pawley had shaken off his most important rival. Sid Green had concluded that Pawley's grassroots party support was unassailable and decided not to contest the leadership. Two candidates came forward: former cabinet minister Russell Doern, who represented the right wing in the party; and Muriel Smith, the candidate of the left. Pawley easily defeated both. As the relatively unassuming but highly organized candidate of the middle, Pawley had tapped much of the northern and rural base that had once supported Schreyer.[34]

Pawley's first job following the convention was to reduce the factionalism within the party and smooth over at least some of the hard feelings generated by the leadership bid. While he could do little about Green, and would eventually have a falling out with Russell Doern, he managed to effect a very productive working relationship with Muriel Smith.[35]

Winning the Election of 1981

On the eve of the 1977 election, the Manitoba NDP had 13,000 memberships. On the eve of the 1981 election, Pawley's rebuilding efforts had paid off as memberships almost doubled to 23,000. In addition, a number of vital new candidates had come forward to seek nominations, and Pawley went into the campaign with a reinvigorated team as well as a powerful party organization. The party's deficit of $250,000 had been wiped out, and new money collected for the war chest.[36] In the words of political scientist Paul Thomas, Pawley had taken "a party that was little more than a personality cult to Ed Schreyer and created a fighting machine" in three short years.[37]

As the new leader of the party, Pawley did not make the mistake of some long-time party veterans by assuming the NDP's interests and values were identical to those of all Manitobans. Like Schreyer, he believed the key to political victory lay in the NDP's ability to appeal beyond its traditional base and reach out directly to disenchanted Liberal voters as well as individuals without formal party affiliations. Indeed, the one constant in the Manitoba political arena is the extent to which the middle ground is aggressively contested by numerous political parties, and Pawley felt he had to position himself as a moderate in order to make the NDP attractive to non-NDP members.

Pawley was greatly aided in his efforts to grab votes from the centre by his antagonist, Premier Sterling Lyon. A leader with a confrontational demeanour whose addiction to the rhetoric of a newly emerging neoconservative right-wing was always on display, Lyon did little to help his own electoral cause.[38] Practicing the politics of polarization, Lyon's blunt manner alienated many voters in the uncommitted middle. Seizing on this, Pawley painted Lyon's government as an extreme, neoconservative threat to Manitoba's moderate political culture and even its way of life. Often the legacy of the Schreyer government was invoked by Pawley to draw a distinction between what his party had to offer and what Lyon's government sought to take away—minority rights, linguistic equality and compassionate government.[39]

From the beginning, Pawley was underestimated. The media generally assumed that Lyon, a colourful—even flamboyant—leader in contrast to the understated NDP leader, would win the election without much difficulty. More importantly, many in the province had jumped to the conclusion that Pawley was a weak leader because of the noisy defection of Sid Green. Despite Pawley's efforts to keep his party united following his election as leader, he could not keep Green in the party tent. Instead, Green and his allies formed a new party—the Progressive Party—that attacked the NDP in general and Pawley in particular, and threatened to take votes both from the base of the party and the undecided middle. The silver lining for Pawley was that much of the factionalism in the party suddenly disappeared with Green's departure.[40]

What the media and even the Conservatives did not see was the powerful party and electoral organization Pawley had built up since Schreyer's departure. For his part, Pawley used this ignorance to his advantage, enticing Lyon and the Conservatives into a false confidence, and pushing his own partisans to greater effort.[41] This effort, combined with the damage he had previously inflicted on Lyon's competency at managing government finances during the prior legislative session, convinced Pawley that the NDP could win the election. Moreover, in a time of economic recession, he discovered that many Manitobans shared his critique of Lyon's mega-project approach to economic development as being fundamentally flawed as well as ineffective.[42]

When the election was called, Pawley laid out a diverse platform which promised, among other things, to freeze tuition fees, upgrade and expand day care facilities, create a Crown-owned oil company, and restore rent controls—a popular policy originally introduced during the Schreyer administration but eliminated by Lyon.[43] Pawley also pledged to bring interest rate relief to homeowners suffering from stagflation—double-digit interest rates during a recession. The Conservatives initially attacked the idea of interest rate relief but they were thrown on the defensive by the popularity of the proposal. To counter this, they reversed their stance by offering an even more generous program of interest rate relief, thereby further undercutting their reputation as fiscally responsible managers. Finally, Pawley took advantage of Lyon's preoccupation with the difficult and time-consuming negotiations over the new constitution to make the Conservative Premier look increasingly out of touch with the issues affecting average Manitobans.[44]

On election night, November 17, 1981, Pawley saw his efforts to restore his party succeed. For the first time in living memory, a sitting government in Manitoba was defeated after only one term. Moreover, Pawley was pleased with the rout of Sid Green's Progressive Party.[45] In a province where razor-thin majorities are the rule rather than the exception, the NDP's 34 seats, compared to the Conservatives' 22 seats, constituted a thumping majority. Polarized along regional and class lines, the NDP was elected in north Winnipeg and the less prosperous rural areas to the north and east of the city, while the Conservatives remained entrenched in "affluent south Winnipeg" and the "highly fertile" southwest part of the province.[46] The popular vote had been tighter with the NDP receiving slightly more than 47% and the Conservatives slightly less than 44%. At less than 7% of the popular vote, the Liberals were shut out of the Manitoba legislature for the first time.[47] It was a powerful mandate for the new Premier whose organizational ability and perseverance in ending the factionalism within his party had made it all possible. In stark contrast to the conventional wisdom of the time, not anyone could have beaten the Progressive Conservatives under Sterling Lyon.[48] It required a dedicated and motivated party under a highly strategic leader in order to prevent nature from taking its course and giving the incumbent government a second term. Pawley delivered on both counts.

Incremental Progress in the Face of Adversity

The Pawley government was sworn in on November 30, 1981. Immediately, the new Premier set about selecting his cabinet with two criteria in mind. First, he needed ministers capable of taking on substantial policy responsibilities in a politically charged atmosphere. Second, they had to be the kind of individuals who could complement, rather than replicate, his own strengths and weaknesses. Although he consulted members, he made the final selection based upon a hard-headed view of how well any individual member fit these two criteria. Invariably, Pawley disappointed some veteran members of the legislature including Russell Doern, a former cabinet minister under Schreyer. Despite threats by some, including Doern, to quit, Pawley refused to reconsider his decision. As a consequence, one backbencher, Henry Carroll from Brandon, quit the caucus to sit as an independent but this simply spurred other caucus members to call for Carroll's resignation from the party.[49]

Pawley believed that good leadership required strategic delegation: too little delegation and he would be personally strong but unable to concentrate on "developing vision and ensuring coordination"; too much delegation and he would not be able to steer the government in the direction he desired.[50] Ultimately, Pawley wanted a "true" cabinet government in which all ministers' voices would be heard as they offered their reasoned assessments and, if need be, their "gut instincts" on the hard choices facing the new government. All the while each minister had to be willing to take personal responsibility for the collective decisions of cabinet. Pawley saw himself as the team captain of his government, and he preferred to exercise his power as premier through quiet persuasion and respectful discussion in the cabinet room.[51] In his view, too much emphasis on the leader would weaken the caucus and the party grassroots.[52] The actual style of cabinet decision-making was to talk and talk until a rough consensus was reached. Sometimes, this meant going around the cabinet table three times, as each minister voiced an opinion or concern, before finally reaching a decision.[53]

Pawley also took control of the machinery of government and the bureaucracy in order to implement his broad-ranging policy agenda. To that end, he replaced the Clerk of the Executive Council, Derek Bedson, with Michael Decter. Bedson had worked for successive administrations since 1958, including the Schreyer government, but was considered to be too sympathetic to the Conservatives by the NDP rank-and-file. Decter, on the other hand, was considered to be sympathetic to the government's agenda by virtue of having served as the director of Schreyer's central planning secretariat. Not having a particularly keen interest in public administration, Pawley felt perfectly at ease leaving most machinery of government issues in Decter's capable hands. In his role as the government's chief civil servant, Decter opted not to recreate the large central planning unit that had held sway during the Schreyer years. Instead, Pawley's government was to rely more heavily on line departments to develop and implement new policy initiatives rather than any central planning body in the Premier's own department.[54]

In its first Speech from the Throne in February 1982, the Pawley government set out its ambitious agenda of new initiatives. Yet, when it came time to table the spring budget, the recession, already a year old, had hit its nadir in both Canada and Manitoba. The agricultural sector was slumping, business investment was lagging, and interest rates were out of control. It seemed that no sector of the Manitoba economy was spared. Major projects, including a potash mine and a uranium smelter, were put on hold by companies suffering the effects of the recession. These fiscal realities forced Pawley to delay the more expensive aspects of his reform agenda, but even this was not enough to forestall a looming deficit, and Pawley was compelled to introduce new revenue measures, including a high-income surtax and a "Health and Education" payroll tax.[55]

Reshuffling priorities and shelving promises in response to the worsening economic picture is a thankless job for any politician, especially when it occurs early in a first term. Still, Pawley felt that something visible, even if not overly expensive, had to be done in the face of the recession. He believed in the basic Keynesian logic that during a recession or depression, the rate of private investment (and therefore the rate of employment) was artificially low due to a generalized lack of confidence in the future, and that the government could restore some of this confidence by priming the pump of the provincial economy through direct investment.[56] When Pawley announced a $200-million Jobs Fund program, it was to be, in effect, the only major new spending initiative for 1982. The opposition charged that only 10% of the fund involved "new" money, and Pawley admitted that about one-half of this money was simply reallocated from existing government programs. However, within a year, the recessionary fog began to lift. While Pawley pointed to the provincial Jobs Fund as the key to success, Manitoba's preferential access to federal funding via one of the Trudeau government's most powerful regional ministers, Lloyd Axworthy, may have been at least as important as any single provincial initiative in the province's remarkable economic recovery.[57] Owing to its highly diversified economy, Manitoba benefited more than most provinces from the turnaround. But just when Pawley was getting ready to kick-start his original agenda with the new revenues flowing into the treasury, his plans were derailed by what would prove to be a protracted and emotionally scarring debate over French-language rights.[58]

The Language Crucible

As Frances Russell points out in her book *The Canadian Crucible*, Manitoba has always played a central role in the country's disputes over language rights.[59] Although English was declared the official language of the province in 1890, subsequent provincial administrations tried to accommodate the vigorous French-speaking communities of Manitoba, mainly concentrated in St. Boniface and the historic French and Métis towns around Winnipeg. Given the sense of historic injustice felt by many Franco-Manitobans as a result of 1890, however, the legal status of the French language was bound to surface periodically. That it would do so in the early 1980s was perhaps inevitable given the Parti Québécois victory in Quebec in 1976 and the subsequent passage of vigorous language laws protecting the French language in that province, as well as the debates over the protection of language in the constitutional negotiations that dominated the federal-provincial agenda after 1976.

The immediate origins of the French-language crisis during the Pawley administration could be traced to 1976 when Georges Forest from St. Boniface challenged a parking ticket written in English on the grounds that the ticket should have been printed in French as well as English. The case eventually wound its way to the Supreme Court of Canada, which in 1979 upheld Forest's contention. As a consequence, the Lyon government began the task of translating all statutes and some other official documents into French. The process went slowly; so in 1980, Roger Bilodeau, a Winnipeg lawyer, challenged a speeding ticket on the grounds that the statute on which it was based had not been translated. By the time of the Pawley government, the Bilodeau case was headed for the Supreme Court and a real possibility loomed that the court would question the legality of all English-language legislation passed since 1890.[60] To avoid this outcome, the Pawley government sought a negotiated solution involving Bilodeau, the Société Franco-Manitobaine, and the federal government that involved translating 400 laws (out of approximately 4,500 laws) over 10 years at an estimated cost of $3.5 million, while expanding some French-language services beyond the courts and the legislature, to key ministries and agencies within government. For its part, the federal government agreed to pay $2.35 million to Manitoba to help cover the cost of translation. On this basis, Bilodeau agreed to delay his court action.[61]

To Pawley, the negotiated agreement seemed the most reasonable and workable solution under the circumstances. He even met with opposition leader Sterling Lyon to explain the nature of the compromise before it became public in the hope and expectation that Lyon would not light the political fuse to the explosive language issue. Instead, the meeting gave Lyon the ammunition he needed to launch an external as well as internal assault on the government.[62] Lyon understood that the nature of the issue was so divisive that dissent could be expected even from certain members of Pawley's own caucus and he planned to take full advantage of the fractures within the NDP as well as fan the flames of widespread anti-French sentiment in Manitoba.

Unfortunately for Pawley, Lyon was deadly accurate in his political calculations. On the proposed settlement, Pawley immediately faced dissenters within his own caucus, the most vocal and powerful of whom was Russell Doern. Still angry at his exclusion from cabinet, Doern broke ranks and openly criticized what he perceived to be a policy of "entrenched bilingualism." Doern felt so strongly that he purchased newspaper advertisements denouncing Pawley's compromise and would later write a book about the struggle within the Pawley government.[63]

When the amendment to the Manitoba Act was finally brought before the legislature, all hell broke loose. Pawley was not helped by the fact that Prime Minister Trudeau, then very unpopular in Manitoba, had announced the settlement unilaterally, pre-empting the opportunity for Pawley to prepare the public for the implications of the settlement.[64] Seizing on the chaos, Lyon led his members out of the House and demanded that municipalities be allowed to hold public hearings on the legislation. After two months of making no progress in the House, Pawley relented and allowed the public hearings to proceed. Controlled by the opposition and fuelled by the vehement attitudes of groups opposed to the amendment, the hearings proved to be an unmitigated disaster for the government, spurring negative national and local media stories. By the end of October a number of municipalities, including Winnipeg, had held plebiscites on the amendment, and soundly rejected the "Pawley compromise."

Frustrated but still eager to resolve the issue, Pawley made one further concession. In order to meet some of the more reasonable objections that had been raised during the long debate, he watered down his original legislation and brought the amended version before the House at the end of the year. But this last-ditch effort seemed to make things worse. On one side, many Franco-Manitobans felt they had compromised enough in the first round, while on the other side, opponents were encouraged at what they perceived as a retreat by the government, and now pushed to obtain a complete surrender on French-language rights.[65]

By this time, Lyon had been replaced by a more conciliatory Conservative leader, Gary Filmon. No matter. He too rejected this newest compromise, leading the opposition through prolonged episodes of bell-ringing in the House. The protest outside the legislature turned ugly. Now faced with death and bomb threats, Pawley and three of his ministers were placed under 24-hour police protection. Such hostile and undemocratic tactics on the part of anti-Francophone elements within Manitoba only served to reinforce Pawley's determination to get the legislation through the House.[66] His government raised motions of closure, attempted caps on the bell-ringing, and called upon speaker Jim Walding to allow the House to continue its business without the opposition. All efforts were futile, however, and Pawley was forced to let the bill die.[67] Although the Premier was no stranger to political defeat, he was horrified by the wellspring of bigotry unleashed by the language crisis and he was disappointed in an opposition that took political advantage of such base feelings. He would have preferred to have been able to pass the legislation on principle and then be defeated in a general election on the issue rather than be defeated in the House on a set of procedural technicalities.[68]

The impasse led to the federal government's decision to refer the Manitoba language issue to the Supreme Court of Canada. In its final decision delivered in early November 1985, the Supreme Court gave the Manitoba government until the end of 1988 to translate all of its current laws and regulations into French (in effect, allowing them temporary force), and an additional two years to translate those laws passed since 1890 but no longer in force. Pawley put the best face possible on a decision he had long tried to avoid, preferring to communicate in a prepared statement that he was "pleased that the language reference has been resolved without further delay or contention" and confident that "all Manitobans" welcomed the opportunity to allow his government to get on with "job creation, tax reform and fighting back federal cuts in transfer payments to the province of Manitoba for health and education."[69]

Changing the Political Channel: The Election of 1986

Pawley had been trying to change the political channel for months before the Supreme Court decision but without success. Now he thought he could finally move on. The acrimony generated by the language debacle had just about destroyed his government's popularity and his own image as an effective Premier. He needed time to rebuild from what polling indicated was less than 20% support for his government.[70] His stated plan was to get his government refocused on the economy through a number of initiatives.[71] His more hidden strategy was to eschew controversial policies of any type in order to avoid losing any more support, while emphasizing the bread-and-butter issues attractive to the majority of voters. It was a strategy borne of extreme caution, one that was highly criticized by the left wing both inside and outside the Manitoba NDP. In a stinging editorial in *Canadian Dimension*, the Pawley government was praised for its good management of the economy and for raising the minimum wage, reforming labour legislation, addressing violence against women, improving daycare, and supporting the arts. However, these "timid" and "partial" steps were seen to be insufficient, nothing more than camouflage for an administration that was deemed a "dull, uninspiring government, as lacking in imagination as it is in political courage." From this perspective, the Pawley government was simply refusing to test the "limits of what was possible."[72]

Of course, Pawley disagreed with this assessment. His scars from the language debate were evidence enough of what it meant to test the limits of what was possible, even among core supporters of the NDP. On one point he could agree, however. The French-language crisis had sapped enormous time and energy from his government, and he needed to lead his troops away from the destructiveness of the language debate and focus on issues in which it would be possible to make tangible progress.[73]

Due to the large deficit, and the continued downgrading of the province's credit rating, Pawley had to ensure that any new initiatives were also low-cost. This meant addressing issues beyond the "jobs agenda" such as freedom of information legislation and the introduction of pay equity in the public sector. In addition, his government negotiated an agreement with Manitoba physicians to end the practice of extra-billing as stipulated under the newly passed Canada Health Act. However, the centrepiece of Pawley's comeback strategy was the most bread-and-butter issue of all, the construction of the Limestone hydroelectric project.[74]

Limestone's origins lay in the hydroelectric potential of Manitoba's huge expanse of northern waterways and the desire by successive governments to ensure the profitability of its Crown-owned utility, Manitoba Hydro. After successfully negotiating a sale of 500 megawatts of power annually from 1993 until 2005 to Northern States Power (NSP) of Minneapolis, and with further export deals in the making, Pawley decided to proceed earlier than planned with the construction of a major hydroelectric generating station. As the project would create hundreds of well-paid construction jobs in the building phase, the government introduced a hiring preference policy favouring Aboriginal and northern residents to ensure the project benefited both the region and the people most in need. Pawley also announced an Alberta-style "Heritage Fund" that would be financed from hydro exports to the United States, even though these revenues would not flow to the government for years.[75]

The announcement of the Limestone project, and all that went with it, helped to generate a new sense of optimism in Manitoba after years of recession and bickering over language issues. It also was the first major victory for a Premier desperately trying to get his party ready for an election. Pawley continued to read the tea leaves through the first weeks of January 1986. By early February, he knew the time was right to call an election. The polls showed Gary Filmon and the Conservatives ahead by a slight margin but Pawley felt his only shot at election success lay in taking immediate advantage of the new sense of optimism in the province.

If anything, the political changes that had emerged since Pawley's election as Premier went against the NDP. He could no longer count on the Conservatives polarizing voters.

Indeed, Filmon was doing precisely the opposite by appealing to moderates throughout the province, allowing splinter groups such as the Confederation of Regions (COR) and the Western Canada Concept to draw up the more radical right-wing vote. In addition, Pawley had to contend with a newly invigorated Liberal Party under the leadership of Sharon Carstairs. For the first time in 20 years, the Liberals planned to run candidates in every seat.[76]

With the crowding of the electoral middle, Pawley realized that he needed more than optimism to win the election and put his faith in a reliable perennial—Manitobans' frustration with the federal government. He chose as his campaign slogan "Stand Up for Manitoba," accused Ottawa of letting Manitoba down by lowering social program transfer payments through indexing Established Programmes Financing (EPF) and reducing equalization payments. Although the Mulroney government had been in office less than two years, the Prime Minister was losing popularity and Pawley knew he would strike a responsive chord with a "bash the feds" campaign.[77]

During the campaign, Pawley mobilized the troops, wringing every drop of energy possible from the party in order to snatch victory from the jaws of defeat. In the process, he saw that his earlier organization work was again paying dividends. He was also helped by the positive economic news which showed a net gain in population for the first time in years. As he loved repeating on doorsteps and through the media, Manitobans no longer needed to leave the province to pursue their careers: "our sons and daughters are coming home, to work."[78]

When the results came in on March 18, 1986, Pawley was delighted. The NDP had recovered from its near-fatal position of less than 20% support to an astounding 41.4% of the popular vote. Although this produced a razor thin majority of 30 seats against 27 opposition seats, this could only be considered a major-victory in the circumstances. Pawley's decision to avoid controversial policy issues after the language crisis while focusing on the economy in the months before the election had proven itself. Now, with a fourth victory since 1969, the NDP could lay claim to its status as a governing party.

Losing Momentum in the Second Term

Pawley set to work immediately, first forming a cabinet with four new ministers, including Gary Doer, a former public sector union leader and future Premier, and Elijah Harper, an Aboriginal member who would later make history in defeating the Meech Lake Accord in the Manitoba legislature. Unfortunately for Howard Pawley, however, any excitement he may have felt concerning his renewed mandate was short-lived. Rather than optimism, successive crises came to characterize his short second term. In some ways, the Pawley government seemed cursed, as its original policy agenda coming out of the election was buffeted by external events and allegations of scandal.

First off the mark was a concerted opposition and media attack on one of Pawley's most trusted ministers, Wilson Parasiuk. After some bad press for personally benefiting from a tax break that his party had criticized in the past, Parasiuk was then accused of a conflict of interest between his public responsibilities as a minister of the Crown and his private business affairs. The affair would generate so much media attention that Pawley was forced into ordering a judicial enquiry. Although Parasiuk was exonerated, the government was thrown off its game plan, and before it could get back on track, it faced yet another crisis thereby losing "momentum when it was most required."[79]

The next in line was the MTX affair. A subsidiary of Crown-held Manitoba Telephone Systems (MTS), MTX was established to market telecommunications equipment abroad, mainly in Saudi Arabia. When it was revealed that MTX had made large losses in the country, as well as bribed Saudi officials in the course of its business, the operations of the company became the centre of a scandal. Pawley ordered an independent managerial review by Coopers & Lybrand, which revealed the fact that MTS had been dangerously lax in its management of MTX. There was also evidence that the minister responsible, and cabinet, exercised virtually no control over MTS and MTX.[80] Admitting that improved accountability and cabinet oversight was required, the Pawley government enacted the Crown Corporation Accountability Act in 1987.[81] In reflecting on this episode many years later, Pawley wished that he had introduced this law much earlier and nipped some of his Crown corporation problems in the bud.[82]

Then along came the CF-18 debacle. In October 1986, Pawley along with all Manitobans were shocked when the federal government announced the decision to award a billion-dollar Canadian Forces maintenance contract for its fleet of CF-18 fighter jets to Montreal-based Canadair rather than to Winnipeg-based Bristol Aerospace. Despite Bristol's lower-price and technically superior bid, the Mulroney administration's concerns about Quebec and national unity won the day, and the federal government awarded the contract—and the employment that went with it—to a Quebec-based firm. Aside from the economic value of the contract, the decision acted like a body blow to Winnipeg's aspirations as a major aerospace centre in Canada. Manitobans were joined in their outrage by all western Canadians who felt that the Mulroney government had intervened in the decision in return for what was perceived as blatant political support in Quebec.[83]

Although he knew the CF-18 decision was likely irreversible, Pawley wanted Brian Mulroney to feel Manitoba's outrage. He led a delegation of business, labour and farm leaders as well as politicians including the mayor of Winnipeg to protest the decision in Ottawa. On the home front, everyone, including the Conservative opposition, united in attacking Ottawa over the decision. Seemingly unfazed, the federal government stuck to its guns, and in the process created a backlash that would come back to haunt Mulroney's government and generate ill feelings among western Canadians towards Ottawa and Quebec for years afterwards.

If these problems were not enough, difficulties with another Crown corporation arose in 1986, only to become a full-fledged political crisis the following year. Unfortunately for Pawley, the problems involved the one state-run corporation with which he had been intimately associated from its inception—the Manitoba Public Insurance Corporation (MPIC). In addition to rumours of lavish company parties and accusations of political interference in rate-setting, MPIC reported a loss of $37 million in reinsurance, a part of its business that had been losing money for a decade although this was not reported until the Annual Report of 1987. To address the loss, MPIC hiked up car insurance rates by 24%, triggering a political storm from which Pawley never recovered.[84]

While these problems were buffeting the government, Pawley did his best to implement social justice agenda such as protecting choice of sexual orientation in its human rights legislation (the first jurisdiction in Canada to do so), streamlining labour legislation to facilitate adjudicated resolutions in cases where collective bargaining negotiations were at an impasse, and creating a seniors' income protection plan. Major social policy changes included the expansion of day care and a children's rural dental care program. In addition, the Pawley government passed a new environment act that, for its time, was the most advanced and comprehensive in the country.[85] Finally, despite holding serious reservations about the Meech Lake Accord, Pawley put these aside to support the agreement in the hope that it would bring Quebec back into the constitutional family. Years later, Pawley concluded that he should have refused to sign the Meech Lake Accord unless it was expanded to include the recognition of Aboriginal rights.[86] With the exception of Meech Lake (which was the subject of an intense national debate and therefore of great media interest), the local media tended to focus on the government's domestic economic agenda, and in particular on its presumed missteps and problems associated with its public investments.

Resignation and the Quick Skid into Defeat

When the legislature convened in February 1988, the publicity surrounding the scandals had taken its toll. Popular sentiment was clearly against the government, which now faced a reinvigorated Progressive Conservative opposition that under Gary Filmon had replaced Lyon's propensity for polarization with a more moderate and conciliatory approach. The Pawley government still had 28 supporters, not including the Speaker, compared to 26 for the Conservatives and one for the Liberals. This was a fragile one-person majority, dependent on each NDP caucus member sticking with the government on every substantive vote in the legislature. Pawley knew he had to reach out to some of his more disaffected members in order to avoid defeat in the House. In an effort to placate one particularly unhappy caucus member, he asked Jim Walding to move the motion to accept the Throne Speech. Walding agreed, but for reasons which Pawley did not anticipate.

Jim Walding had been a backbencher for 16 years. While Walding felt he should have been appointed a minister, neither Schreyer nor Pawley thought he was cabinet material. In 1981, Pawley gave him the consolation position of Speaker but his management of the House was highly criticized by both government and opposition. Then, in 1986, just after Walding resigned from the Speaker's Chair, one of Pawley's own aides challenged Walding's renomination. Bitter and angry, Walding knew he had a perfect opportunity for revenge when Pawley requested that he move the motion on the Throne Speech. In a long and passionate speech, Walding turned on his own government, attacking its handling of MPIC and other public companies and investments, all designed to question Pawley's leadership. The opposition was delighted by the turn of events although Walding, to almost everyone's surprise, did not leave the government at that time. Instead, he waited two more weeks and then at the moment when he could cause maximum damage, joined the opposition in a non-confidence vote against the budget. Thus, on March 8, 1988, less than two years into its second term, the Pawley government fell at the hands of one of its own members.[87] Despite Walding's previous antics, Pawley was shocked. He knew Walding was unhappy but had been informed by one of Walding's confidants the same day that he was 98% sure that Walding would support the government.[88] As late as the day before the vote, Walding himself had told the media that he would vote in favour of the budget.[89] Describing his government's fall that day as the "worst day of [his] life," Pawley called a press conference to announce that a general election would be held.[90] Then, to everyone's great surprise, he announced his own resignation and his wish that a successor be chosen before the election.

Why did Howard Pawley step down? The decision did not seem to fit with the personality of the man. Having persevered for years in the political wilderness helping build the CCF/NDP, having piloted through controversial legislation such as public auto insurance, and after having steered his own government through the treacherous shoals of the language crisis to a second term of government, he simply walked away from the job. The quiet but tough-as-nails political boxer looked like he was ending his career by "backing away from a fight."[91]

Pawley resigned because of his desire to give his party what he thought would be the only chance at survival in the next election. His own popularity had taken a pounding after the automobile insurance rate hike, and he concluded that he was now a liability in terms of the party's re-election. As the lightning rod, he felt he could divert at least some of the public's anger from a new leader. He also had in his mind the Schreyer nomination campaign in 1969 and how this had reinvigorated the party, gambling that the NDP could repeat this earlier success. Even if an election victory was unlikely, he felt his departure would at least allow his party to obtain enough seats in the house to be an effective opposition, and therefore a real threat in any subsequent election.[92]

Before a shocked and disappointed caucus, Pawley explained how the public's anger over the auto insurance rate hike had become fixed on himself, and that the NDP could take advantage of the situation by selecting a new leader as quickly as possible.[93] At the end of March, Gary Doer was selected as leader of the party and had less than four weeks to organize and lead a campaign against the Conservatives and Liberals. But unlike the Schreyer experience of picking a new leader in the midst of a campaign, the publicity surrounding Doer's selection was not enough to turn around the prevailing negative perception of the government—there had been too many mishaps and just not enough progress shown in the second term of the government's life. The election results on April 27, 1988, were categorical. Having lost the confidence of a majority of Manitobans, the party dropped down to 12 seats, garnering only 23% of the popular vote. Filmon's Progressive Conservatives came out on top with 25 seats and 38% of the vote. But the real surprise was Carstairs' Liberals who, capitalizing on some voters' antipathy to the NDP, had wooed back the moderate middle with 35% of the vote, gaining 20 seats and official opposition status.

Life after Premiership

When Howard Pawley stepped down as party leader, he had no intention of leaving electoral politics permanently. His first love was federal politics. As a young man, he had yearned to be an MP in Ottawa. If Ed Schreyer had not asked him to step into the provincial contest of 1969, he would have continued to work on the federal level. In November 1988, just eight months after he resigned as Premier, he entered politics one last time as the federal NDP candidate for Selkirk. But it was too soon after the provincial election. The residual anger over his government's auto insurance rate hike dogged him through the race, and the Liberal candidate managed to split the anti-Conservative vote, preventing Pawley from defeating the incumbent Conservative member.[94]

After the election, Pawley attempted a return to law practise as an associate partner with Baker, Zivot & Co. in Winnipeg. Not surprisingly, the work seemed mundane compared to the job of Premier. Nor did it carry the excitement he had experienced while building a firm with his wife Adele. He quickly abandoned law in favour of an academic career. In 1990, he was appointed an associate professor of Political Science at the University of Windsor and the Pawley family moved from Manitoba to Ontario. Somewhat to his surprise, he discovered that he enjoyed teaching students at least as much as he had ever enjoyed politics.[95] In 1993, he was named the Paul Martin Professor in Political Science and Law at the University of Windsor. He also took temporary leaves of absence to be a visiting professor at the University of Waterloo and the University of Washington.

Pawley also became heavily involved in community organizations as well as a leading figure in national non-profit organizations such as the Canadian Liver Foundation, the Council for Canadian Unity, the Windsor Art Gallery and the Douglas-Coldwell Foundation. He also served as vice-president of the Canadian Civil Liberties Association for a term.[96] In 2002, he became the vice-chair of the Canadian Broadcast Standards Council and, in 2003, the president of the Harry Crowe Foundation for the Canadian Association of University Teachers. In 2006, he became a member of the newly established Essex-St. Clair Local Health Integrated Network board of directors.[97]

Assessment and Conclusion

When Howard Pawley assumed government in 1981, political scientist Allen Mills said that while the new Premier was not charismatic and preferred consensus to confrontation, he nevertheless understood "astutely what makes for success in a social democracy."[98] Pawley's achievements as Premier, particularly those realized in his first term, bore out this prescient judgment. His policy successes, like the man himself, were sober solutions devoid of hype and flash—solid efforts at progressive reform intended to build in part on the earlier gains made in the Schreyer administration.

Howard Pawley offered Manitobans an appealing alternative to the polarizing, neoconservative politics offered by Sterling Lyon. Pawley's policy achievements were in many ways remarkable given that they were achieved during a period marked by stagflation, a searing debate over language and identity, and the growing strength of the neoconservative agenda. Perhaps his most important legacy, however, was his rebuilding the NDP into a formidable government party, a capable critic while preparing for government in opposition, and a competent government while in power. This party organization, based on grassroots support, was able to survive the major defeat of 1988, robust enough to regain official opposition status and permanent enough to regain government a little over a decade later. In many respects, the NDP's endurance as an effective party of government can be traced back to Pawley's momentous organizational efforts from 1979 until 1981.

Notes

The author would like to thank Devon Anderson for her research assistance, Scott MacNeil for his research assistance as well as critical review of an earlier draft, and Paul Thomas for his careful review of a later draft. He is indebted to Barry Ferguson and Robert Wardhaugh for their very useful editorial suggestions and to Howard Pawley for agreeing to an extensive interview. The author takes full responsibility for any remaining errors or omissions.

1. Howard Pawley presentation, DVD recording of Premiers' Symposium (unedited), University of Manitoba, November 13, 1999 (hereafter referred to as Pawley presentation).
2. *Winnipeg Free Press* (November 30, 1981): 25.
3. Howard Pawley, "Governing Manitoba: Reflections of a Premier," in Maureen Mancuso, Richard G. Price and Ronald Wagenburg (eds.), *Leaders and Leadership in Canada* (Toronto: Oxford University Press, 1994), 118. *Toronto Star* (March 10, 1988): A20.
4. Interview of Howard Pawley by author (hereafter referred to as Pawley interview), Winnipeg, August 24, 2006.
5. Entry for Howard Russell Pawley in *Canadian Who's Who* (Toronto: University of Toronto Press, 2001), 1009.
6. Pawley, "Governing Manitoba," 118.
7. Nelson Wiseman, "The Character and Strategy of the Manitoba CCF, 1943 to 1959," *Prairie Forum* 4, no. 1 (1979): 27–34.
8. *Winnipeg Free Press* (January 15, 1979): 4. Pawley, "Governing Manitoba," 118. Pawley interview.
9. Gad Horowitz, *Canadian Labour in Politics* (Toronto: University of Toronto Press, 1968), 219.
10. Nelson Wiseman, *Social Democracy in Manitoba: A History of the CCF–NDP* (Winnipeg: University of Manitoba Press, 1983), 89.
11. Wiseman, *Social Democracy in Manitoba*, 91, 97–101, 152. James A. McAllister, *The Government of Edward Schreyer: Democratic Socialism in Manitoba* (Montreal: McGill-Queen's University Press, 1984), 104.
12. Wiseman, *Social Democracy in Manitoba*, 97.
13. Horowitz, *Canadian Labour in Politics*, 219. Pawley interview.
14. Peter Carlyle-Gordge, "The Quiet, Competent Way to the Top," 25. Pawley interview.
15. Pawley interview.

16. *Toronto Star* (March 10, 1988): A20.

17. Pawley presentation, November 13, 1999.

18. Pawley interview.

19. *Toronto Star* (March 10, 1988): A20.

20. Russell Doern quoted in Peter Carlyle-Gordge, "The Quiet, Competent Way to the Top," *Maclean's* (November 30, 1981): 25. Also see Russell Doern, *Wednesdays are Cabinet Days* (Winnipeg: Queenston House, 1981).

21. "Interview: Harry Enns and Len Evans: Two Longtime Manitoba MLAs," *Canadian Parliamentary Review* 19, no. 2 (1996). Pawley interview.

22. Howard Pawley and C. Lloyd Brown-John, "Transitions: The New Democrats in Manitoba," in Donald J. Savoie (ed.), *Taking Power: Managing Government Transitions* (Ottawa: Institute of Public Administration of Canada and Canadian Centre for Management Development, 1993), 178.

23. Pawley, "Governing Manitoba," 119.

24. Interview, Michael Decter, January 4, 2005.

25. Interview with Edward R. Schreyer by Gregory P. Marchildon, Winnipeg, August 24, 2006.

26. Pawley interview.

27. Ibid.

28. *Winnipeg Free Press* (January 15, 1979): 1.

29. Sidney Green, *Rise and Fall of a Political Animal: A Memoir* (Winnipeg: Great Plains Publications, 2003), 159–60. Pawley, "Governing Manitoba," 119.

30. *Winnipeg Free Press* (January 15, 1979): 1.

31. Rand Dyck, *Provincial Politics in Canada: Towards the Turn of the Century* (Scarborough: Prentice Hall Canada, 1996), 384.

32. Pawley interview.

33. Douglas as quoted by Pawley in "Governing Manitoba," 120.

34. Pawley interview. As Pawley himself explained in the interview, he was seen more in the middle of the party spectrum at that point, although he had previously been positioned more in the left wing of the party.

35. Ibid.

36. Peter Carlyle-Gordge, "The Quiet, Competent Way to the Top," 25.

37. Paul Thomas quoted in Thomas Hopkins, "Upset in Manitoba," *Maclean's* (November 30, 1981): 24.

38. Harold Chorney and Phillip Hansen, "Neo-Conservatism, Social Democracy and 'Province-Building': The Experience of Manitoba," *Canadian Review of Sociology and Anthropology* 22, no. 1 (1985): 1–29.

40. David K. Stewart and Jared Wesley, "Sterling Lyon," in this volume..

42. Pawley interview. Green, *Rise and Fall of a Political Animal.*

43. Pawley interview.

44. *Canadian Annual Review of Politics and Public Affairs 1981*, 396–401. Interview, Michael Decter.

45. *Canadian Annual Review of Politics and Public Affairs 1982*, 256–60.

46. *Canadian Annual Review of Politics and Public Affairs 1981*, 396–98, 402–03. *Canadian Annual Review of Politics and Public Affairs 1982*, 257.

47. Green's new Progressive Party only managed to get 1.8% of the popular vote. In Green's own words, his party had been "soundly thrashed" by Pawley's NDP machine. Green, *Rise and Fall of a Political Animal*, 177.

48. Chorny and Hansen, "Neo-Conservatism, Social Democracy and 'Province-Building,'" 15.

49. Thomas Hopkins, "Upset in Manitoba," *Maclean's*, November 30, 1981, 22.

50. See Wiseman, *Social Democracy in Manitoba*, 151.

51. *Canadian Annual Review of Politics and Public Affairs 1981*, 404. *Canadian Annual Review of Politics and Public Affairs 1982*, 283.

52. Pawley, "Governing Manitoba," 122–24.

53. Ibid., 130–31.

54. Interview, Michael Decter.

55. This was according to Len Evans. See "Interview: Harry Enns and Len Evans, Two Longtime Manitoba MLAs."

56. Pawley and Brown-John, "Transitions," 169. See chapter 9 (the Pawley years) in Christopher Dunn, *The Institutionalized Cabinet: Governing the Western Provinces* (Montreal and Kingston: McGill-Queen's University Press, 1995).

57. *Canadian Annual Review of Politics and Public Affairs 1982*, 260–63.

58. Pawley interview, August 24, 2006.

59. On Lloyd Axworthy's powerful role, see Herman Bakvis, *Regional Ministers: Power and Influence in the Canadian Cabinet* (Toronto: University of Toronto Press, 1991).

58. *Canadian Annual Review of Politics and Public Affairs 1983*, 260–63.

59. Frances Russell, *The Canadian Crucible: Manitoba's Role in Canada's Great Divide* (Winnipeg: Heartland Associates, 2003).

60. On the historical background and the legal details, see Raymond Hébert, *Manitoba's French-language Crisis: A Cautionary Tale* (Montreal and Kingston: McGill-Queen's University Press, 2004), Russell, *The Canadian Crucible*, as well as the special issue of the *Manitoba Law Journal* 15, no. 3 (1986) devoted to the crisis.

61. Andrew Nikiforuk, "Manitoba's Fight over French," *Maclean's* (October 3, 1983): 14–15.

62. Interview, Michael Decter.

63. Russell Doern, *The Battle over Bilingualism: The Manitoba Language Question* (Winnipeg: Cambridge Publishers, 1985). Andrew Nikoforuk, "Manitoba's Fight over French," 14.

64. Pawley interview, August 24, 2006.

65. *Canadian Annual Review of Politics and Public Affairs 1984*, 87–88.

66. Pawley interview, August 24, 2006.

67. *Canadian Annual Review of Politics and Public Affairs 1984*, 82–85.

68. Interview, Michael Decter.

69. Pawley statement quoted in *Montreal Gazette* (November 5, 1985): B1.

70. Dyck, *Provincial Politics in Canada*, 415. Pawley interview.

71. Pawley, "Governing Manitoba," 125.

72. *Canadian Dimension* (July/August 1985): 2.

73. Pawley interview.

74. *Canadian Annual Review of Politics and Public Affairs 1985*, 332–35.

75. Ibid., 74, 332–35.

76. *Canadian Annual Review of Politics and Public Affairs 1986*, 286.

77. Ibid., 287.

78. Pawley quoted in the *Ottawa Citizen* (March 20, 1986): A9.

79. Pawley and Brown-John, "Transitions," 173.

80. *Canadian Annual Review of Politics and Public Affairs 1986*, 290–91.

81. Pawley interview.

82. Pawley presentation, November 13, 1999.

83. Tom Flanagan, "From Riel to Reform (and a Little Beyond): Politics in Western Canada," *American Review of Canadian Studies* 31, no. 4 (2001): 623–38. *Canadian Annual Review of Politics and Public Affairs 1986*, 293–94.

84. *Canadian Annual Review of Politics and Public Affairs 1987*, 308–09.

85. Pawley interview. Pawley presentation.

86. Pawley presentation.

87. Beverly Bosiak, "By One Vote: The Defeat of the Manitoba Government," *Canadian Parliamentary Review* 12, no. 1 (1989). See also Ian Stewart, *Just One Vote: From Jim Walding's Nomination to Constitutional Defeat* (Winnipeg: University of Manitoba Press, 2009).

88. Pawley interview.

89. Bosiak, "By One Vote."

90. Pawley presentation.

91. *Toronto Star* (March 10, 1988): A20.

92. Pawley interview.

93. Ibid.

94. Ibid.

95. Ibid.

96. *Canadian Who's Who 2001* (Toronto: University of Toronto Press, 2001), 1009.

97. Pawley interview, and personal curriculum vitae.

98. Allen Mills quoted in Peter Carlyle-Gordge, "The Quiet, Competent Way to the Top," 25.

Gary Filmon

1988–1999

BARRY FERGUSON

Gary Albert Filmon, 1988–1999

Gary Filmon's premiership was remarkable for rethinking longstanding Manitoba public policy. As a party leader, he pulled the Manitoba Progressive Conservative party, whose rural leaders were veering into neo-conservatism, and whose urban leaders had drifted into reactionism, into the liberal democratic centre through careful organization and patient effort. Once he attained power, he controlled the governmental apparatus and refashioned major economic and social institutions in significant ways, in contrast to Manitoba's reputation for public policy conservatism. He attacked the fiscal crisis that affected Canadian governments sooner than most provinces. He responded to the era of free trade and national deregulation in ways that enhanced the economy and sustained rather than gutted social and other public services. Finally, the governments he led reversed the slow decline that the old "gateway to the west" had experienced from the 1940s to the 1980s.

Education and First Careers

Gary Filmon was born in Winnipeg on August 24, 1942. He grew up in the city's working-class and multicultural North End. His father worked in the garment industry and his mother in the Eaton's catalogue office. No inheritance of status or wealth would make his career. He attended local public schools and graduated in 1960 from the brand-new Sisler High School. He was an outstanding student and athlete, a leader of his high school basketball team that won the Winnipeg championship in 1960.[1] Filmon proceeded to the University of Manitoba just as university education in Canada was opening to talented young people of all social classes. While engineers did not have reputations in the 1950s and 1960s as bookworms, they did work hard and had excellent professional prospects. He graduated in 1964 with a Bachelor of Science in Engineering, specializing in civil engineering.

In 1967, Filmon completed a Master's degree in Civil Engineering, a rare academic achievement. His graduate work involved writing a thesis entitled "An Investigation of the Diversion of Northern Manitoba Waters into Lake Winnipeg." It was part of a set of investigations conducted by the University of Manitoba Faculty of Engineering in collaboration with the federal department of Energy, Mines and Resources into hydro development and water diversion. He had entered the world of consulting engineering in 1964, working for a Saskatchewan-Manitoba company, Underwood & McLellan and Associates. He did well and was appointed Brandon-area manager in 1967 after three years working on hydraulics in the Winnipeg area.[2]

Earlier, in November 1963, Gary Filmon married a classmate, Janice Wainwright, in Westworth United Church. Janice Filmon also graduated in 1964 from the University of Manitoba, where she earned a BSc in Home Economics. A social worker for a time and later a community activist, Mrs. Filmon was throughout her husband's career a vigorous campaigner and, by Filmon's consistent testimony, a crucial advisor.[3] Janice and Gary Filmon had four children.

Civic Business and Politics

In 1969, Gary Filmon changed careers. He became executive director of two commercial colleges, Success Commercial College and Angus School of Commerce, owned by his father-in-law, H.C. Wainwright, a former Hudson's Bay Company manager. The two institutions trained young adults for secretarial, bookkeeping and other administrative duties, filling an educational void that for decades the public sector did not serve. Filmon was active in the Winnipeg community. He became president of the University of Manitoba Alumni Association in June 1975 and in October won a seat on Winnipeg City Council.[4] Filmon ran against five other candidates on the south-side Queenston Ward under the banner of the Independent Citizens' Election Committee, a so-called free enterprise alignment of Liberals and Conservatives who emphasized urban development and neighbourhood preservation. It dominated the unwieldy city council of 50 representatives against a handful of New Democratic Party (NDP) and other factions. He was an effective, visible member of Council, quickly getting chosen as a policy chair, developing the city's six-day garbage cycle, and emerging as a possible mayoralty candidate.

The Move to Provincial Politics

In 1979, Filmon received the Progressive Conservative (PC) party nomination in the River Heights riding and won handily in the ensuing by-election. It was one of three that constituted a test of Premier Lyon's administration. The three by-elections replicated the split affinities of Winnipeg, electing Liberal June Westbury, New Democrat Vic Schroeder, and new Conservative, Gary Filmon. He took over from Sidney Spivak, a former Tory leader and a cabinet minister in the Lyon government who resigned to take a run at federal politics. Filmon remained on the backbenches for two years. He was elevated to the cabinet in January 1981 when Lyon shook up the cabinet. For 10 months, Filmon served as minister of Consumer and Corporate Affairs and Minister of the Environment with responsibilities for insurance regulation and housing.[5]

The Lyon government was soundly defeated in the November 1981 election by a resurgent NDP, led by Howard Pawley. The NDP had fed successfully on the collapse of the provincial Liberals, who were shut out of the Legislature. Politics in Manitoba seemed to be polarizing for the first time in decades.[6]

The Pawley government decided that it must respond to a series of court challenges and federal pressure over the status of the French language in Manitoba. In 1979, the Supreme Court of Canada repudiated Manitoba's 1890 annulment of official bilingualism. Manitoba had to face this decision and growing francophone community pressures for minority educational and government services in line with the original Manitoba Act and the new Charter of Rights and Freedoms. The cabinet decided that the best move was to undertake a constitutional amendment of the Manitoba Act to restore French-language rights and establish a base for the delivery of government services to the francophone community.[7]

At the outset, the Pawley government assumed that its approach was uncontroversial. Both the strategy of constitutional amendment and the tactics of minimal public consultation soon revealed that the question was politically explosive. When the government's proposals were announced in May 1983, they sparked a ferocious reaction from Lyon's PCs. The NDP government was either unwilling or unable to clarify the details behind the constitutional amendment and its consultations with francophone organizations, notably the *Société francomanitobaine* (SFM). The Tories were relentless in their use of legislative procedures to block the initiative. Public opinion was inflamed and both political partisans and interest groups were happy to throw matches onto the pyre of opinion. In the spring of 1983, the SFM offices were firebombed. In the fall of 1983, 22 municipalities, including the City of Winnipeg, had agreed to hold a "plebiscite" on the constitutional amendment. In these plebiscites, three-quarters of voters opposed the proposals.[8]

Party Leadership and Opposition Leader

In the midst of the political crisis he helped to create, Sterling Lyon announced that he would vacate the PC leadership. A convention was called for December 1983 where three younger MLAs ended up running. All were described as "low-key" or "bland" by the media, but their approaches to public issues were new for Manitoba. The candidates were Gary Filmon, Brian Ransom, and Clayton Manness. Ransom, age 43, and Manness, 36, were part of a new wave of neo-conservative rural Tories who were well educated, successful, and iconoclastic. In contrast, 41-year-old Filmon was a PC rarity with his urban perspective and moderate policies. Attesting to his team's organizational skills, Filmon tweaked Ransom for the leadership on the second ballot with Manness a distant third. Filmon was for some time surrounded by rural sceptics within his caucus but his organization and cumulative electoral success dispersed the dissidents.[9]

Filmon's immediate objectives included reshaping the PC party and calming an aggressive caucus in a polarized legislature. Revitalizing the party was the easy part. Bringing down the heat of public debate was a different matter.

The NDP changed tactics but not goals in the French-language dispute in the fall of 1983 by bringing in a conciliatory Andy Anstett, in place of the confrontational Roland Penner to pilot the legislation. Anstett engaged in much-needed legislative committee work and consultations with franco-manitoban groups, local governments and labour unions. Filmon and his ablest ally, the veteran Bud Sherman, were willing to break the impasse through negotiations with Pawley and Anstett. Despite Filmon's milder tone, caucus took its cue from Lyon and fought the amendment using every legislative tactic at its disposal.

The Opposition sapped the legislature of its energy throughout January and February 1984. They engaged in an extraordinary 12-day walkout starting in mid-February. During the extended boycott, the Speaker, Jim Walding, and party leaders on both sides, tried to negotiate an end to the walkout. Walding rejected inordinate pressure from the Premier to call for a vote despite Walding's ruling that it would have been against the rules of Parliament. But nothing worked. Facing the prospect of running out of "supply," and exasperated by the sheer vituperation of the entire debate, the government panicked and announced that the House would be prorogued as of February 27.[10]

A result of prorogation was that the quest for linguistic justice reverted to the Supreme Court of Canada for adjudication. In June 1985, the Court announced its decision on a "reference" from Manitoba. The Court made three crucial points. Firstly, the failure of the Manitoba legislature since 1890 to conduct business, print its proceedings, and proclaim laws in both English and French meant that its enactments and decisions were, in effect, "invalid and of no force or effect." Secondly, the Court held that actual invalidity "would create a legal vacuum with consequent legal chaos in the Province of Manitoba." Manitoba required a reasonable period of time to comply with the constitutional requirements. Finally, the Court ordered the province to comply with its bilingual constitution, including translation of all previous legislation, regulations, and delegated legislation starting in 1890.[11] The Supreme Court's decision effectively ended the crisis. It restored the linguistic rights of francophones in Manitoba but also made clear that the process of implementing French-language rights would not plunge the province into legal chaos or fiscal crisis.

Gary Filmon interpreted the Supreme Court's ruling as a refutation of the NDP's proposals including federal political intervention by his PC counterpart, Brian Mulroney. "That's what people want," Filmon told the *Globe and Mail* in March 1984. The decision "has only confirmed what we have known since 1979," that "the laws of Manitoba must be printed and published in both English and French." He concluded that the "wounds will heal but the NDP Administration must be responsible for opening them." The NDP was weakened and bitter, while the PCs were clearly divided between their federal and provincial wings and Filmon and Mulroney never reconciled.[12]

The 1986 Election Disappointment

Over the next two years, both parties avoided the language issue. The NDP recovered politically while the PCs stalled. When the election was called for March 18, 1986, Filmon's campaign was eased by the retirements of two icons of the Lyon regime, Sterling Lyon himself and Brian Ransom, strengthened by borrowing the Ontario Tory tactician John Laschinger, and smoothed over by a new centrist policy package. Filmon continued to argue that the PCs were not a right-wing party although he denied being a Red Tory. "We huddle around the middle of the political spectrum," he stated. During the campaign, Filmon avoided what he described as the promise-a-day approach of Pawley and concentrated on two major policy statements. The first was a "program for people." This lengthy social program included increases to health and social services of 6.5% in the next fiscal year, 2.5% more than the Pawley government had proposed. The second was a five-part economic development strategy, emphasizing assistance to small business, agriculture and resource industries. This program was based on the PC plan to save Manitoba from "drowning in a sea of government red tape, paperwork and regulations" that stymied growth.[13]

Party leaders avoided references to the French-language dispute, although Filmon informed his candidates that the party position was to abide by the 1985 Supreme Court reference. He admitted that it was a "no-win" issue for all parties but combatively added that he was prepared to declare PC policy whereas Pawley avoided it. Neither Filmon nor Pawley shone on the campaign trail, whereas new Liberal leader Sharon Carstairs flourished.[14]

The March 18, 1986 election returned Pawley and the NDP to power with 30 seats and 41% of the popular vote. The result produced a narrow legislative majority of 3. Filmon led his party to a stronger position with 26 seats, a gain of 3, from 40% of the popular vote. Ominously, new Liberal leader Sharon Carstairs was elected and the party doubled its popular vote to 14%, almost all in the crucial Winnipeg area. Voter turnout was "normal" at 69%.[15] Filmon had re-positioned the PCs as a more competitive party than in 1981. He had to worry that a restive rural party base would reject his moderate stance and disappointing finish when he faced the inevitable leadership review. Sterling Lyon made sure there was discontent by claiming that Filmon had not been aggressive enough during the campaign. Filmon pointed out that only once in Manitoba history had a government not been given a second term. He did not have to add that Sterling Lyon had led that government.[16]

The re-elected Pawley government looked forward to an easier second term, but it faced difficult conditions that provided fodder for Filmon. Manitoba's economy began to experience the downturn that had hit the other western provinces and the provincial deficit began to soar just as federal fiscal transfers from the Mulroney government were being trimmed. The province's inability to deal with Ottawa was underlined in the fall of 1986 when the Mulroney cabinet overturned the tendering process in the award of a large defence industry contract that should have gone to Winnipeg's Bristol Aerospace. Manitoba's own "problem Crowns" (Winnipeg bus-maker, Flyer Industries, Brandon agricultural firm, McKenzie Seeds, and The Pas forest products complex, Manfor Industries) which had bedeviled a succession of governments for two decades, also became more vulnerable and costly. Finally, two successful provincial government enterprises exhibited signs of internal mismanagement and governmental laxity. The first, Manitoba Public Insurance Corporation, or Autopac, was flourishing but nonetheless raised its rates by over 20% in 1985. This action caused a furor. The second, Manitoba Telephone System, had created an overseas subsidiary, MTX, which had lost $25 million in a venture that indicated a lack of business acumen. In both cases, the PCs were able to attack the government for failures of oversight and even managerial competency, very telling matters in Manitoba.[17]

By February 1988, the Pawley government was vulnerable. One veteran MLA, Larry Desjardins, had previously decided to quit politics and he resigned on schedule. Another veteran, Jim Walding, held both personal and policy grievances against Pawley. He then signaled that he was opposed to the large deficit budget that Finance minister Vic Schroeder brought down. When the PCs brought a motion of non-confidence, they gained Walding's vote (and that of Liberal Sharon Carstairs). The government was defeated.[18]

Pawley resigned the NDP leadership and did not contest the election. In the aftermath, the NDP contemplated bleak prospects. Party insiders spoke darkly of Tory tampering or even bribery to explain the departure of Desjardins and the defection of Walding.[19] (No proof of undue or illegal actions has ever been offered.) The party began the election campaign by choosing a new leader from a group of five, including party veteran Harry Harapiak from The Pas and party newcomer Gary Doer from Winnipeg. Doer prevailed over Harapiak after three ballots.

Minority Government 1988

Gary Filmon was expected to win or else. He had received a narrow endorsement at the PC party's 1987 convention. He was not seen as sufficiently conservative for some rural MLAs and activists. But he presided over a solid organization and won the review. By 1988, the party was strong, with far higher membership and election contributions than the usually well-supported and well-funded NDP. Throughout his leadership, the PC party had buoyant membership, contributors and finances.[20]

For Filmon, the campaign focused on avoiding mistakes. Described as "courteous and mild-mannered," Filmon restated his claims of 1986 that the Progressive Conservatives were "socially progressive" but "fiscally conservative." He made no major policy pronouncements and tried to curtail the efforts of the Liberals and NDP to portray his party as reactionary and his leadership as uncertain. The revitalized Liberals under Sharon Carstairs ran a whirlwind campaign centred on Winnipeg while the demoralized NDP found that Gary Doer was a stabilizing force. It was relatively easy to portray the NDP as having run a "reign of error" but it was hard to puncture the bubble lifting the Liberals in Winnipeg.[21]

In the end, Filmon's PCs held all but one of their 1986 seats, retaining 25 from 38% of the popular vote. Carstairs's Liberals surged to 20 seats and 35% of the vote while Doer's NDP, recovering from disastrous early indicators, won 12 seats with 24% of the vote. Voter turnout was the heaviest in some time at 74% of electors.[22]

Gary Filmon became Premier with a tenuous minority government. A sign of the limited PC mandate was that Filmon himself came within 125 votes of being defeated in the Winnipeg riding of Tuxedo. A warning of struggles to come was the election night proclamation by Liberal leader Sharon Carstairs that "Meech Lake is dead."[23]

Filmon set to work crafting a cabinet and a legislative agenda that would allow the minority government to survive. A number of moderate urban PCs were defeated by the upstart Liberals while more radical rural members were re-elected. Filmon pegged the fiscal conservatives Clayton Manness as minister of Finance and Don Orchard as minister of Health. A court reporter, James McCrae from Brandon, was appointed Attorney-General while teacher-farmer Len Derkach from rural Roblin-Russell, was appointed minister of Education. The PCs elected three female MLAs in 1988, part of a female contingent of nine, 14% of the legislature. All three were appointed to cabinet, Charlotte Oleson as minister of Community Services, Gerrie Hammond, partisan but committed to gender rights, as minister of Labour and Bonnie Mitchelson as minister of Culture. (Among other things, Hammond undertook the task of educating the Tory caucus in the ways of gender equality during her time in office.) Finally, for the crucial position of Speaker, Filmon tabbed a rural MLA, Denis Rocan. A bilingual farmer-businessman, Rocan faced the challenge of being firm and fair during a minority legislature in the aftermath of a decade in which the Speaker's autonomy had been challenged.

Budgetary Priorities

The new government began with a summer session. The elegant stone Manitoba Legislative Building can become unbearably hot in summer and no government dares to splurge on air-conditioning, so work is done quickly. Filmon set out the government's main goals through the first Throne Speech. Lieutenant-Governor George Johnson announced that "Manitobans are concerned that economic growth in recent years has relied upon an unhealthy and unsustainable level of public sector spending which has left a legacy of high debt and taxes and a growing burden of debt service costs." The Speech set out the nub of the analysis for successive Filmon governments: "This legacy threatens our ability to fund the public programs Manitobans want and deserve. It also threatens the investment and job creation potential of our economy...."[24]

In the budget brought down two weeks later, Clayton Manness warned that the province was at a crossroads, "facing decisions that seriously affect our future prosperity and quality of life." This vulnerability had occurred because Manitoba's economic expansion "has relied upon an unsustainable level of public sector spending which has left a legacy of high debt, high taxes, and a growing burden of debt-service costs." Manness warned that "this legacy threatens the public programs Manitobans want and Manitobans deserve."[25]

Manness laid out a program that carried Filmon governments forward for a decade. The large debt created a growing deficit that was increasingly costly to service (taking well over 10% of budgetary spending). It crowded out government spending on social services, and dragged down the prospects of future economic expansion. Manitoba's new government was notable not for sounding a more conservative message, but for its essentially centrist liberal commitments to reduce the deficit reduction and preserve social programs. Doer's NDP group did not rally to a Liberal motion of non-confidence in the budget in 1988. Gary Filmon was given the opportunity to govern.

Filmon strongly supported the Free Trade Agreement (FTA) of 1988. He dismissed Doer's worry that the FTA would lead to compulsory water sales to the United States. He bristled at Carstairs's concern that Canadian institutions ranging from medicare to the Wheat Board would be undermined. When Carstairs suggested Filmon was "ostrich-like," he responded that she was "Chicken-Little-like."[26]

As early as 1989, Filmon declared that "Manitoba's Government is back under control" based on tight management and spending controls. The second Budget Address asserted that "both Opposition parties tried to scare Manitobans into believing that we would cut the services on which they depend... This has not happened. This will not happen. Instead, we have maintained and strengthened social programs."[27] Manness also announced the creation of a "Fiscal Stabilization Fund" with $200 million, which would enable government to deal with such fiscal problems as declining federal contributions to social services. The Filmon governments took pride in the Stabilization Fund over the ensuing years, both adding to it and using it to cover subsequent cuts from Ottawa. No one pointed out that it owed its origins to an initiative of Pawley's last Finance minister, Eugene Kostyra, who had begun a fund in 1988. Again, the NDP supported the budget while the Liberals did not.

The Filmon government quickly moved on the "problem Crowns." Pawley had sold bus-maker Flyer Industries to a Dutch company that turned New Flyer into an international leader. Filmon's team had to hustle to sell pulp and lumber manufacturer Manfor, and arranged a successful transfer to Montreal-based RePap Enterprises Inc. that had some success in turning around the money-losing company despite turmoil in the forest industry. The government had more trouble with McKenzie Seeds, but disposed of it in the mid-1990s. In addition, the government sold off three small enterprises—ManOil, Manitoba Data Services, and the Queen's Printer. These sales garnered some income, reduced debt exposure and signified a new approach to the business of government.[28]

The Manitoba economy felt the effects of a slow-down that had already hit the other western provinces. The early 1990s witnessed a recession in which the Manitoba economy shrank for two years running. Population growth stalled throughout the late 1980s and the 1990s. Unemployment began to rise from the 7–8% level in the late 1980s to between 8% and 10% in the early to mid-1990s before beginning a slide downward to 5% by the end of the decade. Housing construction and prices, particularly in the key Winnipeg market, abruptly slowed down after 1987–88 and remained flat throughout the following decade. Interest rates, which affected everything from public finance to consumer spending, began a steady rise. Rates moved above 11% by 1988 and rose to the 14% range by the early 1990s before slowly coming down to the 7–8% level by the end of the decade. A similar dreary pattern pertained to agriculture and mining in the late 1980s and early 1990s, but a strong recovery began by the mid-1990s.[29]

In this atmosphere of decline, provincial fiscal prospects were parlous across the Prairies. In Saskatchewan, the election of an NDP regime led by Roy Romanow in 1991 led to an aggressive attack on a debt and deficit situation that was arguably more severe than Manitoba's. In Alberta, working from a vastly different fiscal and economic base, a crisis of major debt and ballooning deficits was dealt with internally by the ruling PCs by replacing moderate Don Getty with the more ruthless Ralph Klein in 1993. Saskatchewan and Alberta gained more national attention for their campaigns to end deficit spending and curtail provincial debt. Under Filmon, Manitoba had taken on these tasks by the end of the 1980s and did so in a more nuanced fashion.[30]

Manitoba and the Defeat of the Meech Lake Accord

The issue that galvanized Filmon's government was the Meech Lake Accord, a controversial constitutional reform package. Based on an initiative of Prime Minister Mulroney to gain Quebec's signature to the 1982 Constitution, the country's First Ministers agreed on the Accord in the spring of 1987. Meech Lake expressed the minimum demands for adherence expressed by Quebec Premier Robert Bourassa, whose federalist Liberals had replaced the sovereignist Parti Québécois in December 1985.[31] Meech Lake was not radical, reflecting a classical or mildly decentralist version of federalism rather than a centralist or unitary approach to government. Indeed, the swift agreement of the eleven First Ministers suggested that the Accord would become law within three years and that Quebec, the option of separatism irrelevant, would truly join the newly reoriented Canada.

The declaration of Quebec as a "distinct society" became the key point of contention. First, it raised the suspicions of various provincial Liberal parties, who saw it as a threat to everything from Quebec's treatment of minorities to the dream of Senate reform. Second, it stimulated a fierce critique from former Prime Minister Pierre Trudeau, who interpreted it as a sign of ethnic nationalism and a threat to the Charter of Rights. The unlikely synergy of Trudeau, on one hand, and provincial party leaders on the other, fed a growing opposition that led three provinces—New Brunswick, Newfoundland and Manitoba—to balk at the agreement. Howard Pawley had not brought Meech to the Manitoba legislature prior to his defeat.

Filmon's government initially accepted Meech, despite Carstairs's opposition. Filmon knew that Doer's NDP, though uneasy about it, would go along. On December 16, 1988, the Premier introduced the Meech Lake proposals for legislative approval. To emphasize a less partisan style and to remind NDP members of their support, Filmon quoted Howard Pawley ("a renewed spirit of good will and reconciliation") and cited federal NDP leader, Ed Broadbent. Filmon emphasized that the Accord did not weaken the role of the central government and that it clarified federal-provincial roles, and "makes it possible for Quebec to rejoin the Canadian family" without undermining the rights of women or Aboriginals expressed in the Charter.[32]

Three days later, after a decision by Quebec Premier Boursassa to use the "notwithstanding" clause of the Charter of Rights and Freedoms to override minority language guarantees in the case of outdoor English-language signage, Filmon rose in the House to withdraw the Manitoba legislation. Filmon again cited Pawley to argue that the Accord "made it a fundamental obligation of all governments to protect minority language rights," that the Quebec decision "violates the spirit" of the Accord, and therefore that its adoption would not be wise "and may invite a very negative anti-Quebec backlash." Both Opposition leaders supported Filmon and both urged the Premier to explore ways to deal with the "flaws" in the Accord (Doer) or to negotiate a "better accord" (Carstairs).[33]

Within weeks, Manitoba created a legislative "Task Force on the 1987 Constitutional Accord." The Task Force was chaired by Wally Fox-Decent, a University of Manitoba political studies professor best known as a labour negotiator. The Task Force claimed its hearings were "the most extensive in Canada" on the topic, including 300 presentations and 40 written reports.[34] The Task Force report of October 1989 urged Canada's First Ministers to "reconsider the amendments" in the Accord. It recommended no less than six amendments. Perhaps the most important was a "Canada Clause" which would supplement the declaration of the distinct society clause with similar declarations about Canada's Aboriginal peoples and its multicultural identity. Other amendments aimed at further entrenching the Charter of Rights and Freedoms, ensuring that Senate reform would be pursued, turning attention to Aboriginal matters at First Ministers' conferences, and canceling the limitation on the federal spending power.[35]

After accepting the Report, Filmon declared that "the Accord as it now stands cannot and will not be approved by the Manitoba legislature."[36] He had an all-party consensus that reflected public opinion. He had the basis for negotiating with Ottawa as one of the "gang of three" dissenters on the Accord. While Manitoba's position was more critical than New Brunswick's as expressed by new Premier Frank McKenna, it was not as dismissive as the views of Newfoundland's dogmatic new Premier Clyde Wells.

The federal government consulted with the dissenting provinces and met with all the Premiers in May and June 1990 to try to find ways to either amend or supplement the

Accord. Frank McKenna came up with the term "companion accord" for a package that would accommodate the Manitoba and New Brunswick concerns if not the Newfoundland position, yet preserve the original Meech Lake tenets.

Gary Filmon stuck tenaciously to his all-party strategy, which became most clear in early June when Mulroney called the First Ministers to Ottawa for a last-ditch effort to save Meech. Filmon brought Carstairs and Doer with him and insisted on consulting with them. A "Canada Clause," the primacy of the Charter, Senate reform, recognition of Aboriginal peoples, assurances about Ottawa's fiscal support for social programs, were all wrapped into the companion accord that was agreed upon at the last moment when Ontario's Premier, David Peterson, sacrificed some Ontario seats in a reformed Senate for the Atlantic and Western provinces. The Accord seemed to be saved on June 10, 1990, when Filmon, McKenna and Wells agreed to take it and the companion accord to their legislatures for approval.

Filmon had warned that Manitoba's approval required considerable legislative time, but Mulroney was nonetheless jubilant that his last-moment "roll of the dice" would work.[37] When Filmon rose in the legislature on June 15, 1990 to propose the adoption of the Accord and its companion resolution, he well knew that there was shaky support on all sides. New Brunswick had already passed the Accord and its companion resolution but Newfoundland was waiting upon Manitoba. A key legislative procedure meant that unanimous assent would be required to get through the legislative stages by the three-year Meech Lake deadline of June 23. Filmon was surprisingly unruffled when NDP MLA Elijah Harper, a First Nations leader, refused to grant unanimity. Harper was a lone figure throughout the two weeks of debate, grasping an eagle feather as he expressed his opposition to Meech on behalf of Canadian Aboriginal peoples. They felt that Meech had been passed ahead of the entrenchment of Aboriginal rights promised in 1982.

When the legislature finally considered the revised Accord on June 20, 1990, public hearings clogged the legislature for several days. Mulroney and Bourassa criticized Filmon for not invoking closure or finding another device to choke off proceedings. He responded tartly that Mulroney "wants to ignore and subvert the process and that's wrong." He was irked that federal officials and politicians were using "tactics of fear and manipulation" to squeeze Manitoba. He argued that Manitoba should put aside the "anger all of us feel over [Mulroney's] manipulation," concluding that "this is better than nothing at all." Committee hearings and legislative debate continued but by June 22 Manitoba was nowhere close to holding the vote. Filmon raised the prospect of continuing if Ottawa would indicate that a loophole could be found to the June 23 deadline. But both Quebec and Canada rejected that proposal. Newfoundland Premier Clyde Wells took the Manitoba delays as the occasion to renege on his reiterated promise to hold a vote in the provincial House of Assembly. Meech Lake indeed was dead.[38]

In the aftermath, there was a sense nationally that the failure might well lead to the political loss of Quebec. Manitoba and Newfoundland were blamed by the advocates of Meech, above all by a bitterly disappointed Prime Minister Mulroney. Mulroney later reserved his harshest criticisms for Pierre Trudeau and especially Clyde Wells.[39]

Gary Filmon was remarkably calm about the results but uncharacteristically blunt about the cause of the failure, which lay with the federal government. Manitoba had been subjected to undue pressures that had created "wounds" in the relationship with Ottawa. He admitted that he would "forgive, yes; forget, no." He concluded that a new way to address constitutional issues would be essential in future. It may have consoled him that the *Winnipeg Free Press* agreed with him that Meech Lake had failed due to Ottawa's "political and bureaucratic blunders."[40]

As time passed, Filmon's strategy of insisting upon a common Manitoba approach redounded to his credit. While it was clear that the government's minority standing dictated this consensual approach, it was also clear that Filmon was doing everything possible to avoid dividing Manitobans on a very controversial matter. There would be no repeat of the French language constitutional debate and its bitter results. Filmon ended up enhancing his standing for his approach.

1990 Election and a Slender Majority

Filmon saw a favourable moment to fight an election and Manitobans went to the polls on September 11, 1990. It followed a languid late summer campaign that seemed devoid of passion. Although still perceived as capable rather than exciting, Filmon was unquestionably in charge of his party and the most popular party leader. PC election signs asked voters to support the "Filmon Team," with the PC colours and name serving as secondary identifiers. Polls indicated that it was Filmon's personal standing that was crucial. A two-day "strike" by some physicians, reflecting the Manitoba Medical Association's unhappiness over negotiations with a parisimonious provincial government, did not stick to the Premier and almost certainly emphasized the government's message that restraint was going to be applied to everyone. Doer was a dynamic campaigner and shored up the NDP by emphasizing its role as the defender of social programs. His attacks went too far when he tried to align Filmon with Mulroney. Carstairs was as energetic as ever but big spending promises at the last moment did little to enhance the Liberal position. Her party's conservative social policy stances helped to bolster Tory claims to moderation. Filmon countered opposition charge by arguing that Manitoba "must continue to stand up to federal Canada when they introduce policies which favor central Canada at the expense of the rest of us." Government policy had demonstrated that, whatever their instincts, Filmon's PC party was not going to attack social programs.[41]

When the ballots were counted, 69% of eligible electors turned out to give the PCs a bare majority with 30 seats from 42% of the popular vote, a gain of 5 seats and 4%. (The PCs received 206,000 votes in each election.) The NDP surged to 20 seats, a gain of 8, from 29% of the vote, while the Liberals sagged to 7 seats (losing 13) from 28% of the vote.[42] Despite Filmon's popularity, he had struggled for support in the city of Winnipeg. While both the PCs and NDP had solid funding for the election and strong party organizations and membership, the Liberals slipped badly in funding and organization. The trend seemed to suggest a return to two-party predominance.[43]

New Government, Same Agenda

The cabinet in 1990 was unchanged at major posts such as Finance (Manness), Health (Orchard), Education (Derkach) and Attorney-General (McCrae). There was a new approach to social services as a consolidated department of Family Services was now headed by the steady Harold Gilleshammer, a teacher from Minnedosa. Despite the retirements of Charlotte Oleson and Gerrie Hammond, there were now five females in the PC caucus and a total of 11 female MLAs, nearly one-fifth of the legislature. Bonnie Mitchelson remained minister of Culture, Heritage and Citizenship with the added responsibilities of the Status of Women, while Linda McIntosh became minister of Consumer and Corporate Affairs. Two years later, Clayton Manness moved to Education, newcomer Eric Stefanson, who replaced Hammond in Winnipeg's Kirkfield Park, was appointed to Finance, while Jim McCrae moved to Health in place of Don Orchard, and newcomer Rosemary Vodrey moved into Justice after a brief spell in Education, the first of several cabinet moves for a minister who drew criticism wherever she went.

Filmon had a working majority of two once the Speaker was removed from the divisions. Denis Rocan was reappointed Speaker and continued to preside with iron-willed impartiality. During the government's term in office, the balance of power shifted. Prominent MLAs from each party departed, including Liberal luminaries, Gulzar Cheema, Jim Carr and Sharon Carstairs. Also departing were two Conservative MLAs, Ed Connery and Harold Neufeld, who made it clear they were not happy with government policy. Neither departure led to widespread disaffection with Filmon's leadership. Connery was replaced in Portage la Prairie by Brian Pallister, but Neufeld's departure from Winnipeg Rossmere led to a loss of one seat to the NDP during a five-riding by-election campaign in September 1993. The one-seat loss meant a razor-thin majority that had to be managed carefully.

Recessionary Times and Budgetary Cuts

The first majority government Throne Speech was wary about immediate prospects and alerted Manitobans to the economic downturn. The government committed itself to restructuring public finances and refocusing economic activity. By 1991 the government admitted that the country was in major recession and warned that the economic base of Manitoba would be remade by global changes. Throughout the term, there was a strong emphasis on preserving "quality health, education and social services available to all."[44] Filmon had emphasized the link between fiscal stability and social spending in 1989 when he pointed out "the greatest danger to health care and other social services comes from fiscal instability." During the 1990 Budget debate he indicated that the government's top priority was long-term growth: "We cannot afford to be all over the map as we come to grips with the economic challenges before us. We have to focus our efforts on one goal and one goal alone, and that goal must be long-term economic health in our province."[45]

The effects of the recession were serious in Manitoba and included two years in which the provincial economy shrank. Manitoba's vaunted "balanced economy," with its mixture of agriculture, natural resources and manufacturing, was as dependent on inter-provincial as international trade until the mid-1990s, unlike other Western Canadian provinces but similar to Ontario. Most economic indicators were gloomy throughout the first half of the 1990s. To make matters worse, the federal government was engaged in further cuts to fiscal transfers, which provided the revenues for 60% of spending. Manitoba's capacity to deliver health care, social services, and post-secondary education was weakened.[46]

Manness presided over increasingly stringent fiscal controls and in 1993 he brought down a budget he described bluntly as "hard-hitting" There were new fees for government services, growing reliance on lottery revenues (like most provinces), but a freeze on personal income taxes. The 1993 cuts were deep and most visible in a multi-year set of controls on public sector workers—which also applied to non-governmental public sector institutions like the courts, colleges and universities. The 10 days without pay and reduced services began in July 1993 and continued for five years. They were quickly dubbed "Filmon Fridays."[47] Undoubtedly unpopular throughout the public sector, the Filmon Fridays were a major sign that the government was serious about controlling public spending. Civil servants groused, doctors, nurses and teachers bitterly complained, while provincial court judges unsuccessfully took the government to court to protest the impingement on their independence.

By 1994, there were already signs of economic recovery, manifested in declining unemployment, significant expansion in interprovincial and especially international trade (thanks to the FTA) and easing of interest rates. Filmon had been an early defender of the FTA, though less keen on North American Free Trade (NAFTA) with Mexico. A strong and growing trade surplus with the United States became apparent by the mid-1990s. Agricultural prices firmed up and agricultural, natural resources (especially hydro-electicity), and manufacturing exports surged. Agricultural processing expanded and farming conditions began to improve. Rural Manitoba seemed to be the first area to feel the benefits of free trade and provincial capital spending in areas like roads.[48]

Constitutional and Aboriginal Matters

Constitutional reform did not end with Meech Lake. In December 1990, a second "Constitutional Task Force" chaired by Wally Fox-Decent was constituted. The hearings were once again extensive and the committee both consulted with the populace and crafted a report that aimed to overcome the "frustration and sense of alienation" Manitobans felt while providing a strong contribution to the "difficult constitutional negotiations that lie ahead." The Task Force reported in October 1991. It reflected the concerns that had emerged in 1990 for a "Canada Clause" and support for the Charter, Aboriginal rights and multiculturalism, as well as commitments to governmental reform in areas like the Senate and Supreme Court selections.[49]

Ottawa conducted a number of reviews in 1991 and 1992. In September 1992, it came up with the Charlottetown Accord, which would be put to a national referendum. The Accord was a busy text of three pages with seven major provisions, in effect a complicated fine-tuning of the 1982 Constitution and certain measures of Meech Lake.[50] Manitoba should have been pleased, the Premier pointed out, since most of the provincial Task Force recommendations were in the Accord.

Most of Manitoba's federal and provincial political leaders did support Charlotttetown, including Doer but not Carstairs, who broke with her own party. Manitoba's Aboriginal leaders argued against it. Gary Filmon, who campaigned unenthusiastically, claimed that he detected a shift towards the Accord in the last days of the campaign. Voting day of October 27, 1992 saw a surprisingly broad rejection in six provinces, including Manitoba and the other western provinces as well as Nova Scotia and Quebec. In Manitoba, 61.2% voted no, a higher proportion than Quebec (56.7%) or the national total of 54.4%.[51]

The aftermath was swift. Filmon stated that it had been an "honest attempt" at reform but admitted it had "failed." He was one of the first political leaders to argue that it was time to put away constitutional issues. "We just have to get on with other business," he said and noted "I'll be urging the PM to have a first minister's conference on the economy as soon as possible."[52]

A more intense legal issue gripped the province in 1991. It concerned the treatment of Aboriginal people in the Manitoba justice system. In its last days, the Pawley government had created the Aboriginal Justice Inquiry (AJI) whose terms of reference focused on "the state of conditions with respect to aboriginal people in the justice system in Manitoba." The AJI was prompted by two controversial cases. In one, the brutal murder in The Pas of a young Aboriginal woman, Helen Betty Osborne, had been unresolved for 16 years until 1987 due to widespread public refusal to cooperate with the RCMP investigation. In the other, J.J. Harper, a prominent Aboriginal leader, had been killed during a routine investigation and the circumstances were obscured to protect the Winnipeg Police Service. The AJI, led by provincial jurists Alvin Hamilton and Murray Sinclair, took three years and exposed police actions and legal policy to intense scrutiny.

The AJI Report of September 1991 was a carefully researched examination not only of the two criminal cases but also the institutional framework of a "justice system [that] has failed Manitoba's aboriginal people on a massive scale." The AJI Report made recommendations under 12 headings and nearly 300 items. They ranged from "aboriginal and treaty rights," the court and police systems, the "child welfare" and "young offenders" systems, and a "strategy for action." Most controversially, the Report recommended an "aboriginally controlled justice system" and its final "strategy for action" called for systematic "affirmative action."[53]

The governmental response was ponderous. Justice Minister Jim McCrae indicated a determination to work with Aboriginal organizations. In January 1992 the province set up working groups to deal with the key areas such as Native and northern affairs, natural resources, family services, and justice matters. It also indicated that it was "endorsing many meaningful recommendations" from the AJI. Filmon himself emphasized that the negotiating process would take some time, while minister for Aboriginal Affairs Jim Downey argued from the outset that the issues that had taken decades to develop and had a federal dimension that would not be solved quickly.

New initiatives were begun in Aboriginal child welfare and health treatment measures, recognition of Métis rights, and the start of negotiations over treaty land and natural resource rights. But the government stated in December 1992 that recommendation of a separate Aboriginal justice system "was not a recommendation that we are in a position to accept." As a result, other recommendations tied to an Aboriginal justice system were moot. The government was not going embrace the full AJI report.

On the tenth anniversary of Harper's death, in response to Opposition probes, Premier Filmon reported a lengthy list of items that represented the government's support for AJI recommendations. The subjects ranged from Treaty Land Entitlement agreements with all 26 Manitoba bands through reformed court practices and Native healing circles to Aboriginal recruitment in law enforcement services. His listing was wide-ranging, though it was not a complete report on the fate of the recommendations. Whatever progress was made, the government had not clearly communicated either the extent of its adoption of AJI recommendations or its support to the Aboriginal community.[54]

Reforming Education

When it turned to social policy making after 1990, the Filmon government undertook two major undertakings, in education and in health services.

Manitoba's school system, like many in the 1990s, underwent a major curricular reassessment. Prompted by public concern over declining standards of achievement and behaviour, as well as the budget squeezes that governments experienced, provincial departments of education engaged in a serious effort to tighten curricular standards and codes of student behaviour that had been relaxed considerably during the 1970s and 1980s. While the changes were not implemented without agitation (teachers were suspicious of provincial exams, parents fought against school closures), the government did overhaul both pedagogy and practices. Under the rubric of "renewing education," Manitoba embraced a tighter curricular focus, greater inclusivity, more parental consultations through school-based Parent Advisory Councils, and province-wide examinations including national competency tests in reading, math and science. Most of the changes were carried out by administrative reform rather than legislative action.[55]

To deal with school board organization, the government turned to a commission of inquiry chaired by former Winnipeg mayor William Norrie. The inquiry conducted public consultations, examined enrolment trends, and identified areas for economizing, particularly whether the number of divisions was too many and too expensive to support the delivery of a "quality education."[56] The commission found that, despite public respect for teachers, there were concerns about the capacity of school boards to provide everything from proper transportation to effective programs against a backdrop of increasing school taxes. Among a long list of recommendations for greater administrative supervision by district authorities and principals, full recognition of "open boundaries" and greater parental "choice," the commission supported a reduction in the number of school divisions from 57 to 21, including a cut of the greater Winnipeg area's 10 divisions to 4. But it admitted that administrative savings would not be great, and it did not even indicate whether property taxes should remain an important part of school funding.[57] In the end, the government was hesitant and there was a very limited reduction from 57 to 54 divisions during the 1990s.

The government also vowed in 1990 to tackle the post-secondary educational system.

The government appointed former Premier Duff Roblin to head a "University Educational Review Commission" which reported in December 1993. Like reviews of post-secondary systems in other provinces, the Roblin Report was not particularly sympathetic to the post-secondary institutions, particularly universities. It queried the priorities, efficiencies and effectiveness of the university sector, complaining about too little teaching, too much self-government, too little unfocussed research, and insufficient control by boards of governors. It was somewhat better disposed towards the college system, supporting their efficiencies and recommending a doubling of college spaces within the decade.[58] The governmental response was tepid but it announced that it would move to create a new governing structure to replace the current University Grants Commission. In the meantime, the province began a two-decade policy of setting guidelines for post-secondary tuition fees, limiting universities to small increases.[59]

Francophone Education

The Filmon government had further unfinished business from the 1980s regarding French-language education. The recognition of francophone education equality within the system was given a boost by Canada's adoption of section 26 of the Charter of Rights and Freedoms in 1982, which guaranteed English or French minority language education rights in each province. From that point on, the issue was not whether but how to design an appropriate system for French-language education.[60]

The Filmon government was dissatisfied with the vacillation that had occurred during the Pawley years but wanted legal clarification before extending French-language schooling. In 1988, the Attorney-General of Manitoba referred the specific meaning of minority language rights to the Manitoba Court of Appeal, which rendered its determination in 1990. The Manitoba Court did not rule decisively or clearly, stating only that the province must provide French-language education in a "distinct setting." In other words, French-language schooling should be provided but it could be within larger English-language schools and administrative control could be within larger English-language school boards. This "partial victory" for the francophone Fédération Provinciale des Comités de Parents (FPCP) was a signal to the province to deliver better institutional services than the Department of Education had contemplated.[61]

Premier Filmon was committed to a resolution that satisfied the francophone community, but the movement towards effective action took a further four years. In August 1990, the minister of Education, Len Derkach, created a Task Force on Francophone School Governance headed by former federal public servant Edgar Gallant. The Gallant Task Force came up with a solution, starting with a separate provincial francophone school board with both specific educational and broader cultural goals.[62] The government hesitated, apparently due to backbench opposition. In early 1992, new minister of Education Rosemary Vodrey announced government policy based on a very loose interpretation of the Gallant Report. The FPCP opposed it for not implementing a francophone-centred and controlled school division. The province tried to move ahead with an "Implementation Support Team," but it had no clear blueprint.

The FPCP sought a reference from the Supreme Court of Canada, freezing provincial action until the Court did its work. It did so in March 1993. It made three key points. First, there were strong francophone educational rights. Second, these required both a "distinct setting" and parental "right of management and control." Third, the Court stated that the province must move "without delay."[63]

Filmon expressed satisfaction that the Supreme Court had clarified the administrative requirements. He renewed his commitment to move quickly and noted that the province wanted to allow parents at each school to vote on whether to join the new division. The province created a new Implementation Support Team, chaired by retired Manitoba Justice Alfred Monnin. Manitoba then created a strong, autonomous school division to support francophone schools, the *division scolaire franco-manitobaine*. The new *division scolaire* governed 20 schools and some 4,200 students when it began operation in September 1994, and drew $15 million in start-up funds (which Filmon complained was inadequate compared to the amounts granted smaller francophone divisions in Alberta and Saskatchewan) from the federal Official Languages Commission. [64] But the injustices of the past were repaired.

Controlling Health Care Costs

Health care was a contentious matter throughout the 1990s. Even before Manness's 1993 benchmark budget, the province had struggled to control medical costs and it battled publicly with the Manitoba Medical Association over doctors' fees and the Manitoba Nurses Union (MNU) over nursing salaries.

The most significant public battle was with the nursing profession in 1990–91. Negotiations in the fall of 1990 between the MNU and the umbrella Manitoba Health Organizations were difficult, nurses seeking a large salary increase of 15% per year for both registered nurses and practical nurses as well as greater stability of employment and inputs into health care. The government refused and warned that increased labour costs would be taken out of the Health and other departmental budgets. The MNU declared a strike on January 1, 1991. The province's 9,500 nurses spent a month on strike in an unusually cold winter. Manitobans experienced disruptions, delays, and unease as hospital services were rationed. When a settlement was reached, it provided healthy salary increases of 11% for practical nurses and 14% for registered nurses over two years, but the increases were not matched by greater security of tenure. Nurses spent the rest of the decade in a dreary slog of salary roll-backs, limited hours of work and heavier demands. When the next contract was negotiated, nurses were reported to be "afraid to strike" and accepted cuts and lay-offs. Practical nurses were particularly affected and later felt the sting of privatization. The toll of strong fiscal controls was heavy throughout the decade in a pattern common across Canada.[65]

The province was convinced that better management of medical services would lead to improvements in controlling costs and patient care. During the 1990s, the reorganization of hospitals, the centralization of services, and the introduction of new managerial techniques and technologies were investigated. There were cuts to acute care beds starting in 1992 that amounted to 10% of the total in the large Winnipeg region. These cuts led to incessant public debate on issues ranging from the burdens on staff to medical effectiveness and, above all, waiting lists. Sober analysis conducted at regular intervals throughout the decade, as bed closures increased to almost 25% of the 1990 total by 1998, made it clear that the medical experience of most patients for almost all illnesses from diagnosis to treatment actually improved throughout the decade and Manitoba's record was one of the best in Canada.[66]

But there were problems. The most significant were reports about the failure of the pediatric cardiac surgery unit at Winnipeg's Health Sciences Centre. The start of the new unit resulted in the deaths of 12 infants. These deaths were a shock and indicated a system under stress. The situation led in 1995 to a provincial coroner's inquiry by Justice Murray Sinclair of the Manitoba Provincial Court. His recommendations included compensation to families, major reorganization of medical treatment and greater caution in recruiting physicians and implementing new programs. Later still, another provincial commission under the auspices of public administration professor Paul Thomas was called into the "implementation" of the original inquiry's recommendations. From inquiry to completion, the process took 13 years.[67]

Balanced Budgeting and the Election of 1995

In 1994, new Finance minister Eric Stefanson declared that Manitoba had come through the recession, made the necessary adjustments, and was positioned for economic recovery. He argued that Manitoba's fiscal regime made it one of the cheapest places to do business in North America. In early 1995, he announced that Manitoba had moved into an era—unprecedented for over 20 years—of surplus budgets. He also proposed balanced-budget legislation to ensure an escape from the high-debt trap. The Throne Speech reiterated the good news and emphasized that social programs were now secure. If there were dangers ahead, hinted the Throne Speech read by new Lieutenant-Governor Yvon Dumont, they lay in the areas of street crime and youth gangs, which the government poked away at over time, but the core social programs and the economic base of the province were strong.[68]

With these positive signs, the Filmon government went to the polls in the spring of 1995. "Team Filmon" (the party label was very faint) once again campaigned for the election on April 25, 1995. The Filmon team faced a determined NDP that campaigned with vigor, backed by health care and education unions as well as Gary Doer's considerable skills. The Liberals had an articulate new leader, Paul Edwards, but he was undone by declining membership, limited funds, and the burden of the new federal Liberal government. The PC campaign depended on the Premier's credibility and his popularity, which ran far ahead of the party and the other two leaders, neither of whom were lacking in energy or ideas. Still, one newspaper story described the election as "The Bland Leading the Bland." Filmon emphasized his reputation for moderation in conducting the campaign. "I like to think I'm consistent," he told the *Globe and Mail*. "That's who I am. I'm a Progressive Conservative. I'm fiscally conservative but I'm a progressive on people issues. I don't think I could be either a red or blue Tory... I'm right in the middle, honestly." He reiterated the message in a flattering feature story in the *Winnipeg Free Press* that made clear that he was undisputed head of the government.[69]

The election was a modestly successful "three-peat" for the Filmon government, which won a clear majority with 31 seats and 43% of the popular vote. The NDP's popular vote rose to 33% and it added 3 seats to hold 23. Both parties took votes from the Liberals who nonetheless held 24% of the popular vote but fell below official party status with just 3 seats, excluding Paul Edwards, who resigned the leadership. Voter turn-out remained a steady 69%, a sign of neither apathy nor excitement. Gary Filmon had triumphed but had not routed the opposition as Winnipeg in particular remained highly competitive to all three parties.[70]

The cabinet was not rejuvenated and may have weakened, although ministers moved to new posts. Manness and Orchard did not contest the election. Eric Stefanson had already proven he was a solid as minister of Finance. Newcomer Vic Toews was a capable if provocative former prosecutor who recaptured Rossmere in north Winnipeg and took over Labour. Most ministers remained in their posts, although Linda McIntosh moved to Education. Another notable change was the nomination of Louise Dacquay as Speaker in place of Denis Rocan, who returned to the backbench. The number of women elected to the legislature remained the same at 11, and the five Tory MLAs were all returned.

The Manitoba economy continued to improve. Over the next four years, unemployment fell, interest rates declined, international trade (above all to the United States) grew rapidly, and agriculture, natural resources and manufacturing experienced brisk demand and rising prices. Even net provincial population was beginning to grow, as the combination of economic recovery and an important new federal-provincial immigrant recruitment program allowed the province to tout its attractions abroad.

All told, the "Manitoba Advantage"—as Filmon and Stefanson described the fiscal and economic climate of the province throughout the third term—showed that the province was embarking on a period of greater well-being.[71] Filmon joined a succession of federal Trade Missions abroad and promoted the province's "advantage" to international economic events. On the other hand, there was very limited official acknowledgement that 1995 was the 125th anniversary of Manitoba's entry into Confederation and nothing emphasized the austere side of the Filmon government more than this peculiar reticence.

Limits to the Recovery

If the economic momentum and the social outlook were changing, specific circumstances were less propitious. In particular, three developments in the mid-1990s showed that governing Manitoba posed plenty of challenges.

The first and most important was the federal government's decision to fundamentally alter its support for provincial social programs. After more than a decade of federal-provincial tussles, Ottawa moved unilaterally to end the two longstanding programs that supported medicare, social welfare, and post-secondary education and replace them with a single "Canada Health and Social Transfer." For Manitoba, highly dependent on Ottawa for its expenditures, it meant a 10% cut in funding. Health Care and Family Services, which together accounted for nearly half of the province's budget, had to economize even more than they had from the previous round of federal cuts starting in 1992–93. The government did not pass on the full cuts to departmental budgets for Health, Family Services or higher education, but looked for even stricter ways to economize in those portfolios as well as sacrifice other departments. Over the next three years, restrictions were the order of the day, and the ramifications made for acrimonious public debate over social services.[72]

The government had to deal with these serious cuts while conveying the positive message that, thanks to fiscal restraint and the new balanced-budget legislation, Manitoba was on a course of economic recovery. In the budget prior to the election, Stefanson had argued that Manitoba was "on the threshold of a period of unparalleled prosperity and opportunity" despite the "profound changes" Ottawa had imposed. This mixed message was reiterated for the next four years.[73]

The second issue was the future of the Winnipeg Jets hockey team, a potent public issue in a city concerned about its status and visibility as an economic and cultural centre. The National Hockey League decided to expand into the southern United States, which put an intolerable burden on the eight Canadian cities, particularly small-market ones like Quebec and Winnipeg, due to escalating salaries, outmoded arenas, limited corporate sponsorships and small television markets.

The Premier was active in promoting private sector interest in building a new arena and refinancing the hockey team while limiting provincial exposure. He made it clear, however, that the province would not be put into the position of paying for or guaranteeing a $100 million arena project. As he put it, "while our government could be a modest participant in a long term solution, the taxpayers of Manitoba could not and should not be the primary funder of any long-term solution." Despite this, Manitoba did fall into the peculiar Winnipeg structure of public-private partnerships in professional sports, and it partly funded Jets operations during the team's last two seasons, though Filmon argued that the "investment" raised equivalent revenues. In 1996, the Jets were sold to Phoenix, Arizona owners who offered a new arena and corporate support. The loss of the Jets was a symbolic one insofar as it indicated that Winnipeg and Manitoba were no longer part of the major league sports industry.[74]

The third shock was the 1995 Quebec referendum. The sovereigntist movement recovered after Meech and Charlottetown with the return to power in September 1994 of the Parti Quebecois under Jacques Parizeau. He was committed to a quick referendum on "national sovereignty." The rest of Canada, including Manitoba, looked on benignly during the first stage of the 1995 referendum campaign, since initial support for separation was relatively low. Filmon was confident that the benefits of the federation were self-evident and the costs of separation too great. But the combination of massive cuts in federal support to the provinces announced in May 1995 and the replacement of the pedantic Parizeau by the charismatic Lucien Bouchard as leader of the pro-sovereignty campaign transformed the situation. By referendum day, October 30, 1995, polls suggested a disaster for Canada. Federal and provincial leaders, including Gary Filmon, were shaken by the prospects of a

Quebec government unilaterally declaring independence. When the ballots were counted, a tiny plurality just over 1% of voters kept Quebec in Canada.[75]

The aftermath was decisive. The federal cabinet was reinvigorated and passed a "Clarity Bill" that insisted upon a high threshold and a clear question prior to any provincial secession. Manitoba convened yet another Task Force on constitutional issues, chaired yet again by Wally Fox-Decent. Entitled "Your Canada, Your Voice," the report committed Manitoba to efforts designed to assure Quebeckers that the federation remained its best option and that any changes to the federal system would respect provincial rights and Quebec's uniqueness. Thus informed, Manitoba supported a federal-provincial initiative, the Calgary Declaration of September 1997. The Declaration was a "lite" version of the Charlottetown Accord, expressing the fundamental goals of consultation before constitutional change, the inclusion of Aboriginal peoples in changes, the recognition of Quebec's distinctiveness, and the centrality of the division of powers between the two levels of government. Filmon's view was that specific constitutional change was less important than the recognition of the principles behind Canadian federalism and the distinctive place of Quebec in Canada.[76]

The Privatization of the Manitoba Telephone System (MTS)

Undoubtedly the most contentious action the Filmon government undertook after its re-election was the decision to sell the government-owned MTS. Most provincial governments had over the course of the 20th century built up large public enterprises. In Manitoba's case, the largest were in communication (MTS) and energy (Manitoba Hydro). During the 1980s and 1990s, federal and provincial governments engaged in the review and often the privatization of many of these large businesses. Ottawa privatized Petro-Canada and Canadian National Railways, while several provinces sold off their large Crown corporations.

In May 1996 the Premier announced that the government planned to put the company up for sale via a stock offering. The reasons for the sale were strong. MTS had entered a new competitive telecommunications era but it was small and deeply in debt. A year-long series of assessments led to the conclusion that MTS had to change dramatically and privatization was the best solution to preserve the telecommunications sector and public finances alike.

The news was not a total surprise. The minister responsible for MTS, steady cabinet veteran Glen Findlay, had explained in September 1995 that the old era of monopoly operations and provincial control had ended. The federal government had taken over the area of telecommunication including telephony in the 1980s and national competition in telephone, internet and television service was shaking the industry. Findlay and Filmon reviewed the issues on a number of occasions over the next several months. Competition was national (affecting 70% of MTS business), rates were set by a federal regulator, and MTS had a high debt ratio (over 80% of its equity value). Filmon's position was clear. The new dynamics of economic development required privatization because that was in the best interests of the people and government of Manitoba.[77] He reiterated these arguments during heated Question Periods throughout the spring of 1996. He "unequivocally" denied that there had been any consideration of the sale prior to or right after the 1995 election.[78]

The opposition intensified its attacks on the government as time wore on and it sensed public unease and political gain. The attacks included charges that the government had hidden its privatization plan prior to the election, misled the public during the period of review in 1995–96, and concocted the plan in order to reward its business friends. They also argued that the sale could subject Manitobans to the loss of jobs, higher phone charges, worse service and loss of control over the system.

Just as the legislation was about to be passed in November 1996, the issue devolved into a vicious battle of parliamentary procedure. The backdrop lay in changes to legislative procedures agreed upon in December 1995 after five years of discussion. The changes meant that the legislature worked from a fixed annual agenda with greater opportunities for the government to present its program and more time for the opposition to criticize and change but not filibuster legislation.

During the debates, several MLAs on both sides moved from sharp exchanges to taunts and insults beneath the hearing of the Speaker or the Hansard recording system. Worse, the Speaker, who was already viewed by the opposition as peremptory in response to their points of order (and who was prone to a certain rigidity in her rulings in order to keep to the new rules), became the object of opposition outrage. Her rulings in insisting on maintaining the legislative program led to numerous points of order and an opposition motion calling for her resignation.[79]

The battle over privatization was pivotal in that it, far more than other issues, raised the temper of conflict between government and opposition dramatically. Filmon and Doer were often bruising debaters but the MTS affair soured the legislature. Doer, though no wallflower, relied on aggressive colleagues, particularly Tim Sale and Steve Ashton, to attack the government. Opposition attacks drew out Filmon's combative side and diminished his well-earned reputation as cool and analytical. The temper of the legislature remained tense into 1997 and Speaker Dacquay had to face another opposition demand for her resignation when the legislature resumed in March.[80]

Other economic and social policy developments were less contentious. Filmon had championed new industry in the form of call centres throughout the 1990s. Though derided at times, this new industry did over the long run create a lot of jobs and considerable managerial expertise in telecommunications. The government also stepped in to broker further private investment when the Pine Falls Paper Co., which had been partly employee-owned and provincially-financed since 1994, faced a refinancing crisis. The company was sold in 1998 to Quebec-based Tembec Inc., saving employee jobs and investments while the pulp and paper business lurched away from one of its regular crises. On the other side, Manitoba Hydro actually expanded its reach in early 1999. Hydro moved into a new area with its acquisitions of Centra Gas Ltd., the dominant natural gas supplier in the province.[81] More generally, Filmon pointed to the continuing boom of natural resources and agricultural trade to the United States as well as sustained growth in agricultural processing and livestock production that created prosperity in rural regions. The province did not hesitate to provide some financial aid and infrastructure support, with both economic and political benefits.

Reorganization in Health Care and Higher Education

Major reviews of social services led to large-scale reorganization in the late 1990s. If the immediate aftermath of federal cuts in 1995–96 were a shock, after 1997 the province was in a position to ease restraints and even increase social service spending due to the strong provincial recovery. Even before the recovery was solidifying, Filmon pointed out that "of every new dollar that we have spent in this province in the last eight years, 90 cents has gone to the three departments of Health, Education and social services – Family Services – and that is priority setting."[82]

The government moved to contract out a portion of home care services. The government position was that the unavoidable cost-squeeze created by Ottawa's cuts meant that all aspects of health care must become more efficient. Allowing 25% of home care services by private businesses was one area where a public-private partnership was appropriate. A strike by home care workers in the spring of 1996 dramatized the issue. The province tried other ventures in its efforts to economize health care costs, encouraging a centralized food and laundry service for nine Winnipeg health centres. The Urban Shared Services Corporation went through a difficult transition particularly in 1997 with problems in the delivery of palatable hospital food, much to the government's embarrassment.[83]

The province implemented a major change in the management of health care in 1996–97. The province created a provincial system of 11 Regional Health Authorities (RHAs). Each regional authority consisted of hospital and other medical and nursing treatment facilities. The RHAs varied from the tiny and isolated Churchill system in the north through mid-size authorities like the Brandon and Assiniboine systems in the southwest to the powerful Winnipeg system. They were knit together and coordinated with the resources of the provincial department of Health and depended heavily on the deep medical research, diagnostic and teaching resources of Winnipeg and the University of Manitoba.

The RHAs each had an administrative board with considerable community and professional input as well as a core of medical practitioners and facilities. Successive ministers of Health argued that the new structure provided the guarantee of local and regional medical care. When he brought down the RHA legislation in May 1997, Darren Praznik pointed out that the new regional system countered the loss of federal funding, created efficiencies to offset the ever-increasing costs of medical treatment, provided clear provincial standards for treatment and, finally, devised a coordinated approach to health care across the province. Manitoba moved into the late 1990s with a more coordinated health care system and, by most measures, delivered health care in ways that consistently put it not just at the Canadian mean but in many aspects in the top two or three among the provincial systems.[84] In addition, the pivotal Health Sciences Centre in Winnipeg was rebuilt despite restraint from a decaying edifice to a shining complex. Nonetheless, it was a system that had problems, ranging from food services to periodic emergency ward delays. The phrase "hallway medicine" entered the lexicon.

In post-secondary education, Manitoba created a new agency to replace the old University Grants Commission. The Council for Post-Secondary Education (COPSE) raised the concern that it would lead to more provincial interference in post-secondary education.

But it represented less a threat to the much-vaunted autonomy of the institutions than a force for greater coordination of their initiatives. The change was hardly dramatic, but it did involve thinking about post-secondary education as a system, including colleges as well as universities, and pointed to a more balanced college/university system and between large and small institutions. That move was followed by the chartering of a consolidated private university, Canadian Mennonite University, in 1998, a sign that post-secondary education was emerging from two decades of austerity.[85]

Red River Flood

If 1997 was a key year for the consolidation of major provincial initiatives, it was also a year in which a catastrophic flood inundated the Red River Valley. Manitoba is prone to flooding and major flooding had occurred earlier in the decade on the Souris, Assiniboine, and Saskatchewan river systems. The fertile Red River Valley is susceptible to flooding on a spectacular scale and extraordinary winter snows and a heavy spring blizzard led to an extreme flood danger. The threat was worse than the 1950 crisis. The danger was more than the level of protection provided by the Winnipeg Floodway completed in 1968. When the flood crest moved north during April 1997, it inundated Fargo and Grand Forks as well as vast rural areas. Downtown Grand Forks was simultaneously inundated by water and almost destroyed by a vast fire, which shocked North America and braced Manitoba for the worst.

The provincial response pressed into service emergency measures and natural resources personnel as well as provincial and civic government workers to coordinate and support the thousands of rural and urban residents threatened by flooding. The federal government ordered 8,500 military personnel to assist the province and the communities in their labour. As the relentless flood crest pressed on, residents of a dozen communities and thousands of farmhouses in the way of the flood from the border north to Winnipeg worked to strengthen or construct dikes. Winnipeg augmented its flood protection system by constructing dikes using six million sandbags to supplement the city's "primary dike" while the province built an extension dike, the Brunkild Extension, for 20 miles west from the permanent dam at the southern edge of the city. When the flood crest hit the city on May 2, the floodway and the city's primary dike held, the sandbagging held, the Brunkild Extension held, eight communities protected by ring-dikes remained secure, and Manitobans trod softly for a month lest the waters breach the barriers. At its greatest extent, the flood created a 1,800 km lake, dubbed the Red Sea, extending from Winnipeg to North Dakota.[86] There had been major damage to hundreds of properties. The town of Ste. Agathe south of Winnipeg, not prone to flooding and therefore not protected by a ring-dike, was inundated and the Winnipeg suburban enclave of Grande Pointe was flooded.

The provincial government earned its share of credit yet also drew a certain amount of criticism. Some of it was for the very measures that saved the city of Winnipeg, the flood protection system that spread the Red Sea and caused damage to Ste. Agathe, Grande Pointe, and many private houses and farmsteads. That required patient explanation and the offer of compensation. Compensation was offered and accepted but it was criticized for being insufficient. The province tripled disaster relief funds, waived the 20% deductible and interpreted costs generously.[87]

In the aftermath, concerns ranged from whether better weather forecasting was possible to whether more effective flood prevention could be built. There was little doubt that flood protection would have to be extended farther and that it would require national and international cooperation. The province was an active participant in the ensuing reviews and planning, which began almost immediately. In the end, claims were settled, reviews were done, and a confident Manitoba began to plan for enhanced flood protection.[88]

The Trying of Gary Filmon

In June 1998, a political scandal blew up. During the 1995 election, a small group of Progressive Conservative party strategists decided to support a fringe-party candidate in the riding of Interlake, in order to split the vote and win the seat. The move failed. Their plot, illegal under the Manitoba Elections Act and possibly under other Criminal Code legislation, was attacked by the NDP at the time. A post-election investigation by Elections Manitoba found no evidence of the plot, since no one was willing to corroborate the charges. Three years later, investigative journalists did find willing complainants and the government found itself dealing with a serious matter. When the opposition raised the issue, government officials including Filmon at first ignored it and claimed it was a specious matter disposed of by the 1995 investigation. However, the news exposés charged that the Premier's chief of staff, Taras Sokolyk, who had been the campaign chair in 1995, had been part of the Interlake scheme. Sokolyk resigned from his position. The seriousness of the situation led Filmon to call a commission of inquiry headed by retired Chief Justice of the Manitoba Court of Appeal, Alfred Monnin. The Inquiry hearings in late 1998 revealed the details of the scheme and received rapt media attention.[89]

Monnin reported in March 1999. He found that in the riding of Interlake, party officials had induced and funded a candidate to run in order to split the vote. This group included both Sokokyk and Julian Benson, secretary of the Treasury Board. When Filmon became aware of Benson's involvement during inquiry hearings, he demanded and received Benson's resignation. Monnin also found that other senior PC officials provided a small amount of funding for two other fringe candidates in the ridings of Dauphin and Swan River, though they had not induced those candidates to run. The question of the Premier's involvement in and knowledge of the events became the key political issue, eagerly investigated by the opposition and the media. In his testimony, Filmon reiterated his longstanding position that he knew nothing about the chicanery and acted promptly in 1998 to deal with the matter.

Monnin gained public attention with his hyperbolic language in describing the scheme of the five PC officials, two of whom lost their jobs. His recommendations were minuscule since the offenses under the Elections Act occurred beyond the period when Elections Act offenses were punishable. He found that no PC elected member, above all the Premier, were aware of or aided either the plot or the cover-up, and he noted that Filmon had dealt with the matter swiftly when the revelations were made in June 1998.[90]

Filmon apologized to the legislature on the first day of the new session, stating he had misled the assembly, albeit unintentionally, regarding the actions of five people including staff and PC party members. He also apologized to the Association of Manitoba Chiefs for the manipulations of Aboriginal candidates. In both instances, he emphasized his utter disdain for the practices as well as his total absence of knowledge of the plots.[91] Although exonerated, Filmon had to deal with the consequences of being the prime focus of his party's organizational and governmental structure. The leader of Team Filmon was vulnerable, not to any actual charges, which were easy to dismiss, but to the more indirect ones that he somehow enabled political tricksters to operate under his gaze. For a politician who had built a reputation on strict discipline, the burden of the Monnin Inquiry was a heavy one.

The 1999 Session and Election

Meanwhile, the government brought down yet another positive budget promising further economic expansion and expansion to social services, so long subject to tight controls. The budget address of the new minister of Finance, Harold Gilleshammer, was slightly discordant because, unlike the thematic ones of his predecessors Manness and Stefanson, it had no specific direction or message. The 1999 budget was so uncontroversial that Gary Doer led the NDP to support the government, clearly a sign he was repositioning his party away from persistent criticism to a positive mode.

The Throne Speech, delivered by the new Lieutenant-Governor, Peter Liba, emphasized that the government had restored the province's fiscal base and rebuilt its managerial capacities. It gushed that the province was at a "critical junction" in moving into an era of expansion and emphasized that the expansion of social services was now possible due to the strong economic base and the partial restoration of federal supports. It was a brief and optimistic pre-election speech.[92]

The short spring session ended on July 6, and an election was called for September 21. In the meantime, the province enjoyed an international celebration as Winnipeg hosted the 1999 Pan-American Games, the second-largest multi-sports event in the world calendar. The civic and provincial organizational capacity, supported as usual by the extraordinary volunteer spirit of the province, performed effortlessly, and the Games were a success. The Games were the latest in a series of international championships hosted over the previous four years including the World Curling Championship and the World Junior Hockey tournament. Everywhere in the province, from the economic boom to the signs of cultural life, the province was in a more buoyant mood than a decade earlier. Even disquieting issues, such as increased criminal gang activity and continuing high child-poverty levels, though much debated in the legislature, were not borne out by measures of crime rates or social assistance claims.

The campaign was, for the most part, conducted without incident. The parties concentrated their efforts on the vital organization by neighbourhood and community, leaving the headlines to the leaders, who no doubt realized that the fourth election they fought would be the last for one. Doer stumped the province with his usual enthusiasm and made it clear that "today's NDP" was a moderate centrist movement. He embraced the tenets of contemporary social democracy as found in such places as Roy Romanow's

Saskatchewan and Tony Blair's Britain. If doctrinaire socialists complained, Doer, a "Filmon of the Left" in embracing the centre, had no time for their approach as he positioned the NDP as an alternate government.

Filmon was as energetic as ever, demonstrating his mastery of the intricacies of government and once again led Team Filmon rather than the PC party. He spent a great deal of time helping prominent community activists to seek election in Winnipeg's north side ridings. Continued opposition charges about tight-fisted health spending and allusions to the vote-splitting scandal certainly put pressure on Filmon to justify the previous three terms and that was probably the toughest part of the campaign. He focused on one key announcement, delivered towards the end of the campaign. The Premier vowed that Manitoba had turned such a sharp corner that he could promise a $1 billion fiscal bonus. This 50/50 promise consisted of a $500 million tax reduction and a $500 million increase in health and education spending. The largesse was surprising, but Filmon was confident that the growing economy and imminent revisions to fiscal federalism were about to put Manitoba in a strong position for the first time in years. But it was a tough sell to change the message and his image from being the master of restraint to a manager of expansion.

The electorate was as divided as usual, polling indicating that voting preferences were in equilibrium, with only the steady decline of the Liberals providing a pool of new electors. Election day revealed a slight shift in voters, particularly in Winnipeg where more Liberals moved to the NDP than to the PCs, and Manitobans did not grant Gary Filmon a fourth term. The final results saw 45% support the NDP of Gary Doer and 41% support the Conservatives of Gary Filmon.[93]

Filmon conceded quickly and, after an appropriate time for reflection, indicated that he would not carry on as opposition leader or party leader. He resigned as opposition leader in May 2000, formally left the legislature in September, and the party that he had brought to credible, moderate leadership had to find a new way. None of the leading candidates—Eric Stefanson and Darren Praznik were the most prominent—from the Filmon era chose to run and the party was off on a new and uncertain direction under legislative newcomers.

Conclusion

As befitted an engineer, Gary Filmon undertook a methodical approach to politics and government and he made sure that the party and government he led dealt head on with the major problems and priorities that the province faced.

Filmon took a political party that consisted of capable if narrow rural agribusiness interests and nostalgic urban Tories and remade it into a centrist party focused on a realistic appraisal of Manitoba's economic and social needs. He became Premier at a time when Manitoba had clearly fallen behind the other western provinces, more comfortable with praising itself for its social and economic equilibrium than expanding social or economic opportunity. It had long since abandoned a leading role among the provinces or taken a positive stance on most national issues. The two dominant provincial leaders of the 1960s and 1970s, Duff Roblin and Ed Schreyer, had to cajole the province simply to catch up in building economic and political institutions that most provinces, above all the western ones, had long since developed. Later, whether it was Lyon's ineffectual denunciation of Trudeau's constitutional reforms or Pawley's passive acceptance of the Trudeau and Mulroney governments' constitutional projects, the province had become a passenger not a crew-member on the Canadian ship of state.

Governmentally, Filmon was determined to concentrate first on economic issues, then on administrative changes, and finally on social service renewal. Whether this was the best approach may be debated, but it was arrived at after a serious assessment of how to shore up a province that was stagnating in a number of ways. Filmon's governments undertook a reappraisal of provincial fiscal policy that was remarkable in that it was both serious and effective without becoming ideological or misleading.

The 1988 government, aided and abetted by its minority situation, bucked intense federal pressure to change the constitution—and in the process risked the federation's equilibrium. The 1990 and 1995 governments undertook major efforts at reorganizing provincial structures, notably in health care with the regional health authorities and in telecommunications with privatization, in both cases re-engineering the structures of a province that shrank from admitting that major changes were necessary. Finally, they maintained a commitment to deliver the system of social services that did not move towards the abandonment of major redistribution and collective services, though their rationing of money and services was at times unnecessarily penny-pinching and mean.

Gary Filmon put together a strong political and governmental organization in the late 1980s that reset the atmosphere in Manitoba. Filmon himself has gone on to ply a post-electoral career from his Winnipeg home. Energetic and avid about business, totally committed to a life in Manitoba, he remained a mainstay of the Winnipeg and western Canadian business community. He served as a business consultant and corporate director (including to the flourishing Manitoba Telecom in recent years), as well as chair of the most discrete of federal agencies, the Security Services Review Committee. He never intervened publicly in provincial politics.

Notes

For help with research, thanks go to several talented History students at the University of Manitoba, Carl Klassen, Nathan Hoeppner, and Jennifer Rutkair, who provided invaluable assistance. Thanks, too, to Don Leitch, former Clerk of Executive Council, and W.H. Remnant, former Clerk of the Legislature, for taking the time to talk in general about the Filmon administrations.

1. For general background on Winnipeg and Manitoba, see Ruben Bellan, *Winnipeg First Century* and W.L. Morton, *Manitoba: A History* (revised edition); information on Gary Filmon is found in "Profile of Gary Filmon," *Winnipeg Free Press*, April 18, 1995, *Canadian Parliamentary Guide*, 2000, as well as older stories in the *Winnipeg Free Press*.

2. *Winnipeg Free Press*, November 15, 1967, "Tory Filmon Banks on Good Business Sense," *Globe and Mail*, December 28, 1985, A8, "Profile of Gary Filmon, *Winnipeg Free Press*, April 18, 1995, University of Manitoba Libraries, author search.

3. *Winnipeg Free Press*, November 9, 1963,*Canadian Parliamentary Guide*, 2000.

4. *Winnipeg Free Press* November 15, 1967, June 21, 1969.

5. *Winnipeg Free Press*, various issues 1979–81.

6. Christopher Adams, *Politics in Manitoba: Parties, Leaders, and Voters* (Winnipeg: University of Manitoba Press, 2009), especially 43–46.

7. There are two excellent studies of this period. A reliable popular study of the long history of Manitoba's denial of French-language rights and French-language education is found in Frances Russell, *The Canadian Crucible* (Winnipeg: Heartland, 2003). I have followed the more detailed academic monograph, a splendid work by Raymond Hebert, *Manitoba's French Language Crisis* (Toronto: University of Toronto Press, 2004), passim.

8. Ibid.

9. Contemporary summaries are "Other Prized Candidates Said No: 3 Bland Men Seek Lyon's Job," *Globe and Mail*, December 10, 1983, 12, "Tory Filmon Banks on Good Business Sense," *Globe and Mail*, December 28, 1983, A8. A quick overview of the PCs is found in Christopher Adams, *Politics in Manitoba*, especially 46–48.

10. Hebert, *Manitoba's French Language Crisis*, Ian Stewart, *Just One Vote: From Jim Walding's Nomination to Constitutional Defeat* (Winnipeg: University of Manitoba Press, 2009), 50–59, "Manitoba Tories Raise Letter in language Debate," *Globe and Mail*, February 16, 1984, N5, "Speaker Rejects Bid for Vote," *Globe and Mail*, February 22, 1984, P8, *Winnipeg Free Press*, miscellaneous, January–February 1984.

11. Supreme Court of Canada, Re Manitoba Language Rights [1985] 1 SCR 721, File No. 18606, June 11, 12, 13, 1984; June 13, 1985. See http://csc.lexum.umontreal.ca/en for 1985. The lead signature on the Supreme Court decision was from Chief Justice Brian Dickson. The Chief Justice had studied, practiced and judged law in Manitoba for many years until his elevation to the Supreme Court in 1973. The Court knew the Manitoba context. Dickson's careful reasoning in both confuting Manitoba's law and leading it out of its dilemma is explained in Robert J. Sharpe and Kent Roach, *Brian Dickson: A Judge's Journey* (Toronto: University of Toronto Press, 2003), 415n22.

12. "Manitoba PC Chief Assails Mulroney," *Globe and Mail*, March 15, 1984, P1, "A Manitoba Odyssey," *Globe and Mail*, 14 June 1985, P6, Filmon quoted in "Federal Aid in Law Translation Will Be Needed," *Globe and Mail*, June 14, 1985, P1, and "Manitoba Ruling Hailed as Landmark for Minority Rights," *Montreal Gazette*, June 14, 1985, A1, Brian Mulroney, *Memoirs* (Toronto: McClelland & Stewart, 2007), 285–88.

13. "In Manitoba Tory Bike in Middle of Road," *Globe and Mail*, January 21, 1986, A7, "First Major Election Statement," *Globe and Mail*, February 24, 1986, A8, "Manitoba Tory Leader Trying to Lose Party's Blue-Suited, Tight-Fisted Image," *Toronto Star*, February 26, 1986, A9, "Manitoba Tories Woo Small Business," *Globe and Mail*, March 3, 1986, A5.

14. "Burned Once, Manitoba Leaders Skirt Language Rights," *Toronto Star*, March 5, 1986, A18. A deft summary of the election is in Stewart, *Just One Vote*, 129–32.

15. Elections Manitoba, "Statement of Votes, 1986."

16. "Manitoba Re-elects the NDP," *Globe and Mail*, March 19, 1986, A1, "Pawley's NDP Wins Manitoba Vote," *Toronto Star*, March 19, 1986, A1, " Carstairs's Manitoba Win," *Toronto Star*, March 20, 1986, A16.

17. "West Furious Over Rigged F-18 Contract" *Ottawa Citizen*, November 1, 1986, A1; the F-18 contract was a front-page story for days throughout Canada; a year earlier Manitoba had experienced another sign of its declining regional importance when CN Rail transferred both operational authority and senior administrative positions from Winnipeg to Edmonton; "Primed to Oust the Socialists," *Globe and Mail*, December 13, 1984, P8, "Money-Losing Crown Firms Haunt the NDP in Manitoba," *Globe and Mail*, February 26, 1985, P3; "Five Top officials Ousted Over Manitoba Telephone Fiasco," *Globe and Mail*, November 22, 1986, A4, "Pawley Hauls in Reins on Crown Companies after MTX Write-off," *Globe and Mail*, February 6, 1987.

18. The fall of the Pawley government is examined carefully in Stewart's *Just One Vote*.

19. See Stewart, *Just One Vote*.

20. "Filmon Gains PC Vote of Confidence" *Globe and Mail*, April 13, 1987, A4, Elections Manitoba, Annual Reports, Summary of Contributions, 1988 and subsequent years.

21. "New Manitoba Premier," *Ottawa Citizen*, April 29, 1988, A9, "Tory Spending Cuts Will Be Modest Filmon Pledges," *Globe and Mail*, April 22, 1988, "Manitoba Tories Quiet on Policy Details," *Ottawa Citizen*, March 23, 1988, D19, "Filmon's Blunders Set Tone," *Windsor Star*, March 19, 1988, A6.

22. Elections Manitoba, "Statement of Votes 1988."

23. "Manitoba Tories Squeak to Victory," *Globe and Mail*, April 27, 1988, A1, "Meech Lake is Dead, Carstairs Declares," *Ottawa Citizen*, April 28, 1988, A3.

24. Hansard, July 21, 1988.

25. Ibid., August 8, 1988.

26. Ibid., July 22, 1988, November 20, 1989, see also "Filmon Backs Free Trade Despite Carstairs Threat," *Winnipeg Free Press*, May 21, 1990, 15.

27. Ibid., June 5, 1989.

28. "Report on the Netherlands: Flyer Takes Off Under New Dutch Owner," *Globe and Mail*, May 9, 1988, B20, "Opposition Parties Blast Sale of Manfor to Repap," *Montreal Gazette*, March 14, 1989, C12, "Manitoba Sells Off Data Firm for $22 Million," *Globe and Mail*, March 16, 1990, B8, "Sale of Regal Delays Deal for Seed Firm," *Toronto Star*, September 16, 1994, B3.

29. See Manitoba Budget Addresses, 1988, 1989, 1990, etc. for information on everything from government revenue and expenditure to unemployment rates. Reliable data on public finance has been confirmed from, Statistics Canada, "Public Sector Statistics: Financial Management System," annual catalogue 68-213-XIB. Information on interest rates, unemployment and housing starts and sales is digested at the UBC Centre for Urban Economics and Real Estate, "Housing and Real State Data Site" http://cuer.sauder.ubc.ca/cma/index.html

30. Good brief explanations are found in Gregory Marchildon, "Roy Romanow," in Gordon Barnhart (ed.), *Saskatchewan Premiers of the Twentieth Century* (Regina: 2004), 367–72, Doreen Barrie, "Ralph Klein," in Bradford J. Rennie (ed.), *Alberta Premiers of the Twentieth Century* (Regina: CPRC, 2004), 261–67.

31. The five precepts of the Accord were to declare that Quebec was a "distinct society" within Canada, to restore Quebec's veto over constitutional amendment, to recognize the provinces' constitutional role in immigration, to provide clearer means for provinces to "opt-out" of joint federal-provincial spending programs, and to provide clear provincial input into appointments to the Supreme Court of Canada and Senatorial appointments; a clear account of the constitutional issues, proposals and agreements from the 1970s to the 1990s is found in David Milne, *The Canadian Constitution*, third edition (Toronto: Lorimer, 1993).

32. Hansard, December 16, 1988.

33. Ibid., December 19, 1988.

34. W. Fox-Decent, Chair, *Report on the 1987 Constitutional Accord* (Winnipeg, 1989), 1–4, quotation 80; the committee consisted of Liberals Sharon Carstairs and Jim Carr (Liberal deputy leader), NDPer Gary Doer, and Tories Jim McCrae, the Attorney General, Gerrie Hammond, Minister of Labour and Responsible for the Status of Women, and Darren Praznik, a young backbencher serving as the Premier's legislative assistant.

35. Report on the 1987 Constitutional Accord, 72–79.

36. "Manitoba Report Demands Major Changes to Meech, *Globe and Mail*, October 24, 1989, A1.

37. Carol Goar wrote a fine account at the time in the *Toronto Star*: "How the Leaders Made a Deal," June 11, 1990, A13. A clear account of the negotiations remains Milne, *The Canadian Constitution*. As for Gary Filmon, he admitted that along with Carstairs and Doer, Manitoba "did not get everything we wanted. But we did achieve some success in every one of our areas of concern.... I believe we have achieved enough to close this chapter of our constitutional history" ("Leaders Advice: Hold Nose, Swallow," *Winnipeg Free Press*, June 12, 1990, 1).

38. "Parties Rife with Dissent over Meech," *Winnipeg Free Press*, June 12, 1990, 1, "Harper's No Puts Brakes on Meech," *Winnipeg Free Press*, June 13, 1990, 1, "Manitobans Clog Road to Meech," *Winnipeg Free Press*, June 14, 1990, 1, "Heat Turned Up as Meech Debate Begins," *Winnipeg Free Press*, June 21, 1990, 1, "Hope for Meech Dim in Manitoba," *Globe and Mail*, June 21, 1990, A8, "Constitutional Accord Likely Took Its Last Breath in Manitoba Today," *Toronto Star*, June 22, 1990, A18.

39. A good summary of the tensions surrounding Meech Lake and the aftermath as viewed by leading politicians, bureaucrats and academics, including Sharon Carstairs though not Gary Filmon, is found in Robert Bothwell, *Canada and Quebec: One Country, Two Histories* (Vancouver: UBC Press, 1998), Ch. 10 and Ch. 11; for Mulroney's reaction see Brian Mulroney, *Memoirs*, 767–94.

40. "Manitoba Premier Forgives, Won't Forget Federal Tactics," *Ottawa Citizen*, June 24, 1990, C5, "The Wrong Way to Die," *Winnipeg Free Press*, June 23, 1990, 18.

41. "Doctors' Union Optimistic Deal to End Strike in Sight" *Winnipeg Free Press*, September 27, 1990, 1, "Manitoba Election: Three Good Reasons to Vote," *Ottawa Citizen*, August 9, 1990, A14, "Manitoba Poll Predicts Narrow Tory Majority," *Globe and Mail*, September 7, 1990, A6, "Premier Gary Filmon Needs to Add Only Five More Seats to Win a Majority," *Globe and Mail*, September 8, 1990, D2, "Mr. Filmon and Weaker Options," *Globe and Mail*, September 10, 1990, A12.

42. See Elections Manitoba, Statement of Vote, 1990.

43. See Elections Manitoba, Annual Reports, Summary of Contributions, 1988–1995.

44. Lieutenant-Governor George Johnson, Throne Speech, Hansard, October 11, 1990, 3–4.

45. Clayton Manness, Budget Address, Hansard, October 24, 1990, 375ff. Gary Filmon, Hansard, June 1989, November 1990.

46. See Manitoba Finance, Budgets and Economic Outlooks. International and international trade for the period was covered by Statistics Canada, "Interprovincial Trade in Canada 1984–1996," Catalogue No. 15-546-XIE.

47. Clayton Manness, Budget Address, Hansard, April 6, 1993. See also "Tough Problems, Limited Options: Manness," *Winnipeg Free Press*, March 28, 1993, "Manitoba Government's Hard Hitting Budget," *Globe and Mail*, April 7, 1993, A4, "Unpaid 'Filmon Fridays' Make Return Appearance,"

Winnipeg Free Press, March 15, 1994, B1, "Goodbye to Filmon Fridays," *Globe and Mail*, July 30, 1998, A8, "The Filmon Fridays End Tomorrow," *Winnipeg Free Press*, July 20, 1993, A3.

48. "Filmon Backs Free Trade Despite Carstairs Threat," *Winnipeg Free Press*, May 21, 1988, 15, "Filmon Skeptical Three-way Deal Helps Manitoba," *Winnipeg Free Press*, March 26, 1992, A17, Gary Filmon, Hansard, March 17–18, 1992, July 5, 1993, "Province Applauds NAFTA," *Winnipeg Free Press*, December 3, 1993, A1; trade data is found in the annual Budget Papers.

49. W. Fox-Decent, Chair, *Report of the Manitoba Constitutional Task Force* (Winnipeg, Constitutional Task Force, 1991); the task force consisted of Liberal Jim Carr, NDP members Jean Friesen and Oscar Lathlin, and PC members Jim McCrae, Darren Praznik and Shirley Render.

50. It included a Canada Clause (Quebec's distinctiveness, multiculturalism), adjustments to the division of powers (granting more exclusivity to certain provincial areas), a declaration on Aboriginal self-government, Parliamentary reform (elected Senate), changes to the selection of Supreme Court judges, clarification on constitutional amendment, and a "social charter" regarding the role of government; details and a clear summary are in Milne, *The Canadian Constitution*.

51. "Debating the Constitution: Sharon Carstairs/Lloyd Axworthy," *Winnipeg Free Press*, September 27, 1992, A7, "The Consensus Report," ibid., October 3, 1992, A14, "Mercredi Demand Gets No," ibid., October 18, 1992, A1, "Don't Vote, Harper Tells Natives," ibid., October 22, 1992, A1, "Filmon Feels Shift to Yes," ibid., October 26, 1992, A1, "No! in Manitoba," ibid., October 27, 1992, A1.

52. "Weak Prairie Campaign Weakens Vote," *Financial Post*, October 27, 1992, 26, "No! in Manitoba," *Winnipeg Free Press*, October 27, 1992, A1.

53. A.C. Hamilton and C.M. Sinclair, *Report of the Aboriginal Justice Inquiry of Manitoba* (Winnipeg: Government of Manitoba, 1991), "Terms of Reference," 1, Ch. 17 and Appendix 1. A gossipy journalistic account of J.J. Harper's death and its impact on the Winnipeg Police Service is Gordon Sinclair's *Cowboys and Indians: The Shooting of J.J. Harper* (Toronto: McClelland & Stewart, 1999).

54. Hansard: McCrae, December 6, 1991, McCrae, February 20, 1992, Filmon, May 6, 1992, Downey, June 22, 1992, McCrae, June 22, 1992, McCrae, December 8, 1992, Filmon, March 9, 1998. The Doer government created an "Aboriginal Justice Implementation Commission" in 1999 that signed off in 2008: resolution did take a very long time.

55. Manitoba Education and Training, *Renewing Education/New Directions, I: A Blueprint for Action II: A Foundation for Excellence* (Winnipeg, July 1994, June 1995). Two professorial evaluations are: Alma Harris, "Successful School Improvement in the United Kingdom and Canada," *Canadian Journal of Educational Administration and Policy* 15 (April 13, 2000), Benjamin Levin and Jonathan Young, "The Origins of Educational Reform: A Comparative Perspective," *Canadian Journal of Educational Administration and Policy* 12 (January 19, 1999), both at www.umanitoba.ca/publications/cjeap/

56. Thomas Fleming, "Provincial Initiatives to Restructure Canadian School Governance in the 1990s," *Canadian Journal of Educational Administration and Policy* 11 (November 28, 1997), www.umanitoba.ca/publications/cjeap/

57. W. Norrie, chair, "Final Report & Recommendations, Manitoba School Divisions/Districts Boundaries review Commission" (Winnipeg, 1997).

58. "University Educational Review Commission: Doing Things Differently" (Winnipeg, December 1993). The College system grew very slowly throughout the 1990s and 2000s and has yet to double either its total or proportion of post-secondary enrolments in the province.

59. Hansard, June 24, 1994.

60. I rely on the meticulous study of the matter by Michiel Behiels, *Canada's Francophone Minority Communities: Constitutional Renewal and the Winning of School Governance* (Montreal: McGill-Queen's University Press, 2004), 195–244.

61. Ibid., 213–17.

62. E. Gallant, Chair, *Report of the Manitoba Task Force on Francophone Schools Governance* (Winnipeg: Manitoba Education and Training, 1991).

63. Supreme Court of Canada, Reference re Public Schools Act (Man.), s. 79(3), (4) and (7), [1993] 1 S.C.R. 839 March 4, 1993. See http://csc.lexum.umontreal.ca/en for 1993, "Let Francophones Control Schooling, Manitoba Ordered," *Globe and Mail,* 5 March 5, 1993, A4, and Behiels, 236-239.

64. "Filmon to allow Manitoba parents to vote on new francophone school division," *Ottawa Citizen,* 18 May 1993, D14, Behiels, ibid. 231-242, Filmon in Hansard, March 1993.This francophone schoool division continues and flourishes.

65. "Hospitals Cope on Day One of Strike" and "Little Hope Seen For Early Break," *Winnipeg Free Press,* January 2, 1991, 1,. "Union Advises Nurses to Reject Offer," *Winnipeg Free Press,* January 15, 1991, 1. "Nurses Afraid to Strike," *Winnipeg Free Press*, January 18, 1993, A9, "Head Nurses Out, Non-Union Jobs In," *Winnipeg Free Press*, May 5, 1994, B2. A fascinating depiction of the 1990s is found in a short history of the Manitoba Nurses Union found on the organization's website: http://www.manitobanurses.ca/about-us/history.html

66. A series of assessments conducted by the Manitoba Centre for Health Policy examined the situation. N.P. Roos and E. Shapiro, "Monitoring the Winnipeg Hospital System: The First Report 1990–92," 1994, M. Brownell, N.L. Roos and C. Burchill, "Monitoring the Winnipeg Hospital System, 1990–91 through 1996–97," 1999, C. De Coster et al., "Waiting Time for Surgery in Manitoba," 1998. All are accessible at the Centre's web-site: http://www.umanitoba.ca/medicine/units/mchp/ and go to "publications."

67. "Report of the Manitoba Pediatric Cardiac Surgery Inquest: an Inquiry into Twelve Deaths at the Winnipeg Health Science Center, 1994": http://www.pediatriccardiacinquest.mb.ca; "Report of the Review and Implementation of the Report of the Pediatric Cardiac Surgery Inquest," 2002, final review 2008. http://www.gov.mb.ca/health/cardiac/. The reader may decide whether health care policy-making and review is a morass of difficulties or excessive bureaucratization. Similar problems are found in every jurisdiction.

68. Lieutenant-Governor Yvon Dumont, Throne Speech, Hansard, April 7, 1994, December 1, 1994. Eric Stefanson, Budget Address, April 20, 1994, March 9, 1995.

69. "The Prospects for Mr. Filmon," *Globe and Mail*, March 21, 1995, A22, "Provincial Election Campaign Begins," *Kingston Whig-Standard*, March 23, 1995, 5, "Its Bland Leading the Bland," *Montreal Gazette*, April 5, 1995, B8, "Manitoba Premier Takes PC Out of the Party," *Globe and Mail*, April 17, 1995, A3 (quotation), "Profile of Premier Filmon," *Winnipeg Free Press*, April 18, 1995.

70. Elections Manitoba, "Statement of Vote 1995." See also "Filmon Three-Peats: Popular Premier, Balanced Budget," *Winnipeg Free Press*, April 26, 1995, A1.

71. Throne Speech, Hansard, March 3, 1997.

72. Filmon acknowledged the critical problem shortly after the election. See Hansard, June 7, 1995. There is a vast scholarly literature, but I have relied on the budgets of Manitoba and Canada for the period. The federal Department of Finance web site has very clear information regarding "The Fiscal Balance" with "fiscal reference tables" for each province, which show quite clearly how serious

the cuts were during the 1990s, particularly in 1995, and how generous the fiscal turn-around was starting in 1999–2000, when Ottawa offered a new fiscal regime and vastly increased resources to the provinces. That major change did not benefit the Filmon government. See http://www.fin.gc.ca/facts-faits/fbcfacts-eng.asp.

73. Eric Stefanson, Budget Address, Hansard, March 15, 1995, Throne Speech (Lieutenant-Governor Dumont), Hansard, May 23, 1995.

74. See Filmon in Hansard, June 24, 1994, and an excellent Doer-Filmon debate in Hansard May 24, 1995. There is a good book on the subject by Jim Silver, *Thin Ice: Money, Politics and the Demise of an NHL Franchise* (Halifax: Fernwood, 1996).

75. See Filmon-Doer exchange May 18, 1994. "No Deals with Quebec: Filmon," *Winnipeg Free Press*, April 27, 1995, B9, "Filmon Touts Improved Canada," *Winnipeg Free Press*, October 25, 1995, A3, Filmon in Hansard, October 31, 1995. "Changes Crucial Filmon Says," *Winnipeg Free Press*, November 3, 1995, A3.

76. Members were key NDP MLAs Oscar Lathlin and Eric Robinson (former First Nations band leaders), Liberal Neil Gaudry (a francophone) and Tories Merv Tweed, Shirley Render and Vic Toews; Gary Filmon, "Government Resolution: Manitoba Task Force on Canadian Unity," Hansard, March 18, 1998.

77. As is all too common in Manitoba, this important subject has not been the subject of serious sustained scholarly analysis, though there is plenty of partisan academic pamphleteering. The debate can be followed in the Legislature. Filmon's most succinct defence of the MTS sale was in Hansard, May 2, 1995. Gary Filmon, "MTS Sale Right for Manitobans," *Winnipeg Free Press*, December 5, 1996, A15, cf. Gary Doer, "MTS Sale Angers Manitobans," *Winnipeg Free Press*, December 8, 1995, A19. The *Winnipeg Free Press* supported privatization: "The End of the World? Not Quite," November 30, 1996, A12. For the national perspective see Laurence Mussio, *Telecom Nation: Telecommunications, Computers, and Governments in Canada* (Montreal and Kingston: McGill-Queen's University Press, 2001).

78. Hansard, Committee on Public Utilities and Natural Resources, September 26, 1995, Glen Findlay (minister responsible), Tom Stefanson and Bill Fraser (MTS executives) and Steve Ashton (opposition). In one bizarre part of the debate, Ashton spent a great deal of time arguing that MTS board of directors' fees, which were being raised to $7,500 per year, were becoming too high, a sign of Manitoba posturing over public sector expenses. MTS was a $1 billion company. Doer and Filmon argued over the possible sale of MTS, Hansard December 8, 1995, they reviewed the situation in an Executive Committee Meeting months later, see Hansard, April 18, 1996.

79. The matter may be followed in Hansard, November 19–21, 26–28.

80. Hansard, March 3–4, 1997. The usually cool *Globe and Mail* described the legislative conflict as full of "histrionics": "Manitoba Bill Gets Approval Amid Threats, Histrionics," November 29, 1996, A4.

81. "Pine Falls Paper Looks to Celebrate Busy First Year," *Financial Post*, June 27, 1995, 24, "Tembec to Buy Pine Falls Paper," *Globe and Mail*, January 17, 1998, B2, "Westcoast to Sell Centra Gas to Manitoba Hydro for $245 m.," *National Post*, March 11, 1999, C4, "Utility Board Approves of Hydro's Take-over of Centra Gas," *Sudbury Star*, August 3, 1999, B3.

82. Filmon in Hansard, April 17, 1996.

83. "Home-Care Strike Widens" *Winnipeg Free Press*, April 22, 1996, A4, "Manitoba Home Care Strike Over," *Globe and Mail*, May 18, 1996, A9, Canadian Union of Public Employees, "Cooking Up a

Storm: Shared Food Services in the Health Care Sector," Research Branch Study, March 1996," N. Roos et al., "A Look at Home Care in Manitoba," Manitoba Centre for Health Policy and Evaluation, August 2001, http://www.umanitoba.ca/medicine/units/mchp/ and go to "publications."

84. Praznik in Hansard, May 27, 1997. See Manitoba Health, "A Planning Framework to Promote, Preserve and Protect the health of Manitobans," February 1997, www.gov.mb.ca/health/rha/planning.pdf. For assessments of Manitoba's treatment record and the health outcomes for Manitobans see the Romanow Report on national health care, Canada, Commission on "The Future of Health Care in Canada, Interim Report, Final Report" (Ottawa: February and November 2002), archived at: http://www.collectionscanada.gc.ca/webarchives/20071115024341/www.hc-sc.gc.ca/english/care/romanow/index1.html. See also the many reports of the Manitoba Centre for Health Policy Research and Evaluation, http://www.umanitoba.ca/medicine/units/mchp/ and go to "publications."

85. See Council on Post-Secondary Education, First Annual Report, 1997.

86. Information on the flood is vast starting with the CBC archives on the subject, including *Canadian Geographic* and the special reports on the subject prepared by the International Joint Commission of Canada and the United States. Informative picture-books on Red River floods are J.M. Bumsted, *Floods of the Centuries: A History of Flood Disasters in the Red River Valley, 1776–1997* (Winnipeg: Great Plains, 1997), Winnipeg Free Press, *A Red Sea Rising: The Flood of the Century* (Winnipeg: Free Press, 1997), and J. MacDonald, S. Sandrel and T. Thomson, *Faces of the Flood* (Toronto: Stoddard, 1997). A study that puzzles over whether the Red River flood was a disaster or an error is Ashley Shelby, *Red River Rising: The Anatomy of a Flood and the Survival of an American City* (St. Paul: Borealis, 2003).

87. Doer attacked Filmon relentlessly over compensation. see Hansard, November 28, 1997; contrast an earlier much more civil exchange on the impact of flooding in Hansard, May 12, 1997.

88. A good review is the International Joint Commission review: International Joint Commission, "Flood Protection for Winnipeg," Parts I and II, December 1999, Part III, March 2000.

89. Hansard, June 22–23, 1998; the *Winnipeg Free Press* coverage was extensive, but see "PCs Yield, Call Vote Inquiry," June 26, 1998, A1, "'Rather Thin' Allegations Led to Inquiry," November 3, 1998, A1, "What Filmon Knew," November 26, 1998, A1, "Clearly Unethical," March 30, 1999, A10; see also "Filmon Denies Knowledge of Alleged Scheme," *Globe and Mail*, November 26, 1998, A4.

90. Alfred M. Monnin, *Report of the Commission of Inquiry into Allegations of Infractions of the Elections Act and the Elections Finance Act during the 1995 Manitoba General Election* (Winnipeg, 1999), 13, 25–31, 54–55, 65–67.

91. Hansard, April 6, 1999, "Filmon Apologizes to Manitoba Chiefs," *Winnipeg Free Press*, April 9, 1999, A3.

92. Throne Speech, Hansard, April 6, 1999.

93. Campaign summaries from the *Globe and Mail* were most helpful (though the *Winnipeg Free Press* provided a great deal of detail, it was too close to be entirely helpful for this essay): see "Not Much Decided in Inconclusive Manitoba Debate," September 8, 1999, A3, "The Two Garys Both Optimistic," September 18, 1999, A4, "50/50 Campaign," September 22, 1999, A11. Election results are from Elections Manitoba, "Statement of Vote 1999"; see also Christopher Adams's useful summary in *Politics in Manitoba*.

Gary Doer

KARINE DUHAMEL AND
BARRY FERGUSON

Gary Albert Doer, 1999–2009

On August 27, 2009, Gary Doer shocked Manitoba by announcing that, after 10 years as Premier, he was going to leave office. Two days later, Conservative Prime Minister Stephen Harper surprised Canadians by announcing that Gary Doer would be Canada's next ambassador to the United States. Although astonishing, his transition from politician to diplomat is consistent with a career in politics spent negotiating among factions by piloting a middle course and a premiership that led him to national prominence and many ties with American politicians and officials. Doer's political.*modus operandi* consisted of a deft touch as a careful manager, an approach characterized by conciliation not confrontation. The legacy of Doer's premiership may not be clear for some time, yet it appears to be apparent even now that his approach represented a significant break from the fiercely partisan politics of the previous three decades. From his years in trade union administration to a career as one of Manitoba's most popular Premiers, Doer's policy initiatives focused on garnering the broadest possible support while incurring the most minor political price. In short, Doer's approach steered the Manitoba New Democratic Party closer to the centre than perhaps ever in its history. Like other provincial Premiers before him, Doer's challenge was to act as both a leader of a partisan organization as well as a Premier governing on behalf of the entire province. Doer was both a politician and a mediator who skilfully managed to maintain a strong sense of public opinion and to sustain the government agenda during each of his three terms.

Life Before Politics

Gary Albert Doer was born in Winnipeg on March 31, 1948 and grew up in the prosperous south side suburb of River Heights, distant socially and politically from the north side neighbourhoods that comprised the NDP's heartland. He attended an elite Roman Catholic school, St. Paul's High School, a Jesuit-run, fee-paying institution that stressed high academic achievement, sports participation and community service alike. In 1969, Gary Doer enrolled in the Faculty of Arts at the University of Manitoba. He also joined the Zeta-Iota chapter of the Tau Kappa Epsilon fraternity, although frat membership was and is not common at the University of Manitoba. Doer left university after his first year and did not return to complete a degree. He found employment first as a Youth Counsellor at the Vaughn Street Detention Centre and then at the Manitoba Youth Treatment Centre. In a relatively short period of time, Doer rose from being a Youth Counsellor to becoming deputy superintendent of the Manitoba Youth Centre.

Doer also became involved with the Manitoba Government Employees Association (MGEA), which became in 1992 the Manitoba Government Employees Union and then the Manitoba Government and General Employees Union (MGEU) in 2000.[1] In 1977, he was elected one of four vice presidents. In 1979 at age 31, he was elected president of MGEA, a position he retained until 1986. During his tenure as president of MGEA, the union worked to "co-ordinate provincial and national bargaining strategies, establish a provincial employees' daycare centre, and win pay equity legislation in the provincial civil service."[2] During the 1970s and 1980s, the union also grew substantially in membership. The union's own history notes that from the mid-1970s onwards, the MGEA grew steadily, expanding to recruit members working in health care facilities, arts organizations, universities and social service agencies, including a merger in 1982 with the Institutional Employee Union. Although he was not involved in partisan politics, as the head of a dynamic public sector organization, Gary Doer acquired a public profile and considerable experience in labour-management issues and public policy. One major foray into politics in this period was during the poisonous debate in 1983 over entrenching French-language rights and services. Doer's MGEA had not been consulted by the Pawley government in its failed efforts to provide constitutional redress for Manitoba's francophones. The MGEA might have been drawn into the vicious debates that divided the province, since the impact on public sector workers was significant. Instead, Doer and his executive maintained a positive view about the goals of the initiative and, after insisting on consultations that had been overlooked by the government, gained the support of a potentially-restive membership.[3] Doer also acquired a range of community ties as a director of the community-owned Winnipeg Blue Bombers football club, a member of the Board of Governors at the University of Manitoba, a vice president of the Manitoba Special Olympics, and board member of the innovative Winnipeg arts organization, the Prairie Theatre Exchange.

The Move into Politics

By the time Gary Doer ran for the NDP in 1986, by all accounts it was not the only party that noticed his skills and courted him. He was not, however, active in NDP or other party politics at that time. In 1986, his situation would change and he won the nomination in the NDP stronghold of Concordia. This was a predominantly working-class riding on the north side of a Winnipeg that has been divided socially and politically by the Assiniboine River into its NDP and working class north and Tory and middle class south. Doer was well-placed to win by running in an area with a solid base built by Peter Fox, a long-serving NDP stalwart who had decided on retirement. Doer was a rarity in 1986, a prominent recruit for a government that was not very popular and running with a shaky record. The anemic election theme, "Stand Up for Manitoba," was a clear allusion to Pawley's vain protest against the federal government of Brian Mulroney, which was widely perceived to have robbed the province's aeronautics industry of a major defence contract, and perhaps to its strong record of public-sector led economic growth in areas like hydroelectric development. Doer easily won in Concordia with 54% of the popular vote. The general election results were much closer, but the NDP under a beleaguered Howard Pawley narrowly retained power with 30 seats, a loss of 4, from 42% of the popular vote. The NDP government faced an official opposition Progressive Conservative party led by a new leader, Gary Filmon, hamstrung still by internal party quarrels, but which had gained 3 seats to hold 27 and 41% of the vote. Both parties lost votes in Winnipeg to the Liberals under new leader Sharon Carstairs, who was the sole Liberal elected to the House.[4]

The slim NDP majority meant that the government and its new ministers would have to be adept at pursuing its legislative agenda from a weaker base than the solid majority it had enjoyed between 1981 and 1986. Throughout its first mandate, it had struggled to complete its legislative program, notably over entrenching French-language and educational rights. Experienced in the give-and-take of collective bargaining, Doer was well prepared for the contentious legislature of 1986.

Doer was put to work as minister of Urban Affairs. In 1987, he was handed additional cabinet responsibilities, including Crown Investments, the Manitoba Telephone Act and the Manitoba Liquor Control Commission. The responsibilities he was assigned were at the centre of the problems the Pawley government faced by 1986. It had to deal with serious charges by the opposition of failures to control the management of Crown corporations as well as deal with a crisis of legitimacy that public ownership and interventionist government experienced at that time in Manitoba and throughout Canada. Doer's success was measured by his capacity to neutralize the crisis if not undo the damage created by the overseas contracts of a subsidiary of the Manitoba Telephone Systems through careful inquiry and reversal of some policies. Doer's skills were also shown by his ability to deflect the ideological critique of public ownership by correcting errors in the management of Autopac, the provincial public vehicle insurance corporation. He succeeded by effective reforms and by emphasis on responsible, prudent management of all of the Crown investments he oversaw. Just as he was not tainted by the impact of the nasty political environment surrounding the debate over French language rights and public services in 1983 and 1984, which was carried by veterans on both sides of the Legislature, neither was he harmed by charges of dilatory or incompetent management made against veteran members of the second Pawley government. As a new face, Doer was open to new directions and opportunities within the party—and opportunity was to arise two years later.

Howard Pawley's government fell in March 1988. It had been reduced to a one-vote majority when party mainstay, Laurent Desjardins, resigned in February 1988, after alerting the Premier the previous year that he intended to resign. But the precipitating event occurred when NDP backbencher Jim Walding voted against his party's budget. By the time the government fell, it had been worn down by years of contention in the Legislature and indeed within the party itself. The issues ranged from the failed extension of French language rights and other constitutional matters (Pawley had endorsed the 1987 Meech Lake Accord despite a great deal of internal party hostility to it) to the management of fiscal affairs in the province (intensified by the plunge into large provincial deficits in the mid-1980s).

Jim Walding's political rebellion was the culmination of a growing political and personal conflict between the disaffected MLA and the beleaguered Premier. Speaker of the Legislature during the first Pawley government, Walding had been a key member of the caucus since his first electoral victory in 1971. He had represented a south side riding (St. Vital) and moderate social democracy during the Schreyer years and under Pawley. He had also promoted reforms in the conduct of legislative business, including formal recognition of the Speaker's neutrality, during his years as Speaker. His own neutrality had been challenged by NDP and Tory MLAs alike during the vicious debates of 1983 and 1984. By 1988,

Walding was alienated from his caucus, due to the Premier's refusal to pursue reform of the role of Speaker, his disappointment at not getting a cabinet post in 1986, his resentment at being threatened by operatives from the Premier's Office in his own St. Vital riding, and his opposition to the deficit budgets brought down by Finance Minister Vic Schroeder.[5] Once the government fell, an election was called and the Premier, surprisingly, announced his own retirement from politics. The NDP was faced with organizing a leadership convention and fighting an election at the same time.

Party Leader and the 1988 Election

These were the unpromising circumstances in which Gary Doer ran for party leadership. He ran against four others, three cabinet veterans and a seasoned backbencher. Andy Anstett, a former civil servant and policy wonk, had been a member of the Legislature between 1981 and 1986 representing the Springfield riding east of Winnipeg. He served as minister of Municipal Affairs and Government House Leader but had been defeated in 1986. Harry Harapiak, a school principal and farmer, had a good reputation within the party, serving as minister of Natural Resources and then Agriculture. He represented northern riding of The Pas, which the NDP saw as a crucial part of its industrial and agricultural base. Maureen Hemphill, a strong feminist and activist, was elected in the north end Winnipeg riding of Logan in 1981 and was re-elected in 1986. She served as minister of Education in the first Pawley government but was relegated to minor portfolios in the 1986 government. Finally, Conrad Santos, a university teacher of political science and a party eccentric, had run for the New Democrats in the 1970s and was elected to the legislature for the heavily-immigrant Winnipeg riding of Burrows in 1981, an important party beach-head.

The convention was held just three weeks after the Pawley government fell. Doer may have had the most limited NDP credentials, but he drew the support of several influential cabinet ministers as well as Manitoba MPs. It is certainly notable that the Manitoba Federation of Labour also supported his bid.[6] The contest took three ballots. Doer and Harapiak were the front-runners, with Anstett and Hemphill trailing and Santos an also-ran. Doer led each of the first two ballots, the other candidates were forced to drop off, and on the third-ballot run-off, Doer defeated Harapiak. By no means was the 21-vote margin of victory a decisive one. Yet Doer was the victor: a moderate urban party newcomer had defeated a moderate hinterland party veteran.

The new leader had to move immediately to the election battle. Gary Doer refused to accept the title of "Premier," arguing that the premiership should be earned and not inherited. The political climate of the 1988 election was highly charged, concerned not only with the dreary legislative and personal conflicts and the revelations of administrative failure that had brought down Pawley but also momentous national issues, notably the Canada-US Free Trade Agreement and the controversial Meech Lake constitutional reforms. The former challenged deeply held NDP policy favouring tariff protection on behalf of jobs for Canadian industrial workers while the latter threatened the party's equally firm belief in a strong federal government.

Provincially, Doer was not expected to win. Internal party polls actually led party insiders to worry that the party could be almost destroyed in the legislature. In the end, a surge in support for a somewhat unlikely group, the Liberals and leader Sharon Carstairs, was most decisive in shaping the results. The Liberal surge held, the NDP recovered somewhat, but it was the Conservatives, led by their still-beleaguered leader, Gary Filmon, who won.

The election of 1988 produced a minority government. The Progressive Conservatives ended up with 25 seats from 38% of the popular vote, concentrated in their southwestern Manitoba rural base and south Winnipeg urban redoubt. The Liberals took an astonishing 20 seats and 35% of the vote, concentrated in Winnipeg, and the NDP won a surprising 12 seats and 23% of the vote, based as usual in Winnipeg's north side and the rural and industrial north of the province.[7] Despite the loss of official opposition status, Doer had competently managed the election and warded off disaster. The election of 1988 was a reprieve for Doer and the NDP. Afterward, his role was to lead the third party in the provincial Legislature, a role that partially shielded him from the divisive issues of the late 1980s while he honed his own political skills and rebuilt an NDP that had been thoroughly gutted by the end of Pawley's years in office.

Shortly after the election, Gary Doer took an important step in his personal life when he married Virginia Devine. A former schoolteacher and a former Howard Pawley staffer in the earlier 1980s, Devine also maintained a strong autonomous career by co-founding and serving as a principal in Viewpoints Research Ltd., a market and opinion research company that conducts surveys for business, employee associations and labour unions as well as non-profit organizations in Manitoba and throughout Canada. Devine and Doer became the parents of two daughters.

Between 1988 and 1990, the provincial Conservatives governed in a political environment that remained highly volatile. The provincial legislature had to deal with such issues as the constitutional fallout of the Meech Lake Accord of 1987, and the pressures on provincial government programs created by increasing deficit/debt problems intensified by federal government initiatives. Doer demonstrated his considerable parliamentary and strategic skills during the contentious debates in the Legislature throughout this period and he also was also successful in increasing his party's credibility that had been in decline in the mid-1980s. He made sure that the NDP was not drawn into any critical legislative divisions that would plunge the province into a quick election, arguing that the Filmon government had been duly elected and deserved the chance to do so. While critical of most of the Tory agenda and quick in debate against Filmon and the government, Doer and his caucus emerged as a constructive organization and freed itself from the rancorous legislative politics of the Lyon-Pawley era.

Doer also did well from the prolonged debate about the controversial Meech Lake constitutional reform package. Premier Filmon consistently sought an all-party approach to the momentous but increasingly unpopular reform package by working with both opposition parties and their leaders. The government relied on public hearings and an all-party report in 1989 and then drew both opposition leaders into the negotiations during early 1990 when the federal government of Brian Mulroney made a last push to revise Meech Lake in order to get it approved by the three hold-out provinces—Manitoba, New Brunswick and Newfoundland. Doer's NDP was as lukewarm as the Premier and the Conservatives (and probably the citizens of Manitoba), but he was not as hostile to or as compromised by the final effort to salvage an agreement as Liberal leader Sharon Carstairs had been. Like Filmon, Doer appeared measured and statesmanlike in the efforts during 1989 and 1990 to pass the reform package. He was equally poised when a member of his caucus, Elijah Harper, refused the unanimous consent that would have seen the Manitoba legislature approve the Accord by the 23 June 1990 deadline assigned by the federal government. Elijah Harper's principled stance, based on the resolute opposition to the Accord in the Aboriginal community that he both represented and hailed from, was understandable and, in Manitoba at least, supported.

The 1990 Election: Leader of the Official Opposition

In the wake of the June collapse of the constitutional reform package, and the conclusion of the lengthy legislative session, the Premier sought an election and it was duly called for September 1990. This time Gary Filmon won a slender majority. The Progressive Conservatives increased their seat total from 24 to 30 and received 42% of the popular vote. The Liberals, whose leader, Sharon Carstairs, had been diminished by the furor over efforts to save the Meech Lake Accord that she had once denounced and then supported, were reduced to third place with 7 seats but still held 28% of the popular vote. The NDP, however, won 20 seats and 29% of the popular vote. For Doer, the return to Official Opposition status was a victory of sorts and an opportunity to further show he deserved the Premiership.

As leader of the Official Opposition after 1990, Doer bore down in defence of social policies but did not get drawn into pointless votes of confidence. The NDP had even supported the Tory budget of 1990. Doer and his caucus were effective and at times sharp in their criticism of cutbacks and administrative reorganization in both health and education that resulted from Filmon's strong emphasis on deficit reduction. Doer also drew attention to the province's child poverty rates and high unemployment, and in 1993 opposed the withdrawal of funding from public advocacy and local community groups.[8] He also opposed the PC government's general disdain for public ownership and its pursuit of privatization. Resuming his role as a voice for constitutional reform, he announced in 1992 that the NDP caucus supported the provincial government position in favour of the Charlottetown Accord. Again, Filmon had had recourse to an all-party task force whose report had formed the basis for provincial support and was reflected in the content of the Accord. This new Accord, which was a last-ditch effort by the federal government to salvage meaningful constitutional reform pitched at Quebec and to meet the Aboriginal community's constitutional goals, was defeated in the national referendum of October 1992, and defeated in Manitoba and five other provinces. Doer's views on Quebec, as demonstrated during the Meech Lake and Charlottetown debates, were that Quebec required recognition of its distinctiveness within Canada but that there should be no erosion of Ottawa's fiscal responsibilities to the provinces.[9] It was easy enough for Doer to support the later 1997 Calgary Declaration, the effort of the Chrétien government to recognize Quebec and accept greater respect for provincial areas of responsibility since it also entrenched federal fiscal responsibilities to the provinces.

Despite Doer's sustained advocacy between 1990 and 1995 of issues such as health care management and fiscal responsibility in such areas as social welfare and education and post-secondary education, the NDP was still tagged as spendthrift and profligate, In addition to his plans for neighbourhood health organizations, Doer also pledged to negotiate with pharmaceutical companies to reduce the cost of prescription drugs, as well as to create a new group of health care providers called nurse practitioners.[10] Doer also promised a balanced budget with no personal or sales tax increases over four years and indicated that he would cut nearly $119 million from government programs to fund health, education, and job creation.[11] No amount of NDP criticism could counter the Progressive Conservative government's appearance of careful governance through determined restraint and widely-felt cuts in the public sector, including the controversial "Filmon Fridays", compulsory ten-day layoffs that affected and disaffected thousands of public sector employees.

The 1995 Election: Another Term in Opposition

The April 1995 election sustained Filmon's Conservatives in office, but strengthened Doer's NDP as the Official Opposition. The Conservatives received 43% of the popular vote and won 31 seats, while the NDP received 33% of the vote and 23 seats, and the Liberals, under a new Leader, Paul Edwards, held on to 24% of the vote but won just 3 seats.[12] Edwards was not elected and, despite his political skills, did not stick around as leader. The Filmon approach with its emphasis on fiscal responsibility (including the first balanced budget in 20 years), and a campaign focussed yet again on the managerial competency and trustworthiness of the leader rather than the party, was successful, but the Doer approach and the NDP's emphasis on preserving and strengthening social programs, above all, public health insurance, also resonated with the electorate.

In his second term as Opposition Leader, Doer continued to attack the Filmon government over cuts to education, health and social welfare programs. Filmon's government came to be seen as maintaining a course of restraint into the late 1990s that was beginning to seem excessive to the large urban population of Winnipeg in the midst of a turn-around in economic circumstances and expectations. In addition to criticizing the government for sometimes-significant flaws in health care and social services, Doer was presented with other issues that highlighted party differences. In health care, for example, some service cuts and programs simply appeared as mean-spirited and ineffectual, as in a botched move to centralize hospital food preparation. Doer's NDP opposed labour legislation championed by the contentious new minister of Labour, Vic Toews. One bill made the certification of trade unions much more difficult, while another sought to prevent union dues from being directed to a political party. Since there were strong institutional links between labour unions and the NDP and a trend among trade unionists to support the NDP in Manitoba—not a guaranteed tendency in Canada by any means—Doer and his party argued that these measures were simple harassment.[13]

A more crucial political issue was the surprise if not stunning decision by the Filmon government, announced in December 1995, to privatize the Manitoba Telephone System. Not surprisingly, Doer opposed the privatization.[14] Deeply informed about the strengths and limits of MTS and other publicly owned corporations, Doer could mount a highly plausible critique of privatization, both as a business strategy and as a political process. In particular, the NDP was able to chip away at the claims the Filmon government made about the economic benefits of privatization. Doer and his colleagues emphasized such factors as the potential loss of top-quality jobs in Manitoba as well as the rather brazen benefits to financial services brokers in the privatization process. Doer was equally critical about the process of privatization, hammering away at the point that the matter had not even been hinted at in the 1995 election platform of the Filmon team. The extremely contentious debate about privatization once again revealed Doer's strong debating skills.

Throughout his time in opposition, Doer was adept at the skilful thrust-and-parry of Question Period. He was well-briefed, strong in debate and, equally significantly, led a caucus that had its fair share of serious-minded, highly-informed and hard-working MLAs, almost all of whom owed their political life to Doer's revival of the provincial NDP, at a time when its federal counterpart was nearly obliterated even in Manitoba. All of this was on display during the MTS debate and after as the NDP seemed to gain new force by the end of the 1990s.

By 1999, the government had come under fire for failing to convince voters that it could turn in a new direction despite an increasingly prosperous provincial economy. Filmon simply could not convince voters that the PCs were serious about the government's new spending initiatives after years of practicing restraint. The Tories could not quite capture the mood at a time when the economic gloom, like fiscal restraint from Ottawa, was lifting across Canada. Doer had credibility in making promises about restoring social spending and fiscal responsibility after a decade of disciplined, careful and plausible policy proposals as well as a decade of effective criticism of the Filmon governments.

More pointedly, the NDP was handed the benefit of an old-fashioned political scandal. The news media disinterred a piece of political skullduggery pertaining to fringe candidates running in the Interlake riding, and the financing of two other fringe candidates during the 1995 election.[15] The media turned the story, which had run during the 1995 campaign, into an exposé that suggested Progressive Conservatives' culpability at the highest level. Three independent candidates from an unregistered party called Independent Native Voice had received encouragement and financial assistance to run campaigns from Progressive Conservative officials. In one riding, Interlake, the candidate had in effect been put up to run and financed by Conservative plotters. This plan was devised as a measure intended to split the vote in the riding to ensure an NDP defeat. In the Legislature and out, Doer demonstrated his usual high level of debating skills and called for a judicial inquiry, to which Filmon quickly agreed. The ensuing inquiry documented how the Interlake candidate had been induced to run by both local and senior Progressive Conservatives, and funding massaged by a group including Julian Benson, Secretary of the Treasury Board and a sometime-PC activist, and Taras Sokolyk, the Premier's Chief of Staff and senior political advisor. Their involvement cast a shadow on the Premier and the government, despite every indication that he had nothing to do with either the scheme or the later efforts at a cover-up.[16]

The Triumph of 1999: Premier at Last

When Manitoba went to the polls in September 1999, the NDP campaigned with restored credibility and renewed vigour. The NDP platform represented the style if not the themes used by other successful social democratic parties at the time. Like the NDP under Roy Romanow and Lorne Calvert in Saskatchewan (and unlike a succession of NDP Premiers in BC at the time), Doer emphasized administrative efficiency and moderate policies rather than dramatic policy shifts or highly partisan initiatives. It bore similarities of rhetoric and substance to Tony Blair's success with the so-called Third Way model in Great Britain. The themes of fiscal responsibility, a mixed private-public approach to economic development, the nurturing of social programs and the efficient administration of government were all characteristics of successful social democratic parties elsewhere and they fit perfectly with Doer's NDP.[17] "Today's NDP," as the party billed itself during the campaign, was comfortable in pledging it would sustain Manitoba's balanced budget legislation while pursuing the efficient allocation of current social services. If these pledges irritated "socialist" adherents in the party (as it did in Manitoba and everywhere else that social democracy was being rebuilt at the turn of the century), it also removed the sting of those, like the Manitoba Tories, who charged that the NDP would be fiscally irresponsible. Doer promised to hold the line on taxes while continuing to be a vociferous defender of public medical care, including the elimination of "hallway medicine."[18] He promised a 10% tuition freeze and investment in the province's colleges.[19] Doer's middle-of-the-road approach had convinced the public that, in addition to the NDP's traditional emphasis on social programs, there could be added a focus on economic management.

Filmon campaigned with his usual efficiency but even his usual, focused platform—notably key fiscal promises of $500 million in new spending and $500 million in tax cuts—was effectively criticized by Doer and the NDP. The NDP benefited greatly from the implosion in Winnipeg of the provincial Liberal party (after Edwards the leadership was a mess, feisty Winnipeg riding MLAs Kevin Lamoureux and Garry Kowalski left the caucus, respected St. Boniface MLA Neil Gaudry had died, and factionalism did the rest). The campaign seemed close but when the votes were counted, the Doer machine won 32 seats and 45% of the vote to form a majority government.[20] The Tories were reduced to 24 seats and the Liberals to 1. In addition to holding its traditional base, the NDP had started to make gains in ridings in west and south Winnipeg that it had not held in the recent past.[21]

Gary Doer was sworn in as Premier on October 5, 1999. He also took the position of minister of Federal-Provincial Relations, which he held throughout his premiership. While

Doer was the first union leader to be elected as Premier of Manitoba, his victory speech foreshadowed what had by this time characterized his political career: his ability to steer in the middle of the road. As he proclaimed in his victory speech, "Manitobans have chosen to move into the next century with business, labour, government and people working together for the benefit of all our citizens."[22] Quoted by the *Ottawa Citizen* as stating "I am not Howard Pawley," Doer made it clear from the outset he would not lead a tax-and-spend government.[23]

The NDP under Doer stuck to a limited number of themes throughout its years in office. Each throne speech, for example, included overtures to business as well as to labour, emphasized investment in infrastructure as well as social spending concentrated on health care and education, and identified goals in Aboriginal policy initiatives, public safety and crime prevention, and the environment. While the NDP pursued core social democratic themes over Doer's three terms, each term was also characterized by a special focus on one or more at election time or during the mandate. The first term (1999–2003) focused on rebuilding the social policy projects in areas like health care, local government and labour relations that the NDP saw as its core programs. But the new government also spent time building bridges to sectors like the business community and the post-secondary education system that would not provide any direct political payoff. The second term (2003–07) concentrated on education, public safety, capital projects and the environment. The third term (2007–09) appears at this time to represent largely a continuation of themes already broached, but seemingly without a particular focus, perhaps a reflection of the international financial crisis that broke in 2008.

The first term was the chance for Gary Doer to prove that his moderate economic and political management strategy would be implemented. For a start, the NDP had a solid majority and diverse talents. Not only were there several exceptionally capable veterans from the Opposition years like Becky Barrett, Dave Chomiak, Jean Friesen and Gord Mackintosh in Winnipeg ridings and Steve Ashton, Oscar Lathlin, Eric Robinson and Rosann Wowchuk from northern ridings, but the party had attracted new MLAs, notably Greg Selinger in francophone St. Boniface and Ron Lemieux in rural LaVerendrye. All of these people were given roles in key cabinet posts. The 1999 caucus represented a step forward in the representation of groups previously underrepresented and often discriminated against in public and private life, including Aboriginal people, women, and individuals who were openly gay. It was particularly notable that 9 of 32 MLAs were female. It was more than just symbolic that the Minister of Intergovernmental [Municipal] Affairs, Jean Friesen, was also appointed deputy-premier. Subsequent elections would see the female proportion of the NDP's elected slate increase slightly; the 12 female MLAs of 36 MLAs elected in 2007 comprise the highest proportion of any caucus in Canada.

A less divisive approach towards governance was struck at the outset of the Doer regime. The Filmon administration had moved at the end of its term in office to reform the selection of speakers and presented legislation ceding the choice of the office of Speaker to the Legislature. Following the 1999 election, the process was implemented and the veteran NDP MLA for Point Douglas, George Hickes, was elected and he presided over a successful legislative term. The Nunavut-born Hickes has won re-election in the two subsequent legislatures. One of the sources for bitter partisan antagonism during the legislative sessions of the 1980s and 1990s was removed once the House itself selected its own presiding officer.

Under the key term, balance, Doer sought to appeal to both business and unions at the same time. Based on 1999's Speech from the Throne, the government established a new Lower Tax Commission to review all taxation issues and pledged to provide tax cuts across the board, for businesses large and small, and for individuals.[24] Tax reductions were an important component of Doer's economic strategy in the first term, and after. In subsequent years, the Doer government provided significant tax reductions to individual taxpayers and to small business. In addition, important corporate tax reductions and increases in eligible personal amounts pleased both business and individuals. The government's ability, even in relatively tough economic times, to paint its situation as relatively stable, has been key to ensuring that its long-term vision, articulated in the first term, remains undisturbed.

In building bridges with business, Doer attempted to implement key tenets of the new more moderate forms of social democracy, epitomized but by no means copied from New Labour in Great Britain. Economically, the Doer government professed its intention to enhance the competitive climate in Manitoba to promote investment that would benefit every citizen in one way or another, rhetoric hardly distinguishable from the Filmon era. Beginning in 1999 and in the 10 successive throne speeches that followed, from 2000 to 2008, the Doer government aimed at tax reductions for business and individuals.

One of the first measures the new government dealt with was a program to implement the 1991 Aboriginal Justice Commission, which the NDP had regularly attacked the Filmon government for substantively shelving. In October 1999, Justice Minister Gord Mackintosh and Aboriginal Affairs Minister Eric Robinson announced an Aboriginal Justice Implementation Commission would be created. This Commission, co-chaired by law professor Wendy Whitecloud and lawyer-academic Paul Chartrand, completed its work in 2001 and did set the stage for a fairly multi-directional provincial set of initiatives on the legal, political and economic issues that the 1991 Commission had addressed.[25] Provincial legislative changes resulted in areas ranging from child welfare, Métis rights to justice matters, but not in the most controversial matter of 1991, which was the creation of a separate Aboriginal justice system. The government would claim that changes in legal areas such as closer work with local communities and the creation of separate child and family services to Aboriginal communities and in economic areas like the province's approach to resource development and revenues on Aboriginal lands cumulatively made major changes.

The Doer government's Labour minister, Becky Barrett, put in place a number of changes in the first term, including easing the terms for unions to obtain certification as well as giving employees increased powers to move disputes to binding arbitration. Although business leaders opposed the changes, the government argued that the bill was far less contentious than opponents made it out to be.[26] Shortly thereafter, the government opposed a call by its own party to introduce legislation that would ban replacement workers in the case of a strike.[27] Labour complained about Barrett's and Doer's moderation, but ignored the crucial fact that the reforms had negated the stringent legislation passed by the previous regime. Later, the government passed campaign financing reform that banned both corporate and trade union contributions to party finances, a measure that actually sustained one of the Filmon era "reforms" (limiting trade union funding) while extending them to the other side.

The new government took an incremental approach to minimum wage legislation, a core social democratic policy that has faced either malign neglect or outright hostility in Canada in the past 30 years. The government implemented regular if modest increases. The provincial minimum wage was increased to $6.25 from $6.00 in November 2000 and increased by 25¢ per hour annually for several years. By April 2005, the minimum wage had increased to $7.25 per hour, a figure that still fell far short of a true living wage, but which represented a commitment to regular increases.[28] The increases accelerated to semi-annually and as of late 2009 the minimum wage stood at $9.00 per hour. Typically, the government's minimum wage policy was strongly criticized by anti-poverty activists and business advocacy organizations alike.

The government made a serious move at administrative reform in the restructuring of educational administration through a program of school district amalgamation, long a touchy subject in Manitoba. In 2000, the minister of Education, Training and Youth, Drew Caldwell, wrote to the divisions informing them of the province's plan and urging them to consider voluntary amalgamation, and in 2001 the government announced formally its intention to proceed with the plan that was intended to curb school taxes through efforts to save administrative costs while preserving programs.[29] Described as the "modernization" of school boundaries, the plan drew on many of the proposals contained in a 1994 study done for the previous government as the province faced a long-term decline in the school-age population, particularly outside Winnipeg and the Red River Valley. Two voluntary division amalgamations among the 57 districts occurred in the late 1990s, when Norwood merged with St. Boniface and Tiger Hills and Pembina Valley became the Prairie Spirit School Division, but many of the province's divisions were not sold on the idea.[30] Continuing pressure after 2000 led to further reductions, and the total number of school divisions was reduced to 38. The impact of amalgamation was surprisingly uncontroversial, though it provoked continuing eruptions in the case of the amalgamation of the suburban Winnipeg division of Transcona with the semi-rural Springfield division. While school taxes have generally been contained, the financial savings to districts have not been dramatic. In fact, one report claims that the savings have averaged only 2.6%, or half a million dollars, per division due to upward wage harmonization and equalization of working conditions in amalgamated areas.[31] In the end, that report concluded that "the time and energy spent on the amalgamation process would have been better directed towards meaningful educational reform."[32] Other points of criticism included the government's effort to promote Early Years education and greater parental involvement in schools while eliminating early-year province-wide testing. In all of these areas, critics maintain that the effect on pupils' learning has not been assessed positively.

Another key area in the first term was to emphasize the priority of health care, an issue around which Doer had rallied support from the public and professional groups, notably nurses, during his time in opposition. The commitment was signalled by the appointment of one of the most effective MLAs, Dave Chomiak, as Minister of Health, which he held for five years. In 2000, the government announced a Physician Recruitment and Retention Plan. According to the most recent Minister of Health, Theresa Oswald, this plan has resulted in a net increase of over 300 doctors since 2000, and a record net gain of 57 doctors for 2009.[33] Since 1999, the plan has included increasing the number of medical school spaces, attempting to break down barriers in accrediting foreign-trained physicians, and rebating tuition up to 60% to encourage medical students to pursue their careers within the province.

Recruiting doctors was not, however, the only reform program. In its bid to end so-called "hallway medicine" within six months of the government's 1999 majority, meaning the practice of housing in-patients in hallways even during treatment, Doer pledged an initial $135 million increase in health-care spending, including a significant expansion to Manitoba's largest hospital, the Winnipeg Health Sciences Center.[34] Other measures included expanding health services in the north through the Aboriginal Health Strategy, announced in 1999's Speech from the Throne, as well as training more nurses and diagnostic technicians. This theme persisted well beyond the first term, proving that health care was able to provide a great deal of political mileage for Doer. During its first term, the Doer government not only made health care a fiscal priority, but the Premier also stood up for the national basis of the health care system in Canada and raised his profile across the nation.

In a 2002 presentation to the Royal Commission on the Future of Health Care in Canada, Doer announced that it was time to end the "blame game" between Ottawa and the provinces. Further, he stressed the importance of the federal "moral and financial muscle" in improving and updating Medicare, especially in jurisdictions like Manitoba. The Premier argued that "We need a strong federal partner with the energy and resources to sustain and innovate in a national health care system."[35] Health spending increased during Doer's second term as Premier, greatly assisted by large increases to the federal share undertaken by the Chrétien and Martin governments, ensuring that Manitoba's per capita health spending would remain the highest in Canada for the seventh consecutive year, as of 2004.[36] Most recently, provincial support for health care was extended to individual citizens with the announcement of a new Caregivers Tax Credit of up to $1,020 per year for those who care for family members in the home.[37] In all of the measures to strengthen the health care system, the Doer governments benefited a great deal from the actions of the federal government. It created in 2003 a separate Canada Health Transfer to deliver funding to the provinces. This new fiscal package led to substantial increases in federal transfers to the provinces beyond the more generous transfers that had begun in the late nineties after more than a decade of contraction.

Despite the government's new initiatives, however, the health system continued to be criticized for the way in which money was being allocated, especially in recent years when the growth of federal transfers has slowed. For example, in 2006 nurse practitioners criticized the government for failing to fund enough jobs to hire nurse practitioner graduates despite 2005 legislation making it legal for them to work in the province. Jane MacDonald, then co-chair of the Nurse Practitioner Association of Manitoba, argued that each nurse practitioner could handle upward of 500 patients and that their employment could significantly ease nursing shortages.[38] Conservative health critic Myrna Driedger accused the Doer government of only going halfway, then "hitting the snooze button," leaving many qualified health professionals out of work.[39] There have also been concerns put forward by provincial Liberals and Progressive Conservatives about various aspects of the health care system including the need to improve northern maternity care,[40] address the shortage of health care aides,[41] address the reduction of emergency surgeries at community hospitals,[42] redress the lack of attention to mental health issues,[43] and, pointedly, the resurgent problem of "hallway medicine."[44] Government spending in health care was generally seen as the realization, or at least partial fulfillment, of key NDP election promises in the first term, though the government continued to discuss the issue and to infuse dollars in its second and third terms.[45]

Re-election and Recommitment

After a term just short of four years, Doer called a provincial election for June 2003. The 2003 platform, "much accomplished, much to do," emphasized continuities with the first term. Policy initiatives included reducing fees and income taxes, hiring more nurses and doctors, reducing wait lists for medical procedures, improving law enforcement and education, and taking a cautious approach to regulating the economy.[46] In addition, however, Doer's NDP emphasized the themes of education, public safety and the environment. In his own riding of Concordia, Doer won resounding support from over three-quarters of the voters. The NDP was well-funded and focussed in its campaign and it also benefitted from the continued collapse of the provincial Liberals and the failure of the Conservatives under new leader, Stuart Murray, to seriously attack the NDP record. The NDP increased its appeal in Winnipeg into ridings on the south side that had previously been part of the Conservatives' urban bastion. Doer's NDP cruised to re-election, winning a very strong majority with 35 seats and more than 49% of the popular vote.[47]

Doer's second term saw greater activism in the expansion in the province's post-secondary institutions. In 2004, the government pledged to create the University College of the North in The Pas and Thompson. This institution was designed to promote training and education in several critical areas, including media, nursing and midwifery, and other in-demand careers,[48] in addition to providing much-needed training and educational opportunities in Manitoba's north—factors particularly affecting the large and young Aboriginal population of the region.

Higher education also provided more "populist" spending, with substantial expansions beginning in 1999 to technical and vocational education that took on increasing significance after 2003. Manitoba's technical schools were encouraged and funded to grow. Such specific programs as a Technical Vocational Initiative, which created an additional 4,000 apprenticeship spaces in 2007 alone, provided further evidence of the focus on technical training for future economic growth.[49] Using provincial capital funds, Winnipeg's Red River College created a second campus located in the elegant Exchange District of the downtown, and expanded its large, partially-subterranean suburban campus.

The Doer government also appealed to Manitoba's university and college students with a tuition freeze starting in 1999 and a later post-graduate tuition rebate program, regular extensions to student loans and bursaries, and awards for post-graduate students across the province. The tuition and bursary policies controlled post-secondary educational costs and contributed to the large enrolment increases of the past decade in post-secondary institutions (more, however, at the university level than the economically vital technical-vocational level). The objection of university leaders—that the tuition freeze limited their capacity to deliver new programs, particularly strong from the University of Manitoba—had very limited traction with government or the public.[50]

A great deal of post-secondary expansion occurred during the Doer decade. The University of Winnipeg, under the Presidency of Lloyd Axworthy, the former Chrétien cabinet minister who was selected in 2004, was a visible collaborator with the province in an audacious program of physical expansion, including new buildings in such areas as the sciences and fine arts, and it has become a large, highly visible campus in downtown Winnipeg. The University of Manitoba has also been refurbished by new construction and revitalized by new hirings, benefiting from substantial new capital funds, including the lion's large share of two large capital assistance programs during the decade, as well as regular increases in provincial and federal funding for research programs. All four public universities, including Brandon and St. Boniface, have been reshaped and renewed, at the level of new hiring and new facilities, based on resources that were simply unavailable throughout the fiscally constrained 1990s.[51] A notable sign of the Doer government's commitments and tendency to stay the course in its post-secondary policy was the creation in 2003 of a separate department of Advanced Education and the continuous tenure of the minister, Dianne McGifford, through all three governments, a rarity in a government where almost all ministers have been reshuffled regularly.

Alongside new investment in post-secondary education, Doer's second term also focused on public safety, particularly in Winnipeg's core, through new spending on additional police officers and safety personnel, as well as new measures designed to increase the prosecution of gang members, both so-called juvenile gangs and also local branches of international motorcycle gangs. In 2003, the government established a special Gang Prosecution Unit, which was expanded once again in 2005.[52] The problem remains difficult in Manitoba as it is elsewhere in Canada. The province also bore down on child pornography in 2006. The emphasis on public safety was accompanied by increasingly strict Safe Schools legislation and an expansion of various preventative or rehabilitative programs such as the Take Back the Streets, Lighthouse and other programs. Other measures, marketed as pertaining to health and safety, were addressed in the most recent term. These included a ban on a smoking and hand-held cell-phone use in motor vehicles in 2008.[53] Like health and education spending, government investment in the area of safety, broadly defined, was promoted by successive Doer governments as an agenda for all people, fulfilling at least in part the promise of populism that his mandates successively seemed to fulfill.

The government's second term saw a more active development and enunciation of Doer's environmental goals. In addition to the consistent social democratic theme of emphasizing spending in services deemed most important to Manitobans, the Doer government claimed a commitment to the environment. Each of the three Doer governments emphasized an element—land management in the first, water resources in the second, and air quality in the third, most notably a pledge to meet Kyoto greenhouse gas emission standards within five years. Second term Throne Speeches consistently articulated the need for green investment and spending, as well as the cleanup of existing industries and of Lake Winnipeg, prone to fish-harming algae blooms caused by excess farm fertilizer applications throughout its drainage basin as well as Winnipeg's effluent overflows.

Not only did Doer pursue a "green" agenda through a partnership approach, but he also focused on the economic advantages of pursuing a green agenda. A journalist who has covered Manitoba politics for years noted, "Doer continually pushes the idea that hydro power could do for Manitoba what oil has done for Alberta—create an economic boom and attract jobs and people to every corner of the province."[54] Doer argued, "You either build what you've got as strengths, like Alberta has done with oil … or we're going to continue to be a mediocre province. Our strength is hydro and renewable resources."[55] During his tenure as Premier, the government developed numerous policies and plans to support a "greener" sustainable province at the same time as focusing on the economic advantages of green policy. For example, in June 2009, the Premier gave the keynote address at the Energy and Climate Forum of the Canadian American Business Council in Washington, DC, where he addressed such issues "as the growing need for renewable energy, the business opportunities associated with alternative power development and new green technology, as well as the need for Canada and the United States to work together on issues related to energy security."[56] This third approach to dealing with environmental issues was representative of Doer's overall management style. Indeed, in an interview, he highlighted a key part of his overall political strategy with regard to climate change legislation, one that reflected his approach as a manager of public opinion. As he stated, "The best strategy is to talk about the kids and the impacts of climate change on their future. Try a populist approach—with some people you are never going to win on the arguments."[57]

Provincial electric power development proceeded carefully during the last decade under the auspices of Manitoba Hydro, an arms-length Crown corporation. Manitoba Hydro had to contend with increasing environmental and social issues pertaining to northern water diversion and dam-building projects from the 1960s to the 1980s, particularly regarding adverse or disappointing socio-economic impacts on First Nations in the Churchill River and Nelson River drainage basins. The company sold Manitoba's excess electrical power very successfully and profitably into the adjacent areas of the United States, while continuing the decades-long effort, with the provincial government, to negotiate power sales to the potentially voracious Ontario market. Manitoba Hydro undertook one hydro-electric project, the Wuskwatim generating station on the Burntwood River (part of the Nelson River system that has been the focus of northern hydro-electric projects since the late 1950s), and one wind-power project at St. Leon in southern Manitoba. Wuskwatim will generate 200 megawatts of power when completed in 2010, while St. Leon was completed in 2005 and generates about 100 megawatts. Manitoba Hydro also pressed the province to decide upon the location of a new major Direct-Current transmission line to more effectively deliver surplus power to the United States. This so-called BiPole III project was directed by the province to be located on the west side of Lake Winnipeg rather than the more economical east side route precisely because the environmental impact of the latter would be worse and it would draw national and international environmental protests that could threaten future electrical sales. The Crown corporation was entrenched as a vital state enterprise under the NDP government, signified by the construction between 2005 and 2008 of a major new downtown 22-storey headquarters for Hydro, a much-touted "green" building.[58]

Water management, including flood control in the Red River Valley and other river systems in Manitoba, are extremely important matters in the province. The Doer government well knew that the capacity of government to manage drainage basin flows has long been critical to the success of provincial governments with the agricultural community, with local governments and with First Nations. The matter is central to contemporary Manitoba and a Ministry of Water Stewardship was created in 2003 from the former Ministry of Conservation and other agencies, and prominent members of cabinet, first Steve Ashton and continuing since 2007 with Christine Melnick, have held the portfolio. The majority of the work consists of the regulation of water flows, freshwater fisheries and environmental controls, the latter a major challenge in the province since the Filmon government began to encourage very large-scale hog-farm operations after the Free Trade Agreement opened big opportunities in agri-business, which the Doer government sustained although it tried to address the environmental problems the large plants created.

One major test case for the Doer governments was flood control in the Red River Valley, which remains one of the richest agricultural regions in Canada. The entire flood plain remains seriously prone to flooding, which is particularly acute in the case of urban areas, above all the city of Winnipeg.

The origins of this project lay in the aftermath of the 1997 Red River "flood of the century," which had fully stressed the existing capacities of the floodway system completed in 1968. By 1999, after the Filmon government had borne somewhat unfair criticisms for its emergency response in 1997 and its post-flood compensation program (including from Gary Doer), provincial, local and national officials had implemented a full-scale review of the floodway system. Under the auspices of the International Joint Commission (IJC), which manages Canadian-American boundary issues, detailed consulting engineering reports recommended expanding the capacity of the floodway from protecting against a one-in-100-year to a one-in-700-year risk for the entire Red River Valley. Once the IJC report was accepted both by the adjoining states (North Dakota and Minnesota) and the province of Manitoba, it was up to the respective federal and state/provincial governments of the two countries to proceed. Manitoba took the initiative with the federal Liberal governments between 2001 and 2005 to develop joint funding for the massive project.[59]

The province authorized the long-planned expansion to the Winnipeg Floodway with the creation in March 2004 of the Winnipeg Floodway Authority. The project cost more than $700 million and resulted in a major expansion in the capacity of flood protection for the City of Winnipeg and upstream communities as well as major upgrades to existing structures, such as the floodway mechanisms, dykes and drainage works and roadways.[60]

In the subsequent five years, the Authority supervised the reconstruction and expansion of the Floodway up to the one-in-700-year level of protection as well as expanded upstream community protection to such places as Ste. Agathe and the Roseau River First Nation, each of which had been hit by the flood of 1997 and later spring floods. Other communities on the Red River were already protected by ring dikes. As of September 2009, the new floodway had been mostly completed up to the new standards, and its regulatory authority had begun to expand to include authority over a long-awaited but controversial all-weather highway to be constructed along the "east side" of Lake Winnipeg to link a series of First Nations with the existing all-weather highway system.[61]

Doer's role as minister of Federal-Provincial Relations cannot be underestimated in the welter of departmental and inter-governmental negotiations within Canada and dicey negotiations with not only the Bush administration in United States but the hyper-vigilant and powerful federal senators from North Dakota as well as state officials. The result was the successful launch of a joint Manitoba-Canada project run by the provincially operated Floodway Authority. Manitoba's NDP government was successful in cooperating with Ottawa's Liberal government through the mediation between the Premier and the province's federal cabinet ministers. Doer's management of the matter, as well as that of responsible cabinet ministers including successive ministers of Water Stewardship, was all the more important because it was conducted against a backdrop of continuing and longstanding Manitoba concerns about North Dakota/United States water and flood control projects dating from the 1950s and the massive Garrison Dam on the Missouri River, which led to proposals to divert water into the Hudson Bay drainage basin.

One project that resurfaced after 1999 was a plan by the state of North Dakota to divert "foreign" water from land-locked Devil's Lake into the Red River system and ultimately Lake Winnipeg. This diversion had been looming for years due to the relentless expansion of Devil's Lake and resulting loss of agricultural land, which was a major issue in agricultural North Dakota. The diversion concerned Manitobans over the potential for the introduction of new aquatic species, water-borne contaminants, and excessive water volumes in the Red River. The careful and persistent efforts of Gary Doer in meetings with North Dakota and United States officials, as well as in regular meetings between the Prairie Premiers and upper state Governors, led to a limited program of water diversion accompanied by a filtration system that allayed most concerns when the diversions began in 2005.[62]

Doer's green policies also reached beyond Manitoba's and even Canada's borders. Under his tutelage, Manitoba became a national leader addressing climate change. For example, in 2005, *Business Week* magazine ranked Premier Doer as one of 20 international political leaders who stood out for their efforts concerning climate change, specifically concerning his government's goal to reduce gases that cause global warming. The magazine noted that "Under Doer, sustainable development has become an economic lynchpin in the Canadian province of Manitoba. His action plan on climate change aims to shrink GHGs by 23%, or almost four times the Kyoto target."[63] *Business Week* ranked the government of Manitoba to be the most resourceful and creative regional government concerning climate change and specifically made note of Manitoba's commitment to reduce greenhouse gases and how this commitment was also the centerpiece of the province's economic development plan.[64] In one of the key events of Doer's tenure, the provincial government passed legislation in 2008 that required "Manitoba to meet its Kyoto commitment by 2012 and set long-term goals for further greenhouse gas (GHG) reductions by 2020 and 2025."[65]

In addition to being a strong supporter of Kyoto, Doer also pursued regional agreements in support of the environment, including the Midwestern Regional Greenhouse Gas Reduction Accord signed with seven American governors in November 2007.[66] As he stated in a 2005 interview with The Climate Group, Doer believed provincial-state cooperation was one of the keys to implementing Kyoto, despite the federal government's reluctance to sign on to the accord: "For us in North America, faced with the reality that the US President is not going to ratify Kyoto, it is really important for provinces and states to work together and to continue to celebrate the positive opportunities around climate change strategies."[67]

The 2007 Election and the Third Term

While Doer's first two terms featured clear policy directives, 2007 marked a departure in the government's approach to marketing. In 2007, Doer and the NDP chose to focus their platform ("Forward, Not Back," highly evocative of one New Labour manifesto) in ways designed to counter voter fatigue and the time-for-a-change appeal of the Opposition Tories. The campaign themes sustained the familiar priorities of health, the environment, education, tax cuts, public safety, improving Manitoba's highway infrastructure, and maintaining Manitoba Hydro as a public institution, reiterating many of the themes of earlier campaigns, but emphasizing that successful governance was cumulative rather than immediate.[68] Perhaps, at this point, the NDP and Doer himself felt that their record should speak for itself, and that to depart from what had become a highly successful blend of policy and personality would be detrimental to the party. Indeed: on May 22, 2007, Manitobans went to the polls and elected 36 New Democratic Party MLAs. The Conservative Party managed to win 19 seats under new leader Hugh McFadyen, a net loss of one, while the Liberals, again led by Jon Gerrard, held steady at just two seats.[69] The election result confirmed that Doer's leadership and personal appeal, as well as the incremental approach to policy-making, continued to win voters. Voter turnout for this election was also low at 57%, demonstrating that Manitobans were following a national trend towards political apathy. Doer's personal draw had helped his party remain in power and he had matched Duff Roblin's previously unique achievement in winning three successive majorities.

The post-election course of the government was to hold steady to its 2007 pledges. The 2008 Throne Speech featured tax reductions across the board, a new 4-year plan for an additional $4.7 billion in spending in areas of health, housing, transportation, drinking water and wastewater, campus upgrades, an emphasis on Aboriginal educational training, a plan to ban government health care premiums in the province, a ban on smoking in cars, and a new Wetlands initiative, among other projects.[70]

The enduring strategy of a balanced approach to governance was also shown in the 2008 Speech from the Throne. Written during the start of an international financial panic, the Speech stated that "This is not a time to retreat from our balanced policies or from our long-term growth strategy. Indeed, it is more important than ever to expand the skills base of our workforce and invest in strategic capital projects and innovation. By staying the course we will add stability to our economy and position Manitoba more strongly for the economic recovery."[71] In other words, spending money to make money, as well as attempting to provide individual Manitobans with the capital to keep the province's economy stable, represented one key way in which Doer's NDP maintained its social-democratic stance in the first term and beyond.

In dealing with the challenges of Aboriginal affairs, Gary Doer, throughout all three terms, followed the same model as he did for business. He attempted to draw upon the principles of resource partnerships and management with Aboriginal people, particularly in Manitoba's north. Still, the variety of hydro-electric projects were not without controversy, despite the aim to develop Manitoba's largely impoverished North while capitalizing on her natural resources. As Martin Thibault and Steven Hoffman explain in one key study, Manitoba Hydro continues to develop "business-only partnerships" on a community-by-community basis that has been very controversial for many First Nations groups, who see this approach as a mere continuation of a long-standing and exploitative colonial process.[72] On August 14, 2009, members of the Nisichawayasihk Cree Nation near Nelson House blocked construction access to the Wuskwatim Dam project at Taskinigup Falls on the Burntwood River. Protesters argued that Hydro was not honouring its agreement to hire band members as workers, while Manitoba Hydro maintained it had done so, hiring about 44 workers from that particular band of about 300 Aboriginal workers onsite. While the debate over the relative merits and demerits of both Manitoba Hydro and the government's approach to such agreements merits careful consideration, it can be noted that the Doer government continues to assert that its support for hydro development was good for Aboriginal people and for their communities but that many Aboriginal groups continue to dispute that claim.

In addition to investment in the resources of the north, Gary Doer pursued other initiatives designed to appeal to Aboriginal peoples. These included, most significantly, investments in post-secondary education and infrastructure. As early as 1999, Doer was promoting a new Aboriginal Education Strategy. Then, in 2004, he announced Manitoba's first Aboriginal midwife and nurse education program, as well as the creation of the University College of the North. The 2006 Throne Speech announced a round of new building in the north, as well as the expansion of University College of the North. The 2007 speech announced even further investment, plus the intention of the government to look into how to increase First Nations peoples' graduation rates.

The Doer governments avoided serious charges of incompetence or scandal beyond the usual harsh rhetoric that Opposition parties, other levels of government, or interest groups inevitably raise. Nevertheless, a couple of major issues emerged in recent years. At the outset of the 2007 election, the Crocus Fund issue was constantly in the media. The Crocus Investment Fund was a labour-sponsored venture capital fund that focused on investing chiefly in provincial enterprises. In 2005, the Board of Directors of the Crocus Investment Fund resigned and the Fund entered into financial protection and ceased operations.[73] The aftermath left many Manitobans wondering exactly where their money had gone[74] and the government faced a storm of Opposition criticism and veiled charges. The Progressive Conservatives argued that the government had ignored all signs of trouble, putting at risk the investments of more than 30,000 Manitobans and capital valued at about $150 million. Doer's NDP managed to emerge relatively unscathed and rejected a formal inquiry into the matter by insisting that it had done nothing wrong.[75] The government argued that the regulatory system, through reports by the Auditor-General and the Manitoba Securities Commission, had worked and that the normal course of winding up the affairs of the Crocus Fund would lead to an appropriate level of reimbursement from the Fund, which had already provided tax benefits to investors and was a known risky investment. What could have been a political nightmare for the NDP government ended up being a battle that individual Manitobans had to fight over in court, out of the political spotlight.[76]

More recently, an election financing issue resurfaced from the past. It was claimed that in 1999, NDP brass were responsible for altering 13 election financial returns, excluding the official agents, in order to cash in more rebates. In essence, the primary whistle-blower, former agent Jim Treller, alleged that full-time unionized workers were counted as expenses rather than donations-in-kind, thus inflating the assumed rebatable costs of the campaign. Donations-in-kind are not rebated, while actual expenses are. While the party repaid its debts as required, the issue came under public scrutiny in a June 2009 question period, though most of the questions—and the blame—were focused on Finance Minister Greg Selinger.[77] While the issue could have been debated in a court of law, the NDP chose to repay the $76,000 it was alleged to have improperly billed rather than to face a court battle.

In a 2006 interview with the Metropolitan Corporate Counsel, Doer elaborated on Manitoba's "business-friendly" climate, emphasizing how his government had cut business tax by half since the start of his mandate and cultivated partnerships with business on the international scene. As he pointed out, "We have in the last five years had the largest inflow of private sector investment ever."[78] Such measures paid significant dividends to the Doer government, quelling criticism from business people while preserving the NDP's image as a party in service of regular, working Manitobans. Business leaders, in fact, applauded many of Doer's initiatives, including the promotion of immigration for the province's labour pool, his support of new northern hydro projects and his advocacy of a new north-south corridor for free trade between Manitoba and Mexico, initiatives that were not applauded as much in labour or working circles.[79]

The Resignation and the Succession

In the midst of the government's continuing and consistent pursuit of its strategies in 2009, the province absorbed the double surprise of Doer's resignation and his appointment to Washington. While Doer claimed that it would represent the first time in his life he had ever had to be diplomatic,[80] his comments only spoke to his insistence that he remained the ordinary guy with a big job. Clearly, his skills at political brokerage, his 10 years of considerable success in managing a government and his many ties with political figures in the United States as well as Canada all represented many opportunities and situations to be diplomatic, from reconciling business and labour to managing both minor and major scandals. Moreover, the fact that he was named to the post by the Conservative Prime Minister, Stephen Harper, further reflects the legacy of brokerage and Third Way balance that Doer had achieved.

What the immediate future holds for the Manitoba New Democratic Party is difficult to predict, but relevant to an evaluation of Gary Doer's premiership. Three candidates stood up, a relative newcomer to cabinet, Andrew Swan, and the two cabinet veterans, Greg Selinger and Steve Ashton. Swan, a Winnipeg lawyer, soon withdrew despite his good record in cabinet and capable public presentations. Selinger and Ashton then duelled for the leadership.

Ashton had represented the northern riding of Thompson since he was first elected at age 25 in 1981. He held an MA in Economics, and had a record as a traditional NDP activist, a champion of the "north" as well as a key cabinet minister. In the Doer governments, he served variously as minister of Highways, Conservation, Labour, Water Stewardship and Inter-governmental Affairs (responsible for provincial-municipal relations in Manitoba). Selinger, a former academic (with a degrees in Social Work from the University of Manitoba, Public Administration from Queen's, and a PhD from the London School of Economics), was first elected to the Legislature in 1999 in the francophone St. Boniface riding. He had held the Finance ministry for all 10 years of the Doer government as well as the portfolios for French Language Services and Crown Corporations. Selinger easily won the leadership and assumed the premiership on October 19, 2009. While political leaders can change direction, there is every indication that Selinger will maintain the broad policy approaches adhered to by the Doer governments of which he was such a key part. If he does represent an extension of Doer's approach rather than a new one, his premiership will have almost certainly shown that there was a link between Doer's style of politics and the political culture of the province.[81]

An Assessment

In the 2000s, Manitoba has moved away from the world of fierce partisanship and limited expectations for governmental effectiveness that characterized the previous three decades into one in which it is possible to realize a broad consensus and to accept the importance of stable governmental capacity to focus the energies of all sectors and regions of the province. If the latter proves to be the case, then Manitoba will have in a sense returned to a political culture very much like the "progressive/populist" world of the mid-20th century, where politics was conceived of as effective administration and all groups were represented by the "administration." Unlike that world, however, where the segmentation of ethnic, racial, and gender groups was the rule, it would seem that contemporary Manitoba may well have embraced an inclusive democratic ethos for the first time in its history.

Gary Doer's movement from Opposition to Government proved relatively seamless, as his transition from provincial politics to the diplomatic arena has been thus far. His electoral success was built on the practices of a politician more comfortable as a manager carefully giving directives than in espousing wild rhetoric or promises. As the Manitoban "everyman," Doer charmed voters with his particular blend of pragmatic administration and personal appeal. A masterful orator with great public presence, Doer relied on consensus-building as the hallmark of his administrative style. A leader among the Premiers and in national forums, and not just because of his seniority, Doer was also a consensus-builder among them and one to whom they looked to emulate, at least in terms of personal popularity and success at the polls. His overtures to the business community, to the educational community and to the environmental agenda all represented his ability to give everyone at least some measure of what they sought.

Retiring at a time when a fourth term seemed in reach, due to the government's strengths and the Opposition's drift, Doer's legacy among party activists is much different than among the majority of Manitoba's voters. His policy of gradualism rather than transformation has been constant. Doer's legacy has been to leave today's NDP more pragmatic and less program-driven than ever before, appearing at times to respond to the broadest portion of the electorate instead of implementing policy according to the agenda of the party core. This is not to state that political partisanship has diminished, but rather that the approach to politics on Doer's part has included a serious effort to appeal to all parts of the electorate in all parts of the province rather than concentrate on a core of loyal voters and the party's traditional areas of support.

For these reason, Doer's approach represents both mixed policy and mixed results. At the same time, it has been success in a practical sense: Doer and the Manitoba NDP worked successfully over three terms of government for incremental change in a way that strongly suggests the adoption of many Third Way principles, alongside a particular tradition of prairies populism, of contact with the majority, that has worked well throughout Manitoba's political history. As early as 2000, in a speech to an audience at the Queen's University School of Policy Studies, Doer highlighted what was and remained the centrepiece of his electoral and governing strategy, presenting what he called a "balanced vision," one that appealed not only on the basis of tax cuts but of providing additional services in simple terms with which the public could find little fault. As he explained, "The public would rather hear five commitments you can keep than a hundred and five promises, only some of which are kept."[82] The three administrations that Doer led, to reiterate a crucial point, proceeded to govern by increment rather than by transformation, ensuring that their moves were supported by a strong plurality of Manitoba's voters.

Notes

In the preparation of this essay, we would like to thank Dr. Kim Speers, formerly in the Department of Political Studies at the University of Manitoba, for her advice on and contribution to our analysis.

1. "MGEU History," Manitoba Government and General Employees' Union. Accessed July 25, 2007: http://www.mgeu.mb.ca/18.

2. Allen Mills, "Doer, Albert Gary." *The Canadian Encyclopaedia*. Accessed May 12, 2008: http://www.thecanadianencyclopedia.com/index.cfm?PgNm=TCE&Params=A1ARTA0009621.

3. Raymond Hebert, *Manitoba's French-Language Crisis* (Toronto: University of Toronto Press, 2004), 107, 151–52.

4. Elections Manitoba, Statement of Vote 1986, Christopher Adams, *Politics in Manitoba: Parties, Leaders, and Voters* (Winnipeg: University of Winnipeg, 2008), 48, 126.

5. See Ian Stewart, *Just One Vote: From Jim Walding's Nomination to Constitutional Defeat* (Winnipeg: University of Manitoba Press, 2009).

6. For further information on the relationship between the NDP and unions, see: Harold Jansen and Lisa Young, "Solidarity Forever? The NDP, Organized Labour, and the Changing Face of Party Finance in Canada," Paper presented to the Annual Meeting of the Canadian Political Science Association (London, Ontario, June 2–4, 2005), 5–6.

7. Elections Manitoba, Statement of Vote 1988. See also Christopher Adams, *Politics in Manitoba*.

8. Paul Samyn, "NDP Itching to Hit Hustings," *Winnipeg Free Press*, November 14, 1994. See also: "Tories Pull Plug on Agencies," *Winnipeg Free Press*, March 16, 1993.

9. "'No' will Doom Canada, PM Warns," *Financial Post*, September 29, 1992: 6.

10. Alice Krueger, "New Role Favored in Care," *Winnipeg Free Press*, April 11, 1995.

11. Alice Krueger, "Doer Sets Spending Priorities," *Winnipeg Free Press*, March 24, 1995.

12. Elections Manitoba, Statement of Vote 1995.

13. Alice Krueger, "Union Workers Can Say No," *Winnipeg Free Press*, April 13, 1996: A4.

14. Hansard, Second Session of the Thirty-Sixth Legislature, Vol. 74, "Oral Question Period: Manitoba Telephone System" (October 31, 1996). Accessed June 12, 2009: http://www.gov.mb.ca/hansard/hansard/2nd-36th/vol74/h074_3.html.

15. For additional information, see: Doug Smith, *As Many Liars: The Story of the 1995 Manitoba Vote-Splitting Scandal* (Winnipeg: Arbeiter Ring, 2003).

16. David Kuxhaus, "Who Bankrolled Native Candidate in '95 campaign?," *Winnipeg Free Press*, June 24, 1998: A1; David Kuxhaus, "PCs Yield, Call Vote Inquiry," *Winnipeg Free Press*, June 26, 1998, A1; David Kuxhaus, "Vote Charge Haunts Tories NDP Cemands Probe," *Winnipeg Free Press*, June 23, 1998: A1.

17. John F. Conway, *The West: The History of a Region in Confederation*, 3rd. ed. (Halifax: Lorimer: 2005), 375.

18. CBC, "Doer Rallies Candidates on Day One," August 17, 1999. Accessed April 30, 2008: http://www.cbc.ca/news/story/1999/08/17/mb_ndpdayone081799.html.

19. Frances Russell, "NDP Tries Out a New Tune," *Winnipeg Free Press*, December 18, 1998: A14; Brian Cole, "Doer's Democrats," *Winnipeg Free Press*, December 22, 1998: A10; Frances Russell, "Doer Crosses His Fingers," *Winnipeg Free Press*, May 12, 1999: A14.

20. Douglas Nairne, "Manitoba Poll Shows NDP and Tories in Dead Heat," *Globe and Mail*, September 17, 1999: A1; Douglas Nairne, "Doer to Gain from Liberals' Pain," *Winnipeg Free Press*, September 17, 1999: A1; Douglas Nairne, "It's Premier Doer! Collapse of Liberal Vote Swings Province to NDP," *Winnipeg Free Press*, September 22, 1999: A1, "NDP Wins Tight Race with Tories in Manitoba," *Globe and Mail*, September 22, 1999: A1.

21. Elections Manitoba, Statement of Vote 1999. See also Christopher Adams, *Politics in Manitoba*, 125–31.

22. David Roberts, "Doer Takes the Stage as Manitoba's New Premier," *Globe and Mail*, October 6, 1999: A1.

23. "Doer Comes Out Swinging," *Ottawa Citizen*, September 23, 1999: A3.

24. Press Release, "Speech from the Throne Says Economy at a Strategic Junction." Accessed August 31, 2009: http://www.gov.mb.ca/chc/press/top/1999/04/1999-04-06-01.html.

25. "Manitoba Set to Act on Aboriginal Inquiry" Winnipeg Free Press, October 11, 1999: A3; see the web-pages of the Aboriginal Justice Implementation Commission: http://www.ajic.mb.ca/

26. David Kuxhaus, "Premier Tries to Placate Business Riled by Contentious Labour Law Changes," *Winnipeg Free Press*, August 2, 2000: A1.

27. "Premier Won't Ban Replacement Workers," *Winnipeg Free Press*, March 8, 2004: A5.

28. "Manitoba Bumps Up Minimum Wage in the Province by 25 Cents an Hour," *Canadian Press*, November 29, 2000: 20:55; "Survival Above All" [editorial], *Winnipeg Free Press*, December 29, 2001: A14. Also, see Dennis Howlett, "The Call for a Living Wage: Activists Fighting for Fair Wages Across the Country," *Canadian Dimension* (May 1, 2005): 25. Accessed May 12, 2009: http://www.gov.mb.ca/labour/standards/doc,minimum-wage,factsheet.html. The minimum wage in Manitoba rose to $9.00 on October 1, 2009.

29. 2001 Speech from the Throne, November 13, 2001. Accessed August 31, 2009: http://www.gov.mb.ca/legislature/hansard/3rd-37th/vol_01/h01.html.

30. Thomas Fleming, "Provincial Initiatives to Restructure Canadian School Governance in the 1990s," *Canadian Journal of Educational Administration and Policy* 11 (November 8, 1997). Accessed February 1, 2010: www.umanitoba.ca/publications/cjeap/.

31. Frontier Center for Public Policy, Backgrounder, "Manitoba's School Board Amalgamations—Before and After," June 2005. Accessed September 1, 2009: http://www.fcpp.org/pdf/FB036AmalgamationCostSavingsIllusory.pdf.

32. Ibid.

33. Press Release: "Tenth Straight Year for Physician Increases in Manitoba—Oswald," http://news.gov.mb.ca/news/index.html?item=6460.

34. David Roberts, "Manitoba Raises Health-care Spending," *Globe and Mail*, May 11, 2000: A2.

35. Gary Doer, *Presentation to the Commission on the Future of Health Care in Canada*, March 6, 2002: 12. Accessed June 7, 2009: http://www.gov.mb.ca/health/documents/doer.pdf.

36. Mia Rabson, "Manitoba Tops Nation in Health Spending," *Winnipeg Free Press*, December 9, 2004: A12.

37. 2008 Speech from the Throne, 20 November 2008, Winnipeg, Manitoba. Accessed August 14, 2009: http://www.gov.mb.ca/throne.html.

38. CBC News, "Nurse Practitioners Blame Province for Job Shortage," August 31, 2006. Accessed June 7, 2009: http://www.cbc.ca/canada/manitoba/story/2006/08/30/nurse-practitioner.html.

39. Ibid.

40. Progressive Conservative Party of Manitoba, "NDP Ignore Northern Maternity Care," May 27, 2009. Accessed June 15, 2009: http://pcmanitoba.com/newsroom/northern-maternity-care.html.

41. Progressive Conservative Party of Manitoba, "Record High Shortage of Health Care Aides," May 6, 2009. Accessed June 15, 2009: http://www.pcmanitoba.com/newsroom/shortage-of-health-care-aides.html.

42. The Progressive Conservative Party of Manitoba, "NDP Surgery Cutbacks Put Patients at Risk," February 25, 2009. Accessed June 15, 2009: http://www.pcmanitoba.com/Newsroom/ndp-surgery-cutbacks-put-patients-at-risk.html.

43. Liberal Party of Manitoba, "NDP Callously Disregards Mental Health of Manitobans," May 20, 2009. Accessed June15, 2009: http://mlp.manitobaliberals.ca/?p=539.

44. Liberal Party of Manitoba, "Timely Access to Quality Care a Right for All Manitobans," December 4, 2007. Accessed June 15, 2009: http://mlp.manitobaliberals.ca/?p=391.

45. For information on the various health announcements made by the Doer government since 2003, see: Manitoba Health, "News Releases," Accessed June 14, 2009: http://www.gov.mb.ca/health/newsreleases/index.html.

46. Daniel Lett, "Doer Touts 5-point Plan," *Winnipeg Free Press*, May 6, 2003: A1.

47. Elections Manitoba, *Results of the 2003 General Election.* Accessed June7, 2009: http://www.elections.mb.ca/en/Results/general_election_38_static.html.

48. News Release: "Throne Speech Focuses on Managing Growth, Meeting Challenges," November 22, 2004. Accessed February 14, 2010: http://www.gov.mb.ca/chc/press/top/2004/11/2004-11-22-01.html.

49. News Release: "2007 Throne Speech Highlights," November 20, 2007. Accessed February 14, 2010: http://www.gov.mb.ca/chc/press/top/2004/11/2004-11-22-01.html.

50. Benjamin Levin, *Commission on Tuition Fees and Post-Secondary Education in Manitoba*, Winnipeg, March 31, 2009: http://www.postsecondarycommission.mb.ca/pdfs/commision_final_report_en.pdf. Accessed December 15, 2009.

51. See: Government of Manitoba, Press Release: "Manitoba Government Continues Track Record of Affordable, Accessible Post-Secondary Education: McGifford," April 22, 2009; Helen Fallding, "NDP Will Try to Minimize Budget Pain," *Winnipeg Free Press*, January 21, 2002: A9.

52. News Release: "Throne Speech Pledges Further Action on Water, Energy, the Economy and Youth," November 20, 2003. Accessed February 14, 2009: http://www.gov.mb.ca/chc/press/top/2003/11/2003-11-20-02.html. News Release: "Throne Speech Highlights Clean Energy, Emergency Preparedness," October 27, 2005. Accessed August 14, 2009: http://www.gov.mb.ca/chc/press/top/2005/10/2005-10-27-02.html .

53. 2006 Speech from the Throne. Accessed August 14, 2009: http://www.gov.mb.ca/legislature/hansard/5th-38th/vol_01/h01.html . See also Speech from the Throne, November 20, 2008. Accessed August 14, 2009: http://www.gov.mb.ca/throne.html.

54. Steve Lambert, "Manitoba NDP Premier Looking to Leave Legacy of Clean Energy," May 22, 2007. Accessed June 12, 2009: http://www.redorbit.com/news/business/942922/manitobans_go_to_the_polls_in_vote_that_will_determine/index.html.

55. Ibid.

56. CTV Winnipeg, "Doer to Pitch Hydro as Keynote Speaker," June 19, 2009. Accessed June 20, 2009: http://winnipeg.ctv.ca/servlet/an/local/CTVNews/20090618/wpg_doer_speech_090618/20090618?hub=WinnipegHome

57. Gary Doer, interview with The Climate Group, March 8, 2005. Accessed June 6, 2009: http://www.theclimategroup.org/news_and_events/gary_doer/.

58. Sources Froschauer etc., MB Hydro annual reports, StatCan, Interprovincial and International Trade.

59. KGS Group for International Joint Commission, "Flood Protection for Winnipeg," Parts I & II, December 1999, Part III, March 2000. Accessed December 14, 2009 at Winnipeg Floodway Authority website: http://www.floodwayauthority.mb.ca.

60. Winnipeg Floodway Authority Annual Report 2007. Accessed December 14, 2009.

61. Ibid., 2009. Accessed December 14, 2009.

62. Government of Manitoba, Water Stewardship. "Potential Transboundary Water Projects." Accessed February 1, 2010: http://www.gov.mb.ca/waterstewardship/water_info/transboundary/potential.html. See also Michael Byers, "Canada's Man in Washington Brings Expertise to Water File," *Toronto Star*, September 8, 2009.

63. "Table: Individual Achievers," *Business Week*, Accessed May 12, 2008: http://www.businessweek.com/magazine/content/05_50/b3963417.htm .

64. Ibid. For more information on the Government of Manitoba's climate change plan and measures in comparison to other western provinces, see: David Gordon and Kimberly Speers, "Climate Change in Local and Provincial Governments in Western Canada: A Bunch of Hot Air?" Canadian Political Science Association Annual Conference (Vancouver, British Columbia, June 2008).

65. Press Release: "Manitoba First in North America to Propose Legislation of Kyoto Commitment," April 11, 2008. Accessed June 17, 2009: http://news.gov.mb.ca/news/index.html?archive=2008-04-01&item=3509.

66. Accessed June 7, 2009: http://www.midwesternaccord.org/. See also John Ibbitson, "Regions Take Action as Federal Leaders Dither," *Globe and Mail*, November 16, 2007: A24.

67. Doer, interview with The Climate Group.

68. Mia Rabson, "700 new Nurses Pledged," *Winnipeg Free Press*, April 24, 2007: A5.

69. Elections Manitoba, *Official Results*. Accessed November 3, 2009: http://www.electionsmanitoba.ca/en/Results/general_election_39_static.html.

70. 2008 Speech from the Throne, November 20, 2008, Winnipeg, Manitoba. Accessed August 14, 2009: http://www.gov.mb.ca/throne.html .

71. Ibid.

72. For more on the agreements between the provinces of Manitoba and Quebec and First Nations people concerning the development of large hydroelectric projects in their territories, see: Martin Thibault and Steven Hoffman (eds.), *Power Struggles: Hydro Development and First Nations in Manitoba and Quebec* (Winnipeg: University of Manitoba Press, 2008.)

73. Crocus Investment Fund, "News." Accessed June 12, 2009: http://www.crocusfund.com/about/news.asp.

74. CBC News, "Final Settlements Reached in Lawsuit Against Crocus Investment Fund," April 22, 2009. Accessed June 15, 2009: http://www.cbc.ca/canada/manitoba/story/2009/04/22/mb-crocus-settlement.html. About 34,000 Manitobans had more than $150 million invested in Crocus, a labour-sponsored venture-capital fund that had a mandate to invest in Manitoba companies.

75. Martin Cash, "No Crocus Error, Premier Maintains," *Winnipeg Free Press*, May 10, 2006: A10.

76. CBC News, "Final Settlements Reached in Lawsuit…," April 22, 2009. Accessed June 15, 2009.

77. Mary Agnes Welch, "Selinger Feared Election Fallout: Finance Minister Demanded Letter to Absolve Him from 1999 Dispute," *Winnipeg Free Press* June 4, 2009: A5.

78. The Hon. Gary Doer, "Manitoba—The Ideal Business Location Now and Into the Future," *Metropolitan Corporate Counsel* (March 2006): 29. Accessed June 7, 2009: http://www.metrocorpcounsel.com/ pdf/2006/March/29.pdf.

79. Cy Gonick, "Gary Doer's Manitoba," *Canadian Dimension*, June 3, 2007. Accessed June 7, 2009: http://canadiandimension.com/articles/1785.

80. Mia Rabson and Bartley Kives, "Doer Named New U.S. Ambassador: Flight to Churchill in 2007 Launched Discussion." *Winnipeg Free Press,* August 28, 2009.

81 While there has been no clear change in governmental style, the new Selinger government responded to the international financial and business crisis that began in 2008 in its March 2010 Budget by moving the province into a five-year deficit program, which will require changes to the "balanced budget" legislation and a commitment to return to fiscal balance by 2014–15. See www.gov.mb.ca/ finance/budget2010/.

82. Gary Doer, "Policy Challenges for the New Century," Speech at Queen's University School of Policy Studies, Donald Gow Memorial Lecture, 2000, 9. Accessed June 6, 2009: http://www.queensu.ca/sps/ conferences_events/lectures/donald_gow/00lecture.pdf .

Appendix: Manitoba Election Results, 1870–2007

1870
15 Government
9 Opposition

1874
12 Government
12 Opposition

1878
13 Government
11 Opposition

1879
18 Government
6 Opposition

1883
22 Government
16 Opposition

1886
19 Government
16 Opposition

1888
28 Liberals
5 Conservatives
5 Others

1892
25 Liberals
14 Conservatives
1 Other

1896
32 Liberals
5 Conservatives
3 Others

1899
26 Conservatives
14 Liberals

1903
31 Conservatives
9 Liberals

1907
28 Conservatives
13 Liberals

1910
28 Conservatives
13 Liberals

1914
28 Conservatives
21 Liberals

1915
40 Liberals
5 Conservatives
4 Others

1920
21 Liberals
7 Conservatives
12 United Farmers
11 Labour
4 Others

1922
27 United Farmers
7 Liberals
6 Conservatives
6 Labour
9 Others

1927
29 Progressives
15 Conservatives
7 Liberals
3 Farmer/Labour
1 Other

1932
38 Progressives
10 Conservatives
5 Farmer/Labour
2 Others

1936
23 Liberal Progressives
16 Conservatives
7 Cooperative Commonwealth Federation
5 Social Credit
4 Others

1941
25 Liberal Progressives
14 Conservatives
3 Cooperative Commonwealth Federation
3 Social Credit
10 Others

1945
26 Liberal Progressives
13 Conservatives
10 Cooperative Commonwealth Federation
2 Social Credit
4 Others

1949
29 Liberal Progressives
10 Progressive Conservatives
7 Cooperative Commonwealth Federation
11 Others

1953
35 Liberal Progressives
12 Progressive Conservatives
5 Cooperative Commonwealth Federation
2 Social Credit
3 Others

1958
26 Progressive Conservatives
19 Liberal Progressives
11 Cooperative Commonwealth Federation
1 Other

1959
36 Progressive Conservatives
11 Liberal Progressives
10 Cooperative Commonwealth Federation

1962
36 Progressive Conservatives
13 Liberals
7 New Democrats
1 Social Credit

1966
31 Progressive Conservatives
14 Liberals
11 New Democrats
1 Social Credit

1969
28 New Democrats
22 Progressive Conservatives
4 Liberals
1 Social Credit
2 Others

1973
31 New Democrats
21 Progressive Conservatives
5 Liberals

1977
33 Progressive Conservatives
23 New Democrats
1 Liberal

1981
34 New Democrats
23 Progressive Conservatives

1986
30 New Democrats
26 Progressive Conservatives
1 Liberal

1988
25 Progressive Conservatives
20 Liberals
12 New Democrats

1990
30 Progressive Conservatives
20 New Democrats
7 Liberals

1995
31 Progressive Conservatives
23 New Democrats
3 Liberals

1999
32 New Democrats
24 Progressive Conservatives
1 Liberal

2003
35 New Democrats
20 Progressive Conservatives
2 Liberals

2007
36 New Democrats
19 Progressive Conservatives
2 Liberals

SOURCES: compiled from *Historical Statistics of Canada*, 2nd edition, Series Y302-387 and *Elections Manitoba Statement of Vote*, "Summary of Results"

Index

A

Abbott, J.J.C., 11, 95

Aberdeen, Lord, 96

Aberhart, William, 182-83

Aboriginal Education Strategy, 411

Aboriginal Health Strategy, 404

Aboriginal Justice Implementation Commission, 402

Aboriginal Justice Inquiry (AJI), xvi, 369-70

Aboriginal peoples, 273, 284, 297, 376, 405; constitutional goals of, 397; as displaced, 290, 295; and flood control, 408; hiring policy for, 344; and hydro projects, 407; and justice system, 369-70, 402; midwife/nurse education program, 411; mistreatment of, xvi; and natural resources, 369, 402, 411; policy initiatives for, 401; rights of, 347, 364-65, 368; welfare of, 274, 369

Acceptable Mean: The Tax Rental Agreements, 1941-1962, The, 235

Adams, Christopher, xx, 384, 390, 415

Adams, Paul, 324, 329

aeronautics industry, 393

agrarian revolt, 145, 168

Agrarian Revolt in Western Canada: A Survey Showing American Parallels, The, 159–62

Agricultural Credit Corporation, 314

agriculture, xvi, 48, 99, 174, 250, 286, 340, 359, 363, 367, 374; credit facilities for, 243; difficulties of, 168, 170, 177; as economic base, x, xiii, 72; as scientific, 167

Aikins, J.A.M., 112, 130, 133, 135

Aikins, James, 61, 63

Albert College, 118

Alberta Premiers of the Twentieth Century, xx, 385

alcohol. *See* liquor

Alexander Begg's Red River Journal and Other Papers, 44

Alien Investigation Board, 148-49

Allan, Hugh, 27

Allen, Richard, 145, 159

Allen, Ted, 312

Alternative Fueled Systems Inc., 300

Alturas Oil and Gas Reserves Ltd., 300

aluminum smelter, 319

ambulance services, 298

amnesty: for Métis resisters, 2, 4–5, 7, 10–11, 15, 23–25, 37, 52

Anderson, Charles, 138

Anderson, David Bishop, 49

Anglican Church, 58; land holdings of, 20

Anglophones, ix–x, xvii, 14, 23

Angus L. Macdonald: A Provincial Liberal, 235

Angus School of Commerce, 357

Anstett, Andy, 324, 329, 358, 395

appliances, electric, 221

Archbishop A.-A. Taché of St. Boniface: The "Good Fight" and the Illusive Vision, 104–6

Archibald, Adams G., ix–x, 6–7, 9, 11, 15–16, 24–26, 28, 37, 52; and amnesty for Métis resisters, 4–5; and coalition government, 3; as establishing provincial institutions, 33; and private property, 19; and relations with Métis, 20–21, 23; resignation of, 10; and responsible government, 2

Archibald, Elizabeth, 3

Archibald, Samuel, 3

Armstrong, J.W. Dr., 144, 152

Arthur Meighen, 191

Artibise, Alan, 158

As Long as the Rivers Run: Hydroelectric Development and Native Communities in Western Canada, 304

As Many Liars: The Story of the 1995 Manitoba Vote-Splitting Scandal, 415

As the World Wags On, 137

Ashdown, J.H., 58

Ashton, Steve, 377, 389, 401, 408, 413

Asper, Izzy, 297

assimilation, xiv, 129, 135. *See also* immigrants

Assiniboine College, 246

Association of Manitoba Chiefs, 381

Association of Manitoba Liberals, 83

Association Saint-Jean-Baptiste de Manitoba, 15

asylum charge (Norquay), 60

Atkinson, Robert, 44

automobile insurance, 268, 335; as compulsory, 292; as public, 284, 292–93, 301, 319, 348; rates for, 347–49, 360

Autonomy Bills of 1905, 100

Autopac, 295, 298, 314, 360, 394; bill for, 292–93, 335

Axworthy, Lloyd, 316, 323, 341, 352, 406

B

baby boom, 245

Baker, Marilyn, 158

Baker, Paula, xix

Baker, Zivot & Co., 349

Bakker, Peter, 45

Bakvis, Herman, 352

Baldwin, Robert, 118

Bank of Canada, 181

bankruptcy: protection for farmers, 298; as provincial danger, 195

Bannatyne, A.G.B., 4, 7, 35–36

Barnhart, Gordon L., xx, 385

Barrett, Becky, 401–2

Barrett vs. the City of Winnipeg, 92–95

Barrie, Doreen, 385

Bartlett's Canada: A Pre-Confederation Journey, 44

Battle over Bilingualism: The Manitoba Language Question, The, 352

Battling for a Better Manitoba: A History of the Provincial Liberal Party, 158, 208

Beard, Gordon, 270

Beauchemin, André, 7, 11, 13

Beaulieu, Paul, 302

Beck, J. Murray Sir, 158, 162

Bedson, Derek, 269–70, 291, 340

Begg, Alexander, 7, 31–32, 35–37, 42, 45–46

Behiels, Michiel, 388

Bell Telephone Company, xi, 127

Bellan, Ruben, 45, 103, 383

Bend, Robert (Bobby), 232

Bennett, R.B., 177–80, 185–86, 308, 312, 319, 325

Bennett, W.A.C., 312

Benson, Julian, 380, 400

Bercuson, David, J., 160

Berger, Carl, 159–60

Beveridge, William Sir, 247

biculturalism, 38

bigotry: towards French & Catholics, xv

bilingualism, 38, 233, 254, 268, 323, 342, 357

Bill 56, 292

Bilodeau, Roger, 341–42

BiPole III project, 408

Bird, Curtis J. Dr., 7, 16–17, 28, 35

Black, F.M., 170

Blackburn, R.D., 292

Blain, Eleanor M., 45

Blair, Tony, 382, 400

Blakeney, Allan, 325

Blanchard, Jim, xix

Bland, Salem, 130, 161, 163

Blue Cross, 238

Board of Grain Commissioners, 130

Board of Grain Examiners, 119

Board of Railway Commissioners, 156, 175

Board of Trade (Winnipeg), 35

Boles, Christie & Lyon, 309

Booze: A Distilled History, 138

Booze: When Whiskey Ruled the West, 115

Borden, Robert Sir, 127–28, 132, 137, 144

Borden administration, 113, 121, 127, 132; union government of, 144, 148, 168

Bosiak, Beverly, 353

Bothwell, Robert, 210, 386

Bouchard, Lucien, 375

Boulic, Marcel, 241

boundary expansion, xi, 13, 39, 42, 58, 73, 82–83, 142; of constituencies, 54; in the north, 127, 133

Bourassa, Robert, 363, 365

Bowell, Mackenzie, 96–98, 109

Bowen, C.P., 103

Boy Scouts, 222

Boyd, Alfred T., ix–x, 5–8, 28, 52

Boyens, Ingebor, 328

Bracken, Alberta, 166

Bracken, Alice, 169, 188

Bracken, Doug, 168

Bracken, Ephraim, 166

Bracken, George, 168

Bracken, Gordon, 168

Bracken, John, xii–xiv, 155–57, 167–71, 175, 181, 185–86, 194–98, 214, 216, 308; death of, 188; diversification policies of, 177; non-partisanship and coalition government, 166, 173, 206; progressivism of, 187; and relations with Ottawa, 178–80, 182–84; resignation of, 188; and scandal, 176; and schools, 172

Bracken, John administration, xiii, 176, 232; as non-partisan coalition, 171–72, 179, 184, 188

Bracken-Garson-Campbell coalition government, 216

Brackenism, 166, 173

Bradley, Gordon, 269

Brandon College, 215, 247

Brandon Mail, The, 90

Brandon Sun, 89–90

Brandon University, 247, 300

Brandon University Research Fund, 157

Brawn, Dale, 25–27

Brian Dickson: A Judge's Journey, 234, 384

bribery, 87–88

Bristol Aerospace, 346, 360

British American Grangers of Manitoba, 36

British North America Act of 1867, xi, 94, 196, 200–201, 208, 227

Broadbent, Ed, 364

Brockville Collegiate, 166–67

Brodie, Janine, 326

Bronfman Dynasty, 138

Brophy case, 95

Brown, Curtis, xix

Brown, Edward, 128, 130, 132, 142, 144, 154

Brown, George, 3

Brown, Robert Craig, 114, 159–60

Brownell, M., 388

Brown-John, C. Lloyd, 303, 351–53

Brownsey, Keith, 305, 327

Brownstone, Meyer, 291, 304

Bruce, Alice, 168

Bruce, John, 7

Brunkild Extension, 379

Bryce, George, 109, 114

Buddick, Georgina, 269, 279, 281

buffalo hunt, 33, 48–50

Building Trades Protection Act, 133, 135

Bumsted, J.M., 158, 223, 234, 302, 327–28, 390

Bunn, Thomas, 16, 28

Burchill, C., 388

Burke, Joseph, 74–75, 85

Burley, David, 45

Burns, James McGregor, 300, 305

Burns, R.M., 235

Burrows, T.A., 156

Bush administration, 409

Business Week, 409–10

C

Cabinets and First Ministers, xx, 327

Cadbury, George, 291

Caldwell, Drew, 403

Calgary Declaration of September 1997, 376, 398

call centres, 377

Calvert, Lorne, 400

Cameron, Douglas Sir, 135, 143

Cameron, J.D., 95, 97, 102

Cameron, Malcolm C., 81

Cameron, Neil, 170

Camp, Dalton, 230, 255–56

campaign financing, 403

Campbell, Alexander, 22

Campbell, Colin, 123–24, 127, 130, 132–33

Campbell, Douglas L., xii–xiv, 181, 214–17, 224–28, 230, 244, 249, 258, 264–65; as conservative, 219, 232–33, 308, 320; death of, 233; and electrification, 221; and flood protection, 222–23; legacy of, 219, 233; and modernization, 220

Campbell, Douglas L. administration: as coalition, 206, 248; as Liberal-Progressive, 242; reforms of, 229, 231

Campbell, Gladys, 215, 220, 233

Campbell, Howard, 215

Campbell, Howard Wells (Wellie), 215

Campbell, Isaac, 135

Campbell, Mary, 214, 233

Campbell, Maude, 215

Campbell, May, 215

Campbell, Tena, 215

Camplinson, 228

Canada 1874–1896: Arduous Destiny, 65, 105–6, 114

Canada 1896–1921: A Nation Transformed, 114

Canada 1922–1939: Decades of Discord, 161

Canada and Quebec: One Country, Two Histories, 386

Canada and the Métis, 1869–1885, xix, 24, 26, 28, 44–45

Canada Clause, 364–65, 368

Canada Company of Upper Canada, 20

Canada Grain Act 1912, 130

Canada Health Act, 344

Canada Health and Social Transfer, 374

Canada Health Transfer, 404

Canada Since 1945, 210

Canadair, 346

Canada's Francophone Minority Communities: Constitutional Renewal and the Winning of School Governance, 388

Canada-US Free Trade Agreement, 395

Canadian American Business Council, 407

Canadian Annual Review [of Public Affairs] (1901–1938), 132, 138, 158–62

Canadian Annual Review of Politics and Public Affairs (1960–), 278–279, 326, 328–29, 351–52

Canadian Biographical Series: Thomas Greenway, 102

Canadian Broadcast Standards Council, 349

Canadian Civil Liberties Association, 349

Canadian Club, 200

Canadian Constitution, The, 385

Canadian Council of Agriculture, 153, 168

Canadian Crucible: Manitoba's Role in Canada's Great Divide, The, xix, 328, 341, 352, 384

Canadian Dimension, 343, 352

Canadian Labour Congress, 286

Canadian Labour in Politics, 350

Canadian Liver Foundation, 349

Canadian Magazine, 127

Canadian Mennonite University, 379

Canadian National Railway, 376, 385

Canadian Northern Railway, xi, 99, 124, 135

Canadian Northern Railway, The, 104, 137–38

Canadian Pacific Railway, xii, 27, 43, 57, 60, 63, 65, 67, 88, 93, 98, 140; and farmers' grievances, 119; freight rates of, 104, 124; as monopoly, vii, ix, 43, 59, 61, 73–74, 82–83, 86, 99, 121; and new railway construction, xi; and provincial railway charters, 61–62, 89; scandal of, 36, 38

Canadian Party, 13, 24, 34, 42, 52

Canadian Prairies: A History, The, xix, 233, 302, 305

Canadian Provincial Politics: The Party Systems of the Ten Provinces, xix, 161, 302, 326

Canadian Shield Foundation, 300

Canadian Wheat Board, 172, 285

Canadian Who's Who, 350, 353

Cannadine, David, xix

Caregivers Tax Credit, 404

Careless, J.M.S., 45

Carling, Isaac, 80, 102

Carling, John, 80, 102

Carlyle-Gordge, Peter, 350–51, 353

Carodoc Academy, 70

Carr, Jim, 367, 386–87

Carroll, Henry, 340

Carstairs, Sharon, 345, 348, 359–62, 364–67, 369, 386, 393, 396–97

Cartier, George Sir, 3–7, 10–11, 25–26, 30, 55

Cartwright, Richard Sir, 81, 102

Carty, R. Kenneth, xx

Cass-Beggs, David, 233, 295

Catholics. *See* Roman Catholics

Celaphon Oil & Gas Corporation, 300

cell-phone use in vehicles, 406

census, 6, 34, 42

Centennial History of Manitoba, The, 65, 138, 159, 260

Centra Gas Ltd., 377

CF-18 fighter jets, 346

Chaffee, Anna Urania, 30

Chamberlain, Joseph, 127

Charlottetown Accord, 321, 368–69, 375–76, 397

Charter of Rights and Freedoms, 316, 321–22, 325, 357, 364–65, 368, 371

Charter Revolution and the Court Party, The, 328

Chartrand, Paul, 402

Cheema, Gulzar, 367

Cherniak, Saul, 271, 294, 336–37

Chevrier, Horace, 120

Chicago, University of, 182, 238

Child Welfare Act, 152

children: adoption laws for, 243; rural dental care program for, 347; welfare of, 178, 402

Chomiak, Dave, 401, 404

Chorney, Harold, 326–28, 351–52

Chrétien, Jean, 406

Chrétien, Jean administration, 398, 404

Church of England, 49

Churchill Forest Industries (CFI), 251–52, 256–57, 272, 295–97

Churchill River drainage basin, 407

Civil Service Commission, 146, 241

Clague, R.E., 104

Clarity Bill, 376

Clark, Joe, 256, 316

Clark, Lovell C., xix, 24, 26, 45, 105–6

Clarke, Henry Joseph, ix–x, 2, 7–12, 16–17, 20–21, 28, 36, 39, 53; and French support, 34, 37; non-confidence vote in, 13, 37, 41

Clarke, Henry Joseph administration, 53

Cliffe, Charles, 90

Clifford Sifton: Volume I, The Young Napoleon 1861–1900, 67, 102–6, 115

Clifford Sifton: Volume II, A Lonely Eminence, 159

Clifford Sifton in Relation to His Times, 67

climate change, 409–10; legislation for, 407

Climate Group, The, 410

Clubb, W.R., 169–70, 176

coal steal (Norquay), 60

coalition government, 166, 179, 184, 188, 195–96, 200, 206, 215–16, 239, 248–49. *See also* union government

Coates, Colin, 115

Coates, Ken, 158

Cockshutt Plough Company, 332

Code Civile, 16

Coldwell, George, 130, 135; school amendments of, 133

Coldwell, William, 7

Collected Writings of Louis Riel, The, 24

collective bargaining, 186, 347, 394

Collège de Montréal, 4

College de Saint-Hyacinthe, 6

Colombo Plan, 248

Committee on Health, Education and Social Policy, 293

Committee on Reconstruction and Re-establishment, 197

commodity shortages, 298

Community Service and Economic Development committee, 318

Confederation, 3, 11, 14, 23, 30–31, 38, 65, 108, 127; agreements of, 182, 195, 202–3; as called into question, 48, 62, 177; and control of provincial resources, 174; inequities of, 194, 204–5, 374; Manitoba's status in, 64, 73, 81, 85; and party politics, 137; terms of, 71

Confederation of Regions (COR), 233, 345

Connery, Ed, 367

Connor, Ralph, x

conscription, 144, 185–87

conservation, 243, 297

Conservative Anti-Disallowance Association, 74

Conservative National Leadership Convention 1927, 135

Conservative Party, federal, 71, 110, 125, 153, 185–86, 194, 196; and CPR, 65

Conservative Party, provincial, 8, 34, 64, 87, 122, 132–33, 147; as centrist party, 241–42, 245, 258, 272; and coalition, 180; and contributions to, 125–26, 135, 143; as formalized, 59–60; as old-line party, 284, 308–11, 348, 405, 410; rebuilding of, xiv, 238, 312; rifts in, 110, 114

Consolidated Motor Company, 135

constitution: as bilingual, 359; patriation of, 252, 308, 316; reforms to, xviii, 268, 272, 321, 395–97

Constitutional Task Force, 368

Conway, John F., 415

Cook, Ramsay, 114, 159–60, 163

Cooke, Ellen, 66

Co-operative Commonwealth Federation (CCF), 181, 185, 187, 197, 205, 209, 284, 332–34, 348

cooperatives, consumer, 147

Coopers & Lybrand, 346

Coordination of Post-War Planning: Advisory Committee, 197

Copps, Sheila, 325

Cornish, Frank E., 39–41, 53

Council of the Exchange, 119

Council for Canadian Unity, 349

Council for Post-Secondary Education (COPSE), 378

Court of Queen's Bench of Manitoba: A Biographical History, The, 25–27

cow scheme, 147

Cowan, W., 45

Cowboys and Indians: The Shooting of J.J. Harper, 387

Craig, Richard, 170, 173

Craik, Donald, 268, 273, 317

Creighton, Donald, 48–49, 65, 67, 105–6

Crerar, T.A., 168–69, 179

crime, xvi, 373, 401. *See also* gangs

Crisis, Challenge and Change: Party and Class in Canada, 326

Critical Years, Canada 1857–1873, The, 45

Crocus Investment Fund, 412

crop insurance program, 240, 244

Crop Production in Western Canada, 168

Cross, William, xx

Crowe, Harry Foundation for the Canadian Association of University Teachers, 349

Crown corporation, 376, 394

Crown Corporation Accountability Act in 1987, 346

Crow's Nest Pass freight rates, 154

Crunican, Paul, 106

Cunningham, Robert, 7, 28

Cuthbert, Ella Mae, 308

Cuthbert, Sterling Rufus, 308

D

Dacquay, Louise, 374, 377

Dafoe, Chris, 272

Dafoe, John W., 67, 125, 129, 134, 155, 161, 170, 183, 196, 209, 254, 260–61

Dafoe-Sifton Correspondence 1919–1927, The, 163

Dale, Arch, 131

Davidson, John, 123

Davis, Adelaide, 30, 44

Davis, Charles, 30, 44

Davis, Della, 35

Davis, Elizabeth, 43

Davis, Robert A., ix–x, 14–15, 30–31, 33–34, 36–37, 39; activism of, 35, 41; and alliances among groups, 40, 53; and political stability, 41; resignation of, 54; retirement of, 43; and support for French, 42–43

Davis, Robert A. administration, 41

Davis, Thomas Priestley, 30

Davis, William, 215, 321, 325

Davis House, 32–33, 35

Davis Sr., Thomas, 30

Davis-Royal administration, 41–42, 46

Dawson, R. MacGregor, 162

day care, 319, 339, 344, 347

De Coster, C., 388

de Volpi, C.P., 44

debt, provincial, 43, 195, 198; costs to service, 362; repayment plan for, 218–19

Decline of Politics: The Conservatives and the Party System, 1901–1920, The, 114, 138, 159

Decter, Michael, 303, 340, 351–52

Delorme, Pierre, 7, 13

Dembsky, E.P., 102

Demill, Adelaide, 118

Demill, M.E., 119

democracy, parliamentary, 308

deregulation, national, 356

Derkach, Len, 361, 367, 371

Desbarats, Peter, 230

Desjardins, Laurent, 271, 275, 289, 292–93, 297, 360, 394

Development of Education in Canada, The, 28

Development of Education in Manitoba, The, 28, 138, 160

Devil's Lake diversion, 409

Devine, Virginia, 396

Dick, Lyle, 191

Dictionary of Canadian Biography, 24–26, 44–46, 102–03, 114, 137

Dictionary of Canadian Biography Online, 76–77, 137

Dictionary of Manitoba Biography, 158, 302

Diefenbaker, John, 186, 229, 242, 249, 255, 261, 286, 308–9, 316

Diefenbaker, John administration, 227, 252

direct legislation, 133, 142, 145–46

division scolaire franco-manitobaine, 372

Dixon, Fred J., 143, 171

Doer, Gary, xviii, 348, 360–62, 382, 386, 405, 408; and Accords, 364–65, 369, 397; conciliatory nature of, 392, 394, 409, 414; as defender of social programs, 366; economic strategy of, 402; and energy, 407; and French language rights, 393; and green policies, 409–10; and health care, 403–4; leadership of, 301, 345, 373, 410; legacy of, 392, 414; and privatization, 377, 381, 389–90, 395–96; and Quebec as distinct society, 398; and relations with business, 412; and relations with Ottawa, 409; resignation of, 413; and social democracy, 284, 400–401, 411

Doer, Gary administration, xiv, xvi, 259, 412–14; and Aboriginals, 387; and education, 406; and flood control, 408; and health care, 404–5; and hydro development, 411; campaign themes of, 405, 410; mandate of, 406; and social democracy, 403, 407; and tax reductions, 402

Doern, Russell, 233, 315, 326–27, 335, 337, 340, 342, 351–52

Domestic Goods: the Material, the Moral, and the Economic in the Postwar Years, 234

Dominion Alliance (temperance), 123

Dominion Elevator Company, 119, 135

Dominion-Provincial Conference, 195, 197, 199–202, 210

Dominion-Provincial Tax Suspension Agreements of 1942, 200

Donnelly, Murray S., xx, 25, 45, 199, 208–11, 326

Douglas, T.C., 206, 233, 286, 291–92, 301, 332–33, 335, 337

Douglas-Coldwell Foundation, 349

Dower Act, 145

Downey, Jim, 369

Drew, George, 187, 203–5, 216, 242, 309

Driedger, Myrna, 405

drugs, prescription, 294, 298, 398

Drummond, Ian, 210

Dry Farming in Western Canada, 168

Dubuc, Joseph, 4, 6–7, 12–14, 24–25, 37–40

Dufferin, Lord, 39

Dumont, Yvon, 373
Dunlop, W.J., 126
Dunn, Christopher, xx, 279, 303, 316–17, 326, 352
Duplessis, Maurice, 182, 203
Durkin, Douglas, xii
Dyck, Rand, xix, 303–4, 323, 326–28, 351–52

E
Eadie, James A., 137
Early Years education, 403
Eastern Manitoba Development Board, 266
Eastern Townships: A Pictorial Record, The, 44
economic development, xvii, 38, 245, 293, 359;
    as balanced with environment, 297; business
    involvement in, 268, 318; and green policies,
    410; as national promise, 55; in northern
    regions, 284; private-public approach to,
    400; public spending on, 239, 250, 257, 276,
    310; and the railways, 42, 65, 172; through
    privatization, 376
economic policy: Keynesian influence on, 297
economy, 197, 199, 345, 368
Ed Schreyer: A Social Democrat in Power, 302
Edmonton Chamber of Commerce, 200
education, 15, 22, 171, 250, 259, 367, 405, 410;
    dual system for, 18; French-language, xv;
    funding deficit for, 270; investment in, 247;
    policy for, 370; public spending for, 202, 230,
    239, 247, 253, 401; reform of, 90, 246, 403;
    Roman Catholic, xv. *See also* school system
education, post-secondary, 256, 368, 370, 374, 398,
    406, 411; expansion of, xv, 405; facilities for,
    243; as a system, 378–79; tuition fees for, 371
Education Act, 129
Edwards, Paul, 373–74, 398
1812 Settlement, 54
Eldridge, James, 303
elections: financing of, 412; laws for, 112; riots
    during 1872, 35
electoral boundaries: drawing of, 6, 228;
    redistribution of, 22, 214, 228, 290. *See also*
    redistribution
Electoral Divisions Act 1969, 274
*Electoral Realignments: A Critique of an American
    Genre,* 326
electricity production: distribution network for,
    226; monopoly on, 224; provision of, 220;
    reorganization and expansion of, 219. *See also*
    hydroelectric power generation

electrification program, 198, 220–21. *See also* rural
    electrification
Elevator Commission, 131
Emergency War Session, 143
Emmerling's Hotel, 32
employment, full, 198
Energy and Climate Forum, 407
energy, renewable, 407
energy shortages, 298
English, John, 114, 138, 159, 210
English language, 3; as language of instruction, 146,
    148; as official language, 323, 341. *See also*
    Anglophones
English Party, 38, 40–42
Enns, Harry, 268–69, 273–74, 276–79, 281–82
Ens, Gerhard J., 66
environment act, 347
environment issues, 401, 405, 407, 410, 414
Equal Rights Association, 92, 96, 105
Erdoes, Richard, 44
Essex–St. Clair Local Health Integrated Network,
    349
Established Programmes Financing (EPF), 345
Evans, Gurney, 241, 273
Evans, J.H., 157–58
Evans, Len, 352
Evans, Sanford, 171
Ewart, John S. Memorial Fund, 157
Excelsior Motor Works, 120
*Exchange: 100 Years of Trading Grain in Winnipeg,
    The,* 137–38

F
Faces of the Flood, 390
factionalism, 54, 57, 400. *See also* New Democratic
    Party
family allowances, 187, 198
family law reforms, 298, 318, 336
family services, 367, 369, 378
farm income, stabilization of, 204
Farm Loans Act, 147
farm management, 243
farm policy, 286
Farmer, S.J., 184
farmers: bankruptcy protection for, 298; grievances
    against CPR, 119; protest movement of, 59,
    170
Farmers' Platform, 153, 168–69
Farmers' Protective Union of Manitoba, 60, 83, 119

Farmers' Unity League, 180

farmland preservation, xvi

Fashioning Farmers: Ideology, Agricultural Knowledge and the Manitoba Farm Movement, 189

Federal Subsidies to the Provincial Governments in Canada, 67

federal subsidy (transfers) to provinces, 38–39, 41, 55, 64, 82, 201, 404

federalism, 166, 183–84, 188, 254, 363, 375–76, 382–83; reform of, xiii, xviii

Federalism and the Charter, 328

federal-provincial agreements, 204, 254, 270, 272

federal-provincial constitutional conference (1950), 207

Federal-Provincial Financial Arrangements, 318

federal-provincial relations, 201, 267, 269, 364

Fédération Provinciale des Comités de Parents (FPCP), 371–72

female enfranchisement. *See* women

Fenians, 9–10, 36, 108

Fennell, Raymond, 310

Ferguson, Barry, 191, 209

Field, Percy, 126

Filmon, Gary, xvii–xviii, 324, 344–45, 348, 357–58, 360–61, 389–90, 396–98, 402; and Aboriginal relations, 370, 381; and the Accord, 364–65, 369; conciliatory approach of, 343, 347; and economic issues, 363, 373, 383; and federalism, 375–76; and Francophone community, 359, 371–72; and Interlake scheme, 380, 400; leadership of, xiv–xv, 367, 374, 382, 393; and privatization, 377; and public policy, 356; and relations with Ottawa, 366

Filmon, Gary administration, xvi, 256, 363, 370, 389, 396, 401; and flood control, 408; and French language, 371; goals of, 362; and Meech Lake, 364; and privatization, 376–77, 399; and social programs, 362, 373–74, 378, 383, 398

Filmon, Janice, 356

Filmon Fridays, 368, 398

finality clause, 83

Findlay, Glen, 376, 389

Finlay, John L., 25

First Nations. *See* Aboriginal peoples

Fiscal Stabilization Fund, 362

Fisher, Bill, 216

Fisher, James, 83–84

Fisk, Larry John, 103, 158

flag policy, 128–29

Flanagan, Thomas, 28, 353

Flavelle, J.W., 128

Fleming, Thomas, 387, 416

Flin Flon Strike of 1934, 180

flood of 1950, 214, 222, 240, 248; reconstruction after, 221; relief for, 223, 228

flood prevention, 218, 380

flood protection system, 230, 244, 249–50, 379, 409; in Red River Valley, 408

Floods of the Centuries: A History of Flood Disasters in the Red River Valley, 1776–1997, 390

floodway proposal, 249

floodway system, 408–9

Flyer Buses, 314

Flyer Industries, 360, 362

Food and Agricultural Organization of the United Nations, 241

Forbes, Thelma, 274

Forced Growth: Five Studies of Government Involvement in the Development of Canada, 260

Ford, Arthur, 120–21, 130, 137

Forest, Georges, 322, 341

Forest decision, 323–24

forestry-products industry, 250

Forke, Robert, 155

Formidable Heritage: Manitoba's North and the Cost of Development, 1870–1930, xix, 103, 162, 190

Formisano, Ronald P., xix

Fort Garry Hotel, 133

Fox, Peter, 393

Fox-Decent, Wally, 364, 368, 376

Francis, F.H., 75, 85

Francophones, ix, 8, 12, 34, 54, 64, 85; accommodations to, 55–56; constituencies of, 14; and Métis resister amnesty, 2; minority rights of, xi–xii, xvi, 40, 43, 135, 372

free enterprise system, 197–98, 207, 225

free trade, 94, 127, 356, 412

Free Trade Agreement (FTA), 362, 368, 408

freight rates, 83, 86, 93, 121–22, 124, 154, 168, 174, 244; increases in, 59

French language, viii, 23, 54, 284; debate over, 358–59, 366; as language of instruction, 245–46, 254, 258, 295, 371, 384, 394; as official language, xi, xv, 40–42, 84, 90–92; rights to use, 38, 56, 85, 92, 103, 323, 341, 343, 359, 384, 393–94; services in, 298, 342, 357, 393; status of, 121, 322, 357

French Party, 36–39, 41–42, 56–57

French-Canadian Idea of Confederation, 1864–1900, The, 24

Friesen, Gerald A., xviii–xix, xx, 25, 46, 66–67, 71, 103, 199, 209, 233, 284, 302, 305

Friesen, Jean, 26, 387, 401

fur trade, 48–50, 64

Fur Trade Profiles: Five Ancestors of Premier John Norquay, 66

G

Gallant, Edgar, 371

Gallant Report, 371

Game Protection Act, 147

Gang of Eight, 321–22, 325

Gang Prosecution Unit, 406

gangs, 373, 381, 406

Gardiner, Jimmy, 173, 175

Garrison Dam, 409

Garson, Stuart S., xii, xiv, 181–82, 184–86, 194–96, 210, 216–18; death of, 208; and fiscal arrangements, 203–5, 208; and fiscal conservatism, 208; and hydroelectric power, 207; liberalism of, 197; and Rowell-Sirois report, 199; and taxation, 209, 227

Garson, Stuart S. administration: as coalition government, 200, 205–6; as non-partisan, 197

Gaudry, Neil, 389, 400

Gawron, Zenon, 76–77

Gazette, The, 53

Gelley, Thomas, 85

gender equality, 361

General Distributors, 311

George, Dutch, 32

Gerrard, Gary, 158

Gerrard, Jon, 158, 208, 410

Getty, Don, 363

Gibbins, Roger, xviii, xx, 326–27

Giffen, P. James, 209–10

Gilleshammer, Harold, 367, 381

Gilson, J.C. Dr., 240

Girard, Marc-Amable, ix–x, 3, 6–9, 11, 14, 22, 26, 38, 40–41, 57; aid to land vendors, 20–21; and amnesty for Métis resisters, 5; and forming the first ministry, 2; resignation of, 15, 39

Girard, Marc-Amable administration, 14–15, 22, 39, 53

global warming, 410

Globe and Mail, 359, 373

gold mines, 58

Gonick, Cy, 257–58, 260–61, 318–19, 327–28, 419

Gordon, C.W., 130

Gottried, Elizabeth, 285

Goulding, Elizabeth, 220

Goulet, Elzear, 25, 32–33

government: institutions of, 15; instrumentality of, 288

Government Generation: Canadian Intellectuals and the State, 1990–1945, The, 208–10

Government Liquor Commission, 171

Government of Edward Schreyer: Democratic Socialism in Manitoba, The, xix, 303–5, 350

Government of Manitoba, The, xx, 25, 45, 208–11

Government Restructuring and Career Public Services, 303

Graham, Roger, 191

Grain: The Entrepreneurs, 138

grain elevators: as provincially owned, 131, 142

Grain Exchange, 131, 172

Grain Exchange Building, 119

Grain Growers Grain Company, 130–32

Grain Growers Guide, 130–31, 151, 153

Grain Growers movement, 130

grain industry, xi, 59, 131, 204

Granatstein, J.L., 191–92

Grand Trunk Pacific, xi

Grand Trunk Railway, 70

Grangers, 36

Grassby, A.E., 221

Gray, James, 115

Great Depression, 194, 198, 219–20, 264; as economic crisis, 166, 174, 177, 179–82, 188, 195, 200, 208; effects of, 239, 285; provincial response to, viii, xvi; recovery from, 202, 218

Great West Life, 317

Green, Howard, 186

Green, Sidney, 252, 260, 276–77, 282, 287–88, 302–4, 309, 315, 336–39, 351–52

Green, Solomon Hart, 132–33

green policies, 409

green technology, 407

greenhouse gases: Kyoto standards for, 407, 410

Greenway, Elizabeth Heard, 80

Greenway, Emma, 102

Greenway, Thomas, x, xii, 58, 60, 71–72, 75, 82, 86, 91, 96, 104, 106, 125; cabinet of, 85; and charge of bribery, 87–88, 101, 121; death of, 100; as founder of provincial Liberal Party, 63, 80; Francophone support for, 85; political legacy of, 92, 101; and provincial rights, 83–84; and railways, 98; resignation of, 100; and rifts in Liberal Party, 121–22; and schools, 90, 94–95, 97, 99, 105, 129

Greenway, Thomas administration, x–xi, 93, 109, 141; and fiscal practices, 113; and railway matters, 89; and schooling, 110

Greenway Sr., Thomas, 80

Greenway-Sifton regime, x–xi

Gregor, Alexander, 28, 138, 160

Grierson, George A., 143, 152

Grose, Rex, 251–52

Grove, Frederick P., xii

Guest, Hal, 114–15

Gwyn, Richard, 279

H

Haig, John, 171, 190

Half-Breed land Grant Protection Act, 21–22

Hall, D.J., 67, 102–6, 115, 158

"hallway medicine," 378, 400, 404–5

Hamelin, Jean Bishop, 25, 41

Hamilton, Alvin, 66, 369, 387

Hammond, Gerrie, 361, 367, 386

Hansen, Phillip, 326–28, 351–52

Harapiak, Harry, 360, 395

Harper, Elijah, 345, 365, 397

Harper, J.J., 369–70

Harper, Stephen, 392, 413

Harris, Alma, 387

Harris, Mike, 308, 325

Harrison, Abraham, 231

Harrison, David H., ix–x, 63, 70, 84; ambition of, 72, 74–76; resignation of, 75

Harrison, David H. administration, 71, 75

Harrison, George, 75

Harrison, Katherine, 75

Harrison, Milner, 70

Harrison, Thomas, 75

Harvests of War, The, 159

Harvey, Robert, 157

Hatfield, Richard, 321

"have" provinces, 269

"have-not" provinces, 194, 207, 269

Hay, E.H.G.G., 4, 12–15, 20–21, 39, 41

health care aides: shortage of, 405

Health Care and Family Services, 375

health care insurance, 227, 268, 398; premiums for, 292, 411. See also hospital insurance

health care system, 146, 208, 227, 259, 400, 403–4; access to, 291; coordinated approach to, 378; costs of, 372; facilities for, 314, 393; fee-for-service payments to, 293; management of, 372, 398; public spending for, 218, 226, 230, 247, 367–68, 382, 401, 410; reforms to, 294, 301, 405; services of, 199, 370; wait lists for, 405. See also home care services; medicare

Health Insurance and Canadian Public Policy: The Seven Decisions that Created the Canadian Health Insurance System and Their Outcomes, 235, 280

health promotion, 294

Healy, W.J., 50, 66

Heavy Hand of History: Interpreting Saskatchewan's Past, The, xx

Hébert, Raymond, xix, 323, 328, 352, 384, 415

Hedlin, Ralph, 240

Hemphill, Maureen, 395

Henderson, Stephen, 235

Henry, R. Rory, 115

Hepburn, Mitchell, 182–83

Heritage Fund, 344

Heron, Craig, 138

Hickes, George, 401–2

Hiebert, Paul, xiv

highways, 410; construction of, 250, 266

Hill, A.E., 154

Hill, James J., 65

Hilts, Joseph A., 67, 76–77, 101–6

Hincks, Annie, 80

Historical Essays on the Prairie Provinces, 159

History of Manitoba: Its Resources and People, A, 114

History of Perth County, 1825–1902, 76

History of the Canadian Pacific Railway, 67

Hoeschen, Susan, 305

Hoey, Robert, 169–70

Hoffman, Steven, 411, 416

hog-farm operations, 408

Hogg, T.H. Dr., 174, 224, 234

Holmes, John L., 66

home care services, 293–94, 298, 314; contracting out of, 378. *See also* health care system; long-term care

Homeland to Hinterland: The Changing Worlds of the Red River Métis in the Nineteenth Century, 66

homesteads, 81, 119, 215

Hopkins, Thomas, 351–52

Horowitz, Gad, 350

Horwood, V.W., 135

hospital insurance, 226–28, 244, 265; premiums for, 252; private, 226–27. *See also* health care insurance

Hospital Services and Diagnostics Act, 265

hospitals, 243; reorganization of, 372

housing, xvi, 357; construction of, 363; as low-cost, 186

Howard, Thomas, 7, 12, 28, 52–53

Howden, J.H., 130, 135

Howe, C.D., 197, 207

Howe, Joseph, 4, 10, 19, 24–26, 28

Howlett, Dennis, 416

Howlett, Michael, 305, 327

Hoy, Clair, 325

Huband, Charles, 309, 314, 316

Hudson, Albert B., 132, 134, 143, 153, 161

Hudson Bay drainage basin, 409

Hudson's Bay Company, 6, 9, 14, 17, 25, 33, 42–43, 49, 357; influence of, 35; and land registry, 19; monopoly clause of, 86; monopoly of, 36, 50; and taxation, 16

Hudson's Bay Railway, 63, 73, 172, 176

Huel, Raymond, 104–6

Hugh John Macdonald: Manitobans in Profile, 114

Hull, Jeremy, 260, 305, 327

human rights, 332, 347; commission for, 295

Hutton, George, 241, 269

Hydro Board, 232–33

hydroelectric power development, xiii, 268, 290, 314, 393, 411; at Limestone, 344; at Nelson River, 295, 299; in northern regions, 412; at Wuskwatim, 407

hydroelectric power generation, 218, 250, 344; expansion of, 251; potential of, 253; rates for, 319. *See also* power generation

hydroelectricity, 198, 368; nationalization of, 230

I

illness prevention, 293–94

immigrants, 32, 34, 38, 112, 129, 135; American,

128; British, xii; European, xi, 100, 110; German-speaking, 285; Icelanders, x, 51, 89; Ontarian, 33, 51, 119. *See also* assimilation

immigration, xiv, 4, 35, 39, 42, 89, 94, 111, 412

immigration policies, 99, 178

Imperial Canada 1867–1917, 115

Implementation Support Team, 371–72

In Search of Canadian Political Culture, xix

In Subordination: Professional Women in Manitoba, 1870–1970, xix

income taxes. *See* taxes

Independent Citizens' Election Committee, 357

Independent Labour Party (ILP), 181

Indian treaties, 12

inflation, high, 319, 322

information, freedom of: access to, 332; legislation for, 344

Inglis, Alexander I., 158

Ingram, John, 162

Initiative and Referendum Act of 1916, 145

Inkster, Colin, 40–41

Institute of Integrated Energy Systems (UVic), 300

Institutional Employee Union, 393

Institutionalized Cabinet: Governing the Western Provinces, The, xx, 279, 303, 326, 352

insurance. *See* automobile insurance; crop insurance program; health care insurance; hospital insurance

insurance, regulation of, 357

Insurance Bureau of Canada, 293

interest rates, 322, 339–40, 363

Interlake scheme, 380, 399–400

International Electrical Workers' Union, 221

International Ice and Cold Storage Co., 75

International Institute of Sustainable Development, 300

International Joint Commission (IJC), 408

interventionist government (Schreyer), xiv

Irish National Schools Series, 110

Ivens, William, 171

J

Jackson, James A., 25, 48–49, 65, 73, 76–77, 138, 159, 260

Jansen, Harold, 415

Jenson, Jane, 326

Jesuit Estates Act of 1888, 91, 105

Jobs Fund program, 341

Joe Zuken: Citizen and Socialist, 234

John A. Macdonald: The Old Chieftain, 65, 67, 105–6

John Bracken: A Political Biography, xix, 163, 189–92, 208–10

Johnson, Daniel, 269

Johnson, Francis G., 25

Johnson, George Dr., 241, 246, 266–67, 274

Johnson, Thomas H., 132, 134, 143, 152

Johnston, Garson, Forrester and Davison, 194

Johnston, Garson, Forrester, Davison and Taylor, 208

Johnston, J.L., 26

Johnston, William, 70, 76

Jones, Lyman, 85

Jorgensen, Warner, 261

Juba, Stephen, 248

judicial system, 15–16

Just One Vote: From Jim Walding's Nomination to Constitutional Defeat, 353, 384, 415

K

Kasser, Alexander, 251

Keewatin College, 246

Kelly, Thomas, 134–35

Kemp, A.E., 128

Kendle, John, xix, 163, 167–68, 178, 180, 183–84, 189–92, 208–10

Kennedy, F.S., 63

Kennedy, John F., 289

Kent, Tom, 230

Keynes, J.M., 239

Keynesian economic policy, 297, 310, 313, 317. *See also* economic policy

Killam, Justice, 93

King, Mary Jean, 108

Kinnear, Mary, xix

Klein, Ralph, 308, 325, 363

Knopff, Rainer, 322, 328

Knowles, Stanley, 333

Kostyra, Eugene, 362

Kowalski, Garry, 400

Kyoto standards. *See* greenhouse gases

L

labour: legislation for, 344, 347; movement of, xii, 284; as organized, 221, 298, 334; relations with, 48; unions for, 358, 399, 401. *See also* trade unions

Labour Party, 175

Labour Progressive Party, 223

Laird, David, 39

Lake Winnipeg Stewardship Board, 300

Lamb, W. Kaye, 67

Lambert, Geoffrey, 323–24, 328–29

Lamoureux, Kevin, 400

land boom, 83

land grants to old settlers, 28

Langevin, Louis Philippe Archbishop, 96, 129–30

Language of its Own: the Genesis of Michif, the Mixed Cree-French Language of the Canadian Métis, A, 45

languages: controversy over, 332, 345, 348–49; legislation on, 85; minority rights of, xi, xvii, 91, 322, 332, 364; as official, 273. *See also* English language; French language

LaRivière, A.A.C., 62–63, 73–74, 84

Laschinger, John, 359

Lathlin, Oscar, 387, 389, 401

Laurence, Margaret, xvii

Laurier, Wilfrid administration: and farmers, 153

Laurier, Wilfrid Sir, 92, 97–98, 100, 118, 127, 141, 149

Laurier-Greenway Compromise of 1896, 80, 97–98, 129, 134, 141

law reform commission, 295

Lawyers and Laymen of Western Canada, 115

Laycock, David, xix, 161

Le Métis, 10, 13, 32, 34, 53

Leach, R.E.A., 126

Leacock, E.P., 58, 63, 74

Leaders and Leadership in Canada, xx, 350

Leadership, 305

Leavitt, Matilda, 31

Leavitt, W.W., 44

Lebaron, Helen, 31

legal aid, 295

Legislative Council: abolition of, 14, 41

Lemay, Joseph, 7, 13

Lemieux, Ron, 401

Lépine, Ambroise, 5, 11, 15, 33, 57; trial of, 36, 39

Lépine, Baptiste, 57

Levesque, René, 323

Levin, Benjamin, 387

Levine, Allan, 137–38

Levy, Gary, 329

Lewis, Reginald W., 326

Lewis, Stephen, 230

Liba, Peter, 381

liberal capitalism, 80

Liberal Green Book, 187

Liberal Party, federal, 38, 92, 99, 109, 141, 149, 152–53, 173, 206

Liberal Party, provincial, 58–59, 135, 141, 179, 206, 233, 345, 348, 400; and alliances with, 132; as centrist, 313; conservative social policies of, 366; decline of, 284, 316, 405; and farmers' organization, 83; founding of, 80; and Meech Lake Accord, 361; and redistribution, 86; and reforms, 142; and support for citizen initiatives, 133–34; and ties to federal party, 101

Liberal-Conservative Party, 30, 80

liberalism, 175, 197, 206, 233, 301

Liberal-Progressive coalition, 196, 308–10

Life of Lord Strathcona and Mount Royal, The, 24

Lighthouse, 406

Lindquist, Evert, 303

Linteau, Paul-André, 45

liquor: consumption of, 111; referendum on, 171; sales regulations on, 122–23, 135, 171; taxes on, 178

Liquor Control Act, 171

Liquor Control Commission, 207

Lisgar, Lord, 24

livery stable, 140–41

livestock production, 377

Logan, Alexander, 93; and Anglican school funding case, 94–95

London School of Economics, 413

long-term care, 293–94. *See also* home care services

lottery revenues, 368

Lougheed, Peter, 322

Louis Riel, 23–26

Lowe, Robert, 140

Lower Canadian Rebellion of 1837, 21

Lower Tax Commission, 402

Loxley, John, 305

Loyalists (Canadian Party), 52

lumber industry, 99

Luxton, William L., 40, 53, 72, 84, 88

Lyon, David Rufus, 308

Lyon, Sterling R., 241, 264, 266, 274, 291, 299, 309–10, 312–13, 337, 358–59; and Charter, 321–22, 383; and Churchill Forest Industries, 252; and federal-provincial relations, 267; and French language rights, 323, 342; leadership of, xv, 259, 311, 324; legacy of, 324; mega-

project approach of, 339; as neo-conservatist, 316–18, 338, 349; and official language, 323; personality of, 308, 317; and political polarization, xvii, 276, 308, 325, 343, 347, 396; and privatization, 314; resignation of, 324; retirement of, 358

Lyon, Sterling R. administration, 318–19, 322–23, 357; and French language, 341; as neo-conservative, 325; as retrenchment government, 298, 314

M

MacArthur, Duncan, 75

Macdonald, D.A., 135

Macdonald, Daisy, 108

Macdonald, Hugh John, x–xii, 99–100, 108, 125; death of, 114, 122–23; and direct taxation, 113; dislike of politics by, 109; as imperialist, 111; as judge, 135; and schooling, 110; and workers compensation, 132

Macdonald, Hugh John administration, 102, 112, 122

MacDonald, J., 390

MacDonald, Jane, 404

Macdonald, John A., ix, 2–3, 6, 9, 11, 72, 108, 122; and control over provinces, 33–34; death of, 95, 109, 166; and high tariffs, 177; and provincial rights, 83, 92, 194; and railways, 43, 59, 62, 73, 81–82, 86; as reformist, 247; and relations with French, 92; and relations with Norquay, 48–49, 52, 55–57, 59, 61, 64, 67, 74, 84; resignation of, 22, 27, 38; and support for Manitoba Act, 4

Macdonald, John A. administration, 11, 27, 36, 55, 71

Macdonald, R.H., 138

Macdonald, Sanfield, 102

Macdonald Act, 112

Macdonell, G.H., 125

MacFarlane, Robert Dr., 260; Royal Commission on Education, 244–46

machine politics, 125–26, 128, 132, 142, 241

Machray, Robert Archbishop, 65, 122

MacKay, Armour, 266

Mackay, Murdoch, 179

Mackenzie, Alexander, 27, 38–39; and provincial boundaries, 42

Mackenzie, Alexander administration, 14, 22, 39, 56, 173

Mackenzie, William, 99, 101

Mackenzie King, William Lyon, 153–56, 176, 185–86, 206–7; and debt restructuring, 181; and farmers, 183; and financial arrangements with provinces, 204–5; and provincial relations, 174, 182, 201; and resources control, 175; and support for health insurance, 227; and wheat board, 172

Mackenzie King and the Prairie West, 159–60, 162–63, 189–91

Mackintosh, Gord, 401–2

Mackling, Al, 333

MacLean, Campbell, 241

Maclean's magazine, 284

MacNeil, Scott, 210

Mahew, David R., 326

Major, W.J., 176

majoritarianism, 80, 89, 102, 110, 121, 143, 149, 322

Making of the Modern West: Western Canada Since 1945, The, 233

Malcolm, G.H., 152

Management Committee of Cabinet (MCC), 269

Mancuso, Maureen, xx, 350

Manfor Industries, 360, 362

Manitoba: as bilingual province, 308; constitutional subordination of, 71; expansionism of, x

Manitoba Act of 1870, xi, 2–4, 55, 112, 121, 323; amendment to, 18, 342, 357; and communal rights, 21, 23; duality in, 34, 44, 89, 91, 93–94

Manitoba Advantage, 374

Manitoba Agricultural College, xiv, 155, 166, 168–69

Manitoba As I Saw It, 44

Manitoba: A History, xix, 23, 45–46, 65, 76, 102–4, 115, 137–38, 158, 161, 189–90, 208–9, 211, 234, 260–61, 323, 383

Manitoba: The Birth of a Province, 23

Manitoba Centennial celebrations, 241

Manitoba Central Railway, 86–88

Manitoba Club, 133

Manitoba College, 109

Manitoba Co-operative Honey Producers, 206

Manitoba Data Services, 363

Manitoba Development Authority, 269

Manitoba Development Corporation (MDC), 295, 297, 299, 314

Manitoba Development Fund (MDF), 251, 271

Manitoba Elections Act, 94, 109, 380

Manitoba Farm Electrification Enquiry Commission, 198

Manitoba Farmers Union (MFU), 285

Manitoba Federation of Agriculture (MFA), 285

Manitoba Federation of Labour, 395

Manitoba Flood of 1950: An Illustrated History, The, 234

Manitoba Flood Relief Fund, 223

Manitoba Free Press, 17, 53, 70–72, 74–75, 84, 87–88, 91, 93, 104, 120, 125, 128–30, 135, 155, 170

Manitoba Gazette, 91

Manitoba Government Employees Association (MGEA), 392–93

Manitoba Government Employees Union, 392

Manitoba Government and General Employees Union (MGEU), 392

Manitoba Grain Growers' Association, 147, 150, 169

Manitoba Health Organizations, 372

Manitoba Health Plan, 199

Manitoba Health Services Commission (MHSC), 294

Manitoba Historical Society, 109

Manitoba Hospital Insurance Plan, 271

Manitoba Hydro, xiv, 232, 273, 313–14, 344, 376–77, 407–8, 410–11

Manitoba Hydro Commission, 207

Manitoba Law School, 194

Manitoba Liquor Control Commission, 394

Manitoba Medical Association, 272, 366, 372

Manitoba Medical Services Insurance Act, 270–71

Manitoba Milestones, 137, 158

Manitoba Normal School, 333

Manitoba Nurses Union (MNU), 372

Manitoba 125: A History, 211, 327, 328

Manitoba Power Commission (MPC), 196, 216, 219, 221, 224

Manitoba: The Province and the People, 158

Manitoba Public Insurance Corporation (MPIC), 335, 346–47, 360

Manitoba Rural Credit System, 207

Manitoba School Act, 141; bilingual clause in, 148. *See also* Public Schools Act

Manitoba School Question: Majority Rule or Minority Rights, The, xix, 105–6

Manitoba Schools Question, vii, 80, 89, 93–99, 101, 104, 110, 114, 170, 246

Manitoba Securities Commission, 412

Manitoba and Southwestern Railway, 119

Manitoba Special Olympics, 393

Manitoba Sugar Company, 206

Manitoba Telecom, 383

Manitoba Telephone Act, 394

Manitoba Telephone System (MTS), xi, 135, 206, 346, 360, 394; privatization of, xvi, 376, 389, 399

Manitoba, University of, 194, 228, 285–86, 356, 364, 383, 392–93, 413, 415; agricultural school at, 238, 240; Alumni Association at, 357; colleges affiliated with, 246; Duff Roblin chair at, 256, 322; increased funding for, 244, 252, 254; law faculty of, 309, 333; Premiers' symposium at, 259; as provincially controlled, 146; as resource to RHAs, 378; and tuition freeze, 406

Manitoba Western Railway, 42

Manitoba Wheat Pool, 217

Manitoba Youth Treatment Centre, 392

Manitoba-Canada project (floodway), 409

Manitobans for Public Auto Insurance, 335

Manitoba's French-Language Crisis: A Cautionary Tale, xix, 328, 352, 384, 415

Mann, Donald, 99, 101

Manness, Clayton, 358, 361–62, 367–68, 372, 374, 381

Manning, R.F., 125

ManOil, 363

manufacturing, xvi, 374

Marchildon, Gregory P., xx, 277, 302, 350, 385

Margaret McWilliams: An Interwar Feminist, xix

Marital Property Act, 298

Marlborough Hotel, 267

Marlyn, John, xiv

Marshall, Douglas, 302, 304

Martin, Alphonse, 85

Martin, Joseph, xii, 63, 72, 83, 85–86, 90–91, 93, 105, 122; and bribery, 87, 121; and French language, 84; and railways, 87–88; as scapegoat, 104–105

Martin, Paul, 197, 227, 404

Martin, Robert, 326

Marx, Karl, 313

Masters, D.C., 161

maternity care, northern, 405

Mathers, T.G., 135, 143

Mathias, Philip, 260

Maxwell, J.A., 67

Mayers, Barbara Jean, 309

McAllister, James A., xix, 303–5, 350

McCarthy, D'Alton, 89–90, 92, 96, 105

McClung, Nellie, x, 134, 137, 159

McCormack, A.R., xix

McCormick, D., 277

McCrae, James, 361, 367, 369, 386–87

McCutcheon, Brian, 103

McDiarmid, J.S., 179, 217

McDougall, William, 31

McFadden, David H., 123, 125–26

McFadyen, Hugh, 410

McGaw, Samuel, 119

McGee, Thomas D'Arcy, 9

McGifford, Dianne, 406

McGill College, 11

McGill Medical College, 70

McGill University, 30

McGonagil, Elizabeth, 42

McGuinness, Fred, 158

McIntosh, Linda, 367, 374

McKay, Angus, 7, 13

McKay, James, 7, 14, 38, 40–41

McKay, Mary, 238

McKenna, Frank, 364–65

McKenzie, David, 175

McKenzie Seeds, 360, 363

McLean, Stewart E., 241, 246, 266–67

McLenaghen, James, 184

McLeod, Duncan, 170

McLeod, Tommy, 291

McLimont, Andrew, 174

McMicken, Alexander, 36

McMicken, Gilbert, 36

McMillan, Daniel, 119

McMillan, W.W., 119

McNaught, Kenneth, 160

McPherson, Charles D., 152, 216

McPherson, Ewen, 179

McWilliams, Margaret, 137, 158

medical care. *See* health care system

medical insurance. *See* health care insurance; hospital insurance

medicare, xvi, 199, 268–69, 272–73, 276, 314, 362; enabling legislation for, 271; and extra-billing, 344; as national, 252, 292; policy for, 292; premiums, 291; reforms to, 296; updating of, 404. *See also* health care system

Medicare Act, 271

Meech Lake Accord, viii, xvi, 321, 345, 347, 361, 363–66, 368, 375, 386, 394–97

Meighen, Arthur, 185–86, 196, 308–9

Melnick, Christine, 408

Memorandum Re Settlement of School Question, 98

Mennonites, x, 51, 89

Métis cavalry, 31

Métis carts, 50

Métis lands: claims to, 38; conflict over, vii; distribution of, 20; grants to, 20–21; protection of, 54; redistribution of, 3; rights to, 3, 21–22, 34, 36, 89

Métis Lands in Manitoba, 28

Métis people, 18, 53, 295; accommodation to, 2, 110; language of, ix, 5; loyalty of, 9–10; out-migration of, 52; and recognition of rights, 369, 402; violence against, 5, 32

Métis resistance, 6–7, 33, 57. *See also* amnesty

Métis scrip, 52

Metropolitan Corporation of Greater Winnipeg, 248; government of, 248, 294

"Mid-continent and the Peace, The," 197

Midwestern Regional Greenhouse Gas Reduction Accord, 410

migration to western Canada, 24

Military Service Act, 144

Milk Marketing Board, 319

Miller, Cal, 309

Milligan, Frank A., 23, 25–26

Mills, Allen, 349, 353, 415

Milne, David, 385

Minimum Wage Board, 145–46; minimum wage legislation, 403

mining, 363; royalties on companies, 319

Minorities, Schools, and Politics, 160

Mitchelson, Bonnie, 361, 367

Mochoruk, Jim, xix, 103, 162, 190

Moderation League, 171

modernization, 220, 239, 253

Molgat, Gildas, 232, 251, 253, 271

Monarchist League of Canada, 300

Monnin, Alfred, 372, 380, 390

Monnin Inquiry, 380–81

Monoca, A.G., 251

monopoly clause. *See* Hudson's Bay Company

Montague, W.H., 126, 133–35, 143

Morden Fine Foods, 314

Morning Call, The, 73, 88

Morris, Alexander, 2–3, 10; and federal relations, 15, 22, 34; and Métis relations, 39–40; political career, 11; and provincial relations, ix, x, 8–9, 13–14, 23, 37, 42, 55; and responsible government, 12

Morton, Bill, 217

Morton, Desmond, 160

Morton, F.L., 322, 328

Morton, W.L., vii, x, xviii–xx, 23, 32, 44–46, 48–49, 65, 71, 76, 87, 95, 102–4, 115, 120, 137–38, 145, 147, 158–62, 172, 189–90, 194, 205, 208–9, 211, 234, 240, 243, 245–46, 257–58, 260–61, 383

Mothers' Allowance Act, 243

mothers' allowances, xi, 142

Motherwell, W.R., 130, 167

Mott, Morris, 160

Mowat, Farley, 297

Mowat, Oliver, 136, 194

MTX, 346, 360

Muir, E.H., 216

Muir, Robert, 119

Mulroney, Brian, 256, 308, 314, 316, 324–25, 346; 359, 363, 365–66

Mulroney, Brian administration, 345–46, 360, 383; and Meech Lake, 397

multiculturalism, 368, 387

Mulvey, Stewart, 67

Murdoch, Sophia May, 238

Murray, James, 75

Murray, Stuart, 405

Murray, Walter, 171

Mussio, Laurence, 389

N

national adjustment grant, 183

National Deal, The, 326, 328–29

National Electrical Code, 221

National Farmers Union, 286

National Finance Committee, 181

National Hockey League, 375

National Policy, 82–83, 99, 168–69, 177

National Progressive Party, 169

national unity question, 269

nationalism, 364

Native and northern affairs, 369

natural resources, 368–69, 374, 377; control of, 174; development of, xiii–xv, 199, 202, 402; in northern regions, xvi–xvii, 142; rights to, 369; transfer of, 175, 177

Nault, André, 15, 36

Neatby, H. Blair, 162

Nelson River drainage basin, 407

neo-conservatism, xvi, 312, 316–18, 320, 325, 349, 356, 358

nepotism, 299

Netherton, Alex, 305, 313, 317–18, 327–28

Neufeld, Harold, 367

New Democratic Party, xvi, 264, 287, 344–45, 360–61, 363, 381–82, 393, 396–97, 405, 410, 412; and Aboriginal justice, 402; and the Accord, 364; as centrist party, 381, 392; and crown corporations, 408; as emerging from CCF, 334, 348; factionalism within, 337–39, 342, 357, 400; and French language dispute, 358–59; future of, 299, 413; and Interlake scheme, 380; and labour unions, 399, 401; in northern ridings, 395; as pragmatic party, 414; reach of, 338–39, 343; reconstructing of, 332, 349–50; rise of, 259, 275, 284, 335; and social democracy, 400–401, 411; and social programs, 311, 313, 366, 373, 400

New Flyer company, 362

New Party faction, 333–34, 337

Newman, Peter C., 138

Newton, F.Y., 126

Nikiforuk, Andrew, 352

90th Winnipeg Regiment of Rifles, 108, 144

Noel, S.J.R., 125, 138

Nolin, Charles, 40–41, 57

Norquay, John, ix–xi, 8, 22, 40–41, 48, 50, 66, 70, 72, 75, 82, 85; as accused of theft, 71; and alleged breach of trust, 64; ancestry of, 302; and boundary extension, 42; and compromise among minorities, 14, 90; and Conservative Party, 87; and CPR monopoly, 86, 121; death of, 67, 90; and Métis lands, 21; as negotiator, 64; and party system, 60; political life of, 52–54; and provincial rights, 84; and railways, 59, 62, 65, 73–74; and relations with churches, 20; relations with J.A. Macdonald, 56; reputed for moderation, 54; resignation of, 63, 65, 74; and voting system, 55; and wave of prosperity, 58

Norquay, John administration, 48, 57, 59, 61, 70–71, 74, 76, 82, 84; and fiscal practices, 63, 113

Norquay, Joseph, 126

Norquay, Oman, 65

Norquay, Thomas, 51, 67; and provincial power, 102, 103

Norquay Sr., John, 51, 66

Norrie, William, 370, 387

Norris, Tobias C., x–xii, 132, 135, 141–43, 152, 155, 173, 175; and corruption allegation, 168; and French language, 149; impact in province of, 140; and the independents, 150–51; resignation of, 156; and support for war, 144

Norris, Tobias C. administration, xi; coalition government of, 134; and farmers, 150–51, 154, 157, 169; reform measures of, 140, 145–47, 156–57; and veterans benefits, 148

North American Review, 127

North American Free Trade Agreement (NAFTA), 368

Northern Elevator Company, 119

Northern Magus, The, 279

Northern Pacific and Manitoba Railway (NPM), 87

Northern Pacific Railway, 61, 65, 73, 86–88, 93, 104, 121, 124

Northern States Power (NSP), 344

North-West Resistance 1885, 108

North-West territories: as annexed, 2, 24, 51; uprising in, 60, 62

Nor'Wester newspaper, 50

Notman, Margaret, 70

Notwithstanding clause, 322, 364

Noxious Weeds Act, 147

Nurse Practitioner Association of Manitoba, 404

nurse practitioners, 398

Nursey, Walter R., 44–46

O

O'Donnell, John Dr., 32, 41, 44

O'Donoghue, W.B., 5, 33, 36

Office of Lieutenant-Governor: A Study in Canadian Government and Politics, The, xx, 23–26

Official Languages Act, 272, 274

Official Languages Act (Manitoba), 323

Official Languages Commission, 372

Ogilvie, A.W., 58

Ogilvie Floor Mills, 119

Ogletree, Francis, 14–15, 39, 41, 214

oil company, Crown owned, 339

old settler faction, 54, 57, 64

old-age pensions, 186–87, 201, 208, 243–44, 252

Oleson, Charlotte, 361, 367

Oliver, Frank, 124

ombudsman service, 295

One Canada: Memoirs of the Right Honourable John G. Diefenbaker, 261

Ontarian Protestants, 54; as dominant in Manitoba, 121

Ontario Agricultural College (OAC), 167–68

Ontario democracy, x, 49

Ontario Hydro, 128, 219

Ontario Hydro-Electric Power Commission, 174, 224

On-to-Ottawa Trek, 180

OPEC oil crisis, 297

"Operational Productivity," 268, 273

Orange Lodge, 8, 92, 95, 123, 132, 134–35; incorporation of, 59

Orangemen, 10, 33, 39, 59

Orchard, Don, 361, 367, 374

Order of Canada, 208, 256

Order of Manitoba, 256

organized labour. *See* labour

Orlikow, Lionel, 158–59

Osborne, Helen Betty, 369

Ostenso, Martha, xii

Oswald, Theresa, 404

Ottawa (as federal seat), 23, 368; and CF-18 decision, 346; and CPR monopoly, 86; and economic development, xviii; and federal initiatives, xv; and fiscal arrangements with provinces, 174, 178, 200–203, 205, 207–8, 254, 375, 378, 398; and health care, 270–71, 404; and hospital insurance, 265; and land decisions, 34, 38, 42; and Meech Lake, 364–65; and minority rights, 97; and privatization, 376; and provincial relations, 13, 41, 49, 57, 71, 81–82, 195–97, 268, 272, 345, 366; and railway control, 61–62, 74, 102; and resource development, xiii, 174; and social programs, 374; and stabilization fund, 362

Ottawa Citizen, 325, 401

Owram, Doug, 201–2, 208–10

P

Pacific Scandal, 13

Page of the History of the Schools in Manitoba During Seventy-Five Years, A, 104

Pajares, Roland, 115

Paler, Sid, 265

Pallister, Brian, 367

Pan-American Games 1999, 381

Pannekoek, Frits, xix, 44

paper industry, 251

Papers of the Eighteenth Algonquian Conference, 45

Parasiuk, Wilson, 345–46

Parent Advisory Councils, 370

parish system, 18, 22, 33–34

Parisien, Norbert, 33

Parizeau, Jacques, 375

Parker, W.J., 217

Parliament of Women, 134

parliamentary system: reestablishment of, 239; as restored, 259

Parr, Joy, 220, 234

Parti Québécois, 320, 341, 363, 375

partisan politics, 80, 82, 142. *See also* machine politics; party system, provincial

partnerships, public-private, 378

Partridge, E.A., 130–31

party system, provincial, 102, 108, 137, 153, 168–69, 214; as competitive, 239, 258; as multi-party, viii–ix; separation of provincial/federal, 71; as three-parties, xvi; transformation of, 259; as two-party system, viii, x–xi, 57, 59, 65, 114, 366

Paterson Commission, 126

Paterson, George Judge, 126

Paterson, Hugh, 119

Patriation reference, 322

patronage, 118, 125, 128, 132, 135, 137, 218

Patrons of Husbandry, 36

Pattullo, Duff, 183

Paulley, Russ, 274, 287

Pawley, Adele, 334, 349

Pawley, Charysse, 334

Pawley, Christopher, 334

Pawley, Howard, xiv, xvii, xx, 284, 303, 305, 315, 320, 335, 339, 341, 351–53, 362, 401; achievements of, 349–50; and aeronautics industry, 393; as attending Premiers' symposium, 259; and auto insurance, 292, 347; as carrying Schreyer's legacy, 291, 301; and economy, 345; and Francophone issues, 342–44, 358, 371; and a judicial inquiry, 346; and Meech Lake Accord, 364, 383; as moderate social democrat, xv, 337, 347, 349; and recession, 341; as reconstructing the NDP, 332–34, 338; reform agenda of, 298, 336, 340; resignation of, 348–49, 360, 385

Pawley, Howard administration, xv–xvi, 323, 339–40, 345, 359, 394–95; conciliatory approach of, 347; and crown corporations, 346; and economy, 343–44; and French language, 324, 341–42, 357, 393; and justice system, 369; Keynesian values of, 324; non-confidence vote in, 348, 360

Pawley compromise, 342

Payne, Michael, 137

Pearson, Lester, 255, 268, 270, 292

Pedersen, Susan, xix

pemmican, 51

Pendulum of Power; Canada's Federal Elections, 158, 162

Penner, Roland, 358

Pentland, David, 45

Permanent Joint Council of Industry, 146

Peterson, David, 365

Peterson, Thomas, xix, 161, 278–82, 302, 326

Petro-Canada, 376

Pharmacare, 284, 294, 314

Phillips, Alfred T., 27

Phillips, Charles, E., 28

Phillips, Frederick, 119

Physician Recruitment and Retention Plan, 404

physicians: fees of, 293, 372

Pickersgill, J.W., 196, 207–9

Pine Falls Paper Co., 377

Pioneers of Manitoba, 157

Planning and Priorities Committee of Cabinet (PPCC), 269

Political Economy of Manitoba, The, 260, 305, 327

Political Warriors: Recollections of a Social Democrat, 235, 260, 277, 279–80, 304

Politics in Manitoba: Parties, Leaders and Voters, xx, 384, 390, 415, 416

Politics of Survival: The Conservative Party of Canada, 1939–1945, The, 191–92

populism, 111, 414

Populism and Democratic Thought in the Canadian Prairies, 1910–1945, xix, 161

pornography, child, 406

"Port Hope Conservatives," 187

Portage Collegiate Institute, 264, 308

post-flood compensation program, 408

postwar reconstruction, 197–99, 202

potash development, 319

potash mines, 340

poverty levels, child, 381, 397

power generation, 220, 224, 407. *See also* hydroelectric power generation

power grid, western, 319

Power Struggles: Hydro Development and First Nations in Manitoba and Quebec, 418

Prairie Capitalism: Power and Influence in the New West, 234

Prairie Farm Rehabilitation Administration (PFRA), 249

Prairie Home Stock Farm, 81, 101

Prairie Politics and Society: Regionalism in Decline, xx, 326–27

Prairie Theatre Exchange, 393

Pratt, Larry, 234

Praznik, Darren, 378, 382, 386–87

Prendergast, James Émile, 85, 91, 121

Price, Richard G., 350

Priests and Politicians: Manitoba Schools and the Election of 1896, 106

prison system, provincial, 147; probation services, 243

privatization, 376–77, 383, 397, 399. *See also* Crown corporation; Manitoba Telephone System (MTS)

Probyzanski, John, 126

Proceedings and Transactions of the Royal Society of Canada, xx

Progressive Conservative Party, federal, 217, 230, 255

Progressive Conservative Party, provincial, 276, 288, 357, 382, 393, 396–97; as centrist party, 356, 373, 398; decline of, 274; and fiscal responsibility, 412; and Interlake scheme, 380; naming of, xiii, 186, 230; rebuilding of, xiv–xv, 238, 257, 264, 358; rise in popularity by, 299, 337, 339, 347–48, 361; as truly conservative, 266

progressive ideas, American, 132–33

Progressive Party, 215, 338–39, 352

Progressive Party in Canada, The, 159, 162

Progressivism, xii

prohibition, 111, 113, 123–24, 134, 142, 145–46, 150, 171. *See also* temperance movement

Prohibition Act, 112, 123

property, private, 3, 19; rights to, 15, 19, 48, 111; transfers of, 3, 19, 41

property rights, for Métis. *See* Métis lands

Protestants, ix, xii, xiv, xvii, 18, 31, 34

Provinces, xx

provinces, transfers to. *See* federal subsidy

Provincial Agricultural Association, 35

provincial autonomy, 97

*Provincial Politics in Canada: Towards the Turn of the
Century,* xix, 303–4, 326–28, 351–52

provincial rights. *See* rights

Provincial Savings Bank, 147

*Provincial State in Canada: Politics in the Provinces
and Territories, The,* 305, 327

Provincial and Territorial Legislatures in Canada, 329

Pryke, K.G., 24

Public Accounts Committee, 134–35, 143

public debt. *See* debt, provincial

public safety, 401, 405–6, 410

Public Schools Act, 95, 98, 128–29, 133–34. *See
also* Manitoba School Act

public sector: and pay equity, 344

public spending, 239, 251, 258

public transit, 248

Public Utility Board (PUB), 274

public welfare, 202

Q

Quebec: as distinct society, 363, 376, 387;
governing system of, 16, 41; and national
unity, 346; referendum in, 375, 397; special
status for, 269, 272

Quebec, A History 1867–1929, 45

Quebec Party, 37

Queen, John, 171, 190

Queen's Printer, 363

Queen's University, 413–14

Quiet Revolution, xv, 254

Quinn, Frank, 304

R

Radical Tories: The Conservative Tradition in Canada,
276

railway charters: federal disallowance of, 59–60,
82–84, 86

railway policy, 23, 56, 58, 65, 98, 112, 121

railways, xi, 48, 57, 71, 94, 122, 222; branch
lines of, 43, 59, 61, 103, 124; competition
for, 124; construction of, 56, 101, 110, 121,
124; development of, ix–x, 38, 42–43, 99;
extensions of, 82, 93; land grants for, 42,
113; provincial legislation for, 60, 74, 86; as
transcontinental, 55, 81, 87

Ransom, Brian, 358–59

Rasmussen, Ken, 303

Rasporich, A.W., 233

Rea, J.E., 87, 98, 102, 104

Reagan, Ronald, 308, 314

real estate. *See* property, private

Rebellion of 1837, 7

Rebuilding Canadian Party Politics, xx

recession, 332, 344, 367, 373; effects of, 340;
global, 308

Red Cross, 222–23

Red River College, 246, 405

Red River Colony, ix; annexation of, 31

Red River flood: of 1950, xiv, 221, 223; of 1997,
379–80, 408. *See also* flood

Red River Floodway, 249, 259; as National Historic
Site, 250. *See also* floodway

Red River Resistance of 1870, vii, 32

*Red River Rising: The Anatomy of a Flood and the
Survival of an American City,* 390

Red River Settlement, 23, 32, 49–51, 66, 90

Red River Valley Board, 223

Red River Valley flood control, 408. *See also* flood
control

Red River Valley Railway (RRVR), 62–63, 73–74,
87–88

Red River Valley Railway (RRVR) Act, 72–73

Red Sea Rising: The Flood of the Century, A, 390

Redistribution Act, 13, 37, 40, 53, 125

redistribution of electoral districts, 14, 42, 56, 86,
228. *See also* electoral boundaries

Referendum Act, 123

Reform Association, 83–84

Reform Party, 233, 300

*Reformers, Rebels, and Revolutionaries: The Western
Canadian Radical Movement, 1899–1919,* xix

Regehr, T.D., 103–4, 137–38

Regina, University of, 302, 350

Regional Health Authorities (RHAs), 378

*Regional Ministers: Power and Influence in the
Canadian Cabinet,* 352

regionalism, xviii

relief payments to provinces, 195. *See also* Great
Depression

remedial legislation, 96–98, 110

Render, Shirley, 387, 389

Rennie, Bradford J., xx, 385

rent controls, 339

rentalsman service, 295

RePap Enterprises Inc., 362

Report of the Aboriginal Justice Inquiry of Manitoba, 387

Report of the Commission of Inquiry into Allegations of Infractions of the Elections Act and the Elections Finance Act during the 1995 Manitoba General Election, 390

Report on Supply of Electrical Energy in the Province of Manitoba, 224

representation, dual, 14–15, 34, 38, 44

representation by population, 54

resistance movement 1869–1870, 31, 34, 39, 44, 48–49, 52. *See also* Métis resistance

responsible government, 2, 11, 15, 22–23, 34, 36, 38, 42, 102, 312, 321

retirement, mandatory, 232

Reynolds, Janelle, 44

Rhodes Smith, Charles, 217, 224

Richards, John, 234

Richardson, James, 311

Rideau Hall, 121

Riel, Louis, 4, 7–8, 23, 26, 48–49, 57, 65; amnesty for, 52; arrest of, 5, 11; as extremist, 34; harassment of, 36; leadership of, 10, 12, 39; meeting Robert Davis, 32; Provisional Government of, 5–6, 9, 20, 24, 31, 33, 37, 42, 51, 293; and responsible government, 11; supporters of, 2, 25, 38–39; uprising of, 62

rights: of Aboriginals, 347; of Catholics, 94, 96; of Francophones, 96; of language choice, 272, 338; of minorities, 91, 96–98, 143, 322, 338, 371; of province, 65, 71, 82–84, 90, 92–94, 101, 194, 203–4, 376; to schooling, xvii, 96; of women, 332. *See also* property, private

Riley, George, 317

Rise and Fall of Canadian Farm Organizations, The, 302

Rise and Fall of a Political Animal: A Memoir, 260, 282, 302–4, 351–52

Ritchot, Father, 9, 26

River Road: Essays on Manitoba and Prairie History, 66

Roach, Kent, 234, 328, 384

road system, provincial, 147, 172; construction of, 243, 251. *See also* highways

Robarts, John P., 255, 268

Robert Laird Borden, A Biography, vol. II: 1914–1937, 159

Robin, Martin, xix, 161, 302

Robinson, Eric, 389, 401–2

Robinson, Svend, 325

Roblin, Adelaide, 121

Roblin, Arthur, 119

Roblin, Charles, 135, 238

Roblin, David, 118

Roblin, Deborah, 118

Roblin, Duff, 235, 241, 243, 260–61, 266, 277, 289, 302, 309, 316–17, 320, 326, 328, 382; achievement of, 258, 410; as activist, 264; appointment to Senate, 256; death of, 259; and drawing of electoral boundaries, 228; and flood control, 223, 248–50; and health care, 265, 276; and hydro development, 232; interventionist program of, 310; leadership of, 275, 286; legacy of, 259, 268; and loans to industry, 271–72; and modernization, 238–39; and national PC leadership, 255–56, 267; and need-based funding, 222; and public policy, 252–54; and public spending, 247; as rebuilding PC party, xiv, 229–31, 238, 240, 242, 245; reforms of, 313; and report on post-secondary institutions, 371; resignation of, 256; and shared services, 246

Roblin, Duff administration, 244–45, 248, 251–52, 257; legacy of, 259; as progressive, 258; and schools, 245

Roblin, Duff Professorship in Canadian Government, 256

Roblin, George, 135

Roblin, James Platt, 118

Roblin, John P., 118

Roblin, Philip, 118

Roblin Report, 371

Roblin, Rodmond P., xi–xii, 83, 88, 109, 119–20, 125, 133; achievements of, 137; and conspiracy to defraud, 114, 118, 135; death of, 135; and farmers, 131–32; leadership of, 100; and patronage, 118, 142; and prohibition, 112, 123; and railways, 104, 121; resignation of, 135, 143; and schools, 122, 129, 134; and spread of telephone, 127–28; and two-party system, x

Roblin, Rodmond P. administration, xi, xv, 124, 142–43, 156, 317; policies of, 146; and prohibition, 130; and scandal, 176

Roblin, W.L., 135

"Roblin's Folly," 249

Robson, Hugh Amos, 163, 173, 175–76, 179

Rocan, Denis, 361, 367, 374

Rogers, Robert, 123, 125–26, 130–32, 137, 142–43, 155–56

Roman Catholic Church, 8, 89; land holdings of, 20; and schools, 122

Roman Catholics, ix, xi–xii, 9, 18, 26, 34, 85, 94

Romanow Report, 390

Romanow, Roy, 363, 381, 400

Ronaghan, N.E.A., 24–25, 66

Roos, N.P., 388

Roosevelt, Franklin Delano, 289

Rose, John, 76

Ross, Arthur, 240

Ross, Hugh R., 118, 137

Ross, James, 7

Rothney, G.O., 25, 28

Rowell-Sirois Commission, 182–83, 200–201, 207, 209; implementation of, 184; report of, 195, 197–98

Royal Alexandra Hotel, 133

Royal Canadian Mounted Police (RCMP), 369

Royal Commission on Adult Education in 1945, 199

Royal Commission on Dominion-Provincial Relations, 182, 195

Royal Commission on the Future of Health Care in Canada (2002), 404

Royal, Joseph, 3, 7–8, 10, 12–14, 17–18, 27, 37–41, 53, 55–57, 103

Royal Winnipeg Ballet, xvii

Rupert's Land: legal tradition of, 16

Rural Credits Act, 147

rural electrification, xiv, 198–99, 207, 214, 216, 218–21, 224, 230. *See also* electrification program

Rural Life. Portraits of the Prairie Town, 209–10

Russell, Frances, xix, 323, 328, 341, 352, 384

Russell, Peter H., 322, 328

Russell House, 55, 121

S

Safe Schools legislation, 406

Sale, Tim, 377

Saloons of the Old West, 44

Salt, William, 135

Salvation Army, 222

Sandrel, S., 390

Sanger, J.W., 235

Santos, Conrad, 395

Saskatchewan Coal Mining and Transportation Company, 58, 60

Saskatchewan Energy Conservation and Development Authority, 300

Saskatchewan Government Insurance Office, 292, 335

Saskatchewan Grain Growers, 169

Saskatchewan Liberal Association, 206

"Saskatchewan Mafia," 291

Saskatchewan Power Commission, 295

Saskatchewan Premiers of the Twentieth Century, xx, 385

Saskatchewan Stock Breeders' Association, 167

Saskatchewan, University of, 167, 171

Saunders Aircraft company, 299, 314

Savoie, Donald J., 303, 351

Sayer, Guillaume, 50

Saywell, John T., xx, 23–26

Scarth, W.B., 58, 62–63, 67

Schmidt, Louis, 7, 28, 38

Schofield, F.H., 138

school attendance, 18, 134, 142, 146

school boards, 85, 122, 245

school boundaries, 403

school districts, 18; amalgamation of, 244–45, 254, 403

school legislation, 17, 85, 93, 129

school rights. *See* rights

school system: as bilingual, 99, 129, 132, 134–35, 141, 146, 148, 156; as Catholic, xi, 19, 42, 91, 98, 129; as denominational, 89–90, 92–94; as dual, 23, 54, 90, 103; French language teacher's training, 298; as national, 94, 98, 110; as Protestant, xi, 129; public funding for, 18, 93, 129, 370, 403; as separate, 89–92, 95, 100, 295, 301, 319; as technical, 405; as unilingual, xi, 149

schools policy, 141

Schreyer, Adele, 334

Schreyer, Edward, xvi–xvii, 232–33, 285, 310–11, 313–17, 351; and auto insurance, 293; centre-left philosophy of, 288; and Churchill Forest Industries, 251, 296; as dynamic, 264, 274–75; farm policy of, 286; and health care, 294; idealism of, 300; interventionist government of, xiv–xv; leadership of, 301, 320, 333, 335, 337–38, 340, 347–49, 382; legacy of, 287, 291, 295, 300; and medicare, 292; as multicultural symbol, 284; and the New Party, 334; at Premiers' symposium, 259; and public funding, 297; reform agenda of, 297; and relations with business, 290; resignation of, 299, 336; as social democrat, 289, 394; and wage-and-price controls, 298

Schreyer, Edward administration, 232, 252, 290, 340; administrative structures of, 317–18, 332, 335; and compulsory auto coverage, 292; and Crown corporations, 314; Keynesian values of, 324; leadership during, 299; legacy of, 338–39, 349; and public funding, 296; reforms of, 300; and social policy, 294; unicity framework of, 248, 295

Schreyer, John, 285

Schreyer, Lily, 299

Schroeder, Vic, 357, 360, 395

Schultz, John Christian, 4, 6–8, 33–34, 39, 41, 52, 58, 67, 91, 95

Schulz, Herb, 285, 302–3

Schulz, Jacob (Jake), 285, 302

Schulz, Lily, 285

Scott, R.W., 23

Scott, Thomas, 33; execution of, 2, 5, 11, 15, 23–24, 31, 36, 39, 52, 57

Scowen, P.H., 44

Seager, Allen, 161

Security Services Review Committee, 383

Seeing Canada Whole: A Memoir, 209

self-government, 40; constitutional principles of, 2

Selinger, Greg, 401, 412–13

Selkirk, Lord, 54

Senate, reform of, 363–65

seniors' income protection plan, 347

separatism, 363. See also sovereigntist movement

Setter, Elizabeth, 49

settlement policy, 174

Seven Sisters power agreement, 174–76

Shaftesbury, 247

Shapiro, E., 388

shared services proposal, 246

Sharp, Paul F., 144, 159–62

Sharpe, C.A., 158

Sharpe, Robert J., 234, 384

Shelby, Ashley, 390

Sheppard, Robert, 316, 321–22, 325–29

Sherman, Bud, 358

Shields, Carol, xvii

Shilliday, Gregg, 211, 327

Shore, Frederick J., 45, 66

Shuttleworth, Charles, 265

Sifton, Clifford, x, xii, 80, 83, 93–99, 101, 104–5, 111–13, 120, 122, 124

Sifton, John, 234

Sifton, Victor, 122

signage, in English, 364

Sigurdson, Richard, 321

Silcox, J.B. Reverend, 123

Silver, A.I., 24, 26

Silver, Jim, 260, 305, 327, 389

Sinclair, C.M., 387

Sinclair, Gordon, 234, 387

Sinclair, Murray, 66, 369, 373

Size, C.F., 128

Smart, James, 83, 85, 90–91, 105–6

Smith, David E., xviii, xx

Smith, Donald A., 6, 14, 21, 24, 28, 35–36, 41–42, 67, 97

Smith, Doug, 234, 415

Smith, Muriel, 337

Smith, Peter J., 233

Smith's bill, 28

Snug Little Flock: The Social Origins of the Riel Resistance, 1869–1870, A, xix, 44

Social Credit Party, 181

social democracy, xiii, xv–xvi, 284, 288–89, 301, 312–13, 337, 349, 400–402, 407; policies of, 403, 411

Social Democracy in Manitoba: A History of the CCF-NDP, 260, 276–78, 281–82, 302–3, 305, 328, 350, 352

social gospel movement, 145, 332

social policy, xv–xvi, 250, 253, 294; reform of, xiii

social security, 194, 197–98, 247

social service programs, 198, 205, 289, 359, 366–68, 373–74, 400; expansion of, 319, 381; fiscal support for, 365; modernizing of, 318; preservation of, 362, 398; renewal of, 383; reorganization of, 378; spending on, 362, 378; transfer payments for, 345

social welfare system, xvi, 205, 398

socialism, 265, 301

socialized medicine. See medicare

Société franco-manitobaine (SFM), 323, 342, 358

Sokolyk, Taras, 388, 400

soldiers: relief tax for, 178. See also veterans

South Western Colonization Railway, 82

sovereigntist movement, 375. See also separatism

Speaking for Myself: Politics and Other Pursuits, 235, 256, 259–61, 277, 302, 328

Speers, Les Mrs., 157

Spence, Jean Norquay, 49

Spivak, Sidney, 241, 258, 271, 275, 297, 310–13, 315–17, 357

Sprague, Douglas N., xix, 24, 26, 28, 44–45

SSHRC Research Grants Program, 157

St. Boniface College, 323

St. Francis College, 30

St. John's College, 49, 58, 238

St. Laurent, Louis, 206–7, 216, 222, 227, 229

St. Laurent, Louis administration, xiv, 217

St. Paul's College, 157, 286

"Stand Up for Manitoba," 345, 393

Standard, 40

Stanfield, Robert, 255–56, 266

Stanley, George F.G., 23–26

Stefanson, Eric, 367, 373–75, 381–82

Steinkopf, Maitland, 241

Stephen, George, 61–63, 67

Stephens, D.W., 235

Stevens, H.H., 186

Stevenson, Kate, 70

Stewart, Charles, 83

Stewart, David K., 351

Stewart, Ian, 353, 384, 415

Stinson, Lloyd, 228–29, 231, 235, 243, 260, 277, 279–80, 304

Story of Manitoba, 138

Stream Runs Fast, My Own Story, The, 137, 159

Strom, Harry, 273

Stubbs, Roy St. George, 115

Success Commercial College, 357

suffrage: universal manhood, 86. *See also* women

Supreme Court of Manitoba Bill, 16

Supreme Court on Trial: Judicial Activism or Democratic Dialogue, The, 328

Sutherland, Hugh, 87

Sutherland, John, 12, 20

Swainson, Donald, 159

Swan, Andrew, 413

Swan, Ruth, 26, 44–46, 66

Symbol in Stone: The Art and Politics of a Public Building, 158

T

Taché, Alexandre-Antonin, 5–8, 10–11, 20, 24–25, 39, 42, 57, 85, 91–92, 96, 104

Take Back the Streets, 406

Taking Power: Managing Government Transitions, 303, 351

Talbot, P.A., 170

tariff policy, 84

tariffs, 142; as high, 82–83, 99, 153, 168, 177

Tarte, Israel, 98

Task Force on Francophone School Governance, 371

Task Force on the 1987 Constitutional Accord, 364

taxation, 16–17, 239, 258, 273; as direct, 113, 200; as fair, 198; as progressive, 198, 289; as regressive, 296; as unjust, 203

taxes, 257, 400; on business profits, 155; on corporations, 205, 412; cuts to, 410; on gasoline, 152, 171; as general revenue, 296; as high, 362; on payroll for health and education, 340; on personal income, 152, 155, 178, 205, 292, 368, 405; rates of, 319; reduction in, 402; reforms to, 343; relief from, 314; on sales, 254, 256–57, 398; for schools, 403

tax-rental agreements, 270

Taylor, Charles, 276

Taylor, Fawcett, 171, 175–76, 309

Taylor, Jeffery, 189

Taylor, Malcolm G., 235, 280

Technical Vocational Initiative, 405

Technopulp, 251

Telecom Nation: Telecommunications, Computers, and Governments in Canada, 389

telecommunications: and privatization, 383

telegraph cable, trans-Atlantic, 51

telephone system, provincial, 127; publicly owned, 142. *See also* Manitoba Telephone System (MTS)

Tembec Inc., 377

temperance movement, 123, 130, 132, 135. *See also* prohibition

Ten Years in Winnipeg: A Narration of the Principal Events in the History of the City of Winnipeg, 44–46

Thatcher, Margaret, 308, 314

Thatcher, Ross, 273

The Pas forestry development policy, 252

Thibault, Martin, 411, 416

Thin Ice: Money, Politics and the Demise of an NHL Franchise, 389

thin red line scandal, 126

Thirty-Five Years in the Limelight: Sir Rodmond P. Roblin and His Times, 137

Thomas, Paul, xix, 324, 329, 338, 350–51, 373
Thompson, Harriet (Tommie), 264
Thompson, John Herd, 159, 161
Thompson, John Sir, 95–96
Thomson, T., 390
Thornton, Robert S. Dr., 144, 148–49, 152
Timson, Judith, 305
Toews, Eric, 374, 389
Toews, Miriam, xvii
Toews, Vic, 398
Topper, Emily, 194
Toronto Board of Trade, 293
Toronto, University of, 70, 108, 233
Toryism, reformist, 247
Toward Defining the Prairies: Region, Culture and History, 115
trade, international, 374
trade unions: certification of, 398. *See also* labour
Trades and Labour Congress, 221, 227
Trades and Labour Council, 133
trading posts, 48
transfer agreement, 174
transfer payments, 202; to provinces, 16, 201
transportation, xvi–xvii, 38, 411
treaty land: negotiations on, 369
Treaty Land Entitlement agreements, 370
Treller, Jim, 412
Troyer, Warner, 260
Trudeau, Pierre, xv, 256, 284, 299, 310–11; and constitutional issues, 273–74, 321–22, 383; and Gang of Eight, 325; and Manitoba Act amendment, 342; and medicare, 271–72; and Meech Lake Accord, 364–65; and Quebec as distinct society, 363; and wage-and-price controls, 298
Trudeau, Pierre administration, 336, 341, 383
Trudeaumania, 256, 284
True, Susan Augusta, 31, 34–35, 44
Truthwaite, Isabella, 66
Truthwaite, Jacob, 66
tuition fees, 339, 371; rebate program for, 406. *See also* education, post-secondary
Tupper, Charles Sir, 98, 108–10, 112, 115
Tupper, John Stewart, 108
Turgeon Commission on natural resource transfer, 177
Turnbull, Norman, 184
Turner, Ronald D., 218, 234
Tweed, Merv, 389

Tyrwhitt, Janice, 44

U
Underwood & McLellan and Associates, 356
unemployment, 178, 363, 368, 374, 397; insurance for, 186
Unemployment Relief Act, 178
Union of the Canadas 1841–1857, The, 45
union government, 144, 150, 156; and high tariffs, 153. *See also* coalition government
unions. *See* trade unions
United Church, 308
United College, 247, 285, 309, 333
United Farmers of Alberta, 151, 169
United Farmers of Manitoba (UFM), xii–xiii, 150–51, 153–55, 169–73, 215–16, 232; government of, 140, 166
United Farmers of Ontario, 169
United Grain Growers, 133, 264
United States: boundary issues with, 408; and energy agenda, 407–8, 410; relations with, 12, 284; and trade, 377
universities. *See* education, post-secondary
University College of the North, 405, 411
University Educational Review Commission, 371
University Grants Commission, 371, 378
Upper House: dual representation in, 39
uranium smelter, 340
urban crime. *See* crime
urban development, 310, 357
urban ridings, 230. *See also* redistribution
Urban Shared Services Corporation, 378
urban transportation, xvi. *See also* transportation
urban unemployment. *See* unemployment
urbanization, 214
utilities, public, 127–28, 135

V
Vajcner, Mark E., 208
Valpy, Michael, 316, 321–22, 325–29
Van Horne, W.C., 61–62
Vankoughnet, Agnes Gertrude, 108
Vary, Vincent, 214
Vaughn Street Detention Centre, 392
veterans: benefits for, 148. *See also* soldiers
Victoria, University of, 300
View from the Ledge: An Insider's Look at the Schreyer Years, A, 302
Viewpoints Research Ltd., 396

Villard, Henry, 86–87
Viner, Jacob, 182–83
Vodrey, Rosemary, 367, 371

W
Wade, F.C., 83, 97
wage-and-price controls, 298–99, 301
Wagenburg, Ronald, 350
wages, minimum, 344; legislation for, 403
Wainwright, H.C., 357
Wainwright, Janice, 356
Waite, Peter B., 48–49, 65, 105–6, 114
Walding, Jim, 343, 347–48, 358, 360, 394–95
Waldram, James B., 304
Walker Theatre, 134
Wallace, William, 44
Wallbridge, Chief Justice, 60
War Measures Act, 301
war movement, anti-Vietnam, 284
Wardhaugh, Robert A., 115, 159–60, 162–63,
    189–91, 209
Warnes, F.W., 119
Wartime Elections Act, 148–49
Washington, University of, 349
wastewater, 411
water, drinking, xvi, 362, 408–9, 411
Water Control and Conservation Branch, 266
Waterloo, University of, 349
Wednesdays are Cabinet Days, 326–27, 351
Weir, Bill, 264
Weir, Cameron, 264
Weir, Enid, 264
Weir, James Dixon, 264
Weir, John, 264
Weir, Leslie, 264
Weir, Maude, 264
Weir, Patrick, 264
Weir, Tommie, 269
Weir, Walter, xiv, xvii, 241, 284, 288, 308; and
    Churchill Forest Industries, 251; credibility of,
    266; death of, 275–76; as fiscal conservative,
    xv, 258, 264–65, 276, 289, 320; and hydro
    development, 232, 290; leadership of,
    268–70, 287; and medicare, 270–72, 292;
    and provincial roads, 266; and relations with
    Ottawa, 273; retirement of, 311; retrenchment
    policies of, 310
Weir, Walter administration, 252, 275; as
    conservative, 291

Welch, Alex, 184
welfare state, 205, 247, 318
Wells, Clyde, 364–65
Wemyss, John, Mrs., 75
Wesley, Jared J., 324, 326, 329, 351
West: The History of a Region in Confederation, The,
    415
West and the Nation: Essays in Honour of W.L.
    Morton, The, 159–60
West: Regional Ambitions, National Debates, Global
    Age, The, xx
Westbury, June, 357
western alienation, 34
Western Canada Concept, 345
Western Immigration Boom, vii
Western Labour News, 149
western land boom, 81
Wetlands initiative, 411
What is History Now?, xix
wheat: as economic basis, x, 48, 174; as export, 171,
    176; international marketing of, 172; prices
    for, 95, 99, 131, 178, 183
Wheat Board, 171, 183, 362
wheat pools, provincial, 172, 178
White, Graham, xx, 317, 327, 329
White Paper on Health, 293
Whitehead, Charles, 125
Whitney, James, 128
Whyte, William, 88
Wiebe, Rudy, xiv
Wilberforce, 247
William Lyon Mackenzie King: A Political Biography,
    162
William Lyon Mackenzie King, vol. II, 1924–1932:
    The Lonely Heights, 162
Williams, James, 114
Williamson, W.J., 126
Willis, Errick F., 181, 217, 238, 240
Willson, Beckles, 24
Wilson, Ian, 278
Wilson, Keith, 28, 102, 114, 160
Wilton, J.W., 149
Windsor Art Gallery, 349
Windsor, University of, 349
Winkler, Howard, 159
Winkler, Valentine, 144, 152; cow scheme of, 147
Winning the Second Battle: Canadian Veterans and the
    Return to Civilian Life, 1915–1930, 160
Winnipeg, xii, xiv; incorporation of, 17, 35, 37

Winnipeg Blue Bombers, 393
Winnipeg Board of Trade, 103
Winnipeg City Hydro, 219, 224–26
Winnipeg Electric Company (WEC), 174–76, 219, 223–26
Winnipeg First Century: An Economic History, 45, 103, 383
Winnipeg Floodway Authority, xv, 379, 409
Winnipeg Folk Festival, xvii
Winnipeg Free Press, 40, 183, 196, 216–18, 225–27, 229–30, 243, 246, 254, 267, 270, 272, 288, 290, 309, 315, 366, 374
Winnipeg General Hospital (WGH), 226
Winnipeg General Strike, The, 161
Winnipeg General Strike of 1919, vii, xi, 146, 149, 168, 173
Winnipeg Grain and Produce Exchange, 118–19, 130
Winnipeg Health Sciences Centre, 373, 378, 404
Winnipeg Hydro, 220, 226
Winnipeg: An Illustrated History, 158
Winnipeg Jets hockey team, 375
Winnipeg 1912, xix
Winnipeg Piano, 221
Winnipeg Police Service, 369
Winnipeg School Board, 133
Winnipeg Strike: 1919, The, 160–61
Winnipeg Sun, 90
Winnipeg Tribune, 128, 181, 183, 188, 225, 230, 243, 273
Winnipeg, University of, 247, 285, 299, 312, 333, 406
Wiseman, Adele, xiv
Wiseman, Nelson, vii, xix, 241, 260, 276–78, 281–82, 288, 302–3, 305, 320, 328, 350, 352
Wolseley, Garnet Colonel, 51
Wolseley Expedition, 32, 108
women, 325, 344; suffrage for, xi–xii, 112, 132, 134–35, 142, 145
Women of Red River: Being a Book Written from the Recollections of Women Surviving from the Red River Era, 66
Wood, Henry Wise, 151
Woods Milling Company, 119
Woodsworth, J.S., 332
Woodworth, J.E., 58
workers' compensation benefits, 244
Workmen's Compensation Act, 132, 135, 146, 243
World Curling Championship, 381

World Junior Hockey, 381
World War I, xi, xii, 150, 194; demands of, 144, 147; farming communities prior to, 130; governments during, 140, 156; as spurring social movements, 215; and subsequent recession, 168, 197
World War II, xiv, 140, 183, 194, 220, 238, 247
Wowchuk, Rosann, 401
Wright, Glenn, 160
Wuskwatim Dam project, 407, 411

Y
York boats, 33, 48
York Factory, 65
Young, Jonathan, 387
Young, Lisa, xx, 415
"Your Canada, Your Voice," 376

Z
Zelizer, Julian, xix
Zuken, Joe, 225

Contributors

RAYMOND B. BLAKE is professor of history at the University of Regina and one of the authors of a new two-volume history of Canada, "Narrating a Nation: Canadian History Pre-Confederation" and "Narrating a Nation: Canadian History Post-Confederation," as well as the recently-published *From Rights to Needs: A History of Family Allowances in Canada, 1929–92*.

JIM BLANCHARD is a librarian in the Elizabeth Dafoe Library at the University of Manitoba. His area of interest is Manitoba and Winnipeg history and he has published work dealing with agricultural and cultural topics. He has published two books on Winnipeg during the early 20th century: *Winnipeg 1912* and, most recently, *Winnipeg's Great War: the City Comes of Age*.

DAVID BURLEY is a social historian, and currently a senior scholar at the University of Winnipeg, having just retired as professor of History. His recent publications include *Living on Furby: Narratives of Home Winnipeg, 1880–2005*, co-authored with Mike Maunder, and "Winnipeg and the Landscape of Modernity, 1945–1975" in the book *Winnipeg Modernism 1945–1975*.

KARINE DUHAMEL is a PhD candidate in History at the University of Manitoba, where she holds a Joseph-Armand Bombardier CGS doctoral scholarship. Her work is in Canadian political and social history and her dissertation is on aboriginal activism in Canada and the United States between 1960 and 1975.

GERALD FRIESEN teaches History at the University of Manitoba. His recent publications include *Citizens and Nation: An Essay on History, Communication, and Canada* and the co-authored (with Royden Loewen) *Immigrants in Prairie Cities: Ethnic Diversity in Twentieth-Century Canada*.

BARRY FERGUSON teaches Canadian History at the University of Manitoba. His teaching and research interests have concentrated on the 20th century. Recent publications include *Recent Social Trends in Canada, 1960–1999* (McGill-Queen's University Press, 2005) and "Social Cohesion in Canada" in *The Tocqueville Review* 30, no. 2 (2009).

RORY HENRY is policy secretary to cabinet in the Government of Manitoba. He has written previously on the concepts and practices of empire in Australia and Canada and has completed a PhD in History on that subject at the Australian National University.

GREGORY MARCHILDON is professor in the Johnson-Shoyama Graduate School of Public Policy at the University of Regina, where he holds a Canada Research Chair in Public Policy and Economic History. He has published many books and articles related to health care in Canada, western agricultural and environmental history, and on business and political history.

JIM MOCHORUK is a professor of History at the University of North Dakota, where he teaches Canadian, U.S. and British History. His publications include *"Formidable Heritage": Manitoba's North and the Cost of Development, 1870–1930* and the forthcoming book co-authored with Rhonda Hinther, *Re-Imagining Ukrainian-Canadians: History, Politics and Identity*.

MORRIS MOTT is a professor of History at Brandon University, and concentrates on Canadian and Western Canadian history. His publications include many articles on the history of sports, including " 'Tough To Make It:' The History of Professional Team Sports in Manitoba," in John Welsted, John Everitt, Chris Stadel (eds.), *The Geography of Manitoba: Its land and its people.*

JAMES MUIR is assistant professor of History and Law at the University of Alberta. His research and publications, which encompass the intersection of law, colonialism, and the economy, range from 18th-century Nova Scotia and colonial Canada more generally to legal and political developments in the 20th-century prairie provinces.

W. H. W. NEVILLE is a senior scholar at the University of Manitoba where he was long-time department head and professor of Political Studies. His interests have included Manitoba politics and urban politics.

KEN RASMUSSEN is associate director of the Johnson Shoyama Graduate School of Public Policy at the University of Regina. He has published numerous articles in the area of administrative history and public administration and most recently co-authored a book with Luc Juillet entitled *Defending a Contested Ideal: Merit and the Public Service Commission, 1908–2008.*

DAVID STEWART is professor and head of the Department of Political Science at the University of Calgary. His research interests are in Canadian politics, political parties and provincial politics. He has published in journals such as *Political Parties, Publius* and the *Canadian Journal of Political Science.* He is the co-author of *Quasi-Democracy: Parties and Leadership Selection in Alberta* and *Conventional Choices: Maritime Leadership Politics.*

RUTH SWAN is an independent historian and author in Winnipeg, Manitoba; she has published extensively on 19th-century Manitoba, particularly on the origins of the Red River Valley Metis, in various periodicals and books, including *Prairie Forum, Manitoba History* and the *Dictionary of Canadian Biography.*

JASON THISTLETHWAITE is a PhD candidate in Global Governance at the University of Waterloo's Balsillie School of International Affairs (BSIA), a SSHRC doctoral fellow and a Balsillie Fellow. He completed a master's degree in Political Science at the University of Western Ontario. Jason's dissertation research is focused on explaining the politics behind the financial sector's response to climate change.

ROBERT WARDHAUGH is associate professor of Canadian History at the University of Western Ontario. He specializes in Canadian political and prairie history and is author of *Mackenzie King and the Prairie West* and *Behind the Scenes: The Life of William Clifford Clark.*

JARED WESLEY is an assistant professor of Political Studies at the University of Manitoba. His research interests surround Western Canadian politics, parties, and elections, all of which are captured in his forthcoming book, *Code Politics: Campaigns and Cultures on the Canadian Prairies.*

Also in the series:

Alberta Premiers of the Twentieth Century

edited by Bradford J. Rennie

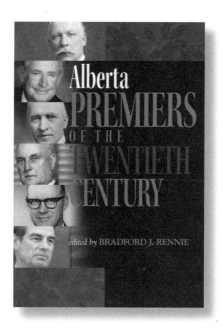

ISBN 978-0-88977-151-2
$24.95

Available online at **cprcpress.ca** or from your favourite retailer

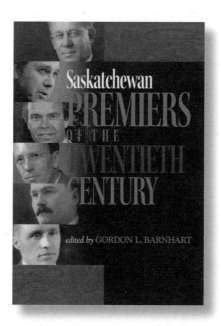